The Yorkshire County Cricket Club Limited

Registered Number 28929R

YEARBOOK
2020

122nd EDITION

Editor:
GRAHAM HARDCASTLE
Production Editor:
JAMES M. GREENFIELD

Records and Statistics
Yorkshire First Eleven:
JOHN T POTTER
Yorkshire Second Eleven:
HOWARD CLAYTON

Official Photographers:
SIMON WILKINSON, ALEX WHITEHEAD
and ALLAN MCKENZIE. *SWpix.com*

Published by
THE YORKSHIRE COUNTY CRICKET CLUB LTD
EMERALD HEADINGLEY CRICKET GROUND
LEEDS LS6 3BU
Tel: 0843 504 0344   Fax: 504 3099
Internet: http://www.yorkshireccc.com
e-mail: cricket@yorkshireccc.com
Auditors: Garbutt & Elliott Audit Limited
Medical Officer: Dr NIGEL MAYERS, MBChB, MRCGP
Burley Park Medical Centre, 273 Burley Road, Leeds LS4 2EL

The opinions expressed by contributors are not necessarily those of the Board.

1

TELEPHONE AND FAX NUMBERS

EMERALD HEADINGLEY CRICKET GROUND

Tel: 0344 504 3099
Fax: 0113 278 4099

NORTH MARINE ROAD, SCARBOROUGH **Tel: 01723 365625**
Fax: 01723 364287

SHIPTON ROAD, YORK **Tel: 01904 623602**

ST GEORGE'S ROAD, HARROGATE **Tel: 01423-525000**

© The Yorkshire County Cricket Club Ltd 2019

Produced by:

Great Northern Books
PO Box 1380, Bradford, BD5 5FB
www.greatnorthernbooks.co.uk

ISBN: 978-1-912101-22-1

CONTENTS

Colour Plates — Facing Pages 32 and 256

3

Officers for 2019

THE BOARD

Mr R A SMITH TD, DL (Chairman)
Mr S WILLIS
Mr M D MOXON (Director of Cricket)
Mr M ARTHUR Chief Executive)
Ms K MATHEW
MR HANIF MALIK OBE
MR S N HARTLEY
MR P HUDSON (Company Secretary)

MEMBERS' COMMITTEE

Chairman: Mr G GREENFIELD

ELECTED MEMBERS

Ms C EVERS   Ms P BEESLEY
Mr H RAY

APPOINTED MEMBERS

Mr G GREENFIELD   Mr A KILBURN
Mr R LEVIN   Mr C WOODTHORPE

ARCHIVES COMMITTEE

Chairman: Mr C HARDY

Dr P E DUNN   Mr P E DYSON
Mr J M GREENFIELD   MR C HARDY
Mr B K SANDERSON   Mr D WARNER

Changes announced after February 10 will be recorded in the 2021 edition of the Yorkshire County Cricket Club Yearbook

Officials of the Yorkshire County Cricket Club

President	President (Continued)	Chairman (Continued)	Captain (Contd)
T R Barker 1863	Harold 'Dickie' Bird OBE 2014-15	R A Smith TD, LLB, DL 2002-5	A B Sellers 1933-1947
M J Ellison 1864-97	John H Hampshire 2016-17	C J Graves 2005-15	N W D Yardley 1948-1955
Lord Hawke 1898-1938	Richard A Hutton 2017-18	S J Denison 2015-18	W H H Sutcliffe 1956-1957
Rt Hon Sir F S Jackson 1939-1947	*Treasurer*	R A Smith TD, LLB, DL 2018-	J R Burnet 1958-1959
T L Taylor 1948-1960	M J Ellison 1863-1893	*Captain*	J V Wilson 1960-1962
Sir W A Worsley Bart 1961-1973	M Ellison, jun 1894-1898	R Iddison 1863-1872	D B Close 1963-1970
Sir K Parkinson 1974-1981	Chas Stokes 1899-1912	J Rowbotham 1873	G Boycott 1971-1978
N W D Yardley 1981-1983	R T Heselton 1913-1931	L Greenwood 1874	J H Hampshire 1979-1980
The Viscount Mountgarret 1984-1989	A Wyndham Heselton 1932-1962	J Rowbotham 1875	C M Old 1981-1982
Sir Leonard Hutton 1989-1990	M G Crawford 1963-1979	E Lockwood 1876-1877	R Illingworth 1982-1983
Sir Lawrence Byford QPM, LLD, DL 1991-1999	J D Welch 1980-1984	T Emmett 1878-1882	D L Bairstow 1984-1986
R A Smith TD, LLB, DL 1999-2004	P W Townend 1984-2002	Hon M B (Lord) Hawke 1883-1910	P Carrick 1987-1989
David Jones CBE 2004-6	*Chairman* A H Connell, DL 1971-1979	E J R H Radcliffe 1911	M D Moxon 1990-1995
Robert Appleyard 2006-8	M G Crawford 1980-1984	Sir A W White 1912-1918	D Byas 1996-2001
Brian Close CBE 2008-10	H R Kirk 1984-1985	D C F Burton 1919-1921	D S Lehmann 2002
Raymond Illingworth CBE 2010-12	B Walsh, QC 1986-1991	Geoff Wilson 1922-1924	A McGrath 2003
Geoffrey Boycott OBE 2012-13	Sir Lawrence Byford CBE, QPM, LLD, DL 1991-1998	A W Lupton 1925-1927	C White 2004-6
	K H Moss MBE 1998-2002	W A Worsley 1928-1929	D Gough 2007-8
	G A Cope 2002	A T Barber 1930	A McGrath 2009
		F E Greenwood 1931-1932	A W Gale 2010-16

Captain (Continued)	Secretary (Continued)	Company Secretary	Chief Executive
G S Ballance 2017-18	**F C (Sir Fredk.) Toone** 1903-1930	**C Hartwell** 2011-14	**Colin J Graves** 2012-13
S A Patterson 2018-	**J H Nash** 1931-1971	**P Hudson** 2014-	**Mark Arthur** 2013-
D J Willey 2020- (T20 only)	**J Lister** 1972-1991	*Chief Executive*	
Secretary	**D M Ryder** 1991-2002	**C D Hassell** 1991-2002	
Geo Padley 1863	*Company Secretary*	**Colin J Graves** 2002-5	
J B Wostinholm 1864-1902	**B Bouttell** 2002-5	**Stewart Regan** 2006-10	

Warrior's centenary honoured

On Armistice Day in November two Northern Cricket Society members, Brian Sanderson and Michael Pulford, visited Harrogate to mark the centenary of the death of Yorkshire batsman James Rothery, an opener who played in two Championship-winning teams — 1905 and 1908.

Rothery, who became the third and final Yorkshire cricketer to lose his life to the Great War after Major Booth and Fairfax Gill, volunteered for the military in 1915, aged 39. He was shot in the left arm in 1917 during fighting near Loos in France. Complications arose, which became long-standing, and he died on June 2, 1919, after septicaemia set in.

Yorkshire debutant with a record

Days after signing for Yorkshire in early November on a four-year contract Dawid Malan posted the fastest *T20* international century by an England batsman in a landslide win over New Zealand at McLean Park, Napier.

Malan struck 103 from 51 balls as England racked up their highest *T20* score, 241-3 in a 76-run win. England went on to win a series decided by a Super Over in Auckland, 3-2.

A SEASON NEVER TO FORGET — AND A CURIOUS EXCITEMENT

Cards on the table. I am not a Yorkshireman. But Yorkshire Cricket means so much to me after just over a decade covering the *White Rose* for a trio of regional newspapers and, most recently, the club.

There is just something about watching cricket in this county. I have even taken to wearing the odd flat cap! It may not always go right, and there have been downs along with the ups in recent years, though the passion for the game remains undiminished.

By Graham Hardcastle

My first season covering Yorkshire came in 2008, writing for the *Bradford Telegraph and Argus*, the *York Press* and the *Northern Echo*. The last two years have seen me work as club journalist.

I take over the Editor's role from David Warner, who has been — and continues to be — a huge help since replacing him as correspondent for the three aforementioned papers. For that, I thank him greatly.

He is one of a handful of people who I want to namecheck for their help and contributions, not only to this publication but to the general coverage of Yorkshire Cricket. James Greenfield's excellent work in laying out the pages goes unnoticed but is crucial, while the year-round work of James Coldman, Sam Gascoyne and Treve Whitford, who make up the club's media department, is exceptional. I also extend my thanks to all of the contributors to this book.

On the field, 2019 was one English Cricket will never forget. A first ever World Cup win and an enthralling drawn *Ashes*. That is why this *Yearbook* has more of an international flavour than usual, highlighted by Ben Stokes being the cover photograph. Yorkshire's summer was mixed, but for me there were signs of progression in the Championship. Dawid Malan's arrival will hopefully add to more standout performances from the up-and-comers, and more silverware will follow shortly.

I hope you enjoy the summer ahead, which includes the new Hundred. My view on that? Cautiously excited. The level of criticism has surprised me. Give it a chance. It could be fun.

2020

MEMBERSHIPS ON SALE NOW

COUNTY FIXTURES — 2020

SPECSAVERS COUNTY CHAMPIONSHIP — Division 1
(All four-day matches)

Date			Opponents	Venue
SUN	**12-15**	**APRIL**	**GLOUCESTERSHIRE** ....**HEADINGLEY**	
Sun	19-22	April	Essex ....Chelmsford	
SAT	**25-28**	**APRIL**	**SURREY** ....**HEADINGLEY**	
Fri	1-4	May	Hampshire ....Southampton	
FRI	**15-18**	**MAY**	**KENT** ....**HEADINGLEY**	
Fri	22-25	May	Northamptonshire ....Northampton	
SUN	**14-17**	**JUNE/JULY**	**LANCASHIRE** ....**SCARBOROUGH**	
SUN	**28-1**	**JUNE**	**ESSEX** ....**HEADINGLEY**	
Sun	5-8	July	Gloucestershire ....Cheltenham	
SUN	**23-26**	**AUGUST**	**WARWICKSHIRE** ....**SCARBOROUGH**	
SAT	**29-1**	**AUG/SEPT**	**SOMERSET** ....**TAUNTON**	
TUE	**8-11**	**SEPTEMBER**	**LANCASHIRE** .... **OLD TRAFFORD**	
MON	**14-17**	**SEPTEMBER**	**HAMPSHIRE** ....**HEADINGLEY**	
Tue	22	September	Surrey ....The Oval	

ROYAL LONDON ONE-DAY CUP

SUN	**19**	**JULY**	**NOTTINGHAMSHIRE** ....**SCARBOROUGH**	
FRI	**24**	**JULY**	**WARWICKSHIRE** ....**SCARBOROUGH**	
Sun	26	July	Derbyshire ....Chesterfield	
Fri	31	July	Glamorgan ....Newport	
Sun	2	August	Leicestershire ....Leicester	
TUE	**4**	**AUGUST**	**NORTHAMPTONSHIRE** ....**YORK**	
THU	**6**	**AUGUST**	**SURREY** ....**YORK**	
Sun	9	August	Somerset ....Taunton	
Thu	13	August	Quarter-Finals ....TBC	
Sun	16	August	Semi-Finals ....TBC	
Sat	19	September	Final ....Trent Bridge	

VITALITY BLAST

FRI	**29**	**MAY**	**DURHAM** ....**HEADINGLEY**	
Sun	31	May	Nottinghamshire ....Trent Bridge	
Wed	3	June	Birmingham Bears ....Edgbaston	
THU	**4**	**JUNE**	**LANCASHIRE** ....**HEADINGLEY**	
Sun	7	June	Worcestershire ....Worcester	
WED	**10**	**JUNE**	**DERBYSHIRE** ....**HEADINGLEY**	
FRI	**12**	**JUNE**	**NORTHAMPTONSHIRE** ....**HEADINGLEY**	
Fri	19	June	Durham ....Riverside	
Sat	20	June	Derbyshire ....Chesterfield	
Thu	25	June	Leicestershire ....Leicester	
FRI	**26**	**JUNE**	**WORCESTERSHIRE** ....**HEADINGLEY**	
THU	**2**	**JULY**	**BIRMINGHAM BEARS** ....**HEADINGLEY**	
Fri	10	July	Lancashire ....Old Trafford	
SUN	**12**	**JULY**	**LEICESTERSHIRE** ....**HEADINGLEY**	
Tue	18-21	August	Quarter-Finals ....TBC	
Sat	5	September	Semi-Finals and Final ....Edgbaston	

OTHER MATCHES

THU	**2-4**	**APRIL**	**LEEDS/BRADFORD MCCU** ....**HEADINGLEY**	
			(FIRST-CLASS)	
Fri	17	July	Northumberland ....TBC	
			One-Day National County 50-over Friendly)	

INTERNATIONAL MATCHES PLAYED AT HEADINGLEY

TUE	**7**	**JULY**	**THIRD IT20 ....ENGLAND V. AUSTRALIA**
SAT	**29**	**AUGUST**	**FIRST IT20 ....ENGLAND V. PAKISTAN**

NORTHERN SUPERCHARGERS IN THE HUNDRED (MEN'S)

Sat	18	July	Manchester Originals ....Old Trafford
MON	**20**	**JULY**	**OVAL INVINCIBLES ....HEADINGLEY**
Thu	23	July	London Spirit ....Lord's
SUN	**26**	**JULY**	**BIRMINGHAM PHOENIX ......HEADINGLEY**
THU	**30**	**JULY**	**SOUTHERN BRAVE ....HEADINGLEY**
Sat	1	August	Welsh Fire ....Sophia Gardens
WED	**5**	**AUGUST**	**MANCHESTER ORIGINALS ...HEADINGLEY**
Mon	10	August	Trent Rockets ....Trent Bridge

NORTHERN SUPERCHARGERS IN THE HUNDRED (WOMEN'S)

Thu	23	July	London Spirit ....Lord's
Sun	26	July	Oval Invincibles ....South Northumberland CC
Thu	30	July	Welsh Fire ....Bristol
Sat	1	August	Trent Rockets ....Derby
WED	**5**	**AUGUST**	**MANCHESTER ORIGINALS ....HEADINGLEY**
SUN	**9**	**AUGUST**	**SOUTHERN BRAVE ....YORK**
TUE	**11**	**AUGUST**	**BIRMINGHAM PHOENIX ....YORK**

SECOND ELEVEN CHAMPIONSHIP

Tue	14 -17	April	Gloucestershire ....Bristol
Mon	20-23	April	Durham ....TBC
MON	**4-7**	**MAY**	**LANCASHIRE ....HEADINGLEY**
Mon	11-14	May	Middlesex ....TBC
Mon	8-11	June	Warwickshire ....TBC
Mon	22-25	June	Nottinghamshire Lady Bay Sports Ground, West Bridgford
MON	**29-2**	**JUNE/JULY**	**LEICESTERSHIRE ....WEETWOOD**
MON	**3-6**	**AUGUST**	**NORTHAMPTONSHIRE ....HARROGATE**
Mon	10-13	August	Glamorgan ....TBC
Mon	17-20	August	Derbyshire ....Derby
TUE	**1-4**	**SEPTEMBER**	**WORCESTERSHIRE ....HEADINGLEY**
MON	**7-10**	**SEPTEMBER**	**SURREY ....YORK**
MON	**14-17**	**SEPTEMBER**	**LANCASHIRE ....SCARBOROUGH**

SECOND ELEVEN TROPHY

Tue	14	July	Lancashire ....Old Trafford
Thu	16	July	Durham ....Marske-By-Sea
Tue	28	July	Lancashire ....TBC
Wed	29	July	Lancashire ....TBC

SECOND ELEVEN TWENTY20

MON	**18**	**MAY**	**NORTHAMPTONSHIRE ....DONCASTER TOWN**
Wed	20	May	Worcestershire ....Kidderminster
Thu	21	May	Birmingham ....TBC
Mon	25	May	Nottinghamshire ....TBC
TUE	**26**	**MAY**	**LANCASHIRE ....WEETWOOD**
			(Two games)
WED	**27**	**MAY**	**DERBYSHIRE ....BARNSLEY**
TUE	**2**	**JUNE**	**LEICESTERSHIRE .........MIDDLESBROUGH**
Thu	4	June	Durham ....TBC
			(Two games)
Thu	18	June	Semi-Finals and Final ....Arundel.

YORKSHIRE ACADEMY IN THE YORKSHIRE LEAGUE

Sat	25	April	Harrogate	Harrogate
SAT	**2**	**MAY**	**WOODHOUSE GRANGE**	**WEETWOOD**
SAT	**9**	**MAY**	**ACOMB**	**HEADINGLEY**
Sat	16	May	Scarborough	Scarborough
SAT	**23**	**MAY**	**CASTLEFORD**	**WEETWOOD**
Mon	25	May	Driffield	Driffield
Sat	30	May	Clifton Alliance	Clifton Alliance
SAT	**6**	**JUNE**	**SHERIFF HUTTON BRIDGE**	**WEETWOOD**
Sat	13	June	Dunnington	Dunnington
Sun	14	June	Harrogate	Harrogate
Sat	27	June	York	Clifton Park
SAT	**4**	**JULY**	**DRIFFIELD**	**WEETWOOD**
SAT	**11**	**JULY**	**HARROGATE**	**WEETWOOD**
Sat	18	July	Woodhouse Grange	Woodhouse Grange
Wed	22	July	Sheriff Hutton Bridge	Sheriff Hutton Bridge
Sat	25	July	Acomb	Acomb
SAT	**1**	**AUGUST**	**SCARBOROUGH**	**WEETWOOD**
Sat	8	August	Castleford	Castleford
SAT	**15**	**AUGUST**	**CLIFTON ALLIANCE**	**WEETWOOD**
SAT	**29**	**AUGUST**	**DUNNINGTON**	**WEETWOOD**
Mon	31	August	Stamford Bridge	Stamford Bridge
SAT	**5**	**SEPTEMBER**	**YORK**	**WEETWOOD**

YORKSHIRE ACADEMY FRIENDLIES

Sun	12	April	Worcestershire	Kidderminster
SUN	**19**	**APRIL**	**LANCASHIRE**	**WEETWOOD**
TUE	**21**	**APRIL**	**DURHAM**	**MIDDLESBROUGH**
WED	**22**	**APRIL**	**DURHAM**	**MIDDLESBROUGH**
Tue	30	June	Cheshire	Away
SUN	**5**	**JULY**	**LANCASHIRE**	**WEETWOOD**
Sat	11-13	July	Durham	Away
SUN	**12**	**JULY**	**NOTTINGHAMSHIRE**	**WEETWOOD**
WED	**15**	**JULY**	**DERBYSHIRE**	**WEETWOOD**
TUE	**4-6**	**AUGUST**	**LANCASHIRE**	**WEETWOOD**
TUE	**18-20**	**AUGUST**	**NOTTINGHAMSHIRE**	**WEETWOOD**
TUE	**25-27**	**AUGUST**	**DERBYSHIRE**	**WEETWOOD**

YORKSHIRE IN VITALITY WOMEN'S COUNTY T20

Fri	8	May	Essex	Essex TBC
Fri	8	May	Middlesex	Essex TBC
Mon	25	May	Berkshire	Staffordshire TBC
Mon	25	May	Staffordshire	Staforsshire TBC
Sun	7	June	Northamptonshire)	Wellingborough
Sun	7	June	Worcestershire	Wellingborough
SUN	**21**	**JUNE**	**SCOTLAND**	**HARROGATE**
SUN	**21**	**JUNE**	**NOTTINGHAMSHIRE**	**HARROGATE**

YORKSHIRE WOMEN'S FRIENDLIES

Sun	26	April	Durham/Northumberland	South Northumberland
Sun	3	May	Nottinghamshire	Away

TOP DELIVERIES MAKE
VERY SPECIAL SUMMER

By Geoff Cope

Early in my first year as Yorkshire president in 2019 I arranged a lunch at Emerald Headingley for the club's staff in recognition of all their hard work as they prepared for a massive summer ahead.

I am delighted to report that all of their energies up to that point — and throughout the months which followed — bore much fruit and helped us to go into the current year with our reputation enhanced throughout the cricketing world.

At the start of last season the club was assiduously working towards staging four World Cup games and an *Ashes* Test, plus all the domestic fixtures. In addition, the magnificent new Emerald Stand, which would transform the appearance of this historic ground, was poised to be opened. All of this was about to be delivered, and I can now say without hesitation that we enjoyed an excellent delivery!

It is all a far cry from 20 years ago when a new square was needed on a tired old ground which was under threat from the TCCB of losing its staging agreement for Test cricket.

Now the Test pitch and the whole of the square have been relaid by our splendid groundsman of the year, Andy Fogarty, and his staff, and we have a superb stadium supported by Leeds City Council and Caddick Construction, with Dr Keith Howard providing the naming rights. A quality delivery indeed, which has brought worldwide acclaim.

Although we missed out on trophies last season I am not alone in being able to look back on several outstanding fixtures, one of them being at York which was hosting only its second Championship match in Yorkshire's history. It was a great game of cricket, well organised and on a good wicket. Although Warwickshire won narrowly in the end, we could so easily have enjoyed a victory. I wish York CC all the very best for this season's festival.

Then there were the two splendid Championship games at Scarborough, both resulting in richly deserved triumphs for the *White Rose*. The first was an epic win by 123 runs against old rivals Surrey, which was achieved in the very last over of a game which produced 300-plus runs in each of the first three innings. It was followed up at the

Festival with a stirring win by 143 runs over Nottinghamshire, Yorkshire turning the tables in dramatic style after slumping to 38-5 on the first morning.

Once again the Festival was a wonderful occasion, and it remains the best cricket festival in the world.

For sheer nail-biting excitement in a grand finale finish few Test Matches can compare with England's one-wicket *Ashes* victory at Emerald Headingley

GOLDEN DAYS: President Cope, right, presents David Moorhouse with Yorkshire County Cricket Club's award for his 50 years of membership.

when Ben Stokes played an astonishing innings which contained the best of Test, county and *T20* batting all rolled into one.

One major factor in all of these matches is the outstanding work of our award-winning groundsmen in Andy Fogarty at Headingley, John Dodds at Scarborough with his ECB Outground of the Year Award for the fifth time in eight seasons, and Jonathan Corcoran at York, who was mentioned in the outgrounds awards. Neither must we forget Richard Robinson at Weetwood and all other groundstaff members for their excellent work.

Looking ahead, I feel confident that Chief Executive Mark Arthur and his management team will continue to receive recognition for all the hard work they put in. While 2019 was a busy highlight year with the World Cup and the *Ashes* Test, 2020 will not be on the same level as Emerald Headingley only hosts two *T20* internationals. But there is also the arrival of *The Hundred* competition, a new concept and which we hope will be successful.

As for the team, we have heard the word "'transition" used a lot recently, and I hope they continue to learn and go from strength to strength. We have got some very fine players in our squad, and they should be aware that if they work hard at their game there are places up for grabs internationally — and that should be the ambition of each and every one of them.

YORKSHIRE MUST GET
ON THE FRONT FOOT

By Graham Hardcastle

If Yorkshire's 2019 summer were to be summed up as a school pupil's report it would probably read along the lines of: "Signs of progress, but plenty of room for improvement."

While the home international campaign will never be forgotten, given the thrills and spills with both red ball and white, the *White Rose* season will be one that does not linger too long in the memory.

There were definite signs of encouragement in the County Championship, both individually and teamwise, despite heavy September defeats against Somerset at Taunton and Kent at Emerald Headingley, the latter — by 433 runs — Yorkshire's heaviest ever in terms of runs in first-class cricket.

If you undertook a straw poll of supporters with the question *"Did Yorkshire progress in the Championship this summer?"* the results would be split. This writer believes there was, but more of that later.

Let us deal with the obvious disappointments first, the Royal London one-day Cup and the Vitality Blast. No poll needed. Things have to get better after two group-stage exits left us watching the Lord's final and finals day from armchairs rather than the Mound Stand or the Hollies.

Yorkshire were always on the back foot in the Blast, with Paul Dyson going into more detail on pages 18-19, but they weren't a million miles away from qualifying in the end — two points behind and with a better net run rate than fourth-placed Worcestershire, who went on to reach the final and were beaten by Essex. Had Yorkshire beaten Nottinghamshire at Trent Bridge on the final Sunday of the group stage when they needed six off the last five balls they would have snuck into the quarter-finals.

Royal London One-Day Cup

A campaign of fine margins

The Vikings won only two of their eight group games, losing three and playing out two ties.

That campaign was definitely a case of fine margins. After beating Leicestershire by 213 runs in their home opener they tied the next game against Warwickshire, the first of two white-ball ties between the two counties through the summer, and lost by one run to Lancashire two days later. A further tie came against Derbyshire, when the Falcons benefited from a *Duckworth Lewis Stern* revised target of 225 from 22 overs after Yorkshire's innings had been curtailed at 308-2 from 40 overs. Further defeats against Nottinghamshire and Worcestershire ended Yorkshire's hopes of a top-three finish.

Five batsmen topped the 200-run mark without reaching 300, with Gary Ballance's 294 the best of them, just pipping the 290 from Tom Kohler-Cadmore, who had an impressive season across all formats, his Championship tally of runs boosted by a superb final-week unbeaten century against Warwickshire.

Winter signing Mat Pillans led the way for the bowlers with 16 wickets, including five on his one-day debut for the county in that big home win against Leicester on the opening day in April. He bowled with good pace and variation.

County Championship

Ballance high five in centuries

There is still significant scope for improvement ahead of the 2020 summer — consistency being at the top of the list. That is fully accepted by the coaching staff. But a developing side showed encouraging signs.

Their tally of five victories matched the 2016 haul when they almost pipped Middlesex to the title at Lord's; it bettered 2017 and matched 2018. They beat defending champions Surrey at Scarborough in a hard-fought game with a nail-biting finish; they hammered pre-game leaders Somerset at Emerald Headingley, and they had the better of an early-season rain-affected home clash with eventual champions Essex.

Away wins at Hampshire and Kent in April and May showed the team's character to fight back from adversity after difficult starts. They must, if they are to elevate themselves to title contenders, get on the front foot early on more often. Too often were they having to fight back.

The two September landslide defeats against Somerset at Taunton and Kent at Headingley took some of the gloss off a positive Division One campaign, no doubt about that.

The innings home victory over Somerset in July, inspired by 10 wickets in the match for the fabulous short-term overseas signing Keshav Maharaj, was arguably the performance of the season. But the Scarborough win over Surrey ran it close. That came as Steven Patterson's side defended a 318 target in 83 overs and claimed five wickets for six runs in 35 balls either side of tea on day four. Surrey slipped

from 157-2 to 163-7 and to 194 all out inside 82 overs, Duanne Olivier getting Gareth Batty caught in the slips with 10 balls left.

The standout performers were Ballance and South African left-arm spinner Maharaj, who claimed 38 wickets in only five games plus two swashbuckling half-centuries down the order.

Ballance started the season like a house on fire with four centuries in the first four Division One games — making it five in a row dating back to the final game of 2018, a win against Worcestershire at New Road.

His form understandably tailed off, but not alarmingly so by any stretch, and he was the obvious candidate

TOM KOHLER-CADMORE: His first taste of one-day captaincy and a notable Championship performer.

to scoop the player-of-the-year awards, having scored 975 runs. He was the second leading run-scorer in Division One behind Warwickshire opener Dom Sibley, whose tally of 1,324 earned him an England Test touring place over the winter.

Kohler-Cadmore, who was given his first taste of captaincy at the end of the one-day Cup and through the Blast, was a notable Championship performer with 828 and 30 outfield catches. His last-week 165 not out in a rain-affected draw at Edgbaston was Yorkshire's highest score of the season. The ex-Worcestershire man took 42 catches across all formats in 2019, the majority at first slip.

Adam Lyth finished with 804 runs, leaving Yorkshire with three of the top nine run-scorers in Division One.

Olivier was Yorkshire's leading Championship wicket-taker with 43, five ahead of compatriot Maharaj. But Olivier admitted that there is significant scope for personal improvement in 2020.

NEEDLE STUCK DESPITE
WHITE ROSE RECORDS

By Paul E Dyson

For the third consecutive season Yorkshire finished fifth in the North Group, and thereby just failed to qualify for the quarter-finals. Unlike the previous two seasons, however, the side rarely looked like qualifying, even being in danger of finishing with the wooden spoon.

The county saved its best form for the last four games, winning three and crucially losing to Nottinghamshire by three runs, having needed six from five balls to win. The final two victories were the only two successive wins. Yorkshire, who finished two points behind Worcestershire in fourth place and with a better net run-rate, the first separator for teams on level points, were not helped by the weather, which caused four abandonments — a county record. Group winners and runners-up Lancashire and Nottinghamshire also had four abandonments, so that cannot be used as a reason for some of the poor performances.

Only one of the first 10 games ended in victory, although there was an authentic tied match with Birmingham Bears when both sides scored 177-4. Derbyshire completed its usual double – for the third successive season – each defeat by a convincing margin. At Chesterfield the hosts won by five wickets, but it could have been much worse. Yorkshire plummeted to 77-6 before Jordan Thompson, striking his first half-century for the first team in any format, and Jonny Tattersall shared a seventh-wicket stand of 66 from 40 balls. Even worse than the defeat, in many respects, was Matthew Fisher dislocating his right (bowling) shoulder when fielding on the boundary. Despite it being the campaign's second match he did not feature again, having also broken his thumb warming up for the same game. When Derbyshire came to Emerald Headingley there was no rescue act from the lower-order batsmen, and an all-out total of 152 confirmed a 55-run defeat.

A total of 19 players were used in the 10 matches — in 2018 it was 17 in 14 — and only three played throughout. These were the top three in the batting order: Adam Lyth, Tom Kohler-Cadmore and David Willey, although Willey dropped down to No.4 in one match. Kohler-Cadmore with 435 runs at 62.14 and Lyth with 379 at 37.90 were easily Yorkshire's best performers, Kohler-Cadmore's tally being the fourth-best in the county's 17 seasons in the format. Next was Willey, but some

What a lift: congratulations for Jack Shutt, who returned the second-best figures in Yorkshire's *T20* history.

way behind with 136 — he scored 446 two years ago. The openers shared two century stands and always scored at a fast pace, their average strike-rate being almost 150. They, Thompson and West Indian overseas wicketkeeper batsman Nicholas Pooran — who appeared in only three games — were the only players to make a half-century.

Surprisingly, Lyth was also the leading bowler; his 12 wickets came at an average of 12.25 and he had figures of 5-31 against Nottinghamshire at Trent Bridge.

This was not the best bowling of the season: that accolade belonged to Jack Shutt, who in his debut season in any format returned the second-best figures in Yorkshire's history of 5-11 against Durham at Chester-le-Street. Amazingly, his four overs included 14 dot balls.

Shutt and South African Keshav Maharaj, who came into the side for all of the last five games, were the only bowlers to concede fewer than seven runs per over. Josh Poysden would have strengthened the spin bowling but, like Fisher, appeared in only the first game after suffering a fractured skull while throwing to loanee Dom Bess in the indoor nets. The pacemen were all inconsistent. Four of Willey's nine wickets came in the last-but-one match; Tim Bresnan took eight wickets, but did not bowl on a regular basis, and Duanne Olivier and Mat Pillans each appeared in only five games. Skipper Steven Patterson played himself only once, and Kohler-Cadmore led the side in the remaining nine matches.

At the first time of asking Lyth scored the 21 needed to break Andrew Gale's record for the highest aggregate for Yorkshire in this format — his tally now stands at 2,619 and he also became the first player, fielder or wicketkeeper, to take 50 catches. He now has 53 – 10 ahead of Gary Ballance. Bresnan extended his own two records: 118 appearances, seven more than Lyth, and 118 wickets, eight more than Adil Rashid who missed the whole campaign due to injury. Bresnan is the only Yorkshire player to have appeared in all 17 seasons of the competition.

"Could do better" is a familiar phrase to summarise Yorkshire's *T20* form. They have qualified for the quarter-finals only twice in the last 12 seasons. Can 2020 bring a different outcome for the *White Rose*?

TROPHY SO NEAR AS COLTS
BAT AWAY PENALTY

By John Virr

The season began in Scarborough with a two-day "friendly" against Lancashire, followed by the first competitive action at the same venue against the same opponents. This first of six one-day Trophy games was won handsomely, and was followed by three victories and two losses.

The suspended points deduction from 2018 — brought about by a bat-size infringement — was successfully bypassed as Yorkshire finished joint top of the North Group with Durham, securing a home semi-final courtesy of a better net run-rate. The semi-final also took place at Scarborough but, despite compiling a competitive total, Yorkshire saw Kent run out worthy winners. Kent then beat Durham in the final.

In the seven Trophy games Will Fraine made 343 runs, averaging 49, and Jordan Thompson 209 runs alongside his 12 wickets at 15.92.

Fraine continued his fine form in the red-ball format, making 420 Championship runs at an average of 70, including two centuries and a top score of 157 not out against Worcestershire at Kidderminster. All agreed that his call-up to the first team was fully deserved.

The Championship saw Yorkshire finish second in the North Group, missing out on the final by only two points despite being the only county to win three games, with four drawn and one lost — to table-toppers Leicestershire. Yorkshire had the third-highest number of bowling bonus points but the lowest number of batting points, a complete reversal of 2018. Other than Fraine, only Thompson exceeded 200 runs.

On the bowling front Jared Warner achieved the only five-for, taking 5-22. also at Kidderminster, among his 13 wickets. Ed Barnes took 12, and the two spinners, Josh Poysden and Jack Shutt, 11 each.

Several red-ball friendlies also took place, enabling Thompson, with 457, and Tom Loten to reach 400-plus runs, while Barnes took 15 wickets and Thompson 14. The late season three-day friendly at Hove against Sussex saw Matthew Revis and Loten share a second-wicket partnership of 221 against a very experienced attack – Loten made 115 while Revis advanced to 177, a performance that fully merited the Howard Clayton Performance of the Year Award and contributed to a first-team

MATTHEW REVIS: 177 earned Performance of the Year Award

Championship debut against Kent at Emerald Headingley, opening the batting alongside Adam Lyth in the absence of the injured Fraine.

The T20 campaign was less successful, Yorkshire finishing fourth. There were six wins from 12 games, five being lost and one abandoned.

Tim Bresnan made 236 runs without being dismissed, and Jack Leaning had a fine all-round series with 327 runs at 40.88 and 14 wickets at 16.71.

Around a third of all available playing days were rain-affected, eight full days being lost and a further 11 interrupted. Across all formats 36 players were used, including seven teenagers.

Besides Fraine making his first-team appearances, congratulations are sent to Revis and Loten for their first-class debuts – also to Loten, Thompson, Warner and Ben Birkhead, who made their List A debuts.

I am aware that Bilal Anjam, Karl Carver and Matthew Taylor are leaving. They are sent our thanks and best wishes for the future.

John Virr is the Yorkshire Second Eleven Scorer

He's got high hopes...

"I feel that after all the hard work and inconsistencies we've had in the last three years, we should start to see our rewards for that in the next two years." — *Yorkshire Coach Andrew Gale.*

TOP-OF-THE-CLASS SCHOLARS
MOVE INTO BIG SCHOOL

By Graham Hardcastle

First-class debuts for Matthew Revis and Tom Loten in the final two Championship matches were definitely highlights for the Academy.

Revis, 17, opened alongside Adam Lyth in the heavy home defeat against Kent. He scored nine and nought, but batting for an hour and a quarter in the first innings will have done him the world of good. There will have to be bigger scores to follow, but looking comfortable against a seam attack led by veteran Darren Stevens was certainly an encouraging start on his first-team bow.

Academy captain Loten, who turned 21 in January, then replaced him for the season-ending draw at Warwickshire, scoring a polished 58 batting at No.3. He had made his first-team debut in a rained-off one-day game earlier in the season without batting or bowling.

Academy coaches Ian Dews and Richard Damms will tell you that results are certainly not the be-all-and-end-all when assessing an Academy season. Of course they are important, but disjointed team selection due to things like school exams can make finding a winning formula tricky.

So, a major goal is making sure that they help players to progress to the next level. Revis and Loten are the prime examples, as is wicket-keeper/batsman Harry Duke, 18. He scored 758 runs and claimed 48 dismissals behind the stumps for teams such as Yorkshire Under-17s, Academy, the second team and the ECB Elite Player Development Under-17s North side, including three fifties and a hundred.

At the end of the year he was called up by England Under-19s for a tour to the Caribbean and debuted in Antigua alongside county colleague George Hill, another Academy product but with slightly more experience. Wakefield-born Duke said: "It's a massive honour getting selected for your country at any level. It's my first call-up.

"I joined the Academy in 2017, and it's improved my game massively. To get the coaching from the likes of Richard Damms, Ian Dews and Rich Pyrah, and then to train with the first team, it's a massive opportunity. To play for the Academy on a Saturday, it's definitely improved all of our games."

HARRY DUKE: Getting his hands on national honours

GEORGE HILL: Academy Player of the Year Award

Two former Academy products to break into first-team cricket in 2019 were spinners Jack Shutt and James Logan. Both returned hauls of five and four wickets in T20 and Championship cricket.

The Academy finished mid-table in the 2019 Yorkshire Premier League North, a competition won by a Sheriff Hutton Bridge side including Matthew Fisher, Karl Carver and Ed Barnes.

Yorkshire won seven league games. An impressive 55-run away success over runners-up Woodhouse Grange in August stands out, a success built on a dogged bowling display defending a target of 168. New-ball seamer Harrison Quarmby and the spin of Harry Sullivan led the way with three wickets apiece. The Academy also reached the semi-final of the league's T20 competition.

Hill won the Academy Player of the Year Award, scoring 514 runs from 10 appearances, with four fifties and a century, averaging 57.11 . He also chipped in with seven wickets.

Left-handed Revis actually made his first-team debut on the back of a fine 177 in a second-team friendly against Sussex at Hove. "At the start of the year the goal I set out was just to play regular second-team cricket," said the Sedbergh School pupil, a fine breeding ground for Yorkshire players Hill and Harry Brook.

"You always think getting into the first team is a long way off, but

23

getting the call was a great honour. Getting that selection gives me a lot of motivation — if you do put in performances they are going to be rewarded. To make my debut last season at 17 was a great honour, and something I'll never ever forget.

"When I was 13 or 14 I came to the ground for T20s and was watching people like Tim Bresnan and Gary Ballance, Adam Lyth as well. To debut alongside them, it made it more special."

YORKSHIRE ACADEMY BATTING IN YORKSHIRE LEAGUE NORTH

Player	I.	N.O.	Runs	H.S.	Avge	100s	50s	Balls Faced	Strike Rate	4s	6s	Ct/St
G C H Hill	10	1	514	122	57.11	1	4	498	103.21	42	13	8
M L Revis	11	0	412	78	37.45	0	4	533	77.30	49	0	11
F J Bean	14	2	402	74*	33.50	0	4	612	65.69	45	2	5
J H Wharton	17	1	505	85	31.56	0	5	864	58.45	51	4	5
Vikram Sharma	2	0	61	60	30.50	0	1	64	95.31	6	1	0
Arjun Ramkumar	12	3	253	48*	28.11	0	0	369	68.56	27	2	1
T W Loten	9	2	176	50*	25.14	0	1	323	54.49	10	0	5
A Greaves	5	1	83	40	20.75	0	0	93	89.25	8	2	2
D J Leech	11	2	172	36*	19.11	0	0	206	83.50	16	0	1
H G Duke	16	2	255	40	18.21	0	0	481	53.01	21	0	20/6
H Harding	8	1	121	23	17.29	0	0	224	54.02	4	1	1
E Booth	7	3	69	23*	17.25	0	0	207	33.33	7	0	1
J R Sullivan	13	4	113	29	12.56	0	0	133	54.59	7	0	5
W Luxton	6	2	44	23	11.00	0	0	13	33.08	2	0	0
J Mukherjee	3	1	12	6	6.00	0	0	124	92.31	0	0	1
H Quarmby	7	4	8	4	2.67	0	0	42	19.05	0	0	2
H A Sullivan	6	3	4	2*	1.33	0	0	45	8.89	0	0	6
A Kay	1	1	6	6*	—	0	0	5	120.00	0	0	3/0

Yash Yagadia did not bat

YORKSHIRE ACADEMY BOWLING IN YORKSHIRE LEAGUE NORTH

Player	Overs	Mdns	Runs	Wkts	Avge	Best	5wI	Econ.	Strike Rate
H Quarmby	106.3	13	423	22	19.23	3-15	0	3.97	29.05
G C H Hill	41	5	151	7	21.57	2-28	0	3.68	35.14
H Harding	87.5	9	327	15	21.80	4-21	0	3.72	35.13
J R Sullivan	88.3	5	480	21	22.86	5-73	1	5.42	25.29
H A Sullivan	131.1	15	484	21	23.05	4-31	0	3.69	37.48
A Greaves	19	2	104	4	26.00	2-21	0	5.47	28.50
D J Leech	78.5	7	293	11	26.64	3-37	0	3.72	43.00
J Mukherjee	14	1	54	2	27.00	1-14	0	3.86	42.00
E Booth	45.3	4	204	6	34.00	2-21	0	4.48	45.50
T W Loten	49	5	156	4	39.00	2-41	0	3.18	73.50
M L Revis	19	2	69	0	—	—	0	3.63	—

Yorkshire Academy Statistician: Andrew Hinchliffe

NOAH'S FLOOD OF RUNS
AS UNDER-13s WIN AGAIN

By Jim Love

After the magnificent summer of 2018 the weather did us no favours, with almost a fifth of the programme cancelled and unable to be rearranged. When the sun did shine the Under-15s A team reached the final of the Royal London National Championship, where they were beaten by a good Surrey side. A third final triumph in three years was not to be, but nevertheless a good season for the Under-15s A side.

The Under-15s Development side suffered most with the weather, with half their fixtures lost. This was due to opposition sides not having staff available to rearrange dates, which was quite frustrating.

The Under-14s A side had a lean season, although several boys put in good performances. As a team it did not quite happen. The Development side had a good year, several boys playing A team cricket. The Under-13s A side once again won the Northern Counties Championship, with the Development team winning 11 of their 12 matches and pushing the A team boys.

The Under-12s A side had a good season, losing two matches, with the Development side losing one. The Under-11s and Under-10s sides now play as Phoenix and Tykes, and they enjoyed good seasons, the "inter matches" being very competitive. They also played some county opposition, where Yorkshire did very well.

Mention should be made of Noah Kelly, who scored over 1,000 runs for both the Under-13s and Under-14s in an outstanding season. Teams frequently play against sides who are one or two years older as Yorkshire strive to challenge their players with better fixtures.

Selected to play for North of England Under-15s were Rhys Ditta, Matthew Weston, Harry Allinson, Clark Doughney and Yash Vagadia.

Next season will see the introduction of Under-12s Tykes and Phoenix, which will reflect the ECB Development Framework. Thanks go to all our county age-group managers, coaches, parents, officials and to clubs who allow us use of their excellent facilities.

RODRIGUES SPARKLES — BUT DIAMONDS MISS SILVER

By Kevin Hutchinson

Yorkshire Diamonds embarked on the 2019 campaign knowing it would be the last time they would participate in the Kia Super League . It was announced pre-tournament that the competition would make way for the women's version of *The Hundred* from 2020, news that received a mixed reaction among supporters who had embraced the original concept about to enter a fourth season.

The appointment of Women's World Cup winner and former England captain Danielle Hazell as head coach heralded a change of direction for the side, who sought to improve on three fifth-place finishes, and the announcement of the 15-strong squad included a number of new faces. Among them was Indian teenager Jemimah Rodrigues, who may have been less well known than the more flamboyant recent Ashes winner Alyssa Healy, but would steal the hearts of all Diamonds followers with her thrilling on-field exploits and modest countenance off it. Lauren Winfield retained the captaincy, but she was dealt an early blow with the news that England team-mate Katherine Brunt would miss the start, and as it transpired the whole, of the competition as she recuperated from injury following a busy international workload.

With the training base established once again at St Peter's School, York, and a couple of practice games behind them, the side stepped out under lights and in front of the Sky cameras at Emerald Headingley, beginning their campaign against defending champions Surrey Stars. Leg-spinner Helen Fenby produced a KSL career best 4-20, and New Zealand international Leigh Kasperek, the third of the overseas contingent, impressed on her debut with three wickets as the 2018 winners were restricted to what appeared to be a manageable 130. At the halfway stage of the reply victory looked on the cards, but the hosts lost their way and four wickets in the final two overs resulted in defeat by nine runs.

Heavy defeats to Loughborough Lightning and Western Storm sandwiched a first taste of success, which came against *Roses* rivals Lancashire Thunder at Liverpool. A half-century from skipper Winfield and useful contributions from both Healy and Hollie Armitage, returning

Turning point: Jemimah Rodrigues dives to catch international teammate Harmanpreet Kaur and set the Diamonds on a roller-coaster ride to victory over the *Red Rose*.

to the side having missed the previous season through injury, set the home side a target of 152. Rodrigues's diving catch on the boundary to dismiss international teammate Harmanpreet Kaur was the turning point that started a roller-coaster ride to a victory sealed with five balls and nine runs to spare. Despite a maiden half-century at Loughborough from Rodrigues, the first half of the season ended with a second defeat to the previous year's beaten finalists.

In stark contrast to the away washout against Surrey 12 months earlier Woodbridge Road, Guildford, was bathed in sunshine when Rodrigues found the cover boundary to seal the points with a ball to spare. Healy again laid down a solid foundation by passing 30 for the third time in six innings as the Diamonds chased down 121 to beat the reigning holders on their home soil for the first time. That was the first half of a road trip that took in Southampton and a first meeting with the Southern Vipers.

Under the lights of the Ageas Bowl the sides produced a gripping spectacle for both those in attendance and the TV audience. England's Danni Wyatt threatened to take the game away with a half-century off 22 deliveries, but the visitors fought back. Katie Levick with 2-17 from four overs, including the wicket of Wyatt, and Kasperek with four wickets, three in the final over, helped to claw back the total to 127-9 after the home side had been 62-0 at the end of the first six.

Armitage and Rodrigues looked to have manoeuvred the side into a position of strength with 22 needed from 23 balls, but for a second time in front of the Sky cameras the visitors conspired to lose a game that was there to be won, the reply unravelling in the last couple of overs as a three-run defeat ensued.

With three games remaining and the chance of a first appearance at Finals Day fading the squad turned up at North Marine Road, Scarborough, for the return *Roses* clash. They were dealt a further blow when a second of their England contingent, Katie George, withdrew during the warmup due to injury. Lancashire posted a challenging 164 despite three wickets from Alice Davidson-Richards, 74 coming in a stand between the Indian Kaur and homegrown Ellie Threlkeld. They were separated when Kaur was dismissed in almost identical fashion to the west coast encounter, Rodrigues adding to a growing highlight reel of exceptional catches. Australia's Healy then came into her own for the first time in the tournament as a mixture of precision and pure power produced an innings of 77 from 38 balls in which she amassed a dozen fours and three sixes. Winfield was happy to play the supporting role as she contributed 16 to a century opening partnership inside nine overs.

The baton was taken up once again by the Indian teenager, who saw the side through to a *Roses* double, her 43 including four boundaries in the last-but-one over to keep alive hopes of a top-three finish with two games to go. Clifton Park staged the penultimate match of the group stage, with eventual finalists Southern Vipers the visitors. This was on the same day that Ben Stokes rescued England from a seemingly impossible position in the *Ashes* at Headingley, but those present 25 miles along the A64 in York were treated to an equally exceptional batting performance as a diminutive 18-year-old right-hander from Mumbai produced the fastest ever KSL century and the Diamonds set a competition record for the highest successful run chase.

Three wickets from Davidson-Richards could not prevent the visitors from reaching 184-4, and when the hosts lost their captain to the second ball of the reply the signs were ominous. Rodrigues kept the crowd spellbound, becoming the first Diamond to score a hundred, accomplishing the feat off 51 balls. An over later the winning run came as Linsey Smith scampered a single off the last ball of the match, sparking celebrations tempered only slightly by the knowledge that failure to collect a bonus point extinguished hopes of progression beyond the group stage.

The match at Taunton against a Western Storm side boasting a 100 per cent winning record from their nine matches would be the last for the Diamonds, and rain for most of the day and into the early evening threatened a disappointing conclusion. Thankfully, the weather relented to allow a 10-over contest. Another rapid-fire half-century from Rodrigues, which took her final KSL tally to 401 runs at an average of 57.28 and a strike rate of 149.62 left the eventual champions chasing slightly more than 10 an over to keep their perfect record intact.

Levick was exemplary, conceding seven runs from her two overs, and in a final over not without drama Beth Langston held her nerve as the visitors won by five runs.

Victories in four of their last five matches was a measure of the progress made under Hazell and assistant coach Melvyn Betts, and a record of five wins and five losses gave a best-ever fourth-placed finish.

But it was impossible to escape the fact that had chances been taken in either the opening game at Headingley or the match at the Ageas Bowl the Diamonds would have proved suitable adversaries for any of the sides in the season finale at Hove.

Leading run-scorer: Diamonds skipper Lauren Winfield in action against Surrey Stars.

So what of the Kia Super League, a competition introduced to increase competitive opportunities for the country's best players and to widen the appeal of women's cricket? No one can argue that it has not been a success, the Diamonds support increasing year on year with crowds in excess of 400 a regular feature of their home games in a county dominated by the men's game.

In terms of personal performances Winfield finished as the club's leading all-time run-scorer with 627 and Levick the leading wicket-taker with 29. Using on-field results alone to measure the contribution the Diamonds have made to women's cricket in Yorkshire would be misleading. Their value in terms of supporter engagement and promotion of the game have been outstanding, and all involved, not least the excellent general manager, Jane Hildreth, should be very proud.

Kevin Hutchinson is the Yorkshire Diamonds scorer and Competitions and Records Secretary, Hunters ECB Yorkshire Premier League North

ENGLAND'S GLORY BLOOMED FROM *WHITE ROSE* GARDEN

By Graham Hardcastle

As Jonny Bairstow, Adil Rashid and Joe Root celebrated wildly on the Lord's outfield after England's remarkable, heart-stopping victory over New Zealand in the World Cup final in mid-July their county were reflecting with pride. A job well done.

England's star trio had been brought up through *White Rose* ranks to achieve something that is likely to be a once-in-a-career moment. A World Cup win on home soil.

Also, Yorkshire could look back on hosting four World Cup group fixtures, which all proved memorable occasions in their own way, including England's nervy low-scoring defeat against Sri Lanka. India, Pakistan, the West Indies and Afghanistan twice all visited Headingley.

Yorkshire Chief Executive Mark Arthur said: "I thought the atmosphere in the ground at Emerald Headingley was something we haven't experienced before, because it was a different type of atmosphere to Yorkshire v. Lancashire, say, in a T20. "Bar a small incident outside the ground in the Pakistan v. Afghanistan game the integration of the participating countries was superb.

"For me, probably the best atmosphere was the India v. Sri Lanka game, our last one. It was wonderful to see all the Indian supporters in their blue shirts. Their enthusiasm for the game becomes infectious."

As an MCC member Arthur was at the World Cup final, which finished in a tie after both the 50-over innings and then the Super Over. England won on count back of most boundaries scored in the day. Many believe it was one of the most remarkable moments in sporting history, let alone just cricket.

"I remember where I was in 1966," Arthur said. "I remember where I was in 2003 for the Rugby World Cup — watching my lad play Saturday morning football. I'll certainly remember where I was for this one. It was the greatest sporting moment I've witnessed live."

Bairstow, Rashid and Root came up through the Yorkshire ranks to be world stars, but the World Cup could have had a positive impact on a number of other *White Rose* up-and-comers with the county having to provide a plethora of net bowlers for each training days prior to games.

Perhaps not an up-and-comer, but leg-spinner Josh Poysden's experi-

Leg-spinners' union: Josh Poysden, right, meets Rashid Khan, the world's number one ranked *T20* international bowler, during a net session at Emerald Headingley.

ence of bowling alongside Afghanistan star Rashid Khan and picking his brains illustrates that point perfectly: "When I was younger and more inexperienced I did a lot of net bowling, especially at the England guys, whenever I could," Poysden explained. "When I've been in Sydney in the winters I've bowled at the Big Bash teams and New South Wales.

"I just thought with the World Cup being at Headingley and Rashid Khan being around, 'Right, this is a good chance for me to pick the brains of someone at the top of their game in international cricket and also around the world in *T20*'. I spoke to Andrew Gale because he knows Phil Simmons, Afghanistan's coach, through his Level Four training to see if he could put me in touch with Rashid.

"When I came in Rashid came over and introduced himself. It was an invaluable hour bowling with him and chatting to him. I've been really lucky in my career so far. I've been able to pick the brains of people like Shane Warne, Stuart MacGill, Imran Tahir and Samuel Badree. With Rashid, we just talked about everything. Just bowling together, you can have that informal chat. He was just amazing to be honest. He was so open with his information, and he's such a nice guy."

Ok, we may not have seen England win a game at Headingley on the way to glory. But, no doubt, Yorkshire played its part in a tournament we will never forget.

ICC World Cup 2019
England v. Sri Lanka

Played at Headingley, Leeds, on June 21, 2019

Sri Lanka won by 20 runs

Toss won by Sri Lanka — Sri Lanka 2 points, England 0 points

SRI LANKA

* F D M Karunaratne, c Buttler b Archer	....	1
§ M D K J Perera, c Ali b Woakes	....	2
W I A Fernando, c Rashid b Wood	....	49
B K G Mendis, c Morgan b Rashid	....	46
A D Mathews, not out	....	85
B M A J Mendis, c and b Rashid	....	0
D M de Silva, c Root b Archer	....	29
N L T C Perera, c Rashid b Archer	....	2
I Udana, c Root b Wood	....	6
S L Malinga, b Wood	....	1
N Pradeep, not out	....	1
Extras lb 4, w 6	....	10
Total (9 wkts, 50 overs)	....	232

FoW: 1-3 (Karunaratne), 2-3 (M D K J Perera), 3-62 (Fernando), 4-133 (B K G Mendis), 5-133 (B M A J Mendis), 6-190 (de Silva), 7-200 (N L T C Perera), 8-209 (Udana), 9-220 (Malinga)

	O	M	R	W
Woakes	5	0	22	1
Archer	10	2	52	3
Wood	8	0	40	3
Stokes	5	0	16	0
Ali	10	0	40	0
Rashid	10	0	45	2
Root	2	0	13	0

ENGLAND

J M Vince, c B K G Mendis b Malinga	....	14
J M Bairstow, lbw b Malinga	....	0
J E Root, c M D K J Perera b Malinga	....	57
* E J G Morgan, c and b Udana	....	21
B A Stokes, not out	....	82
§ J C Buttler, lbw b Malinga	....	10
M M Ali, c Udana b de Silva	....	16
C R Woakes, c M D K J Perera b de Silva	....	2
A U Rashid, c M D K J Perera b de Silva	....	1
J C Archer, c N L T C Perera b Udana	....	3
M A Wood, c M D K J Perera b Pradeep	....	0
Extras lb 1, w 5	....	6
Total (47 overs)	....	212

FoW: 1-1 (Bairstow), 2-26 (Vince), 3-73 (Morgan), 4-127 (Root), 5-144 (Buttler), 6-170 (Ali), 7-176 (Woakes), 8-178 (Rashid), 9-186 (Archer), 10-212 (Wood)

	O	M	R	W
Malinga	10	1	43	4
Pradeep	10	1	38	1
de Silva	8	0	32	3
N L T C Perera	8	0	34	0
Udana	8	0	41	2
B M A J Mendis	3	0	23	0

Man of the Match: S L Malinga

Umpires: M Erasmus and P Wilson — Scorers: J T Potter and P J Rogers
Third: B N J Oxenford — Fourth: P R Reiffel — Match Referee: R B Richardson

SMASH AND GRAB: Joe Root, whose 57 against Sri Lanka was second only to Ben Stokes's 82 as England lost by 20 runs. Joe has scored more runs for England in World Cup matches than any other Yorkshireman with 758, and his tally of 20 World Cup catches is an England record way ahead of his nearest rival, Paul Collingwood, of Durham, with 13. Only Ricky Ponting, of Australia, has more on 28.

ONE OF OUR OWN: Adil Rashid, who was one of three Yorkshire players in England's World Cup winning team alongside Joe Root and Jonny Bairstow. The leg-spinning all-rounder, with 2-45 from 10 overs, came so near to performing a World Cup hat-trick on his home ground against Sri Lanka. Adil and Test captain Root shared five catches.

MAN OF THE MOMENT: Jofra Archer, who later bowled England to glory with a stunning Super Over in the final against New Zealand at Lord's, in action during the group-stage loss to Sri Lanka. **BELOW:** Spectators embrace as Pakistan scrape home against Afghanistan.

EYES ON THE PRIZE: A fine study of Virat Kohli, one of the world's most outstanding batsmen and captain of the much-fancied India. They won their Yorkshire fixture against Sri Lanka handsomely, but they were to be knocked out in the semi-finals by New Zealand.

ALL A BLUR FOR AUSTRALIA: Josh Hazlewood runs in during the fourth and final day of the Third Specsavers *Ashes* Test. The New South Welshman claimed nine wickets in the match, including first-innings figures of 5-30 as England were bowled out for 67.

ASHES EPIC AT EMERALD HEADINGLEY

BIRDSEYE VIEW: The *Ashes* arena seen from the back of the top tier of the Emerald Stand, which was opened with the 2019 summer feast of international cricket very much in mind.

TALKING OF FEASTS: The Emerald Suite is set for the opening *hors d'oeuvre*. One of the stunning features of the new stand, it sits in the middle of the cricket and rugby pitches with fantastic views of both.

FIVE-FOR: Yorkshire's Jonny Bairstow, who was to snare four scalps in Australia's first innings and another in the second.

REMEMBER ME? Left-arm spinner Jack Leach, without whom the Ben Stokes heroics of the last day would not have been possible.

MIRACLE OF BEN STOKES: One of eight sixes smashed by the Herculean all-rounder during one of the greatest innings ever played. England were 1-0 down before the Third Test, and were then bowled out for 67 in the first innings. They were reduced to 286-9 chasing 359, but Stokes, with 135 not out, shared an unbroken stand of 76 with last-man Jack Leach to square the series with a remarkable victory.

Shock of the tournament

Emerald Headingley's first World Cup fixture in 20 years did not disappoint as a superb bowling performance ensured that Sri Lanka produced the shock of the tournament so far by strangling title favourites England in an old-school ODI.

Angelo Mathews struggled for timing during a 115-ball 86 not out, the top score after the visitors had elected to bat. Avishka Fernando's swashbuckling 49 off 39 balls from No.3 was the feature innings, having only just come into the side.

BEN STOKES: One of four sixes

England, chasing 233, then fell 21 short at 212 all out as Lasith Malinga rolled back the years with four wickets and part-time off-spinner Dhananjaya de Silva struck three times in nine balls to secure only a second win in six.

Adil Rashid, with 2-45 from 10 overs, was on a hat-trick on his home ground, while he and Joe Root shared five catches.

Sri Lanka were 3-2 and never looked like they had enough after three wickets apiece for pace duo Jofra Archer and Mark Wood. Rashid removed the Mendises, Kusal and Jeevan.

A win for England would have been their fifth in six group matches, and would have put them on the verge of the semi-finals. Instead, they were undone by veteran fast bowler Malinga, who removed Jonny Bairstow and Root on the way to 4-43.

Bairstow was trapped lbw in the first over for his second golden duck of the tournament, while Root was caught behind down the legside off Malinga for 57, having reached 50 for the fifth time in six innings, including two centuries.

England were in charge at 170-5 in the 39th over, with Moeen Ali hitting Dhananjaya for six, only to try needlessly to repeat the dose next ball and fall caught at long-off.

Wickets fell all too regularly, but Ben Stokes — four sixes in an unbeaten 82 — raised hopes with some late hitting from 186-9.

Saturday, June 29. Pakistan (230-7) beat
Afghanistan (227-9) by three wickets.

Pakistan survived a scare to beat the competition's minnows as they chased down a challenging target with only two balls to spare to maintain their slim hopes of semi-final qualification, something which did not eventuate. Pakistan fell to 81-3 and 156-6 in front of a fervent sellout crowd. With 48 off six overs needed Afghanistan were in the hunt, only for captain and seamer Gulbadin Naib to concede 18 off the 46th over to all but decide the contest, with Imad Wasim on the way to an unbeaten 49. Earlier, precocious 19-year-old quick Shaheen Shah Afridi took 4-47 for Pakistan.

Thursday July 4. West Indies (311-6) beat
Afghanistan (288) by 23 runs.

West Indies celebrated Chris Gayle's final World Cup appearance by ending a run of five successive defeats, at least closing a disappointing campaign on a high against an Afghanistan side who finished bottom with nine straight losses. Shai Hope's measured 77 underpinned a big total to which Gayle contributed seven. Yorkshire fans were given a glimpse of Nicholas Pooran, the dynamic left-hander who would soon join them for the early stages of the Vitality Blast. In a spirited reply wicketkeeper-batsman Ikram Alikhil hit 86, the highest World Cup score by an 18-year-old, eclipsing a record once set by Sachin Tendulkar.

Saturday July 6. India (265-3) beat
Sri Lanka (264-7) by seven wickets.

India secured top spot in the group with a routine win, and Rohit Sharma became the first man to score five centuries in a single World Cup. It was one of three centuries in the match. Former Sri Lanka captain Angelo Mathews hit 113 to recover his side from 55-4. Rohit, 103, then put on 189 for the first wicket with K L Rahul, who top-scored with 111. It was the highest opening stand in the competition, and it set up a win achieved with 6.3 overs to spare.

ICC World Cup 2019
Pakistan v. Afghanistan

Played at Headingley, Leeds, on June 29, 2019

Pakistan won by 3 wickets

Toss won by Afghanistan   Pakistan 2 points, Afghanistan 0 points

AFGHANISTAN

Rahmat Shah, c Babar Azam b Imad Wasim	. . . .	35
* Gulbadin Naib, c Sarfaraz b Shaheen Afridi	. . . . . .	15
Hashmatullah Shahidi, c Imad Wasim b Shaheen Afridi		0
§ Ikram Alikhil, c M Hafeez b Imad Wasim	. . . .	24
Asghar Afghan, b Shadab Khan	. . . .	42
Mohammad Nabi, c M Amir b Wahab Riaz	. . . .	16
Najibullah Zadran, b Shaheen Afridi	. . . .	42
Samiullah Shinwari, not out	. . . .	19
Rashid Khan, c Fakhar Zaman b Shaheen Afridi	. . . . .	8
Hamid Hassan, b Wahab Riaz	. . . .	1
Mujeeb ur Rahman, not out	. . . .	7
Extras lb 8, w 10		18
Total (9 wkts, 50 overs)	. . . .	227

FoW: 1-27 (Gulbadin Naib), 2-27 (Hashmatullah Shahidi), 3-57 (Rahmat Shah), 4-121 (Asghar Afghan), 5-125 (Ikram Alikhil), 6-167 (Mohammad Nabi), 7-202 (Najibullah Zadran), 8-210 (Rashid Khan), 9-219 Hamid Hassan

	O	M	R	W
Imad Wasim	10	0	48	2
Mohammad Amir	10	1	41	0
Shaheen Afridi	10	0	47	4
Mohammad Hafeez	2	0	10	0
Wahab Riaz	8	0	29	2
Shadab Khan	10	0	44	1

PAKISTAN

Fakhar Zaman, lbw b Mujeeb ur Rahman	. . . .	0
Imad ul Haq, st Ikram Alikhil b M Nabi	. . . .	36
Babar Azam, b M Nabi	. . . .	45
Mohammad Hafeez, c H Shahidi b Mujeeb ur Rahman		19
Haris Sohail, lbw b Rashid Khan	. . . .	27
§ * Sarfaraz Ahmed, run out (N Zadran/Ikram Alikhil)		18
Imad Wasim, not out	. . . .	49
Shadab Khan, run out (G Naib/Ikram Alikhil)	. . . .	11
Wahab Riaz, not out	. . . .	15
Shaheen Afridi		
Mohammad Amir Did not bat		
Extras b 1, lb 4, w 5	. . . .	10
Total (7 wkts, 49.4 overs)	. . . .	230

FoW: 1-0 (Fakhar Zaman), 2-72 (Imam ul Haq), 3-81 (Babar Azam), 4-121 (Mohammad Hafeez), 5-142 (Haris Sohail), 6-156 (Sarfaraz Ahmed), 7-206 (Shahid Khan)

	O	M	R	W
Mujeeb ur Rahman	10	1	34	2
Hamid Hassan	2	0	13	0
Gulbadin Naib	9.4	0	73	0
Mohammad Nabi	10	0	23	2
Rashid Khan	10	0	50	1
Samiullah Shinwari	8	0	32	0

Man of the Match: Imad Wasim

Umpires: N J Llong and P Wilson   Scorers: J T Potter and J R Virr
Third: C B Gaffaney   Fourth: I J Gould   Match Referee: B C Broad

ICC World Cup 2019
Afghanistan v. West Indies

Played at Headingley, Leeds, on July 4, 2019

West Indies won by 23 runs

Toss won by West Indies   West Indies 2 points, Afghanistan 0 points

WEST INDIES

C H Gayle, c Ikram Alikhil b Dawlat Zadran		7
E Lewis, c M Nabi b Rashid Khan		58
§ S D Hope, c Rashid Khan b M Nabi		77
S O Hetmyer, c sub (Noor Ali Zadran) b Dawlat Zadran		39
N Pooran, run out (I Alikhil/S Shirzad)		58
* J O Holder, c Dawlat Zadran b S Shirzad		45
C R Brathwaite, not out		14
F A Allen, not out		0
K A J Roach		
S S Cottrell		
O Thomas	Did not bat	
Extras lb 4, w 9		13
Total (6 wkts, 50 overs)		311

FoW: 1-21 (Gayle), 2-109 (Lewis), 3-174 (Hetmyer), 4-192 (Hope), 5-297 (Pooran), 6-297 (Holder).

	O	M	R	W
Mujeeb ur Rahman	10	0	52	0
Dawlat Zadran	9	1	73	2
Sayed Shirzad	8	0	56	1
Gulbadin Naib	3	0	18	0
Mohammad Nabi	10	0	56	1
Rashid Khan	10	0	52	1

AFGHANISTAN

* Gulbadin Naib, c Lewis b Roach		5
Rahmat Shah, c Gayle b Brathwaite		62
§ Ikram Alikhil, lbw b Gayle		86
Najibullah Zadran, run out (Hetmyer/Brathwaite)		31
Asghar Afghan, c Holder b Brathwaite		40
Mohammad Nabi, c Allen b Roach		2
Samiullah Shinwari, c Hetmyer b Roach		6
Rashid Khan, c Holder b Brathwaite		9
Dawlat Zadran, c Cottrell b Brathwaite		1
Sayed Shirzad, c Allen b Thomas		25
Mujeeb ur Rahman, not out		7
Extras lb 2, w 10, nb 2		14
Total (50 overs)		288

FoW: 1-5 (Gulbadin Naib), 2-138 (Rahmat Shah), 3-189 (Ikram Alikhil), 4-194 (Najibullah Zadran), 5-201 (Mohammad Nabi), 6-227 (Samiullah Shinwari), 7-244 (Asghar Afghan), 8-255 (Dawlat Zadran), 9-255 (Rashid Khan), 10-288 (Sayed Shirzad).

	O	M	R	W
Cottrell	7	0	43	0
Roach	10	2	37	3
Thomas	7	0	43	1
Holder	8	0	46	0
Allen	3	0	26	0
Brathwaite	9	0	63	4
Gayle	6	0	28	1

Man of the Match: S D Hope

Umpires: C B Gaffaney and N J Llong   Scorers: J T Potter and J R Virr
Third: I J Gould   Fourth: P Wilson   Match Referee: B C Broad

ICC World Cup 2019
Sri Lanka v. India

Played at Headingley, Leeds, on July 6, 2019

India won by 7 wickets

Toss won by Sri Lanka   India 2 points, Sri Lanka 0 points

SRI LANKA

* F D M Karunaratne, c Dhoni b Bumrah		10
§ M D K J Perera, c Dhoni b Bumrah		18
W I A Fernando, c Dhoni b Pandya		20
B K G Mendis, st Dhoni b Jadeja		3
A D Mathews, c Sharma b Bumrah		113
H D R L Thirimanne, c Jadeja b Yadav		53
D M de Silva, not out		29
N L T C Perera, Pandya b Kumar		2
I Udana, not out		1
S L Malinga		
C A K Rajitha	Did not bat	
Extras b 4, lb 2, w 8, nb 1		15
Total (7 wkts, 50 overs)		264

FoW: 1-17 (Karunaratne), 2-40 (M D K J Perera), 3-53 (Mendis), 4-55 (Fernando), 5-179 (Thirimanne), 6-253 (Mathews), 7-260 (N L T C Perera).

	O	M	R	W
Kumar	10	0	73	1
Bumrah	10	2	37	3
Pandya	10	0	50	1
Jadeja	10	0	40	1
Yadav	10	0	58	1

INDIA

K L Rahul, c M D K J Perera b Malinga		111
R G Sharma, c Mathews b Rajitha		103
* V Kohli, not out		34
R R Pant, lbw b Udana		4
H H Pandya, not out		7
§ M S Dhoni		
K D Karthik		
R A Jadeja	Did not bat	
B Kumar		
K Yadav		
J J Bumrah		
Extras lb 1, w 5		6
Total (3 wkts, 43.3 overs)		265

FoW: 1-189 (Sharma), 2-244 (Rahul), 3-253 (Pant).

	O	M	R	W
Malinga	10	1	82	1
Rajitha	8	0	47	1
Udana	9.3	0	50	1
N L T C Perera	10	0	34	0
de Silva	6	0	51	0

Man of the Match: R G Sharma

Umpires: I J Gould and P Wilson   Scorers: J T Potter and J R Virr

Third: C B Gaffaney   Fourth: N J Llong   Match Referee: B C Broad

STOKES AND LEACH UNITE A RIVEN ENGLAND

By Paul Edwards

It was the Sunday afternoon when the Western Terrace danced and sang; the afternoon when those enjoying hospitality in the Emerald Stand put down their wine glasses and watched in euphoric disbelief; the afternoon when journalists with hundreds of Tests on their clocks put their hands to their heads in the Press Box and wondered what in hell they could write about this. But who could blame them? It was the afternoon when no one really had a clue what was going off out there.

Except, of course, for this ginger bloke, who seemed to have everything under perfect control; who batted as if he had been placed on earth precisely for such occasions as this; who detached himself from the growing mass fervour and calmly chatted with his bespectacled partner. And when all was done Ben Stokes at Headingley was silently placed alongside Roger Federer at Wimbledon and Tiger Woods at Augusta among those sportsmen who regard a sport's great theatre as their proper workplace.

Mortals claimed sanctuary in the facts. They discovered that Stokes and Jack Leach had added 76 runs for England's last wicket in precisely an hour and their stand was the second-highest for the 10th wicket to win a Test Match in the fourth innings. Stokes had hit seven sixes in the partnership to finish unbeaten on 135. Five of those blows came straight from the Chester-le-Street academy but two, a switch-hit and a ramp, had been refined in Rajasthan.

If Sunday's cricket had illustrated the precious glory of five-day cricket it had also shown the extent of cross-fertilisation between the game's longest and shortest formats. Leach, without whom none of it would have been possible, had kept out 17 balls, scoring a single off the last of them, a nudge followed by a scamper down the pitch which he reprised in fading light late on Sunday evening.

He had also hurtled madly down the wicket on another occasion in the stand with Stokes and would have been run out by yards had Nathan Lyon not dropped Pat Cummins's throw. No matter. By the end of the day Somerset's No.11 was no longer a folk-hero only in the West Country; the cloth with which he cleaned his glasses had its own Twitter account.

All smiles: England captain Joe Root and Australia's Tim Paine share a joke before the toss. The tourists came to the Test 1-0 up, having won at Edgbaston and drawn at Lord's. This was to be a week neither man would ever forget.

But amid that eruption of joy on Sunday afternoon and the delighted realisation that yet another *Ashes* Test at Emerald Headingley had been an occasion to treasure it was easy to forget the previous three days of the game and the contribution they had made to the type of contest American playwright David Mamet might have had in mind when he talked about a "correctly structured drama".

On Thursday, in lowering gloom and after early rain, Jofra Archer had taken 6-45 to bowl out Australia for 179. David Warner's 61 was to be his only half-century of the series and Stokes had been the weak link in England's attack, conceding 45 runs in his nine overs.

On Friday the tourists' total had been made to seem formidable when England were dismissed for 67 in 27.5 overs and Stokes's shot to get out had been the worst of a bad bunch. It seemed of little moment, some thought, that he had chosen the way of the warrior and had bowled 16 consecutive overs that evening. Australia's advantage was 283 runs at close of play, and the following morning's headline writers came in off their long runs.

On Saturday afternoon another full house watched England begin their pursuit of 359 to level the series. Joe Root, batting with immense discipline, finished the day unbeaten on 75. Stokes, displaying comparable self-restraint, had faced 50 balls and was two not out. Rarely has a cricketer "batted for tomorrow" to greater effect. At the same time hardly anyone was thinking quite that way on Saturday evening, although Vic Marks was so prescient in Sunday's *Observer* that one wondered exactly what they put in the scrumpy down in Somerset. "Nagging away at the back of the mind is the thought, 'This is Headingley'", he wrote. "Extraordinary things happen here in the fourth innings..."

The super-optimists might have added that on two occasions in less than 40 years those things had happened to Australia's cricketers. Such thoughts may not have impinged on Stokes, who later admitted that his dinner on Saturday had consisted of a "knock-off Nando's" followed by two raisin-and-biscuit Yorkie bars.

If only it had been cow pie and spinach.

Sunday morning is warm and glorious. Buoyed by the possibility of an England victory, spectators fill the stands early and the anthems are roared out with passion. But Root, the putative hero, goes early, well caught at slip by Warner off Lyon. Something else is happening, though, and it surprises even those who have watched many Headingley Tests. The crowd is cheering each run England score, even the leg-byes. At no time in the day's cricket will that cauldron be removed from the heat.

Jonny Bairstow bats brightly but makes only 36 before edging Josh Hazlewood to Marnus Labuschagne. To the delight of the large band of gloriously good-natured Australian supporters under the scoreboard the *Ashes* slip away from England as wickets are squandered. In mid-afternoon Leach marches out to bat. Ben Stokes is on 61, and his life is about to change for ever.

And that is where this report could end, except that this very great Test Match had an afterlife. It began most obviously in the Press conferences, where Tim Paine was both courteous and appreciative in defeat. Then Root admitted that he was unable to explain his side's victory in the fourth innings and unwilling to excuse their batting in the first.

That evening the post-match discussions continued in even more animated style in The Skyrack and The Original Oak on Headingley Lane. Some 200 miles away in London sports editors were redrawing most of their pages and experiencing that special frisson of excitement that comes to all journalists when there is a tale to tell.

The Times even chose to mock its Saturday headline:

"We may have given the impression in Saturday's *Times* that Joe Root's England side had 'No fight, no idea, no hope' after they were bowled out for a dismal 67 in their first innings. We now recognise that they are among the finest battling sides this country has ever produced. We are happy to make this clear."

But as the days passed it became plain that this had been something of a people's triumph, and one imagines Stokes was pleased by that. Stories came in of people stopping car journeys for hours to ensure that they could listen to the cricket; of the bloke who stole away from a wedding in Galway to find out the score (fortunately he was not the bridegroom).

At Nerja on the Costa del Sol Lancashire's former skipper, Warren Hegg, was enjoying the final afternoon of his holiday and listening to the commentary from Headingley some 1,600 miles away.

By the time England's victory was secure a group of mystified German tourists who had watched Hegg's reaction to events reached the conclusion that if this was how the British behaved, it really was time their country left the European Union.

A similar thread was picked up by the *Daily Telegraph* cartoonist Blower two days after the game.

As Britain struggled to manage its departure from the EU he drew a smiling Stokes leaving the negotiating table and approaching Boris Johnson with a "Brexit Deal" in his hand.

JONNY BAIRSTOW
Bright second-innings 36

"And they also agreed to pay you the £39 billion," read the cricketer's speech balloon.

Most beguilingly of all, perhaps, there was the story of the fellow struggling to score the Bank of England's match at Hyde Heath where Andy Stokes was making a rather fine 80 while his namesake was winning the Headingley Test.

And so it went on. When rain interrupted the first day of the Test at Emirates Old Trafford BBC TMS devoted something like 90 minutes to listeners' tales of where they had been and what they had been doing during the climax to that game in Leeds. The "sense of public joy", to borrow Tony Harrison's phrase, seemed inexhaustible, and in those hot, late August days it was not absurd to think that cricket had managed to unite a riven nation.

As for Stokes and Leach, those memories will stay with them for far longer than they play the game. And as for the children who watched that last hour they now have their own Headingley Test to cherish and something to which they can aspire. Maybe that is the best thing about the whole business.

Third Specsavers Ashes Test Match
England v. Australia

Played at Emerald Headingley, Leeds, on August 22, 23, 24 and 25, 2019

England won by 1 wicket at 4.17pm on the Fourth Day

Toss won by England

Close of play: First Day, Australia 179 all out; Second Day, Australia 171-6 (Labuschagne 53*, Pattinson 2*); Third Day, England 75-2 (Root 75*, Stokes 2*)

AUSTRALIA	First Innings		Second Innings	
D A Warner, c Bairstow b Archer		61	(2) lbw b Broad	0
M S Harris, c Bairstow b Archer		8	(1) b Leach	19
U T Khawaja, c Bairstow b Broad		8	c Roy b Woakes	23
M Labuschagne, lbw b Stokes		74	run out (Denly/Bairstow)	80
T M Head, b Broad		0	b Stokes	25
M S Wade, b Archer		0	c Bairstow b Stokes	33
* § T D Paine, lbw b Woakes		11	c Denly b Broad	0
J L Pattinson, c Root b Archer		2	c Root b Archer	20
P J Cummins, c Bairstow b Archer		0	c Burns b Archer	6
N M Lyon, lbw b Archer		1	b Archer	9
J E Hazlewood, not out		0	not out	4
Extras b 4, lb 2, w 5, nb2		13	Extras b 5, lb 13, w 2, nb 7	27
Total		179	Total	246

FoW: 1-12 (Harris), 2-25 (Khawaja), 3-136 (Warner), 4-138 (Head), 5-139 (Wade), 6-162
1st (Paine), 7-173 (Pattinson), 8-177 (Cummins), 9-177 (Labuschagne), 10-179 (Lyon)

FoW: 1-10 (Warner), 2-36 (Harris), 3-52 (Khawaja), 4-97 (Head), 5-163 (Wade), 6-164
2nd (Paine), 7-215 (Pattinson), 8-226 (Cummins), 9-237 (Labuschagne), 10-246 (Lyon)

	O	M	R	W		O	M	R	W
Broad	14	4	32	2	Archer $	14	2	40	2
Archer	17.1	3	45	6	Broad	16	2	52	2
Woakes	12	4	51	1	Woakes	10	1	34	1
Stokes	9	0	45	1	Leach	11	0	46	1
					Stokes $	24.2	7	56	3

$ Archer unable to complete his 9th over:
It was finished by Stokes

ENGLAND	First Innings		Second Innings	
R J Burns, c Paine b Cummins		9	b Warner b Hazlewood	7
J J Roy, c Warner b Hazlewood		9	b Cummins	8
* J E Root, c Warner b Hazlewood		0	c Warner b Lyon	77
J L Denly, c Paine b Pattinson		12	c Paine b Hazlewood	50
B A Stokes, c Warner b Pattinson		8	not out	135
§ J M Bairstow, c Warner b Hazlewood		4	c Labuschagne b Hazlewood	36
J C Buttler, c Khawaja b Hazlewood		5	run out (Head)	1
C R Woakes, c Paine b Cummins		5	c Wade b Hazlewood	1
J C Archer, c Paine b Cummins		7	c Head b Lyon	15
S C J Broad, not out		4	lbw b Pattinson	0
M J Leach, b Hazlewood		0	not out	1
Extras lb 3		3	Extras b 5, lb 15, w 10, nb 1	31
Total		67	Total (9 wkts)	362

FoW: 1-10 (Roy), 2-10 (Root), 3-20 (Burns), 4-34 (Stokes), 5-45 (Denly),
1st 6-45 (Bairstow), 7-54 (Woakes), 8-56 (Buttler), 9-66 (Archer), 10-67 (Leach)

FoW: 1-15 (Burns), 2-15 (Roy), 3-141 (Denly), 4-159 (Root), 5-245 (Bairstow),
2nd 6-253 (Buttler), 7-261 (Woakes), 8-286 (Archer), 9-286 (Broad)

	O	M	R	W		O	M	R	W
Cummins	9	4	23	3	Cummins	24.4	5	80	1
Hazlewood	12.5	4	30	5	Hazlewood	31	11	85	4
Lyon	1	0	2	0	Lyon	39	5	114	2
Pattinson	5	2	9	2	Pattinson	25	9	47	1
					Labuschagne	6	0	16	0

Man of the Match: B A Stokes

Umpires: C B Gaffaney and J S Wilson   Scorers: J T Potter and J R Virr

Third: H D P K Dharmasena   Fourth: R T Robinson   Match Referee: J Srinath

DID All-ROUND STAR ECLIPSE
THE LEGENDS OF 1981?

By David Warner

Emerald Headingley's reputation for hosting some of the greatest Test Matches ever played was further enhanced last summer with England's one-wicket win over Australia when Ben Stokes firmly set the seal on his superstar status.

Many felt that his unbeaten 135 and heart-stopping last-wicket stand of 74 with Jack Leach earned him the accolade of achieving England's greatest solo performance either at Leeds or anywhere else.

It is difficult to present a strong case against that, but not impossible, particularly if you are old enough to remember with clarity the *Ashes* Test at Headingley 38 years earlier when England triumphed by 18 runs after being forced to follow-on — and at one stage tottering on 135-7, still 92 runs in arrears.

The thousands watching last year's epic who were too young to recall the 1981 battle would naturally assume that Stokes's heroics were beyond compare, but older heads could point out gently that in the first confrontation England had not just one genuine hero, but two in Ian Botham and the late Bob Willis.

There were similarities in both games in that England's first innings batting was dire, Mike Brearley's team being bungled out for 111 in reply to 401-9 declared, and Joe Root's side suffering even greater embarrassment — skittled for 67 following Australia's modest 179.

But even at the time of the follow-on 290 runs behind Botham had already made an impression with ball and then bat. Entering the match stripped of the captaincy, he claimed a wicket with his third delivery and ended with 6-95 — and then top-scored with 50 in England's anaemic reply. Willis so far had done nothing to suggest that he would eventually stake claim to an equal share in Botham's glory. He went wicketless in the first innings at a cost of 72 runs in 30 overs.

Famously, at 135-7 following on, the bookies were offering odds of 500-1 against an England win — and even 1,000-1 would not have appeared generous.

Now Botham began to make his move, slowly at first as Graham Dilley dominated the early part of the eighth-wicket stand of 117 in 80 minutes, peppering the cover boundary in a career-best 56.

Botham, having hosted a barbecue for his teammates the previous night, soon realised that the gods were looking down on him and that he could do no wrong. By the time last man Willis succumbed early on the final morning Botham had blasted an unbeaten 149. After Dilley's departure Yorkshire's Chris Old weighed in with a gallant 29 out of 67 for the ninth wicket. Now in full flow, Botham slashed to third man to bring him his century, his last 64 runs coming from 17 shots with 14 fours, a six and two singles. And Twenty20 cricket in those days was not even a glimmer in the eyes of the ECB!

Although Australia's bowling had gone to pieces during the Botham onslaught they were still clear favourites to make the 130 they needed to win, and at 56-1 they seemed to be home and dry.

Suddenly, just before lunch, Willis wrenched the spotlight off Botham and on to himself as Brearley brought him on at the Kirkstall Lane End to bowl down the hill. Charging in with a demonic look in his eye and aware of nothing but the opponent 22 yards down the pitch he captured three for none in 11 balls.

From then on it seemed destined that England could do nothing other than win. Old flattened Allan Border's stumps, and in the next over Willis had John Dyson caught behind mistiming a hook. Rodney Marsh threatened a revival until he, too, attempted to hook Willis and fell to a marvellously judged catch just inside the rope by Dilley.

It became 76-8 in the same over as Geoff Lawson edged to Bob Taylor to give the England and Derbyshire wicketkeeper a world record, his 1,271 first-class dismissals overtaking J T Murray's haul.

Ray Bright and Dennis Lillee gave the England fans palpitations with a last-gasp fightback, but Willis summoned up an untapped reserve of strength to wipe out both of them, the crowd giving out a mighty roar and swarming on to the ground.

So England's greatest moment remained unquestioned and unchallenged until Stokes immortalised himself last summer. Let us compromise and say that England 1981 began to turn the screw much earlier than England 2019, but that the Stokes-Leach unbroken match-winning last wicket stand of 76 was the biggest heart-stopper of all.

The brute strength and sheer genius of Stokes and the unwavering nerve of Leach broke Australia. A dropped catch, a simple run-out fluffed, sixes brushing outstretched fingers, an absurd lbw review leaving them without another chance when a far better appeal was rejected. The thousands who packed Headingley to witness these champagne moments were lucky indeed; those among them who were also at Headingley in 1981 were more fortunate still.

ENTER BATSMAN WITH MORE THAN 10,000 IN THE TANK

By Graham Hardcastle

When, last September, Andrew Gale reflected on the season just gone and looked ahead to 2020 he spoke of the need for quality batting reinforcements, albeit cautiously.

"Experienced batters with 10,000 first-class runs don't just fall off trees," he said.

Thankfully, six or seven weeks later England batsman Dawid Malan had been signed on a four-year contract. Malan, 32, with 15 Test caps and a current England T20 player, arrived from Middlesex with a little over 11,000 to his name.

"I've had 13 happy and suc-

DAWID MALAN: Joining the great

cessful seasons with Middlesex," he said. "However, this feels like the right time to embrace a new challenge, and I'm excited by the prospect of joining one of the great county clubs."

Yorkshire's batting stocks had already been diminished by homegrown Championship winner Jack Leaning's departure to Kent on a three-year deal. Leaning played a significant part in back-to-back titles in 2014 and 2015, ironically prevented from winning three in a row by Malan and Middlesex on that famous final day at Lord's in 2016.

Leaning, Bristol-born but York-raised, scored 1,387 Championship runs from 25 appearances in 2014 and 2015, including three hundreds. As a 21-year-old in that second season he won a number of young-player-of-the-year awards, including becoming the 12th Yorkshireman to win the Cricket Writers' Club's award, joining a list including Fred Trueman, Sir Geoffrey Boycott and Joe Root.

He has been unable to build on that success, with first-team appearances far less frequent in most recent seasons: "Looking back, the easiest two years of my career have been the first two," he said. "That's a bit strange for a young lad coming into a professional environment, but it's so easy to play without fear.

"It gets tougher from then, because teams work you out. It's been a challenge, and I'd have liked to have played more. But now I feel like I'm getting to the stage where there's not really a scenario I haven't been in, whether it's playing in front of 20,000 at Old Trafford or playing a Championship game to win a title. I'll take nothing but fond memories away from Yorkshire. It's my childhood club. I've played here since I was 10."

Another from the York area who played his part in those Championship successes, Karl Carver, was one of three players released alongside Bilal Anjam and Matthew Taylor, neither of whom had made a first-team appearance. Left-arm spinner Carver debuted in 2014 and played five Championship matches in all, one each in 2014 and 2015. Across all three formats he made 30 competitive first-team appearances.

Fast bowler Josh Shaw, who took 14 wickets in 13 first-team appearances, including eight first-class outings between 2016 and 2019, left Headingley to join Gloucestershire, where he had enjoyed a number of loan spells. The bustling seamer will return to his home county immediately in 2020 — the two counties playing out the opening Championship fixture of the season.

Malan was Yorkshire's only domestic recruit ahead of the new season, though overseas signings included the return of powerful West Indian wicketkeeper-batsman Nicholas Pooran for the Vitality Blast. Pooran played three times last season. but is inked in for a longer stay this year.

The return of South African Test spinner Keshav Maharaj, albeit only for a brief early-season spell of Championship cricket, is a huge boost. The left-armer claimed 38 wickets in an exceptional five-game spell last summer. He will hopefully lay the platform for Indian off-spinner Ravichandran Ashwin to build on. One of the world's best spin bowlers, 33-year-old Ashwin, who has previously played for Worcestershire and Nottinghamshire, is closing in on 400 Test wickets.

KARL CARVER
FIRST-CLASS MATCHES FOR YORKSHIRE
BATTING AND FIELDING

Seasons	M	I	NO	Runs	HS	Avge	100s	50s	Ct
2014-18	8	13	6	108	20	15.42	0	0	4

BOWLING

Seasons	Matches	Overs	Mdns	Runs	Wkts	Avge	Best	5wI	10wM
2014-18	8	157.4	44	543	18	30.16	4-106	0	0

LIST A CRICKET FOR YORKSHIRE
BATTING AND FIELDING

Seasons	M	I	NO	Runs	HS	Avge	100s	50s	Ct
2015-18	15	4	4	52	35*	—	0	0	2

Seasons	Matches	Overs	Mdns	Runs	Wkts	Avge	Best	4wI
2015-18	15	81	2	440	14	31.42	3- 5	0

TWENTY20 CRICKET FOR YORKSHIRE
BATTING AND FIELDING

Seasons	M	I	NO	Runs	HS	Avge	100s	50s	Ct
2015-18	10	2	1	2	2	2.00	0	0	5

BOWLING

Seasons	Matches	Overs	Mdns	Runs	Wkts	Avge	Best	4wI
2015-18	10	22	0	208	8	26.00	3-40	0

JACK ANDREW LEANING

FIRST-CLASS MATCHES FOR YORKSHIRE
BATTING AND FIELDING

Seasons	M	I	NO	Runs	HS	Avge	100s	50s	Ct
2013-19	68	108	11	2955	123	30.46	4	16	52

BOWLING

Seasons	Matches	Overs	Mdns	Runs	Wkts	Avge	Best	5wI	10wM
2013-19	68	116.4	19	455	8	56.87	2-20	0	0

LIST A CRICKET FOR YORKSHIRE
BATTING AND FIELDING

Seasons	M	I	NO	Runs	HS	Avge	100s	50s	Ct
2012-19	47	40	7	1024	131*	31.03	2	5	24

BOWLING

Seasons	Matches	Overs	Mdns	Runs	Wkts	Avge	Best	4wI
2012-19	47	38	0	204	7	29.14	5-22	1

TWENTY20 CRICKET FOR YORKSHIRE
BATTING AND FIELDING

Seasons	M	I	NO	Runs	HS	Avge	100s	50s	Ct
2013-19	52	45	11	952	64	28.00	0	2	25

BOWLING

Seasons	Matches	Overs	Mdns	Runs	Wkts	Avge	Best	4wI
2013-19	52	4	0	45	1	45.00	1-15	0

JOSH SHAW

FIRST-CLASS MATCHES FOR YORKSHIRE
BATTING AND FIELDING

Seasons	M	I	NO	Runs	HS	Avge	100s	50s	Ct
2016-19	8	11	2	144	42	16.00	0	0	1

BOWLING

Seasons	Matches	Overs	Mdns	Runs	Wkts	Avge	Best	5wI	10wM
2016-19	8	157.5	23	617	12	51.41	3-58	0	0

TWENTY20 CRICKET FOR YORKSHIRE
BATTING AND FIELDING

Seasons	M	I	NO	Runs	HS	Avge	100s	50s	Ct
2015-18	5	2	1	1	1	1.00	0	0	1

BOWLING

Seasons	Matches	Overs	Mdns	Runs	Wkts	Avge	Best	4wI
2015-18	5	13	0	138	2	69.00	2-39	0

'BOOF' TO SUPERCHARGE HEADINGLEY HUNDRED

By Graham Hardcastle

Darren Lehmann loved his time at Yorkshire — even if he admits that it left him with a dented bank balance.

The Australian earned legendary status during a seven-year spell at Emerald Headingley between 1998 and 2006, scoring 14,599 runs across all formats and winning the Championship title in 2001.

Lehmann, nicknamed "Boof", will be back in the county this year as coach of the Northern Superchargers in the ECB's new 100-ball competition.

A majestic left-hander widely regarded as the county's greatest ever overseas player, Lehmann scored 34 centuries, 84 fifties and posted a top score of 339 in his

DARREN LEHMANN
Challenged Hirst

final innings against Durham at Headingley in late 2006. It remains the second highest score in the *White Rose*'s first-class history, falling only two short of George Hirst's 341 away at Leicestershire in 1905.

"Over the eight or nine years I had an absolute ball there," he said with a smile that evoked memories of his laidback attitude which endeared him to teammates, coaches and members alike, if not the opposition bowlers he regularly toyed with.

"When I first went there they were still training in whites, and you weren't allowed to wear ear-rings. You had to be shaven every day or you got fined. I got fined every day for the first month of my contract because I had a beard and ear-rings. It was certainly an eye opener in that respect. But the people up there, they really look after you. They're salt of the earth folk who are very passionate about the game."

Lehmann's runs record included 8,871 in 88 Championship matches at 68.76. It was no surprise when he highlighted his favourite memory of his time with the county: "Winning the Championship for the first time in 30-odd years stands out above the rest. We won it against Glamorgan at Scarborough, which is a great spot."

HOLMES'S STAR SHINES
IN THE WRONG SEASON

By Anthony Bradbury

In 1920, the second season after the Great War, normality returned to first-class cricket. Championship games were again played over three days, and those matches were to be the predominant cricket of the summer with no Tests planned. The leading teams were to be Middlesex, Surrey, Lancashire and Yorkshire. All participants played a different number of games, and the Championship was decided on taking a percentage of points obtained over points possible.

Yorkshire will have been disappointed to finish fourth, having been the winners in 1919. They won 15 games out of 28, and took 81 points from a possible 120, giving them a percentage of 67.50. Champions Middlesex had a percentage of 77, and poor Derbyshire, losing 17 out of 18 games and having the other match abandoned, scored no points.

Yorkshire's amateur captain was Mr David Cecil Fowler Burton, in the second of his three years in nominal charge ahead of Wilfred Rhodes. The team usually included Percy Holmes and Herbert Sutcliffe as opening batsmen, with David Denton to follow. Denton had first played for Yorkshire in 1894, and 1920 was his last season. His 676 matches for Yorkshire were to be exceeded only by Rhodes and George Hirst, each still playing in 1920, though Hirst only returned to the side after coaching duty at Eton.

Roy Kilner was another solid batsman, in time to become a Test player. Rhodes and Abe Waddington did the bulk of the bowling, Rhodes taking 143 Championship wickets at 12.90, and Waddington, another left-armer, 137 at 16.35. Between them they bowled nearly 2,000 overs. The cautious Emmott Robinson became a fine all-rounder, and Arthur Dolphin behind the stumps was another strong presence. A newcomer, George Macaulay, made little impression. His time would come in 1921.

The star batting performer of the Yorkshire summer was Percy Holmes. He was unlucky that no Tests were being played in 1920, for he scored 2,144 runs for his county at an average of 54.97, and this year was far superior to his younger partner, Herbert Sutcliffe. When Holmes scored 302 not out for Yorkshire against Hampshire he made the highest score of the summer. At that time only J T Brown and Hirst had scored triple centuries for Yorkshire, a feat never accomplished by Sutcliffe, Len Hutton or Geoffrey Boycott.

Holmes also struck two centuries in a drawn match against Lancashire at Old Trafford — 126 and 111*. This was the first time twin centuries had been scored in a *Roses* match, and Holmes had been watched by 58,000 paying spectators.

The other Lancashire fixture was at Bradford, and here Robinson took the personal honours. Yorkshire scored 208 and Lancashire replied with 165. Yorkshire seemed to fail with only 144, and Lancashire needed 188 to win.

On the eve of the second day, they had scored 44 without loss, and at lunch on the third day needed 52 to win with six wickets in hand. Robinson, who had taken the four earlier wickets, struck again in rapid succession.

Lancashire went from 136-4 to 162-9, and Robinson had taken all five wickets with right-arm inswingers. He had now taken nine wickets in the innings. But, with only 25 still needed for a Lancashire victory, there could be no soft bowling from the other end to allow Robinson the chance of "All 10". The last man was duly stumped three runs later off Kilner. Robinson's figures were 31 overs, 15 maidens, 36 runs , nine wickets. He was never to better that analysis, but of course he was given his Yorkshire cap.

PERCY HOLMES: Superior even to Sutcliffe, and unlucky that no Tests were played.
(Photo: Mick Pope Archive)

Despite the ultimate excitement of that Lancashire match the game of the season was probably the one against Middlesex, again at Bradford, in mid-August. Both teams knew that a win or a loss was crucial to County Championship chances. Middlesex batted first, and were shot out for 105, Rhodes taking 7-53. Yorkshire were doing no better when six wickets were down for 69, but the captain, Mr Burton, and wicket keeper Dolphin, came together and put on a precious 93 runs. Dolphin's

52 was his highest score of the year.

So Yorkshire ultimately garnered 169 runs, a lead of 64. Middlesex then batted well to make 261. Yorkshire's difficult target was to be 198 — without Kilner, who had left the ground through illness.

All must have seemed lost when Yorkshire declined to 140-8 with the last available pair at the crease — Mr Rockley Wilson, back home from his teaching appointment at Winchester College, and fast bowler Waddington.

With increasing excitement at the ground they chipped away at the runs needed. When four were needed to tie the game Waddington drove a ball straight down the wicket. No fielder could have stopped a boundary, but the ball struck the opposite stumps and no run was taken. A few inches either way would have made all the difference.

Later in the over, perhaps attempting a similar shot, Waddington was bowled and Middlesex had won by four runs. A different result would have made the Championship race very tight indeed.

The Annual Report from Yorkshire CCC was in quietly satisfied mode. Four team members had been selected for the 1920/21 tour to Australia — Dolphin, Rhodes, Waddington and E R Wilson. Yorkshire Secretary Mr F C Toone was to be tour manager.

EMMOTT ROBINSON: So near to a clean sweep against the *Red Rose*
(Photo: Mick Pope Archive)

Two hundred thousand people had come through the gates in 1920, a huge increase on 1919. There were 3,100 members, considered good at that time, and the finances were in decent order. In 1921 there was to be an Australian Test at Headingley and matches against the Australians at Bradford and Sheffield.

No clouds troubled the Yorkshire horizon.

YORKSHIRE'S FIRST CLASS
HIGHLIGHTS OF 1920

Wins by an innings (8)

Yorkshire (585-3 dec) defeated Hampshire (131 and 219) by an innings and 235 runs
at Portsmouth

Derbyshire (103 and 93) lost to Yorkshire (419-6 dec) by an innings and 223 runs
at Sheffield

Worcestershire (80 and 87) lost to Yorkshire (377-5 dec) by an innings and 210 runs
at Sheffield

Yorkshire (270) defeated Northamptonshire (57 and 40) by an innings and 173 runs
at Northampton

Yorkshire (316) defeated Leicestershire (119 and 69) by an innings and 128 runs
at Hull

Worcestershire (162 and 205) lost to Yorkshire 472-3 dec) by an innings and 105 runs
at Worcester

Derbyshire (74 and 74) lost to Yorkshire (219-3 dec) by an innings and 71 runs
at Derby

Gloucestershire (60 and 114) lost to Yorkshire (229) by an innings and 55 runs
at Gloucester

Win by 10 wickets (1)

Nottinghamshire (215 and 157) lost to Yorkshire (324 and 50-0) at Leeds

Totals of 400 and over (3)

585-3 dec v. Hampshire at Portsmouth
472-3 dec v. Worcestershire at Worcester
419-6 dec v. Derbyshire at Sheffield

Opponents dismissed for under 100 (16)

40	v. Northamptonshire at Northampton	74	v. Derbyshire at Sheffield
51	v. Northamptonshire at Bradford		— 2nd innings
54	v. Warwickshire at Harrogate	80	v. Worcestershire at Sheffield
57	v. Northamptonshire at Northampton	81	v. MCC at Scarborough
60	v. Gloucestershire at Gloucester	87	v. Worcestershire at Sheffield
67	v. Northamptonshire at Bradford	91	v. Sussex at Leeds
69	v. Leicestershire at Hull	93	v. Derbyshire at Sheffield
74	v. Derbyshire at Sheffield	93	v. Warwickshire at Birmingham
	— 1st innings	99	v. Essex at Southend-on-Sea

Century Partnerships (20)

For the 1st wicket (4)

347	P Holmes and H Sutcliffe	v. Hampshire at Portsmouth
191	P Holmes and H Sutcliffe	v. Middlesex at Lord's
126	H Sutcliffe and P Holmes	v. Worcestershire at Worcester
101	H Sutcliffe and P Holmes	v. Gloucestershire at Huddersfield

For the 2nd wicket (2)

193	H Sutcliffe and D Denton	v. Worcestershire at Worcester
109	P Holmes and D Denton	v. Hampshire at Portsmouth

Century Partnerships *(Continued)*

For the 3rd wicket (4)

236	H Sutcliffe and R Kilner	v. Nottinghamshire at Nottingham
150	D Denton and R Kilner	v. Kent at Maidstone
144	P Holmes and R Kilner	v. Derbyshire at Derby
107	D Denton and R Kilner	v. MCC at Scarborough

For the 4th wicket (5)

149	R Kilner and W Rhodes	v. Derbyshire at Sheffield
133	R Kilner and W Rhodes	v. Worcestershire at Sheffield
128 *	P Holmes and W Rhodes	v. Hampshire at Portsmouth
119 *	D Denton and W Rhodes	v. Worcestershire at Worcester
114	P Holmes and W Rhodes	v. Essex at Dewsbury

For the 5th wicket (1)

126	R Kilner and E Robinson	v. Warwickshire at Birmingham

For the 6th wicket (4)

117	R Kilner and D C F Burton	v. Derbyshire at Sheffield
108	E Robinson and N Kilner	v. Warwickshire at Birmingham
116	G H Hirst and E Robinson	v. Leicestershire at Leicester
147	H Sutcliffe and E Robinson	v. Essex at Southend-on-Sea

Centuries (17)

P Holmes (7)

302 *	v. Hampshire at Portsmouth
149	v. Middlesex at Lord's
145 *	v. Northamptonshire at Northampton
141	v. Essex at Dewsbury
126	v. Lancashire at Manchester — 1st innings
111 *	v Lancashire at Manchester — 2nd innings
104	v. Derbyshire at Derby

H Sutcliffe (4)

131	v. Hampshire at Portsmouth
125 *	v. Essex at Southend-on-Sea
112	v. Worcestershire at Worcester
107	v. Nottinghamshire at Nottingham

R Kilner (3)

206 *	v. Derbyshire at Sheffield
121	v. Warwickshire at Birmingham
137	v. Nottinghamshire at Nottingham

D Denton (2)

209 *	v Worcestershire at Worcester
145	v. Kent at Maidstone

W Rhodes (1)

167	v. Nottinghamshire at Leeds

5 wickets in an innings (34)

A Waddington (13)

7 - 18	v. Northamptonshire at Northampton — 2nd innings
7 - 21	v. Warwickshire at Harrogate
7 - 25	v. Leicestershire at Hull — 2nd innings
6 - 24	v. Northamptonshire at Bradford — 1st innings
6 - 30	v. Northamptonshire at Northampton — 1st innings
6 - 64	v. Essex at Dewsbury
6 - 96	v. Kent at Maidstone
5 - 30	v. Northamptonshire at Bradford — 2nd innings
5 - 34	v. Worcestershire at Sheffield
5 - 38	v. Gloucestershire at Gloucester
5 - 49	v. Leicestershire at Hull — 1st innings
5 - 59	v. Warwickshire at Birmingham
5 - 82	v. Leicestershire at Leicester

W Rhodes (12)

8 - 39	v. Sussex at Leeds
7 - 24	v. Derbyshire at Derby
7 - 36	v Cambridge University at Cambridge
7 - 53	v. Middlesex at Bradford
6 - 28	v. Worcestershire at Sheffield
6 - 46	v. Surrey at Sheffield
6 - 73	v. Hampshire at Portsmouth — 2nd innings
5 - 16	v. Northamptonshire at Bradford
5 - 20	v. Essex at Dewsbury
5 - 47	v. Middlesex at Lord's
5 - 56	v. Hampshire at Portsmouth — 1st innings
5 -113	v. Kent at Maidstone

E R Wilson (5)

6 - 29	v. MCC at Scarborough
6 - 62	v. Middlesex at Bradford
5 - 20	v. Hampshire at Portsmouth
5 - 29	v. Surrey at The Oval
5 - 49	v. Sussex at Leeds

G G Macauley (2)

6 - 47	v. Worcestershire at Worcester
5 - 50	v. Gloucestershire at Gloucester

E Robinson (2)

9 -36	v. Lancashire at Bradford
5 -20	v. Derbyshire at Derby

10 wickets in a match (6)

W Rhodes (5)

11 - 44	(4-20 and 7-24)	v. Derbyshire at Derby
11 -129	(5-56 and 6-73)	v. Hampshire at Portsmouth
10 - 80	(3-44 and 7-36)	v. MCC at Scarborough
10 -139	(6-46 and 4-93)	v. Surrey at Sheffield
10 -151	(7-53 and 3-98)	v. Middlesex at Bradford

E R Wilson (1)

10 -92	(4-63 and 6-29)	v. MCC at Scarborough

10 wickets in a match (6)

W Rhodes (5)

11 - 44	(4-20 and 7-24)	v. Derbyshire at Derby
11 -129	(5-56 and 6-73)	v. Hampshire at Portsmouth
10 - 80	(3-44 and 7-36)	v. MCC at Scarborough
10 -139	(6-46 and 4-93)	v. Surrey at Sheffield
10 -151	(7-53 and 3-98)	v. Middlesex at Bradford

E R Wilson (1)

10 -92	(4-63 and 6-29)	v. MCC at Scarborough

3 catches in an innings (3)

A Dolphin (1)

3   v. Kent at Maidstone

P Holmes (1)

3   v. MCC at Scarborough

W Rhodes (1)

3   v. Leicestershire at Leicester

3 dismissals in an innings (2)

A Dolphin (2))

4 (3ct, 1st)   v. Kent at Maidstone
3 (0ct, 3st)   v. Hampshire at Portsmouth

5 catches in a match (1)

A Dolphin (1)

5 (2 + 3)   v. Kent at Maidstone

Debuts (5)

In **First Class cricket (4):** W D Featherby, G G Macaulay, A Judson and M Leyland
Yorkshire (1): H P Ward

Caps (1): E Robinson

World Cup jewel in Headingley crown

Emerald Headingley saw a combined attendance of 66,637 across the four World Cup matches in 2019. Three of the games were classed as ticket sellouts aside from Afghanistan v. West Indies. The variance in crowd figures comes from hospitality.

England v. Sri Lanka 17,590, Pakistan v. Afghanistan 17,734, Afghanistan v. West Indies 14,238 and Sri Lanka v. India 17,075.

100 YEARS AGO

YORKSHIRE AVERAGES 1920

ALL FIRST-CLASS MATCHES

Played 30   Won 17   Lost 6   Drawn 7

County Championship: Played 28   Won 15   Lost 6   Drawn 7

BATTING AND FIELDING *(Qualification 10 completed innings)*

Player	M.	I.	N.O.	Runs	H.S.	100s	50s	Avge	ct/st
P Holmes	30	45	6	2144	302*	7	6	54.97	28
R Kilner	28	36	2	1240	206*	3	5	36.47	19
H Sutcliffe	30	45	3	1393	131	4	7	33.16	15
D Denton	30	43	3	1324	209*	2	9	33.10	9
W Rhodes	29	39	3	983	167*	1	7	27.30	30
G H Hirst	15	20	2	449	81	0	4	24.94	10
E Robinson	30	38	9	644	74	0	4	22.20	19
A Dolphin	30	32	8	429	52	0	3	17.87	32/28
D C F Burton	28	33	3	497	65	0	3	16.56	8
N Kilner	22	25	2	325	73	0	1	14.13	10
A Waddington	28	30	8	188	26	0	0	8.54	24

Also played

Player	M.	I.	N.O.	Runs	H.S.	100s	50s	Avge	ct/st
A W White	2	2	0	60	55	0	1	30.00	0
M Leyland	1	1	0	10	10	0	0	10.00	1
E R Wilson	9	11	3	77	39*	0	0	9.62	7
G G Macaulay	10	12	5	47	15*	0	0	6.71	8
C P Whiting	2	3	0	20	14	0	0	6.66	1
E Oldroyd	2	3	0	5	4	0	0	1.66	1
H P Ward	1	1	1	1	10*	0	0	—	1
W E Blackburn	1	2	1	1	1*	0	0	—	1
W D Featherby	2	0	0	0	—	0	0	—	0
A Judson	1	0	0	0	—	0	0	—	0

BOWLING

(Qualification 10 wickets)

Player	Overs	Mdns	Runs	Wkts	Avge	Best	5wI	10wM
W Rhodes	982.4	291	2008	156	12.87	8- 39	12	5
E R Wilson	432.2	178	696	49	14.20	6- 29	5	1
A Waddington	966	258	2334	140	16.67	7- 18	13	3
G H Hirst	132.3	37	308	15	20.53	3- 19	0	0
E Robinson	589.2	194	1267	60	21.11	9- 36	2	0
G G Macaulay	171.2	31	558	24	23.25	6- 47	2	0
R Kilner	353.2	122	667	27	24.70	4- 10	0	0

Also bowled

Player	Overs	Mdns	Runs	Wkts	Avge	Best	5wI	10wM
C P Whiting	39	2	174	6	29.00	3- 31	0	0
P Holmes	1	1	0	0	—	0- 0	0	0
A Judson	1	0	5	0	—	0- 5	0	0
W D Featherby	4	1	12	0	—	0- 12	0	0
W E Blackburn	14	2	55	0	—	0- 55	0	0

SUMMER LIGHT FADES
TO A DARK WINTER

By Anthony Bradbury

Following the dire Championship season of 1969, when Yorkshire finished at a then all-time low of 13th in the Championship table, matters could surely only improve in 1970? Improvement did take place in the first-class matches, but there was to be little satisfaction in either form of one-day cricket, and the year ended on a sensational — and many thought wholly unwise — move with the unexpected dismissal of Brian Close from captaincy of the first XI and membership of that team.

In the Championship they still had a strong squad of players, with Geoffrey Boycott, John Hampshire, Philip Sharpe, Doug Padgett and Close as top-order batsmen, Richard Hutton a quality all rounder, Chris Old and Tony Nicholson as premier fast bowlers, and Don Wilson and Geoff Cope as spin bowlers.

That left a wicketkeeping position to fill following the retirement of Jimmy Binks and a need for other support when more senior players were called into the Test side or were injured.

Neil Smith was initially the first choice wicketkeeper. But the red-haired David Bairstow, still a schoolboy, had been spotted as an emerging talent and was given his debut in June 1970 on the day that he took an A-level examination. His skill and exuberance soon made him an automatic choice for the side that he then represented and eventually captained in the next 20 years. Long-term recruits as batsmen were harder to find. Barrie Leadbeater played a few matches in 1970, as did John Woodford and Andrew Dalton. Richard Lumb, who played just once (run out in his first innings) eventually became a fine opening batsman, but that was not to be in 1970.

On the bowling front Cope did really well, increasing his tally of Championship wickets from 37 in 1969 to 75 and being awarded his county cap in August. He celebrated with a run of five wickets for no runs at Colchester against Essex, including a hat-trick of premier Essex batsmen. Mike Bore, a left-arm bowler, took 23, and at season's end Phil Carrick, 18, a slow left-armer, had his first games, taking eight match wickets at Scarborough against MCC. He was to grace the Yorkshire side over the next 23 seasons and to follow Bairstow as captain.

With that squad Yorkshire hoped to succeed, and they easily won their first game against Derbyshire. A mini slump followed, including a 10-wicket defeat by Lancashire, for whom Yorkshire old boy Barry Wood scored a century.

Wood was to score another century in the return match later in the season — no doubt much to his satisfaction.

Yorkshire then had a revival of fortunes, including three wins in five games, and became Championship hopefuls.

Boycott, having been caught off a long hop on 99 in a further game against Derbyshire, made no mistake in scoring 260 not out in seven hours against Essex, the same

Rare slip: Philip Sharpe puts one down off Geoff Cope against Hampshire to the surprise of young wicketkeeper David Bairstow. Geoff is now Yorkshire President...and is the umpire Ron Aspinall?
(Photo: Mick Pope Archive)

game in which Cope excelled. This was to be Boycott's highest ever score, so a magical triple century eluded him.

The season then slightly ebbed away with a sequence of drawn matches. Welcome victories against Surrey and Somerset could not achieve an overtaking of Kent and Glamorgan at the top of the Championship table. Kent had been bottom at the end of July, and they had a remarkable run of success to become champions. Lancashire were third and Yorkshire, to their chagrin, finished one point behind those great rivals to finish in fourth position.

Yorkshire had won eight games and lost five. Significantly, Lancashire, winning only six games, had 29 more batting-bonus points than Yorkshire to edge them ahead of their rivals.

Alas, in the Gillette Cup Yorkshire, who had won the title in 1969, were eliminated in the first round of the 1970 competition, bowled out for 76 runs by Surrey on April 25, and lost by 58 runs. That match was at Harrogate, and at one point snow stopped play. Robin Jackman, of Surrey, took seven wickets in his 12 overs.

The John Player League was now in its second season and becoming very popular as a 40-overs-per-side game. Yorkshire never got out of the

Ultimatum: Captain Brian Close said he was given 10 minutes by Cricket Chairman Brian Sellers, left, to decide whether to resign or be sacked after 22 years with the club.
(Photos: Mick Pope Archive)

traps. They lost their first four matches, including to Glamorgan by one run and then to Hampshire at Hull by the enormous margin of 141 runs, when the masterly Barry Richards scored 155 not out. Yorkshire won only five of their 16 games, the last two abandoned, and finished 14th.

If the season ended with some regrets, then worse was to follow. In November the career of Close at Yorkshire was abruptly terminated. The Yorkshire *Yearbook* for 1971 containing a report on 1970 included this paragraph: "After long and careful consideration your Committee decided not to reappoint D B Close as First-Team Captain for 1971, and in view of this decision it was also decided that he should no longer be a playing member of the team." There followed some words of appreciation for the services of Close over the previous 22 years followed by the sentence "G Boycott and D Wilson have been appointed Captain and Vice-Captain respectively for the forthcoming season."

Close subsequently wrote that he was given 10 minutes by Brian Sellers, chairman of the Cricket Committee, to decide whether to resign or to be dismissed. The twin decisions on the captaincy of the Yorkshire team as made by the Committee were to stimulate misery and ructions in Yorkshire cricketing circles for years to come. Much later, in 2008, Brian Close CBE became President of Yorkshire County Cricket Club, a position never held by Sellers.

The dark days that began in late 1970 will never be easily forgotten.

YORKSHIRE'S FIRST CLASS HIGHLIGHTS OF 1970

Wins by an innings (4)

Yorkshire (450-4 dec) defeated Essex (236 and 123) by an innings and 101 runs at Colchester

Yorkshire (306) defeated Somerset (111 and 165) by an innings and 30 runs at Hull

Derbyshire (107 and 111) lost to Yorkshire (238) by an innings and 20 runs at Bradford

Hampshire (144 and 139) lost to Yorkshire (288-9 dec) by an innings and 5 runs at Sheffield

Totals of 400 and over (2)

450-4 dec v. Essex at Colchester
411 v. Northamptonshire at Northampton

Opponents dismissed for under 100 (None)

Century Partnerships (11)

For the 1st wicket (2)

153	G Boycott and P J Sharpe	v. Middlesex at Scarborough
114	G Boycott and P J Sharpe	v. Sussex at Leeds

For the 2nd wicket (2)

118	P J Sharpe and D B Close	v. Northamptonshire at Northampton
104	J D Woodford and D E V Padgett	v. Warwickshire at Birmingham

For the 3rd wicket (1)

109	G Boycott and D E V Padgett	v. Derbyshire at Chesterfield

For the 4th wicket (3)

116	D E V Padgett and G A Cope	v. Hampshire at Sheffield
124	J H Hampshire and R A Hutton	v. Derbyshire at Chesterfield
111*	R A Hutton and J H Hampshire	v. Lancashire at Manchester

For 5th wicket (3)

134	J H Hampshire and D B Close	v. Somerset at Hull
118	D E V Padgett and R A Hutton	v. Nottinghamshire at Sheffield
103	D E V Padgett and R A Hutton	v. Leicestershire at Leicester

Centuries (10)

G Boycott (2))

260*	v. Essex at Colchester
148	v. Kent at Leeds

J H Hampshire (2)

120*	v. Derbyshire at Chesterfield
107	v. Leicestershire at Leicester

D E V Padgett (2)

108	v. Nottinghamshire at Sheffield
106	v. Hampshire at Sheffield

P J Sharpe (2)

120	v. Middlesex at Scarborough
108	v. Kent at Sheffield

Centuries *(Continued)*

   D B Close (1)

      128   v. Northamptonshire at Northampton

   R A Hutton (1)

      104   v. Derbyshire at Bradford

5 wickets in an innings (13)

   G A Cope (4)

      7- 36   v. Essex at Colchester
      6- 55   v. Surrey at Bradford
      6- 81   v. Somerset at Taunton
      5- 87   v. MCC at Scarborough

   R A Hutton (2)

      6- 81   v. Nottinghamshire at Nottingham
      6- 83   v. Middlesex at Lord's

   A G Nicholson (2)

      5- 82   v. Derbyshire at Chesterfield
      5- 116 v. Lancashire at Leeds

   C M Old (2)

      5- 14   v. Derbyshire at Bradford
      5- 44   v. Surrey at Bradford

   M K Bore (1)

      5- 51   v. Northamptonshire at Northampton

   P Carrick (1)

      6- 85   v. MCC at Scarborough

   D Wilson (1)

      5- 41   v. Cambridge University at Cambridge

10 wickets in a match (2)

   G A Cope (1)

      10- 80 (3-44 and 7-36)   v. Gloucestershire at Middlesbrough

   R A Hutton (1)

      10-122 (4-39 and 6-83)   v. Middlesex at Lord's

3 catches in an innings (9)

   D L Bairstow (5)

      4   v. Gloucestershire at Bradford
      4   v. Kent at Sheffield
      4   v. Middlesex at Lord's
      3   v. MCC at Scarborough
      3   v. Somerset at Hull

   P J Sharpe (2)

      3   v. Gloucestershire at Bradford
      3   v. Hampshire at Sheffield

   R A Hutton (1)

      4   v. Surrey at Bradford

   J H Hampshire (1)

      3   v. Essex at Colchester

3 dismissals in an innings (3)

D L Bairstow (2))

    4 (3ct, 1st)   v. MCC at Scarborough
    3 (2ct, 1st)   v. Middlesex at Scarborough

N Smith (1)

    4 (2ct, 2st)   v. Warwickshire at Birmingham

5 catches in a match (3)

D L Bairstow (3)

    6 (4 + 2)   v. Kent at Sheffield)
    5 (4 + 1)   v. Gloucestershire at Bradford)
    5 (3 + 2)   v. MCC at Scarborough

Debut (4)

In First Class cricket: N Smith, D L Bairstow, D Schofield and P Carrick

Cap awarded: G A Cope

Yorkshire's big seven for the Hundred

Seven Yorkshire men's players are to appear in this summer's Hundred, the ECB's new 100-ball competition.

Tom Kohler-Cadmore, Adam Lyth, Adil Rashid and David Willey will all play for the Emerald Headingley-based Northern Superchargers, while Jonny Bairstow and Joe Root will represent Welsh Fire and Trent Rockets respectively. New signing Dawid Malan will also play for the Rockets.

This number could rise, with each of the eight teams able to add a wildcard selection, rewarding early-season county form, to their current squads.

Yorkshire Coach Andrew Gale will be an assistant coach of the Superchargers, meaning Rich Pyrah will lead Yorkshire through their 50-over campaign.

Spinner takes turn at the rugby

Yorkshire leg-spinner Josh Poysden was spotted by the TV cameras celebrating as England's rugby-union team brushed aside the All Blacks in Yokohama, Japan, in October. Poysden was holidaying in nearby Tokyo, where his fiancee, Caitlin, was on a six-month secondment as part of her law traineeship.

YORKSHIRE'S LIST A
HIGHLIGHTS OF 1970

Win by 100 or more runs (None)

Totals of 250 and over (None)

Match aggregates of 450 and over (1)

471   Yorkshire 235-6 lost to Nottinghamshire 236-8 by 2 wickets at Sheffield

Century Partnerships (3)

For 1st wicket (1)

114   G Boycott and D E V Padgett v. Sussex at Middlesbrough

For 2nd wicket (1)

114   D E V Padgett and P J Sharpe v. Leicestershire at Leicester

For 3rd wicket (1)

114   D E V Padgett and J H Hampshire v. Nottinghamshire at Sheffield

Centuries (1)

J H Hampshire (1)

108   v. Nottinghamshire at Sheffield

4 wickets in an innings (5)

M K Bore (2)

4-21   v. Sussex at Middlesbrough

4-21   v. Worcestershire at Worcester

A G Nicholson (1)

4-39   v. Surrey at Scarborough

C M Old (1)

4-31   v. Leicestershire at Leicester

J D Woodford (1)

4-23   v. Northamptonshire at Northampton

3 catches in an innings (1)

D L Bairstow (1)

3   v. Sussex at Middlesbrough

3 dismissals in an innings (1)

D L Bairstow (1)

4 (3ct + 1st) v. Sussex at Middlesbrough

List A Debuts (4): N Smith, D L Bairstow, D Schofield and P Carrick

YORKSHIRE AVERAGES 1970

ALL FIRST-CLASS MATCHES

Played 26   Won 10   Lost 5   Drawn 11

County Championship: Played 24   Won 8   Lost 5   Drawn 11

BATTING AND FIELDING *(Qualification 10 completed innings)*

Player	M.	I.	N.O.	Runs	H.S.	100s	50s	Avge	ct/st
G Boycott	21	34	4	1558	260*	2	11	51.93	9
J H Hampshire	21	34	5	1079	120*	2	4	37.20	20
D B Close	20	28	2	949	128	1	6	36.50	19
P J Sharpe	24	38	1	1149	120	2	7	31.05	33
D E V Padgett	24	38	4	1042	108	2	6	30.64	14
R A Hutton	26	38	6	875	104	1	4	27.34	26
C M Old	19	22	5	433	92*	0	1	25.47	10
D L Bairstow	19	24	5	334	36	0	0	17.57	43/6
J D Woodford	10	17	0	275	51	0	1	16.17	4
A G Nicholson	23	21	10	173	24*	0	0	15.72	5
G A Cope	26	29	8	327	66	0	2	15.57	11
D Wilson	16	18	2	238	48	0	0	14.87	5
Also batted									
B Leadbeater	6	9	1	299	89*	0	2	37.37	5
A J Dalton	6	9	1	174	47*	0	0	21.75	2
P Carrick	3	3	1	36	32	0	0	18.00	2
N Smith	7	11	5	82	20	0	0	13.66	4/3
R G Lumb	1	2	0	21	17	0	0	10.50	0
M K Bore	10	9	4	50	21*	0	0	10.00	5
C Johnson	2	3	1	20	15	0	0	10.00	1
R Smith	1	1	0	2	2	0	0	2.00	0
D Schofield	1	1	1	1	1*	0	0	—	0

BOWLING *(Qualification 10 wickets)*

Player	Overs	Mdns	Runs	Wkts	Avge	Best	5wI	10wM
C M Old	489.4	118	1232	65	18.95	5 -14	2	0
R A Hutton	619.1	152	1597	74	21.58	6 -81	2	1
P Carrick	84.3	14	312	14	22.28	6 -85	1	0
G A Cope	878.5	282	2111	83	25.43	7 -36	4	1
D Wilson	553.5	195	1255	47	26.70	5 -41	1	0
M K Bore	279	94	648	23	28.17	5 -51	1	0
A G Nicholson	792.2	229	1939	65	29.83	5 -82	2	0
Also bowled								
D B Close	34	10	95	2	47.50	1 -31	0	0
J H Hampshire	15	4	69	0	—	0 - 8	0	0
D Schofield	20	9	53	0	—	0 -25	0	0
J D Woodford	19	5	47	0	—	0 - 0	0	0
C Johnson	7	2	20	0	—	0 -11	0	0
P J Sharpe	2	0	4	0	—	0 - 1	0	0
D E V Padgett	1	0	3	0	—	0 - 3	0	0

YORKSHIRE AVERAGES 1970

LIST A

Played 17   Won 5   Lost 10   No result 2

BATTING AND FIELDING *(Qualification 4 completed innings)*

Player	M.	I.	N.O.	Runs	H.S.	100s	50s	Avge	ct/st
G Boycott	14	13	0	487	98	0	5	37.46	5
J D Woodford	14	12	4	228	69*	0	1	28.50	6
D E V Padgett	16	15	1	337	68	0	2	24.07	5
J H Hampshire	14	14	2	279	108	1	0	23.25	6
R A Hutton	17	13	5	170	44	0	0	21.25	4
P J Sharpe	15	14	0	234	60	0	1	16.71	6
B Leadbeater	8	8	0	130	34	0	0	16.25	2
D B Close	10	9	0	141	28	0	0	15.66	3
C M Old	12	8	2	56	16	0	0	9.33	2
D Wilson	10	10	2	66	21	0	0	8.25	3
A G Nicholson	15	6	2	27	12*	0	0	6.75	1
D L Bairstow	10	7	1	19	15	0	0	3.16	9/1
Also batted									
J C Balderstone	2	2	0	35	25	0	0	17.50	0
G A Cope	9	5	3	33	13	0	0	16.50	1
A J Dalton	5	4	1	47	13*	0	0	15.66	1
N Smith	7	2	1	5	5	0	0	5.00	2
R G Lumb	1	1	0	1	1	0	0	1.00	0
M K Bore	3	2	2	15	14*	0	0	—	4
D Schofield	2	0	0	0	—	0	0	—	1
P Carrick	1	0	0	0	—	0	0	—	0
C Johnson	1	0	0	0	—	0	0	—	0
R Smith	1	0	0	0	—	0	0	—	0

BOWLING *(Qualification 4 wickets)*

Player	Overs	Mdns	Runs	Wkts	Avge	Best	4wI	RPO
M K Bore	24	4	70	9	7.77	4-21	2	2.91
A G Nicholson	105.1	18	358	18	19.88	4-39	1	3.40
J D Woodford	69.2	5	319	14	22.78	4-23	1	4.60
C M Old	85	14	339	14	24.21	4-31	1	3.98
R A Hutton	118.1	13	521	19	27.42	3-11	0	4.40
D Wilson	79	4	354	11	32.18	2-22	0	4.48
Also bowled								
J H Hampshire	4	1	22	1	22.00	1-22	0	5.50
D B Close	20	3	69	3	23.00	3-27	0	3.45
D E V Padgett	4	0	25	1	25.00	1-25	0	6.25
P Carrick	8	0	37	1	37.00	1-37	0	4.62
G Boycott	23	0	121	2	60.50	1-34	0	5.26
D Schofield	16	2	88	1	88.00	1-27	0	5.50
G A Cope	44	2	199	2	99.50	2-43	0	4.52
P J Sharpe	0.4	0	11	0	—	0-11	0	16.50

BOYS' MIGHTY ROAR THAT DROWNED THE SPEEDWAY

By Jeremy Lonsdale

At the distance of almost 100 years it is hard to appreciate quite how popular cricket was in Yorkshire in the 1920s. Crowds after the First World War were well above pre-war levels, and over 200,000 people watched Yorkshire home matches for several seasons in a row.

Matches on certain Bank Holidays were extraordinary events, with mounted police stationed inside the grounds to keep crowds back and thousands turned away. On occasions the gates at Bradford and Sheffield were overwhelmed, and people got in without paying.

By the end of the decade things returned to a more normal state as the great Championship-winning side of 1922-25 slowly broke up, with Arthur Dolphin and Abe Waddington retiring in 1927 and Roy Kilner dying tragically the following year. Yorkshire were in transition, and many people had less money to spare at a time of economic depression.

Despite this, one remarkable event highlights just how popular cricket in general and the Yorkshire side in particular, remained, when on the night of Monday, June 17, 1929, more than 25,000 boys attended an evening of mass cricket coaching led by William Worsley, the Yorkshire captain, and senior professional Wilfred Rhodes, all finished off with the noise and excitement of speedway racing.

The event was organised and heavily publicised by the *Sheffield Independent* and *Sheffield Mail* newspapers at a time when there was anxiety in Sheffield about its lack of contribution to the Yorkshire XI and when the need for new blood in the *White Rose* team was a subject of wide debate.

The coaching session was held at the new Owlerton Speedway track on the Monday evening of Yorkshire's match with Nottinghamshire at Sheffield. Speedway had been launched as a commercial sport in England the previous year, and it immediately attracted enthusiastic crowds. The Owlerton venue was chosen because it had extensive banking so that everyone had an unrestricted view, and it was equipped with numerous loudspeakers which allowed the coaching commentary to be heard everywhere. The centre of the track was a skating rink, but matting was put down so that nets could be set up.

Yorkshire CCC got behind the plans, and F C Toone, the Yorkshire Secretary, and George Hirst both gave the event their blessing, although Hirst was still coaching at Eton College and could not attend.

Captain Worsley suggested that some boys should be brought onto the matting for individual tuition, and the Sheffield Schools' Sports Association identified six suitable lads in advance. Invitations were sent out to all boys over 10 at schools in Sheffield and district, while those in the Scouts and Boys' Brigades movements were asked to apply for tickets through their clubs.

In the week running up to the event the sponsoring papers whipped up excitement about what they thought was the first time cricket coaching on this scale had ever been organised. They speculated that among those present there might be another Hirst or Rhodes. Most boys who attended were part of organised parties, and this helped the papers to stress that no parent need worry about their child's safety.

On the Monday night, trams from Fitzalan Square were the easiest means of getting to the track, along with a special service from Bridge Street from 6.30pm onwards. During the afternoon many boys who were not attending through their schools besieged the Sheffield newspaper offices for individual tickets, and then crammed onto tramcars in scenes conductors claimed were unprecedented even for local football matches.

By the start about 25,000 were packed into the stadium, reportedly making a noise like "the roar of surf on a beach of pebbles". Events started at 7.30pm, when the Yorkshire players appeared to an enormous ovation and were introduced by Captain Worsley. The players involved were Percy Holmes, Edgar Oldroyd, Rhodes, Emmott Robinson, George Macaulay, Arthur Mitchell, Arthur Wood and Frank Dennis. Captain Worsley read out messages from Herbert Sutcliffe and Maurice Leyland, who were in Birmingham playing in the first Test against South Africa.

Rhodes then went into the net, and demonstrated a series of strokes against the bowling of Macaulay, Dennis and Robinson. The coaching covered all aspects of the game including how to hold a bat, maintain a proper stance and use good footwork; how to hold the ball and different types of bowling as well as fielding and wicketkeeping. Holmes also demonstrated some strokes before Rhodes moved on to bowling, explaining how to grip the ball for swerve and spin. The crowd followed the instruction intently, with Worsley's instructions and commentary heard clearly for most of the time above the chatter and cheering.

After these demonstrations the boys selected by Sheffield and District Schools' Sports Association came out for instruction, with Rhodes pointing out their errors and advising on changes in approach before the boys showed their strokes standing on the speedway track. In the meantime Mitchell demonstrated good fielding technique, and Wood showed how to take the ball behind the wicket.

After about 90 minutes the coaching ended, and the tempo changed as the speedway riders came out to the combined roar of engines and the voices of thousands of boys. Six riders connected with the Sheffield track were involved, including "Smoky" Stratton, the venue manager, and local celebrities "Clip" Crawshaw and Jack Barber. Each rider did some demonstration laps before two heats and the final began, and afterwards a failed attempt was made to break the track lap record.

At the end of the evening there was a rush for autographs from the cricketers and riders alike. One speedway rider said there were so many requests that he had used a rubber stamp, and boys without albums pleaded to have signatures stamped on their hands. Another lad told a reporter that he had asked for the signature on his forearm, as he did not expect his mother to wash that far up next day!

Then, long queues of excited boys were marshalled outside by their teachers and crammed back onto the trams waiting to take them home.

The Yorkshire players left the track once the crowds had cleared, and were dined by the management of the *Sheffield Independent*. They were reportedly overwhelmed by the experience, as were the riders, one of whom claimed he had never heard the noise of his engine drowned out by a crowd before.

Holmes said it was the most thrilling and inspiring night he had ever experienced, and nothing had affected him as much as the enthusiasm of the boys. Other members of the side were quoted as saying that they "would not have missed it for anything in the world".

The overwhelming memory of everyone involved was the noise made by so many voices. Local reporters thought it was doubtful whether the speedway track or Hillsborough had ever resounded to such noise as heard when the cricketers appeared, when Mitchell hit a ball onto the roof of the grandstand, and when the riders finally brought the evening to a close around 10 o'clock.

The night had been a remarkable success, helped by perfect warm mid-summer weather. Thrilled by its efforts, the *Sheffield Independent* modestly called it probably "the greatest demonstration of cricket ever seen in any city". It was, wrote one reporter, "another indication of how deeply English people love the great summer game, and the Yorkshire players did some fine propaganda work, which I hope, will bear fruit in the future."

Despite the unusual distraction the Yorkshire side returned to Bramall Lane next morning and beat Nottinghamshire by five wickets in the early afternoon. Whether much work was done in schools around Sheffield the next morning is another matter.

EYRE MAY HAVE GONE ON TO CAPTAIN YORKSHIRE IF...

By Michael Pulford

Lancashire-born Charles Eyre, captain of Harrow in 1902 and Cambridge in 1906, was invited by Lord Hawke to play for Yorkshire in 1904, having hit 72 for the university against them that season, the offer coming despite it being known that Eyre was born outside the county. His qualification for Yorkshire was one of residence as the family home had been at Sheffield, where his father was Archdeacon, since Eyre was 12. Unfortunately, Eyre had a prior Cambridge cricketing engagement and could not accept the invitation, which would have made him the first non-Yorkshire-born player to represent the county in the 20th Century.

Two years later, in 1906, he had even greater success for Cambridge against Yorkshire, scoring 153, taking five catches and leading the university to a staggering 305-run victory, Yorkshire's record runs defeat until 1994. A truly memorable match for Eyre yet, very surprisingly, this does not appear to have prompted Hawke to repeat the invitation.

Following his time at Cambridge, he embarked upon a teaching career, firstly at Elstree and then back at Harrow, playing occasional club matches in summer holidays but no more first-class cricket. Sad to relate, like many of his generation Eyre's life was cut short serving in the Great War.

The first of Eyre's two notable scores against Yorkshire came in his second appearance for Cambridge, the opening game of 1904. He was an attacking batsman, and this was a typically positive performance. Old Ebor (Alfred Pullin) observed in *The Athletic News*: "At present he is essentially a hitter in front of the wicket, but he watches the ball so well that he is sure to develop other strokes", adding, "I rather think he will establish a name for himself before his Varsity career is over. Two or three innings like the one he played on Friday will doubtless secure an invitation to play in the Yorkshire XI when the university term is over."

Two scores of 80 that season, against Warwickshire and Surrey, did indeed keep his name in Hawke's mind, though Eyre's attacking instinct may also have led to a number of cheap dismissals.

Old Ebor was not merely an important and long-standing chronicler of Yorkshire's affairs, but was also close to Hawke. So the following comments about Eyre's background and eligibility in match reports of the Cambridge-Yorkshire fixture are especially interesting: "Eyre, as the reader will doubtless know, is a Sheffielder, and though I believe not born in the county he fulfils the definition which prevails in Yorkshire cricket circles of a Yorkshire qualification."

In *The Yorkshire Evening Post* he commented: "Eyre, one of the opening pair of batsmen today, is a son of Archdeacon Eyre, of Sheffield, and can be considered qualified to play for Yorkshire under the county's established policy, even though he was not born within the shire." His place of birth, Liverpool, was not given in either report, perhaps because Old Ebor did not yet know that fact.

Yorkshire's tradition of fielding Yorkshire-born cricketers is worthy of greater research and comment, but it suffices here to state that Hawke was actually prepared to choose men who, like himself, were born outside the county but had affiliations with Yorkshire through family background and residence — usually amateurs.

Eyre's invitation came a week after the 1904 Varsity match, Sheffield's *Yorkshire Telegraph and Star* reporting on Friday, July 8, that Hawke had made efforts that afternoon to "secure the help of C H Eyre, the Cambridge Blue, for at least the first of the three matches which are to be played in the South during the next 10 days".

But, the following Monday, the *Sheffield Daily Telegraph* reporter, Looker-On, revealed: "I learn from a letter which Mr Eyre has been good enough to send me that he is unable to make the team for the Hampshire match, having some time ago promised to go with his university to Ireland. He naturally regrets very much this compulsory inability to assist Yorkshire."

Eyre took on the role of CUCC Honorary Secretary in 1905 and, after overcoming an illness which limited his appearances for the university XI that summer, he went on a North American MCC tour when the term was over. He had become a member of the MCC the previous year.

Then, in 1906, he was appointed Cambridge captain. His first match in charge was against Yorkshire — the previously mentioned record defeat — and his 153 was particularly noteworthy as it was against a bowling attack which included Hirst, Rhodes and Haigh. It was an innings not without luck, however, as he was almost out three times before reaching 50. His five catches, all taken in the slips, included Hirst, Rhodes and Hawke. Quite a haul.

The *Lancashire Daily Post* erroneously and ironically referred to Eyre as "a son of the shire of broad acres" for he was in fact born at the quaintly named St Michael-in-the-Hamlet district of Liverpool during his father's lengthy period of ministry in the city. This information must have become known for *The Yorkshire Post*, *The Daily Mail of Hull* and *The Leeds and Yorkshire Mercury* all referred to this "dual qualification" for Yorkshire and Lancashire, the *Mercury* stating: "He has at all events Yorkshire associations."

The *Yorkshire Post* said: "That he will have the refusal of another opportunity to assist the county may be taken for granted, and on his form yesterday his services would undoubtedly be valued by Yorkshire."

The *Athletic News* said: "Such an achievement would excite the admiration of the opposing captain, Lord Hawke." The public acknowledgment of Eyre's qualification for Lancashire prompted

Opening at Lord's: Charles Eyre, left, walks out with Geoffrey MacLaren for Harrow v. Eton in 1902. Geoffrey was the younger brother of Archie MacLaren, who captained Lancashire and England and whose 424 was the highest score in first-class cricket until 1923 and a record in English cricket until 1994.
(Photo: Jenny Kean Archive)

Old Ebor to write: "I am wondering whether any enterprising member of the Red Rose body will give him an invitation to play in their team."

Yet, at the close of the university season, he was not reported as receiving a further invitation to play for Yorkshire or for Lancashire despite places becoming available in Yorkshire's middle-order. It is unlikely that he would have held down a place in Yorkshire's side on merit — though this could be said of many of Hawke's successors as Yorkshire captain — but etiquette of the time suggested that, as Cambridge University captain, he would have been accorded a further invitation to play. Indeed, as Hawke was 44 he might have been expected to consider Eyre, among others, as a future captain. Birth in Yorkshire was not a prerequisite for the captaincy as Hawke was Lincolnshire-born and his successor, Everard Radcliffe, was born in Devon.

Why was a further invitation not forthcoming? Was Hawke disappointed that two years earlier Eyre had chosen an end-of-season tour with Cambridge rather than appearances for Yorkshire? On the other hand, might it have been that the greater publicity and detail given to his birth outside the county boundary told against him? In 1904 it was merely stated by Old Ebor that he was born elsewhere, but in 1906 this was specified as being in Lancashire. So was it just possible that his birth in another first-class cricket county — and the arch-rival at that! — caused Hawke to overlook him?

A further factor might have been that Hawke in such cases preferred the player to have a Yorkshire family connection, but neither of Eyre's parents were from the county. His lack of involvement in Yorkshire club cricket may also have been a disadvantage. He seems to have made only one club appearance in Sheffield, and I have not come across a record of him ever playing for the Yorkshire Gentlemen, the common route Yorkshire amateurs took to the county XI. Though it should be noted their base was in York, some distance from Sheffield.

All could have been reasons, but a greater one may have been that Eyre had made it known he would not be available to play first-class cricket following his time at university. Old Ebor hinted at this in reports from the Cambridge-Yorkshire match of 1906, firstly stating on the opening day: "I do not know whether Eyre will be able to give attention to county cricket when his university days are over." Then, perhaps after making enquiries, writing the following day: "I believe it is doubtful whether he will be able to take up cricket seriously once his university days are concluded."

This must have been because Eyre could not have reasonably asked his family to financially support him as an amateur cricketer, as his status demanded, and he needed to find paid employment to maintain himself after his studies. He came from a very large family with eight siblings, and this had helped him to obtain financial help in the way of scholarships at both Harrow and Cambridge, while none of his six sisters had married and they, also in keeping with the times, remained at home and dependent on parents.

It transpired that Eyre intended to be a schoolmaster, and would be unable to play much first-class cricket in the future. Moreover, in order to progress his teaching career he studied for an MA, which did not necessitate him actually being at Cambridge, but which will have taken up a lot of his spare time until completed in 1910, and perhaps prevented him being able to commit himself to play county cricket in the summer holidays, as was the practice of some schoolmasters.

After a brief period as a master at Elstree School he returned to Harrow and established himself as an integral member of the staff and community. He encouraged cricket there, and he was recorded as playing some club matches during the holidays, including for MCC XIs.

At the outbreak of war in August 1914 Eyre immediately volunteered for the Army and joined the 2nd King's Royal Rifle Corps, receiving a commission and becoming a 2nd Lieutenant "On Probation".

He was in Sheffield the following month, along with all his brothers and sisters, for the consecration and dedication of two memorials to his father and mother, who had both died in 1912. He also attended a meeting of the Sheffield Sports Club, participating in a discussion about military training.

He was ordered to France in Christmas week 1914 and was immediately on trench work near the German lines. Letters to Harrow say he experienced shell-fire and saw casualties and German prisoners, though he had occasional times of relief — early morning runs, rides and even cricket.

For King and country: Acting Captain Charles Eyre, who was killed on the first day of the Battle of Loos in 1915.
(Photo: Jenny Kean Archive)

In September 1915 Eyre was shot through the head while, as acting captain, he led his men towards the enemy lines in an attempt to cut through barbed wire on the first day of the battle of Loos. He was 32. His body was recovered, and his grave is at Dud Corner Cemetery, Loos.

A Special Memorial Service was held at Harrow School on October 3, 1915, for Eyre and two other masters killed that year. Later that month he was one of a number of soldiers with Sheffield connections remembered in a Memorial Service at Sheffield Parish Church. In 1920 eight Masters' Stalls in oak were installed at Harrow Chapel to commemorate the three teachers who lost their lives, while his name is inscribed on at least five war memorials at places which were important in his life: St Michael-in-the-Hamlet Church, Liverpool; Elstree School; Harrow School; Pembroke College, Cambridge, and Lord's Cricket Ground.

AUSSIE STARS DO LIKE TO BE BESIDE THE SEASIDE

By Graham Hardcastle

**Last of the Summer Wickets — Tales from the Scarborough Cricket Festival   By John Fuller   *(Great Northern Books £9.99*

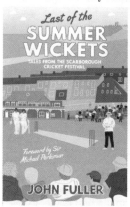

The summer of 2019 was almost the perfect time for John Fuller to release his second book. As Emerald Headingley was awash with international cricket, at domestic level this was the summer of outgrounds.

While North Marine Road hosted its usual two County Championship matches, York's Clifton Park superbly hosted its maiden first-class fixture and the city's first since 1890. Places such as the Isle of Wight and Sedbergh also saw Hampshire and Lancashire host games.

Not only this, but as Fuller signed copies of his excellent book, which delves deeper into Scarborough life than just bat and ball, Yorkshire were securing pulsating wins over Surrey and Nottinghamshire in front of his eyes.

The editor of the website *CricketYorkshire.com* centres his book around the 2018 Festival fixture against Worcestershire, and he has spoken to all manner of folk intrinsically linked to one of county cricket's great venues. Some you will know, many you won't.

Sir Michael Parkinson has written the foreword, and we learn that Parky's first taste of the Scarborough Festival came while working as a 14-year-old potato peeler!

Jason Gillespie describes visits to Scarborough as the "highlight of the summer". Darren Lehmann also speaks about one of the greatest innings seen at North Marine Road, his 191 in a Sunday League match against Nottinghamshire in 2001, days after the Championship title was sealed against Glamorgan at the same venue.

After celebrations it is fair to say Yorkshire's squad weren't quite in peak condition, and the Australian legend described how he went out to bat with a free mind and got "lucky".

The book is a light read, the sort you could pick up and put down as you sit on the Popular Bank listening to roars of delight as home boundaries are cover-driven or groans as opposition bowlers snare wickets.

Just A Few Lines...the unseen letters and memorabilia of Brian Close   By David Warner   *(Great Northern Books £20*

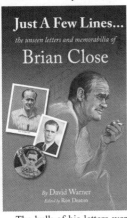

Fresh never-seen-before material on the early cricket and soccer careers of Brian Close is revealed in a book out soon penned by cricket writer and former Yorkshire CCC *Yearbook* Editor David Warner.

Close's feats on the cricket field are legendary and well documented, but even those who knew him well will be surprised to learn of a previously undisclosed side to his character.

He was a compulsive and prolific letter-writer at a time he was making his mark both for Yorkshire and England and as a soccer player on the books of Leeds United, Arsenal and Bradford City.

The bulk of his letters were sent to his former schoolmate and best friend, John Anderson, and they give a fascinating account of his triumphs and tribulations on and off the field, including his debut season with Yorkshire and his first Test tours of Australia and Pakistan. His adventures on National Service in the Army are also packed with incident and drama.

Scores of Brian's letters and other cricket memorabilia have been saved, and now form part of the Brian Close Collection which was purchased last year by the Yorkshire Cricket Foundation.

It is from meticulous research into this collection that the book has been written and lavishly illustrated, many of the photographs never having been seen before. It has been meticulously edited by Yorkshire cricket historian Ron Deaton, a well known figure at Headingley and a consistent contributor of archive material to the *Yearbook*.

To order the book go to www.gnbooks.co.uk or call 01274-735056 or the Yorkshire CCC shop.

BOB WILLIS, LEGEND OF 1981

By Graham Hardcastle

Robert George Dylan Willis MBE may not have played for Yorkshire, but his impact on cricket within the county was huge.

One of the ECB's catchlines is *Inspiring a Generation*, and that is exactly what the late ex-England fast bowler did to *White Rose* supporters with his contribution in the Miracle of 1981 Ashes Test at Headingley.

Sunderland-born Bob Willis, who died on December 4, 2019, aged 70, became a popular pundit who called a spade a spade — surely a quality of a Yorkshireman — after taking 325 wickets in 90 Tests between 1971 and 1984.

A tall and wiry seamer, who battled through surgery on both knees in his mid-twenties, the former Surrey and Warwickshire paceman captained England in 18 Tests.

His Test best of 8-43 from 15.1 overs came at the perfect time.

Defending a 130 target in the third Test at Headingley in 1981, with Australia 1-0 up, Willis demolished the Aussies for 111.

Without Ian Botham's second-innings century, which dragged England back from the brink of defeat, Willis could not have done what he did. But there was no denying that his was one of the greatest bowling performances witnessed at Leeds.

Following a career which yielded 1,320 wickets — 899 of them first-class victims — Willis, also a lover of music, worked as a commentator and pundit for BBC and Sky TV.

His most famous role was as the face of the often hard-hitting Cricket Verdict/Debate show on Sky, reviewing every day of England Tests.

He was on duty in August to assess Ben Stokes's sensational unbeaten 135 as England beat Australia to level the 2019 Ashes at 1-1, the only rival to '81 as Headingley's greatest Test.

"Naturally, his unbeaten 135 will be compared to Ian Botham's 149 at Headingley 38 years ago — and let me tell you, Ben's is the better knock," Willis told his viewers.

He was England's fourth-leading Test wicket-taker at the time of his death, but his contribution to English cricket extends way beyond that.

Coup de grâce: Bob Willis rips out Ray Bright's middle stump to complete his analysis of 8-43 as England level the *Ashes* series at Headingley in 1981 after following on.
(Photo: Gary Longbottom)

DAVID DRABBLE

By David Warner

Yorkshire CCC Vice-President and former long-serving committee member David Drabble, right, died on October 17, 2019, aged 82, after a long illness.

Former England captain Michael Vaughan and Yorkshire CCC Chairman Robin Smith, were among those to pay tribute to David who, along with his father, George, formed the Sheffield Cricket Lovers' Society in 1960.

David's outstanding service to cricket was recognised by the ICC in April 2010 when he received the ICC Centenary Medal from ECB Chief Executive David

Collier. It was just over half-a-century ago, in the spring of 1969, that David was elected to the Yorkshire Committee as a Sheffield district representative, and he gave 22 years of continuous service before stepping down under the rules of the club and then being elected a Vice-President in recognition of his work. He began by serving on the grounds and membership subcommittee, becoming its chairman in 1985. He was also a member of the public-relations subcommittee for several years up to 1980, and from 1986 to 1990 he was a member of the powerful seven-man management committee.

Following its formation in 1960 the Sheffield Cricket Lovers' Society became one of the most prominent cricket societies in the county with its regular meetings attracting a variety of speakers from all over the country. In its early days David planned and organised cricket tours all over the country and abroad. Society chairman Dave Longley said: "He was a remarkable organiser with a photographic memory, and was meticulous in everything he did."

David Tunbridge, a former Yorkshire CCC Committee member who also represented Sheffield, said: "Over the past 50 years that I have known David he was a tremendously loyal and valued friend. David and I travelled all over the country watching Yorkshire since 1972 through good times and bad. David was an admirer of the batting prowess of Geoffrey Boycott and Darren Lehmann, in particular."

As society secretary David organised hundreds of dinners, and always engaged high-quality celebrity speakers. His organising skills were outstanding, and helped to raise the society's profile to one of the most prestigious in the country.

Dorothy Betts, who succeeded David as secretary when he was in failing health, said: "As well as in Sheffield his passing will be felt in the corridors of power at Yorkshire CCC, where he was a well-known member and friend of the club."

Vaughan, who was brought up in Sheffield and whose prodigious talents as a schoolboy were first spotted by Yorkshire when he was playing on the outfield at Abbeydale Park during the interval of a Championship match, tweeted: "Such a sad day...David did so much for cricket in South Yorkshire."

Yorkshire Chairman Smith said: "As well as serving Yorkshire with great distinction he was a leading figure in cricket in South Yorkshire, and he will be much missed throughout the county."

David leaves a widow, Anne, a son and daughter and six grandchildren. His funeral service took took place at Dronfield Parish Church on November 4.

SIR DAVID JONES CBE

Sir David Jones CBE, left, a former President of Yorkshire County Cricket Club, died on December 29, 2019, at the age of 76.

Sir David, who lived in Ilkley, served as President in 2004 and 2005, taking over the reins from Robin Smith, who was ending his term of office in that role, and later being succeeded by Bob Appleyard, the former Yorkshire and England bowler.

Sir David, who transformed Next from a failing business into the third biggest fashion chain in the UK, serving first as Chief Executive and then Chairman, took great pride in his surprise election as Yorkshire President, and although his strenuous business life that meant he kept a generally low profile he was a keen follower of Yorkshire's fortunes, both on and off the field. He joined Next in 1986 from the Grattan catalogue business, and he also went on to hold board positions with Morrisons Supermarket Group and JJB Sports.

Yorkshire Chairman Smith, said: "Sir David Jones was the first Yorkshire President to come from a commercial background, where he had turned the Next retail chain into one of the most successful businesses on UK high streets. He also put Next into a leading position in mail-order retailing, the precursor to today's internet shopping.

"His astute guidance during his Presidential term was greatly valued at the time and, with the benefit of hindsight, can be seen now to have influenced the formation of the club's current business model.

"However, my main admiration for Sir David arises from his indefatigable courage over many years in the face of adversity. He was diagnosed with Parkinson's disease in his 30s and, fearing that it might be viewed negatively, he kept it secret from his colleagues while he pursued his outstandingly successful business career.

"Latterly, he had been hospitalised for some months following a fall, but he continued to talk with enthusiasm about the future. David Jones was an exceptional man and a true friend of Yorkshire cricket.

He leaves a widow, Ann, three children, Alison, Richard and Stuart, and five grandchildren, Jamie, William, Charlie, Harry and Ryan. His funeral service was held on January 16, at the Priory Church of St Mary and St Cuthbert, at Bolton Abbey.

ERIC SUTTON

Eric Sutton, a founder member of the Yorkshire CCC Players' Association, died in St. James's Hospital, Leeds, on May 26, 2019, aged 87. Born in Otley on January 29, 1932, Eric kept wicket several times for Yorkshire Seconds from the mid-1950s until the early 60s, playing alongside many who would become household names and Championship winners with the county.

He began his cricket with Menston CC in the Aire-Wharfe League before moving into the Bradford League, where he enjoyed spells with Lidget Green, Farsley, Salts and Yeadon.

Eric was also a fine rugby player, turning out for Otley RUFC before being signed by Bradford Northern, where he spent three seasons from 1955, playing in 49 matches and scoring 12 tries. He then had spells with Batley and Dewsbury.

He left a widow, Shirley, a son and two daughters. His funeral service took place at Rawdon Crematorium.

JOHN ASHMAN

Robert John Ashman, who played in one match for Yorkshire in 1951, died in Willow Lodge Care Home, Chichester, on March 4, 2019, aged 92. Born in Rotherham on May 20, 1926, Robert spent his early career with Bowling Old Lane in 1946 before turning out for Sheffield United three years later.

He played for Yorkshire Seconds from 1946 to 1950 and his only first-team appearance came the following year against Surrey at Headingley, when he scored 0 not out and claimed two wickets in each innings, twice dismissing Arthur McIntyre.

He then returned to the second team, and after a year out in 1952 he joined Worcestershire, where he stayed for two seasons, playing in 33 first-class matches and taking 60 wickets.

The Players

Steven Andrew PATTERSON
Right-hand batsman, right-arm medium-fast bowler
Born: Beverley, October 3, 1983

First-Class Cricket:
Debut: v. Bangladesh A at Leeds, 2005
Highest score: 63* v. Warwickshire at Leeds, 2016
Best bowling: 6-40 v. Essex at Chelmsford, 2018

One-Day:
Highest score: 25* v. Worcestershire at Leeds, 2006
Best bowling: 6-32 v. Derbyshire at Leeds, 2010

T20:
Highest score: 3* v. Derbyshire at Leeds, 2010
Best bowling: 4-30 v. Lancashire at Leeds, 2010

Autograph

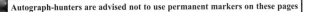

Joe Edward ROOT
Right-hand batsman, right-arm off-spin bowler
Born: Sheffield, December 30, 1990

First-Class cricket:
Debut: v. Loughborough MCCU at Leeds, 2010
Highest score: 254 for England v. Pakistan at Manchester, 2016
Highest for Yorkshire: 236 v. Derbyshire at Leeds, 2013
Best bowling: is 4-5 v. Lancashire at Manchester, 2018

One-Day:
Highest Score: 133* for England v. Bangladesh at The Oval, 2017
Highest for Yorkshire: 83 v. Warwickshire at Birmingham, 2017
Best bowling: 3-52 for England v. Ireland at Lord's, 2017
Best bowling for Yorkshire: 2-14 v. Kent at Leeds, 2012

T20:
Highest score: 92* v. Lancashire at Manchester, 2016
Best bowling for England: 2-9 v West Indies at Kolkata, 2016-17
For Yorkshire: 1-12 v. Warwickshire at Leeds, 2011

Autograph

Autograph-hunters are advised not to use permanent markers on these pages

Gary Simon BALLANCE

Left-hand batsman, leg-break bowler
Born: Harare, Zimbabwe, November 22, 1989

First-Class Cricket:
Debut: v Kent at Canterbury, 2008
Highest score: 210 for Mid-West Rhinos v.
Southern Rocks at Masvingo, Zimbabwe, 2011-12
For Yorkshire: 203* v. Hampshire at West End,
Southampton, 2017

One-Day:
Highest score: 156 v. Leicestershire at Leeds,
2019

T20:
Highest score: 79 v. Birmingham at Birmingham,
2018

Autograph

Jonathan Marc BAIRSTOW

Right-hand batsman, wicket-keeper
Born: Bradford, September 26, 1989

First-Class Cricket:
Debut: v Somerset at Leeds, 2009
Highest score: 246 v. Hampshire at Leeds, 2016

One-Day:
Highest score: 174 v, Durham at Leeds, 2017

T20:
Highest score: 102* v. Durham
at Chester-le-Street, 2014

Autograph

Timothy Thomas BRESNAN

Right-hand batsman, right-arm medium-fast bowler
Born: Pontefract, February 28, 1985
First-Class cricket:
Debut: v. Northamptonshire at Northampton, 2003
Highest score: 169* v. Durham
at Chester-le-Street, 2015
Best bowling: 5-28 v. Hampshire at Leeds, 2018
One-Day:
Highest score: 95* v. Nottinghamshire
at Scarborough, 2016
Best bowling: 5-48 for England v. India
at Bangalore, 2011
Best bowling for Yorkshire: 4-25 v. Somerset
at Leeds, 2005
T20:
Highest score: 51 v. Lancashire
at Manchester, 2015
Best bowling: 6-19 v. Lancashire at Leeds, 2017

Autograph

Tom KOHLER-CADMORE

Right-hand batsman, right-arm off-break bowler
Born: Chatham, August 19, 1994

First-Class Cricket:
Debut: For Worcestershire v. Hampshire
at West End, Southampton, 2014
Debut for Yorkshire: v. Somerset
at Scarborough, 2017
Highest score: 176 v. Leeds/Bradford MCCU
at Weetwood, Leeds, 2019

One-Day:
Highest score: 164 v. Durham at Chester-le-Street,
2018

T20:
Highest score: 127 for Worcestershire v. Durham
at Worcester, 2016
For Yorkshire: 96* v. Leicestershire at Leicester,
2019

Autograph

David Jonathan WILLEY

Left-hand batsman, left-arm fast-medium bowler
Born: Northampton, February 28, 1990
First-Class cricket:
Debut: for Northamptonshire v. Leicestershire
at Leicester, 2009
Debut for Yorkshire: v. Nottinghamshire
at Nottingham, 2016
Highest score: 104* for Northamptonshire
v. Gloucestershire at Northampton, 2015
Highest for Yorkshire: 46 v. Warwickshire at York,
2019
Best bowling: 5-29 for Northamptonshire
v. Gloucestershire at Northampton, 2011
For Yorkshire: 3-55 v. Surrey at Leeds, 2016
One-Day:
Highest score: 167 for Northamptonshire v. Warwickshire at Birmingham, 2013
Highest for Yorkshire: 131 v. Lancashire at Manchester, 2018
Best bowling: 5-62 for England Lions v. New Zealand A at Bristol, 2014
For Yorkshire: 4-47 v. Derbyshire at Derby, 2018
T20:
Highest score: 118 for Yorkshire v. Worcestershire at Leeds, 2017
Best bowling: 4-7 for England v. West Indies at Basseterre, 2019
For Yorkshire: 4-18 v. Northamptonshire at Leeds, 2019

Autograph

Adam LYTH

Left-hand batsman, right-arm medium bowler
Born: Whitby, September 25, 1987
First-Class cricket:
Debut: v. Loughborough UCCE at Leeds, 2007
Highest score: 251 v. Lancashire
at Manchester, 2014
Best bowling: 2-9 v. Middlesex at Scarborough,
2016
One-Day:
Highest score: 144 v. Lancashire at Manchester,
2018
Best bowling: 1-6 v Middlesex at Leeds, 2013
T20:
Highest score: 161 v. Northamptonshire
at Leeds, 2017
Best bowling: 5-31 v. Nottinghamshire
at Nottingham, 2019

Autograph

Autograph

Adil Usman RASHID

Right-hand batsman, leg-break bowler
Born: Bradford, February 17, 1988

First-Class cricket:
Debut: v. Warwickshire at Scarborough, 2006
Highest score: 180 v Somerset at Leeds, 2013
Best bowling: 7-107 v. Hampshire
at Southampton, 2008

One-Day:
Highest score: 71 v. Gloucestershire at Leeds, 2014
Best bowling: 5-27 for England v.Ireland
at Bristol, 2017
Best bowling for Yorkshire: 5-33 v. Hampshire
at Southampton 2014

t20:
Highest score: 36* v Uva Next
at Johannesburg, 2012/13
Best bowling: 4-19 v. Durham at Leeds, 2017

Benjamin Oliver COAD

Right-hand batsman, right-arm fast-medium bowler
Born: Harrogate, January 10, 1994

First-Class Cricket:
Debut: v. Durham at Chester-le-Street, 2016
Highest score: 48 v. Surrey at Scarborough, 2019
Best bowling: 6-25 v. Lancashire at Leeds, 2017

One-Day:
Highest score: 9 v. Hampshire at West End, 2018
Best bowling: 4-63 v. Derbyshire at Leeds, 2017

t20:
Highest score: 2* v. Northamptonshire
at Northampton, 2015
Best bowling: 2-24 v. Northamptonshire
at Northampton, 2015

Autograph

Dawid Johannes MALAN

Left-hand batsman, leg-break bowler
Born: Roehampton September 3, 1987

First-Class cricket:
Debut: for Boland v Border at Paarl, 2006
Highest score: 199 for Middlesex v. Derbyshire
at Derby, 2019
Best bowling: 5-61 for Middlesex v. Lancashire
at Liverpool, 2012

One-Day:
Highest score: 185* for England Lions v. Sri Lanka
at Northampton, 2016
Best bowling: 4-25 for Prime Doleshwar Sporting Club
v. Partex Sporting Club at Savar, Bangladesh, 2014

T20:
Highest score: 117 for Middlesex v. Surrey at The
Oval, 2019
Best bowling: 2-10 for Middlesex v. Essex at Lord's 2009

Autograph

Harry Charrington BROOK

Right-hand batsman, medium-pace bowler
Born: Keighley, February 22, 1999

First-Class Cricket:
Debut: v. Pakistan A at Leeds, 2016
Highest score: 124 v. Essex at Chelmsford, 2018
Best bowling: 1-54 v. Somerset
at Scarborough, 2017

One-Day:
Highest score: 103 v. Leicestershire at Leeds, 2019
Best bowling: 0-19 v. Worcestershire at
Worcestershire, 2019

T20:
Highest score: 44 v. Durham at Leeds, 2018
Best bowling: 0-13 v. Nottinghamshire at
Nottingham, 2018

Autograph

Duanne OLIVIER

Right-hand batsman, right-arm fast bowler
Born: Groblersdal, South Africa, May 12, 1992

First-Class cricket:

Debut: for Free State v. North West
at Potchefstroom, 2011
Debut for Yorkshire: v. Leeds/Bradford MCCU
at Weetwood, Leeds, 2019
Highest score: 72 for Free State v. Namibia
 at Bloemfontein, 2014
Highest score for Yorkshire: 24 v. Kent at Leeds,
2019
Best bowling: 6-37 for South Africa v. Pakistan
at Centurion, 2018
Best bowling for Yorkshire: 5-96 v.
Nottinghamshire at Nottingham, 2019

One-Day:

Highest score: 25* for Knights v. Lions at Kimberley, 2018
Highest score for Yorkshire: 8* v. Nottinghamshire at Nottingham, 2019
Best bowling: 4-34 for Knights v Lions at Kimberley, 2018
Best bowling for Yorkshire: 1-44 v. Lancashire at Leeds, 2019

T20:

Highest score: 15* for Jozi Stars v. Nelson Mandela Bay Giants at Johannesburg, 2018
Highest score for Yorkshire: 1 v. Lancashire at Leeds, 2019,
and 1 v. Derbyshire at Leeds, 2019
Best bowling: 4-28 for Free State v. South West Districts at Oudtshoom, 2013
Best bowling for Yorkshire: 2-29 v. Worcestershire at Leeds, 2019

Autograph

Jonathon Andrew TATTERSALL

Right-hand batsman, leg-break bowler
Born: Harrogate, December 15, 1994

First-Class Cricket:

Debut: v. Hampshire at West End, Southampton,
2018
Highest score: 135* v. Leeds/Bradford MCCU
at Weetwood, Leeds, 2019

One-Day:

Highest score: 89 v. Hampshire at West End,
Southampton, 2018

T20:

Highest score: 53* v. Durham at Leeds, 2018

Autograph

Matthew David FISHER

Right-hand batsman, right-arm fast-medium bowler
Born: York, November 9, 1997

First-Class Cricket:
Debut: v. Nottinghamshire at Nottingham, 2015
Highest score: 47* v. Kent at Leeds, 2019
Best bowling: 5-54 v. Warwickshire at Leeds, 2017

One-Day:
Highest score: 36* v. Worcestershire
at Worcester, 2017
Best bowling: 3-32 v, Leicestershire at Leeds, 2015

T20:
Highest score: 17* v. Birmingham at Birmingham,
2018
Best bowling: 5-22 v. Derbyshire at Leeds, 2015

Autograph

Matthew James WAITE

Right-hand batsman, right-arm fast medium bowler
Born: Leeds, December 24, 1995

First-Class Cricket:
Debut: v. Somerset at Taunton, 2017
Highest score: 42 v. Nottinghamshire at
Nottingham, 2018
Best bowling: 5-16 v. Leeds/Bradford MCCU
at Weetwood, Leeds, 2019

One-Day:
Highest score: 71 v. Warwickshire
at Birmingham, 2017
Best bowling: 4-65 v. Worcestershire
at Worcester, 2017

T20:
Highest score: 19* v. Glamorgan at Cardiff, 2016
Best bowling: 1-6 v. Glamorgan at Cardiff, 2016

Autograph

James Edwin Graham LOGAN

Left-hand batsman, slow left-arm orthodox bowler
Born: Wakefield, October 12, 1997

First-Class Cricket:
Debut: v. Worcestershire at Worcester, 2018
Highest score: 20* v. Warwickshire at York, 2019
Best bowling: 4-22 v. Warwickshire at York, 2019

One-Day:
Awaits debut

T20:
Awaits debut

Autograph

William Alan Richard FRAINE

Right-hand batsman, right-arm medium pace bowler
Born: Huddersfield, June 13, 1996

First-Class Cricket:
Debut: For Durham MCCU v. Gloucestershire at
Bristol, 2017
Debut for Yorkshire: v. Essex at Leeds, 2019
Highest score: 106 v. Surrey at Scarborough, 2019

One-Day:
Highest score: 13 for Nottinghamshire v.
Lancashire at Manchester, 2018
Awaiting Yorkshire debut

T20:
Highest score: 16 v. Durham at Chester-le-Street,
2019

Autograph

Joshua Edward POYSDEN

Left-hand batsman, leg-break bowler
Born: Shoreham-by-Sea, August 8, 1991

First-Class Cricket:
Debut: for Cambridge MCCU v Essex at
Cambridge, 2011
Debut for Yorkshire: v. Lancashire at Manchester,
2018
Highest score: 47 for Cambridge MCCU v. Surrey
at Cambridge, 2011
Highest score for Yorkshire: 20 v. Lancashire
at Manchester, 2018
Best bowling: 5-29 for Warwickshire v. Glamorgan
at Birmingham, 2018
Best bowling for Yorkshire: 3-128 v. Worcestershire
at Scarborough, 2018

One-Day:
Highest score: 10* for Unicorns v. Gloucestershire at Wormsley, 2013
Highest score for Yorkshire: 1 v. Lancashire at Leeds, 2019, and 1 v. Nottinghamshire
at Nottingham, 2019
Best bowling: 3-33 for Unicorns v. Middlesex at Lord's 2013
Best bowling for Yorkshire: 2-31 v. Leicestershire at Leeds, 2019

T20:
Highest score: 9* for Warwickshire v. Northamptonshire at Northampton, 2016
Has not batted for Yorkshire
Best bowling: 4-51 for Warwickshire v. Derbyshire at Birmingham, 2015
Best bowling for Yorkshire: 2-26 v. Lahore Qalandars at Abu Dhabi 2018

<u>*Autograph*</u>

Jordan Aaron THOMPSON

Left-hand batsman, right-arm medium-pace bowler
Born: Leeds, October 9, 1996

First-Class Cricket:
Debut: v. Surrey at Guildford, 2019
Highest score: 34 v. Surrey at Guildford, 2019
Best bowling: 2-28 v. Warwickshire at York, 2019

One-Day:
Has not batted
Best bowling: 0-43 v. Durham at Leeds, 2019

T20:
Highest score: 50 v. Derbyshire at Chesterfield,
2019
Best bowling: 3-23 v. Derbyshire at Leeds, 2018

<u>*Autograph*</u>

Matthew William PILLANS

Right-hand batsman, right-arm fast bowler
Born: Westville, South Africa, July 4, 1991

First-Class Cricket:
Debut: for Northerns v North West at Pretoria, 2012
Debut for Yorkshire: v. Nottinghamshire
at Nottingham, 2018
Highest score: 56 for Leicestershire v.
Northamptonshire at Northampton, 2017
Highest score for Yorkshire: 8 v. Nottinghamshire
at Nottingham, 2018
Best bowling: 6-67 for Dolphins v. Knights
at Durban, 2015
Best bowling for Yorkshire: 2-34 v. Leeds/Bradford
MCCU at Weetwood, Leeds, 2019

One-Day:
Highest score: 31 v. Worcestershire
at Worcester, 2019
Best bowling: 5-29 v. Leicestershire at Leeds, 2019

T20:
Highest score: 34* for Leicestershire v. Warwickshire at Leicester, 2017
Highest score for Yorkshire: 8 v. Lancashire at Leeds, 2019
Best bowling: 3-15 for KwaZulu-Natal Inland v. Northerns at Bloemfontein, 2015
Best bowling for Yorkshire: 1-25 v. Birmingham at Birmingham, 2019

Autograph

Jack William SHUTT

Right-hand batsman, right-arm off-break bowler
Born: Barnsley, June 24, 1997

First-Class Cricket:
Awaiting debut

One-Day:
Awaiting debut

T20:
Highest score: 0* v. Lancashire at Leeds, 2019
Best bowling: 5-11 v. Durham at Chester-le-Street ,
2019

Autograph

Thomas William LOTEN

Right-hand batsman, right-arm medium-fast bowler
Born: Huddersfield, June 13, 1996

First-Class Cricket:
Debut: v. Warwickshire at Birmingham, 2019
Highest score: 58 v. Warwickshire at Birmingham, 2019

One-Day:
Awaiting debut

T20:
Awaiting debut

Autograph

Matthew Liam REVIS

Right-hand batsman, right-arm medium-fast bowler
Right-hand batsman, right-arm medium-pace bowler
Born: Steeton, November 15, 2001

First-Class Cricket:
Debut: v. Kent at Leeds, 2019
Highest score: 9 v. Kent at Leeds, 2019

One-Day:
Awaiting debut

T20:
Awaiting debut

Autograph

YORKSHIRE'S FIRST-CLASS HIGHLIGHTS OF 2019

Wins by an innings (3)

Leeds/Bradford MCCU (119 and 219) lost to Yorkshire (489-8 dec) by an innings and 151 runs at Weetwood, Leeds

Yorkshire (520) defeated Somerset (196 and 251) by an innings and 73 runs at Headingley, Leeds

Yorkshire (553-7 dec) defeated Hampshire (302 and 208) by an innings and 44 runs at West End, Southampton

Totals of 400 and over (4)

553-7 dec	v. Hampshire at West End, Southampton
520	v. Somerset at Headingley, Leeds
489-8 dec	v. Leeds/Bradford MCCU at Weetwood, Leeds
469	v. Kent at Canterbury

Century Partnerships (13)

For 1st wicket (1)

116	A Lyth and W A R Fraine	v. Surrey at Scarborough

For 2nd wicket (3)

184	T Kohler-Cadmore and T W Loten	v. Warwickshire at Birmingham
108	A Lyth and G S Ballance	v. Nottinghamshire at Scarborough
101 *	A Lyth and G S Ballance	v. Essex at Leeds

For 3rd wicket (5)

253 *	G S Ballance and J E Root	v. Nottinghamshire at Nottingham
199	G S Ballance and T Kohler-Cadmore	v. Somerset at Leeds
182	G S Ballance and J E Root	v. Hampshire at West End, Southampton
141	G S Ballance and T Kohler-Cadmore	v. Hampshire at Leeds
127	A Lyth and T Kohler-Cadmore	v. Essex at Leeds

For 4th wicket (1)

188	G S Ballance and J A Leaning	v. Kent at Canterbury

For 5th wicket (1)

213	T Kohler-Cadmore and J A Tattersall	v. Leeds/Bradford MCCU at Weetwood

For 6th wicket (1)

121	J A Tattersall and T T Bresnan	v. Nottinghamshire at Scarborough

For 8th wicket (1)

105	H C Brook and K A Maharaj	v. Somerset at Leeds

Centuries (12)

G S Ballance (5)

    159   v. Kent at Canterbury
    148   v. Hampshire at West End, Southampton
    111   v. Somerset at Leeds
    101 * v. Nottinghamshire at Nottingham
    100   v. Hampshire at Leeds

T Kohler-Cadmore (3)

    176   v. Leeds/Bradford MCCU at Weetwood, Leeds
    165 * v. Warwickshire at Birmingham
    102   v. Somerset at Leeds

H C Brook (1)

    101   v. Somerset at Leeds

W A R Fraine (1)

    106   v. Surrey at Scarborough

J E Root (1)

    130 * v. Nottinghamshire at Nottingham

J A Tattersall (1)

    135 * v. Leeds/Bradford MCCU at Weetwood, Leeds

5 wickets in an innings (9)

K A Maharaj (4)

    7- 52   v. Somerset at Leeds
    6- 95   v. Nottinghamshire at Scarborough
    5- 54   v. Somerset at Taunton — 1st innings
    5- 122 v. Somerset at Taunton — 2nd innings

D Olivier (2)

    5- 96   v. Nottinghamshire at Nottingham
    5- 108 v. Kent at Leeds

B O Coad (1)

    6- 52   v. Kent at Canterbury

S A Patterson (1)

    5- 81   v. Surrey at Guildford

M J Waite (1)

    5- 16   v. Leeds/Bradford at Weetwood, Leeds

10 wickets in a match (2)

K A Maharaj (2)

    10-127 (7-52 and 3-75)   v. Somerset at Leeds
    10-176 (5-54 and 5-122)   v. Somerset at Taunton

3 catches in an innings (7)

T Kohler-Cadmore (4)

6	v. Kent at Canterbury
4	v. Hampshire at West End, Southampton — 2nd innings
3	v. Leeds/Bradford MCCU at Weetwood, Leeds
3	v. Hampshire at West End, Southampton — 1st innings

J A Tattersall (3)

4	v. Nottinghamshire at Scarborough
3	v. Leeds/Bradford MCCU at Weetwood, Leeds
3	v. Hampshire at West End, Southampton

5 catches in a match (4)

T Kohler-Cadmore (2)

7 (3 + 4)	v. Hampshire at West End, Southampton
6 (6 + 0)	v. Kent at Canterbury

J A Tattersall (2)

6 (4 + 2)	v. Nottinghamshire at Scarborough
5 (3 + 2)	v Hampshire at West End, Southampton

3 dismissals in an innings (None)

Debuts (8)

In First Class cricket (3): J A Thompson, M L Revis and T W Loten
In First Class cricket for Yorkshire (5): D Olivier, D M Bess, W A R Fraine, K A Maharaj and A Y Patel

Capped: T Kohler-Cadmore

Drink to Leaning and the Three Bears

Jack Leaning, now with Kent, put his name to Jack's Batch 34, a blond ale with a citrus finish, according to the Old Mill Brewery, for whom he is a brand ambassador.

Old Mill, based in Snaith, linked up with Leaning in 2019, with 5p from every pint sold donated to the Three Bears Foundation, a charity linked to Pancreatic Cancer. Other Yorkshire players who have done similarly have included Head Coach Andrew Gale and Sir Geoffrey Boycott.

FIRST CLASS FACTFILE

Compiled by John T Potter

Versus Leeds/Bradford MCCU at Weetwood, Leeds

1. This was the first First Class match to be played at Weetwood Sports Ground, Leeds. The last new ground Yorkshire visited in the United Kingdom for a First Class match was John Walker's Ground, Southgate, to play Middlesex in 2006
2. March 31 was the earliest date on which Yorkshire had started a First Class match in England. In 2014 they started on April 1.
3. D Olivier made his First Class debut for Yorkshire and took his 400th First Class wicket.
4. M J Waite's 5-16 was his maiden five-wicket haul in an innings.
5. T Kohler-Cadmore's 176 was his highest First Class score.
6. J A Tattersall's 135* was his maiden First Class century.
7. S T Ashraf's 62 was his maiden First Class fifty.

SPECSAVERS COUNTY CHAMPIONSHIP

Versus NOTTINGHAMSHIRE at Nottingham

1. D Olivier made his Championship debut for Yorkshire.
2. B O Coad took his 100th Championship wicket.
3. G S Ballance's 101* was his second century in two years at Trent Bridge.
4. Yorkshire's second-innings third-wicket unbroken partnership of 253 by G S Ballance and J E Root was their highest against Nottinghamshire for this wicket, passing by one run the partnership of D E V Padgett and D B Close at Nottingham in 1959.

Versus HAMPSHIRE at West End, Southampton

1. G S Ballance's 148 was his third Championship century in consecutive matches and Yorkshire's 100th century against Hampshire.
2. G S Ballance and J E Root added 182 for the third wicket, which meant that they had added 435 runs in consecutive innings.
3. Hampshire's ninth-wicket partnership of 131 in their second innings was the highest for this wicket on this ground.
4. I G Holland was a concussion replacement for Hampshire. It was the first time this had happened in a Yorkshire match.
5. Yorkshire's win by an innings was their 28th against Hampshire but only their second in Southampton, the first being in 1898.

SPECSAVERS CHAMPIONSHIP FACTFILE *(Continued)*

Versus KENT at Canterbury

1. D M Bess made his First Class debut for Yorkshire.
2. F J Klaassen made his Championship debut for Kent.
3. G S Ballance's 159 was his fourth century in consecutive Championship matches.
4. Yorkshire's last victory at Canterbury was in 2001.

Versus HAMPSHIRE at Leeds

1. G S Ballance's 100 was his fifth century in consecutive Championship matches, his second this season against Hampshire, and his sixth in all to join H Sutcliffe as having scored the most centuries for Yorkshire against Hampshire.

Versus ESSEX at Leeds

1. W A R Fraine made his First Class debut for Yorkshire.
2. Essex's W E L Buttleman made his First Class debut.
3. G S Ballance's run of centuries in successive Championship matches came to an end.

Versus SURREY at Guildford

1. J A Thompson made his First Class debut.
2. Surrey's J L Smith made his Championship debut and his First Class debut in English cricket.
3. The first day saw no play because of rain, and in the match 823 minutes were lost to the weather.
4. This was Yorkshire's third visit to Guildford: they have lost two and drawn one.

Versus WARWICKSHIRE at York

1. This was only the second First Class match to be played by Yorkshire in York. The first, in 1890, was at Wigginton Road against Kent, and the second was this game at Clifton Park.
2. This was Yorkshire's first new home ground since Abbeydale Park, Sheffield, in 1974.
3. S A Patterson passed a total of 2,000 Championship runs.
4. T R Ambrose passed a total of 10,000 Championship runs.
5. J E G Logan's 4-24 was a First Class career-best.

SPECSAVERS CHAMPIONSHIP FACTFILE *(Continued)*

Versus SURREY at Scarborough

1. K A Maharaj made his First Class debut for Yorkshire.
2. Maharaj became the fourth overseas player to play for both *Roses* counties, but unlike S M Katich, J S Lehmann and G J Maxwell who had all played for Yorkshire first he played for Lancashire first.
3. W A R Fraine's 106 was his maiden First Class century.
4. G S Ballance passed personal totals of 7,000 Championship runs and 11,000 First Class runs.
5. Surrey lost the last eight wickets in their second innings for 37 runs.
6. This was Yorkshire's first win at Scarborough since 2016, when they defeated Nottinghamshire.

Versus ESSEX at Chelmsford

1. Yorkshire took their first batting point at Chelmsford in three matches.
2. S R Harmer took his 50th Championship wicket of the season.
3. This was Yorkshire's third match in three years to last for only three days.

Versus SOMERSET at Leeds

1. G S Ballance with 111, T Kohler-Cadmore, 102, and H C Brook, 101, gave Yorkshire their first three centuries in an innings against Somerset.
2. S A Patterson took his 400th First Class wicket, all for Yorkshire.
3. T D Groenewald also took his 400th First Class career wicket.

Versus NOTTINGHAMSHIRE at Scarborough

1. J A Tattersall's 92 was his Championship highest score.
2. T T Bresnan passed a personal total of 6,500 First Class runs.
3. Yorkshire achieved two wins in a season at Scarborough for the first time since 2015.
4. This was the first time since 2012 that a team winning at Scarborough did not go on to win the Championship.
5. Nottinghamshire lost and were relegated...is this the new pattern a Scarborough?

Versus SOMERSET at Taunton

1. A Lyth passed a total of 10,000 First Class runs for Yorkshire. Could he be the last to do this?
2. J H Davey's 5-21 was a First Class career-best.
3. K A Maharaj took his second haul of 10 wickets in a match against Somerset: 10-127 at Leeds and 10-176 at Taunton.
4. G S Ballance passed a total of 1,000 First Class runs for the season.
5. This match finished in three days. The last time Yorkshire finished in three days at Taunton was 2002.

Versus KENT at Leeds

1. M L Revis made his First Class debut for Yorkshire, and became the first Yorkshire cricketer born in the 21st Century.
2. A Y Patel made his First Class debut for Yorkshire.
3. D I Stevens's 237 was a First Class career-best. He became Kent's highest scorer against Yorkshire, surpassing D P Fulton's 207 at Maidstone in 1998. Stevens was the fifth oldest to score a double-century and the second oldest at 43 years and 142 days to do the double of scoring a double-century and taking 10 wickets in a match, which he had done the previous week against Nottinghamshire at Trent Bridge. W G Grace at 46 years and 303 days did that double in 1895.
4. Kent's sixth-wicket partnership of 346 by S W Billings and D I Stevens achieved the following records:
   Highest sixth-wicket partnership for Kent against any opposition, highest by any team against Yorkshire and a record for Emerald Headingley, Leeds.
6. S W Billings with 138 and 122* became only the second cricketer to score a century in each innings in a match at Headingley, the other being S D Hope in 2018 for West Indies against England.
7. The margin of victory, 433 runs, was Kent's largest by runs and Yorkshire's heaviest defeat by runs.

Versus WARWICKSHIRE at Birmingham

1. T W Loten made his First Class debut
2. T Kohler-Cadmore's 165* was his Championship best for Yorkshire. He also passed 1,000 First Class runs for the season.
3. No play was possible because of rain after tea on the first day and the next three days.

MCCU University Match — First Class
Leeds/Bradford MCCU v. Yorkshire

Played at Weetwood Sports Ground, Leeds, on March 31 and April 1 and 2, 2019

Yorkshire won by an innings and 151 runs at 3.04pm on the Third Day

Toss won by Leeds/Bradford MCCU

Close of play: First Day, Yorkshire 164-3 (Kohler-Cadmore 64*, Leaning 20*); Second Day, Leeds/Bradford MCCU 91-3 (Dahl 31*, Ashraf 30*)

LEEDS/BRADFORD MCCU

	First Innings			Second Innings	
J L Haynes,	lbw b Waite	20		lbw b Coad	18
T Cornall,	b Olivier	10		lbw b Olivier	9
O R Batchelor,	c Tattersall b Waite	2		c Tattersall b Coad	15
* A E C Dahl,	c Lyth b Coad	46		b Olivier	36
S T Ashraf,	b Waite	24		st Tattersall b Leaning	62
D A Ironside,	lbw b Waite	0		c Kohler-Cadmore b Patterson	18
§ J Read,	c Leaning b Olivier	5		c Kohler-Cadmore b Pillans	15
A J Neal,	c Tattersall b Waite	0		b Pillans	15
J B Fallows,	c Tattersall b Coad	1		absent ill	0
J B R Holling,	b Coad	0		(9) c Kohler-Cadmore b Waite	13
S Cantwell,	not out	1		(10) not out	21
	Extras b 1, lb 1, nb 8	10		Extras b 5, lb 3, nb 4	12
	Total	119		Total	219

FoW: 1-36 (Cornall), 2-40 (Batchelor), 3-49 (Haynes), 4-88 (Ashraf), 5-88 (Ironside)
1st 6-93 (Read), 7-102 (Neal), 8-118 (Dahl), 9-118 (Holling), 10-19 (Fallows)
FoW: 1-30 (Haynes), 2-30 (Batchelor), 3-30 (Cornall), 4-99 (Dahl), 5-134 (Ironside)
2nd 6-163 (Ashraf), 7-177 (Read), 8-180 (Neal), 9-219 (Holling)

	O	M	R	W		O	M	R	W
Coad	10.5	4	21	3	Coad	16	5	37	2
Olivier	14	4	38	2	Olivier $	10.4	5	30	2
Patterson	9	4	17	0	Patterson	10	3	28	1
Waite	12	5	16	5	Waite	13	5	41	1
Pillans	4	1	25	0	Leaning	11	0	32	1
					Lyth $	3.2	1	9	0
					Pillans	10	1	34	2

$ Olivier unable to complete his 10th over.
It was finished by Lyth

YORKSHIRE

A Lyth,	lbw b Cantwell	12
H C Brook,	c Read b Holling	17
G S Ballance,	c sub (S F G Bullen) b Neal	39
T Kohler-Cadmore,	c sub (S F G Bullen) b Ironside	176
J A Leaning,	b Neal	20
§ J A Tattersall,	not out	135
M J Waite,	c Read b Neal	15
* S A Patterson,	c Neal b Haynes	39
M W Pillans,	c Fallows b Ironside	3
B O Coad,	not out	10
D Olivier	Did not bat	
	Extras b 8, lb 7, nb 8	23
	Total (8 wkts dec)	489

FoW: 1-31 (Brook), 2-31 (Lyth), 3-119 (Ballance), 4-165 (Leaning), 5-378 (Kohler-Cadmore)
6-406 (Waite), 7-475 (Patterson), 8-478 (Pillans)

	O	M	R	W
Fallows	17	5	43	0
Cantwell	24	4	88	1
Holling	18	3	98	1
Neal	22	3	77	3
Haynes	20	0	94	1
Dahl	8	0	54	0
Ironside	3	0	20	2

Umpires: P J Hartley and N J Pratt   Scorers: J T Potter and C N Rawson

Leeds/Bradford MCCU v. Yorkshire

Chill as Yorkshire warm up

The opening first-class match proved a more successful warm-up for some of Yorkshire's players than spectators, who had to endure a bracing wind throughout.

The students had fielded a full team of first-class debutants in defeat at Derby the week before, having had no opportunity to take the waterlogged field against Yorkshire in 2018. They elected to bat and enjoyed a reasonable morning.

Yorkshire fielded their new Kolpak signing, Duanne Olivier, who took two wickets opening with Ben Coad (3-21), but Matthew Waite produced the standout performance. Building on encouraging winter performances and pre-season tour in South Africa his career-best of 5-16 came in 12 miserly overs.

MATTHEW WAITE
Stand-out bowler

He moved the ball just enough, and with Tim Bresnan and Matthew Fisher injured it was reassuring to see a strong performance from a fourth seamer as the hosts were bowled out for 119. Yorkshire's batsmen all made starts, but only two prospered.

Newly capped Tom Kohler-Cadmore began uncertainly before blossoming as his innings progressed. The first of his three sixes damaged a pavilion window, his double-century stand for the fifth wicket with Jonny Tattersall ending any prospect of a second chance for Yorkshire's other batsmen. Yorkshire decided to bat for as long as possible, posting 489-8 declared. Tattersall, like Waite, had enjoyed the pre-season tour, and he built on it with a composed unbeaten maiden century. Kohler-Cadmore holed out for 176, but Steven Patterson batted brightly for 39 before a tea-time declaration on day two came with a lead of 370.

The MCCU side put up a better fight in the second innings with 219 all out. Indifferent light compelled the use of spin in the last 20 minutes of day two, and light rain delayed the start of day three. The last five wickets fell in two sessions, and there was an injury scare for Olivier as he slipped in the foot holes. Saad Ashraf's 62 came within seven runs of the highest score by a Leeds/Bradford player against Yorkshire. Nearly 90 minutes into the afternoon Kohler-Cadmore's third slip catch of the day ended proceedings with injured last man Josh Fallows unable to bat.

Specsavers Championship Division 1, 2019

Captain: S A Patterson

*Captain

§ Wicket-Keeper

Figures in brackets ( ) indicate position in 2nd Innings batting order,
where different from 1st Innings

DETAILS OF PLAYERS WHO APPEARED FOR YORKSHIRE IN 2019
(ALL FIRST-CLASS MATCHES)

Player	Date of Birth	Birthplace	First-Class debut for Yorkshire	Date Capped
S A Patterson	October 3, 1983	Beverley	August 3, 2005	May 16, 2012
G S Ballance	November 22, 1989	Harare, Zim	July 11, 2008	Sept 4, 2012
T T Bresnan	February 28, 1985	Pontefract	May 14, 2003	July 19, 2006
A Lyth	September 25, 1987	Whitby	May 16, 2007	Aug 22, 2010
J E Root	December 30, 1990	Sheffield	May 10, 2010	Sept 4, 2012
J A Leaning	October 18, 1993	Bristol	June 21, 2013	Aug 13, 2016
D J Willey	February 28, 1990	Northampton	May 1, 2016	Aug 13, 2016
B O Coad	January 10, 1994	Harrogate	June 20, 2016	Sept 18, 2018
T Kohler-Cadmore	April 19, 1994	Chatham	July 3, 2017	Feb 28, 2019
D Olivier	May 9, 1992	Groblersdal, South Africa	March 31, 2019	Mar 31, 2019
K A Maharaj	February 7, 1990	Durban, South Africa	June 30, 2019	June 30, 2019
A Y Patel	October 21 1988	Bombay (now Mumbai)	September 16, 2019	Sept 16, 2019
M D Fisher	November 9, 1997	York	April 19, 2015	
J Shaw	January 3, 1996	Wakefield	June 20, 2016	
H C Brook	February 22, 1999	Keighley	June 26, 2016	
M J Waite	December 24, 1995	Leeds	June 9, 2017	
J A Tattersall	December 15, 1994	Harrogate	June 20, 2018	
J E Poysden	August 8, 1991	Shoreham-by-Sea	July 20, 2018	
M W Pillans	July 4, 1991	Westville, South Africa	September 4, 2018	
J E G Logan	October 12, 1997	Wakefield	September 24, 2018	
D M Bess	July 22, 1997	Exeter	May 14, 2019	
W A R Fraine	June 13, 1996	Huddersfield	June 3, 2019	
J A Thompson	October 9, 1996	Leeds	June 10, 2019	
M L Revis	November 15, 2001	Steeton	September 16, 2019	
T W Loten	January 8, 1999	York	September 23, 2019	

Match-By-Match Reports   **ANDREW BOSI**

103

Specsavers County Championship Division 1
Nottinghamshire v. Yorkshire

Played at Trent Bridge, Nottingham, on April 6, 7, 8 and 9, 2019

Match drawn at 5.02pm on the Fourth Day

Toss: None. Yorkshire opted to field

Nottinghamshire 12 points, Yorkshire 9 points

Close of play: First Day, Nottinghamshire 324-5 (Clarke 109*, Moores 11*); Second Day, Yorkshire 206-5 (Root 56*, Tattersall 4*); Third Day, Nottinghamshire 329-5 (Clarke 97*, Patel 23*)

First Innings	NOTTINGHAMSHIRE	Second innings	
B T Slater, c Tattersall b Olivier	76	c Lyth b Coad	2
B M Duckett, c Waite b Patterson	43	c Lyth b Olivier	61
C D Nash, lbw b Waite	21	c Root b Olivier	75
J M Clarke, b Olivier	112	not out	97
* S J Mullaney, c Lyth b Olivier	31	b Waite	52
S R Patel, c Brook b Patterson	11	(7) not out	23
§ T J Moores, c Ballance b Olivier	27	(6) c Tattersall b Waite	1
P Coughlin, c Tattersall b Patterson	46		
S C J Broad, lbw b Olivier	0		
L J Fletcher, c Kohler-Cadmore b Patterson	3		
J T Ball, not out	15		
Extras b 10, lb 10, w 1, nb 2	23	Extras b 6, lb 4, w 2, nb 6	18
Total	408	Total (5 wkts dec)	329

Bonus points — Nottinghamshire 4, Yorkshire 2   Score at 110 overs: 368-8

FoW: 1-75 (Duckett), 2-125 (Nash), 3-172 (Slater), 4-226 (Mullaney), 5-249 (Patel),
1st 6-329 (Clarke), 7-358 (Moores), 8-358 (Broad), 9-375 (Fletcher), 10-408 (Coughlin).
2nd 1-4 (Slater), 2-94 (Duckett), 3-196 (Nash), 4-278 (Mullaney), 5-300 (Moores).

	O	M	R	W		O	M	R	W
Coad	28	4	96	0	Coad	13	2	57	1
Olivier	28	8	96	5	Olivier	14	1	66	2
Waite	22	4	91	1	Patterson	14	2	52	0
Patterson	30.3	7	78	4	Root	11	1	57	0
Root	12	1	27	0	Waite	16	0	71	2
					Lyth	2	0	16	0

First Innings	YORKSHIRE	Second Innings	
A Lyth, c Fletcher b Ball	81	b Ball	21
H C Brook, lbw b Broad	30	c Nash b Ball	2
G S Ballance, b Fletcher	7	not out	101
J E Root, c Mullaney b Patel	73	not out	130
T Kohler-Cadmore, c Coughlin b Broad	22		
J A Leaning, b Fletcher	0		
§ J A Tattersall, b Fletcher	9		
M J Waite, c Mullaney b Patel	22		
* S A Patterson, c Mullaney b Patel	4		
B O Coad, not out	26		
D Olivier, c Moores b Broad	7		
Extras b 6, lb 2, nb 2	10	Extras b 9, lb 12, nb 2	23
Total	291	Total (2 wkts)	277

Bonus points — Yorkshire 2, Nottinghamshire 3

FoW: 1-39 (Brook), 2-70 (Ballance), 3-153 (Lyth), 4-194 (Kohler-Cadmore), 5-195 (Leaning),
1st 6-215 (Tattersall), 7-253 (Root), 8-256 (Waite), 9-265 (Patterson), 10-291 (Olivier).
2nd 1-19 (Brook), 2-24 (Lyth).

	O	M	R	W		O	M	R	W
Broad	20.3	4	56	3	Ball	18	3	73	2
Ball	17	3	67	1	Broad	11	2	20	0
Coughlin	13	1	49	0	Coughlin	13	1	58	0
Fletcher	20	5	64	3	Fletcher	8	3	10	0
Mullaney	3	0	16	0	Patel	25.2	3	81	0
Patel	9	2	31	3	Duckett	3	0	14	0

Umpires: D J Millns and R J Warren   Scorers: J T Potter and R Marshall

Nottinghamshire v. Yorkshire

A whole new ball game

Yorkshire followed the convention of recent seasons by inserting the opposition in April. But it was too cold for swing, and the switch to a ball with a less pronounced seam gave it little impact on a straw-coloured pitch.

The attack made little headway against a succession of batsmen raised in other counties, and many of the wickets they did take were to unforced errors. On the second morning Yorkshire bowled better, Duanne Olivier taking two wickets in an over.

Steven Patterson found his rhythm after a disappointing opening spell, as he and Olivier took nine of the 10 wickets in the Nottinghamshire total of 408. Olivier was notably quicker than any of Yorkshire's bowlers this season or last in returning 5-96, but he would need to bowl a fuller length to prosper in English conditions.

Yorkshire's reply of 291 was founded on a solid half-century from Adam Lyth, but surprisingly he holed out 19 short of three figures. Joe Root (73) was lucky to survive chances on eight and 44. His dismissal five short of the follow-on was the start of a mini-collapse to Samit Patel's left-arm spin, probably introduced to retrieve a slow over-rate.

DUANNE OLIVIER
Quickest quick

Yorkshire trailed by 117. An early wicket fell to Ben Coad, but the game was soon beyond their reach. Their prime objective was to restrict runs to delay the declaration, which came at 329-5. In the last hour of day three in light far worse than what had ended play earlier the day before they kept Joe Clarke off strike, preventing him from completing his second century of the match that night, leaving him stranded on 97.

The need to win dictated that Yorkshire must face the first over, and with both openers gone before the opening bowlers were rested an uphill battle beckoned. Third-wicket pair Gary Ballance and Root proved equal to the task, sharing an unbeaten stand of 253. Ballance was more fluent than in the first innings, and he did not give a chance until after tea as he accelerated towards three figures. Root's first Yorkshire hundred in three years was chanceless.

Specsavers County Championship Division 1
Hampshire v. Yorkshire

Played at the Ageas Bowl, West End, Southampton, on April 11, 12, 13 and 14, 2019
Yorkshire won by an innings and 44 runs at 2.40pm on the Fourth Day

Toss won by Yorkshire   Yorkshire 23 points, Hampshire 4 points

Close of play: First Day, Yorkshire 310-3 (Ballance 120*, Patterson 5*); Second Day, Hampshire 74-3 (Northeast 19*, Abbott 1*); Third Day, Hampshire 54-5 (Rossouw 2*, Dawson 12*)

YORKSHIRE

A Lyth, c McManus b Edwards		67
H C Brook, b Edwards		5
G S Ballance, c McManus b Berg		148
J E Root, b Dawson		94
* S A Patterson, c Dawson b Berg		34
T Kohler-Cadmore, lbw b Dawson		41
J A Leaning, not out		77
§ J A Tattersall, c Vince b Dawson		52
M J Waite, not out		5
B O Coad		
D Olivier	Did not bat	
Extras b 4, lb 17, w 4, nb 6		31
Total (7 wkts dec)		554

Bonus points — Yorkshire 4, Hampshire 1   Score at 110 overs: 371-3

FoW: 1-21 (Brook), 2-109 (Lyth), 3-291 (Root), 4-371 (Ballance), 5-445 (Patterson), 6-445 (Kohler-Cadmore), 7-540 (Tattersall)

	O	M	R	W
Edwards	21	3	78	2
Abbott	25	5	84	0
Barker	30	6	90	0
Berg	27	3	92	2
Dawson	60	4	184	3
Weatherley	1	0	5	0

HAMPSHIRE

	First Innings		Second Innings	
J J Weatherley, c Tattersall b Olivier		2	c Kohler-Cadmore b Patterson	9
* J M Vince, c Kohler-Cadmore b Coad		5	lbw b Patterson	11
A K Markram, c Ballance b Leaning		45	c Tattersall b Waite	7
S A Northeast, c Tattersall b Olivier		99	c Kohler-Cadmore b Patterson	0
K J Abbott, c Ballance b Coad		19	(6) lbw b Waite	3
R R Rossouw, b Waite		33	(5) lbw b Coad	5
L A Dawson, c Root b Leaning		57	c Kohler-Cadmore b Olivier	92
§ L D McManus, c Kohler-Cadmore b Patterson		27 **		
G K Berg, c Tattersall b Olivier		0	(8) c Kohler-Cadmore b Coad	0
K H D Barker, not out		9	c Tattersall b Patterson	64
F H Edwards, c Kohler-Cadmore b Patterson		0	not out	0
** I G Holland			(9) lbw b Coad	0
Extras b 14, nb 10		24	Extras b 4, lb 6, w 1, nb 6	17
Total		302	Total	208

Bonus points — Hampshire 3, Yorkshire 3

** *I G Holland was a concussion replacement for L D McManus*

FoW: 1-7 (Vince), 2-11 (Weatherley), 3-70 (Markram), 4-87 (Abbott), 5-138 (Rossouw),
1st   6-247 (Dawson), 7-264 (Northeast), 8-274 (Berg), 9-302 (McManus), 10-302 (Edwards)
FoW: 1-22 (Weatherley), 2-23 (Vince), 3-29 (Northeast), 4-31 (Markram), 5-41 (Abbott),
2nd   6-55 (Rossouw), 7-59 (Berg), 8-59 (Holland), 9-190 (Barker), 10-208 (Dawson)

	O	M	R	W		O	M	R	W
Coad	23	6	65	2	Coad	17	8	27	3
Olivier	21	3	89	3	Olivier	16.4	5	50	1
Patterson	19.3	8	36	2	Patterson	18	5	47	4
Waite	10	0	35	1	Waite	11	1	38	2
Root	12	0	43	0	Root	8	0	31	0
Leaning	9	2	20	2	Leaning	1	0	5	0

Umpires: J H Evans and A G Wharf   Scorers: J T Potter and K R Baker

Scoreboard pressure triumphs

GARY BALLANCE: His 1,000-run ground

The hosts topped the table after being invited by Essex to bat on a belter of a wicket and going on to win by an innings, but Steven Patterson was not so profligate.

Yorkshire won first use of another benign surface, Adam Lyth batting beautifully for 67 before Gary Ballance and Joe Root resumed their partnership so crucial at Trent Bridge — they put on 182 for the third wicket as Hampshire were obliged to focus on slowing the scoring rate, delaying the second new ball and finally frustrating Root, who fell for 94.

Ballance posted a superb 148, and incredibly went beyond 1,000 first-class runs at this venue in only his eighth match for Yorkshire and England. Jack Leaning and Jonny Tattersall contributed further half-centuries before the declaration came on 554-7, Yorkshire's first score of 500-plus in the Championship since 2016.

Hampshire had to face 26 overs in indifferent light late on day two. Eventually Patterson was obliged to turn to the spin of Root and Leaning, and it was Leaning who induced a shot to forget three overs before the close from key South African Aiden Markram, who was caught at deep mid-wicket. Leaning struck again on day three to remove Liam Dawson.

Having been asked to follow-on 252 behind shortly after tea, Hampshire were torn apart by brilliant Patterson, who claimed three of five wickets to fall before the close at 54-5. Although Kohler-Cadmore hogged most of the catches off the skipper at first slip — he took seven in the match — there was a good deal of team work in Yorkshire's efforts. Duanne Olivier's pace intimidated batsmen into errors at the other end; Patterson frustrated and Ben Coad and Matthew Waite chipped in.

A ninth-wicket century stand on the final day between Dawson (92) and Keith Barker (64) delayed the inevitable from 59-8. Yorkshire completed an innings win in mid-afternoon, taking them to second in the table ahead of the first break in the season for one-day cricket.

Specsavers County Championship Division 1
Kent v. Yorkshire

Played at The Spitfire Ground, St Lawrence, Canterbury, on May 14, 15, 16 and 17, 2019
Yorkshire won by 172 runs at 5.14pm on the Fourth Day

Toss won by Yorkshire   Yorkshire 20 points, Kent 5 points

Close of play: First Day, Kent 130-4 (Crawley 73*, Robinson 14*); Second Day, Yorkshire 166-3 (Ballance 57*, Leaning 11*); Third Day, Kent 34-3 (Klaassen 3*, Bell-Drummond 0*)

YORKSHIRE

First Innings		Second Innings	
A Lyth, c Renshaw b Podmore	0	c Robinson b Claydon	44
H C Brook, c Podmore	29	c Robinson b Klaassen	13
G S Ballance, c Robinson b Klaassen	11	b Bell-Drummond	159
T Kohler-Cadmore, c Podmore b Milnes	28	c Crawley b Bell -Drummond	28
J A Leaning, run out (Kuhn)	17	lbw b Milnes	69
§ J A Leaning, lbw b Claydon	29	c Robinson b Milnes	19
T T Bresnan, c Crawley b Milnes	0	b Claydon	23
D M Bess, b Milnes	25	c Klaassen b Podmore	34
* S A Patterson, run out (Claydon)	23	b Claydon	0
B O Coad, c Crawley b Bell - Drummond	7	c Dickson b Podmore	35
D Olivier, not out	21	not out	0
Extras b 4, lb 6, nb 10	20	Extras b 13, lb 11, w 1, nb 20	45
Total	210	Total	469

Bonus points — Yorkshire 1, Kent 3

FoW: 1-0 (Lyth), 2-35 (Ballance), 3-47 (Brook), 4-87 (Leaning), 5-96 (Kohler-Cadmore),
1st 6-96 (Bresnan), 7-126 (Bess), 8-166 (Tattersall), 9-181 (Coad), 10-210 (Patterson).
FoW: 1-33 (Bess), 2-82 (Lyth), 3-139 (Kohler-Cadmore), 4-327 (Leaning), 5-361 (Ballance),
2nd 6-374 (Tattersall), 7-416 (Bresnan), 8-416 (Patterson), 9-460 (Bess), 10-469 (Coad)

	O	M	R	W		O	M	R	W
Podmore	15	5	33	2	Podmore	32.1	11	89	2
Milnes	16	5	63	3	Milnes	28	4	107	2
Klaassen	10	0	44	1	Claydon	27	5	83	3
Claydon	11.2	1	51	1	Klaassen	19	0	88	1
Bell-Drummond	4	2	9	1	Bell-Drummond	13	2	35	2
					Renshaw	11	2	34	0
					Blake	1	0	9	0

KENT

First Innings		Second Innings	
S R Dickson, b Olivier	5	c Brook b Olivier	1
Z Crawley, c and b Patterson	81	lbw b Coad	9
M T Renshaw, c Kohler-Cadmore b Coad	16	b Coad	13
D J Bell-Drummond, c Kohler-Cadmore b Bresnan	3	(5) lbw b Patterson	41
* H G Kuhn, c Kohler-Cadmore b Bresnan	15	(6) c Lyth b Coad	0
§ O G Robinson, c Patterson b Coad	103	(7) c Ballance b Coad	35
A J Blake, c Kohler-Cadmore b Olivier	34	(8) lbw b Leaning	22
H W Podmore, c Kohler-Cadmore b Bess	9	(9) b Coad	29
M E Milnes, c Tattersall b Olivier	6	(10) not out	14
F J Klaassen, c Kohler-Cadmore b Coad	10	(4) c Lyth b Olivier	13
M E Claydon, not out	3	c Brook b Coad	4
Extras b 6, lb 1, nb 10	17	Extras b 3, lb 7, nb 20	30
Total	296	Total	211

Bonus points — Kent 2, Yorkshire 3

FoW: 1-9 (Dickson), 2-38 (Renshaw), 3-51 (Bell-Drummond), 4-71 (Kuhn), 5-157 (Crawley),
1st 6-261 (Blake), 7-272 (Podmore), 8-272 (Milnes), 9-293 (Robinson), 10-296 (Klaassen)
FoW: 1-3 (Dickson), 2-19 (Crawley), 3-30 (Renshaw), 4-84 (Klaassen), 5-89 (Kuhn), 6-118
2nd (Bell-Drummond), 7-142 (Robinson), 8-179 (Blake), 9-207 (Podmore), 10-211 (Claydon)

	O	M	R	W		O	M	R	W
Coad	21	7	66	3	Coad	24.5	6	52	6
Olivier	21	4	82	3	Olivier	25	4	92	2
Bresnan	17	5	47	2	Patterson	19	10	35	1
Patterson	15	5	42	1	Bresnan	2	2	0	0
Bess	13	0	52	1	Bess	16	6	14	0
					Leaning	2	0	8	1

Umpires: M Burns and P R Pollard   Scorers: J T Potter and L A R Hart

Red-ball skills rediscovered

TOM KOHLER-CADMORE
Record six in catches

Yorkshire won first use of another golden-brown wicket, but by lunchtime the scoreboard challenged that decision.

The score of 96-6 owed much to two *one-day* shots and the run-out of Jack Leaning, but Jonny Tattersall, debutant Dom Bess, Steven Patterson and Duanne Olivier clawed their way to 210 all out without anyone reaching 30.

When the fourth Kent wicket went down at 71 Yorkshire were back in the game — and might have secured parity on first innings but for opener Zak Crawley's 81 and a determined 103 from wicketkeeper Ollie Robinson as the fifth and sixth wickets added 190.

Kent fell away. Coad and Olivier claimed three wickets apiece, while Kohler-Cadmore finished with six catches in the innings, five at first slip. Ellis Robinson, against Leicestershire at Bradford in 1938, was the only previous Yorkshire outfielder to take six catches in a first-class innings. Yorkshire now batted with greater circumspection.

Day two closed at 161-3, a lead of 80, but Gary Ballance and Leaning batted through the third morning, the ex-England man completing his third successive Championship hundred just before lunch. Their stand of 188 came within 13 of Yorkshire's best for the fourth wicket at Canterbury. Patterson declared 383 ahead, leaving Kent eight overs to face before the close. Olivier and Coad took three wickets in that time.

Next morning nightwatchman Fred Klaassen and Daniel Bell-Drummond emulated Yorkshire's fourth-wicket pair by batting through the morning. A burst of four wickets threatened to disrupt the tea interval before some more resistance came from the lower order. A calf injury to Tim Bresnan added to the workload, but Bess was even more miserly than Patterson and Leaning grabbed a wicket just before the second new ball. Olivier's hostile pace was a perfect foil for Coad, who led the players from the field after completing a six-wicket haul and victory.

Specsavers County Championship Division 1
Yorkshire v. Hampshire

Played at Emerald Headingley, Leeds, on May 27, 28, 29 and 30, 2019

Match drawn at 6.04pm on the Fourth Day

Toss won by Yorkshire · · · · · · · · · · · · · · · · · · · Hampshire 9 points, Yorkshire 8 points

Close of play: First Day, Hampshire 14-1 (Weatherley 8*); Second Day, Yorkshire 5-0 (Lyth 3*, Brook 1*); Third Day, Yorkshire 207-3 (Ballance 83*, Leaning 17*)

First Innings	YORKSHIRE	Second Innings	
A Lyth, c Weatherley b Barker	18	c Weatherley b Barker	9
H C Brook, b Edwards	17	c Weatherley b Barker	9
G S Ballance, c sub (A H T Donald) b Barker	12	lbw b Crane	100
T Kohler-Cadmore, b Fuller	45	lbw b Holland	69
J A Leaning, c Rahane b Fuller	19	b Barker	41
§ J A Tattersall, c sub (A H T Donald) b Edwards	14	not out	51
D J Willey, c Barker b Edwards	34	not out	26
D M Bess, c Holland b Fuller	6		
* S A Patterson, b Edwards	0		
B O Coad, b Edwards	0		
D Olivier, not out	0		
Extras b 9, lb 3, nb 4	16	Extras b 9, lb 10, nb 8	27
Total	181	Total (5 wkts dec)	332

Bonus points — Hampshire 3

FoW: 1st 1-44 (Brook), 2-50 (Lyth), 3-65 (Ballance), 4-116 (Leaning), 5-131 (Kohler-Cadmore), 6-170 (Tattersall), 7-175 (Willey), 8-175 (Patterson), 9-177 (Coad), 10-181 (Bess)

2nd 1-15 (Brook), 2-20 (Lyth), 3-161 (Kohler-Cadmore), 4-239 (Ballance), 5-268 (Leaning)

	O	M	R	W		O	M	R	W
Barker	16	6	40	2	Barker	26	6	64	3
Edwards	15	4	49	5	Edwards	16	2	68	0
Fuller	13.2	4	51	3	Fuller	15	1	63	0
Holland	12	2	29	0	Holland	17	6	40	1
					Crane	17	2	78	1

First Innings	HAMPSHIRE	Second Innings	
J J Weatherley, c Lyth b Olivier	14	c Willey b Bess	66
O C Soames, lbw b Coad	2	c and b Olivier	0
A M Rahane, st Tattersall b Bess	31	b Coad	0
* S A Northeast, lbw b Coad	50	c Willey b Coad	14
R R Rossouw, c Kohler-Cadmore b Willey	12	not out	54
§ T P Alsop, c Lyth b Olivier	14	(7) not out	3
I G Holland, lbw b Patterson	19	(6) b Bess	14
J K Fuller, not out	54		
K H D Barker, c Kohler-Cadmore b Willey	14		
M S Crane, b Coad	5		
F H Edwards, b Coad	1		
Extras b 9, lb 3, w 1, nb 6	19	Extras lb 5, nb 2	7
Total	235	Total (5 wkts)	158

Bonus points — Hampshire 1, Yorkshire 3

FoW: 1st 1-14 (Soames), 2-32 (Weatherley), 3-80 (Rahane), 4-93 (Rossouw), 5-133 (Alsop), 6-143 (Northeast), 7-180 (Holland), 8-207 (Barker), 9-225 (Crane), 10-235 (Edwards)

2nd: 1-4 (Soames), 2-7 (Rahane), 3-35 (Northeast), 4-137 (Weatherley), 5-153 (Holland)

	O	M	R	W		O	M	R	W
Coad	19.1	7	41	4	Coad	12	2	43	2
Olivier	16	3	54	2	Olivier	9	4	38	1
Patterson	18	7	31	1	Willey	6	1	27	0
Willey	9	1	52	2	Patterson	5	1	20	0
Bess	11	1	37	1	Bess	13	5	24	2
Leaning	1	0	8	0	Leaning	1	0	1	0

Umpires: R J Bailey and N L Bainton · · · · · · · · Scorers: J T Potter and K R Baker

Brave challenge washed out

GARY BALLANCE: Five in five

The first Championship match at Emerald Headingley of 2019 saw a return to frequent rain interruptions, which disrupted the rhythm of Yorkshire's first innings and refreshed that of 37-year-old Fidel Edwards, whose five-wicket haul ensured no home batting points.

There was one wicket before the 6.55pm close, and Yorkshire worked their way through Hampshire's batting on day two. At lunch four bowlers had conceded under two an over, and Hampshire had failed to muster a half-century partnership — Yorkshire had had one — losing seven wickets in securing a first-innings lead. After a lengthy rain delay Yorkshire faced an anxious last session if they took the last two wickets too quickly, but Coad timed it just about right. Adam Lyth, who had tweaked a hamstring taking a sensational catch at second slip, and Harry Brook saw out three overs.

They could not capitalise on day three, but third-wicket pair Gary Ballance and Tom Kohler-Cadmore put on 141 to turn the tide with the first significant stand of the match. Kohler-Cadmore maintained his promising start to the season, and Ballance was unbeaten on 83 when rain brought an early tea and a premature close.

Short but frequent showers disrupted the final morning, but Ballance completed another hundred, his fifth in as many matches dating back to the end of 2018. Only Sir Leonard Hutton (twice) had previously achieved this feat for Yorkshire, including seven in succession in 1947/48.

In the early afternoon, played through light rain, Yorkshire accumulated quick runs and declared to set a target of 279 in 48 overs. Risking the five draw points demonstrated Yorkshire's confidence after dominating what play had been possible since day one.

Early wickets — Coad took his fifth and sixth wickets of the match to remove Indian Ajinkya Rahane and Sam Northeast — compelled Hampshire, who were 35-3 at tea, to focus on five rather than 16 points. With more than a full day's play lost, rain proved the ultimate winner.

Specsavers County Championship Division 1
Yorkshire v. Essex

Played at Emerald Headingley, Leeds, on June 3, 4, 5 and 6, 2019
Match drawn at 4.30pm on the Fourth Day

Toss won by Yorkshire — Yorkshire 11 points, Essex 9 points
Close of play: First Day, Yorkshire 289-6 (Tattersall 20*, Bess 30*); Second Day, Essex 18-1 (Browne 10*, Westley 3*); Third Day, Essex 252-9 (Siddle 39*, S J Cook 0*)

YORKSHIRE

	First Innings			Second Innings	
A Lyth, c Buttleman b Porter			95	not out	56
W A R Fraine, b S J Cook			39	c A N Cook b Porter	0
G S Ballance, run out (S J Cook/Buttleman)			14	not out	51
T Kohler-Cadmore, c Buttleman b S J Cook			83		
J A Leaning, c Harmer b Siddle			3		
§ J A Tattersall, c Buttleman b Bopara			45		
D J Willey, lbw b Harmer			3		
D M Bess, not out			91		
* S A Patterson, lbw b Porter			8		
B O Coad, c A N Cook b Porter			1		
D Olivier, c Harmer b S J Cook			1		
Extras b 1, lb 3, w 1, nb 2			7	Extras	0
Total			390	Total (1 wkt)	107

Bonus points — Yorkshire 3, Essex 2   Score at 110 overs: 325-6

FoW: 1-77 (Fraine), 2-97 (Ballance), 3-224 (Lyth), 4-229 (Leaning), 5-247 (Kohler-Cadmore), 1st 6-252 (Willey), 7-342 (Tattersall), 8-379 (Patterson), 9-387 (Coad), 10-390 (Olivier)
2nd   1-1 (Fraine)

	O	M	R	W		O	M	R	W
Porter	28	6	84	3	Porter	9.5	2	30	1
S J Cook	28.4	6	91	4	S J Cook	10	3	24	0
Siddle	20	3	68	1	Harmer	10	4	22	0
Harmer	33	9	90	1	Westley	4.5	1	14	0
Bopara	16	1	53	1	Bopara	5	2	7	0
					ten Doeschate	1.1	0	5	0
					Lawrence	2	0	5	0

Porter unable to complete his 10th over:
It was finished by ten Doeschate

ESSEX

N J L Browne, lbw b Bess		35
A N Cook, c Kohler-Cadmore b Coad		2
T Westley, c Tattersall b Willey		77
D W Lawrence, c Fraine b Olivier		21
R S Bopara, b Olivier		44
* R N ten Doeschate, c Lyth b Bess		0
S R Harmer, c Lyth b Bess		18
§ W E L Buttleman, c Tattersall b Willey		0
P M Siddle, lbw b Patterson		60
J A Porter, c Kohler-Cadmore b Patterson		0
S J Cook, not out		37
Extras b 5, lb 4, nb6		15
Total		309

Bonus points — Essex 2, Yorkshire 3   Score at 110 overs: 295-9

FoW: 1-3 (A N Cook), 2-97 (Browne), 3-132 (Westley), 4-190 (Lawrence), 5-191 (ten Doeschate), 6-191 (Bopara), 7-197 (Buttleman), 8-213 (Harmer), 9-223 (Porter), 10-309 (Siddle)

	O	M	R	W
Coad	26	7	73	1
Olivier	28	12	74	2
Patterson	17.5	2	69	2
Willey	19	8	39	2
Bess	26	11	45	3

Umpires: N A Mallender and S J O'Shaughnessy   Scorers: J T Potter and A E Choat

Snubbed Willey's best yet

The second successive game at Headingley suffered the same fate — significant rain interruptions — after Yorkshire had established the stronger position.

Will Fraine's torrent of second-team runs was rewarded, and he and Adam Lyth gave Yorkshire their best start of the season with a stand of 77 after Steven Patterson had won his ninth successive toss.

Gary Ballance looked in sublime form, and it was a major setback when he went for a non-existent second run 10 minutes before lunch, Lyth accepting the blame.

The afternoon was enriched by crisp boundaries and an unbroken third-wicket stand approaching 127 between Lyth and Tom Kohler-Cadmore.

DAVID WILLEY: In the swing

Four evening wickets threatened Yorkshire's hopes of reaching 300, but Jonny Tattersall and Dom Bess were equal to the task of keeping out the new ball, taken after 89 overs, and extending their stand next day to 90 and a third batting point. Bess scored more freely, and was seldom troubled, even though conditions on the second morning favoured swing and seam. The last two wickets fell to expansive drives when he was in touching distance of a first Championship ton.

Ben Coad produced a beauty to dismiss Sir Alastair Cook before rain ended play for the day. Essex then moved serenely to 190-3 before a middle order sag to 223-9. Nine overs passed without a run, two of them wicket maidens. David Willey, aided by reverse swing, responded to his England World Cup omission with the best bowling of his Yorkshire first-class career. Peter Siddle was badly missed second ball off Willey by Tattersall, and this cost Yorkshire the chance of enforcing the follow-on (241). Bess bowled tidily, and it was a pleasure to watch him exercising such control on a pitch often regarded as a spinners' graveyard.

Interest in the final day was confined to whether Ballance could extend his run of centuries. Torrential rain at tea curtailed his efforts.

Specsavers County Championship Division 1
Surrey v. Yorkshire

Played at Woodbridge Road, Guildford, on June 10, 11, 12 and 13, 2019
Match drawn at 4.57pm on the Fourth Day

Toss: None. Yorkshire opted to field   Surrey 11 points, Yorkshire 8 points

Close of play: First Day, no play; Second Day, Surrey 290-8 (Clark 7*, Morkel 5); Third Day, Yorkshire 58-1 (Fraine 17*, Ballance 6*)

SURREY

M D Stoneman, c Tattersall b Thompson	61
D Elgar, c Bess b Patterson	24
S G Borthwick, c Lyth b Thompson	21
R S Patel, lbw b Coad	19
* § B T Foakes, b Patterson	62
J L Smith, b Patterson	56
W G Jacks, b Patterson	0
R Clarke, lbw b Coad	13
J Clark, c sub (M D Fisher) b Patterson	26
M Morkel, c Lyth b Coad	5
M P Dunn, not out	2
Extras b 14, lb 2, nb 8	24
Total	313

Bonus points — Surrey 3, Yorkshire 3

FoW: 1-78 (Elgar), 2-98 (Stoneman), 3-142 (Patel), 4-147 (Borthwick), 5-265 (Foakes), 6-265 (Jacks), 7-266 (Smith), 8-285 (Clarke), 9-291 (Morkel), 10-313 (Clark)

	O	M	R	W
Coad	25	4	71	3
Olivier	12	3	42	0
Bess	18	1	62	0
Patterson	26.4	4	81	5
Thompson	19	6	41	2

YORKSHIRE

First Innings		Second Innings	
A Lyth, c Jacks b Clarke	30	not out	15
W A R Fraine, c Foakes b Morkel	25	not out	14
G S Ballance, c Elgar b Morkel	6		
T Kohler-Cadmore, c Foakes b Clarke	14		
J A Leaning, c Foakes b Morkel	4		
§ J A Tattersall, c Clarke b Clark	7		
D M Bess, c Clarke b Clark	0		
J A Thompson, c Morkel b Dunn	34		
* S A Patterson, c Foakes b Clarke	6		
B O Coad, b Morkel	0		
D Olivier, not out	13		
Extras lb 7, nb 2	9	Extras lb 1	1
Total	148	Total (0 wkts)	30

Bonus points — Surrey 3

FoW: 1-51 (Lyth), 2-58 (Ballance), 3-75 (Fraine), 4-79 (Leaning), 5-93 (Tattersall), 1st 6-93 (Bess), 7-93 (Kohler-Cadmore), 8-109 (Patterson), 9-114 (Coad), 10-148 (Thompson)

	O	M	R	W		O	M	R	W
Morkel	16	4	43	4	Morkel	3	1	7	0
Dunn	11	3	26	1	Dunn	4	2	9	0
Clark	8	1	37	2	Clarke	4	2	8	0
Clarke	13	4	35	3	Clark	2.3	1	5	0

Umpires: J W Lloyds and R T Robinson   Scorers: J T Potter and P J Makepeace

114

Surrey v. Yorkshire

River Jordan, Patterson gold

STEVEN PATTERSON
Bowled three in over

A deluge on the first day left the surrounding roads like a river, but the prompt start next morning, following tireless work from the groundstaff, surprised many.

With David Willey unavailable for family reasons Jordan Thompson made his first-class debut for Yorkshire, impressing with two top-order wickets and the most economical figures of the innings.

Yorkshire otherwise made little headway, and a fifth-wicket century stand between Ben Foakes and Surrey Championship debutant Jamie Smith took the home side to a peak of 265-4.

Duanne Olivier was off the field with a hip injury, and skipper Steven Patterson, who was to bowl 24 overs in a day curtailed by bad light, was obliged to take the second new ball. He produced a golden over in which the stumps were hit three times, Foakes playing on as the score slipped to 265-7.

Cloud cover on day three offered more movement, but 20 were added before Patterson claimed his fifth wicket.

Adam Lyth and Will Fraine again shaped well, and produced their second half-century stand before Lyth was out to a well taken low catch. Soon afterwards further prolonged rain ended the day's play.

The groundstaff ensured a prompt start on day four even as the temporary seating around the ground was being carted away. Ballance was out to the day's first ball, a nasty lifting delivery from Morne Morkel. There were batting points at stake, but rain was never far away. Jordan Clark, he of the 2018 *Roses* Old Trafford hat-trick, took his first wickets for Surrey, and the only prolonged resistance came from Thompson.

Arriving shortly before the seventh wicket fell at 93, Thompson defended stoutly until injured last man Olivier came to the crease. He then attacked judiciously enough to take Yorkshire within 16 of the follow-on target and to reduce the number of overs Yorkshire still faced to a possible 38. Lyth and Fraine were rarely troubled, and bad light limited the innings to 81 balls.

Specsavers County Championship Division 1
Yorkshire v. Warwickshire

Played at Clifton Park, York, on June 17, 18, 19 and 20, 2019

Warwickshire won by 3 wickets at 5.38pm on the Fourth Day

Toss: None. Warwickshire opted to field   Warwickshire 21 points, Yorkshire 5 points

Close of play: First Day, Yorkshire 208-8 (Patterson 36*, Logan 0*); Second Day, Warwickshire 192-5 (Hain 23*, Ambrose 11*); Third Day, Yorkshire 178-7 (Leaning 47*, Patterson 9*)

YORKSHIRE

	First Innings		Second Innings	
A Lyth, c Ambrose b Hannon-Dalby	7	c Ambrose b Miles	37
W A R Fraine, c Lamb b Miles	42	lbw b Hannon-Dalby	1
G S Ballance, lbw b Patel	54	c Rhodes b Hannon-Dalby	18
T Kohler-Cadmore, lbw b Miles	0	c Ambrose b Lamb	20
J A Leaning, b Miles	0	lbw b Patel	65
§ J A Tattersall, c Hain b Hannon-Dalby	4	c Ambrose b Hannon-Dalby	17
J A Thompson, lbw b Hannon-Dalby	0	b Patel	2
D J Willey, b Miles	46	st Ambrose b Patel	0
* S A Patterson, b Hannon-Dalby	60	b Hannon-Dalby	9
J E G Logan, not out	20	b Patel	7
B O Coad, b Hannon-Dalby	2	not out	5
Extras b 7, lb 16, w 1	24	Extras b 4, lb 10, nb 16	30
Total	259	Total	211

Bonus points — Yorkshire 2, Warwickshire 3

FoW: 1-8 (Lyth), 2-93 (Fraine), 3-93 (Kohler-Cadmore), 4-93 (Leaning), 5-101 (Tattersall),
1st   6-101 (Thompson), 7-145 (Ballance), 8-205 (Willey), 9-253 (Patterson), 10-259 (Coad)
FoW: 1-3 (Fraine), 2-31 (Ballance), 3-68 (Kohler-Cadmore), 4-97 (Lyth), 5-127 (Tattersall),
2nd   6-134 (Thompson), 7-140 (Willey), 8-179 (Patterson), 9-200 (Logan), 10-211 (Leaning)

	O	M	R	W		O	M	R	W
Hannon-Dalby	26.4	9	76	5	Hannon-Dalby	25	7	61	4
Norwell	20	6	51	0	Norwell	7	2	10	0
Patel	29	7	65	1	Miles	11	1	47	1
Miles	17	3	44	4	Patel	31	8	48	4
					Lamb	7	1	31	1

WARWICKSHIRE

	First Innings		Second Innings	
W M H Rhodes, c Leaning b Coad	28	b Willey	83
D P Sibley, b Patterson	67	c Patterson b Logan	81
R M Yates, c Kohler-Cadmore b Patterson	49	c Willey b Logan	9
S R Hain, c Lyth b Willey	25	c Tattersall b Patterson	8
A J Hose, lbw b Patterson	0	b Logan	24
M J Lamb, c Lyth b Willey	11	b Logan	7
§ T R Ambrose, c Kohler-Cadmore b Willey	39	c Kohler-Cadmore b Thompson	2
C N Miles, c Patterson b Coad	27	not out	0
* J S Patel, c Tattersall b Thompson	5	not out	4
L C Norwell, lbw b Thompson	0		
O J Hannon-Dalby, not out	0		
Extras lb 3	3	Extras lb 1	1
Total	254	Total (7 wkts)	219

Bonus points — Warwickshire 2, Yorkshire 3

FoW: 1-38 (Rhodes), 2-139 (Sibley), 3-148 (Yates), 4-148 (Hose), 5-166 (Lamb),
1st   6-201 (Hain), 7-234 (Miles), 8-250 (Patel), 9-250 (Norwell), 10-254 (Ambrose)
FoW: 1-132 (Rhodes), 2-166 (Yates), 3-181 (Sibley), 4-183 (Hain), 5-202 (Lamb),
2nd   6-213 (Hose), 7-215 (Ambrose)

	O	M	R	W		O	M	R	W
Coad	26	4	83	2	Coad	11	1	33	0
Willey	21.2	3	71	3	Patterson	17	4	36	1
Patterson	23	8	33	3	Willey	13	3	56	1
Logan	8	2	19	0	Thompson	9	0	36	1
Thompson	12	4	28	2	Leaning	3	0	35	0
Leaning	8	2	17	0	Logan	13	4	22	4

Umpires: J H Evans and D J Millns   Scorers: J T Potter and R J Dickinson

Dampener on historic week

JACK LEANING: Model of concentration

Brilliant organisation for Yorkshire's first game at Clifton Park and thrilling cricket were marred only by the result.

Inserted in difficult conditions, Yorkshire lost five wickets for eight runs, slipping from 93-1 to 101-6 after rain meant a midday start. Steven Patterson's 60, three short of his best, later took most plaudits as the last three wickets added 114. Former Yorkshire seamer Oliver Hannon-Dalby finished with five wickets.

In contrast Warwickshire relied on their top orde, but they were aided by drops with Will Rhodes and Rob Yates on one, Yates and Dom Sibley sharing a second-wicket century stand from 38-1. But as day two drew to a close skipper Patterson brought Yorkshire back into the game with three wickets. Three more wickets shared between Jordan Thompson and David Willey in six balls either side of lunch on day three wrapped up Warwickshire's innings and secured a lead of five.

Yorkshire made reasonable progress to tea, when they led by 101 with seven wickets in hand, but in the evening three fell in a misguided attempt to force the pace. Again the last three wickets made useful runs, home boy Leaning a model of concentration in a fifty that lasted longer than a barrel of Jack's Batch 34.

The last-day target of 217 seemed to offer an equal chance to both sides after Hannon-Dalby had recorded a career best nine-for in the match. Unfortunately for the hosts the pace bowlers were unable to break through. Leaning had looked threatening in the first innings, but his familiarity to former teammate Rhodes cost 26 in a key over.

Only when 52 runs were needed was James Logan introduced at the Shipton Road End, earlier used by Jeetan Patel to claim his 700th Warwickshire wicket in all formats at the start of day four.

A stunning Patterson catch at mid-off helped Logan to claim four of six wickets to fall from 181-2 to 215-7, his first in first-class cricket but Warwickshire won this historic encounter with 10 overs remaining.

Specsavers County Championship Division 1
Yorkshire v. Surrey

Played at North Marine Road, Scarborough, on June 30 and July 1. 2 and 3, 2019
Yorkshire won by 123 runs at 5.54pm on the Fourth Day

Toss won by Yorkshire — Yorkshire 22 points, Surrey 7 points

Close of play: First Day, Surrey 48-0 (Stoneman 28*, Elgar 14*); Second Day, Surrey 362 all out; Third Day, Yorkshire 303-9 (Coad 16*, Olivier 0*)

First Innings	YORKSHIRE	Second Innings	
A Lyth, c Smith b Clarke	55	c Foakes b Clarke	68
W A R Fraine, c Foakes b Morkel	106	c Clark b Patel	43
G S Ballance, c Borthwick b Clark	23	lbw b Curran	23
T Kohler-Cadmore, b Clark	5	st Foakes b Batty	42
J A Leaning, c Borthwick b Clark	0	lbw b Clarke	0
§ J A Tattersall, c Foakes b Clark	11	c Clarke b Curran	38
D J Willey, c Stoneman b Curran	19	c Borthwick b Curran	43
K A Maharaj, b Curran	0	c Borthwick b Morkel	10
* S A Patterson, c Clarke b Clark	46	c Patel b Morkel	2
B O Coad, c Patel b Morkel	25	c Foakes b Batty	48
D Olivier, not out	11	not out	11
Extras lb 8, nb 18	26	Extrs lb 8, lb 8	24
Total	327	Total	352

Bonus points — Yorkshire 3, Surrey 3

FoW: 1-116 (Lyth), 2-187 (Ballance), 3-201 (Kohler-Cadmore), 4-205 (Fraine), 5-205
1at (Leaning), 6-231 (Willey), 7-231 (Maharaj), 8-250 (Tattersall), 9-295 (Coad), 10-327 (Patterson)

FoW: 1-94 (Fraine), 2-131 (Ballance), 3-162 (Lyth), 4-168 (Leaning), 5-225 (Kohler Cadmore),
2nd 6-251 (Tattersall), 7-276 (Willey), 8-286 (Maharaj), 9-295 (Patterson), 10-352 (Coad)

	O	M	R	W		O	M	R	W
Morkel	21	5	77	1	Morkel	21	7	61	2
Curran $	18.4	3	84	2	Curran	26	4	90	3
Clarke $	16	3	56	1	Clark	3	0	22	0
Clarke	17.4	1	77	5	Clarke	13	2	36	2
Batty	6	0	25	0	Batty	32.1	5	87	2
					Patel	11	1	40	1

$ Curran was unable to complete his 15th over. It was finished by Clark

First Innings	SURREY	Second Innings	
M D Stoneman c Tattersall b Olivier	100	(2) c Fraine b Maharaj	46
D Elgar, b Coad	24	(1) run out (Willey)	71
S G Borthwick, c Kohler-Cadmore b Willey	24	b Willey	24
R S Patel, c Tattersall b Maharaj	26	c Fraine b Maharaj	9
* § B T Foakes, c Leaning b Coad	40	b Coad	0
S M Curran, c Leaning b Coad	43	c Tattersall b Coad	0
J L Smith, c Lyth b Willey	28	not out	24
R Clarke, c Kohler-Cadmore b Maharaj	26	c Tattersall b Maharaj	0
J Clark, c Lyth b Maharaj	25	b Olivier	1
M Morkel, b Olivier	0	run out (Kohler-Cadmore/Maharaj)	0
G J Batty, not out	9	c Lyth b Olivier	4
Extras lb 1, nb 16	17	Extras b10, lb 5	15
Total	362	Total	194

Bonus points — Surrey 4, Yorkshire 3

FoW: 1-68 (Elgar), 2-110 (Borthwick), 3-182 (Patel), 4-186 (Stoneman), 5-267 (Curran),
1st 6-286 (Foakes), 7-303 (Smith), 8-334 (Clarke), 9-334 (Morkel), 10-362 (Clark)
FoW: 1-93 (Stoneman), 2-136 (Borthwick), 3-157 (Elgar), 4-157 (Foakes), 5-163 (Patel),
2nd 6-163 (Patel), 7-163 (Clarke), 8-180 (Clark), 9-180 (Morkel), 10-194 (Batty)

	O	M	R	W		O	M	R	W
Coad	21	4	60	3	Coad	14	7	30	2
Olivier	25	3	111	2	Olivier	13.2	1	32	2
Patterson	23	5	58	0	Maharaj	33	11	69	3
Maharaj	23.4	5	75	3	Patterson	11	0	32	0
Willey	14	3	55	2	Willey	6	2	16	1
Leaning	1	0	2	0	Leaning	4	4	0	0

Umpires: I D Blackwell and A G Wharf

Scorers: J T Potter and P J Makepeace

Holiday crowd rewarded

Ten minutes from tea on day four Surrey were half way to their 318 target, two wickets down, as a second successive enthralling home fixture drew to a close.

A first innings deficit of 35 was a fair exchange for bowling last, but only when Ben Coad and Duanne Olivier frustrated Surrey on the final morning with a half-century stand did Yorkshire land a psychological blow and post a challenging target in 83 overs.

The first new ball was ineffective in all four innings, but good containing bowling preyed on the minds of third-wicket pair Ryan Patel and Dean Elgar, parted by a calamitous run out of Elgar.

Two more wickets for Coad in what became the last over before tea and two straight afterwards put Yorkshire on top. The eighth wicket consumed 17 overs.

Then a comical run-out of Morne Morkel left Jamie Smith and Gareth Batty 10.5 overs to survive, only for the

WILL FRAINE: Converted his first fifty to a hundred

second new ball to secure victory with 10 balls to go when Olivier had Batty caught at second slip. On day one opener Will Fraine had converted his first first-class half-century to three figures, but the middle-order failed to capitalise on a sound start, and it was left to Steven Patterson to shepherd the tail to add 96 for the last three wickets.

All of the Surrey top nine made a start on day two, but only Mark Stoneman went on to a significant score. Yorkshire took the last six wickets after tea.

Adam Lyth and Fraine opened with 94 at the start of day three to follow their century stand, but the second innings fell away, only Lyth passing 50. Batty had achieved some turn, and spin was introduced early in the fourth innings. New signing Keshav Maharaj bowled mainly from the Trafalgar Square End, where he gained useful bounce, and was key to maintaining the pressure on Surrey as they crumbled from a position of strength.

Specsavers County Championship Division 1
Essex v. Yorkshire

Played at Cloud FM County Ground, Chelmsford, on July 7, 8 and 9, 2019
Essex won by 8 wickets at 4.55pm ont the Third Day

Toss won by Yorkshire   Essex 22 points, Yorkshire 3 points

Close of play: First Day, Essex 122-3 (Westley 52*, Patel 10*); Second Day, Yorkshire 38-3 (Lyth 9*, Brook 4*)

First Innings	YORKSHIRE	Second Innings	
A Lyth, c Browne b Porter	5	lbw b Porter	14
W A R Fraine, c Wheater b Porter	29	b Siddle	3
G S Ballance, b Siddle	8	c Wheater b Siddle	4
T Kohler-Cadmore, lbw b Harmer	16	lbw b Harmer	8
H C Brook, b Harmer	46	lbw b Siddle	12
§ J A Tattersall, c Wheater b Harmer	23	c Lawrence b Harmer	14
M D Fisher, lbw b Harmer	25	lbw b Harmer	16
K A Maharaj, lbw b Harmer	26	b Siddle	85
* S A Patterson, b Siddle	7	c Cook b Porter	4
B O Coad, c Wheater b Beard	14	c Cook b Porter	18
D Olivier, not out	1	not out	7
Extras lb 6, nb 2	8	Extras b 8, lb 16, nb 2	26
Total	208	Total	211

Bonus points — Yorkshire 1, Essex 3

FoW: 1-18 (Lyth), 2-37 (Ballance), 3-43 (Fraine), 4-69 (Kohler-Cadmore), 5-128 (Brook),
1st   6-129 (Tattersall), 7-177 (Maharaj), 8-184 (Patterson), 9-206 (Coad), 10-208 (Fisher)
FoW: 1-10 (Fraine), 2-14 (Ballance), 3-30 (Kohler-Cadmore), 4-52 (Lyth), 5-58 (Brook),
2nd   6-81 (Tattersall), 7-110 (Fisher), 8-129 (Patterson), 9-193 (Maharaj), 10-211 (Coad)

	O	M	R	W		O	M	R	W
Porter	11	1	40	2	Porter	18.4	2	62	3
Siddle	14	1	71	2	Siddle	21	8	32	4
Harmer	18.3	2	76	5	Harmer	24	8	72	3
Beard	6	2	15	1	Beard	8	2	17	0

First Innings	ESSEX	Second Innings	
N L J Browne, c and b Fisher	8	not out	33
A N Cook, c Tattersall b Patterson	27	c Kohler-Cadmore b Patterson	6
T Westley, lbw b Olivier	81	st Tattersall b Maharaj	31
D W Lawrence, c Maharaj b Olivier	15	not out	18
R K Patel, c Fraine b Fisher	35		
* R N ten Doeschate, not out	70		
§ A J A Wheater, c Tattersall b Coad	6		
S R Harmer, b Fisher	3		
P M Siddle, b Maharaj	19		
A P Beard, b Maharaj	41		
J A Porter, c Kohler-Cadmore b Maharaj	0		
Extras b 1, lb 16, nb 6	23	Extras b 2, lb 4	6
Total	328	Total (2 wkts)	94

Bonus points — Essex 3, Yorkshire 2   Score at 110 overs: 308-8

FoW: 1-11 (Browne), 2-57 (Cook), 3-101 (Lawrence), 4-169 (Patel), 5-202 (Westley),
1st   6-219 (Wheater), 7-222 (Harmer), 8-253 (Siddle), 9-328 (Beard), 10-328 (Porter)
2nd   1-22 (Cook), 2-61 (Westley)

	O	M	R	W		O	M	R	W
Coad	19	4	56	1	Fisher	3	1	13	0
Fisher	22	4	59	3	Patterson	8	3	19	1
Patterson	17	7	22	1	Maharaj	8	2	35	1
Maharaj	36	11	93	3	Olivier	2.5	0	21	0
Olivier	19	1	76	2					
Lyth	4	2	5	0					

Umpires: R J Bailey and P R Pollard   Scorers: J T Potter and A E Choat

Outmuscled by the tops

KESHAV MAHARAJ
Face-saving 85

This was the only time throughout the Championship campaign that Yorkshire were soundly beaten.

Defeat had come against Warwickshire a few weeks earlier at York, but the hosts had their chances. Here, they were outmuscled by a title-challenger.

Hitherto this season the first innings at Chelmsford had failed to yield a batting point. Yorkshire, with 208, broke this sequence during the first half of day one as Harry Brook batted nicely for 46 at No.5, having come back into the side following earlier struggles opening.

Matthew Fisher with 25 was also a key contributor to at least gaining respectability after a number of surrendered wickets. Spectators were also feeling the heat — the ice cream was sold out by tea.

Essex demonstrated how to bat in a four-day game, but Yorkshire's seam attack bowled well, led by three wickets for Fisher. When the seventh wicket fell at 222 Yorkshire were back in the game, but captain Ryan ten Doeschate frustrated them with an unbeaten 70 as the hosts posted 328.

Yorkshire did much better in the second innings after Peter Siddle, soon to be called up for the *Ashes*, challenged them with the early dismissals of Will Fraine and Gary Ballance. They sold their wickets dearly, which meant the ball was older and the attack less fresh for Keshav Maharaj to entertain with a face-saving 85. Essex would have to bat again and the game would extend beyond tea on the third day.

South African off-spinner Simon Harmer out-bowled compatriot Maharaj on the ground where he was already approaching 50 wickets in the season — five in the first innings and three in the second.

A victory target of only 92 was achieved for the loss of two wickets, including Sir Alastair Cook off Steven Patterson for the second time in the match. The former England captain fell for six, but he had been dropped on nought. Patterson took the new ball in place of Ben Coad, who was suffering from a sore calf.

Specsavers County Championship Division 1
Yorkshire v. Somerset

Played at Emerald Headingley, Leeds, on July 13, 14, 15 and 16, 2019
Yorkshire won by an innings and 73 runs at 12.43pm on the Fourth Day

Toss: None. Somerset opted to field   Yorkshire 22 points, Somerset 1 point

Close of play: First Day, Yorkshire 282-3 (Kohler-Cadmore 77*, Shaw 0*); Second Day, Somerset 76-4 (Hildreth 36*, Davies 12*); Third Day, Somerset following on 159-4 (Banton 58*, Groenewald 0*)

YORKSHIRE

A Lyth, c Abell b Bess		35
W A R Fraine, c Bess b Brooks		45
G S Ballance, c J Overton b Groenewald		111
T Kohler-Cadmore, c J Overton b C Overton		102
J Shaw, b Groenewald		6
H C Brook, c Azhar Ali b Abell		101
§ J A Tattersall, c J Overton b Brooks		3
M D Fisher, c Banton b Bess		20
K A Maharaj, c J Overton b Bess		72
* S A Patterson, c Davies b Bess		1
D Olivier, not out		2
Extras b 8, lb 12, nb 2		22
Total		520

Bonus points — Yorkshire 3, Somerset 1   Score at 110 overs: 339-5

FoW: 1-80 (Fraine), 2-82 (Lyth), 3-181 (Ballance), 4-305 (Shaw), 5-319 (Kohler-Cadmore), 6-351 (Tattersall), 7-398 (Fisher), 8-503 (Maharaj), 9-506 (Patterson), 10-520 (Brook)

	O	M	R	W
C Overton	28	4	91	1
Brooks	28	2	96	2
Groenewald	26	7	74	2
J Overton	20	3	71	0
Bess	42	11	130	4
Abell	16.1	7	38	1

SOMERSET

First Innings			Second Innings	
* T B Abell, c Brook b Fisher		6	c Tattersall b Fisher	53
Azhar Ali, c Lyth b Fisher		4	lbw b Fisher	41
J C Hildreth, lbw b Maharaj		37	c Patterson b Maharaj	1
T Banton, c Tattersall b Maharaj		5	b Patterson	63
G A Bartlett, c Patterson b Olivier		5	c Lyth b Maharaj	5
§ S M Davies, c Lyth b Maharaj		37	(7) c Olivier b Patterson	24
D M Bess, lbw b Maharaj		7	(8) b Patterson	4
C Overton, c Maharaj		2	(9) lbw b Patterson	23
J Overton, not out		52	(10) lbw b Maharaj	21
T D Groenewald, lbw b Maharaj		15	(6) c Fraine b Fisher	8
J A Brooks, c Kohler-Cadmore b Maharaj		9	not out	2
Extras b 9, lb 5, nb 4		18	Extras b 1, lb 4, w 1	6
Total		196	Total	251

Bonus points — Yorkshire 3

FoW: 1-8 (Abell), 2-31 (Azhar Ali), 3-36 (Banton), 4-49 (Bartlett), 5-85 (Hildreth),
1st   6-101 (Bess), 7-103 (C Overton), 8-138 (Davies), 9-192 (Groenewald), 10-196 (Brooks)
FoW: 1-89 (Azhar Ali), 2-94 (Hildreth), 3-101 (Abell), 4-148 (Bartlett), 5-167 (Groenewald),
2nd   6-188 (Banton), 7-192 (Bess), 8-211 (Davies), 9-239 (J Overton), 10-251 (C Overton)

	O	M	R	W		O	M	R	W
Fisher	11	4	38	1	Fisher	15	3	61	3
Patterson	12	6	30	0	Patterson	20.5	5	54	4
Olivier	14	2	56	2	Olivier	8	2	33	0
Maharaj	26.3	9	52	7	Maharaj	34	11	75	3
Shaw	4	3	6	0	Shaw	4	0	18	0
					Lyth	1	0	5	0

Umpires: M Burns and P J Hartley   Scorers: J T Potter and L M Rhodes

Maharaj spins his magic

Forget the gloves: Yorkshire wicket-keeper Jonny Tattersall looks on as skipper Steven Patterson knocks Tim Banton's off-stump out

The visitors may have been lured into bowling first by an unfulfilled forecast of cloud cover, and it was an hour and three quarters before they struck.

Apart from a minor wobble just before lunch from 80-0 to 82-2 Yorkshire dominated this match.

The opening afternoon saw Gary Ballance at his most imperious, but Tom Kohler-Cadmore was more circumspect as the centuries added a third-wicket 199.

A nightwatchman shortened the tail, and once Keshav Maharaj, who later spun Somerset into trouble, had been dismissed for 72 Harry Brook had to marshal the remainder to secure an excellent first home century. He was last out at 520.

Scoreboard pressure told on Somerset, who were without Lewis Gregory and Jack Leach due to England Lions calls. Before a disappointing crowd on World Cup final day four wickets were taken in the final session and four before lunch next day. Maharaj took the last six to finish with 7-52, the best Yorkshire figures for five years as the leaders were bowled out for 196. Dom Bess had obtained modest turn on day one, though his replacement following a loan spell with the county exploited conditions which belied Headingley's reputation as a spinner's graveyard.

Steven Patterson enforced the follow-on, with Somerset's openers surviving to tea on day three. Again, four wickets fell in the evening. A healthy crowd came to the final day, which lasted for only 90 minutes — quite a few decamped to the second-team game at Stamford Bridge. Surprisingly, Maharaj, who bowled all but seven overs from the Emerald Stand End, took only one more wicket. Patterson claimed his 400th first-class scalp as the victory was wrapped up.

Jack Brooks and Bess were warmly welcomed by their former home crowd. Yorkshire's win cemented third place in Division One, ahead of the long break for T20, while Somerset lost the lead to Essex.

Specsavers County Championship Division 1
Yorkshire v. Nottinghamshire

Played at North Marine Road, Scarborough, on August 18, 19, 20 and 21, 2019

Yorkshire won by 143 runs at 2.03pm on the Fourth Day

Toss: None. Nottinghamshire opted to field   Yorkshire 20 points, Nottinghamshire 3 points

Close of play: First Day, Nottinghamshire 41-0 (Slater 29*, Libby 12*); Second Day, Yorkshire 177-2 (Ballance 52*, Patterson 5*): Third Day, Nottinghamshire 135-5 (Duckett 47*, Patterson-White 16*)

	First Innings	YORKSHIRE		Second Innings	
A Lyth, c Moores b Wood		4	c Coughlin b Patterson-White		81
W A R Fraine, c Nash b Wood		11	lbw b Fletcher		24
G S Ballance, c Libby b Wood		0	c sub (L R Bhabra) b Wood		61
T Kohler-Cadmore, b Wood		0	(5) lbw b Fletcher		59
H C Brook, c Moores b Wood		6	(6) c Ball b Patterson-White		18
§ J A Tattersall, c Moores b Patterson-White		92	(7) c Duckett b Fletcher		7
T T Bresnan, c Moores b Patterson-White		58	(8) c Moores b Fletcher		2
K A Maharaj, b Fletcher		7	(9) c and b Coughlin		35
* S A Patterson, not out		16	(4) c Nash b Coughlin		9
B O Coad, lbw b Patterson-White		7	c Coughlin b Fletcher		11
D Olivier, b Patterson-White		14	not out		4
Extras lb 5, nb 14		19	Extras b 8, lb 2, w 1, nb 16		27
Total		232	Total		338

Bonus points — Yorkshire 1, Nottinghamshire 3

FoW: 1-5 (Lyth), 2-5 (Ballance), 3-7 (Kohler-Cadmore), 4-13 (Brook), 5-38 (Fraine),
1st 6-159 (Bresnan), 7-178 (Maharaj), 8-204 (Tattersall), 9-212 (Coad), 10-232 (Olivier)
FoW: 1-64 (Fraine), 2-172 (Lyth), 3-185 (Patterson), 4-199 (Ballance), 5-232 (Brook), 6-273
2nd (Tattersall), 7-281 (Bresnan), 8-302 (Kohler-Cadmore), 9-320 (Coad), 10-338 (Maharaj)

	O	M	R	W		O	M	R	W
Fletcher	17	2	46	1	Fletcher	27	6	67	5
Wood	17	0	67	5	Wood	13	3	71	1
Ball	13	3	44	0	Ball	21	6	59	0
Coughlin	12	1	36	0	Coughlin	18.3	4	58	2
Patterson-White	17.1	5	34	4	Patterson-White	22	2	73	2

	First Innings	NOTTINGHAMSHIRE		Second Innings	
B T Slater, c Tattersall b Coad		29	c Kohler-Cadmore b Olivier		18
J D Libby, b Olivier		18	c Tattersall b Patterson		11
* C D Nash, c and b Olivier		33	lbw b Maharaj		30
J M Clarke, c Tattersall b Coad		8	c Tattersall b Maharaj		4
B M Duckett, b Maharaj		15	c Fraine b Olivier		75
L A Patterson-White, c Tattersall b Patterson		15	not out		58
§ T J Moores, c Tattersall b Olivier		48	c Fraine b Maharaj		5
P Coughlin, c Brook b Maharaj		0	c Lyth b Bresnan		9
L Wood, c Lyth b Coad		6	b Maharaj		0
LJ Fletcher, c Brook b Olivier		4	lbw b Maharaj		15
J T Ball, not out		1	c Lyth b Maharaj		0
Extras b 4, lb 1, nb 4		9	Extras b 9, lb 5, nb 4		18
Total		184	Total		243

Bonus points — Yorkshire 3

FoW: 1-41 (Slater), 2-65 (Libby), 3-90 (Nash), 4-94 (Clarke), 5-125 (Duckett), 6-131
1st (Patterson-White), 7-132 (Coughlin), 8-173 (Wood), 9-179 (Moores), 10-184 (Fletcher)
FoW: 1-29 (Slater), 2-42 (Libby), 3-51 (Clarke), 4-103 (Nash), 5-181 (Duckett),
2nd 6-187 (Moores), 7-218 (Coughlin), 8-219 (Wood), 9-243 (Fletcher), 10-243 (Ball)

	O	M	R	W		O	M	R	W
Coad	16	3	58	3	Coad	11	2	21	0
Olivier	17	3	60	4	Olivier	15	2	54	2
Maharaj	15	4	49	2	Maharaj	30	7	95	6
Patterson	13	9	12	1	Patterson	11	3	25	1
					Bresnan	10	3	31	1
					Lyth	2	0	3	0

Umpires: D J Millns and M J Saggers   Scorers: J T Potter and R Marshall

Yorkshire v. Nottinghamshire

Scarborough double triumph

Yorkshire completed the Scarborough double two overs into the fourth afternoon.

They had to contend with a damp patch after an uncontested toss, well exploited by Luke Wood in an excellent five-wicket opening spell which left Yorkshire on 38-5.

Jonny Tattersall and Tim Bresnan batted soundly to effect a

KESHAV MAHARAJ: Eight-wicket haul

recovery, steadily accumulating a sixth-wicket century stand. Tattersall fell narrowly short of a maiden Championship century as four of the last five wickets fell to Liam Patterson-White's spin at the Peasholm Park End. Nottinghamshire's openers came through the remaining 17 overs.

Coad found the edge of another Ben, Slater, with the first ball of day two, which proved the most one-sided of the match as the visitors struggled to a 48-run deficit. They then watched Adam Lyth and Gary Ballance, 61, share the second century stand of the match, a fluent alliance in the best batting conditions. Lyth was mortified to steer a loose delivery into backward-point's hands just before the close, falling 19 short of a season's first century.

The visitors displayed better purpose during the last two days, restricting Yorkshire's scoring rate to below three an over for much of day three. The end of the innings left Yorkshire a 44-over evening session with the ball, reduced by two in deteriorating light, in which Duanne Olivier, Steve Patterson and Maharaj took the first five wickets defending a target of 387 — unlikely for a Nottinghamshire team winless and rooted to the foot of Division One.

On the final day, with reduced price admission, Yorkshire needed five wickets and Nottinghamshire 252 runs. Ben Duckett, 75, was snared by a lifting ball from Olivier, and then Maharaj reverted to the Peasholm Park End, working his way to 6-95. The visitors had the satisfaction of surviving to a lunch interval delayed by 15 minutes when the end was nigh. Leading pair Essex and Somerset both won compelling games to leave Yorkshire as title outsiders with three games remaining.

Specsavers County Championship Division 1
Somerset v. Yorkshire

Played at Cooper Associates County Ground, Taunton, on September 10, 11 and 12, 2019
Somerset won by 298 runs at 3.16pm on the Third Day

Toss: None . Yorkshire opted to field   Somerset 19 points, Yorkshire 3 points

Close of play: First Day, Yorkshire 70-3 (Kohler-Cadmore 6*, Patterson 0*); Second Day, Somerset 269-5 (Bartlett 39*; Gregory 38*)

First Innings	SOMERSET		Second Innings	
M Vijay, c Tattersall b Olivier	7		lbw b Maharaj	0
§ S M Davies, c Fraine b Patterson	11		c sub (J A Leaning) b Patterson	4
* T B Abell, b Maharaj	66		lbw b Bresnan	62
J C Hildreth, b Olivier	1		c Brook b Lyth	58
T Banton, c Lyth b Bresnan	2		c Lyth b Maharaj	43
G A Bartlett, c Lyth b Maharaj	12		st Tattersall b Maharaj	47
L Gregory, c Tattersall b Coad	12		b Maharaj	39
D M Bess, c Bresnan b Maharaj	15		b Bresnan	0
R E van der Merwe, lbw b Maharaj	10		c Kohler-Cadmore b Maharaj	30
J Overton, not out	40		b Patterson	18
J H Davey, lbw b Maharaj	0		not out	2
Extras b 12, lb 7, nb 4	23		Extras b 16, lb 4, nb 6	26
Total	199		Total	329

Bonus points — Yorkshire 3

FoW: 1-18 (Davies), 2-31 (Vijay), 3-37 (Hildreth), 4-46 (Banton), 5-70 (Bartlett),
1st 6-85 (Gregory), 7-130 (Bess), 8-148 (van der Merwe), 9-199 (Abell), 10-199 (Davey)
FoW: 1-4 (Vijay), 2-4 (Davies), 3-121 (Hildreth), 4-191 (Banton), 5-191 (Abell), 6-272
2nd (Gregory), 7-273 (Bess), 8-291 (Bartlett), 9-310 (van der Merwe), 10-329 (Overton)

	O	M	R	W		O	M	R	W
Coad	13	4	23	1	Maharaj	36	9	122	5
Patterson	12	4	24	1	Patterson	13.2	1	65	2
Bresnan	10	2	27	1	Olivier	8	1	47	0
Olivier	14	2	52	2	Lyth	9	0	25	1
Maharaj	23.5	7	54	5	Bresnan	17	2	50	2

First Innings	YORKSHIRE		Second innings	
A Lyth, c Davies b Davey	21		c Overton b Davey	1
W A R Fraine, c Davies b Gregory	6		(7) c and b Davey	5
G S Ballance, lbw b Bess	35		c Davies b Overton	23
T Kohler-Cadmore, c Overton b Gregory	14		c Hildreth b Davey	11
* S A Patterson, b van der Merwe	8		(9) not out	24
H C Brook, lbw b Davey	6		(5) b van der Merwe	10
§ J A Tattersall, c Hildreth b van der Merwe	0		(2) c Hildreth b Overton	20
T T Bresnan, c Vijay b Davey	4		(6) run out (Bess)	17
K A Maharaj, c and b van der Merwe	4		(8) lbw b Davey	0
D Olivier, not out	0		c Bess b Davey	4
B O Coad	absent ill	0		absent ill	0
Extras lb 1, nb 4	5		Extras b 4, lb 2, nb 6	12
Total	103		Total	127

Bonus points — Somerset 3

FoW: 1-27 (Fraine), 2-27 (Lyth), 3-70 (Ballance), 4-86 (Kohler-Cadmore), 5-88 (Patterson)
1st 6-92 (Tattersall), 7-98 (Brook), 8-99 (Bresnan), 9-103 (Maharaj)
FoW: 1-7 (Lyth), 2-47 (Bresnan), 3-54 (Tattersall), 4-71 (Brook), 5-94 (Bresnan)
2nd 6-94 (Kohler-Cadmore), 7-94 (Maharaj), 8-103 (Fraine), 9-127 (Olivier)

	O	M	R	W		O	M	R	W
Gregory	10	0	36	2	Gregory	9	4	22	0
Davey	6	2	30	3	Davey	11.2	4	21	5
Overton	3	1	9	0	Bess	4	0	12	0
Bess	6	2	13	1	Overton	6	1	21	2
van de Merwe	8.3	4	14	3	van der Merwe	15	3	45	1

Umpires: M A Gough and M J Saggers   Scorers: J T Potter and L M Rhodes

Yorkshire's chance goes

JONNY TATTERSALL
Promoted to opener

This defeat was as comprehensive as Yorkshire's home victory which had knocked Somerset from the top of the Championship table in July.

In this round, the first of three in September, Somerset regained the lead from Essex and ended the slim title hopes of the *White Rose.*

The pitch looked more worn on day one than on the third day, and its grass covering encouraged Steven Patterson to insert.

Yorkshire began well with six wickets for 85, with Duanne Olivier, demoted to second change, bowling his best spell of the summer so far without significant reward. But home captain Tom Abell, 66, looked a class above and was well supported by the long handle of the tail.

Yorkshire omitted Jack Shutt, who had been in a travelling 14, but Somerset's two frontline spinners obtained prodigious bounce and turn from the River End. When Yorkshire were 70-2, and Gary Ballance batting serenely, the game was finely poised. Dom Bess took only one wicket in the match, but it was the crucial one of Yorkshire's top-scorer. Next morning Yorkshire folded alarmingly to 103-9, with Ben Coad absent ill. Keshav Maharaj opened the bowling with Patterson — and two early wickets had the Cricket Liaison Officer inspecting the pitch at lunch. Thereafter, although Maharaj took five wickets to finish with 10 in the match for the second time against Somerset, he disappointed with too many deliveries directed at leg stump at a quicker pace than deployed by Somerset's spinners.

Abell again excelled, but he fell for 62. Yorkshire took the last five wickets in an hour on the third day to face a 426 target. A knee injury to Will Fraine, suffered in warm-ups, gave Jonny Tattersall the opportunity to open, and up to lunch he acquitted himself well. Ballance again looked serene until a peach of a delivery dismissed him just before the break. Tim Bresnan also batted well until run out.

Pace rather than spin closed out the game to leave Somerset dreaming of a maiden title.

Specsavers County Championship Division 1
Yorkshire v. Kent

Played at Emerald Headingley, Leeds, on September 16, 17, 18 and 19, 2019
Kent won by 433 runs at 12.45pm on the Fourth Day

Toss won by Kent   Kent 24 points, Yorkshire 4 points

Close of play: First Day, Kent 482-8 (Rayner 40*, Milnes 14*); Second Day, Kent 2-0 (Crawley 0*, Bell-Drummond 2*); Third Day, Yorkshire 44-6 (Tattersall 6*, Bresnan 0*)

First Innings	KENT	Second Innings	
Z Crawley, lbw b Olivier	4	lbw b Fisher	15
D J Bell-Drummond, b Fisher	10	b Fisher	7
§ O G Robinson, c Tattersall b Olivier	2	c Tattersall b Olivier	97
F du Plessis, b Olivier	0	c Kohler-Cadmore b Patterson	36
* S W Billings, c Lyth b Olivier	138	not out	122
H G Kuhn, lbw b Olivier	8	run out (Tattersall)	8
D I Stevens, c Revis b Patel	237	c Kohler-Cadmore b Patel	21
O P Rayner, not out	40	run out (Ballance)	1
H W Podmore, b Fisher	0	not out	24
M W Milnes, not out	14		
M E Claydon	Did not bat		
Extras b 6, lb 15, nb 6	27	Extras b 1, lb 3, nb 2	6
Total (8 wkts dec)	482	Total (7 wkts dec)	337

Bonus points — Kent 5, Yorkshire 2

FoW: 1-4 (Crawley), 2-8 (Robinson), 3-8 (du Plessis), 4-22 (Bell-Drummond), 5-39 (Kuhn),
1st   6-385 (Stevens), 7-454 (Billings), 8-455 (Podmore)

FoW: 1-14 (Bell-Drummond), 2-23 (Crawley), 3-101 (du Plessis), 4-225 (Robinson), 5-235
2nd   (Kuhn), 6-297 (Stevens), 7-300 (Rayner)

	O	M	R	W		O	M	R	W
Olivier	24	2	108	5	Olivier	15	2	57	1
Fisher	19	2	79	2	Fisher	12	2	38	2
Patterson	20	4	90	0	Bresnan	11	1	49	0
Bresnan	15	2	58	0	Patterson	12	1	59	1
Patel	15	0	119	1	Patel	20	0	112	1
Lyth	3	1	7	0	Lyth	4	0	18	0

First Innings	YORKSHIRE	Second Innings	
A Lyth, c du Plessis b Stevens	5	lbw b Stevens	9
M L Revis, c Robinson b Milnes	9	lbw b Stevens	0
G S Ballance, lbw b Stevens	4	c du Plessis b Stevens	2
T Kohler-Cadmore, b Milnes	36	c Rayner b Stevens	19
H C Brook, lbw b Milnes	36	c Kuhn b Milnes	13
§ J A Tattersall, c Crawley b Podmore	27	(7) c du Plessis b Bell-Drummond	41
T T Bresnan, b Milnes	4	(8) c Robinson b Stevens	0
M D Fisher, not out	47	(9) c Robinson b Podmore	7
* S A Patterson, b Podmore	4	(6) c Crawley b Milnes	0
D Olivier, lbw b Milnes	10	b Bell-Drummond	24
A Y Patel, b Rayner	20	not out	0
Extras lb 16, nb 10	26	Extras lb 2	2
Total	269	Total	117

Bonus points — Yorkshire 2, Kent 3

FoW: 1-9 (Lyth), 2-17 (Ballance), 3-36 (Revis), 4-95 (Brook), 5-106 (Kohler-Cadmore),
1st   6-141 (Tattersall), 7-194 (Bresnan), 8-220 (Patterson), 9-244 (Olivier), 10-269 (Patel)

FoW: 1-4 (Revis), 2-9 (Lyth), 3-16 (Ballance), 4-43 (Brook), 5-43 (Kohler-Cadmore),
2nd   6-43 (Patterson), 7-46 (Bresnan), 8-81 (Fisher), 9-116 (Olivier), 10-117 (Tattersall)

	O	M	R	W		O	M	R	W
Podmore	21	5	60	2	Podmore	12	3	31	1
Stevens	20	8	50	2	Stevens	18	7	20	5
Claydon	13	3	34	0	Milnes	10	4	24	2
Milnes	21	1	87	5	Claydon	6	0	26	0
Rayner	15	7	21	1	Rayner	6	2	7	0
Bell-Drummond	2	1	1	0	Bell-Drummond	3.2	0	7	2

Umpires: M A Gough and D J Milnes   Scorers: J T Potter and L A R Hart

Yorkshire v. Kent

White Rose pricked deep

Yorkshire lost a contested toss for the first time in two seasons and little went right from there.

Kent chose to take first use of an excellent batting track knowing that they would face a difficult first hour with the 10.30 start.

Duanne Olivier took four wickets and Matthew Fisher beat the bat countless times for one wicket as the visitors fell to 39-5.

Had Sam Billings been run out at the non-strikers end following a firm drive

DARREN STEVENS: The oldest Championship double-centurion for 70 years — and then a five-for.

history would record something very different from a 433-run defeat.

Instead, Darren Stevens at 43 became the oldest double-centurion in the Championship since 1949; Kent recorded their largest stand for the sixth-wicket ever; Billings became the first to score two Championship centuries in a Headingley match, and Yorkshire went down by the largest number of runs in their first-class history.

Yorkshire hoped that Ajaz Patel would take up where Keshav Maharaj had left off, but he struggled to find his length and lacked any variation in pace or angle of delivery. Stevens counter-attacked, and even skipper Steven Patterson was unable to stem the flow. Until the closing few overs only three maidens were bowled after lunch. Kent declared overnight. Matthew Revis held out for 54 balls, and later Fisher survived 150 in making his career-best 47 not out.

Kent were well in front by tea on the third day, with Billings one away from his second century. He batted on in the belief that a harder ball would be needed at 10.30 next day to secure a win, but Stevens took four of six wickets to fall in the 22 overs that remained, Adam Lyth offering no shot to a straight ball and Tom Kohler-Cadmore a forcing shot to one he could have ignored. There was no charge for admission on the last day. Jonny Tattersall, supported by Fisher and Olivier, took the game just beyond the scheduled lunch interval.

Specsavers County Championship Division 1
Warwickshire v. Yorkshire

Played at Edgbaston, Birmingham, on September 23, 24, 25 and 26, 2019

Match drawn at 12.50pm on the Fourth Day

Toss won by Yorkshire   Yorkshire 7 points, Warwickshire 5 points

Close of play: First Day, Yorkshire 261-2 (Kohler-Cadmore 165*). No play on the second, third or fourth day

YORKSHIRE

A Lyth, c Hain b Miles	26
T Kohler-Cadmore, not out	165
T W Loten, c Rhodes b Thomson	58
G S Ballance	
H C Brook	
§ J A Tattersall	
M D Fisher	
D J Willey	
* S A Patterson	
D Olivier	
A Y Patel	
Extras b 5, lb 5, nb 2	12
Total (2 wkts)	261

Bonus points — Yorkshire 2

FoW: 1-77 (Lyth), 2-261 (Loten)

	O	M	R	W
Hannon-Dalby	12	2	47	0
Brookes	11	1	54	0
Miles	10	2	46	1
Patel	20	5	64	0
Thomson	4	0	21	1
Rhodes	7	1	19	0

WARWICKSHIRE

W M H Rhodes
D P Sibley
R M Yates
S R Hain
A T Thomson
§ T R Ambrose
M G R Burgess
H J H Brookes
* J S Patel
O J Hannon-Dalby
C N Miles

Umpires: G D Lloyd and R J Warren   Scorers: J T Potter and M D Smith

TomTom guides the way

Two heavy defeats saw Yorkshire promise end-of-season opportunities for younger players, and they made two changes.

In the event only three players actually took the field, one of these being first-class debutant Tom Loten, the county's Academy captain.

Circumstances could not have been better in which to start a career. The openers had survived the new ball and the 10.30 start. Loten, batting at

TOM KOHLER-CADMORE: 165 not out ended his season as it began

No.3, was joining a partner in Tom Kohler-Cadmore who was scoring freely. Whatever nerves Loten may have felt were invisible to the watching crowd, and until his dismissal on the stroke of tea — with what proved to be the last ball of the match — he gave no chance and it is hard to recall a ball that beat his bat.

At the other end Kohler-Cadmore was ending the season as he began, with a score in excess of 150. He too took few risks and punished any lapse in line or length with crisp drives and pulls on the way to the highest score of the season by a Yorkshire player. He followed Gary Ballance to 1,000 first-class runs for the season in the process.

Torrential rain before the second day, which virtually flooded the outfield, ultimately prevented any further play. Hopes were raised on the final morning as the groundstaff continued to work hard to facilitate play. A win would have taken Yorkshire back to third place in the Championship table, and Warwickshire could have gone above Surrey with at least a draw and some bonus points.

A long discussion with the captains, who were concocting a contrived run chase, followed the first inspection. An hour later another inspection and a shorter conversation ended with the captains shaking hands.

SPECSAVERS COUNTY CHAMPIONSHIP 2019

DIVISION 1

	P	W	L	D	Tied	Abdn	Bonus Points BAT	BOWL	Pen	Points
1 Essex(Div 1, 3)	14	9	1	4	0	0	26	38	0	228
2 Somerset (Div 1, 2)	14	9	3	2	0	0	25	38	0	217
3 Hampshire (Div 1, 5) ...	14	5	3	6	0	0	31	36	1	176
4 Kent (Div 2, 2)	14	5	5	4	0	0	36	36	0	172
5 Yorkshire (Div 1, 4)	**14**	**5**	**4**	**5**	**0**	**0**	**24**	**36**	**0**	**165**
6 Surrey (Div 1, 1)	14	2	6	6	0	0	33	38	0	133
7 Warwickshire (Div 2, 1) .	14	3	6	5	0	0	26	32	0	131
8 Nottinghamshire (Div 1, 6) *										
	14	0	10	4	0	0	16	32	1	67

Abandoned matches — each team takes 5 points

Pen. 1 point deducted for each over short in a match based on a rate of 16 overs per hour

* Relegated to Division 2 for 2020

DIVISION 2

	P	W	L	D	Tied	Abdn	Bonus Points BAT	BOWL	Pen	Points
1 Lancashire (Div 1, 7) * ..	14	8	0	6	0	0	34	41	0	233
2 Northamptonshire (Div 2, 9) *										
	14	5	2	7	0	0	35	38	0	188
3 Gloucestershire (Div 2, 5) *										
	14	5	3	6	0	0	36	36	0	182
4 Glamorgan (Div 2, 10) ..	14	4	3	7	0	0	35	34	1	167
5 Durham (Div 2, 8)	14	5	5	4	0	0	21	36	0	157
6 Sussex (Div 2, 3)	14	4	5	5	0	0	32	35	0	156
7 Derbyshire (Div 2, 7) ...	14	4	6	4	0	0	23	38	0	145
8 Middlesex (Div 2, 4) ...	14	3	5	6	0	0	24	33	2	133
9 Worcestershire (Div1, 8) .	14	3	7	4	0	0	20	37	0	125
10 Leicestershire (Div 2, 6) .	14	1	6	7	0	0	24	32	0	107

Abandoned matches — each team takes 5 points

Pen. 1 point deducted for each over short in a match based on a rate of 16 overs per hour

* Promoted to Division 1 for 2020.

(2018 positions in brackets)

YORKSHIRE AVERAGES 2019

SPECSAVERS COUNTY CHAMPIONSHIP

Played 14   Won 5   Lost 4   Drawn 5

BATTING AND FIELDING
(Qualification 10 completed innings)

Player	M.	I.	N.O.	Runs	H.S.	100s	50s	Avge	ct/st
G S Ballance	14	23	2	975	159	5	3	46.42	4
T Kohler-Cadmore	14	22	1	828	165*	2	3	39.42	30
A Lyth	14	25	2	804	95	0	7	34.95	26
W A R Fraine	8	15	1	393	106	1	0	28.07	8
J A Leaning	8	12	1	295	77*	0	3	26.81	3
J T Tattersall	14	21	1	523	92	0	3	26.15	32/3
H C Brook	10	16	0	353	101	1	0	22.06	7
D Olivier	13	17	11	130	24	0	0	21.66	3
B O Coad	11	14	2	196	48	0	0	16.33	0
S A Patterson	14	20	2	271	60	0	1	15.05	6

Also played

Player	M.	I.	N.O.	Runs	H.S.	100s	50s	Avge	ct/st
J E Root	2	3	1	297	130*	1	2	148.50	2
T W Loten	1	1	0	58	58	0	1	58.00	0
D M Bess	4	5	1	156	91*	0	1	39.00	1
M D Fisher	4	5	1	115	47*	0	0	28.75	1
D J Willey	5	7	1	171	46	0	0	28.50	3
J E G Logan	1	2	1	27	20*	0	0	27.00	0
M J Waite	2	2	1	27	22	0	0	27.00	1
K A Maharaj	5	9	0	239	85	0	2	26.55	1
A Y Patel	2	2	1	20	20	0	0	20.00	0
T T Bresnan	4	8	0	143	58	0	1	17.87	1
J A Thompson	2	3	0	36	34	0	0	12.00	0
J Shaw	1	1	0	6	6	0	0	6.00	0
M L Revis	1	2	0	9	9	0	0	4.50	1

BOWLING
(Qualification 10 wickets)

Player	Overs	Mdns	Runs	Wkts	Avge	Best	5wI	10wM
K A Maharaj	266	76	719	38	18.92	7 -52	4	2
B O Coad	340	82	955	37	25.81	6 -52	1	0
M D Fisher	82	16	288	11	26.18	3 -59	0	0
D J Willey	88.2	21	316	11	28.72	3 -71	0	0
S A Patterson	396.4	111	1050	36	29.16	5 -81	1	0
D Olivier	365.5	66	1390	43	32.32	5 -96	2	0

Also bowled

Player	Overs	Mdns	Runs	Wkts	Avge	Best	5wI	10wM
J E G Logan	21	6	41	4	10.25	4 -22	0	0
J A Thompson	40	10	105	5	21.00	2 -28	0	0
J A Leaning	30	8	96	3	32.00	2 -20	0	0
D M Bess	97	24	234	7	33.42	3 -45	0	0
M J Waite	59	5	235	6	39.16	2 -38	0	0
T T Bresnan	82	17	262	6	43.66	2 -47	0	0
A Lyth	25	3	79	1	79.00	1 -25	0	0
A Y Patel	35	0	231	2	115.50	1-112	0	0
J E Root	43	2	158	0	—	0 -27	0	0
J Shaw	8	3	24	0	—	0 - 6	0	0

YORKSHIRE AVERAGES 2019

ALL FIRST CLASS MATCHES

Played 15   Won 6   Lost 4   Drawn 5

BATTING AND FIELDING

(Qualification 10 completed innings)

Player	M.	I.	N.O.	Runs	H.S.	100s	50s	Avge	ct/st
G S Ballance	15	24	2	1014	159	5	3	46.09	4
T Kohler-Cadmore	15	23	1	1004	176	3	3	45.63	33
A Lyth	15	26	2	816	95	0	7	34.00	27
J A Tattersall	15	22	2	658	135*	1	3	32.90	36
W A R Fraine	8	15	1	393	106	1	0	28.07	8
J A Leaning	9	13	1	315	77*	0	3	26.25	4
H C Brook	11	17	0	370	101	1	0	21.76	7
B O Coad	12	15	3	206	35	0	0	17.16	0
S A Patterson	15	21	2	310	60	0	1	16.31	6

Also played

Player	M.	I.	N.O.	Runs	H.S.	100s	50s	Avge	ct/st
J E Root	2	3	1	297	130*	1	2	148.50	2
T W Loten	1	1	0	58	58	0	1	58.00	0
D M Bess	4	5	1	156	91*	0	1	39.00	1
M D Fisher	4	5	1	115	47*	0	0	28.75	1
D J Willey	5	7	1	171	46	0	0	28.50	3
J E G Logan	1	2	1	27	20*	0	0	27.00	0
K A Maharaj	5	9	0	239	85	0	2	26.55	1
D Olivier	14	17	11	130	24	0	0	21.66	3
M J Waite	3	3	1	42	22*	0	0	21.00	1
A Y Patel	2	2	1	20	20	0	0	20.00	0
T T Bresnan	4	8	0	143	58	0	1	17.87	1
J A Thompson	2	3	0	36	34	0	0	12.00	0
J Shaw	1	1	0	6	6	0	0	6.00	0
M L Revis	1	2	0	9	9	0	0	4.50	1
M W Pillans	1	1	0	3	3	0	0	3.00	0

BOWLING

(Qualification 10 wickets)

Player	Overs	Mdns	Runs	Wkts	Avge	Best	5wI	10wM
K A Maharaj	266	76	719	38	18.92	7 -52	4	2
B O Coad	366.5	91	1013	42	24.11	6 -52	1	0
M J Waite	84	15	292	12	24.33	5 -16	1	0
M D Fisher	82	16	288	11	26.18	3 -59	0	0
D J Willey	88.2	21	316	11	28.72	3 -71	0	0
S A Patterson	415.4	118	1095	37	29.59	5 -81	1	0
D Olivier	390.3	75	1458	47	31.02	5 -96	2	0

Also bowled

Player	Overs	Mdns	Runs	Wkts	Avge	Best	5wI	10wM
J E G Logan	21	6	41	4	10.25	4 -22	0	0
J A Thompson	40	10	105	5	21.00	2 -28	0	0
M W Pillans	14	2	59	2	29.50	2 -34	0	0
J A Leaning	41	8	128	4	32.00	2 -20	0	0
D M Bess	97	24	234	7	33.42	3 -45	0	0
T T Bresnan	82	17	262	6	43.66	2 -47	0	0
A Lyth	28.2	4	88	1	88.00	1 -25	0	0
S R Patel	35	0	231	2	115.50	1-112	0	0
J E Root	43	2	158	0	—	0 -27	0	0
J Shaw	8	3	24	0	—	0 - 6	0	0

ROYAL LONDON ONE-DAY CUP
HIGHLIGHTS OF 2019

WINNERS

Somerset, who beat Hampshire by 6 wickets

Win by 100 or more runs (1)

   Yorkshire (379-7) defeated Leicestershire (166) by 213 runs at Leeds

Totals of 250 and over (4)

379-7	v. Leicestershire at Leeds (won)
310	v. Lancashire at Leeds (lost)
288-2	v. Derbyshire at Leeds (tied — *DLS method*)
270-9	v. Warwickshire at Birmingham (tied)

Match aggregates of 450 and over (5)

621	Lancashire (311-6) defeated Yorkshire (310) by 1 run at Leeds
545	Yorkshire (379-7) defeated Leicestershire (166) by 213 runs at Leeds
540	Warwickshire (270-8) tied with Yorkshire (270-9) at Birmingham
526	Northamptonshire (351) lost to Yorkshire (175-5) by 5 wickets at Northampton *(DLS method)*
512	Yorkshire (288-2) tied with Derbyshire (224-3) at Leeds *(DLS method)*

Century Partnerships (8)

For 1st wicket (1)

   157   A Lyth and T Kohler-Cadmore v. Derbyshire at Leeds

For 2nd wicket (2)

   109   T Kohler-Cadmore and H C Brook v. Northamptonshire at Northampton
   107   A Lyth and H C Brook v. Nottinghamshire at Nottingham

For 3rd wicket (1)

   141*   D J Willey and H C Brook v. Derbyshire at Leeds

For 4th wicket (2)

   211   H C Brook and G S Ballance v. Leicestershire at Leeds
   127   T Kohler-Cadmore and G S Ballance v. Lancashire at Leeds

For 5th wicket (1)

   101   G S Ballance and J A Tattersall v. Leicestershire at Leeds

For 6th wicket (1)

   138   J A Tattersall and T T Bresnan v. Warwickshire at Birmingham

Centuries (2)

G S Ballance (1)

   156   v. Leicestershire at Leeds

H C Brook (1)

   103   v. Leicestershire at Leeds

4 wickets in an innings (2)

S A Patterson (1)

    4-45   v. Worcestershire at Worcester

M W Pillans (1)

    5-29   v. Leicestershire at Leeds

3 catches in an innings (2)

J A Tattersall (2)

    4   v. Lancashire at Leeds

    3   v. Warwickshire at Birmingham

3 dismissals in an innings (1)

J A Tattersall (1)

    4 (3ct + 1st) v. Warwickshire at Birmingham

Debuts (8)

List A (4): B D Birkhead, T W Loten, J A Thompson and J D Warner

For Yorkshire (4): M W Pillans, J E Poysden, D Olivier and W A R Fraine

---

Match-By-Match Reports   PAUL E DYSON

Worcestershire beat Yorkshire on ties

Yorkshire's two Royal London one-day Cup ties in 2019 — against Warwickshire on April 19 and Derbyshire on April 26 — were unusual, but not unique, as Worcestershire will tell you.

In the 1983 John Player League, which the *White Rose* won under Ray Illingworth, the Pears tied three games in a fortnight: against Nottinghamshire on July 10, Lancashire on July 17 and Warwickshire on July 24.

Royal London One-Day Cup

FINAL TABLES 2019

NORTH GROUP

		P	W	L	T	NR/A	PTS	NRR
1	Notts Outlaws (2)	8	6	1	0	1	13	0.619
2	Worcestershire Rapids (1) *	8	6	2	0	0	12	1.083
3	Lancashire Lightning (6) *	8	5	3	0	0	10	0.344
4	Durham (9)	8	4	2	0	2	10	0.472
5	Derbyshire Falcons (5)	8	3	4	1	0	7	-0.070
6	**Yorkshire Vikings (3) ....**	**8**	**2**	**3**	**2**	**1**	**7**	**-0.091**
7	Warwickshire Bears (4)	8	2	5	1	0	5	-0.911
8	Northamptonshire Steelbacks (7)	8	2	6	0	0	4	0.069
9	Leicestershire Foxes (8)	8	2	6	0	0	4	-1.313

SOUTH GROUP

		P	W	L	T	NR/A	PTS	NRR
1	Hampshire Royals (1)	8	7	1	0	0	14	1.020
2	Middlesex Panthers (6) *	8	6	2	0	0	12	0.135
3	Somerset (4) *	8	5	3	0	0	10	0.505
4	Gloucestershire (7)	8	5	3	0	0	10	0.270
5	Sussex Sharks (8)	8	4	4	0	0	8	0.013
6	Glamorgan (9)	8	3	4	0	1	7	-0.298
7	Kent Spitfires (3)	8	2	5	0	1	5	-0.966
8	Essex Eagles (2)	8	2	6	0	0	4	0.325
9	Surrey (5)	8	1	7	0	0	2	-1.007

* Qualified for Quarter-Finals

(2018 group positions in brackets)

Coaching roles for former leg-spinner

Former Essex leg-spinner Tom Craddock has been appointed as a full-time High Performance Coach for the Yorkshire County Age-Group Pathway and Development Squad, while he will also take charge of the women's senior team in 2020.

Craddock, who turns 31 in July and is Huddersfield-born, took 41 wickets in 18 first-class matches between 2011 and 2014. He played second-team cricket for Yorkshire in 2015.

Royal London One-Day Cup — North Group
Yorkshire v. Leicestershire

Played at Emerald Headingley, Leeds, on April 17, 2019
Yorkshire won by 213 runs

Toss won by Leicestershire   Yorkshire 2 points, Leicestershire 0 points

YORKSHIRE

A Lyth, c Horton b Taylor	0
T Kohler-Cadmore, lbw b Taylor	7
D J Willey, c Horton b Taylor	8
H C Brook, c Hill b Ali	103
G S Ballance, c Lilley b Davis	156
§ J A Tattersall, c Hill b Griffiths	58
T T Bresnan, c Taylor b Wright	16
M W Pillans, not out	10
A U Rashid, not out	1
* S A Patterson	
J E Poysden Did not bat	
Extras lb 10, w 8, nb 2	20
Total (7 wkts, 50 overs)	379

FoW: 1-0 (Lyth), 2-15 (Willey), 3-17 (Kohler-Cadmore), 4-228 (Brook), 5-329 (Ballance), 6-362 (Bresnan), 7-369 (Tattersall)

	O	M	R	W
Taylor	10	0	57	3
Wright	10	0	65	1
Lilley	10	0	59	0
Griffiths	8	0	74	1
Davis	9	0	82	1
Ali	3	0	32	1

LEICESTERSHIRE

H E Dearden, b Willey	0
* P J Horton, c Kohler-Cadmore b Patterson	26
A M Lilley, c Bresnan b Willey	25
M J Cosgrove, lbw b Poysden	42
C N Ackermann, b Pillans	19
§ L J Hill, c Willey b Pillans	7
A M Ali, c Lyth b Pillans	26
T A I Taylor, c Rashid b Pillans	12
W S Davis, b Poysden	2
C J C Wright, c Tattersall b Pillans	1
G T Griffiths, not out	0
Extras lb 4, w 2	6
Total (29.3 overs)	166

FoW: 1-1 (Dearden), 2-37 (Lilley), 3-86 (Horton), 4-108 (Cosgrove), 5-118 (Ackermann) 6-132 (Hill), 7-150 (Taylor), 8-164 (Ali), 9-166 (Davis), 10-166 (Wright)

	O	M	R	W
Willey	5	0	26	2
Bresnan	5	0	29	0
Rashid	4	0	24	0
Patterson	3	0	23	1
Pillans	6.3	0	29	5
Poysden	6	0	31	2

Umpires: G D Lloyd and P R Pollard   Scorers: J T Potter and P J Rodgers

Yorkshire batsmen run amok

GARY BALLANCE: Career-best 156

From the perils of 17-3 Yorkshire fashioned a win of such magnitude that the margin was their second-best in List A cricket.

The low point was reached after only 13 balls from Tom Taylor, who took all three wickets, both Adam Lyth — from the game's third ball — and David Willey being dismissed in identical fashion at first slip.

Thereafter Harry Brook and Gary Ballance kept the bowlers at bay for 205 balls, their 211-run stand breaking the county's fourth-wicket record. Although two slips were still in place after the first powerplay had ended Leicestershire's support bowlers wilted under the attack...which became an onslaught once Jonny Tattersall had replaced Brook, who mistimed a pull to end a 105-ball innings that secured his first century in this format.

Once he had reached his own 100 mark Ballance joined in the fun to the extent of making a career-best 156 in 133 balls, many of his 15 fours and six sixes — three of which were struck from consecutive balls — taking advantage of the short boundary on the White Rose Stand side of the ground. He and Tattersall added 101 from a mere 45 balls, Tattersall's 58, with three fours and four sixes, coming from only 29, and Yorkshire powered 142 from the last 10 overs to create a ground record and equal their highest total against a first-class county.

Leicestershire had a mountain to climb. Willey took two wickets in his opening spell, including one with his fourth ball, and though Paul Horton — removed by a good diving catch at cover — and Mark Cosgrove briefly threatened wickets continued to fall regularly. Mat Pillans, on his List A Yorkshire debut, created the most damage: he was the most economical and was well supported by Josh Poysden, another debutant, who took a wicket with his first ball. They took all of the final seven wickets while only 58 runs were added – 213 too few.

Royal London One-Day Cup — North Group
Warwickshire v. Yorkshire

Played at Edgbaston, Birmingham, on April 19, 2019
Match tied

Toss won by Yorkshire   Yorkshire 1 point, Warwickshire 1 point

WARWICKSHIRE

E J Pollock, b Bresnan		4
D P Sibley, c Tattersall b Bresnan		26
S R Hain, st Tattersall b Rashid		40
§ T R Ambrose, c Lyth b Pillans		77
W M H Rhodes, c Tattersall b Pillans		43
L Banks, c Kohler- Cadmore b Poysden		31
C R Woakes, c Kohler-Cadmore b Poysden		12
A T Thomson, not out		23
H J H Brookes, c Tattersall b Pillans		0
G D Panayi, not out		8
* J S Patel	Did not bat	
Extras lb 2, w 4		6
Total (8 wkts, 50 overs)		270

FoW: 1-6 (Pollock), 2-53 (Sibley), 3-93 (Hain), 4-155 (Rhodes), 5-196 (Banks), 6-218 (Woakes), 7-257 (Ambrose), 8-260 (Brookes).

	O	M	R	W
Willey	6	0	44	0
Bresnan	6	0	27	2
Patterson	10	0	41	0
Rashid	10	0	46	1
Poysden	10	0	54	2
Pillans	8	0	56	3

YORKSHIRE

A Lyth, b Brookes		3
T Kohler-Cadmore, b Brookes		9
D J Willey, c Patel b Panayi		40
H C Brook, c Sibley b Woakes		3
G S Ballance, c Sibley b Woakes		4
§ J A Tattersall, b Patel		79
T T Bresnan, c Patel b Woakes		89
A U Rashid, c Pollock b Patel		6
M W Pillans, c Woakes b Brookes		12
* S A Patterson, not out		11
J E Poysden, not out		0
Extras b 2, lb 6, w 6		14
Total (9 wkts, 50 overs)		270

FoW: 1-12 (Kohler- Cadmore), 2-14 (Lyth), 3-29 (Brook), 4-33 (Ballance), 5-89 (Willey), 6-227 (Tattersall), 7-235 (Bresnan), 8-251 (Rashid), 9-268 (Pillans).

	O	M	R	W
Woakes	10	1	47	3
Brookes	10	0	50	3
Panayi	9	0	52	1
Patel	10	0	41	2
Thomson	8	0	53	0
Rhodes	3	0	19	0

Umpires: N L Bainton and I D Blackwell   Scorers: J T Potter and M D Smith

Topsy-turvy bye tie

This game reached a thrilling finale with last man Josh Poysden — against his former county — unable to get his bat onto the last ball from teenaged Henry Brookes to score the two needed for victory...but still alert enough to run a bye and level the scores.

And this at the end of an innings which first went one way — a collapse to 33-4 — and then the other — a century partnership, a sixth-wicket stand of 138 between the youthful Jonny Tattersall, 79 from 81 balls, and the veteran Tim Bresnan, 89 from 88.

They were dismissed within four balls of each other, and the target was then 37 from 27. This became 10 from the last over. Skipper Steven Patterson struck a boundary, but the loss of Mat Pillans to the fourth ball gave Poysden too much to do.

Earlier, on a sun-drenched Good Friday, the hosts had batted steadily on a slowish pitch with no boundary struck from their 10th to 21st overs. The third wicket fell in the 22nd with the 100-mark not yet been reached.

Patterson in particular held the batsmen in check, conceding only 17 from

TIM BRESNAN: 89 from 88

his first seven overs. Tim Ambrose, with 77 from 108 balls, top-scored in a sheet-anchor innings, but former Yorkshire-player Will Rhodes, with 43 from 39 balls, set the necessary acceleration in motion. Late wickets from Pillans and Poysden kept the total down to what was regarded as a gettable target.

As expected Chris Woakes and Jeetan Patel proved to be the bowlers Yorkshire had to be most careful with. It was Woakes along with Brookes who did the early damage and Patel who applied the brakes in the middle of the innings to set up the unforgettable grand finale. It was Yorkshire's fifth List A tie in 980 games and their second against Warwickshire, whom they have not beaten since 2003.

Royal London One-Day Cup — North Group
Yorkshire v. Lancashire

Played at Emerald Headingley, Leeds, on April 21, 2019
Lancashire won by 1 run

Toss won by Lancashire   Lancashire 2 points, Yorkshire 0 points

LANCASHIRE

K K Jennings, c Tattersall b Willey	....	8
H Hameed, c Tattersall b Olivier	....	22
S J Croft, c Tattersall b Willey	....	97
G J Maxwell, c Tattersall b Rashid	....	22
* § D J Vilas, run out (Poysden)	....	21
R P Jones, c Willey b Bresnan	....	65
J J Bohannon, not out	....	55
L J Hurt, not out	....	15
S Mahmood		
G Onions	Did not bat	
M W Parkinson		
Extras lb 2, w 4	....	6
Total (6 wkts, 50 overs)	....	311

FoW: 1-26 (Jennings), 2-40 (Hameed), 3-85 (Maxwell), 4-116 (Vilas), 5-236 (Jones), 6-243 (Croft)

	O	M	R	W
Willey	10	1	51	2
Bresnan	10	0	82	1
Olivier	8	0	44	1
Rashid	10	0	53	1
Pillans	6	0	41	0
Poysden	6	0	38	0

YORKSHIRE

* A Lyth, c Jennings b Maxwell	....	19
T Kohler-Cadmore, b Mahmood	....	97
D J Willey, c Hameed b Mahmood	....	1
H C Brook, lbw b Parkinson	....	24
G S Ballance, c Maxwell b Mahmood	....	72
§ J A Tattersall, run out (Vilas)	....	49
T T Bresnan, c Maxwell b Parkinson	....	11
A U Rashid, c Jones b Onions	....	17
M W Pillans, lbw b Hurt	....	1
D Olivier, not out	....	4
J E Poysden, run out (Vilas/Maxwell)	....	1
Extras b 2, lb 6, w 6	....	14
Total (50 overs)	....	310

FoW: 1-39 (Lyth), 2-42 (Willey), 3-87 (Brook), 4-214 (Kohler-Cadmore), 5-241 (Ballance), 6-265 (Bresnan), 7-290 (Rashid), 8-296 (Pillans), 9-309 (Tattersall), 10-310 (Poysden)

	O	M	R	W
Onions	10	1	50	1
Mahmood	10	1	76	3
Maxwell	7	1	42	1
Hurt	8	0	42	1
Parkinson	10	0	47	2
Bohannon	2	0	12	0
Croft	3	0	33	0

Umpires: M A Gough and R T Robinson   Scorers: J T Potter and C Rimmer

The one that got away

For the second successive match Josh Poysden was required to hit the winning runs from the last ball of an enthralling contest...and again fell short.

He played a ball to deep square-leg, ran the first — but was run out going for a second which would have levelled the scores.

On Easter Sunday, a Family Fun Day at Emerald Headingley of unremitting sunshine and record temperatures, Yorkshire's attempt at overhauling Lancashire was given most impetus

TON-UP DUO: Tom Kohler-Cadmore, left, and Gary Ballance, who put on 127 for Yorkshire's fourth wicket.

by a fourth-wicket 127-run stand between Tom Kohler-Cadmore, who fell three runs short of a century, and Gary Ballance, who struck 72 from 64 balls. Each batsman struck one six, Kohler-Cadmore's sailing spectacularly over the top deck of the North East Stand.

Once more Jonny Tattersall, who had claimed four dismissals for the second consecutive match, supplied the real acceleration, but he left in the last over — also to a run-out — for an enterprising 49 from 29. He struck two fours at the start of that over, from which 16 were needed to win. Earlier the Lancashire skipper, wicketkeeper Dane Vilas, had been asked by the umpires to speak to two of his players following dissent shown after a run-out appeal that was not upheld.

Vilas was brilliantly run out by Poysden with a direct hit to the non-striker's end from short fine-leg, but Lancashire were underpinned by a fifth-wicket stand of 120 between Steven Croft, whose score Kohler-Cadmore would replicate, and Rob Jones, with 65 from 51 balls. Jones hit a career-best, as did the ruthless Josh Bohannon, whose 55 not out from 32 balls was largely responsible for his side reaching 311. Tim Bresnan conceded 41 from the 48th and 50th overs, all to Bohannon to help the *Red Rose* to its first List A victory over the *White Rose* since 2008. New signing Duanne Olivier did not complete his allocation.

Royal London One-Day Cup — North Group
Yorkshire v. Derbyshire

Played at Emerald Headingley, Leeds, on April 26, 2019
Match tied (DLS method)

Toss won by Yorkshire   Yorkshire 1 point, Derbyshire 1 point

YORKSHIRE

T Kohler-Cadmore, c Madsen b Critchley	....	79
A Lyth, c Conners b Rampaul	....	78
D J Willey, not out	....	72
H C Brook, not out	....	59
G S Ballance		
§ J A Tattersall		
J A Leaning		
T T Bresnan	Did not bat	
* S A Patterson		
J E Poysden		
D Olivier		
Extras b 5, lb 8, w 5, nb 2	....	20
Total (2 wkts, 40 overs)	....	308

FoW: 1-157 (Lyth), 2-167 (Kohler-Cadmore)

	O	M	R	W
Madsen	6	0	40	0
Conners	7	0	57	0
Rampaul	8	0	44	1
Reece	5	0	48	0
Hughes	6	0	60	0
Critchley	8	0	46	1

DERBYSHIRE
(Revised target to win: 225 runs off 22 overs)

L M Reece, st Tattersall b Lyth	....	1
* B A Godleman, not out	....	107
W L Madsen, c Leaning b Willey	....	1
J L du Plooy, c Willey b Lyth	....	75
M J J Critchley, not out	....	33
T C Lace		
A L Hughes		
§ H R Hosein	Did not bat	
A K Dal		
S Conners		
R Rampaul		
Extras b 1, w 6	....	7
Total (3 wkts, 22 overs)	....	224

FoW: 1-8 (Reece), 2-10 (Madsen), 3-145 (du Plooy)

	O	M	R	W
Lyth	3	0	27	2
Willey	5	0	41	1
Bresnan	3	0	46	0
Patterson	5	0	45	0
Olivier	4	0	43	0
Poysden	2	0	21	0

Umpires: R J Bailey and P K Baldwin   Scorers: J T Potter and J M Brown

Bowlers put to the sword

Poised to pouch: Yorkshire are looking good as Jack Leaning catches Wayne Madsen.

A three-hour break for rain meant that Yorkshire's innings was concluded after 40 overs and that Derbyshire required 225 from 22 overs to win.

These were the bare facts behind the *White Rose* county's third successive nail-biting conclusion which went down to the last ball. The visitors needed 17 from the final over and then two from the last ball.

To push-start the over skipper Billy Godleman struck David Willey for two boundaries to bring up his third consecutive century — a remarkable achievement and the first Derby batsman to do it.

He failed to strike the winning runs; a bye was scampered, and for the second time in three games Yorkshire had to be content with a tie when they had looked like winning during each innings.

Tom Kohler-Cadmore and Adam Lyth began the day in bright sunshine with a stand of 157, but fell within 10 runs of each other, Lyth's 78 coming from 60 balls. Of the four batsmen to get to the wicket — Willey and Harry Brook shared an unbeaten stand of 141 from a mere 82 balls — only one did not hit a six or have a strike-rate slower than a run-per-ball. Yorkshire were on course for a 400-plus total for their first time against a first-class county when the weather cruelly interrupted.

Play resumed at 5.15pm under floodlights in murky conditions, and Derbyshire were quickly reduced to 10-2. Then came the passage that set up the finale: Godleman, 107 not out from 62 balls with six sixes, and Leus du Plooy (75, 37, five) but who was dropped on 35, put together an explosive 135 in 73 balls. The Yorkshire bowlers suffered considerably from the onslaught. Steven Patterson bowled the last-but-one over and conceded only six runs, but Godleman was equal to the final over's task.

Royal London One-Day Cup — North Group
Nottinghamshire v. Yorkshire

Played at Trent Bridge, Nottingham, on April 28, 2019
Nottinghamshire won by 4 wickets

Toss won by Yorkshire   Nottinghamshire 2 points, Yorkshire 0 points

YORKSHIRE

A Lyth, c Moores b Patel	63
T Kohler-Cadmore, c Duckett b Carter	0
H C Brook, b Carter	39
J A Leaning, c Carter b Pattinson	4
G S Ballance, c Carter b Ball	25
§ J A Tattersall, c Duckett b Ball	19
M J Waite, b Pattinson	32
M W Pillans, c Clarke b Ball	0
* S A Patterson, b Fletcher	6
D Olivier, not out	8
J E Poysden, c Moores b Fletcher	1
Extras b 8, lb 3, w 5	16
Total (42.2 overs)	213

FoW: 1-5 (Kohler-Cadmore), 2-112 (Brook), 3-112 (Lyth), 4-122 (Leaning), 5-156 (Ballance), 6-164 (Tattersall), 7-171 (Pillans), 8-199 (Patterson), 9-205 (Waite), 10-213 (Poysden)

	O	M	R	W
Fletcher	9.2	0	36	2
Carter	8	0	36	2
Pattinson	10	1	42	2
Ball	6	0	32	3
Patel	8	1	39	1
Mullaney	1	0	17	0

NOTTINGHAMSHIRE

C D Nash, c Pillans b Patterson		35
J M Clarke, lbw b Pillans		40
B M Duckett, c Ballance b Pillans		21
J D Libby, c Tattersall b Pillans		0
S R Patel, c Tattersall b Waite		36
* S J Mullaney, not out		54
§ T J Moores, c Olivier b Waite		12
L J Fletcher, not out		2
J L Pattinson		
M Carter	Did not bat	
J T Ball		
Extras b 1, lb 2, w 3, nb 8		14
Total (6 wkts, 34.3 overs)		214

FoW: 1-75 (Nash), 2-98 (Duckett), 3-98 (Libby), 4-121 (Clarke), 5-184 (Patel), 6-211 (Moores)

	O	M	R	W
Waite	4.3	0	32	2
Olivier	7	1	51	0
Patterson	6	1	29	1
Pillans	8	0	57	3
Poysden	7	1	20	0
Leaning	2	0	22	0

Umpires: R J Bailey and B V Taylor   Scorers: J T Potter and R Marshall

Arrowed by the *Outlaws*

The hosts had played four and won four, twice passing the 400-mark, and now they enticed a Family Fun Day crowd of 14,478 — a ground record for a domestic List A fixture.

They went on to a win of such conviction that not only were four wickets remaining when the winning runs were scored, but no fewer than 93 balls were still left.

Yorkshire lost an early wicket, but Adam Lyth at his fluent best made his second successive half-century well-supported by Harry Brook in a rapid century partnership

ADAM LYTH: Fluent for 63

which took the side to a promising 112-1. It was at this total that both batsmen were dismissed within three balls of each other, Lyth's 63 having come from only 54 balls and Brook losing his middle stump to the off-spin of Matt Carter. The middle-order flourished briefly, but the batsmen were often beaten by a pitch of pace and some good bounce, especially from Jake Ball. Matthew Waite in his first game of the campaign held the tail together. but the end came in the 43rd over when nine wickets had fallen for 101 runs.

Chris Nash struck the first ball for four, as Lyth had done, to kickstart Nottinghamshire's innings in a stand with Joe Clarke of 75 from only 66 balls, Clarke making 40 from 28. The partnership ended with a brilliant one-handed diving catch by Mat Pillans at mid-on, and Pillans then weighed in with two wickets in consecutive deliveries, adding a third when he trapped Clarke lbw. The scoreboard was then showing 121-4 to give Yorkshire some hope.

Josh Poysden conceded fewer than three runs per over, and Steven Patterson was his usual economical self, 28 of his 36 balls being dots, but Samit Patel and skipper Steven Mullaney shared a stand of 63, and Mullaney saw his side home with a well-judged captain's innings. His county had swept Yorkshire aside, and justifiably cemented their position at the top of the table.

Royal London One-Day Cup — North Group
Northamptonshire v. Yorkshire

Played at Wantage Road, Northampton, on May 1, 2019
Yorkshire won by 5 wickets (DLS method)

Toss won by Northamptonshire   Yorkshire 2 points, Northamptonshire 0 points

NORTHAMPTONSHIRE

R E Levi, c Brook b Patterson	....	58
R S Vasconcelos, c Lyth b Poysden	....	112
J J Cobb, c Leaning b Poysden	....	58
J O Holder, lbw b Waite	....	36
* A G Wakely, c Leaning b Pillans	....	25
§ A M Rossington, not out	....	45
R I Keogh, lbw b Pillans	....	0
L A Procter, b Olivier	....	4
I G Holland, b Patterson	....	1
N L Buck, run out (Waite/Tattersall)	....	0
B W Sanderson, b Pillans	....	0
Extras lb 3, w 5, nb 4	....	12
Total (49.3 overs)	....	351

FoW: 1-118 (Levi), 2-232 (Vasconcelos), 3-238 (Cobb), 4-288 (Holder), 5-308 (Wakely), 6-309 (Keogh), 7-337 (Procter), 8-348 (Holland), 9-350 (Buck), 10-351 (Sanderson)

	O	M	R	W
Waite	8	0	66	1
Olivier	10	0	69	1
Pillans	9.3	0	65	3
Patterson	10	0	80	2
Poysden	10	0	56	2
Leaning	2	0	12	0

YORKSHIRE
(Revised target to win: 175 runs off 25 overs)

A Lyth, c Vasconcelos b Sanderson	....	16
T Kohler-Cadmore, c and b Holland	....	67
H C Brook, c Cobb b Buck	....	47
G S Ballance, c Sanderson b Keogh	....	28
J A Leaning, c sub (T B Sole) b Holland	....	0
§ J A Tattersall, not out	....	14
M J Waite, not out	....	0
M W Pillans		
* S A Patterson	Did not bat	
D Olivier		
J E Poysden		
Extras w 3	....	3
Total (5 wkts, 24.4 overs)	....	175

FoW: 1-19 (Lyth), 2-128 (Brook), 3-143 (Kohler-Cadmore), 4-161 (Ballance), 5-163 (Leaning)

	O	M	R	W
Buck	5	0	39	1
Sanderson	5	0	15	1
Procter	6	0	42	0
Holland	4.4	0	38	2
Keogh	4	0	41	1

TV Man of the match: R S Vasconcelos

Umpires: J H Evans and M J Saggers   Scorers: J T Potter and T R Owen
Third Umpire: N G B Cook

Nails bitten to victory

JOSH POYSDEN: Quick wickets turned the game

Yorkshire's prospects were looking remote. Northamptonshire were 232-1 in the 35th over on a flat pitch with a fast outfield — and the visitors had to win their last three games to qualify for the knockouts.

Two quick wickets from Josh Poysden turned the innings, and the hosts' last nine wickets fell for only 119 runs. The two main partnerships, 118 and 114, both involved Ricardo Vasconcelos, Poysden's first victim, who struck 112 from 97 balls with 11 fours and three sixes.

Vasconcelos's partners, Richard Levi and Josh Cobb, each made 58. The middle-order kept up the momentum, Jason Holder and skipper Alex Wakely sharing a 50-run stand from 38 balls, but wicket-keeper Adam Rossington, who made 45 not out from 25 balls, could only stand and watch as the last three wickets went down in four balls. Once again Poysden was the most economical of Yorkshire's bowlers and Mat Pillans — already Yorkshire's leading wicket-taker — added three more, but his side had to chase the third-highest total ever scored against it.

Adam Lyth made 16 of Yorkshire's first 19 runs, but fell to former teammate Ben Sanderson. Harry Brook joined Tom Kohler-Cadmore, and the pair made excellent progress towards the target. The threatened rain duly came, but the batsmen steered their team ahead of the *DLS* run-rate so that when the umpires called the players in on 128-1 after 20.5 overs they were in a match-winning position. A lengthy delay saw Yorkshire's target reduced to a further 58 from 31 balls.

Then it rained again, meaning another revised target of 47 from 25 balls. Harry Brook, having made 47 from 38, holed out first ball back to end his 109-run stand with Kohler-Cadmore, but Gary Ballance smote 28 from 11 with three consecutive sixes. Jonny Tattersall supplied the finishing touches when 12 were needed from the last over...and Yorkshire had won with two balls to spare — another nail-biting finish.

Royal London One-Day Cup — North Group
Worcestershire v. Yorkshire

Played at Blackfinch New Road, Worcester, on May 4, 2019
Worcestershire won by 150 runs

Toss won by Worcestershire   Worcestershire 2 points, Yorkshire 0 points

WORCESTERSHIRE

T C Fell, c Pillans b Patterson		31
M H Wessels, c Kohler-Cadmore b Patterson		10
C J Ferguson, lbw b Bresnan		14
G H Rhodes, b Pillans		106
* B L D'Oliveira, c Ballance b Patterson		2
§ O B Cox, c Kohler-Cadmore b Patterson		87
R A Whiteley, b Pillans		16
W D Parnell, not out		9
E G Barnard		
P R Brown	Did not bat	
C A J Morris		
Extras lb 7, w 9, nb 2		18
Total (7 wkts, 50 overs)		293

FoW: 1-30 (Wessels), 3-56 (Fell), 3-57 (Ferguson), 4-62 (D'Oliveira), 5-231 (Cox), 6-272 (Whiteley), 7-293 (Rhodes)

	O	M	R	W
Bresnan	10	0	39	1
Olivier	10	0	55	0
Patterson	9	1	45	4
Pillans	10	0	72	2
Brook	3	0	19	0
Poysden	8	0	56	0

YORKSHIRE

A Lyth, c Cox b Parnell	22
T Kohler-Cadmore, b Parnell	31
H C Brook, lbw b Barnard	0
J A Leaning, b Barnard	24
G S Ballance, lbw b D'Oliveira	9
§ J A Tattersall, c Cox b Barnard	13
T T Bresnan, b Barnard	1
M W Pillans, c Rhodes b Parnell	31
* S A Patterson, c and b D'Oliveira	1
D Olivier, not out	5
J E Poysden, c Cox b Parnell	0
Extras lb 1, w 5	6
Total (33 overs)	143

FoW: 1-46 (Lyth), 2-46 (Brook), 3-67 (Kohler-Cadmore), 4-84 (Leaning), 5-98 (Tattersall), 6-100 (Bresnan), 7-108 (Ballance), 8-118 (Patterson), 9-143 (Pillans), 10-143 (Poysden)

	O	M	R	W
Brown	6	0	50	0
Morris	5	1	12	0
Parnell	7	1	25	5
Barnard	7	0	26	3
Rhodes	2	0	9	0
D'Oliveira	6	1	20	2

Umpires: P K Baldwin and M Burns   Scorers: J T Potter and S M Drinkwater

Worst exit for six years

A poor batting performance on a sluggish, used pitch left *White Rose* hopes of a quarter-final place dashed. Their defeat by 150 runs was Yorkshire's fourth-heaviest in List A cricket, but that did not look likely when Worcestershire were batting slowly and losing wickets.

The hosts were reduced to 62-4 after 91 balls, the last three falling for six runs. Steven Patterson had three of these first four wickets, and Tim Bresnan was bowling very tightly — comfortably the most economical bowler used.

The match turned during a 169-run stand between George Rhodes, son of Steven, former Yorkshire and Worcestershire wicketkeeper, and Ben Cox. Their partnership broke the record for any wicket for their county against Yorkshire.

Cox became the fourth victim

TIM BRESNAN: Kept it tight

of Patterson, who conceded only 22 runs from his first eight overs, when he was caught for 87 from 86 balls. Rhodes then supervised the acceleration — his side had been only 100-4 after 25 overs — as 62 came from the last 41 balls. He was bowled from the last ball of the innings for a maiden first-team century in any format.

Yorkshire's reply began well with an opening partnership of 46, but Wayne Parnell took three wickets to send them tumbling to 67-3. Thereafter wickets fell at very regular intervals, Ed Barnard ripping out the middle-order with three in three overs, and the *White Rose* county found itself on 118-8 in the 28th over. Mat Pillans held Worcestershire at bay briefly but lustily for 31 from 31 balls, but Parnell returned to take his wicket and that of Josh Poysden in successive deliveries to finish with 5-25.

Yorkshire's innings ended with 17 overs still to be bowled. All of their 10 wickets had fallen a for a mere 97 runs and, hence, they failed to qualify for the knockout stages for the first time since 2013.

Royal London One-Day Cup — North Group
Yorkshire v. Durham

Played at Emerald Headingley, Leeds, on May 6, 2019

No result

Toss won by Yorkshire

Yorkshire 1 point, Durham 1 point

DURHAM

B A Raine, c Birkhead b Bresnan		32
S Steel, c Leaning b Bresnan		68
A Z Lees, not out		51
* § C T Bancroft, not out		18
M J Richardson		
J T A Burnham		
M J Potts		
M A Wood	Did not bat	
G J Harte		
B A Carse		
L Trevaskis		
Extras lb 4, w 5, nb 4		13
Total (2 wkts, 34.2 overs)		182

FoW: 1-55 (Raine), 2-159 (Steel)

	O	M	R	W
Bresnan	10	0	36	2
Warner	5	0	32	0
Thompson	5	0	43	0
Leaning	4	0	16	0
Pillans	4.2	0	24	0
Poysden	6	0	27	0

YORKSHIRE

* T Kohler-Cadmore
W A R Fraine
H C Brook
J A Leaning
T W Loten
T T Bresnan
J A Thompson
§ B D Birkhead
M W Pillans
J D Warner
J E Poysden

Umpires: P K Baldwin and D J Millns

Scorers: J T Potter and W R Dobson

Yorkshire v. Durham
Rain boosts the *Red Rose*

Given Yorkshire's inability to qualify for the next stage of the competition, they decided to give first-team debuts to four players: Ben Birkhead, Will Fraine — who had played for Nottinghamshire — Tom Loten and Jared Warner as well as a List A bow to Jordan Thompson.

The county was without any first XI cricket for seven days, so this was a decision which raised a few eyebrows across the Pennines, as a victory for Durham would give them a quarter-final place ahead of Lancashire.

With rain forecast Tom Kohler-Cadmore, skipper at county level for the first time, did the sensible thing and elected to field. Ben Raine and Scott Steel began brightly for Durham, taking advantage of some loose bowling from Warner and Thompson.

TOM KOHLER-CADMORE
Debut as captain

The score had reached 55 from 40 balls when Raine gave a leg-side edge to wicket-keeper Birkhead off Tim Bresnan, who was proving more difficult to get away. This brought Alex Lees to the crease to face his former county for the first time since moving north towards the end of the 2018 season. He came into this match averaging 77.50 in this season's competition, and soon demonstrated his good form. He batted freely, including some good cover-drives, in a 104-run stand with Steel, who was caught at deep square-leg to give Bresnan his second wicket and make the score 159-2 in the 28th over.

Bresnan completed his allocation with excellent figures. The spinners also stemmed the tide, but Lees reached an assured half-century, his fifth in succession. The promised rain arrived after 33.1 overs with the scoreboard showing 179-2. The players managed to return after about three hours, but for seven balls only, and the match was called off at 5.30pm. Yorkshire's first *No Result* in a List A competitive match for three years had spared Lancashire, who advanced to the knockouts.

YORKSHIRE AVERAGES 2019

ROYAL LONDON ONE-DAY CUP

Played 8   Won 2   Tied 2   Lost 3   No Result 1

BATTING AND FIELDING

(Qualification 4 completed innings)

Player	M.	I.	N.O.	Runs	H.S.	100s	50s	Avge	ct/st
G S Ballance	7	6	0	294	156	1	1	49.00	2
J A Tattersall	7	6	1	232	79	0	2	46.40	10/2
H C Brook	8	7	1	275	103	1	1	45.83	1
T Kohler-Cadmore	8	7	0	290	97	0	3	41.42	5
T T Bresnan	6	4	0	117	89	0	1	29.25	1
A Lyth	7	7	0	201	78	0	2	28.71	3
M W Pillans	7	5	1	54	31	0	0	13.50	2

Also played

Player	M.	I.	N.O.	Runs	H.S.	100s	50s	Avge	ct/st
D J Willey	4	4	1	121	72*	0	1	40.33	3
M J Waite	2	2	1	32	32	0	0	32.00	0
A U Rashid	3	3	1	24	17	0	0	12.00	1
J A Leaning	5	3	0	28	24	0	0	9.33	4
S A Patterson	6	3	1	18	11*	0	0	9.00	0
J E Poysden	8	4	1	2	1	0	0	0.66	0
D Olivier	5	3	3	17	8*	0	0	—	1
B D Birkhead	1	0	0	0	—	0	0	—	1
W A R Fraine	1	0	0	0	—	0	0	—	0
T W Loten	1	0	0	0	—	0	0	—	0
J A Thompson	1	0	0	0	—	0	0	—	0
J D Warner	1	0	0	0	—	0	0	—	0

BOWLING

(Qualification 4 wickets)

Player	Overs	Mdns	Runs	Wkts	Avge	Best	4wI	RPO
M W Pillans	52.2	0	344	16	21.50	5-29	1	6.57
D J Willey	26	1	162	5	32.40	2-26	0	6.23
S A Patterson	43	2	263	8	32.87	4-45	1	6.11
T T Bresnan	44	0	259	6	43.16	2-27	0	5.88
J E Poysden	55	1	303	6	50.50	2-31	0	5.50

Also bowled

Player	Overs	Mdns	Runs	Wkts	Avge	Best	4wI	RPO
A Lyth	3	0	27	2	13.50	2-27	0	9.00
M J Waite	12.3	0	98	3	32.66	2-32	0	7.84
A U Rashid	24	0	123	2	61.50	1-46	0	5.12
D Olivier	39	1	262	2	131.00	1-44	0	6.71
J A Leaning	8	0	50	0	—	0-22	0	6.25
J D Warner	`5	0	32	0	—	0-32	0	6.40
J A Thompson	5	0	43	0	—	0-43	0	8.60
H C Brook	3	0	19	0	—	0-19	0	6.33

Fifth Royal London One-Day International
England v. Pakistan

Played at Emerald Headingley, Leeds, on May 19, 2019

England won by 54 runs

Toss won by England

ENGLAND

J M Vince, c Fakhar Zaman b Shaheen Afridi		33
J M Bairstow, c Shaheen Afridi b Imad Wasim		32
J E Root, c Asif Ali b Mohammad Hasnain		84
* E J G Morgan, c Abid Ali b Shaheen Afridi		76
§ J C Buttler, c Abid Ali b Imad Wasim		34
B A Stokes, c Fakhar Zaman b Hasan Ali		21
M M Ali, lbw b Imad Wasim		0
C R Woakes, c Babar Azam b Shaheen Afridi		13
D J Willey, b Shaheen Afridi		14
T K Curran, not out		29
A U Rashid, not out		2
Extras lb 2, w 10, nb 1		13
Total (9 wkts, 50 overs)		351

FoW: 1-63 (Vince), 2-105 (Bairstow), 3-222 (Root), 4-257 (Root), 5-272 (Buttler), 6-272 (Ali), 7-295 (Woakes), 8-310 (Stokes), 9-336 (Willey)

	O	M	R	W
Hasan Ali	10	0	70	1
Shaheen Afridi	10	0	82	4
Mohammad Hasnain	8	0	67	1
Imad Wasim	10	0	53	3
Fakhar Zaman	4	0	23	0
Shoaib Malik	4	0	29	0
Mohammad Hafeez	4	0	25	0

PAKISTAN

Fakhar Zaman, c Root b Woakes		0
Abid Ali, lbw b Woakes		5
Babar Azam, run out (Buttler/Rashid)		80
Mohammad Hafeez, lbw b Woakes		0
* § Sarfaraz Ahmed, run out (Buttler)		97
Shoaib Malik, c and b Rashid		4
Asif Ali, c Stokes b Willey		22
Imad Wasim, c Buttler b Woakes		25
Hasan Ali, c Willey b Woakes		11
Shaheen Afridi, not out		19
Mohammad Hasnain, st Buttler b Rashid		28
Extras lb 3, w 3		6
Total (46.5 overs)		297

FoW: 1-0 (Fakhar Zaman), 2-6 (Abid Ali), 3-6 (M Hafeez), 4-152 (Babar Azam), 5-189 (Shoaib Malik), 6-193 (Sarfaraz Ahmed), 7-232 (Imad Wasim), 8-250 (Asif Ali), 9-250 (Hasan Ali), 10-297 (M Hasnain)

	O	M	R	W
Woakes	10	2	54	5
Willey	9	1	44	1
Curran	6	0	40	0
Stokes	4	0	28	0
Ali	10	0	63	0
Rashid	7.5	0	54	2

Man of the Match: C R Woakes

Umpires: M A Gough and P R Reiffel   Scorers: J T Potter and J R Virr
Third: C B Gaffaney   Fourth: R T Robinson   Match Referee: R B Richardson

VITALITY BLAST HIGHLIGHTS OF 2019

VITALITY BLAST WINNERS

Essex Eagles, who beat Worcestershire Rapids by 4 wickets

Totals of 150 and over (8)

255-2	v. Leicestershire at Leicester (won)	
200-3	v. Birmingham Bears at Birmingham (won)	
187-7	v. Northamptonshire at Leeds (won)	
179-7	v. Worcestershire at Leeds (lost)	
177-7	v. Birmingham Bears at Leeds (tied)	
164-8	v. Derbyshire at Chesterfield (lost)	
161-9	v. Lancashire at Leeds (lost)	
152	v. Derbyshire at Leeds (lost)	

Match aggregates of 350 and over (5)

456	Yorkshire (255-2) defeated Leicestershire (201-4) by 54 runs at Leicester
381	Yorkshire (200-3) defeated Birmingham Bears (181-5) by 19 runs at Birmingham
359	Derbyshire (207-5) defeated Yorkshire (152) by 55 runs at Leeds
356	Yorkshire (177-7) lost to Worcestershire (179-5) by 5 wickets at Leeds
354	Birmingham Bears (177-4) tied with Yorkshire (177-7) at Leeds

Century Partnerships (4)

For 1st wicket (3)

116	A Lyth and T Kohler-Cadmore	v. Leicestershire at Leicester
104	A Lyth and T Kohler-Cadmore	v. Worcestershire at Leeds
102	T Kohler-Cadmore and A Lyth	v. Birmingham Bears at Birmingham

For 2nd wicket (1)

121	T Kohler-Cadmore and N Pooran	v. Leicestershire at Leicester

4 wickets in an innings (3)

A Lyth (1)

    5-31   v. Nottinghamshire at Nottingham

J W Shutt (1)

    5-11   v. Durham at Chester-le-Street

D J Willey (1)

    4-18   v Northamptonshire at Leeds

3 catches in an innings (1)

H C Brook (1)

    4   v. Northamptonshire at Leeds

3 dismissals in an innings (None)

Debuts (7)

T20 (1): J W Shutt

For Yorkshire (6): D M Bess, N Pooran, D Olivier, M W Pillans, K A Maharaj and W A R Fraine

VITALITY BLAST in 2019

NORTH GROUP

		P	W	L	T	NR/A	PTS	NRR
1	Lancashire Lightning (3) *	14	8	2	0	4	20	0.755
2	Notts Outlaws (4) *	14	6	4	0	4	16	0.336
3	Derbyshire Falcons (7) *	14	7	5	0	2	16	0.022
4	Worcestershire (Rapids) (1) *	14	6	5	0	3	15	0.205
5	**Yorkshire Vikings (5)**	**14**	**4**	**5**	**1**	**4**	**13**	**0.339**
6	Durham (2)	14	5	7	0	2	12	-0.049
7	Northamptonshire Steelbacks (9)	14	4	6	0	4	12	-0.543
8	Birmingham Bears (6)	14	4	7	1	2	11	-0.467
9	Leicestershire Foxes (8)	14	4	7	0	3	11	-0.471

SOUTH GROUP

		P	W	L	T	NR/A	PTS	NRR
1	Sussex Sharks (3) *	14	8	3	1	2	19	0.803
2	Gloucestershire (4) *	14	7	3	1	3	18	0.242
3	Middlesex Panthers (9) *	14	7	6	0	1	15	0.216
4	Essex Eagles (7) *	14	5	4	1	4	15	-0.464
5	Kent Spitfires (2)	14	6	6	0	2	14	0.000
6	Somerset (1)	14	6	7	0	1	13	0.448
7	Hampshire Royals (8)	14	5	6	1	2	13	0.021
8	Surrey (5)	14	5	7	1	1	12	-0.246
9	Glamorgan (6)	14	1	8	1	4	7	-1.381

* Qualified for the Quarter-Finals

(2018 group positions in brackets)

Yorkshire quartet in world cups

Yorkshire had four players representing England at two World Cups in the opening months of 2020. George Hill and Harry Duke were part of the men's Under-19 squad in the 50-over competition in South Africa, where they won the Plate final in early February — effectively meaning they were the best team of those who did not reach the quarter-finals of the main event. Katherine Brunt and Lauren Winfield were then in England's senior squad for the Women's T20 World Cup in Australia later in the month. That event was played after this *Yearbook* edition went to print.

Vitality Blast — North Group
Yorkshire v. Nottinghamshire

At Emerald Headingley, Leeds, on July 19, 2019
Match abandoned without a ball bowled

Toss: None   Yorkshire 1 point, Nottinghamshire 1 point
Umpires: I D Blackwell and P J Hartley   Scorers: J T Potter and I J Smith

Derbyshire v. Yorkshire

Played at Queen's Park, Chesterfield, on July 20, 2019
Derbyshire won by 5 wickets

Toss won by Yorkshire   Derbyshire 2 points, Yorkshire 0 points

YORKSHIRE

A Lyth, c Stevens b Rampaul		21
* T Kohler-Cadmore, b van Beek		7
D J Willey, lbw b Watt		6
H C Brook, c Godleman b Watt		7
J A Tattersall, not out		39
G S Ballance, b Watt		5
§ N Pooran, c Madsen b Watt		12
J A Thompson, c Smit b van Beek		50
M D Fisher, c Madsen b Rampaul		9
J E Poysden		
D M Bess	Did not bat	
Extras lb 4, w 4		8
Total (8 wkts, 20 overs)		164

FoW: 1-31 (Lyth), 2-36 (Kohler-Cadmore), 3-40 (Willey), 4-50 (Brook), 5-63 (Ballance), 6-77 (Pooran), 7-143 (Thompson), 8-164 (Fisher)

	O	M	R	W
Stevens	1	0	12	0
Rampaul	4	1	29	2
Madsen	1	0	15	0
van Beek	4	0	22	2
Watt	4	0	19	4
Critchley	3	0	23	0
Reece	2	0	24	0
Hudson-Prentice	1	0	16	0

DERBYSHIRE

F J Hudson-Prentice, c Kohler-Cadmore b Willey		8
* B A Godleman, not out		70
L M Reece, lbw b Bess		19
W L Madsen, lbw b Bess		13
J L du Plooy, c sub (M W Pillans) b Thompson		30
D I Stevens, b Lyth		2
M J J Critchley, not out		14
§ D Smit		
L V Van Beek		
M R J Watt	Did not bat	
R Rampaul		
Extras b 2, lb 2, w 6		10
Total (5 wkts, 19.1 overs)		166

FoW: 1-8 (Hudson-Prentice), 2-46 (Reece), 3-67 (Madsen), 4-132 (du Plooy), 5-137 (Stevens)

	O	M	R	W
Willey	3.1	0	29	1
Fisher	1	0	13	0
Thompson	4	0	38	1
Bess	4	0	30	2
Poysden	3	0	25	0
Lyth	4	0	27	1

Man of the Match: B A Godleman

Umpires: N J Llong and T Lungley   Scorers: J T Potter and J M Brown

Vitality Blast — North Group
Leicestershire v. Yorkshire

Played at The Fischer County Ground, Grace Road, Leicester, on July 23, 2019
Yorkshire won by 54 runs

Toss won by Leicestershire   Yorkshire 2 points, Leicestershire 0 points

YORKSHIRE

A Lyth, c Klein b Parkinson	....	69
* T Kohler-Cadmore, not out	....	96
§ N Pooran, c Dearden b Klein	....	67
H C Brook, not out,	....	6
D J Willey		
G S Ballance		
T T Bresnan		
J A Thompson	Did not bat	
M W Pillans		
D Olivier		
D M Bess		
Extras lb 5, w 10, nb 2	....	17
Total (2 wkts, 20 overs)	....	255

FoW: 1-116 (Lyth), 2-237 (Pooran)

	O	M	R	W
Klein	4	0	40	1
Wright	4	0	49	0
Mike	4	0	57	0
Ackermann	1	0	20	0
Parkinson	4	0	53	1
Dexter	2	0	18	0
Lilley	1	0	13	0

LEICESTERSHIRE

M J Cosgrove, c Ballance b Bess	....	31
N J Dexter, b Olivier	....	25
* C N Ackermann, b Thompson	....	29
A M Lilley, c Brook b Pillans	....	47
§ L J Hill, not out	....	49
H E Dearden, not out	....	5
A M Ali		
B W M Mike		
C F Parkinson	Did not bat	
D Klein		
C J C Wright		
Extras lb 6, w 6, nb 4	....	15
Total (4 wkts, 20 overs)	....	201

FoW: 1-51 (Dexter), 2-82 (Cosgrove), 3-110 (Ackermann), 4-177 (Lilley)

	O	M	R	W
Willey	4	0	23	0
Olivier	4	0	47	1
Pillans	4	0	50	1
Thompson	3	0	19	1
Bess	4	0	45	1
Bresnan	1	0	12	0

Man of the Match: T Kohler-Cadmore

Umpires: B V Taylor and A G Wharf   Scorers: J T Potter and P J Rogers

Vitality Blast — North Group
Yorkshire v. Lancashire

Played at Emerald Headingley, Leeds, on July 25, 2019

Lancashire won by 9 runs

Toss won by Lancashire   Lancashire 2 points, Yorkshire 0 points

LANCASHIRE

A L Davies, c Pooran b Thompson		25
L S Livingstone, c Brook b Shutt		25
S J Croft, c Lyth b Shutt		11
G J Maxwell, c Pooran b Olivier		25
* § D J Vilas, run out (Willey)		43
K K Jennings, not out		16
J J Bohannon, c Willey b Pillans		12
J P Faulkner, not out		0
R J Gleeson		
M W Parkinson	Did not bat	
S Mahmood		
Extras lb 2, w 9, nb 2		13
Total (6 wkts, 20 overs)		170

FoW: 1-45 (Davies), 2-62 (Croft), 3-79 (Livingstone), 4-140 (Maxwell), 5-144 (Vilas), 6-164 (Bohannon)

	O	M	R	W
Willey	4	0	35	0
Bess	1	0	8	0
Olivier	4	0	37	1
Thompson	4	0	25	1
Pillans	3	0	32	1
Shutt	4	0	31	2

YORKSHIRE

* T Kohler-Cadmore, b Mahmood		14
A Lyth, b Croft		0
D J Willey, c Bohannon b Parkinson		32
H C Brook, c Faulkner b Gleeson		30
§ N Pooran, b Mahmood		43
G S Ballance, run out (Gleeson)		4
J A Thompson, not out		15
D M Bess, lbw b Mahmood		0
M W Pillans, lbw b Faulkner		8
D Olivier, run out (Davies/Faulkner)		1
J W Shutt, not out		0
Extras b 4, lb 3, w 7		14
Total (9 wkts, 20 overs)		161

FoW: 1-12 (Lyth), 2-16 (Kohler-Cadmore), 3-78 (Willey), 4-97 (Brook), 5-131 (Ballance), 6-140 (Pooran), 7-140 (Bess), 8-149 (Pillans), 9-151 (Olivier)

	O	M	R	W
Croft	1	0	12	1
Mahmood	4	0	33	3
Gleeson	3	0	25	1
Faulkner	4	0	21	1
Maxwell	4	0	30	0
Parkinson	4	0	33	1

Man of the Match: S Mahmood

Umpires: J H Evans and N A Mallender   Scorers: J T Potter and C Rimmer

Third Umpire: J W Lloyds

Vitality Blast — North Group
Northamptonshire v. Yorkshire

At Wantage Road, Northampton, on July 28, 2019
Match abandoned without a ball bowled

Toss:None

Yorkshire 1 point, Northamptonshire 1 point

Umpires: B J Debenham and N A Mallender

Scorers: J T Potter and T R Owen

Yorkshire v. Worcestershire

Played at Emerald Headingley, Leeds, on August 2, 2019
Worcestershire won by 5 wickets

Toss won by Yorkshire

Worcestershire 2 points, Yorkshire 0 points

YORKSHIRE

A Lyth, c Mitchell b Rhodes		68
T Kohler-Cadmore, c Barnard b Rhodes		40
H C Brook, b Pennington		17
D J Willey, c Wessels b Pennington		3
T T Bresnan, c Barnard b Brown		18
G S Ballance, c Barnard b Brown		4
J A Thompson, b Parnell		0
§ J A Tattersall, not out		14
D M Bess, not out		5
* S A Patterson		
D Olivier	Did not bat	
Extras lb 2, w 6		8
Total (7 wkts, 20 overs)		177

FoW: 1-104 (Kohler-Cadmore), 2-114 (Lyth), 3-133 (Brook), 4-140 (Willey), 5-157 (Ballance), 6-157 (Thompson), 7-161 (Bresnan)

	O	M	R	W
Pennington	4	0	34	2
Parnell	4	0	36	1
Brown	4	0	41	2
Barnard	4	0	36	0
Mitchell	2	0	16	0
Rhodes	2	0	12	2

WORCESTERSHIRE

M H Wessels, c Lyth b Bess		91
M J Guptill, c Patterson b Olivier		5
* C J Ferguson, c Ballance b Lyth		27
W D Parnell, c Brook b Olivier		27
§ O B Cox, not out		9
R A Whiteley, b Willey		0
E G Barnard, not out		4
D K H Mitchell		
G H Rhodes		
D Y Pennington	Did not bat	
P R Brown		
Extras lb 4, w 12		16
Total (5 wkts, 17.3 overs)		179

FoW: 1-28 (Guptill), 2-93 (Ferguson), 3-152 (Wessels), 4-174 (Parnell), 5-175 (Whiteley)

	O	M	R	W
Willey	3.3	0	30	1
Bess	4	0	34	1
Olivier	3	0	29	2
Patterson	2	0	27	0
Thompson	3	0	37	0
Lyth	2	0	18	1

Man of the Match: M H Wessels

Umpires: N G B Cook and J D Middlebrook

Scorers: J T Potter and P M Mellish

Vitality Blast — North Group
Yorkshire v. Birmingham Bears

Played at Emerald Headingley, Leeds, on August 4, 2019

Match tied

Toss won by Yorkshire   Yorkshire 1 point, Birmingham Bears 1 point

BIRMINGHAM BEARS

D P Sibley, c Ballance b Willey		64
§ M G K Burgess, c Tattersall b Olivier		16
S R Hain, c Lyth b Olivier		31
A J Hose, c Tattersall b Shutt		14
W H M Rhodes, not out		22
L Banks, not out		24
A T Thomson		
H J H Brookes		
* J S Patel	Did not bat	
J C Wainman		
F H Edwards		
Extras lb 3, w 3		6
Total (4 wkts, 20 overs)		177

FoW: 1-37 (Burgess), 2-99 (Sibley), 3-124 (Hose), 4-137 (Hain)

	O	M	R	W
Willey	4	0	29	1
Bresnan	1	0	9	0
Bess	4	0	32	0
Thompson	4	0	40	0
Olivier	3	0	31	2
Shutt	4	0	33	1

YORKSHIRE

A Lyth, st Burgess b Patel		40
* T Kohler-Cadmore, not out		76
D J Willey, b Thomson		30
G S Ballance, c Thomson b Brookes		11
H C Brook, b Patel		2
§ J A Tattersall, not out		8
J A Thompson		
D M Bess		
T T Bresnan	Did not bat	
J W Shutt		
D Olivier		
Extras lb 2, w 6, nb 2		10
Total (4 wkts, 20 overs)		177

FoW: 1-88 (Lyth), 2-131 (Willey), 3-148 (Ballance), 4-151 (Brook)

	O	M	R	W
Brookes	4	0	31	1
Edwards	4	0	54	0
Wainman	3	0	31	0
Patel	4	0	21	2
Thomson	4	0	27	1
Rhodes	1	0	11	0

Man of the Match: T Kohler-Cadmore

Umpires: R J Bailey and P R Pollard   Scorers: J T Potter and C Hughes

Vitality Blast — North Group
Lancashire v. Yorkshire

At Emirates Old Trafford, Manchester, on August 9, 2019
Match abandoned without a ball bowled

Toss: None
Umpires: I J Gould and J W Lloyds
Third Umpire: R T Robinson

Yorkshire 1 point, Lancashire 1 point
Scorers: J T Potter and C Rimmer

Yorkshire v. Derbyshire

Played at Emerald Headingley, Leeds, on August 11, 2019
Derbyshire won by 55 runs

Toss won by Yorkshire

Derbyshire 2 points, Yorkshire 0 points

DERBYSHIRE

L M Reece, c Kohler-Cadmore b Willey		11
* B A Godleman, c Tattersall b Thompson		28
W L Madsen, lbw b Bresnan		66
J L du Plooy, lbw b Willey		51
M J J Critchley, c Willey b Bresnan		17
A L Hughes, not out		10
F J Hudson-Prentice, not out		15
§ D Smit		
L V van Beek		
W B Rankin	Did not bat	
R Rampaul		
Extras lb 4, w 3, nb 2		9
Total (5 wkts, 20 overs)		207

FoW: 1-21 (Reece), 2-55 (Godleman), 3-142 (du Plooy), 4-179 (Madsen), 5-181 (Critchley)

	O	M	R	W
Bess	3	0	25	0
Willey	4	0	35	2
Maharaj	4	0	39	0
Olivier	3	0	47	0
Thompson	3	0	25	1
Shutt	1	0	15	0
Bresnan	2	0	17	2

YORKSHIRE

A Lyth, c Smit b Rampaul		28
* T Kohler-Cadmore, c Madsen b van Beek		0
D J Willey, c Hughes b van Beek		11
§ J A Tattersall, lbw b Critchley		17
J A Leaning, c Smit b van Beek		36
T T Bresnan, run out (Godleman)		10
J A Thompson, c Godleman b van Beek		23
K A Maharaj, not out		10
D M Bess, c Godleman b Reece		3
D Olivier, c Madsen b Reece		1
J W Shutt, run out (van Beek/Critchley)		0
Extras lb 3, w 10		13
Total (17.1 overs)		152

FoW: 1-1 (Kohler-Cadmore), 2-31 (Willey), 3-40 (Lyth), 4-75 (Tattersall), 5-89 (Bresnan), 6-134 (Thompson), 7-137 (Leaning), 8-147 (Bess), 9-150 (Olivier), 10-152 (Shutt)

	O	M	R	W
van Beek	3	0	17	4
Rampaul	3	0	33	1
Hudson-Prentice	2	0	21	0
Rankin	2	0	30	0
Reece	4	0	27	2
Critchley	3.1	0	21	1

Man of the Match: W L Madsen

Umpires: B J Debenham and I J Gould

Scorers: J T Potter and J M Brown

Vitality Blast — North Group

Yorkshire v. Durham

At Emerald Headingley, Leeds, on August 16, 2019
Match abandoned without a ball bowled

Toss: None   Yorkshire 1 point, Durham 1 point
Umpires: M Burns and G D Lloyd   Scorers: J T Potter and W R Dobson
Third Umpire: S J O'Shaughnessy

Durham v. Yorkshire

Played at Emirates Riverside, Chester-le-Street on August 23, 2019
Yorkshire won by 14 runs

Toss won by Durham   Yorkshire 2 points, Durham 0 points

YORKSHIRE

* T Kohler-Cadmore, c Clark b Rimmington	52
A Lyth, c Carse b Steel	13
D J Willey, c and b Potts	2
§ J A Tattersall, c Clark b Rimmington	7
J A Leaning, c Adair b Rimmington	39
W A R Fraine, c Short b Potts	16
T T Bresnan, not out	14
J A Thompson, not out	0\
K A Maharaj	
M W Pillans	Did not bat
J W Shutt	
Extras b 1, w 2	3
Total (6 wkts, 20 overs)	146

FoW: 1-16 (Lyth), 2-21 (Willey), 3-37 (Tattersall), 4-112 (Kohler-Cadmore), 5-128 (Leaning), 6-138 (Fraine)

	O	M	R	W
Steel	2	0	6	1
Carse	2	0	23	0
Potts	4	0	32	2
Trevaskis	4	0	28	0
Rimmington	3	0	16	3
Harte	1	0	9	0
Short	4	0	31	0

DURHAM

D J M Short, b Shutt	29
S Steel, c Tattersall b Shutt	49
H R D Adair, c Lyth b Shutt	4
* § P S P Handscomb, c Kohler-Cadmore b Shutt	19
G J Harte, c Willey b Shutt	6
G Clark, c Fraine b Lyth	13
B A Carse, c Maharaj b Leaning	1
B A Raine, c Fraine b Lyth	1
L Trevaskis, c Leaning b Lyth	0
M J Potts, run out (Thompson/Lyth)	1
N J Rimmington, not out	0
Extras lb 6, w 3	9
Total (19 overs)	132

FoW: 1-70 (Short), 2-78 (Adair), 3-106 (Steel), 4-116 (Harte), 5-116 (Handscomb), 6-124 (Carse), 7-128 (Raine), 8-129 (Trevaskis), 9-131 (Clark), 10-132 (Potts)

	O	M	R	W
Willey	2	0	9	0
Bresnan	2	0	21	0
Pillans	1	0	11	0
Thompson	1	0	19	0
Maharaj	4	0	21	0
Shutt	4	0	11	5
Leaning	2	0	15	1
Lyth	3	0	19	3

Man of the Match: J W Shutt

Umpires: MJ Saggers and R J Warren   Scorers: G Maddison and W R Dobson

Vitality Blast — North Group
Nottinghamshire v. Yorkshire

Played at Trent Bridge, Nottingham, on August 25, 2019

Nottinghamshire won by 3 runs

Toss won by Nottinghamshire   Nottinghamshire 2 points, Yorkshire 0 points

NOTTINGHAMSHIRE

J M Clarke, c Shutt b Lyth	50
A D Hales, c Maharaj b Bresnan	7
B M Duckett, c Kohler-Cadmore b Bresnan	2
J D Libby, c Fraine b Lyth	35
§ T J Moores, c Shutt b Lyth	2
* D T Christian, not out	31
S R Patel, c Fraine b Lyth	11
L J Fletcher, c Pillans b Lyth	6
M Carter	
L Wood Did not bat	
H F Gurney	
Extras lb 1, w 3	4
Total (7 wkts, 20 overs)	148

FoW: 1-12 (Hales), 2-16 (Duckett), 3-82 (Libby), 4-98 (Moores), 5-98 (Clarke), 6-136 (Patel), 7-148 (Fletcher)

	O	M	R	W
Lyth	4	0	31	5
Willey	3	0	32	0
Bresnan	3	0	17	2
Thompson	2	0	17	0
Maharaj	4	0	26	0
Shutt	4	0	24	0

YORKSHIRE

A Lyth, c Duckett b Gurney	48
* T Kohler-Cadmore, run out (Patel)	5
D J Willey, b Libby	23
§ J A Tattersall, lbw b Patel	15
J A Leaning, b Fletcher	20
W A R Fraine, c Carter b Gurney	13
T T Bresnan, b Fletcher	5
K A Maharaj, not out	0
J A Thompson, not out	2
M W Pillans	
J W Shutt Did not bat	
Extras lb 3, w 9, nb 2	14
Total (7 wkts, 20 overs)	145

FoW: 1-15 (Kohler-Cadmore), 2-59 (Willey), 3-99 (Lyth), 4-108 (Tattersall), 5-131 (Leaning), 6-137 (Bresnan), 8-143 (Fraine)

	O	M	R	W
Wood	2	0	16	0
Carter	4	0	12	0
Gurney	4	0	29	2
Fletcher	3	0	31	2
Christian	2	0	17	0
Libby	1	0	11	1
Patel	4	0	26	1

Man of the Match: M Carter

Umpires: G D Lloyd and J W Lloyds   Scorers: A Cusworth and R Marshall

Vitality Blast — North Group
Yorkshire v. Northamptonshire

Played at Emerald Headingley, Leeds, on August 25, 2019

Yorkshire won by 80 runs

Toss won by Yorkshire

Yorkshire 2 points, Northamptonshire 0 points

YORKSHIRE

* T Kohler-Cadmore, c Buck b Keogh	....	51
A Lyth, c Wakely b White	....	50
D J Willey, c Faheem Ashraf b White	....	4
H C Brook, c Sole b Keogh	....	38
§ J A Tattersall, c Muzarabani b Buck	....	10
J A Leaning, c Wakely b Faheem Ashraf	....	18
T T Bresnan, c White b Faheem Ashraf	....	8
W A R Fraine, not out	....	1
J A Thompson, not out	....	1
K A Maharaj		
J W Shutt	Did not bat	
Extras b 4, lb 1, w 1	....	6
Total (7 wkts, 20 overs)	....	187

FoW: 1-88 (Lyth), 2-109 (Kohler-Cadmore), 3-113 (Willey), 4-158 (Brook), 5-159 (Tattersall), 6-185 (Bresnan), 7-185 (Leaning)

	O	M	R	W
Cobb	1	0	10	0
Muzarabani	2	0	29	0
Faheem Ashraf	3	0	34	2
Buck	2	0	14	1
Pretorius	2	0	25	0
Keogh	4	0	38	2
White	4	0	18	2
Sole	2	0	14	0

NORTHAMPTONSHIRE

R E Levi, c Brook b Willey	....	19
§ A M Rossington, b Bresnan	....	0
* J J Cobb, c Leaning b Willey	....	1
D Pretorius, c Fraine b Willey	....	9
A G Wakely, c Leaning b Willey	....	7
R I Keogh, b Maharaj	....	11
Faheem Ashraf, c Brook b Bresnan	....	1
T B Sole, not out	....	41
G G White, c Brook b Shutt	....	6
N L Buck, c Brook b Shutt	....	0
B Muzarabani, c Tattersall b Lyth	....	9
Extras lb 1, w 2	....	3
Total (18 overs)	....	107

FoW: 1-19 (Levi), 2-19 (Rossington), 3-26 (Cobb), 4-30 (Pretorius), 5-43 (Wakely), 6-45 (Faheem Ashraf), 7-68 (Keogh), 8-81 (White), 9-82 (Buck), 10-107 (Muzarabani)

	O	M	R	W
Lyth	2	0	21	1
Willey	4	1	18	4
Bresnan	3	0	15	2
Shutt	4	0	27	2
Maharaj	4	0	17	1
Thompson	1	0	8	0

Man of the Match: D J Willey

Umpires: P J Hartley and R T Robinson

Scorers: J T Potter and T R Owen

Vitality Blast — North Group
Birmingham Bears v. Yorkshire

Played at Edgbaston, Birmingham, on August 30, 2019

Yorkshire won by 19 runs

Toss won by Birmingham   Yorkshire 2 points, Birmingham 0 points

YORKSHIRE

* T Kohler-Cadmore, not out		94
A Lyth, c Sibley b Garrett		42
D J Willey, c Rhodes b Green		25
H C Brook, b Rhodes		23
T T Bresnan, not out		3
J A Leaning		
§ J A Tattersall		
W A R Fraine	Did not bat	
M W Pillans		
K A Maharaj		
J W Shutt		
Extras lb 3, w 10		13
Total (3 wkts, 20 overs)		200

FoW: 1-102 (Lyth), 2-137 (Willey), 3-193 (Brook)

	O	M	R	W
Green	4	0	37	1
Wainman	2	0	39	0
Thomson	4	0	39	0
Patel	4	0	34	0
Rhodes	3	0	29	1
Garrett	3	0	19	1

BIRMINGHAM

D P Sibley, lbw b Lyth		37
E J Pollock, c Tattersall b Bresnan		22
C J Green, c Fraine b Bresnan		4
M J Lamb, b Pillans		11
S R Hain, not out		64
W M H Rhodes, b Maharaj		9
A T Thomson, not out		11
§ A J Mellor		
* J S Patel	Did not bat	
G A Garrett		
J C Wainman		
Extras b 4, lb 12, w 7		23
Total (5 wkts, 20 overs)		181

FoW: 1-31 (Pollock), 2-35 (Green), 3-56 (Lamb), 4-100 (Sibley), 5-127 (Rhodes)

	O	M	R	W
Lyth	3	0	31	1
Willey	3	0	33	0
Bresnan	3	0	30	2
Pillans	4	0	25	1
Maharaj	4	1	23	1
Shutt	3	0	23	0

Man of the Match: T Kohler-Cadmore

Umpires: D J Millns and R A White   Scorers: J T Potter and M D Smith

YORKSHIRE AVERAGES 2019

VITALITY BLAST

Played 10	Won 4	Lost 5	Tied 1	Abandoned 4

BATTING AND FIELDING

(Qualification 4 completed innings)

Player	M.	I.	N.O.	Runs	H.S.	100s	50s	Avge	ct/st
T Kohler-Cadmore	10	10	3	435	96*	0	5	62.14	4
A Lyth	10	10	0	379	69	0	3	37.90	4
J A Leaning	5	4	0	113	39	0	0	28.25	3
J A Tattersall	8	7	3	110	39*	0	0	27.50	6
H C Brook	7	7	1	123	38	0	0	20.50	7
D J Willey	10	9	0	136	32	0	0	15.11	3
T T Bresnan	8	6	2	58	18	0	0	14.50	0
G S Ballance	5	4	0	24	11	0	0	6.00	3

Also played

Player	M.	I.	N.O.	Runs	H.S.	100s	50s	Avge	ct/st
N Pooran	3	3	0	122	67	0	1	40.66	2
J A Thompson	9	7	4	91	50	0	1	30.33	0
W A R Fraine	4	3	1	30	16	0	0	15.00	6
M D Fisher	1	1	0	9	9	0	0	9.00	0
M W Pillans	5	1	0	8	8	0	0	8.00	1
D M Bess	6	3	1	8	5*	0	0	4.00	0
D Olivier	5	2	0	2	1	0	0	1.00	0
J W Shutt	7	2	1	0	0*	0	0	0.00	2
K A Maharaj	5	2	2	10	10*	0	0	—	2
S A Patterson	1	0	0	0	—	0	0	—	1
J E Poysden	1	0	0	0	—	0	0	—	0

BOWLING

(Qualification 4 wickets)

Player	Overs	Mdns	Runs	Wkts	Avge	Best	4wI	RPO
A Lyth	18	0	147	12	12.25	5-31	1	8.16
T T Bresnan	15	0	121	8	15.12	2-15	0	8.06
J W Shutt	24	0	164	10	16.40	5-11	1	6.83
D J Willey	34.4	1	273	9	30.33	4-18	1	7.87
D Olivier	17	0	191	6	31.83	2-29	0	11.23
D M Bess	20	0	174	4	43.50	2-30	0	8.70
J A Thompson	25	0	228	4	57.00	1-19	0	9.12

Also bowled

Player	Overs	Mdns	Runs	Wkts	Avge	Best	4wI	RPO
J A Leaning	2	0	15	1	15.00	1-15	0	7.50
M W Pillans	12	0	118	3	39.33	1-25	0	9.83
K A Maharaj	20	1	126	2	63.00	1-17	0	6.30
J E Poysden	3	0	25	0	—	0-25	0	8.33
S A Patterson	2	0	27	0	—	0-27	0	13.50
M D Fisher	1	0	13	0	—	0-13	0	13.00

Second Eleven 2019

PLAYERS WHO APPEARED FOR YORKSHIRE SECOND ELEVEN IN 2019
(excluding First Eleven capped players)

Player	Date of Birth	Birthplace	Type
E Barnes *	November 26, 1997	York	RHB/RFM
H C Brook *	February 22, 1999	Keighley	RHB/RM
K Carver *	March 26, 1996	Northallerton	LHB/SLA
M D Fisher *	January 9, 1997	York	RHB/RFM
W A R Fraine * §	June 13, 1996	Huddersfield	RHB/RM
J E G Logan *	October 12, 1997	Wakefield	LHB/SLA
M W Pillans * §	July 4, 1991	Westville, Kwa-Zulu, Natal, S Africa	RHB/RFM
J E Poysden * §	August 8, 1991	Shoreham-by-Sea, Sussex	LHB/LB
J Shaw *	January 3, 1996	Wakefield	RHB/RFM
J A Thompson *	October 9, 1996	Leeds	LHB/RMF
M J Waite *	December 25, 1995	Leeds	RHB/RMF
J D Warner *	November 14, 1996	Wakefield	RHB/RFM
O R Batchelor §	October 2, 1996	Chelsea	RHB
F J Bean §	April 16, 2002	Harrogate	LHB/WK
Bilal Anjam	January 30, 1999	Rotherham	RHB/OB
B D Birkhead	October 28, 1998	Halifax	RHB/WK
H G Duke	September 6, 2001	Wakefield	RHB/WK
G C H Hill	January 24, 2001	Keighley	RHB/RMF
D J Leech	January 10, 2001	Middlesbrough	RHB/RM
T W Loten	January 8, 1999	York	RHB/RMF
A Ramkumar §	December 26, 2001	Chennai, India	RHB/OB
M L Revis	November 15, 2001	Steeton, Keighley	RHB/RM
J D Shutt	June 24, 1997	Barnsley	RHB/OB
H A Sullivan §	December 17, 2002	Leeds	LHB/SLA
J R Sullivan	August 4, 2000	Leeds	RHB/LB
M A Taylor	December 18, 1997	Wakefield	RHB/RFM
J H Wharton	February 1, 2001	Huddersfield	RHB/OB

* Second Eleven cap

§ Debutants

SECOND ELEVEN HIGHLIGHTS OF 2019

CHAMPIONSHIP

Century partnerships (2)

For the 1st wicket (2)

   164   by W A R Fraine and F J Bean v. Worcestershire at Kidderminster CC

   103   by W A R Fraine and Bilal Anjam v. Derbyshire at York CC

Centuries (2)

  W A R Fraine (2)

     157*   v. Worcestershire at Kidderminster CC

     124   v. Derbyshire at York CC

Ten wickets in a match: – No one achieved this milestone in 2019. The best match return was 8-113 by J W Shutt v. Warwickshire at Stamford Bridge.

Five wickets in an innings (1)

  J D Warner (1)

    5-22 v. Worcestershire at Kidderminster

Five victims in an innings: No one managed this feat in 2019

TROPHY

Century Partnerships (4)

For the 1st wicket (1)

   219   W A R Fraine and H C Brook v. Nottinghamshire at York CC

For the 3rd wicket (2)

   127   J A Thompson and J A Leaning v. Lancashire at Scarborough

   101   W A R Fraine and F J Bean v. Worcestershire at Kidderminster CC

For the 5th wicket (1)

   126   M D Fisher and H G Duke v. Worcestershire at Kidderminster CC

5 wickets in an innings: No one achieved this milestone in 2019. The best match return was 3-10 by E Barnes v Lancashire at Scarborough.

Five victims in an innings: No one achieved this target in 2019.The best return was four catches by Jordan Thompson against Derbyshire at Barnsley.

T20 COMPETITION

Century Partnerships: None recorded in 2019. The highest partnership was 86* by J A Leaning and T T Bresnan against Worcestershire at Weetwood.

Centuries: None recorded in 2019. The highest score was 78* by T T Bresnan v Northamptonshire at Desborough.

5 wickets in an innings (1)

  J A Leaning (1)

    5-18 v. Derbyshire at Glossop CC

Five victims in an innings: None. The best returns were three catches by Josh Poysden v. Worcestershire at Weetwood and three by Jared Warner v. Warwickshire at Weetwood.

FRIENDLY MATCHES

Yorkshire Second Eleven have played 314 such matches from 1862 to the end of 2019, and records now exist for these games.

R W Frank (1900-1914) is the leading run-maker with 1,354 in 51 matches at 23.75. Jonathan Tattersall (1,291 in 34 games at 33.10) is the nearest challenger still playing.

R C Sargent (1911-1921) took 124 wickts at 12.11 in 25 appearances. Karl Carver with 71 wickets is the nearest of the modern generation.

Second Eleven Championship
Yorkshire v Nottinghamshire

Played at Harrogate on April 24, 25 and 26, 2019

Match drawn at 3.20pm on the Third Day

Toss won by Yorkshire   Yorkshire 12 points, Nottinghamshire 9 points

Close of play: First Day, Nottinghamshire (1) 0-1 (C F Gibson 0, L A Patterson-White 0) (1.2 overs);
Second Day: Nottinghamshire (1) 137-9 (J D Cook 5, M A R Cohen 1) (48.2 overs)

First Innings	YORKSHIRE		Second Innings	
W A R Fraine, c Hall b Blathwerick	35		not out	26
F J Bean, lbw b Footitt	8		lbw b Blatherwick	0
T W Loten, lbw b James	75		not out	43
J R Thompson, lbw b Wood	32			
§ B D Birkhead, b Blatherwick	18			
H G Duke, lbw b Footitt	19			
M D Fisher, lbw b Wood	31			
E Barnes, c Hall b Footitt	1			
* J D Warner, lbw b Footitt	0			
K Carver, lbw b Footitt	11			
J W Shutt, not out	0			
M A Taylor				
D J Leech	Did not bat			
Extras b 18, lb 15, w 5, nb 10	48		Extras b 6, lb 4, nb 8	18
Total (68.4 overs)	278		Total (1 wkt, 26 overs)	87

E Barnes joined Sussex on loan during this match. He was replaced by D J Leech.

FoW: 1-29 (Bean), 2-86 (Fraine), 3-175 (Thompson), 4-201 (Loten), 5-209 (Birkhead),
1st 6-233 (Duke), 7-235 (Barnes), 8-235 (Warner), 9-270 (Fisher), 10-278 (Carver)
2nd 1-4 (Bean)

	O	M	R	W		O	M	R	W
Footitt	14.4	2	51	5	Coughlin	8	1	19	0
Wood	16	1	67	2	Blatherwick	6	2	21	1
Blatherwick	15	1	43	2	Cohen	6	1	25	0
Cohen	4	0	19	0	Footitt	6	2	12	0
Cook	11	0	44	0					
Patterson-White	3	0	6	0					
James	5	0	15	1					

NOTTINGHAMSHIRE

S G Budinger, b Fisher	0	
C F Gibson, lbw b Fisher	1	
L A Patterson-White, c Thompson b Leech	24	
* L W James, b Warner	1	
L Wood, c Shutt b Leech	25	
J Schadendorf, lbw b Thompson	15	
§ S J W Hall, b Warner	5	
K S Leverock, b Shutt	41	
J M Blatherwick, b Loten	17	
J D Cook, not out	5	
M A R Cohen, b Warner	1	
M H A Footitt		
P Coughlin	Did not bat	
Extras nb 2	2	
Total (48.3 overs)	137	

FoW: 1-0 (Budinger); 2-1 (Gibson); 3-4 (James); 4-50 (Patterson-White); 5-54 (Wood);
6-69 (Hall); 7-77 (Schadendorf); 8-120 (Blatherwick); 9-136 (Leverock); 10-137 (Cohen)

	O	M	R	W
Fisher	5	1	18	2
Warner	8.3	2	13	3
Thompson	11	4	27	1
Taylor	9	1	29	0
Shutt	6	1	22	1
Leech	5	0	20	2
Loten	4	1	8	1

Umpires: D J Millns and J Pitcher   Scorers: J R Virr and Mrs A Cusworth

Second Eleven Championship
Worcestershire v Yorkshire

Played at Kidderminster CC on May 14, 15 and 16, 2019

Yorkshire won by 258 runs at 4.30pm on the Third Day, the largest margin ever achieved by Yorkshire against Worcestershire in the Second Eleven County Championship.

Toss won by Yorkshire   Worcestershire 5 points, Yorkshire 23 points

Close of play: First Day, Worcestershire (1) 38-2 (M D Lezar 3, M Ahmed 1) (19 overs); Second Day, Yorkshire (2) 199-1 (W A R Fraine 105, A Ramkumar 15) (49 overs)

First Innings	YORKSHIRE			Second Innings	
W A R Fraine, c Finch b Sanders	52			not out	157
F J Bean, c Milton b Finch	11			lbw b Sanders	63
A Ramkumar, c Phagura b Sanders	37			lbw b Finch	35
J A Thompson, c Godsal b Phagura	53			not out	15
M D Fisher, c Beadsworth b Ahmed	9				
§ B D Birkhead, c Sanders b Godsal	8				
H G Duke, b Ahmed	19				
E Barnes, b Sanders	5				
J Shaw, c Milton b Ahmed	37				
* J D Warner, lbw b Phagura	20				
J E Poysden, not out	21				
J W Shutt	Did not bat				
Extras b 3, lb 1, nb 6	10			Extras b 6, lb 11, nb 8	25
Total (83 overs)	282			Total (2 wkts dec, 61.5 overs)	295

FoW: 1-34 (Bean), 2-93 (Ramkumar), 3-104 (Fraine), 4-123 (Fisher), 5-156 (Birkhead),
1st 6-185 (Thompson), 7-199 (Barnes), 8-207 (Duke), 9-250 (Shaw), 10-282 (Warner)
2nd 1-164 (Bean), 2-244 (Ramkumar)

The second-innings first-wicket partnership of 164 is the highes ever record by Yorkshire against Worcestershire in the Second Eleven County Championship.

	O	M	R	W		O	M	R	W
Sanders	14	3	53	3	Sanders	15	1	57	1
Finch	15	2	41	1	Finch	15	2	48	1
Pahgura	14	3	53	2	Pahgura	9.5	0	51	0
Godsal	10	2	47	1	Ahmed	10	0	56	0
Ahmed	24	2	66	3	Godsal	6	1	36	0
Westbury	6	0	18	0	Westbury	6	0	30	0

First Innings	WORCESTERSHIRE			Second Innings	
O E Westbury b Warner	18			b Warner	4
A J Robson, c Thompson b Warner	15			c Fraine b Warner	1
M D Lezar, b Warner	20			lbw b Thompson	13
M Ahmed, b Warner	3			(9) not out	15
* § A G Milton, b Thompson b Hobson	0			(4) lbw b Barnes	32
C E Lea, c Fraine b Warner	4			(5) lbw b Thompson	0
C J Clist, not out	64			(7) lbw b Barnes	5
A W Finch, b Barnes	3			(6) c Birkhead b Shaw	2
B S Phagura, c Fraine b Poysden	46			(8) lbw b Barnes	24
C W G Sanders, c Bean b Poysden	0			b Poysden	17
A Godsal, lbw b Poysden	5			lbw b Shutt	1
S Beadsworth	Did not bat				
Extras lb 16	16			Extras b 4, lb 4, nb 4	12
Total (72.4 overs)	193			Total (51.4 overs)	126

FoW: 1-26 (Robson), 2-35 (Westbury), 3-57 (Ahmed), 4-58 (Lezar), 5-64 (Milton),
1st 6-74 (Lea), 7-84 (Finch), 8-175 (Phagura), 9-185 (Sanders), 10-193 (Godsal)
FoW: 1-2 (Robson), 2-7 (Westbury), 3-27 (Lezar), 4-27 (Lea), 5-30 (Finch),
2nd 6-55 (Clist), 7-93 (Milton), 8-94 (Phagura), 9-125 (Sanders), 10-126 (Godsal)

	O	M	R	W		O	M	R	W
Fisher	8	3	15	0	Fisher	8	3	15	0
Shaw	8	0	31	0	Warner	7	0	21	2
Thompson	13	5	23	1	Shaw	8	1	22	1
Warner	13	3	22	5	Thompson	6	2	9	2
Barnes	4	0	13	1	Barnes	9	2	22	3
Poysden	15.4	1	36	3	Poysden	11	4	17	1
Shutt	11	1	37	0	Shutt	2.4	0	12	1

Umpires: H Adnan and A C Harris   Scorers: R M Wilks and J R Virr

Second Eleven Championship
Leicestershire v. Yorkshire

Played at Kibworth CC on May 21, 22 and 23, 2019
Leicestershire won by an innings and 106 runs at 12.35pm on the Third Day

Toss won by Yorkshire   Leicestershire 24 points, Yorkshire 2 points

Close of play: First Day, Leicestershire (1) 215-3 (S T Evans 101, C F Parkinson 59) (71 overs);
Second Day, Yorkshire (2) 128-6 (B D Birkhead 10) (55.4 overs)

YORKSHIRE

	First Innings			Second Innings	
W A R Fraine, lbw b Klein		14	c Evans b Dexter		12
Bilal Anjam, c Swindells b Davis		29	b Dexter		17
O R Batchelor, b Davis		12	lbw b Dexter		23
J A Thompson, c Bates b Dexter		2	c Swindells b Davis		27
A Ramkumar, c Swindells b Davis		2	c Swindells b Griffiths		29
M D Fisher, lbw b Davis		0	b Davis		0
§ B D Birkhead, lbw b Klein		1	c and b Davis		42
E Barnes, not out		5	c Lilley b Dexter		20
M W Pillans, b Klein		0	lbw b Davis		21
M A Taylor, b Klein		0	lbw b Davis		2
* J E Poysden, c Swindells b Dexter		1	not out		0
J W Shutt	Did not bat				
Extras b 4, nb 2		6	Extras b 6, lb 5, w 1, nb 6		18
Total (32.5 overs)		72	Total (79 overs)		211

FoW: 1-15 (Fraine), 2-48 (Anjam), 3-55 (Thompson), 4-61 (Batchelor), 5-61 (Fisher),
1st 6-62 (Ramkumar), 7-71 (Birkhead), 8-71 (Pillans), 9-71 (Taylor), 10-72 (Poysden)
FoW: 1-27 (Fraine), 2-40 (Anjam), 3-58 (Batchelor), 4-102 (Thompson), 5-104 (Fisher),
2nd 6-128 (Ramkumar), 7-176 (Barnes), 8-196 (Birkhead), 9-206 (Taylor), 10-211 (Pillans)

	O	M	R	W		O	M	R	W
Griffiths	6	2	22	0	Klein	20	5	71	1
Klein	8	3	20	4	Griffiths	15	5	35	1
Dexter	10.5	5	13	2	Dexter	17	7	34	3
Davis	8	3	13	4	Davis	20	6	52	5
					Lilley	7	0	8	0

LEICESTERSHIRE

S T Evans, c Fisher b Thompson		146
§ S J Swindells, b Barnes		12
N J Dexter, lbw b Barnes		2
A M Ali, b Barnes		23
C F Parkinson, c Thompson b Shutt		61
* A M Lilley, c Birkhead b Fisher		47
S D Bates, c Thompson b Poysden		35
D Klein, b Poysden		36
G T Griffiths, not out		1
W S Davis, lbw b Thomspon		2
N Bowley, b Thompson		0
A W G Jones	Did not bat	
Extras b 5, lb 16, w 1, nb 2		24
Total (117 overs)		389

FoW: 1-45 (Swindells), 2-55 (Dexter), 3-114 (Ali), 4-220 (Parkinson), 5-286 (Lilley),
6-342 (Evans), 7-381 (Bates), 8-386 (Klein), 9-389 (Davis), 10-389 (Bowley)

	O	M	R	W
Fisher	20	2	66	1
Pillans	15	3	48	0
Barnes	16	3	50	3
Thompson	17	3	43	3
Taylor	12	1	50	0
Poysden	22	3	60	2
Shutt	15	1	51	1

Umpires: R T Robinson and R P Medland   Scorers: P N Johnsons and J R Virr

Second Eleven Championship
Yorkshire v. Derbyshire

Played at York CC on May 28, 29 and 30, 2019

Yorkshire won by 5 wickets at 5.32pm on the Third Day

Toss won by Yorkshire   Yorkshire 20 points, Derbyshire 4 points

Close of play: First Day, Derbyshire (1) 44-2 (T A Wood 25; J L du Plooy 0) (13 overs); Second Day, Derbyshire (1) 379-9 dec (C R Marshall 71, J P A Taylor 45) (102.5 overs)

DERBYSHIRE
(Second Innings forfeited)

T R McGladdery, lbw b Fisher	16
J J Dinnie, b Pillans	0
T A Wood, lbw b Fisher	117
J L du Plooy, c Fraine b Pillans	0
F J Hudson-Prentice, c and b Logan	74
* § D Smit, c Birkhead b Thompson	13
M R J Watt, c Pillans b M A Taylor	27
C R Marshall, not out	71
S Conners, b Pillans	1
A Karvelas, c Revis b Pillans	1
J P A Taylor, not out	45
D R Williams	Did not bat
Extras b 5, lb 5, nb 4	14
Total (9 wkts dec, 102.5 overs)	379

FoW: 1-0 (J J Dinnie), 2-44 (McGladdery), 3-45 (du Plooy), 4-149 (Hudson-Prentice), 5-176 (Smit), 6-229 (Watt), 7-301 (Wood), 8-302 (Conners), 9-304 (Karvelas)

	O	M	R	W
Fisher	21	6	63	2
Pillans	19	4	73	4
Thompson	13	3	45	1
Barnes	12	3	41	0
Shutt	17	0	64	0
Logan	13	0	43	1
Taylor	7	1	35	1
Bilal Anjam	0.5	0	5	0

YORKSHIRE
(First Innings forfeited)

Fraine, st Smit b Marshall	124
Bilal Anjam, c Smit b Williams	31
F J Bean, lbw b Karvelas	28
* J A Thompson, not out	92
M L Revis, c McGladdery b Karvelas	40
M D Fisher, c Smith b Williams	0
§ B D Birkhead, not out	33
E Barnes	
J E G Logan	
M W Pillans	Did not bat
J W Shutt	
M A Taylor	
Extras b 3, lb 14, nb 18	35
Total (5 wkts, 84.5 overs)	383

FoW: 1-103 (Bilal Anjam), 2-187 (Bean), 3-218 (Fraine), 4-310 (Revis), 5-320 (Fisher)

	O	M	R	W
Taylor	15.5	1	67	0
Conners	12	1	68	0
Karvelas	18	3	77	2
Williams	12	2	67	2
Marshall	12	1	46	1
Watt	15	4	41	0

Umpires: I N Ramage and S Widdup   Scorers: J R Virr and J A Wallis

Second Eleven Championship
Yorkshire v. Durham

Played at Harrogate CC on June 17, 18 and 19, 2019
Match drawn at 6.31pm on the Second Day

Toss won by Yorkshire   Yorkshire 7 points, Durham 9 points

Close of play: First Day, no play; Second Day, Durham (1) 388-6 (S W Poynter 102, W J Weighell 11) (104 overs). There was no play on the Third Day.

DURHAM

M A Jones, lbw b Poysden	....	45
* R D Pringle, b Poysden	....	59
C T Bancroft, lbw b Fisher	....	13
G Clark, b Leech	....	74
G J Harte, b Poysden	....	37
§ S W Poynter, not out	....	102
S J D Bell, lbw b Poysden	....	34
W J Weighell, not out	....	11
N J Rimmington		
L Doneathy	Did not bat	
G H I Harding		
J O I Campbell		
Extras lb 13	....	13
Total (6 wkts, 104 overs)	....	388

FoW: 1-97 (Jones), 2-120 (Bancroft), 3-142 (Pringle), 4-232 (Clark), 5-256 (Harte), 6-337 (Bell)

	O	M	R	W
Fisher	16	7	36	1
Pillans	16	2	58	0
Barnes	15	6	56	0
Leech	12	2	40	1
Taylor	6	0	29	0
Poysden	25	6	92	4
Shutt	14	2	64	0

YORKSHIRE

J H Wharton
Bilal Anjam
F J Bean
H G Duke
M D Fisher
§ B D Birkhead
E Barnes
D J Leech
M W Pillans
* J E Poysden
M A Taylor
J W Shutt

Umpires: I N Ramage and S Richardson   Scorers: J R Virr and G Maddison

175

Second Eleven Championship
Lancashire v. Yorkshire

Played at Aigburth, Liverpool, on July 10, 11 and 12, 2019

Match drawn at 4.14pm on the Second Day

Toss won by Lancashire

Lancashire 11 points, Yorkshire 9 points

Close of play: First Day, Yorkshire (1) 39-2 (J A Leaning 22, G C H Hill 4) (23 overs); Second Day, Lancashire (2) 73-2 (S M O Shah 35, J P Faulkner 16) (25 overs). There was no play on the Third Day.

LANCASHIRE

First Innings		Second Innings	
B D Guest, c Warner b Thompson	33	c Warner b Bresnan	4
S M O Shah, c Leaning b Poysden	32	not out	35
* D J Lamb, c Birkhead b Leaning	71	c Leaning b Waite	16
J P Faulkner, c Thompson b Bresnan	19	not out	16
E B Fluck, c Thompson b Barnes	2		
G P Balderson, c Bresnan b Carver	23		
§ G I D Lavelle, c Leaning b Carver	5		
T W Hartley, c Birkhead b Leaning	1		
J P Morley, lbw b Leaning	0		
R Lord, c Poysden b Leaning	2		
G D Burrows, not out	1		
E H T Moulton	Did not bat		
Extras b 11, lb 6	17	Extras b 1, lb1	2
Total (78.4 overs)	207	Total (2 wkts, 25 overs)	73

FoW: 1-71 (Guest), 2-71 (Shah), 3-112 (Faulkner), 4-117 (Fluck), 5-196 (Lamb)
1st 6-196 (Balderson), 7-199 (Hartley), 8-199 (Morley), 9-203 (Lavelle), 10-206 (Lord
2nd 1-4 (Guest), 2-45 (Lamb)

	O	M	R	W		O	M	R	W
Bresnan	12	4	29	1	Bresnan	6	1	20	1
Warner	9	4	26	0	Warner	3	0	14	0
Waite	4	1	8	0	Waite	6	1	15	1
Poysden	17	2	32	1	Leaning	7	5	16	0
Thompson	12	5	27	1	Thompson	3	0	6	0
Carver	13	4	38	2					
Barnes	6	1	21	1					
Leaning	5.4	2	8	4					

YORKSHIRE

J H Wharton, lbw b Moulton	6
Bilal Anjam, c Lamb b Moulton	2
J A Leaning, b Moulton	24
G C H Hill, c Lavelle b Balderson	31
T T Bresnan, c Lavelle b Burrows	1
M J Waite, c Lavelle b Balderson	13
J A Thompson, not out	34
§ B D Birkhead, b Balderson	0
E Barnes, c Lamb b Morley	10
*J D Warner, c Lavelle b Balderson	2
J E Poysden, c Shah b Morley	0
K Carver	Did not bat
Extras b 5, w 5	10
Total (46.5 overs)	133

FoW: 1-4 (Anjam), 2-20 (Wharton), 3-45 (Leaning), 4-50 (Bresnan), 5-81 (Waite)
6-90 (Hill), 7-90 (Birkhead), 8-103 (Barnes), 9-118 (Warner), 10-133 (Poysder

	O	M	R	W
Burrows	12	4	39	1
Moulton	14	7	24	3
Balderson	10	3	36	4
Hartley	3	0	6	0
Morley	7.5	1	33	2

Umpires: N A Mallender and J P Prince

Scorers: G L Morgan and J R Vir

Second Eleven Championship
Yorkshire v. Warwickshire

Played at Stamford Bridge on July 16, 17 and 18, 2019
Yorkshire won by 88 runs at 5.03pm on the Third Day

Toss won by Yorkshire Yorkshire 24 points, Warwickshire 6 points
Close of play: First Day, Warwickshire (1) 6-1 (N A Hammond 1, M J Lamb 0) (4 overs); Second Day, Yorkshire (2) 79-3 (J H Wharton 28, M J Waite 17) (31 overs)

YORKSHIRE

	First Innings		Second Innings	
J H Wharton, c Hammond b Bethell	59	c Chapman-Lilley b Wightman	47
Bilal Anjam, c Wightman b Hughes	27	lbw b Bethell	14
T W Loten, c Mellor b Hughes	2	(6) st Mellor b Bethell	19
G C H Hill, lbw b Hughes	0	b Furrer	11
M J Waite, c Hammond b Lintott	40	c Lamb b Garrett	50
J A Leaning, c Garrett b Wightman	75	(3) c Hammond b Bethell	6
§ B D Birkhead, c Mellor b Wightman	59	b Garrett	15
E Barnes, st Mellor b Lintott	20	(10) not out	1
J E G Logan, c Mellor b Wightman	5	(8) c Lamb b Bethell	0
* J D Warner, not out	15	(9) c Furrer b Bethell	0
J W Shutt, not out	2	not out	4
M A Taylor	Did not bat		
Extras b 4, lb 1, w 2, nb 16	23	Extras lb 4, w 1	5
Total (9 wkts dec, 98 overs)	327	Total (9 wkts dec, 51 overs)	172

FoW: 1- 59 (Anjam), 2-61 (Loten), 3-61 (Hill), 4-115 (Waite), 5-168 (Wharton),
1st 6-277 (Birkhead), 7-282 (Leaning), 8-310 (Barnes), 9-314 (Logan)
FoW: 1-31 (Anjam), 2-37 (Leaning), 3-55 (Hill), 4-113 (Wharton), 5-144 (Waite),
2nd 6-166 (Birkhead), 7-166 (Loten), 8-166 (Logan), 9-166 (Warner)

	O	M	R	W		O	M	R	W
Furrer	13	2	47	0	Wightman	16	2	34	1
Wightman	17	4	59	3	Furrer	5	0	22	1
Garrett	15	1	57	0	Bethell	16	5	42	5
Hughes	13	3	57	3	Lintott	10	2	54	0
Lintott	23	4	62	2	Garrett	4	1	16	2
Bethell	17	1	40	1					

WARWICKSHIRE

	First Innings		Second Innings	
B J Chapman-Lilley, lbw b Waite	3	c Wharton b Waite	6
N A Hammond, c Leaning b Waite	59	c Birkhead b Warner	2
M J Lamb, lbw b Waite	0	lbw b Shutt	10
* § A J Mellor, lbw b Barnes	66	b Shutt	38
H D Johnson, c Birkhead b Barnes	30		
J G Bethell, c Warner b Shutt	4	c Hill b Leaning	2
B J Griffin, c Warner b Shutt	12	c Birkhead b Barnes	10
J B Lintott, b Hill	17	b Barnes	13
G A Garrett, c Leaning b Shutt	19	b Leaning	33
G W Furrer, b Shutt	8	lbw b Shutt	14
L R D Hughes, not out	0	not out	26
B J Wightman	Did not bat		
R A Jones		(5) c Anjam b Shutt	10
Extras b 12, nb 2	14	Extras b 5, lb 4, nb 6	15
Total (76.3 overs)	232	Total (56 overs)	179

FoW: 1-4 (Chapman-Lilley), 2-6 (Lamb), 3-120 (Hammond), 4-169 (Mellor), 5-176 (Johnson),
1st 6-176 (Bethell), 7-205 (Lintott), 8-205 (Griffin), 9-221 (Furrer), 10-232 (Garrett)
FoW: 1-6 (Hammond), 2-12 (Chapman-Lilley), 3-39 (Lamb), 4-68 (Mellor), 5-77 (Jones),
2nd 6-78 (Bethell), 7-99 (Griffin), 8-102 (Lintott), 9-127 (Furrer), 10-179 (Garrett)

	O	M	R	W		O	M	R	W
Waite	13	7	24	3	Waite	7	4	9	1
Warner	10	1	24	0	Warner	5	0	22	1
Barnes	8	2	32	2	Barnes	8	3	16	2
Taylor	5	3	13	0	Shutt	21	5	70	4
Leaning	18	4	51	0	Leaning	14	4	51	2
Loten	4	0	26	0	Bilal Anjam	1	0	2	0
Shutt	13.3	1	43	4					
Hill	5	0	7	1					

Umpires: N J Pratt and G M Roberts Scorers: J R Virr and R J Dickinson

Second Eleven Championship
Northamptonshire v. Yorkshire

Played at Desborough Town CC on July 30 and 31 and August 1, 2019
Match drawn at 5.21pm on the Third Day

Toss won by Yorkshire   Northamptonshire 9 points, Yorkshire 6 points

Close of play: First Day, Yorkshire (1) 11-1 (J H Wharton 6, T W Loten 4) (6 overs); Second Day, no play.

YORKSHIRE

W A R Fraine, lbw b Neal	0
J H Wharton, b Pereira	38
T W Loten, c Gouldstone b Neal	9
J A Leaning, b Twigger	13
M J Waite, c Bramley b Bhabra	26
M L Revis, b Pereira	12
§ B D Birkhead, lbw b Neal	11
E Barnes, not out	10
J Shaw, c Cronie b Neal	0
* J D Warner, lbw b Twigger	0
K Carver, c Gouldstone b Neal	3
J R Sullivan	Did not bat	
Extras b 1, lb 2	3
Total (52.2 overs)	125

FoW: 1-0 (Fraine), 2-30 (Loten), 3-53 (Leaning), 4-65 (Wharton), 5-91 (Revis), 6-111 (Waite), 7-111 (Birkhead), 8-115 (Shaw), 9-116 (Warner), 10-125 (Carver)

	O	M	R	W
Neal	13	5	32	5
Bhabra	17	9	24	1
Rereira	11.2	4	34	2
Twigger	9	2	27	2
Zaib	2	1	5	0

NORTHAMPTONSHIRE

E N Gay, lbw b Waite	2
B Coddington, c Wharton b Warner	0
S A Zaib, retired hurt	0
* C O Thurston, c Leaning b Warner	28
†H O M Gouldstone, not iut	54
A S B Bramley, c Sullivan b Carver	5
J Cronie, not out	4
B J Bhabra	
A J Neal	
B Claydon	Did not bat
J Twigger	
W J Pereira	
Extras b 4, lb 1, nb 2	7
Total (4 wkts, 25 overs)	100

FoW: 1-2 (Coddington), 2-8 (Gay), 3-44 (Thurston), 4-92 (Bramley)

	O	M	R	W
Waite	5	1	20	1
Warner	5	0	26	2
Shaw	4	2	5	0
Barnes	3	0	23	0
Carver	4	1	9	1
Sullivan	4	1	12	0

Umpires: N L Bainton and M P Dobbs   Scorers: Q L S Jones and J R Virr

SECOND ELEVEN CHAMPIONSHIP 2019

FINAL

Hampshire (343 and 278) beat Leicestershire (187 and 291) by 143 runs

NORTHERN GROUP FINAL TABLE

	P	W	L	D	Tied	Aban.	Bonus Points Bat	Bonus Points Bowl	Ded	Points
1 Leicestershire (6)	8	2	0	6	0	0	19	24	0	105
2 Yorkshire (5)	**8**	**3**	**1**	**4**	**0**	**0**	**10**	**25**	**0**	**103**
3 Nottinghamshire (4)	8	2	0	6	0	0	15	26	0	103
4 Lancashire (3)	8	1	0	7	0	0	19	30	0	100
5 Northamptonshire (8)	8	1	2	5	0	0	18	21	0	80
6 Warwickshire (2)	8	1	3	4	0	0	21	22	0	79
7 Durham (1)	8	0	1	7	0	0	22	22	0	79
8 Worcestershire (9)	8	1	2	5	0	0	14	22	0	77
9 Derbyshire (10)	8	0	2	6	0	0	20	16	0	66

SOUTHERN GROUP FINAL TABLE

	P	W	L	D	Tied	Aban.	Bonus Points Bat	Bonus Points Bowl	Ded	Points
1 Hampshire (2)	9	5	0	4	0	0	24	25	0	149
2 Kent (5)	9	4	1	4	0	0	31	27	0	142
3 Sussex (8)	9	3	1	5	0	0	23	20	0	116
4 Somerset (7)	9	1	1	7	0	0	25	32	0	108
5 MCC Young Cricketers *	9	2	1	6	0	0	23	20	-1.5	103.5
6 Essex (1)	9	2	3	4	0	0	23	28	0	103
7 Glamorgan (3)	9	1	0	8	0	0	19	23	0	98
8 Surrey (4)	9	1	3	5	0	0	21	28	0	90
9 Middlesex (9)	9	1	3	5	0	0	22	25	0	88
10 Gloucestershire (6)	9	0	7	2	0	0	14	23	0	47

Ded. Points deducted for slow over-rates

(2018 group positions in brackets)

*The MCC Young Cricketers played in the Southern Group in 2019, so the Southern sides played nine matches. The MCC Young Cricketers lost 1.5 points for slow over-rates.
The MCC Young Cricketers finished in fifth position in the Northern group in 2018.*

SECOND ELEVEN CHAMPIONS

In the seasons in which Yorkshire have competed. The Championship has been split into two groups since 2009, the group winners playing off for the Championship. These groups were deemed North and South from the 2012 season.

Season	Champions	Yorkshire's Position	Season	Champions	Yorkshire's Position
1959	Gloucestershire	7th	1997	Lancashire	2nd
1960	Northamptonshire	14th	1998	Northamptonshire	9th
1961	Kent	11th	1999	Middlesex	14th
1975	Surrey	4th	2000	Middlesex	5th
1976	Kent	5th	2001	Hampshire	2nd
1977	**Yorkshire**	**1st**	2002	Kent	3rd
1978	Sussex	5th	**2003**	**Yorkshire**	**1st**
1979	Warwickshire	3rd	2004	Somerset	8th
1980	Glamorgan	5th	2005	Kent	10th
1981	Hampshire	11th	2006	Kent	3rd
1982	Worcestershire	14th	2007	Sussex	10th
1983	Leicestershire	2nd	2008	Durham	5th
1984	**Yorkshire**	**1st**	2009	Surrey	A 2nd
1985	Nottinghamshire	12th	2010	Surrey	A 8th
1986	Lancashire	5th	2011	Warwickshire	A 10th
1987	**Yorkshire and Kent**	**1st**	2012	Kent	(North) 9th
1988	Surrey	9th	2013	Lancashire & Middlesex	
1989	Middlesex	9th			(North) 4th
1990	Sussex	17th	2014	Leicestershire	(North) 4th
1991	**Yorkshire**	**1st**	2015	Nottinghamshire	(North) 7th
1992	Surrey	5th	2016	Durham	(North) 5th
1993	Middlesex	3rd	2017	Lancashire	(North) 4th
1994	Somerset	2nd	2018	Durham	(North) 5th
1995	Hampshire	5th	2019	Leicestershire	(North) 2nd
1996	Warwickshire	4th			

SECOND ELEVEN CHAMPIONSHIP
AVERAGES 2019

Played 9   Won 3   Lost 1   Drawn 4

BATTING AND FIELDING
(Qualification 5 innings)

Player	M.	I.	N.O.	Runs	H.S.	Avge	100s	50s	ct/st
W A R Fraine	5	8	2	420	157*	70.00	2	1	4
J A Thompson	5	7	3	255	92*	63.75	0	2	6
T W Loten	3	5	1	148	75	37.00	0	1	0
B D Birkhead	8	9	1	187	59	23.37	0	1	8
F J Bean	4	5	0	110	63	22.00	0	1	1
Bilal Anjam	5	6	0	120	31	20.00	0	0	1
E Barnes	8	8	3	72	20	14.40	0	0	1
M D Fisher	5	5	0	40	31	8.00	0	0	1
J D Warner	5	6	1	37	20	7.40	0	0	4

Also played

Player	M.	I.	N.O.	Runs	H.S.	Avge	100s	50s	ct/st
A Leaning	3	4	0	118	75	29.50	0	1	6
M L Revis	2	2	0	52	40	26.00	0	0	1
A Ramkumar	2	4	0	103	37	25.75	0	0	0
H G Duke	3	2	0	38	19	19.00	0	0	0
J Shaw	2	2	0	37	37	18.50	0	0	0
O R Batchelor	1	2	0	35	23	17.50	0	0	0
G C H Hill	2	3	0	42	31	14.00	0	0	1
J E Poysden	4	4	2	22	21*	11.00	0	0	1
M W Pillans	3	2	0	21	21	10.50	0	0	1
K Carver	3	2	0	14	11	7.00	0	0	-
E G Logan	2	2	0	5	5	2.50	0	0	1
T T Bresnan	1	1	0	1	1	1.00	0	0	1
M A Taylor	5	2	0	2	2	1.00	0	0	0
J W Shutt	6	3	3	6	4*	—	0	0	1
M J Waite	3	4	0	129	50	—	1	0	0
O J Leech	2	0	0	0	—	—	0	0	0
R Sullivan	1	0	0	0	—	—	0	0	1

BOWLING
(Qualification 10 wickets)

Player	Overs	Mdns	Runs	Wkts	Avge	Best	5wI	10wM
J D Warner	60.3	10	168	13	12.92	5-22	1	0
J E Poysden	90.4	16	237	11	21.54	4-92	0	0
E Barnes	81	20	274	12	22.83	3-22	0	0
J W Shutt	100.1	11	363	11	33.00	4-43	0	0

Also bowled

Player	Overs	Mdns	Runs	Wkts	Avge	Best	5wI	10wM
G C H Hill	5	0	7	1	7.00	1- 7	0	0
M J Waite	35	14	76	6	12.67	3-24	0	0
K Carver	17	5	47	3	15.67	2-39	0	0
J A Thompson	75	22	180	9	20.00	3-43	0	0
O J Leech	17	2	60	3	20.00	2-20	0	0
A Leaning	44.4	15	126	6	21.00	4- 8	0	0
T T Bresnan	18	5	49	2	24.50	1-20	0	0
T W Loten	8	1	34	1	34.00	1- 8	0	0
M D Fisher	78	22	213	6	35.50	2-18	0	0
E G Logan	13	0	43	1	43.00	1-43	0	0
M W Pillans	50	9	179	4	44.75	4-73	0	0
J Shaw	20	3	58	1	58.00	1-22	0	0
M A Taylor	39	6	156	1	156.00	1-35	0	0
R Sullivan	4	1	12	0	—	—	0	0
Bilal Anjam	1.5	0	7	0	—	—	0	0

Second Eleven Trophy
Yorkshire v. Lancashire

Played at Scarborough on April 18, 2019
Yorkshire won by 210 runs at 5.01pm

Toss won by Lancashire   Yorkshire 2 points, Lancashire 0 points

YORKSHIRE

W A R Fraine, c Hartley b Lord	....	38
§ B D Birkhead, c Moulton b Gibbon	....	30
J A Thompson, c Aitchison b Hartley	....	86
J A Leaning, c Greenwood b Gibbon	....	74
T W Loten, b Moulton	....	38
M L Revis, lbw b Moulton	....	1
E Barnes, c Parry b Lord	....	8
* J D Warner, b Lord	....	14
M A Taylor, c Aitchison b Lord	....	2
K Carver, not out	....	0
J W Shutt	Did not bat	
Extras b 5, lb 3, w 13, nb 2	....	23
Total (9 wkts, 50 overs)		314

FoW: 1-51 (Birkhead), 2-112 (Fraine), 3-239 (Thompson), 4-268 (Leaning), 5-271 (Revis)
6-294 (Loten), 7-300 (Barnes), 8-308 (Taylor), 9-314 (Warner)

	O	M	R	W
Aitchison	10	0	59	0
Gibbon	7	1	44	2
Moulton	9	0	61	2
Hartley	10	0	46	1
Lord	9	1	61	4
Greenwood	5	0	35	0

LANCASHIRE

J G T Crawley, b Barnes	....	9
E B Fluck, lbw b Barnes	....	1
* § G I D Lavelle, c Revis b Barnes	....	4
S J Perry, lbw b Carver	....	9
S Dorsey, lbw b Thompson	....	20
N A Greenwood, c Birkhead b Warner	....	46
T W Hartley, c Revis b Carver	....	0
E H T Moulton, lbw b Carver	....	2
B J G Gibbon, c Revis b Warner	....	7
B W Aitchison, not out	....	5
R Lord, lbw b Shutt	....	0
Extras w 1	....	1
Total (32 overs)		104

FoW: 1-2 (Fluck), 2-14 (Lavelle), 3-14 (Crawley), 4-37 (Perry), 5-53 (Dorsey)
6-54 (Hartley), 7-87 (Moulton), 8-97 (Greenwood), 9-104 (Gibbon), 10-104 (Lord)

	O	M	R	W
Warner	6	0	20	2
Barnes	5	0	10	3
Taylor	5	0	17	0
Carver	10	0	3	3
Thompson	5	0	1	1
Shutt	1	1	0	1

Umpires: RA White and J Pitcher   Scorers: J R Virr and G L Morgan

Second Eleven Trophy
Yorkshire v. Nottinghamshire

Played at York CC on April 23, 2019
Yorkshire won by 264 runs at 5.11pm

Four records were set in this match: the highest Yorkshire total in the history of the Second
Eleven Trophy, the highest individual score by a Yorkshire player, the highest first-wicket
partnership by a Yorkshire pair and the fifth-highest innings total nationally.

Toss won by Nottinghamshire   Yorkshire 2 points, Nottinghamshire 0 points

YORKSHIRE

W A R Fraine, c Budinger b Patterson-White		92
H C Brook, b Coughlin		144
J A Thompson, c Hall b Coughlin		37
J A Leaning, c sub (J T Schadendorf) b Blatherwick		51
M J Waite, c Hall b Cohen		24
T W Loten, c Patterson-White b Blatherwick		17
§ B D Birkhead, not out		5
E Barnes, not out		0
* J D Warner		
K Carver		
B O Coad	Did not bat	
J W Shutt		
Extras b 2, lb 6, w 24		32
Total (6 wkts, 50 overs)		402

FoW: 1-219 (Fraine), 2-299 (Brook), 3-304 (Thompson), 4-347 (Waite), 5-385 (Leaning),
6-401 (Loten)

	O	M	R	W
Footitt	7	0	62	0
Blatherwick	9	0	82	2
Coughlin	10	0	64	2
Cohen	8	0	75	1
Cook	6	0	51	0
Patterson-White	10	0	60	1

NOTTINGHAMSHIRE

* C D Nash, b Waite		13
L A Patterson-White, c Fraine b Waite		11
S G Budinger, c Birkhead b Waite		14
C F Gibson, lbw b Warner		9
J D M Evison, c Brook b Warner		21
J M Blatherwick, lbw b Carver		16
§ S J W Hall, c Birkhead b Thompson		28
J D Cook, not out		17
M H A Footitt, c Fraine b Leaning		4
M A R Cohen, lbw b Leaning		0
P Coughlin	Absent	
Extras w 5		5
Total (26 overs)		138

FoW: 1-24 (Patterson-White), 2-24 (Nash), 3-40 (Budinger), 4-64 (Gibson), 5-71 (Evison),
6-103 (Blatherwick), 7-123 (Hall), 8-138 (Footitt), 9-138 (Cohen)

	O	M	R	W
Coad	6	1	19	0
Waite	5	0	30	3
Warner	4	0	17	2
Barnes	3	0	21	0
Carver	4	0	26	1
Thompson	3	0	20	1
Leaning	1	0	5	2

Umpires: D J Milns and I G Warne   Scorers: J R Virr and Mrs A Cusworth

Second Eleven Trophy
Durham v. Yorkshire

Played at Brandon CC on May 10, 2019
Yorkshire won by 3 wickets at 5.26pm

Toss won by Durham   Durham 0 points, Yorkshire 2 points

DURHAM

*R D Pringle, c Poysden b Shaw		1
S Steel, c Pillans b Fisher		10
M J Richardson, c Carver b Thompson		32
§ R L Greenwell, b Poysden		47
B A Carse, c Fraine b Poysden		19
§ S W Poynter, lbw b Carver		19
L Doneathy, lbw b Poysden		13
N J Rimmington, c Birkhead b Thompson		6
C Rushworth, b Warner		6
O J Gibson, c sub (J W Shutt) b Thompson		6
F Hussain, not out		1
Extras lb 2, w 6		8
Total (46.5 overs)		168

FoW: 1-1 (Pringle), 2-14 (Steel), 3-79 (Richardson), 4-111 (Carse), 5-131 (Greenwell), 6-149 (Doneathy), 7-149 (Poynter), 8-157 (Rimmington), 9-167 (Gibson), 10-168 (Rushworth)

	O	M	R	W
Fisher	5	1	15	1
Shaw	4	1	11	1
Poysden	10	0	34	3
Warner	5.5	0	27	1
Pillans	3	0	14	0
Thompson	9	0	26	3
Carver	10	1	39	1

YORKSHIRE

W A R Fraine, c Pringle b Rushworth		4
§ B D Birkhead, c Rimmington b Rushworth		2
J A Thompson, b Rimmington		34
M D Fisher, c Poynter b Hussain		33
E Barnes, run out (Rimmington)		26
M W Pillans, b Rushworth		34
J Shaw, c Poynter b Rushworth		0
* J D Warner, not out		17
K Carver, not out		11
T W Loten		
J E Poysden	Did not bat	
Extras b 1, lb 1, w 8		10
Total (7 wkts, 42.5 overs)		171

FoW: 1-6 (Birkhead), 2-15 (Fraine), 3-53 (Thompson), 4-87 (Fisher), 5-129 (Pillans), 6-129 (Shaw), 7-155 (Barnes)

	O	M	R	W
Rushworth	10	2	21	4
Carse	9	0	45	0
Rimmington	5	0	28	1
Hussain	8.5	1	50	1
Pringle	9	1	18	0
Gibson	1	0	7	0

Umpires: N A Mallender and I N Warne   Scorers: G Maddison and J R Virr

Second Eleven Trophy
Worcestershire v. Yorkshire

Played at Kidderminster CC on May 13, 2019
Worcestershire won by 5 wickets at 6.03pm

Toss won by Yorkshire　　　　　　　　　　Worcestershire 2 points, Yorkshire 0 points

YORKSHIRE

W A R Fraine, lbw b Ahmed	.....	67
§ B D Birkhead, b Wilkinson	.....	6
J A Thompson, l;bw b Finch	.....	1
F J Bean, c Breed b Ahmed	.....	74
M D Fisher, not out	.....	99
H G Duke, st Milton b Finch	.....	34
E Barnes, not out	.....	1
J Shaw		
K Carver	Did not bat	
J E Poysden		
* J D Warner		
Extras lb 7, nb 2, w 11	.....	20
Total (5 wkts, 50 overs)		302

FoW: 1-22 (Birkhead), 2-31 (Thompson), 3-132 (Fraine), 174 (Bean), 5-300 (Duke)

	O	M	R	W
Finch	10	0	48	2
Wilkinson	10	0	47	1
Phagura	8	0	59	0
Bragg	7	0	44	0
Breed	2	0	20	0
Ahmed	10	0	48	2
Westbury	3	0	29	0

WORCESTERSHIRE

O E Westbury, lbw b Fisher	.....	7
A J Robson, run out (Fraine/Birkhead)	.....	53
J A Haynes, not out	.....	180
* § A G Milton, c Thompson b Barnes	.....	0
C E Lea, c Poysden b Thompson	.....	22
A W Finch, b Poysden	.....	24
B S Phagura, not out	.....	5
J Breed		
A R Wilkinson	Did not bat	
E D H Bragg		
M Ahmed		
Extras lb 1, w 12	.....	13
Total (5 wkts, 44.3 overs)		304

FoW: 1-30 (Westbury), 2-134 (Robson), 3-135 (Milton), 4-167 (Lea), 5-259 (Finch)

	O	M	R	W
Fisher	8	0	55	1
Shaw	5	0	27	0
Poysden	10	0	75	1
Warner	6	0	32	0
Barnes	6	0	36	1
Thompson	6	0	50	1
Carver	3.3	0	28	0

Umpires: J D Middlebrook and M Qureshi　　　Scorers: Mrs S M Drinkwater and J R Virr

Second Eleven Trophy
Leicestershire v. Yorkshire

Played at Lutterworth CC on May 20, 2019
Leicestershire won by 90 runs at 5.05 pm

Toss won by Yorkshire   Leicesterhire 2 points, Yorkshire 0 points

LEICESTERSHIRE

§ H J Swindells, c Birkhead b Taylor	65
D N Butchart, c Taylor b Leech	18
N J Dexter, c Thompson b Poysden	67
A M Ali, c Fisher b Thompson	24
S T Evans, c Revis b Fisher	1
C F Parkinson, c Revis b Thompson	13
*A M Lilley, c Leech b Poysden	12
D Klein, c Thompson b Carver	11
S D Bates, run out (Barnes/Carver)	2
W S Davis, c Barnes b Thompson	1
G T Griffiths, not out	1
Extras lb 12, w 8	20
Total (49.3 overs)	235

FoW: 1-42 (Butchart), 2-122 (Swindells), 3-182 (Ali), 4-189 (Evans), 5-194 (Dexter), 6-217 (Lilley), 7-229 (Parkinson), 8-232 (Klein), 9-234 (Bates), 10-235 (Davis)

	O	M	R	W
Fisher	8	0	29	1
Barnes	7	1	21	0
Leech	5	1	20	1
Thompson	9.3	0	42	3
Poysden	10	1	67	2
Carver	6	0	30	1
Taylor	4	0	14	1

YORKSHIRE

W A R Fraine, c Ali b Griffiths	6
§ B D Birkhead, b Griffiths	6
J A Thompson, c Lilley b Griffiths	15
M L Revis, b Griffiths	8
A Ramkumar, b Davis	16
M D Fisher, c Lilley b Dexter	8
E Barnes, c Swindells b Griffiths	37
M A Taylor, run out (Klein/Swindells)	15
D J Leech, st Swindells b Parkinson	5
K Carver, not out	7
* J E Poysden, st Swindells b Parkinson	4
Extras w 18	18
Total (32.3 overs)	145

FoW: 1-6 (Fraine), 2-19 (Birkhead), 3-27 (Revis), 4-48 (Thompson), 5-67 (Fisher), 6-69 (Ramkumar), 7-123 (Taylor), 8-127 (Barnes), 9-137 (Leech), 10-145 (Poysden)

	O	M	R	W
Griffiths	10	0	52	5
Klein	7	1	39	0
Dexter	5	1	9	1
Davis	6	0	27	1
Parkinson	4.3	0	18	2

Umpires: T Lungley and J K H Naik   Scorers: P N Johnson and J R Virr

Second Eleven Trophy
Yorkshire v. Derbyshire

Played at Barnsley CC on May 31, 2019
Yorkshire won by 52 runs at 5.55pm

Toss won by Derbyshire   Yorkshire 2 points, Derbyshire 0 points

YORKSHIRE

W A R Fraine, c Watt b Conners	15
§ B D Birkhead, c Smit b Conners	2
Bilal Anjam, c Watt b Hudson-Prentice	31
J A Thompson, c Smit b Gleadall	36
A Ramkumar, lbw b Watt	14
M D Fisher, c Hudson-Prentice b Gleadall	30
E Barnes, b Gleadall	24
M W Pillans, c Smit b J P A Taylor	7
M A Taylor, c Smit b Gleadall	0
K Carver, not out	15
* J E Poysden, c Smit b J P A Taylor	8
Extras lb 9, w 12, nb 6	27
Total (48.3 overs)	209

FoW: 1-17 (Birkhead), 2-21 (Fraine), 3-94 (Thompson), 4-102 (Anjam), 5-121 (Ramkumar), 6-169 (Fisher), 7-176 (Barnes), 8-176 (Taylor), 9-190 (Pillans), 10-209 (Poysden)

	O	M	R	W
J P A Taylor	8.3	0	34	2
Conners	8	1	45	2
Gleadall	10	0	44	4
Hudson-Prentice	6	1	23	1
Watt	10	0	33	1
Marshall	6	0	21	0

DERBYSHIRE

T R McGladdery, c Birkhead b Thompson	16
J J Dinnie, c Birkhead b Fisher	6
T A Wood, c Thompson b Barnes	7
J L du Plooy, lbw b Poysden	38
F J Hudson-Prentice, c Fisher b Thompson	6
* § D Smit, c Thompson b Poysden	33
C R Marshall, c Fraine b M A Taylor	3
A F Gleadall, c Thompson b Barnes	6
S Conners, c Birkhead b Thompson	14
M R J Watt, c Thompson b Poysden	10
J P A Taylor, not out	6
Extras lb 5, w 7	12
Total (42.5 overs)	157

FoW: 1-15 (Dinnie), 2-28 (McGladdery), 3-47 (Wood), 4-54 (Hudson-Prentice), 5-84 (du Plooy), 6-97 (Marshall), 7-122 (Gleadall), 8-128 (Smit), 9-138 (Watt); 10-157 (Conners)

	O	M	R	W
Fisher	8	3	17	1
Pillans	7	1	18	0
Thompson	7.5	1	26	3
Barnes	8	1	29	2
Poysden	9	0	44	3
M A Taylor	3	0	18	1

Umpires: I N Ramage and J Pitcher   Scorers: J R Virr and J A Wallis

Second Eleven Trophy — Semi-Final
Yorkshire v. Kent

Played at Scarborough CC on June 21, 2019
Kent won by 6 wickets at 5.50pm
Toss won by Kent

YORKSHIRE

H C Brook, b Lysaught	8
W A R Fraine, c O'Riordan b MacVicar	121
Bilal Anjam, c Rouse b MacVicar	37
G C H Hill, run out (Dilkes/Cox)	0
§ B D Birkhead, b Watson	11
M D Fisher, c Blake b O'Riordan	15
E Barnes, b Lysaught	41
M W Pillans, c Rouse b O'Riordan	26
K Carver, c Watson b Qayyum	1
M A Taylor, not out	7
* J E Poysden, c Rouse b MacVicar	2
Extras b 4, lb 4, w 17	25
Total (49.3 overs)	294

FoW: 1-28 (Brook), 2-113 (Anjam), 3-117 (Hill), 4-150 (Birkhead), 5-206 (Fraine), 6-214 (Fisher), 7-259 (Pillans), 8-262 (Carver), 9-286 (Barnes), 10-294 (Poysden)

	O	M	R	W
Watson	8	0	58	1
Lysaught	10	1	49	2
Haggett	2	0	8	0
Qayyum	10	0	52	1
MacVicar	9.3	0	62	3
O'Riordan	10	0	57	2

KENT

C J Haggett, c Birkhead b Fisher	1
§ J M Cox, c Birkhead b Pillans	97
S J D Burgess, lbw b Poysden	34
A J Blake, c Anjam b Fisher	139
* A P Rouse, not out	11
I V A Dilkes. not out	0
I Qayyum	
J M Lysaught	
M K O'Riordan	Did not bat
W A MacVicar	
J Watson	
Extras b 4, lb 4, w 6, nb 2	16
Total (4 wkts, 42.1 overs)	298

FoW: 1-22 (Haggett), 2-62 (Burgess), 3-279 (Cox), 4-289 (A J Blake)

	O	M	R	W
Fisher	10	3	60	2
Pillans	9	1	55	1
Barnes	6	0	43	0
Poysden	8.1	0	49	1
Taylor	2	0	28	0
Carver	5	0	39	0
Brook	2	0	16	0

Umpires: I N Ramage and J D Middlebrook   Scorers: J R Virr and A L Bateup

SECOND ELEVEN TROPHY 2019

SEMI-FINALS

Yorkshire (294) lost to Kent (298-4) by 6 wickets (at Scarborough)
Somerset (295) lost to Durham (296-7) by 3 wickets (at Taunton Vale CC)

FINAL

Kent (276) beat Durham (260) by 16 runs at Beckenham

NORTHERN GROUP – FINAL TABLE *(2018 in brackets)*

		P	W	L	Aban/NR	Points	Net Run Rate
1	**Yorkshire (3)**	**6**	**4**	**2**	**0**	**8**	**1.514**
2	Durham (9)	6	4	2	0	8	0.598
3	Warwickshire (1)	6	3	2	1	7	0.297
4	Worcestershire (2)	6	3	2	1	7	0.270
5	Derbyshire (10)	6	3	3	0	6	0.184
6	Northamptonshire (6)	6	2	2	2	6	-0.135
7	Leicestershire (8)	6	2	3	1	5	-0.013
8	Nottinghamshire (7)	6	1	3	2	4	-1.148
9	Lancashire (4)	6	1	4	1	4	-1.522

SOUTHERN GROUP – FINAL TABLE *(2018 in brackets)*

		P	W	L	Aban/NR	Points	Net Run Rate
1	Somerset (2)	6	5	0	1	11	1.272
2	Kent (7)	6	4	2	0	8	0.632
3	Glamorgan (9)	6	3	1	2	8	0.867
4	MCC Young Cricketers (5 in North)	6	3	2	1	7	0.458
5	Essex (4)	6	2	3	1	5	-0.148
6	Hampshire (5)	6	2	3	1	5	-0.227
7	Sussex (10)	6	2	4	0	4	-0.380
8	Surrey (8)	6	2	4	0	4	-0.583
9	Middlesex (1)	6	2	4	0	4	-0.783
10	Gloucestershire (3)	6	1	3	2	4	-0.991

The Unicorns (6th in 2018) did not compete in the 2019 competition.

SECOND ELEVEN TROPHY

PREVIOUS WINNERS

1986	**Northamptonshire**, who beat Essex by 14 runs
1987	**Derbyshire**, who beat Hampshire by 7 wickets
1988	**Yorkshire**, who beat Kent by 7 wickets
1989	**Middlesex**, who beat Kent by 6 wickets
1990	**Lancashire**, who beat Somerset by 8 wickets
1991	**Nottinghamshire**, who beat Surrey by 8 wickets
1992	**Surrey**, who beat Northamptonshire by 8 wickets
1993	**Leicestershire**, who beat Sussex by 142 runs
1994	**Yorkshire**, who beat Leicestershire by 6 wickets
1995	**Leicestershire**, who beat Gloucestershire by 3 runs
1996	**Leicestershire**, who beat Durham by 46 runs
1997	**Surrey**, who beat Gloucestershire by 3 wickets
1998	**Northamptonshire**, who beat Derbyshire by 5 wickets
1999	**Kent**, who beat Hampshire by 106 runs.
2000	**Leicestershire**, who beat Hampshire by 25 runs.
2001	**Surrey**, who beat Somerset by 6 wickets
2002	**Kent**, who beat Hampshire by 5 wickets
2003	**Hampshire**, who beat Warwickshire by 8 wickets
2004	**Worcestershire**, who beat Essex by 8 wickets
2005	**Sussex**, who beat Nottinghamshire by 6 wickets
2006	**Warwickshire**, who beat Yorkshire by 93 runs
2007	**Middlesex**, who beat Somerset by 1 run
2008	**Hampshire**, who beat Essex by 7 runs
2009	**Yorkshire**, who beat Lancashire by 2 wickets
2010	**Essex**, who beat Lancashire by 14 runs
2011	**Nottinghamshire**, who beat Lancashire by 4 wickets
2012	**Lancashire**, who beat Durham by 76 runs
2013	**Lancashire**, who beat Nottinghamshire by 76 runs
2014	**Leicestershire**, who beat Lancashire by 168 runs
2015	**Derbyshire**, who beat Durham by 10 runs
2016	**Lancashire**, who beat Somerset by 10 wickets *(DLS)*
2017	**Yorkshire,** who beat Middlesex by 99 runs *(DLS)*
2018	**Middlesex,** who beat Somerset by 1 wicket
2019	**Kent**, who beat Durham by 16 runs

SECOND ELEVEN TROPHY
AVERAGES 2019

Played 7   Won 4   Lost 3

BATTING AND FIELDING
(Qualification 3 innings)

Player	M.	I.	N.O.	Runs	H.S.	Avge	Strike Rate	100s	50s	ct/st
W A R Fraine	7	7	0	343	121	49.00	100.88	1	2	4
M D Fisher	5	5	1	185	99*	46.25	79.05	0	1	2
J A Thompson	6	6	0	209	86	34.83	98.12	0	1	7
K Carver	7	5	4	34	15*	34.00	68.00	0	0	1
J D Warner	4	2	1	31	17*	31.00	60.78	0	0	0
T W Loten	3	3	0	55	38	27.50	144.73	0	0	0
E Barnes	7	7	2	137	41	27.40	61.71	0	0	1
M W Pillans	3	3	0	67	34	22.33	106.34	0	0	1
A Ramkumar	3	2	0	30	16	15.00	53.57	0	0	0
B D Birkhead	7	7	1	62	30	10.33	70.45	0	0	10
M A Taylor	4	4	1	24	15	8.00	52.17	0	0	1
J E Poysden	5	3	0	14	8	4.67	37.83	0	0	2
Also played										
H C Brook	2	2	0	152	144	76.00	124.59	1	0	1
F J Bean	1	1	0	74	74	74.00	85.05	0	1	0
J A Leaning	2	2	0	125	74	62.50	101.62	0	2	0
Bilal Anjam	2	2	0	68	37	34.00	71.57	0	0	1
H G Duke	1	1	0	34	34	34.00	80.95	0	0	0
M J Waite	1	1	0	24	24	24.00	114.28	0	0	0
O J Leech	1	1	0	5	5	5.00	71.42	0	0	1
M L Revis	2	2	0	9	8	4.50	128.57	0	0	5
G C H Hill	1	1	0	0	0	0.00	—	0	0	0
J Shaw	2	1	0	0	0	0.00	—	0	0	0
W Shutt	2	0	0	0	—	—	—	0	0	0
B O Coad	1	0	0	0	—	—	—	0	0	0

BOWLING
(Qualification 4 wickets)

Player	Overs	Mdns	Runs	Wkts	Avge	Best	4wI	Strike Rate	Econ.
J A Thompson	40.2	1	191	12	15.91	3-26	0	20.16	4.73
J D Warner	21.5	0	96	5	19.20	2-17	0	26.20	4.39
E Barnes	35	2	160	6	26.67	3-10	0	35.00	4.57
J E Poysden	47.1	1	269	10	26.90	3-34	0	28.39	5.70
M D Fisher	39	7	176	6	29.33	2-60	0	39.00	4.51
K Carver	38.3	1	192	6	32.00	3-30	0	38.50	4.98
Also bowled									
A Leaning	1	0	5	2	2.50	2-5	0	3.00	5.00
M J Waite	5	0	30	3	10.00	3-30	0	10.00	6.00
O J Leech	5	1	20	1	20.00	1-20	0	30.00	4.00
J Shaw	9	1	38	1	38.00	1-11	0	54.00	4.22
M A Taylor	14	0	77	2	38.50	1-14	0	42.00	5.50
M W Pillans	19	2	87	1	87.00	1-55	0	114.00	4.57
W Shutt	1	1	0	1	0.00	1-0	0	6.00	0.00
B O Coad	6	1	19	0	—	—	0	3.16	—
H C Brook	2	0	16	0	—	—	0	8.00	—

Second Eleven Twenty20
Yorkshire v. Worcestershire

Played at Weetwood, Leeds, on July 8, 2019
Yorkshire won by by 7 wickets at 1.50pm

Toss won by Worcestershire

Yorkshire 2 points, Worcestershire 0 points

WORCESTERSHIRE

O E Westbury, c Poysden b Bresnan		2
T C Fell, c Waite b Bresnan		5
G H Rhodes, c Poysden b Bresnan		3
J A Haynes, c Barnes b Poysden		5
§ A G Milton, b Thompson		30
J Banton, not out		44
E W H Bragg, c Poysden b Willey		15
* P R Brown, not out		0
M C Davis		
J Dickenson	Did not bat	
L Marshall		
Extras w 1		1
Total (6 wkts, 20 overs)		105

FoW: 1-3 (Westbury), 2-9 (Fell), 3-12 (Rhodes), 4-31 (Haynes), 5-58 (Milton), 6-97 (Bragg)

	O	M	R	W
Willey	4	0	15	1
Bresnan	3	0	8	3
Pillans	4	0	32	0
Poysden	4	0	16	1
Carver	3	0	24	0
Thompson	2	0	10	1

YORKSHIRE

§ B D Birkhead, c Marshall b Davis		2
* D J Willey, c Fell b Bragg		19
J A Thompson, lbw b Banton		6
J A Leaning, not out		27
T T Bresnan, not out		41
E Barnes		
M W Pillans		
J E Poysden	Did not bat	
M J Waite		
G C H Hill		
K Carver		
Extras b 5, nb 6, w 3		14
Total (3 wkts, 12.3 overs)		109

FoW: 1-18 (Birkhead), 2-31 (Willey), 3-48 (Thompson)

	O	M	R	W
Brown	3	0	29	0
Davis	1	0	2	1
Marshall	1	0	13	0
Bragg	1	0	4	1
Rhodes	3	0	24	0
Banton	2	0	19	1
Dickenson	1.3	0	13	0

Umpires: T Lungley and J Pitcher

Scorers : J R Virr and R M Wilks

Second Eleven Twenty20
Yorkshire v. Worcestershire

Played at Weetwood, Leeds, on July 8, 2019
Yorkshire won by by 61 runs at 5.30pm

Toss won by Yorkshire   Yorkshire 2 points, Worcestershire 0 points

YORKSHIRE

§ B D Birkhead, c Bragg b Dickenson		44
* D J Willey, c Milton b Brown		7
G C H Hill, st Milton b Dickenson		33
J A Leaning, not out		44
T T Bresnan, not out		42
J A Thompson		
M W Pillans		
E Barnes		
M J Waite	Did not bat	
K Carver		
J E Poysden		
J D Warner		
Extras lb 1, nb 2, w 7		10
Total (3 wkts, 20 overs)		180

FoW: 1-24 (Willey), 2-89 (Birkhead), 3-94 (Hill)

	O	M	R	W
Rhodes	4	0	27	0
Davis	3	0	44	0
Bragg	3	0	25	0
Brown	4	0	40	1
Marshall	1	0	10	0
Banton	2	0	14	0
Dickenson	3	0	19	2

WORCESTERSHIRE

T C Fell, b Poysden		55
§ A G Milton, c Poysden b Bresnan		3
J A Haynes, c Willey b Bresnan		1
O E Westbury, c Pillans b Leaning		1
G H Rhodes, c Pillans b Poysden		9
J Banton, b Warner		10
* P R Brown, b Poysden		0
E W H Bragg, c Thompson b Warner		7
M C Davis, not out		16
J Dickenson, b Thompson		8
G O Marshall, not out		1
J Miszkowski	Did not bat	
Extras b 4, nb 2, w 2		8
Total (9 wkts, 20 overs)		119

FoW: 1-9 (Milton), 2-16 (Haynes), 3-32 (Westbury), 4-62 (Rhodes), 5-86 (Fell), 6-86 (Brown), 7-86 (Banton), 8-95 (Bragg), 9-117 (Dickenson)

	O	M	R	W
Willey	2	0	12	0
Bresnan	2	0	14	2
Leaning	2	0	14	1
Pillans	4	0	18	0
Poysden	4	1	16	3
Warner	4	0	28	2
Carver	1	0	10	0
Thompson	1	0	3	1

Umpires: T Lungley and J Pitcher   Scorers: J R Virr and R M Wilks

Second Eleven Twenty20
Yorkshire v. Warwickshire

Played at Weetwood, Leeds, on July 15, 2019
Warwickshire won by 4 wickets at 2.18pm

Toss won by Yorkshire

Yorkshire 0 points, Warwickshire 2 points

YORKSHIRE

J A Thompson, c Pollock b Brookes		6
§ B D Birkhead, c Mellor b Wightman		5
G C H Hill, st Mellor b Garrett		13
J A Leaning, c Agar b Brookes		56
T T Bresnan, not out		42
M J Waite, not out		10
E Barnes		
* J D Warner		
J F. Poysden	Did not bat	
K Carver		
M W Pillans		
M L Revis		
Extras lb 2, w 3		5
Total (4 wkts, 20 overs)		137

FoW: 1-12 (Birkhead), 2-14 (Thompson), 3-44 (Hill), 4-119 (Leaning)

	O	M	R	W
Agar	4	0	25	0
Furrer	1	0	10	0
Wightman	3	0	15	1
Brookes	4	0	22	2
Bethell	4	0	26	0
Garrett	4	0	37	1

WARWICKSHIRE

A G Oxley, c Hill b Bresnan		4
* E J Pollock b Carver		64
M J Lamb, c and b Leaning		20
A C Agar, c Warner b Thompson		22
§ A J Mellor, b Leaning		0
E A Brookes, c Warner b Carver		21
H D Johnson, not out		3
J G Bethell, not out		1
G A Garrett		
G W Furrer	Did not bat	
B J Wightman		
N A Hammond		
Extras w 3		3
Total (6 wkts, 19.3 overs)		138

FoW: 1-11 (Oxley), 2-91 (Pollock), 3-91 (Lamb), 4-91 (Mellor), 5-134 (Agar), 6-136 (Brookes)

	O	M	R	W
Leaning	4	0	19	2
Bresnan	3	0	29	1
Thompson	2.3	0	28	1
Poysden	4	0	27	0
Pillans	2	0	11	0
Carver	4	1	24	2

Umpires: N J Pratt and S A Richardson

Scorers: J R Virr and R J Dickinson

Second Eleven Twenty20
Yorkshire v. Warwickshire

Played at Weetwood, Leeds, on July 15, 2019
Yorkshire won by 7 wicktes at 5.41pm

Toss won by Warwickshire   Yorkshire 2 points, Warwickshire 0 points

WARWICKSHIRE

* E J Pollock, c Warner b Leaning		34
A G Oxley, lbw b Carver		21
M J Lamb, c Hill b Leaning		50
E A Brookes, c Hill b Thompson		9
§ A J Mellor, c Waite b Poysden		5
N A Hammond, not out		12
H D Johnson, not out		17
J G Bethell		
G A Garrett		
G W Furrer	Did not bat	
B J Wightman		
A C Agar		
Extras lb 2, w 3, nb 4		9
Total (5 wkts, 20 overs)		157

FoW: 1-35 (Pollock), 2-78 (Oxley), 3-107 (Brookes), 4-122 (Lamb), 5-126 (Mellor)

	O	M	R	W
Bresnan	3	0	22	0
Waite	1	0	14	0
Leaning	3	0	18	2
Pillans	3	0	35	0
Poysden	4	0	26	1
Carver	3	0	19	1
Thompson	3	0	21	1

YORKSHIRE

§ B D Birkhead, b Wightman		15
M L Revis, st Mellor b Bethell		49
J A Thompson, not out		68
J A Leaning, c Hammond b Furrer		13
T T Bresnan, not out		7
G C H Hill		
M J Waite		
J D Warner		
* J E Poysden	Did not bat	
K Carver		
M W Pillans		
E Barnes		
Extras lb 2, w 7		9
Total (3 wkts, 15.5 overs)		161

FoW: 1-48 (Birkhead), 2-82 (Revis), 3-122 (Leaning)

	O	M	R	W
Bethell	4	0	31	1
Wightman	3	0	30	1
Furrer	3.5	0	55	1
Brookes	3	0	32	0
Garrett	2	0	11	0

Umpires: N J Pratt and S A Richardson   Scorers: J R Virr and R J Dickinson

Second Eleven Twenty20
Derbyshire v. Yorkshire

Played at Glossop CC on July 24, 2019
Yorkshire won by 16 runs at 2.25pm

Toss won by Yorkshire   Derbyshire 0 points, Yorkshire 2 points

YORKSHIRE

W A R Fraine, run out (Morgan/Palladino)	....	45
§ B D Birkhead, run out (Marshall/Hosein)	....	41
J A Leaning, not out	....	61
M L Revis, not out	....	15
E Barnes		
K Carver		
T W Loten		
J W Shutt		
J Shaw	Did not bat	
M J Waite		
* J D Warner		
Bilal Anjam		
M A Taylor		
Extras b 1, lb 2, w 10, nb 4		17
Total (2 wkts, 20 overs)	....	179

FoW: 1-84 (Birkhead), 2-112 (Fraine)

	O	M	R	W
Godsdal	4	0	52	0
Palladino	3	0	20	0
Priestley	4	0	34	0
Dal	3	0	25	0
Gleadhall	4	0	24	0
Marshall	2	0	21	0

DERBYSHIRE

* § H R Hosein, lbw b Shaw	....	17
J Redman, c Barnes b Waite	....	1
A K Dal, b Waite	....	0
S R Oldham, b Warner	....	5
T A Wood, c Revis b Shutt	....	11
J Morgan, c Shaw b Waite	....	50
N O Priestley, st Birkhead b Shutt		6
C R Marshall, c Leaning b Barnes		32
A F Gleadhall, not out	....	11
A Godsal, not out	....	4
A P Palladino		
J T Lacey	Did not bat	
Extras lb 9, w 7, nb 10		26
Total (8 wkts, 20 overs)	....	163

FoW: 1-19 (Redman), 2-20 (Dal), 3-20 (Hosein), 4-40 (Wood), 5-46 (Oldham), 6-58 (Priestley), 7-116 (Marshall), 8-158 (Morgan)

	O	M	R	W
Waite	4	0	38	3
Warner	4	0	22	1
Shaw	4	0	28	1
Shutt	4	0	15	2
Leaning	1	0	12	0
Carver	1	0	22	0
Barnes	2	0	17	1

Umpires: P R Pollard and N Ashraf   Scorers: Mrs J E M Hough and J R Virr

Second Eleven Twenty20
Derbyshire v. Yorkshire

Played at Glossop CC on July 24, 2019
Derbyshire won by 58 runs at 5.40pm

Toss won by Derbyshire   Derbyshire 2 points, Yorkshire 0 points

DERBYSHIRE

* § H R Hosein, c Birkhead b Leaning	....	57
T A Wood, c Anjam b Waite	....	31
A K Dal, c Anjam b Shaw	....	19
S R Oldham, c Revis b Leaning	....	4
J Redman, lbw b Leaning	....	0
J Morgan, not out	....	21
J T Lacey, c Birkhead b Leaning	....	9
C R Marshall, lbw b Leaning	....	12
A F Gleadhall, run out (Leaning)	....	2
A Godsal		
A P Palladino	Did not bat	
N O Priestley		
Extras lb 1, w 6, nb 2	....	9
Total (8 wkts, 20 overs)	....	164

FoW: 1-54 (Wood), 2-85 (Dal), 3-115 (Hosein), 4-115 (Redman), 5-116 (Oldham), 6-129 (Lacey), 7-151 (Marshall), 8-164 (Gleadhall)

	O	M	R	W
Waite	3	0	13	1
Warner	3	0	27	0
Shaw	3	0	25	1
Taylor	1	0	15	0
Leaning	4	0	21	5
Barnes	4	0	43	0
Carver	2	0	19	0

YORKSHIRE

§ B D Birkhead, c Dal b Gleadhall	....	5
M L Revis, c Wood b Godsal	....	18
M J Waite, c Lacey b Godsal	....	9
J A Leaning, c Hosein b Godsal	....	3
W A R Fraine, c Hosein b Palladino	....	3
Bilal Anjam, c Marshall b Godsal	....	9
E Barnes, c Marshall b Oldham	....	6
J Shaw, c Gleadall b Godsal	....	9
* J D Warner, c Redman b Dal	....	14
K Carver, b Dal	....	27
M A Taylor, not out	....	2
J W Shutt		
T W Loten	Did not bat	
Extras w 1	....	1
Total (16.5 overs)	....	106

FoW: 1-20 (Birkhead), 2-33 (Revis), 3-33 (Waite), 4-38 (Fraine), 5-40 (Leaning), 6-51 (Anjam), 7-62 (Shaw), 8-64 (Barnes), 9-88 (Warner), 10-106 (Carver)

	O	M	R	W
Gleadhall	2	0	20	1
Palladino	4	0	15	1
Godsal	4	0	19	5
Oldham	3	0	24	1
Dal	2.5	0	15	2
Marshall	1	0	13	0

Umpires: P R Pollard and N Ashraf   Scorers: Mrs J E M Hough and J R Virr

Second Eleven Twenty20
Lancashire v. Yorkshire

Played at Blackpool CC on July 25, 2019
Yorkshire won by 37 runs at 2.18pm

Toss won by Lancashire

Lancashire 0 points, Yorkshire 2 points

YORKSHIRE

W A R Fraine, c Perry b Hameed		57
§ B D Birkhead, c Hameed b Hurt		34
J A Leaning, c and b Hartley		29
M L Revis, b Sutton		4
M J Waite, b Hurt		7
T W Loten, not out		9
Bilal Anjam, not out		9
E Barnes		
J Shaw	Did not bat	
* J D Warner		
K Carver		
Extras lb 2, w 3		5
Total (5 wkts, 20 overs)		154

FoW: 1-73 (Birkhead), 2-102 (Fraine), 3-125 (Revis), 4-129 (Leaning), 5-135 (Waite)

	O	M	R	W
Sanders	3	0	32	0
Sutton	4	0	27	1
Lord	3	0	30	0
Hurt	4	0	22	2
Hartley	4	0	26	1
Hameed	2	0	15	1

LANCASHIRE

S M O Shah, run out (Barnes/Shaw)		17
E B Fluck, c Birkhead b Waite		0
* H Hameed, c Shaw b Carver		21
§ G I D Lavelle, c Leaning b Shaw		8
S J Perry, run out (Fraine)		40
T R Cornall, c Revis b Carver		3
T W Hartley, run out (Shaw/Birkhead)		12
L J Hurt, c Shaw b Anjam		4
C W G Sanders, c Anjam b Barnes		2
O W Sutton, not out		5
R Lord, not out		4
Extras w 1		1
Total (9 wkts, 20 overs)		117

FoW: 1-1 (Fluck), 2-18 (Shah), 3-30 (Lavelle), 4-71 (Hameed), 5-82 (Cornall), 6-91 (Perry), 7-104 (Hurt), 8-108 (Hartley), 9-109 (Sanders)

	O	M	R	W
Waite	3	0	16	1
Warner	2	0	9	0
Shaw	3	0	17	1
Leaning	4	0	17	0
Carver	4	0	31	2
Barnes	2	0	19	1
Bilal Anjam	2	0	8	1

Umpires: N J Pratt and K Fergusson

Scorers: G L Morgan and J R Virr

Second Eleven Twenty20
Lancashire v. Yorkshire

Played at Blackpool CC on July 25, 2019
Match abandoned at 5.20pm. No Result

Toss won by Lancashire

Lancashire 1 point, Yorkshire 1 point

LANCASHIRE

R P Jones, c Shaw b Barnes	....	33
E B Fluck, not out	....	23
* H Hameed, b Barnes	....	1
§ G I D Lavelle, not out	....	3
D Chugtai		
S J Perry		
T W Hartley		
O W Sutton	Did not bat	
C W G Sanders		
L J Hurt		
K N Watson		
Extras lb 1, nb 2	....	3
Total (2 wkts, 7.3 overs)	....	63

FoW: 1-46 (Jones), 2-48 (Hameed)

	O	M	R	W
Waite	2	0	12	0
Warner	1	0	15	0
Shaw	2	0	17	0
Barnes	2	0	16	2
Leaning	0.3	0	2	0

YORKSHIRE

W A R Fraine
§ B D Birkhead
J A Leaning
M L Revis
M J Waite
T W Loten
Bilal Anjam
E Barnes
J Shaw
* J D Warner
K Carver

Umpires: N J Pratt and K Fergusson

Scorers: G L Morgan and J R Virr

Second Eleven Twenty20
Northamptonshire v. Yorkshire

Played at Desborough CC on July 29, 2019
Yorkshire won by 5 wickets at 2.19pm

Toss won by Yorkshire

Northamptonshire 0 points, Yorkshire 2 points

NORTHAMPTONSHIRE

B J Curran, c and b Warner	....	35
* R I Newton, lbw b Waite	....	4
S A Zaib, st Birkhead b Leaning	....	3
C O Thurston, c Carver b Leaning	....	6
L A Procter, not out	....	62
T B Sole, c Barnes b Carver	....	6
B A Hutton, b Barnes	....	10
B D Glover, run out (Anjam)	....	6
§ H O M Gouldstone, run out (Fraine/Leaning)	.....	8
B J Bhabra, c Carver b Waite	....	3
A J Neal, not out	....	0
Extras lb 1, w 4		5
Total (9 wkts, 20 overs)	....	148

FoW: 1-18 (Newton), 2-39 (Zaib), 3-49 (Thurston), 4-56 (Curran), 5-81 (Sole), 6-113 (Hutton), 7-121 (Glover), 8-137 (Gouldstone), 9-141 (Bhabra)

	O	M	R	W
Bresnan	2	0	28	0
Waite	3	0	21	2
Warner	3	0	19	1
Shaw	3	0	14	0
Leaning	4	0	26	2
Carver	3	0	27	1
Barnes	2	0	12	1

YORKSHIRE

W A R Fraine, c Curran b Hutton	....	3
§ B D Birkhead, run out (Zaib/Gouldstone)	....	19
M L Revis, run out (Hutton)	....	21
J A Leaning, b Procter	....	51
T T Bresnan, not out	....	26
M J Waite, c Procter b Hutton	....	5
Bilal Anjam, not out	....	10
E Barnes		
J Shaw	Did not bat	
K Carver		
* J D Warner		
Extras lb 9, w 7	....	16
Total (5 wkts, 19.3 overs)	....	151

FoW: 1-19 (Fraine), 2-29 (Birkhead), 3-85 (Revis), 4-134 (Leaning), 5-141 (Waite)

	O	M	R	W
Hutton	4	0	20	2
Glover	2.3	0	28	0
Procter	4	0	33	1
Neal	3	0	19	0
Sole	2	0	16	0
Bhabra	2	0	9	0
Zaib	2	0	17	0

Umpires: N L Bainton and H S Davies

Scorers: Q L S Jones and J R Virr

Second Eleven Twenty20
Northamptonshire v. Yorkshire

Played at Desborough CC on July 29, 2019
Northamptonshire won by 4 wickets at 5.37pm

Toss won by Northamptonshire　　　　Northamptonshire 2 points, Yorkshire 0 points

YORKSHIRE

W A R Fraine, c Gouldstone b Glover		1
B D Birkhead, c Gouldstone b Hutton		11
§ Bilal Anjam, c Gouldstone b Glover		0
J A Leaning, c Bramley b Bhabra		3
T T Bresnan, not out		78
M J Waite, run out (Thurstone/Gouldstone)		12
T W Loten, not out		15
E Barnes		
J Shaw	Did not bat	
K Carver		
* J D Warner		
Extras b 1, lb 1, w 3, nb 2		7
Total (5 wkts, 20 overs)		128

FoW: 1-3 (Fraine), 2-13 (Anjam), 3-17 (Leaning), 4-26 (Birkhead), 5-63 (Waite)

	O	M	R	W
Glover	3	0	10	2
Bhabra	3	0	27	1
Hutton	4	0	26	1
Neal	2	0	22	0
Zaib	4	0	19	0
Procter	3	0	17	0
Sole	1	0	5	0

NORTHAMPTONSHIRE

C O Thurston, b Bresnan		4
A S B Bramley, b Barnes		60
L A Procter, c Leaning b Bresnan		12
* R I Newton, c Barnes b Leaning		25
B A Hutton, c Warner b Leaning		2
T B Sole, not out		12
S A Zaib, c Fraine b Carver		13
§ H O M Gouldstone, not out		0
B D Glover		
B J Bhabra	Did not bat	
A J Neal		
Extras lb 1		1
Total (6 wkts, 18.1 overs)		129

FoW: 1-5 (Thurston), 2-27 (Procter), 3-75 (Newton), 4-80 (Hutton), 5-115 (Bramley), 6-128 (Zaib)

	O	M	R	W
Waite	2	0	14	0
Bresnan	4	0	15	2
Leaning	4	0	34	2
Shaw	3	0	16	0
Carver	3	0	26	1
Warner	1	0	17	0
Barnes	1.1	0	6	1

Umpires: N L Bainton and H S Davies　　　　Scorers: Q L S Jones and J R Virr

Second Eleven Twenty20
Yorkshire v. Durham

Played at Marske-by-the-Sea on August 5, 2019
Durham won by 29 runs at 2.21pm

Toss won by Yorkshire

Yorkshire 0 points, Durham 2 poiunts

DURHAM

H R D Adair, lbw b Waite	....	0
L Trevaskis, c Shaw b Taylor	....	40
M A Jones, c Waite b Taylor	....	32
S W Poynter, b Shaw	....	70
J W A Burnham, c Loten b Shaw	....	45
G J Harte, run out (Shaw)	....	12
W J Weighell, not out	....	0
* § E J H Eckersley, not out	....	12
O J Gibson		
C Rushworth	Did not bat	
B G Whitehead		
Extras b 2, lb 1, w 4		7
Total (6 wkts, 20 overs)		218

FoW: 1-0 (Adair), 2-65 (Trevaskis), 3-84 (Jones), 4-175 (Poynter), 5-200 (G J Harte), 6-206 (Burnham)

	O	M	R	W
Waite	4	0	32	1
Warner	2	0	24	0
Shaw	4	0	51	2
Barnes	3	0	31	0
Leaning	3	0	38	0
Carver	1	0	11	0
Taylor	3	0	28	2

YORKSHIRE

W A R Fraine, b Trevaskis	....	73
§ B D Birkhead, c Burnham b Gibson	....	6
Bilal Anjam, c Rushworth b Gibson	....	16
J A Leaning, c Trevaskis b Gibson	....	20
M J Waite, c Jones b Trevaskis	....	44
T W Loten, lbw b Harte	....	5
E Barnes, c Poynter b Trevaskis	....	0
J Shaw, c Jones b Burnham	....	2
* J D Warner, not out	....	14
K Carver, c Weighell b Burnham	....	1
M A Taylor, not out	....	2
Extras w 2, nb 4		6
Total (9 wkts, 20 overs)		189

FoW: 1-14 (Birkhead), 2-42 (Anjam), 3-96 (Leaning), 4-143 (Fraine), 5-166 (Waite), 6-167 (Barnes), 7-170 (Loten), 8-174 (Shaw), 9-185 (Carver)

	O	M	R	W
Rushworth	4	0	32	0
Gibson	4	0	39	3
Trevaskis	4	0	45	3
Burnham	4	0	32	2
Harte	3	0	27	1
Whitehead	1	0	14	0

Umpires: N A Mallender and S Widddup

Scorers: J R Virr and G Maddison

Second Eleven Twenty20
Yorkshire v. Durham

Played at Marske-by-the-Sea on August 5, 2019
Durham won by 7 wickets at 5.24pm

Toss won by Yorkshire

Yorkshire 0 points, Durham 2 points

YORKSHIRE

W A R Fraine, c C T Steel b S Steel	49
§ B D Birkhead, c Eckersley b Rushworth	14
Bilal Anjam, b Raine	41
J A Leaning, c Harte b S Steel	20
M J Waite, hit wicket b Rushworth	8
T W Loten, run out (Whitehead)	1
M W Pillans, lbw b Main	7
E Barnes, c Weighell b Rushworth	16
J Shaw, c Eckersley b Main	2
* J D Warner, c Eckersley b Main	0
J W Shutt, not out	2
Extras lb 1, w 3, nb 4	8
Total (20 overs)	168

FoW: 1-22 (Birkhead), 2-97 (Fraine), 3-132 (Anjam), 4-132 (Leaning), 5-134 (Loten), 6-143 (Pillans), 7-160 (Barnes), 8-164 (Waite), 9-165 (Warner), 10-168 (Shaw)

	O	M	R	W
Whitehead	4	0	34	0
Rushworth	4	0	27	3
Main	4	0	33	3
Raine	3	0	30	1
Burnham	1	0	14	0
Harte	1	0	11	0
S Steel	2	0	6	2
C T Steel	1	0	12	0

DURHAM

H R D Adair, c Loten b Shaw	26
S Steel, c and b Pillans	63
B A Raine, c Birkhead b Shaw	7
C T Steel. not out	32
W J Weighell, not out	29
G J Harte	
G T Main	
J T A Burnham	Did not bat
* § E J H Eckersley	
C Rushworth	
B G Whitehead	
Extras b 4, lb 1, w 5, nb 4	14
Total (3 wkts, 17.3 overs)	171

FoW: 1-61 (Adair), 2-88 (Raine), 3-123 (S Steel)

	O	M	R	W
Waite	3	0	36	0
Pillans	2	0	29	1
Barnes	1	0	11	0
Leaning	3.3	0	33	0
Shaw	3	0	17	2
Warner	1	0	12	0
Shutt	4	0	28	0

Umpires: N A Mallender and S Widddup   Scorers: J R Virr and G Maddison

SECOND ELEVEN
TWENTY20 2019

Two matches played against the same opponents at the same venue on the same day.

SEMI-FINALS

| Glamorgan (204-4) | beat Nottinghamshire (99) | by 105 runs |
| Durham (93) | lost to Hampshire (97-5) | by 5 wickets |

FINAL

| Glamorgan (122-7) | beat Hampshire (121-8) | by 1 run |

NORTHERN GROUP – FINAL TABLE *(2018 in brackets)*

		P	W	L	T	Aban/NR	Points	Net Run Rate
1	Nottinghamshire (7)	12	10	2	0	0	20	1.066
2	Durham (2)	12	8	2	0	2	18	1.037
3	Derbyshire (3)	12	7	4	0	1	15	0.826
4	**Yorkshire(6)**	**12**	**6**	**5**	**0**	**1**	**13**	**0.426**
5	Warwickshire (5)	12	6	6	0	0	12	-0.987
6	Lancashire (1)	12	3	6	0	3	9	-0.458
7	Leicestershire (4)	12	4	7	0	1	9	-1.072
8	Northamptonshire (8)	12	3	9	0	0	6	-0.184
9	Worcestershire (9)	12	3	9	0	0	6	-1.435

SOUTHERN GROUP – FINAL TABLE *(2018 in brackets)*

		P	W	L	T	Aban/NR	Points	Net Run Rate
1	Hampshire (3)	12	9	3	0	0	18	1.586
2	Glamorgan (9)	12	7	3	0	2	16	0.915
3	Middlesex (6)	12	8	4	0	0	16	0.463
4	Essex (1)	12	7	4	0	1	15	0.372
5	Sussex (4)	12	6	3	0	3	15	-0.284
6	Somerset (7)	12	7	5	0	0	14	-0.121
7	Gloucestershire (2)	12	6	4	0	2	14	-0.709
8	Surrey (8)	12	2	9	0	1	5	-0.207
9	Kent (5)	12	2	10	0	0	2	-0.722
10	MCC Young Cricketers (*)	12	0	9	0	3	3	-1.078

(*) MCC Young Cricketers finished in 10th position in the Northern group in 2018
Unicorns did not compete in the competition in 2019

PREVIOUS WINNERS

2011	**Sussex**, who beat Durham by 24 runs
2012	**England Under-19s**, who beat Sussex by eight wickets
2013	**Surrey**, who beat Middlesex by six runs
2014	**Leicestershire**, who beat Somerset by 11 runs
2015	**Middlesex**, who beat Kent by four wickets
2016	**Middlesex**, who beat Somerset by two wickets
2017	**Sussex**, who beat Hampshire by 24 runs
2018	**Lancashire**, who beat Essex by 25 runs
2019	**Glamorgan**, beat Hampshire by 1 run

SECOND ELEVEN TWENTY20
AVERAGES 2019

Played 12   Won 6   Lost 5   Abandoned 1

BATTING AND FIELDING

(Qualification 3 innings)

Player	M.	I.	N.O.	Runs	H.S.	Avge	Strike Rate	100s	50s	ct/st
J A Leaning	12	11	3	327	61*	40.87	136.82	0	3	4
J A Thompson	4	3	1	80	68*	40.00	150.94	0	1	1
W A R Fraine	8	7	0	231	73	33.00	144.37	0	2	1
M L Revis	8	5	1	107	49	26.75	109.18	0	0	3
Bilal Anjam	8	8	2	85	41	21.25	108.97	0	0	3
B D Birkhead	12	11	0	197	44	17.90	113.21	0	0	4/2
M J Waite	12	7	1	95	44	15.83	137.68	0	0	3
T W Loten	5	4	2	30	15*	15.00	71.42	0	0	2
J D Warner	11	3	1	28	14*	14.00	121.73	0	0	6
E Barnes	12	3	0	22	16	7.33	129.41	0	0	4
J Shaw	8	3	0	13	9	4.33	100.00	0	0	5
T T Bresnan	6	6	6	236	78*	—	144.78	0	1	4

Also played

Player	M.	I.	N.O.	Runs	H.S.	Avge	Strike Rate	100s	50s	ct/st
G C H Hill	4	2	0	46	33	23.00	97.87	0	0	3
K Carver	11	2	0	28	27	14.00	107.69	0	0	2
D J Willey	2	2	0	26	19	13.00	104.00	0	0	1
M W Pillans	5	1	0	7	7	7.00	140.00	0	0	3
J E Poysden	4	0	0	0	—	—	—	0	0	4
J W Shutt	3	1	1	2	2*	—	100.00	0	0	0
M A Taylor	3	2	2	4	2*	—	80.00	0	0	0

BOWLING

(Qualification 5 wickets)

Player	Overs	Mdns	Runs	Wkts	Avge	Best	Strike Rate	Econ.	4wI
T T Bresnan............	17	0	116	8	14.50	3- 6	12.75	6.82	0
J A Leaning............	33	0	234	14	16.71	5-21	14.14	7.09	1
J E Poysden	16	1	85	5	17.00	3-16	19.20	5.31	0
M J Waite	25	0	196	8	24.50	3-38	18.75	7.84	0
E Barnes	17.1	0	155	6	25.83	2-16	17.16	9.02	0
J Shaw	25	0	185	7	26.42	2-17	21.42	7.40	0
K Carver	25	1	213	7	30.42	2-24	21.42	8.52	0

Also bowled

Player	Overs	Mdns	Runs	Wkts	Avge	Best	Strike Rate	Econ.	4wI
Bilal Anjam	2	0	8	1	8.00	1- 8	12.00	4.00	0
J A Thompson.........	8.3	0	62	4	15.50	1- 3	12.75	7.29	0
J W Shutt	8	0	43	2	21.50	2-15	24.00	5.37	0
M A Taylor	4	0	43	2	21.50	2-28	12.00	10.75	0
D J Willey..............	6	0	27	1	27.00	1-15	36.00	4.50	0
J D Warner.............	21	0	173	4	43.25	2-28	31.50	8.23	0
M W Pillans............	15	0	125	1	125.00	1-29	90.00	8.33	0

Other Second Eleven Matches
Yorkshire v. Lancashire

Played at Scarborough on April 16 and 17, 2019

Lancashire 258 (T W Hartley 54, N A Greenwood 44, M A Taylor 4-41, K Carver 3-30, J D Warner 3-32). **Yorkshire** 335-9 (J A Thompson 103, M L Revis 59, E Barnes 51*, T W Loten 51, T W Hartley 4-85, B W A Aitchisson 3-53

Match drawn Toss: Yorkshire

Durham v. Yorkshire

Played at the Riverside on May 7, 8 and 9, 2019

Durham 294-7 dec (E J H Eckersley 109*, R L Greenwell 52, W R Smith 44). **Yorkshire** 213-6 (J A Thompson 53, B D Birkhead 37, W A R Fraine 35).

Match drawn Toss: Durham

Yorkshire v. Leicestershire *T20*

Played at York CC on August 7, 2019

Yorkshire 162-5 (J A Leaning 49, T T Bresnan 44). **Leicestershire** 113-9.

Yorkshire won by 49 runs Toss: Yorkshire

Yorkshire v. Leicestershire *T20*

Played at York CC on August 7, 2019

Leicestershire 116-9. **Yorkshire** 117-2 (J A Leaning 45*, B D Birkhead 41).

Yorkshire won by 8 wickets Toss: Leicestershire

Derbyshire v. Yorkshire

Played at Belper Meadows CC on August 13, 14 and 15, 2019

Derbyshire 148 (C R Marshall 69, S A Patterson 4-20, D Olivier 3-45). **Yorkshire** 181-7 (M J Waite 42*, J A Leaning 35, H C Brook 35, B J Hutchinson 4-34).

Match drawn Toss: Yorkshire

Yorkshire v. Surrey

Played at York CC on August 27, 28 and 29, 2019

Surrey 326-8 dec (A A P Atkinson 97, C McKerr 57, Z Malik 52, S C Meaker 49, M D Fisher 3-43) and 21-0 dec. **Yorkshire** 39-1 dec. and 216 (M J Waite 45, T W Loten 42, D T Moriarty 6-71).

Surrey won by 92 runs Toss: Surrey

Sussex v. Yorkshire

Played at The County Ground, Hove, on September 10, 11 and 12, 2019

Yorkshire 457-6 dec (M L Revis 177, T W Loten 115, J H Wharton 49, A Sakande 3-90) *Second Innings forfeited.* **Sussex** *(First Innings forfeited)* 430-6 (H Z Finch 221, A G R Orr 85*, T G R Clark 71, J R Sullivan 3-72).

Match drawn Toss: Yorkshire

Yorkshire v. Durham

Played at Scarborough on September 16, 17 and 18, 2019

Yorkshire 222 (T W Loten 64, B D Birkhead 42, J J Bushnell 3-34) and 262-8 dec (J A Thompson 76, F J Bean 40, H G Duke 36, W J Weighell 3-65). **Durham** 206-7 dec (M J Potts 69*, S W Poynter 53) and 282-6 (S J D Bell 109, J J Bushnell 69, T S S Mackintosh 40).

Durham won by 4 wickets Toss: Yorkshire

Yorkshire Premier Leagues Championship — Final
Sheriff Hutton Bridge v. Woodlands

Played at Emerald Headingley, Leeds, on September 21, 2019

Sheriff Hutton Bridge won by 2 runs

Toss won by Sheriff Hutton Bridge

SHERIFF HUTTON BRIDGE

L Foxton, b Muhammad Bilal		1
E Barnes, c Muhammad Bilal b Brice		54
* A Fisher, c Ahmed b Schmulian		75
D Udayanga, c Garner b Brice		13
T Hudson, st Finn b Brice		6
K Carver, not out		38
Mark Fisher, run out (Schmulian)		3
R Robinson, not out		1
A Patel		
§ B Gill	Did not bat	
D Henstock		
Extras b 3, lb 5, w 13		21
Total (6 wkts, 50 overs)		212

FoW: 1-13 (Foxton), 2-123 (Barnes), 3-143 (Udayanga), 4-156 (Hudson), 5-175 (A Fisher), 6-210 (Mark Fisher)

	O	M	R	W
Muhammad Bilal	9	1	29	1
E Richardson	5	0	23	0
Schmulian	9	0	45	1
Brice	15	2	44	3
Ahmed	12	0	63	0

WOODLANDS

S Frankland, c Gill b Barnes		9
T Jackson, c Gill b Henstock		1
B Schmulian, lbw b Carver		16
* C Garner, b Henstock		1
L Collins, c Barnes b Henstock		92
§ G Finn, b Carver		23
S Richardson Jun., c Carver b Udayanga		11
Muhammad Bilal, c Udayanga b Barnes		24
E Richardson, not out		18
K Ahmed, c Hudson b Henstock		3
C Brice	Did not bat	
Extras lb 5, w 4, nb 3		12
Total (9 wkts, 50 overs)		210

FoW: 1-4 (Jackson), 2-17 (Frankland), 3-18 (Garner), 4-60 (Schmulian), 5-99 (Finn), 6-137 (S Richardson), 7-182 (Muhammad Bilal), 8-194 (Collins), 9-210 (Ahmed)

	O	M	R	W
Barnes	11	1	37	2
Henstock	10	2	28	4
Mark Fisher	4	0	31	0
Carver	13	0	64	2
Udayanga	12	3	45	1

Man of the Match: E Barnes

Umpires: Babir Noor and D Oliver   Scorers: G Conway, M Rhodes and J T Potter
Third Umpire: S Widdup

YORKSHIRE DIAMONDS

Captain: Lauren Winfield

General Manager: Jane Hildreth   Head Coach: Danielle Hazell

KIA SUPER LEAGUE 2019 (T20)

2019 WINNERS: Western Storm, who beat Southern Vipers by six wickets
with 6 balls remaining

LEAGUE TABLE

*4 points awarded for a win, plus 1 bonus point for any team that
achieves victory with a run rate 1.25 times that of the opposition*

		P	W	L	T	NR/A	PTS	NRR
1	Western Storm (2)	10	9	1	0	0	39	1.109
2	Loughborough Lightning (1) *	10	7	3	0	0	32	0.792
3	Southern Vipers (6) *	10	4	4	1	1	22	0.425
4	**Yorkshire Diamonds (5)**	**10**	**5**	**5**	**0**	**0**	**20**	**-0.456**
5	Surrey Stars (3)	10	3	6	1	0	16	-0.857
6	Lancashire Thunder (4)	10	0	9	1	0	2	-1.194

* Qualified for Semi-Finals

(2018 group positions in brackets)

YORKSHIRE DIAMONDS 2019 KIA SUPER LEAGUE SQUAD

Player	Date of Birth	Birthplace	Type
L Winfield (Captain)	August 16, 1990	York	RHB, WK
H J Armitage	June 14, 1997	Huddersfield	RHB, LB
K H Brunt	July 2, 1985	Barnsley	RHB, RAMF
A N Davidson-Richards	May 29, 1994	Tunbridge Wells	RHB, RAFM
G K Davis	June 3, 1999	Birmingham	RHB, RAOS
H L Fenby	November 23, 1998	Stockton, Co Durham	RHB, LB
K L George	April 7, 1999	Haywards Heath	LHB, LAM
C L Griffiths	September 19, 1995	Islington, London	RHB, RAFM
A J Healey	March 24, 1990	Gold Coast, Queensland	RHB, WK
B A M Heath	August 20, 2001	Chesterfield	RHB, WK
L M Kasperek	February 15, 1992	Edinburgh	RHB, OB
B A Langston	September 6, 1992	Harold Wood, Essex	RHB, RAM
K A Levick	July 17, 1991	Sheffield	RHB, LB
J I Rodrigues	September 5, 2000	Mumbai, India	RHB, RAOS
L C N Smith	March 10, 1995	Hillingdon	RHB, SLA

Kia Super League
Yorkshire Diamonds v. Surrey Stars

Played at Emerald Headingley, Leeds, on Tuesday, August 6, 2019 *(Day/Night)*
Surrey Stars won by 9 runs

Toss won by Surrey Stars   Yorkshire 0 points, Surrey Stars 4 points

SURREY STARS

L Lee, lbw b Fenby	9
B F Smith, c Armitage b Fenby	20
§ S J Taylor, c and b Kasperek	43
* N R Sciver, c and b Kasperek	24
D van Niekirk, c Rodrigues b Kasperek	16
M Kapp, c and b Smith	5
A Cranstone, run out (Rodrigues)	9
L A Marsh, b Fenby	3
G M Davies, c Rodrigues b Fenby	0
M K Villiers, not out	0
G J Gibbs	Did not bat	
Extras b 1	1
Total (9 wkts, 20 overs)	130

FoW: 1-20 (Lee), 2-31 (Smith), 3-79 (Sciver), 4-108 (Taylor), 5-117 (van Niekerk), 6-121 (Kapp), 7-129 (Marsh), 8-129 (Davies), 9-130 (Cranstone)

	O	M	R	W
Smith	4	0	21	1
Langston	3	0	28	0
Fenby	4	0	20	4
Levick	3	0	18	0
Kasperek	4	0	25	3
Davidson-Richards	2	0	17	0

YORKSHIRE DIAMONDS

* L Winfield, b Sciver	31
§ A J Healey, c van Niekerk b Villiers	31
H J Armitage, st Taylor b Marsh	12
J I Rodrigues, b Marsh	4
C L Griffith, c van Niekerk b Sciver	5
A N Davidson-Richards, run out (Lee)	17
L M Kasperek, c Sciver b Marsh	1
L C N Smith, run out (van Niekerk)	6
B A Langston, run out (van Niekerk)	2
H L Fenby, not out	3
K A Levick, st Taylor b van Niekerk	0
Extras lb 3, w 6	9
Total (19.5 overs)	121

FoW: 1-43 (Healy), 2-59 (Armitage), 3-75 (Rodrigues), 4-89 (Griffith), 5-97 (Winfield), 6-100 (Kasperek), 7-115 (Davidson-Richards), 8-118 (Smith), 9-120 (Langston), 10-121 (Levick)

	O	M	R	W
Kapp	3	0	20	0
Villiers	4	0	21	1
van Niekerk	3.5	0	27	1
Sciver	4	0	25	2
Marsh	4	0	17	3
Smith	1	0	8	0

Player of the Match: L A Marsh

Umpires: N G B Cook and J H Evans   Scorers: K N Hutchinson and S E Robinson
TV Umpire: R J Warren

Kia Super League
Yorkshire Diamonds v. Loughborough Lightning

Played at Emerald Headingley, Leeds, on Sunday, August 11, 2019
Loughborough Lightning won by nine wickets with 40 balls remaining

Toss won by Loughborough   Yorkshire 0 points, Loughborough 5 points

YORKSHIRE DIAMONDS

* L Winfield, lbw b Bryce		9
§ A J Healy, b Matthews		5
H J Armitage, b Gordon		23
J I Rodrigues, c and b Gordon		20
C L Griffith, b Elwiss		12
A N Davidson-Richards, c Matthews b Glenn		27
K L George, not out		13
L M Kasperek, not out		5
L C N Smith		
H L Fenby	Did not bat	
K A Levick		
Extras lb 3, w 4		7
Total (6 wkts, 20 overs)		121

FoW: 1-16 (Healy), 2-30 (Winfield), 3-62 (Rodrigues), 4-69 (Armitage), 5-94 (Griffith), 6-112 (Davidson-Richards)

	O	M	R	W
Bryce	3	1	17	1
Matthews	4	0	25	1
Norris	1	0	8	0
Atapattu	1	0	5	0
Glenn	4	0	17	1
Gordon	4	0	27	2
Gunn	2	0	12	0
Elwiss	1	0	7	1

LOUGHBOROUGH LIGHTNING

H K Matthews, not out		54
§ A E Jones, c Winfield b Smith		12
C J Atapattu, not out		40
* G A Elwiss		
W du Preez		
G L Adams		
J L Gunn	Did not bat	
K E Bryce		
S Glenn		
T Norris		
K L Gordon		
Extras b 2 w 14		16
Total (1 wkt, 13.2 overs)		122

FoW: 1-44 (Jones)

	O	M	R	W
George	2	0	16	0
Smith	2	0	8	1
Fenby	3	0	30	0
Levick	2.2	0	18	0
Kasperek	2	0	16	0
Davidson-Richards	1	0	13	0
Armitage	1	0	19	0

Umpires: R A White and S Redfern   Scorers: K N Hutchinson and K Gerrard

Kia Super League
Lancashire Thunder v. Yorkshire Diamonds

Played at Aigburth, Liverpool, on Tuesday, August 13, 2019
Yorkshire Diamonds won by 9 runs

Toss won by Yorkshire   Lancashire 0 points, Yorkshire 4 points

YORKSHIRE DIAMONDS

* L Winfield, b Ecclestone	....	56
§ A J Healy, b Dunkley	....	30
H J Armitage, b Cross	....	33
J I Rodrigues, c Luus b Cross	....	2
A N Davidson-Richards, b Lamb	....	0
B A M Heath, run out (Ecclestone)	....	9
K L George, not out	....	6
L M Kasperek, not out	....	7
L C N Smith		
H L Fenby Did not bat		
K A Levick		
Extras b 4, lb 1, w 2, nb 1	....	8
Total (6 wkts, 20 overs)	....	151

FoW: 1-68 (Healy), 2-106 (Winfield), 3-124 (Armitage), 4-125 (Davidson-Richards), 5-127 (Rodrigues), 6-139 (Heath)

	O	M	R	W
Lamb	3	0	14	1
Cross	4	0	31	2
Ecclestone	4	0	26	1
Hartley	3	0	33	0
Dunkley	4	0	24	1
McGrath	1	0	10	0
Luus	1	0	8	0

LANCASHIRE THUNDER

T M McGrath, b Fenby	....	14
S Luus, c Davidson-Richards b George	....	5
S R Dunkley, c Heath b Davidson-Richards	....	11
H Kaur, c Rodrigues b Davidson-Richards	....	37
G E B Boyce, run out (George)	....	14
E L Lamb, c Heath b Smith	....	32
E Jones, b George	....	2
S Ecclestone, st Healy b Kasperek	....	13
§ E Threlkeld, c Healy b Levick	....	8
* K L Cross, run out (Kasperek)	....	1
A Hartley, not out	....	0
Extras lb 1, w 2, nb 2	....	5
Total (19.1 overs)	....	142

FoW: 1-20 (McGrath), 2-23 (Luus), 3-69 (Dunkley), 4-83 (Kaur), 5-90 (Boyce), 6-120 (Lamb), 7-124 (Jones), 8-138 (Ecclestone), 9-141 (Cross), 10-142 (Threlkeld)

	O	M	R	W
Smith	4	0	37	1
George	3	0	16	2
Fenby	3	0	22	1
Kasperek	4	0	23	1
Levick	2.1	0	18	1
Davidson-Richards	3	0	25	2

Umpires: T Lungley and I N Ramage Scorers: A M Gregan and K N Hutchinson

Kia Super League
Yorkshire Diamonds v. Western Storm

Played at York Cricket Club, on Thursday, August 15, 2019
Western Storm won by 9 wickets with 31 balls remaining

Toss won by Western Storm   Yorkshire 0 points, Western Storm 5 points

YORKSHIRE DIAMONDS

§ A J Healy, c Sharma b Nicholas		12
* L Winfield, st Priest b Odedra		18
H J Armitage, b Davies		59
J I Rodrigues, c Mandhana b Shrubsole		28
A N Davidson-Richards, run out (Luff)		7
B A M Heath, run out (Luff)		1
K L George, run out (Luff)		3
L M Kasperek, run out (Nicholas)		1
L C N Smith, not out		2
H L Fenby, run out (Luff)		2
K A Levick	Did not bat	
Extras lb 4, w 13, nb 1		18
Total (9 wkts, 20 overs)		151

FoW: 1-18 (Healy), 2-47 (Winfield), 3-107 (Rodrigues), 4-134 (Davidson-Richards), 5-139 (Heath), 6-142 (George), 7-143 Kasperek, 8-147 (Armitage), 9-151 (Fenby).

	O	M	R	W
Nicholas	3	0	24	1
Davies	4	0	29	1
Shrubsole	4	0	16	1
Sharma	3	0	32	0
Odedra	3	0	21	1
Knight	3	0	25	0

WESTERN STORM

§ R H Priest, not out		72
S S Mandhana, c Heath b Davidson-Richards		70
* H C Knight, not out		0
F C Wilson		
S N Luff		
D B Sharma		
N D Dattani	Did not bat	
A Shrubsole		
S B Odedra		
F R Davies		
C Nicholas		
Extras w 9, nb 1		10
Total (1 wkt, 14.5 overs)		152

FoW: 1-133 (Mandhana)

	O	M	R	W
George	3	0	35	0
Fenby	1	0	13	0
Smith	3.5	0	43	0
Kasperek	2	0	19	0
Levick	2	0	15	0
Davidson-Richards	3	0	27	1

Umpires: T Lungley and S Redfern   Scorers: K N Hutchinson and J Slater

Kia Super League
Loughborough Lightning v. Yorkshire Diamonds

Played at Haslegrave Ground, Loughborough, on Sunday, August 18, 2019
Loughborough Lightning won by 6 wickets with 5 balls remaining

Toss won by Yorkshire   Loughborough 4 points, Yorkshire 0 points

YORKSHIRE DIAMONDS

§ A J Healy, c Higham b Matthews		15
* L Winfield, c Adams b Gunn		9
H J Armitage, b Gordon		6
J I Rodrigues, c Matthews b Elwiss		58
A N Davidson-Richards, run out (Glenn)		12
B A M Heath, c Elwiss b Bryce		9
K L George, run out (Gunn)		10
L M Kasperek, run out (Higham)		1
B A Langston, b Matthew		1
L C N Smith, run out (Adams)		1
K A Levick, not out		1
Extras b 1, lb 3, w 2		6
Total (20 overs)		129

FoW: 1-17 (Winfield), 2-29 (Healy), 3-46 (Armitage), 4-81 (Davidson-Richards), 5-106 (Heath), 6-124 (Rodrigues), 7-125 (George), 8-127 (Kasperek), 9-128 (Langston), 10-129 (Smith)

	O	M	R	W
Bryce	4	0	22	1
Matthews	4	0	19	2
Gunn	2	0	15	1
Glenn	3	0	29	0
Gordon	4	0	14	1
Elwiss	3	0	26	1

LOUGHBOROUGH LIGHTNING

H K Matthews, b Levick		24
§ A E Jones, c Heath b Langston		29
C Atapattu, run out (George)		15
* G A Elwiss, lbw b Smith		10
M du Preez, not out		38
G L Adams, not out		9
J L Gunn		
K E Bryce		
S Glenn	Did not bat	
L F Higham		
K L Gordon		
Extras b 1, lb 2, w 6, nb 1		10
Total (4 wkts, 19.1 overs)		135

FoW: 1-49 (Matthews), 2-74 (Atapattu), 3-74 (Jones), 4-111 (Elwiss)

	O	M	R	W
Langston	4	0	17	1
Kasperek	4	0	38	0
Smith	3.1	0	25	1
George	4	0	25	0
Levick	4	0	27	1

Umpires: N J Pratt and I N Ramage   Scorers: K Gerrard and K N Hutchinson

Kia Super League
Surrey Stars v. Yorkshire Diamonds

Played at Guildford, on Tuesday, August 20, 2019
Yorkshire Diamonds won by 5 wickets with one 1 ball remaining

Toss won by Yorkshire　　　　　　　　　　Surrey 0 points, Yorkshire 4 points

SURREY STARS

L Lee, c Armitage b Davidson-Richards	28
B F Smith, b Levick	0
§ S J Taylor, st Healy b Levick	3
* N R Sciver, c Healy b George	5
D van Niekerk, c Rodrigues b Smith	32
M Kapp, not out	39
M K Villiers, b Langston	1
I. A Marsh, not out	1
A Cranstone	
AG Gordon　　　　　　Did not bat	
E Gray	
Extras lb 2, w 10	12
Total (6 wkts, 20 overs)	121

FoW: 1-1 (Smith), 2-15 (Taylor), 3-32 (Sciver), 4-52 (Lee), 5-111 (van Niekerk), 6-112 (Villiers)

	O	M	R	W
Levick	4	0	13	2
Langston	4	0	36	1
George	4	0	20	1
Smith	3	0	17	1
Davidson-Richards	3	0	23	1
Kasperek	2	0	10	0

YORKSHIRE DIAMONDS

§ A J Healy, c Marsh b Gordon	38
* L Winfield, c Taylor b Kapp	7
H J Armitage, run out (Smith)	24
J I Rodrigues, not out	42
A N Davidson-Richards, c van Niekerk b Marsh	8
K L George, c Kapp b Marsh	0
B A M Heath, not out	0
L M Kasperek	
B A Langston　　　　　　Did not bat	
L C N Smith	
K A Levick	
Extras b 2, lb 1, w 2	5
Total (5 wkts, 19.5 overs)	124

FoW: 1-22 (Winfield), 2-62 (Healy), 3-92 (Armitage), 4-119 (Davidson-Richards), 5-120 (George)

	O	M	R	W
Kapp	4	0	18	1
Villiers	2	0	21	0
van Niekerk	4	0	30	0
Sciver	4	0	24	0
Gordon	3	0	13	1
Marsh	2.5	0	15	2

Umpires: H M S Adnan and M Waldron　　　　Scorers: S E Robinson and K N Hutchinson

Kia Super League
Southern Vipers v. Yorkshire Diamonds

Played at The Ageas Bowl, Southampton, on Wednesday, August 21, 2019 *(Day/Night)*
Southern Vipers won by 3 runs

Toss won by Southern Vipers   Southern Vipers 4 points, Yorkshire 0 points

SOUTHERN VIPERS

S W Bates, st Healy b Kasperek		9
D N Wyatt, c Smith b Levick		59
* § T T Beaumont, c Kasperek b Levick		1
T F Brookes, c and b George		17
M E Bouchier, run out (Heath)		1
M Kelly, c Healy b Smith		5
P J Schofield, c Rodrigues b Kasperek		24
F M K Morris, not out		5
A Wellington, c Armitage b Kasperek		0
N E Farrant, st Healy b Kasperek		0
L K Bell	Did not bat	
Extras lb 2, w 4		6
Total (9 wkts, 20 overs)		127

FoW: 1-62 (Bates), 2-69 (Beaumont), 3-79 (Wyatt), 4-81 (Bouchier), 5-90 (Kelly), 6-107 (Brookes), 7-125 (Schofield), 8-126 (Wellington), 9-127 (Farrant)

	O	M	R	W
Langston	4	0	40	0
Kasperek	4	0	16	4
Smith	4	0	27	1
Levick	4	0	17	2
George	4	0	25	1

YORKSHIRE DIAMONDS

* L Winfield, lbw b Bates		23
§ A J Healy, run out (Wyatt)		11
H J Armitage, lbw b Morris		34
J I Rodrigues, b Bates		32
A N Davidson-Richards, c Bell b Farrant		16
K L George, not out		3
B A M Heath, not out		1
L M Kasperek		
B A Langston	Did not bat	
L C N Smith		
K A Levick		
Extras lb 2, w 2		4
Total (5 wkts, 20 overs)		124

FoW: 1-12 (Healy), 2-60 (Winfield), 3-83 (Armitage), 4-120 (Davidson-Richards), 5-122 (Rodrigues)

	O	M	R	W
Farrant	4	0	23	1
Bell	4	0	13	0
Wyatt	3	0	16	0
Wellington	3	0	32	0
Morris	2	0	11	1
Bates	4	0	27	2

Player of the Match: D N Wyatt

Umpires: N L Bainton, A G Wharf and N J Llong (TV umpire)

Scorers: K Rouse and K N Hutchinson

Kia Super League
Yorkshire Diamonds v. Lancashire Thunder

Played at North Marine Road, Scarborough, on Friday, August 23, 2019
Yorkshire Diamonds won by 4 wickets with 7 balls remaining

Toss won by Lancashire   Yorkshire 4 points, Lancashire 0 points

LANCASTER THUNDER

LANCASHIRE THUNDER

T M McGrath, lbw b Davidson-Richards	....	29
S Luus, c Rodrigues b Levick	....	15
S R Dunkley, c Davidson-Richards b Levick	....	8
H Kaur, c Rodrigues b Smith	....	38
§ E Threlkeld, b Davidson-Richards	....	52
E L Lamb, not out	....	7
S Eccleston, not out	....	6
* K L Cross		
A Hartley	Did not bat	
R Fackrell		
N Brown		
Extras lb 1, w 7, nb 1	....	9
Total (5 wkts, 20 overs)	....	164

FoW: 1-32 (Luus), 2-44 (Dunkley), 3-58 (McGrath), 4-132 (Kaur), 5-158 (Threlkeld)

	O	M	R	W
Langston	4	0	31	0
Smith	4	0	23	1
Levick	4	0	19	2
Kasperek	4	0	39	0
Davidson-Richards	4	0	51	2

YORKSHIRE DIAMONDS

* L Winfield, b Eccleston		16
§ A J Healy, c Dunkley b Eccleston	....	77
H J Armitage, run out (Cross)	....	0
J I Rodrigues, not out	....	43
C L Griffith, st Threlkeld b Brown	....	1
B A M Heath, run out (Cross)	....	2
A N Davidson-Richards, st Threlkeld b Cross	....	13
L M Kasperek, not out	....	1
B A Langston		
L C N Smith	Did not bat	
K A Levick		
Extras b 1, lb 1, w 12, nb 1	....	15
Total (6 wkts, 18.5 overs)	....	168

FoW: 1-103 (Healy), 2-103 (Winfield), 3-105 (Armitage), 4-112 (Griffith), 5-115 (Heath),
6-149 (Davidson-Richards)

	O	M	R	W
Lamb	3	0	27	0
Cross	3.5	0	45	1
Eccleston	4	0	18	2
McGrath	1	0	16	0
Hartley	4	0	27	0
Luus	1	0	21	0
Brown	2	0	21	1

Umpires: J E Middlebrook and C M Watts   Scorers: K N Hutchinson and A M Gregan

Kia Super League
Yorkshire Diamonds v. Southern Vipers

Played at York Cricket Club, on Sunday, August 25, 2019
Yorkshire Diamonds won by 4 wickets with 0 balls remaining

Toss won by Yorkshire   Yorkshire 4 points, Southern Vipers 0 points

SOUTHERN VIPERS

S W Bates, c Winfield b Davidson-Richards	. . . .	47
D N Wyatt, c Davidson-Richards b Kasperek	. . . .	42
* § T T Beaumont, c Armitage b Davidson-Richards	.	33
M E Bouchier, not out	. . . .	23
T F Brookes, c Rodrigues b Davidson-Richards	. . . . .	7
A Wellington, not out	. . . .	24
F M K Morris		
P J Schofield		
N E Farrant	Did not bat	
L K Bell		
C E Dean		
Extras b 1, lb 2, w 5	. . . .	8
Total (4 wkts, 20 overs)	. . . .	184

FoW: 1-49 (Wyatt), 2-125 (Beaumont), 3-127 (Bates), 4-141 (Brookes)

	O	M	R	W
Levick	4	0	41	0
Langston	4	0	42	0
Smith	4	0	45	0
Kasperek	4	0	32	1
Davidson-Richards	4	0	21	3

YORKSHIRE DIAMONDS

* L Winfield, c Bates b Farrant	. . . .	0
§ A J Healy, c Morris b Farrant	. . . .	22
J I Rodrigues, not out	. . . .	112
H J Armitage, lbw b Wellington	. . . .	23
B A M Heath, c Bates b Wellington	. . . .	0
A N Davidson-Richards, c Beaumont b Morris	. . . . . .	0
L M Kasperek, c Morris b Bell	. . . .	12
L C N Smith, not out	. . . .	2
G K Davis		
B A Langston	Did not bat	
K A Levick		
Extras b 10, w 2, nb 2	. . . .	14
Total (6 wkts, 20 overs)	. . . .	185

FoW: 1-0 (Winfield), 2-28 (Healy), 3-118 (Armitage), 4-118 (Heath), 5-121 (Davidson-Richards), 6-170 (Kasperek)

	O	M	R	W
Farrant	4	0	27	2
Bell	4	0	33	1
Wyatt	2	0	22	0
Wellington	4	0	31	2
Bates	2	0	25	0
Morris	3	0	26	1
Dean	1	0	11	0

Umpires: H M S Adnan and J D Middlebrook Scorers: K N Hutchinson and J B Godbold

Kia Super League
Western Storm v. Yorkshire Diamonds

Played at Cooper Associates County Ground, Taunton,
on Wednesday, August 28, 2019 *(Day/Night)*
Match reduced to 10 overs per side: Yorkshire Diamonds won by 5 runs

Toss won by Western Storm   Western Storm 0 points, Yorkshire 4 points

YORKSHIRE DIAMONDS

§ A J Healy, c Priest b Davies		7
* L Winfield, c Priest b Davies		12
J I Rodrigues, c Odedra b Davies		60
H J Armitage, run out (Shrubsole)		19
A N Davidson-Richards, not out		2
G K Davis		
B A M Heath		
L M Kasperek	Did not bat	
L C N Smith		
B A Langston		
K A Levick		
Extras lb 2, w 2		4
Total (4 wkts, 10 overs)		104

FoW: 1-19 (Winfield), 2-21 (Healy), 3-100 (Rodrigues), 4-104 (Armitage)

	O	M	R	W
Nicholas	2	0	26	0
Davies	2	0	7	3
Shrubsole	1	0	7	0
Knight	1	0	15	0
Sharma	2	0	20	0
Odedra	2	0	27	0

WESTERN STORM

§ R H Priest, c Rodrigues b Smith		7
S S Mandhana, c Langston b Kasperek		7
* H C Knight, c Winfield b Davidson-Richards		4
F C Wilson, not out		45
S N Luff, not out		31
D B Sharma		
N D Dattani		
A Shrubsole	Did not bat	
S B Odedra		
F R Davies		
C Nicholas		
Extras lb 1, w 2, nb 2		5
Total (3 wkts, 10 overs)		99

FoW: 1-17 (Priest), 2-19 (Mandhana), 3-23 (Knight)

	O	M	R	W
Levick	2	0	9	0
Langston	2	0	21	0
Smith	2	0	14	1
Kasperek	2	0	21	1
Davidson-Richards	2	0	33	1

Umpires: M Newell and T Lungley   Scorers: L M Rhodes and K N Hutchinson

KIA SUPER LEAGUE 2019

YORKSHIRE DIAMONDS AVERAGES

Played 10   Won 5   Lost 5

BATTING AND FIELDING

Player	M	I	N.O.	Runs	H.S.	100s	50s	Avge	S.R.	ct/st
J I Rodrigues	10	10	3	401	112*	1	2	57.28	149.62	9
A J Healy	10	10	0	248	77	0	1	24.80	135.51	5/3
H J Armitage	10	10	0	233	59	0	1	23.30	96.28	4
L Winfield	10	10	0	181	56	0	1	18.10	102.25	3
K L George	6	6	3	35	13*	0	0	11.66	100.00	1
A N Davidson-Richards	10	10	1	102	27	0	0	11.33	87.93	3
L M Kasperek	10	7	3	28	12	0	0	7.00	96.55	3
C L Griffith	3	3	0	18	12	0	0	6.00	56.25	0
L C N Smith	10	4	2	11	6	0	0	5.50	73.33	2
H L Fenby	4	2	1	5	3*	0	0	5.00	100.00	0
B A M Heath	8	7	2	22	9	0	0	4.40	84.61	3
B A Langston	7	2	0	3	2	0	0	1.50	75.00	1
K A Levick	10	2	1	1	1*	0	0	1.00	25.00	0
G K Davis	2	0	0	0	—	0	0	—	—	0

BOWLING

Player	Overs	Mdns	Runs	Wkts	Avge	Best	4wI	Econ
H L Fenby	11	0	85	5	17.00	4-20	1	7.72
A N Davidson-Richards	22	0	210	10	21.00	3-21	0	9.54
L M Kasperek	32	0	239	10	23.90	4-16	1	7.46
K A Levick	31.3	0	195	8	24.37	2-13	0	6.19
L C N Smith	34	0	260	8	32.50	1- 8	0	7.64
K L George	20	0	137	4	34.25	2-16	0	6.85
B A Langston	25	0	215	2	107.50	1-17	0	8.60
H J Armitage	1	0	19	0	—	—	0	19.00

RECORDS SECTION

All records in this section relate to First-Class Yorkshire matches except where stated

HONOURS

County Champions (34)
1867, 1870, 1893, 1896, 1898, 1900, 1901, 1902, 1905, 1908, 1912, 1919,
1922, 1923, 1924, 1925, 1931, 1932, 1933, 1935, 1937, 1938, 1939,
1946, 1959, 1960, 1962, 1963, 1966, 1967, 1968, 2001, 2014, 2015

Joint Champions (2)
1869, 1949

Promoted to Division 1
2005, 2012

Gillette Cup Winners (2)
1965, 1969

Cheltenham & Gloucester Trophy (1)
2002

Benson & Hedges Cup Winners (1)
1987

John Player Special League Winners (1)
1983

Fenner Trophy Winners (3)
1972, 1974, 1981

Asda Challenge Winners (1)
1987

Ward Knockout Cup (1)
1989

Joshua Tetley Festival Trophy (7)
1991, 1992 (Joint), 1993, 1994, 1996, 1997 and 1998

Tilcon Trophy Winners (2)
1978 and 1988

Pro-Arch Trophy (1)
2007-08

Emirates Airlines T20 (2)
2015 and 2016

Second Eleven Champions (4)
1977, 1984, 1991, 2003

Joint Champions (1)
1987

Minor Counties Champions (5)
1947, 1957, 1958, 1968, 1971

Under-25 Competition Winners (3)
1976, 1978, 1987

Bain Clarkson Trophy Winners (2)
1988 and 1994

Second Eleven Trophy (1)
2009

220

YORKSHIRE'S CHAMPIONSHIP CAPTAINS

1867 to 2019

* R Iddison (2)	1867, 1870
Lord Hawke (8)	1893, 1896, 1898, 1900, 1901, 1902, 1905, 1908
Sir Archibald White (1)	1912
D C F Burton (1)	1919
G Wilson (3)	1922, 1923, 1924
A W Lupton (1)	1925
F E Greenwood (2)	1931, 1932
A B Sellers (6)	1933, 1935, 1937, 1938, 1939, 1946
J R Burnet (1)	1959
J V Wilson (2)	1960, 1962
D B Close (4)	1963, 1966, 1967, 1968
D Byas (1)	2001
A W Gale (2)	2014, 2015

Joint Champions

* R Iddison (1)	1869
N W D Yardley (1)	1949

* R Iddison was captain when Yorkshire were Champion county, the County Championship starting in 1890.

RECORDS SECTION INDEX

The County Championship

The County Championship was officially constituted in 1890, and before that Yorkshire were generally considered Champions by the Press in 1867 and 1870, and equal top in 1869. From 1873 the list was generally accepted in the form as it is today.

		Yorkshire's Position
1873	Gloucestershire / Nottinghamshire	7th
1874	Gloucestershire	4th
1875	Nottinghamshire	4th
1876	Gloucestershire	3rd
1877	Gloucestershire	7th
1878	Middlesex	6th
1879	Nottinghamshire/Lancashire	6th
1880	Nottinghamshire	5th
1881	Lancashire	3rd
1882	Nottinghamshire/Lancashire	3rd
1883	Nottinghamshire	2nd
1884	Nottinghamshire	3rd
1885	Nottinghamshire	2nd
1886	Nottinghamshire	4th
1887	Surrey	3rd
1888	Surrey	2nd
1889	Surrey/Lancashire / Nottinghamshire	7th
1890	Surrey	3rd
1891	Surrey	8th
1892	Surrey	6th
1893	**Yorkshire**	**1st**
1894	Surrey	2nd
1895	Surrey	3rd
1896	**Yorkshire**	**1st**
1897	Lancashire	4th
1898	**Yorkshire**	**1st**
1899	Surrey	3rd
1900	**Yorkshire**	**1st**
1901	**Yorkshire**	**1st**
1902	**Yorkshire**	**1st**
1903	Middlesex	3rd
1904	Lancashire	2nd
1905	**Yorkshire**	**1st**
1906	Kent	2nd
1907	Nottinghamshire	2nd
1908	**Yorkshire**	**1st**

		Yorkshire's Position
1909	Kent	3rd
1910	Kent	8th
1911	Warwickshire	7th
1912	**Yorkshire**	**1st**
1913	Kent	2nd
1914	Surrey	4th
1919	**Yorkshire**	**1st**
1920	Middlesex	4th
1921	Middlesex	3rd
1922	**Yorkshire**	**1st**
1923	**Yorkshire**	**1st**
1924	**Yorkshire**	**1st**
1925	**Yorkshire**	**1st**
1926	Lancashire	2nd
1927	Lancashire	3rd
1928	Lancashire	4th
1929	Nottinghamshire	2nd
1930	Lancashire	3rd
1931	**Yorkshire**	**1st**
1932	**Yorkshire**	**1st**
1933	**Yorkshire**	**1st**
1934	Lancashire	5th
1935	**Yorkshire**	**1st**
1936	Derbyshire	3rd
1937	**Yorkshire**	**1st**
1938	**Yorkshire**	**1st**
1939	**Yorkshire**	**1st**
1946	**Yorkshire**	**1st**
1947	Middlesex	7th
1948	Glamorgan	4th
1949	**Yorkshire**/Middlesex	**1st**
1950	Lancashire/Surrey	3rd
1951	Warwickshire	2nd
1952	Surrey	2nd
1953	Surrey	12th
1954	Surrey	2nd
1955	Surrey	2nd
1956	Surrey	7th
1957	Surrey	3rd

CHAMPION COUNTIES SINCE 1873 *(Continued)*

		Yorkshire's Position			*Yorkshire's Position*
1958	Surrey	11th	1989	Worcestershire	16th
1959	**Yorkshire**	**1st**	1990	Middlesex	10th
1960	**Yorkshire**	**1st**	1991	Essex	14th
1961	Hampshire	2nd	1992	Essex	16th
1962	**Yorkshire**	**1st**	1993	Middlesex	12th
1963	**Yorkshire**	**1st**	1994	Warwickshire	13th
1964	Worcestershire	5th	1995	Warwickshire	8th
1965	Worcestershire	4th	1996	Leicestershire	6th
1966	**Yorkshire**	**1st**	1997	Glamorgan	6th
1967	**Yorkshire**	**1st**	1998	Leicestershire	3rd
1968	**Yorkshire**	**1st**	1999	Surrey	6th
1969	Glamorgan	13th	2000	Surrey	3rd
1970	Kent	4th	**2001**	**Yorkshire**	**1st**
1971	Surrey	13th	2002	Surrey	9th
1972	Warwickshire	10th	2003	Sussex	Div 2, 4th
1973	Hampshire	14th	2004	Warwickshire	Div 2, 7th
1974	Worcestershire	11th	2005	Nottinghamshire	Div 2, 3rd
1975	Leicestershire	2nd	2006	Sussex	Div 1, 6th
1976	Middlesex	8th	2007	Sussex	Div 1, 6th
1977	Kent/Middlesex	12th	2008	Durham	Div 1, 7th
1978	Kent	4th	2009	Durham	Div 1, 7th
1979	Essex	7th	2010	Nottinghamshire	Div 1, 3rd
1980	Middlesex	6th	2011	Lancashire	Div 1, 8th
1981	Nottinghamshire	10th	2012	Warwickshire	Div 2, 2nd
1982	Middlesex	10th	2013	Durham	Div 1, 2nd
1983	Essex	17th	**2014**	**Yorkshire**	**Div 1, 1st**
1984	Essex	14th	**2015**	**Yorkshire**	**Div 1, 1st**
1985	Middlesex	11th	2016	Middlesex	Div 1, 3rd
1986	Essex	10th	2017	Essex	Div 1, 4th
1987	Nottinghamshire	8th	2018	Surrey	Div 1, 4th
1988	Worcestershire	13th	2019	Essex	Div 1, 5th

SEASON-BY-SEASON RECORD OF ALL FIRST-CLASS MATCHES PLAYED BY YORKSHIRE 1863-2019

Season	Played	Won	Lost	Drawn	Abd§	Season	Played	Won	Lost	Drawn	Abd§
1863	4	2	1	1	0	1921	30	17	5	8	0
1864	7	2	4	1	0	1922	33	20	2	11	0
1865	9	0	7	2	0	1923	35	26	1	8	0
1866	3	0	2	1	0	1924	35	18	4	13	0
1867	7	7	0	0	0	1925	36	22	0	14	0
1868	7	4	3	0	0	1926	35	14	0	21	1
1869	5	4	1	0	0	1927	34	11	3	20	1
1870	7	6	0	1	0	1928	32	9	0	23	0
1871	7	3	3	1	0	1929	35	11	2	22	0
1872	10	2	7	1	0	1930	34	13	3	18	2
1873	13	7	5	1	0	1931	33	17	1	15	1
1874	14	10	3	1	0	1932	32	21	2	9	2
1875	12	6	4	2	0	1933	36	21	5	10	0
1876	12	5	3	4	0	1934	35	14	7	14	0
1877	14	2	7	5	0	1935	36	24	2	10	0
1878	20	10	7	3	0	1935-6	3	1	0	2	0
1879	17	7	5	5	0	1936	35	14	2	19	0
1880	20	6	8	6	0	1937	34	22	3	9	1
1881	20	11	6	3	0	1938	36	22	2	12	0
1882	24	11	9	4	0	1939	34	23	4	7	1
1883	19	10	2	7	0	1945	2	0	0	2	0
1884	20	10	6	4	0	1946	31	20	1	10	0
1885	21	8	3	10	0	1947	32	10	9	13	0
1886	21	5	8	8	0	1948	31	11	6	14	0
1887	20	6	5	9	0	1949	33	16	3	14	0
1888	20	7	7	6	0	1950	34	16	6	12	1
1889	16	3	11	2	1	1951	35	14	3	18	0
1890	20	10	4	6	0	1952	34	17	3	14	0
1891	17	5	11	1	2	1953	35	7	7	21	0
1892	19	6	6	7	0	1954	35	16	3	16*	0
1893	23	15	5	3	0	1955	33	23	6	4	0
1894	28	18	6	4	1	1956	35	11	7	17	0
1895	31	15	10	6	0	1957	34	16	5	13	1
1896	32	17	6	9	0	1958	33	10	8	15	2
1897	30	14	7	9	0	1959	35	18	8	9	0
1898	30	18	3	9	0	1960	38	19	7	12	0
1899	34	17	4	13	0	1961	39	19	5	15	0
1900	32	19	1	12	0	1962	37	16	5	16	0
1901	35	23	2	10	1	1963	33	14	4	15	0
1902	31	15	3	13	1	1964	33	12	4	17	0
1903	31	16	5	10	0	1965	33	12	4	17	0
1904	32	10	2	20	1	1966	32	16	6	10	1
1905	33	21	4	8	0	1967	31	16	5	10	2
1906	33	19	6	8	0	1968	32	13	4	15	0
1907	31	14	5	12	2	1969	29	4	7	18	0
1908	33	19	0	14	0	1970	26	10	5	11	0
1909	30	12	5	13	0	1971	27	5	8	14	0
1910	31	11	8	12	0	1972	21	4	5	12	1
1911	32	16	9	7	0	1973	22	3	5	14*	0
1912	35	14	3	18	1	1974	22	6	7	9	1
1913	32	16	5	11	0	1975	21	11	1	9	0
1914	31	16	4	11	2	1976	22	7	7	8	0
1919	31	12	5	14	0	1977	23	7	5	11	1
1920	30	17	6	7	0	1978	24	10	3	11	1

Season	Played	Won	Lost	Drawn	Abd§	Season	Played	Won	Lost	Drawn	Abd§
1979	22	6	3	13	1	1999	17	8	6	3	0
1980	24	5	4	15	0	2000	18	7	4	7	0
1981	24	5	9	10	0	2001	16	9	3	4	0
1982	22	5	1	16	1	2002	16	2	8	6	0
1983	23	1	5	17	1	2003	17	4	5	8	0
1984	24	5	4	15	0	2004	16	3	4	9	0
1985	25	3	4	18	1	2005	17	6	1	10	0
1986	25	4	6	15	0	2006	16	3	6	7	0
1986-7	1	0	0	1	0	2007	17	5	4	8	0
1987	24	7	4	13	1	2008	16	2	5	9	0
1988	24	5	6	13	0	2009	17	2	2	13	0
1989	22	3	9	10	0	2010	18	6	2	10	0
1990	?4	5	9	10	0	2011	17	4	6	7	0
1991	24	4	6	14	0	2012	17	5	0	12	0
1991-2	1	0	1	0	0	2013	17	8	2	7	0
1992	22	4	6	12	1	2014	17	8	1	8	0
1992-3	1	0	0	1	0	2015	18	12	1	5	0
1993	19	6	4	9	0	2016	18	5	4	9	0
1994	20	7	6	7	0	2017	15	5	5	5	0
1995	20	8	8	4	0	2018	13	5	5	3	2
1995-6	2	2	0	0	0	2019	15	6	4	5	0
1996	19	8	5	6	0						
1997	20	7	4	9	0		3645	1532	667	1446	40
1998	19	9	3	7	0						

* Includes one tie each season

§ All these matches were abandoned without a ball being bowled, except Yorkshire v Kent at Harrogate, 1904, which was abandoned under Law 9. The two in 1914 and the one in 1939 were abandoned because of war. The four-day match, Yorkshire v. Essex at Leeds in 2018, was abandoned without a ball bowled, but each side received 5 points. All these matches are excluded from the total played.

Of the 1,532 matches won 524 have been by an innings margin, 88 by 200 runs or more, and 134 by 10 wickets. Of the 667 lost 113 have been by an innings margin, 17 by 200 runs or more and 35 by 10 wickets.

ANALYSIS OF RESULTS VERSUS ALL FIRST-CLASS
TEAMS 1863-2019

COUNTY CHAMPIONSHIP

Opponents	Played	Won	Lost	Drawn	Tied
Derbyshire	205	103	19	83	0
Durham	36	16	8	12	0
Essex	165	85	28	52	0
Glamorgan	111	53	13	45	0
Gloucestershire	200	102	43	55	0
Hampshire	175	75	20	80	0
Kent	202	85	40	77	0
Lancashire	261	79	52	130	0
Leicestershire	166	84	15	66	1
Middlesex	235	82	59	93	1
Northamptonshire	142	67	26	49	0
Nottinghamshire	258	93	47	118	0
Somerset	179	92	27	60	0
Surrey	248	87	69	92	0
Sussex	199	85	33	81	0
Warwickshire	194	87	32	75	0
Worcestershire	142	71	22	49	0
Cambridgeshire	8	3	4	1	0
Total	3126	1349	557	1218	2

OTHER FIRST-CLASS MATCHES

Opponents	Played	Won	Lost	Drawn	Tied
Derbyshire	2	1	1	0	0
Essex	2	2	0	0	0
Hampshire	1	0	0	1	0
Lancashire	12	5	3	4	0
Leicestershire	2	1	1	0	0
Middlesex	1	1	0	0	0
Nottinghamshire	2	1	1	0	0
Surrey	1	0	0	1	0
Sussex	2	0	0	2	0
Warwickshire	2	0	0	2	0
Totals	27	11	6	10	0
Australians	55	6	19	30	0
Indians	14	5	1	8	0
New Zealanders	10	2	0	8	0
Pakistanis	4	1	0	3	0
South Africans	17	1	3	13	0
Sri Lankans	3	0	0	3	0
West Indians	17	3	7	7	0
Zimbabweans	2	0	1	1	0
Bangladesh A	1	1	0	0	0
India A	2	0	0	2	0
Pakistan A	2	1	0	1	0
South Africa A	1	0	0	1	0
Totals	128	20	31	77	0

Opponents	Played	Won	Lost	Drawn	Tied
Cambridge University/U C C E	88	42	17	29	0
Canadians	1	1	0	0	0
Combined Services	1	0	0	1	0
Durham MCCU	1	1	0	0	0
England XI's	6	1	2	3	0
Hon. M.B. Hawke's XI	1	0	1	0	0
International XI	1	1	0	0	0
Ireland	3	3	0	0	0
Jamaica	3	1	0	2	0
Leeds/Bradford MCCU	6	3	0	3	0
Liverpool and District*	3	2	1	0	0
Loughborough UCCE	2	1	0	1	0
MCC	155	55	40	60	0
Mashonaland	1	1	0	0	0
Matebeleland	1	1	0	0	0
Minor Counties	1	1	0	0	0
Oxford University	44	21	3	20	0
Philadelphians	1	0	0	1	0
Rest of England	16	4	5	7	0
Royal Air Force	1	0	0	1	0
Scotland**	11	7	0	4	0
South of England	2	1	0	1	0
C. I. Thornton's XI	5	2	0	3	0
United South of England	1	1	0	0	0
Western Province	2	0	1	1	0
Windward Islands	1	0	0	1	0
I Zingari	6	2	3	1	0
Totals	**364**	**152**	**73**	**139**	**0**
Grand Totals	**3645**	**1532**	**667**	**1444**	**2**

*Matches played in 1889, 1891, 1892 and 1893 are excluded. **Match played in 1878 is included

ABANDONED MATCHES (40)

1889	v. MCC at Lord's	1939	v. MCC at Scarborough (due to war)
1891 (2)	v. MCC at Lord's	1950	v. Cambridge University
	v. MCC at Scarborough		at Cambridge
1894	v. Kent at Bradford	1957	v. West Indians at Bradford
1901	v. Surrey at The Oval	1958 (2)	v. Nottinghamshire at Hull
1902	v. Leicestershire at Leicester (AR)		v. Worcestershire at Bradford
1904	v. Kent at Harrogate (Law 9	1966	v. Oxford University at Oxford
	— now Law 10)	1967 (2)	v. Leicestershire at Leeds
1907 (2)	v. Derbyshire at Sheffield		v. Lancashire at Manchester
	v. Nottinghamshire at Huddersfield	1972	v. Australians at Bradford
1912	v. Surrey at Sheffield	1974	v. Hampshire at Bournemouth
1914 (2)	v. England at Harrogate (due to war)	1977	v. Gloucestershire at Bristol
	v. MCC at Scarborough (due to war)	1978	v. Pakistan at Bradford
1926	v. Nottinghamshire at Leeds	1979	v. Nottinghamshire at Sheffield (AP)
1927	v. Kent at Bradford	1982	v. Nottinghamshire at Harrogate
1930 (2)	v. Derbyshire at Chesterfield*	1983	v. Middlesex at Lord's
	v. Northamptonshire at Harrogate*	1985	v. Essex at Sheffield (AP)
1931	v. Sussex at Hull	1987	v. Sussex at Hastings
1932 (2)	v. Derbyshire at Chesterfield	1992	v. Oxford University at Oxford
	v. Kent at Sheffield	2018	v. Leeds/Bradford MCCU at Leeds*
1937	v. Cambridge University at Bradford	2018	v. Essex at Leeds*

* Consecutive matches

ANALYSIS OF RESULTS ON GROUNDS IN YORKSHIRE USED IN 2019

FIRST-CLASS MATCHES

Ground	Played	Won	Lost	Drawn	Tied
Leeds Headingley 1891-2019	466	177 (37.98%)	82 (17.60%)	207 (44.42%)	0 (0.00%)
Scarborough North Marine Road 1874-2019	259	105 (40.54%)	40 (15.44%)	114 (44.02%)	0 (0.00%)
York Clifton Park 2019	1	0 (0.00%)	1 (100.00%)	0 (0.00%)	0 (0.00%)

HIGHEST MATCH AGGREGATES – OVER 1350 RUNS

Runs	Wkts	
1665	33	Yorkshire (351 and 481) lost to Warwickshire (601:9 dec and 232:4) by 6 wkts at Birmingham, 2002
1606	31	Yorkshire (438 and 363:5 dec) lost to Somerset (326 and 479:6) by 4 wkts at Taunton, 2009
1479	28	Yorkshire (405 and 333:4 dec) lost to Somerset (377 and 364:4) by 6 wkts at Taunton , 2010
1473	17	Yorkshire (600:4 dec. and 231:3 dec.) drew with Worcestershire (453:5 dec. and 189:5) at Scarborough, 1995.
1442	29	Yorkshire (501:6 dec. and 244:6 dec.) beat Lancashire (403:7 dec. and 294) by 48 runs at Scarborough, 1991.
1439	32	Yorkshire (536:8 dec. and 205:7 dec.) beat Glamorgan (482: 7 dec. and 216) by 43 runs at Cardiff, 1996.
1431	32	Yorkshire (388 and 312:6) drew with Sussex (398 and 333:6 dec) at Scarborough, 2011
1417	33	Yorkshire (422 and 193:7) drew with Glamorgan (466 and 336:6 dec) at Colwyn Bay, 2003
1406	37	Yorkshire (354 and 341:8) drew with Derbyshire (406 and 305:9 dec) at Derby, 2004
1400	32	Yorkshire (299 and 439: 4 dec.) drew with Hampshire (296 and 366:8) at Southampton, 2007
1393	35	Yorkshire (331 and 278) lost to Kent (377 and 407:5 dec) by 175 runs at Maidstone, 1994.
1390	34	Yorkshire (431:8 dec and 265:7) beat Hampshire (429 and 265) by 3 wkts at Southampton, 1995.
1390	33	Durham (573 and 124:3) beat Yorkahire (274 and 419) by 7 wkts at Scarborough, 2013.
1376	33	Yorkshire (531 and 158:3) beat Lancashire (373 and 314) by 7 wkts at Leeds, 2001
1376	20	Yorkshire (677: 7 dec.) drew with Durham (518 and 181:3 dec.) at Leeds, 2006
1374	36	Yorkshire (594: 9 dec. and 266:7 dec.) beat Surrey (344 and 170) by 346 runs at The Oval, 2007
1373	36	Yorkshire (520 and 114:6) drew with Derbyshire (216 and 523) at Derby, 2005
1364	35	Yorkshire (216 and 433) lost to Warwickshire (316 and 399:5 dec.) by 66 runs at Birmingham, 2006
1359	25	Yorkshire (561 and 138:3 dec.) drew with Derbyshire (412:4 dec. and 248:8) at Sheffield, 1996.
1359	30	Yorkshire (358 and 321) lost to Somerset (452 and 228:0) by 10 wkts at Taunton, 2011
1353	18	Yorkshire (377:2 dec. and 300:6) beat Derbyshire (475:7 dec. and 201:3 dec.) by 4 wkts at Scarborough, 1990.

LOWEST MATCH AGGREGATES – UNDER 225 RUNS
IN A COMPLETED MATCH

Runs	Wkts	
165	30	Yorkshire (46 and 37:0) beat Nottinghamshire (24 and 58 by 10 wkts at Sheffield, 1888.
175	29	Yorkshire (104) beat Essex (30 and 41) by an innings and 33 runs at Leyton, 1901.
182	15	Yorkshire (4:0 dec. and 88.5) beat Northamptonshire (4:0 dec. and 86) by 5 wkts at Bradford, 1931.
193	29	Yorkshire (99) beat Worcestershire (43 and 51) by an innings and 5 runs at Bradford, 1900.
219	30	Yorkshire (113) beat Nottinghamshire (71 and 35) by an innings and 7 runs at Nottingham, 1881.
222	32	Yorkshire (98 and 14:2) beat Gloucestershire (68 and 42) by 8 wkts at Gloucester, 1924.
223	40	Yorkshire (58 and 51) lost to Lancashire (64 and 50)

LOWEST MATCH AGGREGATES – UNDER 325 RUNS
IN A MATCH IN WHICH ALL 40 WICKETS FELL

Runs	Wkts	
223	40	Yorkshire (58 and 51) lost to Lancashire (64 and 50) by 5 runs at Manchester, 1893.
288	40	Yorkshire (55 and 68) lost to Lancashire (89 and 76) by 42 runs at Sheffield, 1872.
295	40	Yorkshire (71 and 63) lost to Surrey (56 and 105) by 27 runs at The Oval, 1886.
303	40	Yorkshire (109 and 77) beat Middlesex (63 and 54) by 69 runs at Lord's, 1891.
318	40	Yorkshire (96 and 96) beat Lancashire (39 and 87) by 66 runs at Manchester, 1874.
318	40	Yorkshire (94 and 104) beat Northamptonshire (61 and 59) by 78 runs at Bradford, 1955.
319	40	Yorkshire (84 and 72) lost to Derbyshire (106 and 57) by 7 runs at Derby, 1878.
320	40	Yorkshire (98 and 91) beat Surrey (72 and 59) by 58 runs at Sheffield, 1893.
321	40	Yorkshire (88 and 37) lost to I Zingari (103 and 93) by 71 runs at Scarborough, 1877.
321	40	Yorkshire (80 and 67) lost to Derbyshire (129 and 45) by 27 runs at Sheffield, 1879.

LARGE MARGINS OF VICTORY – BY AN INNINGS
AND OVER 250 RUNS

Inns and 397 runs	Yorkshire (548:4 dec.) beat Northamptonshire (58 and 93) at Harrogate, 1921
Inns and 387 runs	Yorkshire (662) beat Derbyshire (118 and 157) at Chesterfield, 1898.
Inns and 343 runs	Yorkshire (673:8 dec) beat Northamptonshire (184 and 146) at Leeds, 2003
Inns and 321 runs	Yorkshire (437) beat Leicestershire (58 and 58) at Leicester, 1908.
Inns and 314 runs	Yorkshire (356:8 dec) beat Northamptonshire (27 and 15) at Northampton, 1908. (Yorkshire's first match v. Northamptonshire).
Inns and 313 runs	Yorkshire (555:1 dec) beat Essex (78 and 164) at Leyton, 1932.
Inns and 307 runs	Yorkshire (681:5 dec.) beat Sussex (164 and 210) at Sheffield, 1897.
Inns and 302 runs	Yorkshire (660) beat Leicestershire (165 and 193) at Leicester, 1896.
Inns and 301 runs	Yorkshire (499) beat Somerset (125 and 73) at Bath, 1899.
Inns and 294 runs	Yorkshire (425:7 dec.) beat Gloucestershire (47 and 84) at Bristol, 1964.
Inns and 284 runs	Yorkshire (467:7 dec.) beat Leicestershire (111 and 72) at Bradford, 1932.
Inns and 282 runs	Yorkshire (481:8 dec) beat Derbyshire (106 and 93) at Huddersfield, 1901.
Inns and 280 runs	Yorkshire (562) beat Leicestershire (164 and 118) at Dewsbury, 1903.
Inns and 271 runs	Yorkshire (460) beat Hampshire (128 and 61) at Hull, 1900.
Inns and 271 runs	Yorkshire (495:5 dec) beat Warwickshire (99 and 125) at Huddersfield, 1922.
Inns and 266 runs	Yorkshire (352) beat Cambridgeshire (40 and 46) at Hunslet, 1869.
Inns and 260 runs	Yorkshire (521: 7dec.) beat Worcestershire (129 and 132) at Leeds, 2007.
Inns and 258 runs	Yorkshire (404:2 dec) beat Glamorgan (78 and 68) at Cardiff, 1922. (Yorkshire's first match v. Glamorgan).
Inns and 256 runs	Yorkshire (486) beat Leicestershire (137 and 93) at Sheffield, 1895.
Inns and 251 runs	Yorkshire (550) beat Leicestershire (154 and 145) at Leicester, 1933.

LARGE MARGINS OF VICTORY – BY OVER 300 RUNS

389 runs	Yorkshire (368 and 280:1 dec) beat Somerset (125 and 134) at Bath, 1906.
370 runs	Yorkshire (194 and 274) beat Hampshire (62 and 36) at Leeds, 1904.
351 runs	Yorkshire (280 and 331) beat Northamptonshire (146 and 114) at Northampton, 1947.
346 runs	Yorkshire (594: 9 dec. and 266: 7 dec.) beat Surrey (344 and 179) at The Oval, 2007.
328 runs	Yorkshire (186 and 318:1 dec) beat Somerset (43 and 133) at Bradford, 1930.
328 runs	Yorkshire (280 and 277:7 dec) beat Glamorgan (104 and 105) at Swansea, 2001
320 runs	Yorkshire (331 and 353:9 dec) beat Durham (150 and 214) at Chester-le-Street, 2004
308 runs	Yorkshire (89 and 420) beat Warwickshire (72 and 129) at Birmingham, 1921
308 runs	Yorkshire (89 and 420) beat Warwickshire (72 and 129)
305 runs	Yorkshire (370 and 305:4 dec) beat Hampshire (227 and 143) at Leeds, 2015
305 runs	Yorkshire (282 and 263:4 dec) beat Nottinghamshire (94 and 146) at Scarborough 2016

LARGE MARGINS OF VICTORY – BY 10 WICKETS
(WITH OVER 100 RUNS SCORED IN THE 4th INNINGS)

4th Innings

167:0 wkt	Yorkshire (247 and 167:0) beat Northamptonshire 233 and 180) at Huddersfield, 1948.
147:0 wkt	Yorkshire (381 and 147:0) beat Middlesex (384 and 142) at Lord's, 1896.
142:0 wkt	Yorkshire (304 and 142:0) beat Sussex (254 and 188) at Bradford, 1887.
139:0 wkt	Yorkshire (163:9 dec and 139:0) beat Nottinghamshire (234 and 67) at Leeds, 1932.
138:0 wkt	Yorkshire (293 and 138:0) beat Hampshire (251 and 179) at Southampton, 1897.
132:0 wkt	Yorkshire (328 and 132:0) beat Northamptonshire (281 and 175) at Leeds, 2005
129:0 wkt	Yorkshire (355 and 129:0) beat Durham MCCU (196 and 287) at Durham, 2011
127:0 wkt	Yorkshire (258 and 127:0) beat Cambridge University (127 and 257) at Cambridge, 1930.
119:0 wkt	Yorkshire (109 and 119:0) beat Essex (108 and 119) at Leeds, 1931.
118:0 wkt	Yorkshire (121 and 118:0) beat MCC (125 and 113) at Lord's, 1883.
116:0 wkt	Yorkshire (147 and 116:0) beat Hampshire (141 and 120) at Bournemouth, 1930.
114:0 wkt	Yorkshire (135 and 114:0) beat Hampshire (71 and 176) at Bournemouth, 1948.
114:0 wkt	Yorkshire (135 and 114:0) beat Hampshire (71 and 176)
105:0 wkt	Yorkshire (307 and 105:0) beat Worcestershire (311 and 100) at Worcester, 2015

HEAVY DEFEATS – BY AN INNINGS
AND OVER 250 RUNS

Inns and 272 runs	Yorkshire (78 and 186) lost to Surrey (536) at The Oval, 1898.
Inns and 261 runs	Yorkshire (247 and 89) lost to Sussex (597: 8 dec.) at Hove, 2007.
Inns and 255 runs	Yorkshire (125 and 144) lost to All England XI (524) at Sheffield, 1865.

HEAVY DEFEATS – BY OVER 300 RUNS

433 runs	Kent (482-8 dec and 337-7 dec) defeated Yorkshire (269 and 117) at Leeds, 2019
376 runs	Essex (227 and 334-7 dec) defeated Yorkshire (111 and 74) at Chelmsford, 2017
324 runs	Yorkshire (247 and 204) lost to Gloucestershire (291 and 484) at Cheltenham, 1994.
305 runs	Yorkshire (119 and 51) lost to Cambridge University (312 and 163) at Cambridge, 1906.

HEAVY DEFEATS – BY 10 WICKETS
(WITH OVER 100 RUNS SCORED IN THE 4th INNINGS)

4th Innings

228:0 wkt	Yorkshire (358 and 321) lost to Somerset (452 and 228:0) at Taunton, 2011
148:0 wkt	Yorkshire (83 and 216) lost to Lancashire (154 and 148:0) at Manchester, 1875.
119:0 wkt	Yorkshire (92 and 109) lost to Nottinghamshire (86 and 119:0 wkt) at Leeds, 1989.
108:0 wkt	Yorkshire (236 and 107) lost to Hampshire (236 and 108:0 wkt) at Southampton, 2008
100:0 wkt	Yorkshire (95 and 91) lost to Gloucestershire (88 and 100:0) at Bristol, 1956.

NARROW VICTORIES – BY 1 WICKET

Yorkshire (70 and 91:9) beat Cambridgeshire (86 and 74) at Wisbech, 1867.
Yorkshire (91 and 145:9) beat MCC (73 and 161) at Lord's, 1870.
Yorkshire (265 and 154:9) beat Derbyshire (234 and 184) at Derby, 1897.
Yorkshire (177 and 197:9) beat MCC (188 and 185) at Lord's, 1899.
Yorkshire (391 and 241:9) beat Somerset (349 and 281) at Taunton, 1901.
Yorkshire (239 and 168:9) beat MCC (179 and 226) at Scarborough, 1935.
Yorkshire (152 and 90:9) beat Worcestershire (119 and 121) at Leeds, 1946.
Yorkshire (229 and 175:9) beat Glamorgan (194 and 207) at Bradford, 1960.
Yorkshire (265.9 dec and 191:9) beat Worcestershire (227 and 227) at Worcester, 1961.
Yorkshire (329:6 dec and 167:9) beat Essex (339.9 dec and 154) at Scarborough, 1979.
Yorkshire (Innings forfeited and 251:9 beat Sussex (195 and 55.1 dec) at Leeds, 1986.
Yorkshire (314 and 150:9) beat Essex (200 and 261) at Scarborough, 1998.

NARROW VICTORIES – BY 5 RUNS OR LESS

By 1 run	Yorkshire (228 and 214) beat Middlesex (206 and 235) at Bradford, 1976.
By 1 run	Yorkshire (383 and inns forfeited) beat Loughborough UCCE (93: 3 dec. and 289) at Leeds, 2007.
By 2 runs	Yorkshire (108 and 122) beat Nottinghamshire (56 and 172) at Nottingham, 1870.
By 2 runs	Yorkshire (304:9 dec and 135) beat Middlesex (225:2 dec and 212) at Leeds, 1985.
By 3 runs	Yorkshire (446:9 dec and 172:4 dec) beat Essex (300:3 dec and 315) at Colchester, 1991.
By 3 runs	Yorkshire (202 and 283) beat Somerset (224 and 258) at Taunton, 2017
By 5 runs	Yorkshire (271 and 147:6 dec) beat Surrey (198 and 215) at Sheffield, 1950.
By 5 runs	Yorkshire (151 and 176) beat Hampshire (165 and 157) at Bradford, 1962.
By 5 runs	Yorkshire (376:4 and 106) beat Middlesex (325:8 and 152) at Lord's, 1975
By 5 runs	Yorkshire (323:5 dec and inns forfeited) beat Somerset (inns forfeited and 318) at Taunton, 1986.

NARROW DEFEATS – BY 1 WICKET

Yorkshire (224 and 210) lost to Australian Imperial Forces XI (265 and 170:9) at Sheffield, 1919

Yorkshire (101 and 159) lost to Warwickshire (45 and 216:9) at Scarborough, 1934.

Yorkshire (239 and 184:9 dec.) lost to Warwickshire (125 and 302:9) at Birmingham, 1983.

Yorkshire (289 and 153) lost to Surrey (250:2 dec and 193:9) at Guildford, 1991.

Yorkshire (341 and Inns forfeited) lost to Surrey (39:1 dec and 306:9) at Bradford, 1992.

NARROW DEFEATS – BY 5 RUNS OR LESS

By 1 run	Yorkshire (135 and 297) lost to Essex (139 and 294) at Huddersfield, 1897.
By 1 run	Yorkshire (159 and 232) lost to Gloucestershire (164 and 228) at Bristol, 1906.
By 1 run	Yorkshire (126 and 137) lost to Worcestershire (101 and 163) at Worcester, 1968.
By 1 run	Yorkshire (366 and 217) lost to Surrey (409 and 175) at The Oval, 1995.
By 2 runs	Yorkshire (172 and 107) lost to Gloucestershire (157 and 124) at Sheffield, 1913.
By 2 runs	Yorkshire (179:9 dec and 144) lost to MCC (109 and 216) at Lord's, 1957.
By 3 runs	Yorkshire (126 and 181) lost to Sussex (182 and 128) at Sheffield, 1883.
By 3 runs	Yorkshire (160 and 71) lost to Lancashire (81 and 153) at Huddersfield, 1889.
By 3 runs	Yorkshire (134 and 158) lost to Nottinghamshire (200 and 95) at Leeds, 1923.
By 4 runs	Yorkshire (169 and 193) lost to Middlesex (105 and 261) at Bradford, 1920.
By 5 runs	Yorkshire (58 and 51) lost to Lancashire (64 and 50) at Manchester, 1893.
By 5 runs	Yorkshire (119 and 115) lost to Warwickshire (167 and 72) at Bradford, 1969.

HIGH FOURTH INNINGS SCORES – 300 AND OVER

By Yorkshire

To Win:

406:4	beat Leicestershire by 6 wkts at Leicester, 2005
402:6	beat Gloucestershire by 4 wkts at Bristol, 2012
400:4	beat Leicestershire by 6 wkts at Scarborough, 2005
339:6	beat Durham by 4 wkts at Chester-le-Street, 2013
331:8	beat Middlesex by 2 wkts at Lord's, 1910.
327:6	beat Nottinghamshire by 4 wkts at Nottingham, 1990.*
323:5	beat Nottinghamshire by 5 wkts at Nottingham, 1977.
318:3	beat Glamorgan by 7 wkts at Middlesbrough, 1976.
316:8	beat Gloucestershire by 2 wkts at Scarborough, 2012
309:7	beat Somerset by 3 wkts at Taunton, 1984.
305:8	beat Nottinghamshire by 2 wkts at Worksop, 1982.
305:5	beat Hampshire by 5 wkts at West End, Southampton, 2015
305:3	beat Lancashire by 7 wkts at Manchester, 1994.
304:4	beat Derbyshire by 6 wkts at Chesterfield, 1959.
300:4	beat Derbyshire by 6 wkts at Chesterfield, 1981.
300:6	beat Derbyshire by 4 wkts at Scarborough, 1990.*

To Draw:

341:8	(set 358) drew with Derbyshire at Derby, 2004.
333:7	(set 369) drew with Essex at Chelmsford, 2010
316:6	(set 326) drew with Oxford University at Oxford, 1948.
312:6	(set 344) drew with Sussex at Scarborough 2011
316:7	(set 320) drew with Somerset at Scarborough, 1990.
300:5	(set 392) drew with Kent at Canterbury, 2010

To Lose:

433	(set 500) lost to Warwickshire by 66 runs at Birmingham, 2006
380	(set 406) lost to MCC. by 25 runs at Lord's, 1937.
343	(set 490) lost to Durham by 146 runs at Leeds 2011
324	(set 485) lost to Northamptonshire by 160 runs at Luton, 1994.
322	(set 344) lost to Middlesex by 21 runs at Lord's, 1996.
309	(set 400) lost to Middlesex by 90 runs at Lord's 1878.

*Consecutive matches

By Opponents:

To Win:

479:6	Somerset won by 4 wkts at Taunton, 2009
472:3	Middlesex won by 7 wkts at Lord's, 2014
404:5	Hampshire won by 5 wkts at Leeds, 2006
392:4	Gloucestershire won by 6 wkts at Bristol, 1948
364:4	Somerset won by 6 wkts at Taunton, 2010
354:5	Nottinghamshire won by 5 wkts at Scarborough, 1990
337:4	Worcestershire won by 6 wkts at Kidderminster, 2007
334:6	Glamorgan won by 4 wkts at Harrogate, 1955
329:5	Worcestershire won by 5 wkts at Worcester, 1979
321:6	Hampshire won by 4 wickets at Leeds, 2017
306:9	Surrey won by 1 wkt at Bradford, 1992
305:7	Lancashire won by 3 wkts at Manchester, 1980
302:9	Warwickshire won by 1 wkt at Birmingham, 1983

By Opponents:

To Draw:

366:8	(set 443)	Hampshire drew at Southampton, 2007.
334:7	(set 339)	MCC. drew at Scarborough, 1911.
322:9	(set 334)	Middlesex drew at Leeds, 1988.
317:6	(set 355)	Nottinghamshire drew at Nottingham, 1910.
300:9	(set 314)	Northamptonshire drew at Northampton, 1990.

To Lose:

370	(set 539)	Leicestershire lost by 168 runs at Leicester, 2001
319	(set 364)	Gloucestershire lost by 44 runs at Leeds, 1987.
318	(set 324)	Somerset lost by 5 runs at Taunton, 1986.
315	(set 319)	Essex lost by 3 runs at Colchester, 1991.
314	(set 334)	Lancashire lost by 19 runs at Manchester, 1993.
310	(set 417)	Warwickshire lost by 106 runs at Scarborough, 1939.
306	(set 413)	Kent lost by 106 runs at Leeds, 1952.
300	(set 330)	Middlesex lost by 29 runs at Sheffield, 1930.

TIE MATCHES

Yorkshire (351:4 dec and 113) tied with Leicestershire (328 and 136) at Huddersfield, 1954.
Yorkshire (106:9 dec and 207) tied with Middlesex (102 and 211) at Bradford, 1973.

HIGHEST SCORES BY AND AGAINST YORKSHIRE

Yorkshire versus: —

Derbyshire:	**By Yorkshire:**	**Against Yorkshire:**
In Yorkshire:	677:7 dec at Leeds 2013	491 at Bradford, 1949
Away:	662 at Chesterfield, 1898	523 at Derby, 2005
Durham:		
In Yorkshire:	677:7 dec. at Leeds, 2006	573 at Scarborough, 2013
Away	589-8 dec at Chester-le-Street, 2014	507:8 dec at Chester-le-Street, 2016
Essex:		
In Yorkshire:	516 at Scarborough, 2010	622:8 dec. at Leeds, 2005
Away:	555:1 dec. at Leyton, 1932	521 at Leyton, 1905
Glamorgan:		
In Yorkshire:	580:9 dec at Scarborough, 2001	498 at Leeds, 1999
Away:	536:8 dec. at Cardiff, 1996	482:7 dec. at Cardiff, 1996
Gloucestershire:		
In Yorkshire:	504:7 dec. at Bradford, 1905	411 at Leeds, 1992
Away:	494 at Bristol, 1897	574 at Cheltenham, 1990
Hampshire:		
In Yorkshire:	593:9 dec. at Leeds 2016	498:6 dec at Scarborough, 2010
Away	585:3 dec at Portsmouth 1920	599:3 at Southampton, 2011
Kent:		
In Yorkshire:	550:9 at Scarborough, 1995	537:9 dec at Leeds, 2012
Away:	559 at Canterbury, 1887	580: 9 dec. at Maidstone, 1998
Lancashire:		
In Yorkshire:	590 at Bradford, 1887	517 at Leeds, 2007.
Away	616:6 dec at Manchester, 2014	537 at Manchester, 2005
Leicestershire:		
In Yorkshire	562 { at Scarborough, 1901 { at Dewsbury, 1903	681:7 dec. at Bradford, 1996
Away:	660 at Leicester, 1896	425 at Leicester, 1906

Yorkshire versus: —

	By Yorkshire:	Against Yorkshire:
Middlesex:		
In Yorkshire:	575:7 dec. at Bradford, 1899	527 at Huddersfield, 1887
Away	538:6 dec at Lord's, 1925	573:8 dec at Lord's, 2015
Northamptonshire:		
In Yorkshire:	673:8 dec. at Leeds, 2003	517:7 dec. at Scarborough, 1999
Away	546:3 dec at Northampton, 2014	531:4 dec at Northampton, 1996
Nottinghamshire:		
In Yorkshire:	572:8 dec at Scarborough, 2013	545:7 dec at Leeds, 2010
Away	534:9 dec at Nottingham, 2011	490 at Nottingham, 1897
Somerset:		
In Yorkshire:	525:4 dec. at Leeds, 1953	630 at Leeds, 1901
Away:	589:5 dec at Bath, 2001	592 at Taunton, 1892
Surrey:		
In Yorkshire:	582:7 dec. at Sheffield, 1935	516-7 dec at Leeds, 2017
Away:	704 at The Oval, 1899	634:5 dec at The Oval, 2013
Sussex:		
In Yorkshire:	681:5 dec. at Sheffield, 1897	566 at Sheffield, 1937
Away:	522:7 dec. at Hastings, 1911	597:8 dec. at Hove, 2007
Warwickshire:		
In Yorkshire	561:7 dec at Scarborough 2007	482 at Leeds, 2011
Away:	887 at Birmingham, 1896	601:9 dec. at Birmingham, 2002
	(Highest score by a First-Class county)	
Worcestershire:		
In Yorkshire:	600: 4 dec. at Scarborough, 1995	572:7 dec. at Scarborough 2018
Away:	560:6 dec at Worcester, 1928	456:8 at Worcester, 1904
Australians:		
In Yorkshire:	377 at Sheffield, 1953	470 at Bradford, 1893
Indians:		
In Yorkshire:	385 at Hull, 1911	490:5 dec. at Sheffield, 1946
New Zealanders:		
In Yorkshire:	419 at Bradford, 1965	370:7 dec. at Bradford, 1949
Pakistanis:		
In Yorkshire:	433:9 dec. at Sheffield, 1954	356 at Sheffield, 1954
South Africans:		
In Yorkshire:	579 at Sheffield, 1951	454:8 dec at Sheffield, 1951
Sri Lankans:		
In Yorkshire:	314:8 dec. at Leeds, 1991	422:8 dec. at Leeds, 1991
West Indians:		
In Yorkshire:	312:5 dec. at Scarborough, 1973	426 at Scarborough, 1995
Zimbabweans:		
In Yorkshire:	298:9 dec at Leeds, 1990	235 at Leeds, 2000
Cambridge University:		
In Yorkshire:	359 at Scarborough, 1967	366 at Leeds, 1998
Away:	540 at Cambridge, 1938	425:7 at Cambridge, 1929
Durham MCCU:		
Away:	355 at Durham, 2011	287 at Durham, 2011
Leeds/Bradford MCCU:		
In Yorkshire	543-5 dec at Leeds, 2017	211 at Leeds, 2012
Away	489-8 dec at Weetwood, Leeds, 2019	219 at Weetwood, Leeds, 2019
Loughborough MCCU:		
In Yorkshire:	383:6 dec at Leeds, 2007	289 at Leeds, 2007

Yorkshire versus: —

MCC:

	By Yorkshire:	**Against Yorkshire:**
In Yorkshire:	557:8 dec. at Scarborough, 1933	478:8 at Scarborough, 1904
Away:	528:8 dec. at Lord's, 1919	488 at Lord's, 1919

Oxford University:

| In Yorkshire: | 173 at Harrogate, 1972 | 190:6 dec at Harrogate, 1972 |
| Away: | 468:6 dec. at Oxford, 1978 | 422:9 dec. at Oxford, 1953 |

LOWEST SCORES BY AND AGAINST YORKSHIRE

Yorkshire versus:

Derbyshire:

	By Yorkshire:	**Against Yorkshire:**
In Yorkshire:	50 at Sheffield, 1894	20 at Sheffield, 1939
Away:	44 at Chesterfield, 1948	26 at Derby, 1880

Durham:

| In Yorkshire: | 93 at Leeds, 2003 | 125 at Harrogate, 1995 |
| Away: | 108 at Durham, 1992 | 74 at Chester-le-Street, 1998 |

Essex:

| In Yorkshire: | 31 at Huddersfield, 1935 | 52 at Harrogate, 1900 |
| Away: | 50 at Chelmsford, 2018 | 30 at Leyton, 1901 |

Glamorgan:

| In Yorkshire: | 83 at Sheffield, 1946 | 52 at Hull, 1926 |
| Away: | 92 at Swansea, 1956 | 48 at Cardiff, 1924 |

Gloucestershire:

| In Yorkshire: | 61 at Leeds, 1894 | 36 at Sheffield, 1903 |
| Away: | 35 at Bristol, 1959 | 42 at Gloucester, 1924 |

Hampshire:

| In Yorkshire: | 23 at Middlesbrough, 1965 | 36 at Leeds, 1904 |
| Away: | 96 at Bournemouth, 1971 | 36 at Southampton, 1898 |

Kent:

| In Yorkshire: | 30 at Sheffield, 1865 | 39 { at Sheffield, 1882 / at Sheffield, 1936 |
| Away: | 62 at Maidstone, 1889 | 63 at Canterbury, 1901 |

Lancashire:

| In Yorkshire: | 33 at Leeds, 1924 | 30 at Holbeck, 1868 |
| Away: | 51 { at Manchester, 1888 / at Manchester, 1893 | 39 at Manchester, 1874 |

Leicestershire:

	By Yorkshire:	**Against Yorkshire:**
In Yorkshire:	93 at Leeds, 1935	34 at Leeds, 1906
Away:	47 at Leicester, 1911	57 at Leicester, 1898

Middlesex:

| In Yorkshire: | 45 at Leeds, 1898 | 45 at Huddersfield, 1879 |
| Away: | 43 at Lord's, 1888 | 49 at Lord's in 1890 |

Northamptonshire:

| In Yorkshire: | 85 at Sheffield, 1919 | 51 at Bradford, 1920 |
| Away | 64 at Northampton, 1959 | 15 at Northampton, 1908 (and 27 in first innings) |

Nottinghamshire:

| In Yorkshire: | 32 at Sheffield, 1876 | 24 at Sheffield, 1888 |
| Away: | 43 at Nottingham, 1869 | 13 at Nottingham, 1901 (second smallest total by a First-Class county) |

Yorkshire versus:

	By Yorkshire:	**Against Yorkshire:**
Somerset:		
In Yorkshire:	73 at Leeds, 1895	43 at Bradford, 1930
Away:	83 at Wells, 1949	35 at Bath, 1898
Surrey:		
In Yorkshire:	54 at Sheffield, 1873	31 at Holbeck, 1883
Away:	26 at The Oval, 1909	44 at The Oval, 1935
Sussex:		
In Yorkshire:	61 at Dewsbury, 1891	20 at Hull, 1922
Away:	42 at Hove, 1922	24 at Hove, 1878
Warwickshire:		
In Yorkshire:	49 at Huddersfield, 1951	35 at Sheffield, 1979
Away:	54 at Birmingham, 1964	35 at Birmingham, 1963
Worcestershire:		
In Yorkshire:	62 at Bradford, 1907	24 at Huddersfield, 1903
Away:	72 at Worcester, 1977	65 at Worcester, 1925
Australians:		
In Yorkshire:	48 at Leeds, 1893	23 at Leeds, 1902
Indians:		
In Yorkshire:	146 at Bradford, 1959	66 at Harrogate, 1932
New Zealanders:		
In Yorkshire:	189 at Harrogate, 1931	134 at Bradford, 1965
Pakistanis:		
In Yorkshire:	137 at Bradford, 1962	150 at Leeds, 1967
South Africans:		
In Yorkshire:	113 at Bradford, 1907	76 at Bradford, 1951
Sri Lankans:		
In Yorkshire:	Have not been dismissed. Lowest is 184:1 dec at Leeds, 1991	287:5 dec at Leeds, 1988
West Indians:		
In Yorkshire:	50 at Harrogate, 1906	58 at Leeds, 1928
Zimbabweans:		
In Yorkshire:	124 at Leeds, 2000	68 at Leeds, 2000
Cambridge University:		
In Yorkshire:	110 at Sheffield, 1903	39 at Sheffield, 1903
Away:	51 at Cambridge, 1906	30 at Cambridge, 1928
Durham MCCU:		
Away	355 at Durham, 2011	196 at Durham, 2011
Leeds/Bradford MCCU:		
In Yorkshire	135 at Leeds, 2012	118 at Leeds, 2013
Away		118 at Weetwood, Leeds, 2019
Loughborough MCCU:		
In Yorkshire	348:5 dec at Leeds, 2010	289 at Leeds, 2007
MCC:		
In Yorkshire:	46 { at Scarborough, 1876 at Scarborough, 1877	31 at Scarborough, 1877
Away:	44 at Lord's, 1880	27 at Lord's, 1902
Oxford University:		
In Yorkshire:	Have not been dismissed. Lowest is 115:8 at Harrogate, 1972	133 at Harrogate, 1972
Away:	141 at Oxford, 1949	46 at Oxford, 1956

INDIVIDUAL INNINGS OF 150 AND OVER

**A complete list of all First-class Centuries up to and including 2007
is to be found in the 2008 edition**

J M BAIRSTOW (7)

205	v. Nottinghamshire	Nottingham	2011
182	v. Leicestershire	Scarborough	2012
186	v. Derbyshire	Leeds	2013
161*	v. Sussex	Arundel	2014
219*	v. Durham	Chester-le-Street	2015
246	v. Hampshire	Leeds	2016
198	v. Surrey	Leeds	2016

G S BALLANCE (5)

203 *	v. Hampshire	West End	2017
194	v. Worcestershire	Worcester	2018
174	v. Northamptonshire	Leeds	2014
165	v. Sussex	Hove	2015
159	v. Kent	Canterbury	2019

W BARBER (7)

162	v. Middlesex	Sheffield	1932
168	v. MCC	Lord's	1934
248	v. Kent	Leeds	1934
191	v. Sussex	Leeds	1935
255	v. Surrey	Sheffield	1935
158	v. Kent	Sheffield	1936
157	v. Surrey	Sheffield	1938

M G BEVAN (2)

153*	v. Surrey	The Oval	1995
160*	v. Surrey	Middlesbrough	1996

H D BIRD (1)

181*	v. Glamorgan	Bradford	1959

R J BLAKEY (3)

204*	v. Gloucestershire	Leeds	1987
196	v. Oxford University	Oxford	1991
223*	v. Northamptonshire	Leeds	2003

G BLEWETT (1)

190	v. Northamptonshire	Scarborough	1999

M W BOOTH (1)

210	v. Worcestershire	Worcester	1911

G BOYCOTT (32)

165*	v. Leicestershire	Scarborough	1963
151	v. Middlesex	Leeds	1964
151*	v. Leicestershire	Leicester	1964
177	v. Gloucestershire	Bristol	1964
164	v. Sussex	Hove	1966
220*	v. Northamptonshire	Sheffield	1967
180*	v. Warwickshire	Middlesbrough	1968
260*	v. Essex	Colchester (Garrison Ground)	1970
169	v. Nottinghamshire	Leeds	1971
233	v. Essex	Colchester (Garrison Ground)	1971
182*	v. Middlesex	Lord's	1971
169	v. Lancashire	Sheffield	1971
151	v. Leicestershire	Bradford	1971

INDIVIDUAL INNINGS OF 150 AND OVER *(Continued)*

G BOYCOTT (Continued)

204*	v. Leicestershire	Leicester	1972
152*	v. Worcestershire	Worcester	1975
175*	v. Middlesex	Scarborough	1975
201*	v. Middlesex	Lord's	1975
161*	v. Gloucestershire	Leeds	1976
207*	v. Cambridge University	Cambridge	1976
156*	v. Glamorgan	Middlesbrough	1976
154	v Nottinghamshire	Nottingham	1977
151*	v Derbyshire	Leeds	1979
167	v Derbyshire	Chesterfield	1979
175*	v Nottinghamshire	Worksop	1979
154*	v Derbyshire	Scarborough	1980
159	v Worcestershire	Sheffield (Abbeydale Park)	1982
152*	v Warwickshire	Leeds	1982
214*	v Nottinghamshire	Worksop	1983
163	v Nottinghamshire	Bradford	1983
169*	v Derbyshire	Chesterfield	1983
153*	v Derbyshire	Harrogate	1984
184	v Worcestershire	Worcester	1985

T T BRESNAN (1)

169*	v. Durham	Chester-le-Street	2015

G L BROPHY (1)

177*	v Worcestershire	Worcester	2011

J T BROWN (8)

168*	v Sussex	Huddersfield	1895
203	v Middlesex	Lord's	1896
311	v Sussex	Sheffield	1897
300	v Derbyshire	Chesterfield	1898
150	v Sussex	Hove	1898
168	v Cambridge University	Cambridge	1899
167	v Australians	Bradford	1899
192	v Derbyshire	Derby	1899

D BYAS (5)

153	v Nottinghamshire	Worksop	1991
156	v Essex	Chelmsford	1993
181	v Cambridge University	Cambridge	1995
193	v Lancashire	Leeds	1995
213	v Worcestershire	Scarborough	1995

D B CLOSE (5)

164	v Combined Services	Harrogate	1954
154	v Nottinghamshire	Nottingham	1959
198	v Surrey	The Oval	1960
184	v Nottinghamshire	Scarborough	1960
161	v Northamptonshire	Northampton	1963

D DENTON (11)

153*	v Australians	Bradford	1905
165	v Hampshire	Bournemouth	1905
172	v Gloucestershire	Bradford	1905
184	v Nottinghamshire	Nottingham	1909
182	v Derbyshire	Chesterfield	1910

INDIVIDUAL INNINGS OF 150 AND OVER *(Continued)*

D DENTON *(Continued)*

200*	v Warwickshire	Birmingham	1912
182	v Gloucestershire	Bristol	1912
221	v Kent	Tunbridge Wells	1912
191	v Hampshire	Southampton	1912
168*	v Hampshire	Southampton	1914
209*	v Worcestershire	Worcester	1920

A W GALE (4)

150	v. Surrey	The Oval	2008
151*	v. Nottinghamshire	Nottingham	2010
272	v. Nottinghamshire	Scarborough	2013
164	v. Worcestershire	Scarborough	2015

P A GIBB (1)

157*	v. Nottinghamshire	Sheffield	1935

S HAIGH (1)

159	v. Nottinghamshire	Sheffield	1901

L HALL (1)

160	v. Lancashire	Bradford	1887

J H HAMPSHIRE (5)

150	v. Leicestershire	Bradford	1964
183*	v. Sussex	Hove	1971
157*	v. Nottinghamshire	Worksop	1974
158	v. Gloucestershire	Harrogate	1974
155*	v. Gloucestershire	Leeds	1976

I J HARVEY (1)

209*	v. Somerset	Leeds	2005

LORD HAWKE (1)

166	v. Warwickshire	Birmingham	1896

G H HIRST (15)

186	v. Surrey	The Oval	1899
155	v. Nottinghamshire	Scarborough	1900
214	v. Worcestershire	Worcester	1901
153	v. Leicestershire	Dewsbury	1903
153	v. Oxford University	Oxford	1904
152	v. Hampshire	Portsmouth	1904
157	v. Kent	Tunbridge Wells	1904
341	v. Leicestershire	Leicester (Aylestone Road)	1905
232*	v. Surrey	The Oval	1905
169	v. Oxford University	Oxford	1906
158	v. Cambridge University	Cambridge	1910
156	v. Lancashire	Manchester	1911
218	v. Sussex	Hastings	1911
166*	v. Sussex	Hastings	1913
180*	v. MCC	Lord's	1919

P HOLMES (16)

302*	v. Hampshire	Portsmouth	1920
150	v. Derbyshire	Chesterfield	1921
277*	v. Northamptonshire	Harrogate	1921
209	v. Warwickshire	Birmingham	1922

P HOLMES *(Continued)*

220*	v. Warwickshire	Huddersfield	1922
199	v. Somerset	Hull	1923
315*	v. Middlesex	Lord's	1925
194	v. Leicestershire	Hull	1925
159	v. Hampshire	Southampton	1925
180	v. Gloucestershire	Gloucester	1927
175*	v. New Zealanders	Bradford	1927
179*	v. Middlesex	Leeds	1928
275	v. Warwickshire	Bradford	1928
285	v. Nottinghamshire	Nottingham	1929
250	v. Warwickshire	Birmingham	1931
224*	v. Essex	Leyton	1932

L HUTTON (31)

196	v. Worcestershire	Worcester	1934
163	v. Surrey	Leeds	1936
161	v. MCC	Lord's	1937
271*	v. Derbyshire	Sheffield	1937
153	v. Leicestershire	Hull	1937
180	v. Cambridge University	Cambridge	1938
158	v. Warwickshire	Birmingham	1939
280*	v. Hampshire	Sheffield	1939
151	v. Surrey	Leeds	1939
177	v. Sussex	Scarborough	1939
183*	v. Indians	Bradford	1946
171*	v. Northamptonshire	Hull	1946
197	v. Glamorgan	Swansea	1947
197	v. Essex	Southend-on-Sea	1947
270*	v. Hampshire	Bournemouth	1947
176*	v. Sussex	Sheffield	1948
155	v. Sussex	Hove	1948
167	v. New Zealanders	Bradford	1949
201	v. Lancashire	Manchester	1949
165	v. Sussex	Hove	1949
269*	v. Northamptonshire	Wellingborough	1949
156	v. Essex	Colchester (Castle Park)	1950
153	v. Nottinghamshire	Nottingham	1950
156	v. South Africans	Sheffield	1951
151	v. Surrey	The Oval	1951
194*	v. Nottinghamshire	Nottingham	1951
152	v. Lancashire	Leeds	1952
189	v. Kent	Leeds	1952
178	v. Somerset	Leeds	1953
163	v. Combined Services	Harrogate	1954
194	v. Nottinghamshire	Nottingham	1955

R A HUTTON (1)

189	v. Pakistanis	Bradford	1971

R ILLINGWORTH (2)

150	v. Essex	Colchester (Castle Park)	1959
162	v. Indians	Sheffield	1959

Hon F S JACKSON (3)

160	v. Gloucestershire	Sheffield	1898
155	v. Middlesex	Bradford	1899
158	v. Surrey	Bradford	1904

INDIVIDUAL INNINGS OF 150 AND OVER *(Continued)*

P A JAQUES (7)

243	v. Hampshire	Southampton (Rose Bowl)	2004
173	v. Glamorgan	Leeds	2004
176	v. Northamptonshire	Leeds	2005
219	v. Derbyshire	Leeds	2005
172	v. Durham	Scarborough	2005
160	v. Gloucestershire	Bristol	2012
152	v. Durham	Scarborough	2013

R KILNER (5)

169	v. Gloucestershire	Bristol	1914
206*	v. Derbyshire	Sheffield	1920
166	v. Northamptonshire	Northampton	1921
150	v. Northamptonshire	Harrogate	1921
150	v. Middlesex	Lord's	1926

T KOHLER-CADMORE (2)

176	v. Leeds/Bradford MCCU	Weetwood, Leeds	2019
165*	v. Warwickshire	Birmingham	2019

F LEE (1)

165	v. Lancashire	Bradford	1887

A Z LEES (1)

275*	v. Derbyshire	Chesterfield	2013

D S LEHMANN (13)

177	v. Somerset	Taunton	1997
163*	v. Leicestershire	Leicester	1997
182	v. Hampshire	Portsmouth	1997
200	v. Worcestershire	Worcester	1998
187*	v. Somerset	Bath	2001
252	v. Lancashire	Leeds	2001
193	v. Leicestershire	Leicester	2001
216	v. Sussex	Arundel	2002
187	v. Lancashire	Leeds	2002
150	v. Warwickshire	Birmingham	2006
193	v. Kent	Canterbury	2006
172	v. Kent	Leeds	2006
339	v. Durham	Leeds	2006

E I LESTER (5)

186	v. Warwickshire	Scarborough	1949
178	v. Nottinghamshire	Nottingham	1952
157	v. Cambridge University	Hull	1953
150	v. Oxford University	Oxford	1954
163	v. Essex	Romford	1954

M LEYLAND (17)

191	v. Glamorgan	Swansea	1926
204*	v. Middlesex	Sheffield	1927
247	v. Worcestershire	Worcester	1928
189*	v. Glamorgan	Huddersfield	1928
211*	v. Lancashire	Leeds	1930
172	v. Middlesex	Sheffield	1930
186	v. Derbyshire	Leeds	1930
189	v. Middlesex	Sheffield	1932
153	v. Leicestershire	Leicester (Aylestone Road)	1932
166	v. Leicestershire	Bradford	1932
153*	v. Hampshire	Bournemouth	1932

M LEYLAND *(Continued)*

192	v. Northamptonshire	Leeds	1933
210*	v. Kent	Dover	1933
263	v. Essex	Hull	1936
163*	v. Surrey	Leeds	1936
167	v. Worcestershire	Stourbridge	1937
180*	v. Middlesex	Lord's	1939

E LOCKWOOD *(1)*

208	v. Kent	Gravesend	1883

J D LOVE *(4)*

163	v. Nottinghamshire	Bradford	1976
170*	v. Worcestershire	Worcester	1979
161	v. Warwickshire	Birmingham	1981
154	v. Lancashire	Manchester	1981

F A LOWSON *(10)*

155	v. Kent	Maidstone	1951
155	v. Worcestershire	Bradford	1952
166	v. Scotland	Glasgow	1953
259*	v. Worcestershire	Worcester	1953
165	v. Sussex	Hove	1954
164	v. Essex	Scarborough	1954
150*	v. Kent	Dover	1954
183*	v. Oxford University	Oxford	1956
154	v. Somerset	Taunton	1956
154	v. Cambridge University	Cambridge	1957

R G LUMB *(2)*

159	v. Somerset	Harrogate	1979
165*	v. Gloucestershire	Bradford	1984

A LYTH *(5)*

248 *	v. Leicestershire	Leicester	2012
230	v. Northamptonshire	Northampton	2014
251	v. Lancashire	Manchester	2014
202	v. Surrey	The Oval	2016
194	v. Leeds/Bradford MCCU	Leeds	2017

A McGRATH *(7)*

165	v. Lancashire	Leeds	2002
174	v. Derbyshire	Derby	2004
165*	v. Leicestershire	Leicester	2005
173*	v. Worcestershire	Leeds	2005
158	v. Derbyshire	Derby	2005
188*	v. Warwickshire	Birmingham	2007
211	v. Warwickshire	Birmingham	2009

D R MARTYN *(1)*

238	v. Gloucestershire	Leeds	2003

A A METCALFE *(7)*

151	v. Northamptonshire	Luton	1986
151	v. Lancashire	Manchester	1986
152	v. MCC	Scarborough	1987
216*	v. Middlesex	Leeds	1988
162	v. Gloucestershire	Cheltenham	1990
150*	v. Derbyshire	Scarborough	1990
194*	v. Nottinghamshire	Nottingham	1990

INDIVIDUAL INNINGS OF 150 AND OVER *(Continued)*

A MITCHELL (7)

189	v. Northamptonshire	Northampton	1926
176	v. Nottinghamshire	Bradford	1930
177*	v. Gloucestershire	Bradford	1932
150*	v. Worcestershire	Worcester	1933
158	v. MCC	Scarborough	1933
152	v. Hampshire	Bradford	1934
181	v. Surrey	Bradford	1934

F MITCHELL (2)

194	v. Leicestershire	Leicester	1899
162*	v. Warwickshire	Birmingham	1901

M D MOXON (14)

153	v. Lancashire	Leeds	1983
153	v. Somerset	Leeds	1985
168	v. Worcestershire	Worcester	1985
191	v. Northamptonshire	Scarborough	1989
162*	v. Surrey	The Oval	1989
218*	v. Sussex	Eastbourne	1990
200	v. Essex	Colchester (Castle Park)	1991
183	v. Gloucestershire	Cheltenham	1992
171*	v. Kent	Leeds	1993
161*	v. Lancashire	Manchester	1994
274*	v. Worcestershire	Worcester	1994
203*	v. Kent	Leeds	1995
213	v. Glamorgan	Cardiff (Sophia Gardens)	1996
155	v. Pakistan 'A'	Leeds	1997

E OLDROYD (5)

151*	v. Glamorgan	Cardiff	1922
194	v. Worcestershire	Worcester	1923
162*	v. Glamorgan	Swansea	1928
168	v. Glamorgan	Hull	1929
164*	v. Somerset	Bath	1930

D E V PADGETT (1)

161*	v. Oxford University	Oxford	1959

R PEEL (2)

158	v. Middlesex	Lord's	1889
210*	v. Warwickshire	Birmingham	1896

A U RASHID (3)

157*	v. Lancashire	Leeds	2009
180	v. Somerset	Leeds	2013
159*	v. Lancashire	Manchester	2014

W RHODES (8)

196	v. Worcestershire	Worcester	1904
201	v. Somerset	Taunton	1905
199	v. Sussex	Hove	1909
176	v. Nottinghamshire	Harrogate	1912
152	v. Leicestershire	Leicester (Aylestone Road)	1913
167*	v. Nottinghamshire	Leeds	1920
267*	v. Leicestershire	Leeds	1921
157	v. Derbyshire	Leeds	1925

P E ROBINSON (2)

150*	v. Derbyshire	Scarborough	1990
189	v. Lancashire	Scarborough	1991

J E ROOT (5)

160	v. Sussex	Scarborough	2011
222 *	v. Hampshire	Southampton (West End)	2012
182	v. Durham	Chester-le-Street	2013
236	v. Derbyshire	Leeds	2013
	2013 innings consecutive		
213	v.Surrey	Leeds	2016

J W ROTHERY (1)

161	v. Kent	Dover	1908

J A RUDOLPH (5)

220	v. Warwickshire	Scarborough	2007
155	v. Somerset	Taunton	2008
198	v. Worcestershire	Leeds	2009
191	v. Somerset	Taunton	2009
228*	v. Durham	Leeds	2010

H RUDSTON (1)

164	v. Leicestershire	Leicester (Aylestone Rd)	1904

J J SAYERS (3)

187	v. Kent	Tunbridge Wells	2007
173	v. Warwickshire	Birmingham	2009
152	v. Somerset	Taunton	2009

A B SELLERS (1)

204	v. Cambridge University	Cambridge	1936

K SHARP (2)

173	v. Derbyshire	Chesterfield	1984
181	v. Gloucestershire	Harrogate	1986

P J SHARPE (4)

203*	v. Cambridge University	Cambridge	1960
152	v. Kent	Sheffield	1960
197	v. Pakistanis	Leeds	1967
172*	v. Glamorgan	Swansea	1971

G A SMITHSON (1)

169	v. Leicestershire	Leicester	1947

W B STOTT (2)

181	v. Essex	Sheffield	1957
186	v. Warwickshire	Birmingham	1960

H SUTCLIFFE (39)

174	v. Kent	Dover	1919
232	v. Surrey	The Oval	1922
213	v. Somerset	Dewsbury	1924
160	v. Sussex	Sheffield	1924
255*	v. Essex	Southend-on-Sea	1924
235	v. Middlesex	Leeds	1925
206	v. Warwickshire	Dewsbury	1925
171	v. MCC	Scarborough	1925

INDIVIDUAL INNINGS OF 150 AND OVER *(Continued)*

H SUTCLIFFE *(Continued)*

200	v. Leicestershire	Leicester (Aylestone Road)	1926
176	v. Surrey	Leeds	1927
169	v. Nottinghamshire	Bradford	1927
228	v. Sussex	Eastbourne	1928
150	v. Northamptonshire	Northampton	1929
150*	v. Essex	Dewsbury	1930
173	v. Sussex	Hove	1930
173*	v. Cambridge University	Cambridge	1931
230	v. Kent	Folkestone	1931
183	v. Somerset	Dewsbury	1931
195	v. Lancashire	Sheffield	1931
187	v. Leicestershire	Leicester (Aylestone Road)	1931
153*	v. Warwickshire	Hull	1932
313	v. Essex	Leyton	1932
270	v. Sussex	Leeds	1932
182	v. Derbyshire	Leeds	1932
194	v. Essex	Scarborough	1932
205	v. Warwickshire	Birmingham	1933
177	v. Middlesex	Bradford	1933
174	v. Leicestershire	Leicester (Aylestone Road)	1933
152	v. Cambridge University	Cambridge	1934
166	v. Essex	Hull	1934
203	v. Surrey	The Oval	1934
187*	v. Worcestershire	Bradford	1934
200*	v. Worcestershire	Sheffield	1935
212	v. Leicestershire	Leicester (Aylestone Road)	1935
202	v. Middlesex	Scarborough	1936
189	v. Leicestershire	Hull	1937
165	v. Lancashire	Manchester	1939
234*	v. Leicestershire	Hull	1939
175	v. Middlesex	Lord's	1939

W H H SUTCLIFFE (3)

171*	v. Worcestershire	Worcester	1952
181	v. Kent	Canterbury	1952
161*	v. Glamorgan	Harrogate	1955

K TAYLOR (8)

168*	v. Nottinghamshire	Nottingham	1956
159	v. Leicestershire	Sheffield	1961
203*	v. Warwickshire	Birmingham	1961
178*	v. Oxford University	Oxford	1962
163	v. Nottinghamshire	Leeds	1962
153	v. Lancashire	Manchester	1964
160	v. Australians	Sheffield	1964
162	v. Worcestershire	Kidderminster	1967

T L TAYLOR (1)

156	v. Hampshire	Harrogate	1901

J TUNNICLIFFE (2)

243	v. Derbyshire	Chesterfield	1898
158	v. Worcestershire	Worcester	1900

G ULYETT (1)

199*	v. Derbyshire	Sheffield	1887

M P VAUGHAN (7)

183	v. Glamorgan	Cardiff (Sophia Gardens)	1996
183	v. Northamptonshire	Northampton	1996
161	v. Essex	Ilford	1997
177	v. Durham	Chester-le-Street	1998
151	v. Essex	Chelmsford	1999
153	v. Kent	Scarborough	1999
155*	v. Derbyshire	Leeds	2000

E WAINWRIGHT (3)

171	v. Middlesex	Lord's	1897
153	v. Leicestershire	Leicester	1899
228	v. Surrey	The Oval	1899

W WATSON (7)

153*	v. Surrey	The Oval	1947
172	v. Derbyshire	Scarborough	1948
162*	v. Somerset	Leeds	1953
163	v. Sussex	Sheffield	1955
174	v. Lancashire	Sheffield	1955
214*	v. Worcestershire	Worcester	1955
162	v. Northamptonshire	Harrogate	1957

C WHITE (6)

181	v. Lancashire	Leeds	1996
172*	v. Worcestershire	Leeds	1997
186	v. Lancashire	Manchester	2001
183	v. Glamorgan	Scarborough	2001
161	v. Leicestershire	Scarborough	2002
173*	v. Derbyshire	Derby	2003

K S WILLIAMSON (1)

189	v. Sussex	Scarborough	2014

B B WILSON (2)

150	v. Warwickshire	Birmingham	1912
208	v. Sussex	Bradford	1914

J V WILSON (7)

157*	v. Sussex	Leeds	1949
157	v. Essex	Sheffield	1950
166*	v. Sussex	Hull	1951
223*	v. Scotland	Scarborough	1951
154	v. Oxford University	Oxford	1952
230	v. Derbyshire	Sheffield	1952
165	v. Oxford University	Oxford	1956

M J WOOD (5)

200*	v. Warwickshire	Leeds	1998
157	v. Northamptonshire	Leeds	2003
207	v. Somerset	Taunton	2003
155	v. Hampshire	Scarborough	2003
202*	v. Bangladesh 'A'	Leeds	2005

N W D YARDLEY (2)

177	v. Derbyshire	Scarborough	1947
183*	v. Hampshire	Leeds	1951

YOUNUS KHAN (2)

202*	v. Hampshire	Southampton (Rose Bowl)	2007
217*	v. Kent	Scarborough	2007

CENTURIES BY CURRENT PLAYERS

A complete list of all First-class Centuries up to and including 2007 is to be found in the 2008 edition

J M BAIRSTOW (15)

205	v. Nottinghamshire	Nottingham	2011
136	v. Somerset	Taunton	2011
182	v. Leicestershire	Scarborough	2012
118	v. Leicestershire	Leicester	2012
107	v. Kent	Leeds	2012
186	v. Derbyshire	Leeds	2013
123	v. Leeds/Bradford	Leeds	2014
161*	v. Sussex	Arundel	2014
102	v. Hampshire	Leeds	2015
125*	v. Middlesex	Leeds	2015
219*	v. Durham	Chester-le-Street **	2015
108	v. Warwickshire	Birmingham **	2015

(** consecutive innings)

139	v. Worcestershire	Scarborough	2015
246	v. Lancashire	Leeds	2016
198	v. Surrey	Leeds	2016

G S BALLANCE (26)

111	v. Warwickshire	Birmingham	2011
121*	v. Gloucestershire	Bristol	2012
112	v. Leeds/Bradford MCCU	Leeds	2013
107	v. Somerset	Leeds	2013
141	v. Nottinghamshire	Scarborough	2013
112	v. Warwickshire	Leeds	2013
148	v. Surrey 1st inns	The Oval **	2013
108*	v. Surrey 2nd inns	The Oval **	2013
101	v. Leeds/Bradford MCCU	Leeds **	2014
174	v. Northamptonshire	Leeds	2014
130	v. Middlesex	Lord's	2014
165	v. Sussex	Hove	2015
105	v. MCC	Abu Dhabi	2016
132	v. Middlesex	Scarborough	2016
101*	v. Nottinghamshire	Scarborough	2016
120	v. Hampshire	Leeds	2017
108	v. Hampshire (1st innings)	West End, Southampton	2017
203*	v. Hampshire (2nd innings)	West End, Southampton	2017
109	v. Hampshire	West End, Southampton	2018
104	v. Nottinghamshire	Nottingham	2018
194	v. Worcestershire	Worcester	2018
101*	v. Nottinghamshire	Nottingham	2019
148*	v. Hampshire	West End, Southampton	2019
159	v. Kent	Canterbury	2019
100	v. Hampshire	Leeds	2019
111	v. Somerset	Leeds	2019

T T BRESNAN (5)

116	v. Surrey	The Oval	2007
101*	v. Warwickshire	Scarborough	2007
100*	v. Somerset	Taunton	2015
169*	v. Durham	Chester-le-Street	2015
142*	v. Middlesex	Lord's	2016

H C BROOK (2)

124	v. Essex	Chelmsford	2018
101	v. Somerset	Leeds	2019

CENTURIES BY CURRENT PLAYERS *(Continued)*

W A R FRAINE (1)

106	v. Surrey	Scarborough	2019

T KOHLER-CADMORE (5)

106	v. Nottinghamshire	Nottingham	2018
105*	v. Lancashire	Leeds	2018
176	v. Leeds/Bradford MCCU	Weetwood, Leeds	2019
102	v. Somerset	Leeds	2019
165*	v. Warwickshire	Birmingham	2019

A LYTH (22)

132	v. Nottinghamshire	Nottingham	2008
142	v. Somerset	Taunton	2010
133	v. Hampshire	Southampton	2010
100	v. Lancashire	Manchester	2010
248*	v. Leicestershire	Leicester	2012
111	v. Leeds/Bradford	Leeds	2013
105	v. Somerset	Taunton	2013
130	v. Leeds/Bradford MCCU	Leeds	2014
104	v. Durham	Chester-le-Street	2014
230	v. Northamptonshire	Northampton	2014
143	v. Durham	Leeds	2014
117	v. Middlesex	Scarborough	2014
251	v. Lancashire	Manchester	2014
122	v. Nottinghamshire	Nottingham	2014
113	v. MCC	Abu Dhabi	2015
111	v. Hampshire	Leeds	2016
106	v. Somerset	Taunton	2016
202	v. Surrey	The Oval	2016
114*	v. Durham	Leeds	2016
194	v. Leeds/Bradford MCCU	Leeds	2017
100	v. Lancashire	Leeds	2017
134*	v. Hampshire	Leeds	2018

A U RASHID (10)

108	v. Worcestershire	Kidderminster	2007
111	v. Sussex	Hove	2008
117*	v. Hampshire	Basingstoke	2009
157*	v. Lancashire	Leeds	2009
180	v. Somerset	Leeds	2013
110*	v. Warwickshire	Birmingham	2013
103	v. Somerset	Taunton	2013
108	v. Somerset	Taunton	2014
159*	v. Lancashire	Manchester	2014
127	v. Durham	Scarborough	2015
	(2013 consecutive innings)		

J E ROOT (7)

160	v. Sussex	Scarborough	2011
222 *	v. Hampshire	Southampton (West End)	2012
125	v. Northamptonshire	Leeds	2012
182	v. Durham	Chester-le-Street	2013
236	v. Derbyshire	Leeds	2013
213	v. Surrey	Leeds	2016
130*	v. Nottinghamshire	Nottingham	2019

J A TATTERSALL (1)

135*	v. Leeds/Bradford MCCU	Weetwood, Leeds	2019

CENTURIES

(Including highest score)

112	H Sutcliffe	313	v. Essex	at Leyton	1932
103	G Boycott	260*	v. Essex	at Colchester (Garrison Gd)	1970
85	L Hutton	280*	v. Hampshire	at Sheffield	1939
62	M Leyland	263	v. Essex	at Hull	1936
61	D Denton	221	v. Kent	at Tunbridge Wells	1912
60	P Holmes	315*	v. Middlesex	at Lord's	1925
56	G H Hirst	341	v. Leicestershire	at Leicester (Aylestone Rd)	1905
46	W Rhodes	267*	v. Leicestershire	at Leeds	1921
41	M D Moxon	274*	v. Worcestershire	at Worcester	1994
39	A Mitchell	189	v. Northamptonshire	at Northampton	1926
37	E Oldroyd	194	v. Worcestershire	at Worcester	1923
34	J H Hampshire	183*	v. Sussex	at Hove	1971
34	A McGrath	211	v. Warwickshire	at Birmingham	2009
33	D B Close	198	v. Surrey	at The Oval	1960
30	F A Lowson	259*	v. Worcestershire	at Worcester	1953
29	D E V Padgett	161*	v. Oxford University	at Oxford	1959
29	J V Wilson	230	v. Derbyshire	at Sheffield	1952
28	D Byas	213	v. Worcestershire	at Scarborough	1995
27	W Barber	255	v. Surrey	at Sheffield	1935
26	G S Ballance	203*	v, Hampshire	at West End, Southampton	2017
26	D S Lehmann	339	v. Durham	at Leeds	2006
26	W Watson	214*	v. Worcestershire	at Worcester	1955
25	A A Metcalfe	216*	v. Middlesex	at Leeds	1988
24	E I Lester	186	v. Warwickshire	at Scarborough	1949
23	J T Brown	311	v. Sussex	at Sheffield	1897
23	P J Sharpe	203*	v. Cambridge University	at Cambridge	1960
22	R G Lumb	165*	v. Gloucestershire	at Bradford	1984
22	A Lyth	251	v. Lancashire	at Manchester	2014
22	J Tunnicliffe	243	v. Derbyshire	at Chesterfield	1898
21	Hon F S Jackson	160	v. Gloucestershire	at Sheffield	1898
20	M P Vaughan	183	v. Glamorgan	at Cardiff (Sophia Gardens)	1996
and		183	v. Northamptonshire	at Northampton	1996
19	A W Gale	272	v. Nottinghamshire	at Scarborough	2013
19	C White	186	v. Lancashire	at Manchester	2001
18	J A Rudolph	228*	v. Durham	at Leeds	2010
18	E Wainwright	228	v. Surrey	at The Oval	1899
17	W B Stott	186	v. Warwickshire	at Birmingham	1960
17	N W D Yardley	183*	v. Hampshire	at Leeds	1951
16	K Taylor	203*	v. Warwickshire	at Birmingham	1961
16	M J Wood	207	v. Somerset	at Taunton	2003
15	J M Bairstow	246	v. Hampshire	at Leeds	2016
15	R Kilner	206*	v. Derbyshire	at Sheffield	1920
15	G Ulyett	199*	v. Derbyshire	at Sheffield	1887
15	B B Wilson	208	v. Sussex	at Bradford	1914
14	R Illingworth	162	v. Indians	at Sheffield	1959
13	J D Love	170*	v. Worcestershire	at Worcester	1979
12	R J Blakey	223*	v. Northamptonshire	at Leeds	2003
12	H Halliday	144	v. Derbyshire	at Chesterfield	1950
11	P A Jaques	243	v. Hampshire	at Southampton (Rose Bowl)	2004
11	A Z Lees	275*	v. Derbyshire	at Chesterfield	2013
11	K Sharp	181	v. Gloucestershire	at Harrogate	1986
10	C W J Athey	134	v. Derbyshire	at Derby	1982
10	Lord Hawke	166	v. Warwickshire	at Birmingham	1896
10	F Mitchell	194	v. Leicestershire	at Leicester	1899
10	A U Rashid	180	v. Somerset	at Leeds	2013
9	D L Bairstow	145	v. Middlesex	at Scarborough	1980

9	M G Bevan	160*	v. Surrey	at Middlesbrough	1996
9	L Hall	160	v. Lancashire	at Bradford	1887
9	J J Sayers	187	v. Kent	at Tunbridge Wells	2007
8	W Bates	136	v. Sussex	at Hove	1886
8	M J Lumb	144	v. Middlesex	at Southgate	2006
8	T L Taylor	156	v. Hampshire	at Harrogate	1901
7	J B Bolus	146*	v. Hampshire	at Portsmouth	1960
7	E Robinson	135*	v. Leicestershire	at Leicester (Aylestone Rd)	1921
7	P E Robinson	189	v. Lancashire	at Scarborough	1991
7	J E Root	236	v. Derbyshire	at Leeds	2013
6	E Lockwood	208	v. Kent	at Gravesend	1883
6	R Peel	210*	v. Warwickshire	at Birmingham	1896
6	W H H Sutcliffe	181	v. Kent	at Canterbury	1952
5	T T Bresnan	169*	v. Durham	at Chester-le-Street	2015
5	T Kohler-Cadmore	176	v. Leeds/Bradford MCCU	at Weetwood, Leeds	2019
5	C M Old	116	v. Indians	at Bradford	1974
4	I Grimshaw	129*	v. Cambridge University	at Sheffield	1885
4	S Haigh	159	v. Nottinghamshire	at Sheffield	1901
4	S N Hartley	114	v. Gloucestershire	at Bradford	1982
4	R A Hutton	189	v. Pakistanis	at Bradford	1971
4	J A Leaning	123	v. Somerset	at Taunton	2015
4	A B Sellers	204	v. Cambridge University	at Cambridge	1936
3	G L Brophy	177*	v. Worcestershire	at Worcester	2011
3	P Carrick	131*	v. Northamptonshire	at Northampton	1980
3	A J Dalton	128	v. Middlesex	at Leeds	1972
3	A Drake	147*	v. Derbyshire	at Chesterfield	1911
3	F Lee	165	v. Lancashire	at Bradford	1887
3	G G Macaulay	125*	v. Nottinghamshire	at Nottingham	1921
3	R Moorhouse	113	v. Somerset	at Taunton	1896
3	R M Pyrah	134*	v. Loughborough MCCU	at Leeds	2010
3	J W Rothery	161	v. Kent	at Dover	1908
3	J Rowbotham	113	v. Surrey	at The Oval	1873
3	T F Smailes	117	v. Glamorgan	at Cardiff	1938
3	Younus Khan	217*	v. Kent	at Scarborough	2007
2	M W Booth	210	v. Worcestershire	at Worcester	1911
2	H C Brook	124	v. Essex	at Chelmsford	2018
2	D C F Burton	142*	v. Hampshire	at Dewsbury	1919
2	K R Davidson	128	v. Kent	at Maidstone	1934
2	P A Gibb	157*	v. Nottinghamshire	at Sheffield	1935
2	P J Hartley	127*	v. Lancashire	at Manchester	1988
2	I J Harvey	209*	v. Somerset	at Leeds	2005
2	C Johnson	107	v. Somerset	at Sheffield	1973
2	S A Kellett	125*	v. Derbyshire	at Chesterfield	1991
2	N Kilner	112	v. Leicestershire	at Leeds	1921
2	B Parker	138*	v. Oxford University	at Oxford	1997
2	A Sellers	105	v. Middlesex	at Lord's	1893
2	E Smith (Morley)	129	v. Hampshire	at Bradford	1899
2	G A Smithson	169	v. Leicestershire	at Leicester	1947
2	G B Stevenson	115*	v. Warwickshire	at Birmingham	1982
2	F S Trueman	104	v. Northamptonshire	at Northampton	1963
2	C Turner	130	v. Somerset	at Sheffield	1936
2	D J Wainwright	104*	v. Sussex	at Hove	2008

2	T A Wardall	106	v. Gloucestershire	at Gloucester (Spa Ground)	1892
1	Azeem Rafiq	100	v. Worcestershire	at Worcester	2009
1	A T Barber	100	v. England XI	at Sheffield	1929
1	H D Bird	181*	v. Glamorgan	at Bradford	1959
1	T J D Birtles	104	v. Lancashire	at Sheffield	1914
1	G S Blewett	190	v. Northamptonshire	at Scarborough	1999
1	J A Brooks	109*	v. Lancashire	at Manchester	2017
1	M T G Elliott	127	v, Warwickshire	at Birmingham	2002
1	T Emmett	104	v. Gloucestershire	at Clifton	1873
1	G M Fellows	109	v. Lancashire	at Manchester	2002
1	A J Finch	110	v. Warwickshire	at Birmingham	2014
1	W A R Fraine	106	v. Surrey	at Scarborough	2019
1	J N Gillespie	123*	v. Surrey	at The Oval	2007
1	D Gough	121	v. Warwickshire	at Leeds	1996
1	A K D Gray	104	v. Somerset	at Taunton	2003
1	A P Grayson	100	v. Worcestershire	at Worcester	1994
1	F E Greenwood	104*	v. Glamorgan	at Hull	1929
1	G M Hamilton	125	v. Hampshire	at Leeds	2000
1	P S P Handscomb	101*	v. Lancashire	at Manchester	2017
1	W E Harbord	109	v. Oxford University	at Oxford	1930
1	R Iddison	112	v. Cambridgeshire	at Hunslet	1869
1	W G Keighley	110	v. Surrey	at Leeds	1951
1	R A Kettleborough	108	v. Essex	at Leeds	1996
1	B Leadbeater	140*	v. Hampshire	at Portsmouth	1976
1	J S Lehmann	116	v. Somerset	at Leeds	2016
1	D R Martyn	238	v. Gloucestershire	at Leeds	2003
1	G J Maxwell	140	v. Durham	at Scarborough	2015
1	S E Marsh	125*	v. Surrey	at The Oval	2017
1	J T Newstead	100*	v. Nottinghamshire	at Nottingham	1908
1	L E Plunkett	126	v. Hampshire	at Leeds	2016
1	C A Pujara	133*	v. Hampshire	at Leeds	2015
1	R B Richardson	112	v. Warwickshire	at Birmingham	1993
1	H Rudston	164	v. Leicestershire	at Leicester (Aylestone Rd)	1904
1	A Sidebottom	124	v. Glamorgan	at Cardiff (Sophia Gardens)	1977
1	I G Swallow	114	v. MCC	at Scarborough	1987
1	J A Tattersall	135*	v. Leeds/Bradford MCCU	at Weetwood, Leeds	2019
1	S R Tendulkar	100	v. Durham	at Durham	1992
1	J Thewlis	108	v. Surrey	at The Oval	1868
1	C T Tyson	100*	v. Hampshire	at Southampton	1921
1	H Verity	101	v. Jamaica	at Kingston (Sabina Park)	1935/36
1	A Waddington	114	v. Worcestershire	at Leeds	1927
1	W A I Washington	100*	v. Surrey	at Leeds	1902
1	H Wilkinson	113	v. MCC	at Scarborough	1904
1	W H Wilkinson	103	v. Sussex	at Sheffield	1909
1	K S Williamson	189	v. Sussex	at Scarborough	2014
1	E R Wilson	104*	v. Essex	at Bradford	1913
1	A Wood	123*	v. Worcestershire	at Sheffield	1935
1	J D Woodford	101	v. Warwickshire	at Middlesbrough	1971

SUMMARY OF CENTURIES
FOR AND AGAINST YORKSHIRE 1863-2019

FOR YORKSHIRE				AGAINST YORKSHIRE		
Total	In Yorkshire	Away		Total	In Yorkshire	Away
110	65	45	Derbyshire	57	27	30
32	16	16	Durham	24	13	11
76	34	42	Essex	46	21	25
68	38	30	Glamorgan	23	13	10
87	41	46	Gloucestershire	53	27	26
101	44	57	Hampshire	61	27	34
82	37	45	Kent	64	32	32
117	58	59	Lancashire	116	58	58
97	52	45	Leicestershire	46	23	23
97	49	48	Middlesex	92	38	54
81	35	46	Northamptonshire	53	25	28
131	60	71	Nottinghamshire	86	33	53
105	53	52	Somerset	62	23	39
120	51	69	Surrey	114	41	73
90	42	48	Sussex	77	33	44
106	36	70	Warwickshire	75	29	46
75	32	43	Worcestershire	45	17	28
1	1	0	Cambridgeshire	0	0	0
1576	**744**	**832**	**Totals**	**1094**	**480**	**614**
9	9	0	Australians	16	16	0
9	9	0	Indians	7	7	0
8	8	0	New Zealanders	3	3	0
5	5	0	Pakistanis	1	1	0
9	9	0	South Africans	7	7	0
5	5	0	Sri Lankans	1	1	0
5	5	0	West Indians	6	6	0
1	1	0	Zimbabweans	0	0	0
3	3	0	Bangladesh 'A'	1	1	0
0	0	0	India 'A'	3	3	0
1	1	0	Pakistan 'A'	1	1	0
45	1	44	Cambridge University	20	2	18
2	2	0	Combined Services	0	0	0
1	0	1	Durham MCCU	1	0	1
4	3	1	England XIs	3	2	1
0	0	0	International XI	1	1	0
1	0	1	Ireland	0	0	0
3	0	3	Jamaica	3	0	3
10	8	2	Leeds/Bradford MCCU	0	0	0
1	0	1	Liverpool and District	0	0	0
2	2	0	Loughborough MCCU	1	1	0
1	0	1	Mashonaland	0	0	0
2	0	2	Matabeleland	1	0	1
54	38	16	MCC	52	34	18
39	0	39	Oxford University	11	0	11
6	0	6	Rest of England	15	0	15
9	5	4	Scotland	1	0	1
3	3	0	C L Thornton's XI	4	4	0
0	0	0	Western Province	1	0	1
1	1	0	I Zingari	1	1	0
239	**118**	**121**	**Totals**	**161**	**91**	**70**
1815	**862**	**953**	**Grand Totals**	**1255**	**571**	**684**

FOUR CENTURIES IN ONE INNINGS

			F S Jackson	117
1896	v.	Warwickshire	E Wainwright	126
		at Birmingham	Lord Hawke	166
			R Peel	*210

(First instance in First-Class cricket)

THREE CENTURIES IN ONE INNINGS

			L Hall	116
1884	v.	Cambridge University	W Bates	133
		at Cambridge	I Grimshaw	115
			G Ulyett	124
1887	v.	Kent	L Hall	110
		at Canterbury	F Lee	119
			J T Brown	311
1897	v.	Sussex	J Tunnicliffe	147
		at Sheffield	E Wainwright	*104
			F S Jackson	155
1899	v.	Middlesex	D Denton	113
		at Bradford	F Mitchell	121
			D Denton	105
1904	v.	Surrey	G H Hirst	104
		at The Oval	J Tunnicliffe	*139
			H Sutcliffe	118
1919	v.	Gloucestershire	D Denton	122
		at Leeds	R Kilner	*115
			P Holmes	130
1925	v.	Glamorgan	H Sutcliffe	121
		at Huddersfield	E Robinson	*108
			P Holmes	105
1928	v.	Middlesex	E Oldroyd	108
		at Lord's	A Mitchell	105
			H Sutcliffe	129
1928	v.	Essex	P Holmes	136
		at Leyton	M Leyland	*133
			E Oldroyd	168
1929	v.	Glamorgan	W Barber	114
		at Hull	F E Greenwood	*104
			H Sutcliffe	107
1933	v.	MCC	A Mitchell	158
		at Scarborough	M Leyland	133
			H Sutcliffe	129
1936	v.	Surrey	L Hutton	163
		at Leeds	M Leyland	*163
			H Sutcliffe	189
1937	v.	Leicestershire	L Hutton	153
		at Hull	M Leyland	*118
			L Hutton	137
1947	v.	Leicestershire	N W D Yardley	100
		at Leicester	G.A Smithson	169

KNIGHT OF THE GREENSWARD

PALACE AWAITS: Yorkshire legend Geoffrey Boycott, who was knighted in September by former Prime Minister Theresa May in her resignation honour's list. Sir Geoffrey, who captained the *White Rose* and England, is pictured championing the Be A Hero organ-donor campaign at the Headingley ground he graced on so many occasions, including scoring his 100th first-class hundred in the 1977 *Ashes* Test.

YORKSHIRE 2019: Back Row, left to right: Matthew Taylor, James Logan, Jordan Thompson, Harry Brook, Matthew Waite, Jared Warner, Ed Barnes, Will Fraine and Ben Birkhead. Middle Row: Bilal Anjam, Karl Carver, Josh Shaw, Duanne Olivier, Jack Leaning, Tom Kohler-Cadmore, Ben Coad, Matthew Fisher, Mathew Pillans, Jack Shutt, Josh Poysden, Tom Loten and Jonathan Tattersall. Front Row: Gary Ballance, Adam Lyth, Tim Bresnan, Martyn Moxon, Director of Cricket; Steven Patterson, Captain; Andrew Gale, First Eleven Coach; Adil Rashid, Joe Root, England Test captain, and David Willey.

TESTIMONIAL FOR ADAM LYTH: Yorkshire's left-handed opener who in 2019 joined the select few to have scored more than 10,000 first-class runs for the county, and who also became the club's all-time leading *T20* run-scorer with 2,619. Yorkshire have designated 2020 as a testimonial year for the 32-year-old from Whitby, who has seven Test caps.

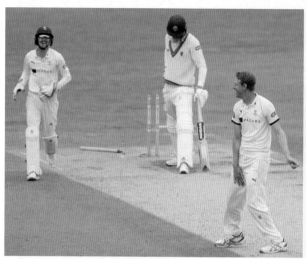

400 UP: Wicketkeeper Jonny Tattersall runs to congratulate Yorkshire captain Steven Patterson on his 400th first-class wicket when he bowls Tom Banton in Somerset's second innings at Emerald Headingley.

UNDER AND OVER: Yorkshire's Harry Brook executes the ramp shot against Northamptonshire Steelbacks in the Vitality Blast.

STANDOUT PERFORMER: South African left-arm spinner Keshav Maharaj, who claimed 38 wickets in only five Championship games for Yorkshire plus two swashbuckling half-centuries down the order.

WICKETKEEPER-BATSMAN: Jonny Tattersall, who became a fixture in Yorkshire's side, hits out against Surrey at Scarborough.

CAPITAL OUTGROUND: Crowds bask in the June sunshine as first-class cricket returns to the city of York for the first time since 1890. York CC and Clifton Park for the first time hosted a County Championship fixture, a pulsating game against Warwickshire which the visitors won deep into the fourth day. This summer the venue will host two Royal London one-day Cup and two women's *Hundred* matches in early August.

OPENING UP: Alyssa Healy, above, hits to leg for Yorkshire Diamonds v. Western Storm at York. Australian wicketkeeper Alyssa, who went in first, bagged five catches and three stumpings in the Kia Super League season as well as totalling 248 runs with a top score of 77.

STRIKE FORCE: Yorkshire's Alice Davidson-Richards, left, and Leigh Kasperek, below, who each totalled 10 wickets. Alice was just ahead in both batting and bowling averages.

YORKSHIRE DIAMONDS 2019. Back Row, left to right: Harrison Allen, Analyst; Melvin Betts, Assistant Coach; Georgia Davis, Alyssa Healy, Helen Fenby, Jane Hildreth, General Manager; Cordelia Griffith, Katie George, Linsey Smith, Pete Sim, Strength and Conditioning Coach, and Ben Coad, YCCC Player. Front Row: Bess Heath, Leigh Kasperek, Beth Langston, Hollie Armitage, Danielle Hazell, Head Coach; Lauren Winfield, Captain; Katie Levick, Alice Davidson-Richards and Jemimah Rodrigues.

		J H Hampshire	*116
1971	v. Oxford University at Oxford	R A Hutton A J Dalton	101 111
1975	v. Gloucestershire at Bristol	G Boycott R G Lumb J H Hampshire	141 101 *106
1995	v. Cambridge University at Cambridge	M D Moxon D Byas M G Bevan	130 181 *113
2001	v. Leicestershire at Leeds	M J Wood M J Lumb D S Lehmann	102 122 104
2001	v. Glamorgan at Scarborough	C White M J Wood D Byas	183 124 104
2007	v. Surrey at The Oval	J A Rudolph T T Bresnan J N Gillespie	122 116 *123
2014	v. Leeds/Bradford MCCU at Leeds	A Lyth G S Ballance J M Bairstow	130 101 123
2016	v. Hampshire at Leeds	A Lyth J M Bairstow L E Plunkett	111 246 126
2019	v. Somerset at Leeds	G S Ballance T Kohler-Cadmore H C Brook	111 102 101

CENTURY IN EACH INNINGS

D Denton	107 and 109*	v. Nottinghamshire at Nottingham, 1906
G H Hirst	111 and 117*	v. Somerset at Bath, 1906
D Denton	133 and 121	v. MCC at Scarborough, 1908
W Rhodes	128 and 115	v. MCC at Scarborough, 1911
P Holmes	126 and 111*	v. Lancashire at Manchester, 1920
H Sutcliffe	107 and 109*	v. MCC at Scarborough, 1926
H Sutcliffe	111 and 100*	v. Nottinghamshire at Nottingham, 1928
E I Lester	126 and 142	v. Northamptonshire at Northampton, 1947
L Hutton	197 and 104	v. Essex at Southend, 1947
E I Lester	125* and 132	v. Lancashire at Manchester, 1948
L Hutton	165 and 100	v. Sussex at Hove, 1949
L Hutton	103 and 137	v. MCC at Scarborough, 1952
G Boycott	103 and 105	v. Nottinghamshire at Sheffield, 1966
G Boycott	163 and 141*	v. Nottinghamshire at Bradford, 1983
M D Moxon	123 and 112*	v. Indians at Scarborough, 1986
A A Metcalfe	194* and 107	v. Nottinghamshire at Nottingham, 1990
M P Vaughan	100 and 151	v. Essex at Chelmsford, 1999
Younus Khan	106 and 202*	v. Hampshire at Southampton, 2007
G S Ballance	148 and 108*	v. Surrey at The Oval, 2013
G S Ballance	108 and 203*	v. Hampshire at West End, 2017

HIGHEST INDIVIDUAL SCORES
FOR AND AGAINST YORKSHIRE

Highest For Yorkshire:
341 G H Hirst v. Leicestershire at Leicester, 1905

Highest Against Yorkshire:
318* W G Grace for Gloucestershire at Cheltenham, 1876

Yorkshire versus:

Derbyshire	*For Yorkshire:*	300 — J T Brown at Chesterfield, 1898
	Against:	270* — C F Hughes at Leeds, 2013
Most Centuries	*For Yorkshire:*	G Boycott 9
	Against:	K J Barnett and W Storer 4 each
Durham	*For Yorkshire:*	339 — D S Lehmann at Leeds, 2006
	Against:	221* — K K Jennings at Chester-le-Street, 2016
Essex	*For Yorkshire:*	313 — H Sutcliffe at Leyton, 1932
	Against:	219* — D J Insole at Colchester, 1949
Most Centuries	*For Yorkshire:*	H Sutcliffe 9
	Against:	F L Fane, K W R Fletcher, G A Gooch and D J Insole 3 each
Glamorgan	*For Yorkshire:*	213 — M D Moxon at Cardiff, 1996
	Against:	202* — H Morris at Cardiff, 1996
Most Centuries	*For Yorkshire:*	G Boycott, P Holmes and H Sutcliffe 5 each
	Against:	H Morris 5
Gloucestershire	*For Yorkshire:*	238 — D R Martyn at Leeds, 2003
	Against:	318*— W G Grace at Cheltenham, 1876
Most Centuries	*For Yorkshire:*	G Boycott 6
	Against:	W G Grace 9
Hampshire	*For Yorkshire:*	302* — P Holmes at Portsmouth, 1920
	Against:	300* — M A Carberry at Southampton, 2011
Most Centuries	*For Yorkshire:*	H Sutcliffe and G S Ballance 6 each
	Against:	C P Mead 10
Kent	*For Yorkshire:*	248 — W Barber at Leeds, 1934.
	Against:	237 — D I Stevens at Leeds, 2019
Most Centuries	*For Yorkshire:*	A McGrath 6
	Against:	F E Woolley 5
Lancashire	*For Yorkshire:*	252 — D S Lehmann at Leeds, 2001
	Against:	225 — G D Lloyd at Leeds, 1997 (Non-Championship)
		206 — S G Law at Leeds, 2007
Most Centuries	*For Yorkshire:*	G Boycott and H Sutcliffe 9 each
	Against:	M A Atherton and C H Lloyd 6 each.
Leicestershire	*For Yorkshire:*	341—G H Hirst at Leicester, 1905
	Against:	218— J J Whitaker at Bradford, 1996
Most Centuries	*For Yorkshire:*	H Sutcliffe 10
	Against:	J J Whitaker and C J B Wood 5 each
Middlesex	*For Yorkshire:*	315*— P Holmes at Lord's, 1925
	Against:	243*— A J Webbe at Huddersfield, 1887
Most Centuries	*For Yorkshire:*	P Holmes and H Sutcliffe 7 each
	Against:	M W Gatting 8

Yorkshire versus

Northamptonshire	*For Yorkshire:*	277* — P Holmes at Harrogate, 1921
	Against:	235 — A J Lamb at Leeds, 1990
Most Centuries	*For Yorkshire:*	H Sutcliffe 5
	Against:	W Larkins 5
Nottinghamshire	*For Yorkshire:*	285 — P Holmes at Nottingham, 1929
	Against:	251* — D J Hussey at Leeds, 2010
Most Centuries	*For Yorkshire:*	G Boycott 15
	Against:	R T Robinson 6
Somerset	*For Yorkshire:*	213 — H Sutcliffe at Dewsbury, 1924
	Against:	297 — M J Wood at Taunton, 2005
Most Centuries	*For Yorkshire:*	G Boycott 6
	Against:	L C H Palairet, IVA. Richards, M E Trescothick 5 each
Surrey	*For Yorkshire:*	255 — W Barber at Sheffield, 1935
	Against:	273 — T W Hayward at The Oval, 1899
Most Centuries	*For Yorkshire:*	H Sutcliffe 9
	Against:	J B Hobbs 8
Sussex	*For Yorkshire:*	311 — J T Brown at Sheffield, 1897
	Against:	274* — M W Goodwin at Hove, 2011
Most Centuries	*For Yorkshire:*	L Hutton 8
	Against:	C B Fry 7
Warwickshire	*For Yorkshire:*	275 — P Holmes at Bradford, 1928
	Against:	225 — D P Ostler at Birmingham, 2002
Most Centuries	*For Yorkshire:*	G Boycott and H Sutcliffe 8 each
	Against:	D L Amiss, H E Dollery, R B Khanhai and W G Quaife 4 each.
Worcestershire	*For Yorkshire:*	274* — M D Moxon at Worcester, 1994
	Against:	259 — D Kenyon at Kidderminster, 1956
Most Centuries	*For Yorkshire:*	M Leyland 6
	Against:	D Kenyon and G M Turner 5 each
Australians	*For Yorkshire:*	167 — J T Brown at Bradford, 1899
	Against:	193* — B C Booth at Bradford, 1964
Most Centuries	*For Yorkshire:*	G Boycott and D Denton 2 each
	Against:	N C O'Neill 2
Indians	*For Yorkshire:*	183* — L Hutton at Bradford, 1946
	Against:	244* — V S Hazare at Sheffield, 1946
Most Centuries	*For Yorkshire:*	M D Moxon 2
	Against:	V S Hazare, VMankad, PR Umrigar D K Gaekwad, G A Parkar and R Lamba 1 each
New Zealanders	*For Yorkshire:*	175 — P Holmes at Bradford, 1927
	Against:	126 — W M Wallace at Bradford, 1949
Most Centuries	*For Yorkshire:*	L Hutton and DB Close 2 each
	Against:	H G Vivian, WM Wallace and J G Wright 1 each
Pakistanis	*For Yorkshire:*	197 — P J Sharpe at Leeds, 1967
	Against:	139 — A H Kardar at Sheffield, 1954
Most Centuries	*For Yorkshire:*	P J Sharpe 2
	Against:	A H Kardar 1

HIGHEST INDIVIDUAL SCORES FOR AND AGAINST YORKSHIRE *(continued)*

Yorkshire versus

South Africans

	For Yorkshire:	156 — L Hutton at Sheffield, 1951
	Against:	168 — I J Seidle at Sheffield, 1929
Most Centuries	*For Yorkshire:*	L Hutton 2
	Against:	H B Cameron, J D Lindsay, B Mitchell, D P B Morkel, I J Seidle, L J Tancred, C B van Ryneveld 1 each

Sri Lankans

	For Yorkshire:	132 — M D Moxon at Leeds, 1988
	Against:	112 — S A R Silva at Leeds, 1988
Most Centuries	*For Yorkshire:*	K Sharp 2
	Against:	S A R Silva 1

West Indians

	For Yorkshire:	112* — D Denton at Harrogate, 1906
	Against:	164 — S F A Bacchus at Leeds, 1980
Most Centuries	*For Yorkshire:*	M G Bevan, D Denton, L Hutton, R G Lumb and A A Metcalfe 1 each
	Against:	S F A Bacchus, C O Browne, S Chanderpaul P A Goodman, C L Hooper and G St A Sobers 1 each

Zimbabweans

	For Yorkshire:	113 — M D Moxon at Leeds, 1990
	Against:	89 — G J Whittall at Leeds, 2000
Most Centuries	*For Yorkshire:*	M D Moxon 1
	Against:	None

Cambridge University

	For Yorkshire:	207* — G Boycott at Cambridge, 1976
	Against:	171* — G L Jessop at Cambridge, 1899
		171 — P B H May at Cambridge, 1952
Most Centuries	*For Yorkshire:*	H Sutcliffe 4
	Against:	G M Kemp 2

Durham MCCU

	For Yorkshire:	139 — J J Sayers at Durham, 2011
	Against:	127 — T Westley at Durham, 2011
Most Centuries	*For Yorkshire:*	J J Sayers 1
	Against:	T Westley 1

Leeds Bradford MCCU

	For Yorkshire:	194 — A Lyth at Leeds, 2017
	Against:	69 — A MacQueen at Leeds, 2012
Most Centuries	*For Yorkshire:*	A Lyth, 3

Loughborough MCCU

	For Yorkshire:	134* — R M Pyrah at Leeds, 2010
	Against:	107 — C P Murtagh at Leeds, 2007
Most Centuries	*For Yorkshire:*	R M Pyrah 2
	Against:	C P Murtagh 1

MCC

	For Yorkshire:	180* — G H Hirst at Lord's, 1919
	Against:	214 — E H Hendren at Lord's, 1919
Most Centuries	*For Yorkshire:*	L Hutton 8
	Against:	R E S Wyatt 5

Oxford University

	For Yorkshire:	196 — R J Blakey at Oxford, 1991
	Against:	201— J E Raphael at Oxford, 1904
Most Centuries	*For Yorkshire:*	M Leyland 4
	Against:	A A Baig and Nawab of Pataudi (Jun.) 2 each

J B Hobbs scored 11 centuries against Yorkshire – the highest by any individual (8 for Surrey and 3 for the Rest of England).

Three players have scored 10 centuries against Yorkshire – W G Grace (9 for Gloucestershire and 1 for MCC). E H Hendren (6 for Middlesex, 3 for MCC and 1 for the Rest of England) and C P Mead (all 10 for Hampshire).

CARRYING BAT THROUGH A COMPLETED INNINGS

Batsman	Score	Total	Against	Season
G R Atkinson	30*	73	Nottinghamshire at Bradford	1865
L Hall	31*	94	Sussex at Hove	1878
L Hall	124*	331	Sussex at Hove	1883
L Hall	128*	285	Sussex at Huddersfield	1884
L Hall	32*	81	Kent at Sheffield	1885
L Hall	79*	285	Surrey at Sheffield	1885
L Hall	37*	96	Derbyshire at Derby	1885
L Hall	50*	173	Sussex at Huddersfield	1886
L Hall	74*	172	Kent at Canterbury	1886
G Ulyett	199*	399	Derbyshire at Sheffield	1887
L Hall	119*	334	Gloucestershire at Dewsbury	1887
L Hall	82*	218	Sussex at Hove	1887
L Hall	34*	104	Surrey at The Oval	1888
L Hall	129*	461	Gloucestershire at Clifton	1888
L Hall	85*	259	Middlesex at Lord's	1889
L Hall	41*	106	Nottinghamshire at Sheffield	1891
W Rhodes	98*	184	MCC at Lord's	1903
W Rhodes	85*	152	Essex at Leyton	1910
P Holmes	145*	270	Northamptonshire at Northampton	1920
H Sutcliffe	125*	307	Essex at Southend	1920
P Holmes	175*	377	New Zealanders at Bradford	1927
P Holmes	110*	219	Northamptonshire at Bradford	1929
H Sutcliffe	104*	170	Hampshire at Leeds	1932
H Sutcliffe	114*	202	Rest of England at The Oval	1933
H Sutcliffe	187*	401	Worcestershire at Bradford	1934
H Sutcliffe	135*	262	Glamorgan at Neath	1935
H Sutcliffe	125*	322	Oxford University at Oxford	1939
L Hutton	99*	200	Leicestershire at Sheffield	1948
L Hutton	78*	153	Worcestershire at Sheffield	1949
F A Lowson	76*	218	MCC at Lord's	1951
W B Stott	144*	262	Worcestershire at Worcester	1959
D E V Padgett	115*	230	Gloucestershire at Bristol	1962
G Boycott	114*	297	Leicestershire at Sheffield	1968
G Boycott	53*	119	Warwickshire at Bradford	1969
G Boycott	182*	320	Middlesex at Lord's	1971
G Boycott	138*	232	Warwickshire at Birmingham	1971
G Boycott	175*	360	Nottinghamshire at Worksop	1979
G Boycott	112*	233	Derbyshire at Sheffield	1983
G Boycott	55*	183	Warwickshire at Leeds	1984
G Boycott	55*	131	Surrey at Sheffield	1985
M J Wood	60*	160	Somerset at Scarborough	2004
J J Sayers	122*	326	Middlesex at Scarborough	2006
J J Sayers	149*	414	Durham at Leeds	2007
A Lyth	248*	486	Leicestershire at Leicester	2012

44 instances, of which L Hall (14 times), G Boycott (8) and H Sutcliffe (6) account for 28 between them.

The highest percentage of an innings total is 61.17 by H. Sutcliffe (104* v. Hampshire at Leeds in 1932) but P Holmes was absent ill, so only nine wickets fell.

Other contributions exceeding 55% are:

59.48%	G Boycott	(138*	v. Warwickshire at Birmingham, 1971)
56.87%	G Boycott	(182*	v. Middlesex at Lord's, 1971)
56.43%	H Sutcliffe	(114*	v. Rest of England at The Oval, 1933)
55.92%	W Rhodes	(85*	v. Essex at Leyton, 1910)

2,000 RUNS IN A SEASON

Batsman	Season	M	I	NO	Runs	HS	Avge	100s
G H Hirst	1904	32	44	3	2257	157	55.04	8
D Denton	1905	33	52	2	2258	172	45.16	8
G H Hirst	1906	32	53	6	2164	169	46.04	6
D Denton	1911	32	55	4	2161	137*	42.37	6
D Denton	1912	36	51	4	2088	221	44.23	6
P Holmes	1920	30	45	6	2144	302*	54.97	7
P Holmes	1925	35	49	9	2351	315*	58.77	6
H Sutcliffe	1925	34	48	8	2236	235	55.90	7
H Sutcliffe	1928	27	35	5	2418	228	80.60	11
P Holmes	1928	31	40	4	2093	275	58.13	6
H Sutcliffe	1931	28	33	8	2351	230	94.04	9
H Sutcliffe	1932	29	41	5	2883	313	80.08	12
M Leyland	1933	31	44	4	2196	210*	54.90	7
A Mitchell	1933	34	49	10	2100	158	53.84	6
H Sutcliffe	1935	32	47	3	2183	212	49.61	8
L Hutton	1937	28	45	6	2448	271*	62.76	8
H Sutcliffe	1937	32	52	5	2054	189	43.70	4
L Hutton	1939	29	44	5	2316	280*	59.38	10
L Hutton	1947	19	31	2	2068	270*	71.31	10
L Hutton	1949	26	44	6	2640	269*	69.47	9
F A Lowson	1950	31	54	5	2067	141*	42.18	5
D E V Padgett	1959	35	60	8	2158	161*	41.50	4
W B Stott	1959	32	56	2	2034	144*	37.66	3
P J Sharpe	1962	36	62	8	2201	138	40.75	7
G Boycott	1971	18	25	4	2221	233	105.76	11
A A Metcalfe	1990	23	44	4	2047	194*	51.17	6

1,000 RUNS IN A SEASON

Batsman		Runs scored	Runs scored	Runs scored
C W J Athey	(2)	1113 in 1980	1339 in 1982	—
D L Bairstow	(3)	1083 in 1981	1102 in 1983	1163 in 1985
J M Bairstow	(2)	1015 in 2011	1108 in 2015	—
G S Ballance	(3)	1363 in 2013	1023 in 2017	1014 in 2019
W Barber	(8)	1000 in 1932	1595 in 1933	1930 in 1934
		1958 in 1935	1466 in 1937	1455 in 1938
		1501 in 1939	1170 in 1946	—
M G Bevan	(2)	1598 in 1995	1225 in 1996	—
R J Blakey	(5)	1361 in 1987	1159 in 1989	1065 in 1992
		1236 in 1994	1041 in 2002	—
J B Bolus	(2)	1245 in 1960	1970 in 1961	—
M W Booth	(2)	1189 in 1911	1076 in 1913	—
G Boycott	(19)	1628 in 1963	1639 in 1964	1215 in 1965
		1388 in 1966	1530 in 1967	1004 in 1968
		1558 in 1970	2221 in 1971	1156 in 1972
		1478 in 1974	1915 in 1975	1288 in 1976
		1259 in 1977	1074 in 1978	1160 in 1979
		1913 in 1982	1941 in 1983	1567 in 1984
		1657 in 1985	—	—
J T Brown	(9)	1196 in 1894	1260 in 1895	1755 in 1896
		1634 in 1897	1641 in 1898	1375 in 1899
		1181 in 1900	1627 in 1901	1291 in 1903
D Byas	(5)	1557 in 1991	1073 in 1993	1297 in 1994
		1913 in 1995	1319 in 1997	—

262

1,000 RUNS IN A SEASON *(Continued)*

Batsman	*Runs scored*	*Runs scored*	*Runs scored*
D B Close .... (13)	1192 in 1952	1287 in 1954	1131 in 1955
	1315 in 1957	1335 in 1958	1740 in 1959
	1699 in 1960	1821 in 1961	1438 in 1962
	1145 in 1963	1281 in 1964	1127 in 1965
	1259 in 1966	—	—
K R Davidson .... (1)	1241 in 1934		
D Denton .... (20)	1028 in 1896	1357 in 1897	1595 in 1899
	1378 in 1900	1400 in 1901	1191 in 1902
	1562 in 1903	1919 in 1904	2258 in 1905
	1905 in 1906	1128 in 1907	1852 in 1908
	1765 in 1909	1106 in 1910	2161 in 1911
	2088 in 1912	1364 in 1913	1799 in 1914
	1213 in 1919	1324 in 1920	—
A Drake .... (2)	1487 in 1911	1029 in 1913	
A W Gale .... (2)	1076 in 2013	1045 in 2015	
A P Grayson .... (1)	1046 in 1994	—	—
S Haigh .... (1)	1031 in 1904	—	—
L Hall .... (1)	1120 in 1887	—	—
H Halliday .... (4)	1357 in 1948	1484 in 1950	1351 in 1952
	1461 in 1953	—	—
J H Hampshire .... (12)	1236 in 1963	1280 in 1964	1424 in 1965
	1105 in 1966	1244 in 1967	1133 in 1968
	1079 in 1970	1259 in 1971	1124 in 1975
	1303 in 1976	1596 in 1978	1425 in 1981
Lord Hawke .... (1)	1005 in 1895	—	—
G H Hirst .... (19)	1110 in 1896	1248 in 1897	1546 in 1899
	1752 in 1900	1669 in 1901	1113 in 1902
	1535 in 1903	2257 in 1904	1972 in 1905
	2164 in 1906	1167 in 1907	1513 in 1908
	1151 in 1909	1679 in 1910	1639 in 1911
	1119 in 1912	1431 in 1913	1655 in 1914
	1312 in 1919	—	—
P Holmes .... (14)	1876 in 1919	2144 in 1920	1458 in 1921
	1614 in 1922	1884 in 1923	1610 in 1924
	2351 in 1925	1792 in 1926	1774 in 1927
	2093 in 1928	1724 in 1929	1957 in 1930
	1431 in 1931	1191 in 1932	—
L Hutton .... (12)	1282 in 1936	2448 in 1937	1171 in 1938
	2316 in 1939	1322 in 1946	2068 in 1947
	1792 in 1948	2640 in 1949	1581 in 1950
	1554 in 1951	1956 in 1952	1532 in 1953
R Illingworth .... (5)	1193 in 1957	1490 in 1959	1029 in 1961
	1610 in 1962	1301 in 1964	—
F S Jackson .... (4)	1211 in 1896	1300 in 1897	1442 in 1898
	1468 in 1899	—	—
P A Jaques .... (2)	1118 in 2004	1359 in 2005	—
S A Kellett .... (2)	1266 in 1991	1326 in 1992	—
R Kilner .... (10)	1586 in 1913	1329 in 1914	1135 in 1919
	1240 in 1920	1137 in 1921	1132 in 1922
	1265 in 1923	1002 in 1925	1021 in 1926
	1004 in 1927	—	—
T Kohler-Cadmore .... (1)	1004 in 2019	—	—

Batsman		Runs scored	Runs scored	Runs scored
A Z Lees	(2)	1018 in 2014	1285 in 2016	—
D S Lehmann	(5)	1575 in 1997	1477 in 2000	1416 in 2001
		1136 in 2002	1706 in 2006	
E I Lester	(6)	1256 in 1948	1774 in 1949	1015 in 1950
		1786 in 1952	1380 in 1953	1330 in 1954
M Leyland	(17)	1088 in 1923	1203 in 1924	1560 in 1925
		1561 in 1926	1478 in 1927	1554 in 1928
		1407 in 1929	1814 in 1930	1127 in 1931
		1821 in 1932	2196 in 1933	1228 in 1934
		1366 in 1935	1621 in 1936	1120 in 1937
		1640 in 1938	1238 in 1939	—
J D Love	(2)	1161 in 1981	1020 in 1983	—
F A Lowson	(8)	1678 in 1949	2067 in 1950	1607 in 1951
		1562 in 1952	1586 in 1953	1719 in 1954
		1082 in 1955	1428 in 1956	—
M J Lumb	(1)	1038 in 2003	—	—
R G Lumb	(5)	1002 in 1973	1437 in 1975	1070 in 1978
		1465 in 1979	1223 in 1980	—
A Lyth	(3)	1509 in 2010	1619 in 2014	1153 in 2016
A McGrath	(3)	1425 in 2005	1293 in 2006	1219 in 2010
A A Metcalfe	(6)	1674 in 1986	1162 in 1987	1320 in 1988
		1230 in 1989	2047 in 1990	1210 in 1991
A Mitchell	(10)	1320 in 1928	1633 in 1930	1351 in 1932
		2100 in 1933	1854 in 1934	1530 in 1935
		1095 in 1936	1602 in 1937	1305 in 1938
		1219 in 1939	—	—
F Mitchell	(2)	1678 in 1899	1801 in 1901	—
R Moorhouse	(1)	1096 in 1895	—	—
M D Moxon	(11)	1016 in 1984	1256 in 1985	1298 in 1987
		1430 in 1988	1156 in 1989	1621 in 1990
		1669 in 1991	1314 in 1992	1251 in 1993
		1458 in 1994	1145 in 1995	—
E Oldroyd	(10)	1473 in 1921	1690 in 1922	1349 in 1923
		1607 in 1924	1262 in 1925	1197 in 1926
		1390 in 1927	1304 in 1928	1474 in 1929
		1285 in 1930	—	—
D E V Padgett	(12)	1046 in 1956	2158 in 1959	1574 in 1960
		1856 in 1961	1750 in 1962	1380 in 1964
		1220 in 1965	1194 in 1966	1284 in 1967
		1163 in 1968	1078 in 1969	1042 in 1970
R Peel	(1)	1193 in 1896	—	—
W Rhodes	(17)	1251 in 1904	1353 in 1905	1618 in 1906
		1574 in 1908	1663 in 1909	1355 in 1910
		1961 in 1911	1030 in 1912	1805 in 1913
		1325 in 1914	1138 in 1919	1329 in 1921
		1368 in 1922	1168 in 1923	1030 in 1924
		1256 in 1925	1071 in 1926	—
E Robinson	(2)	1104 in 1921	1097 in 1929	—
P E Robinson	(3)	1173 in 1988	1402 in 1990	1293 in 1991
J A Rudolph	(4)	1078 in 2007	1292 in 2008	1366 in 2009
		1375 in 2010	—	—

1,000 RUNS IN A SEASON *(Continued)*

Batsman	Runs scored	Runs scored	Runs scored
J J Sayers	(1) 1150 in 2009	—	—
A B Sellers	(1) 1109 in 1938	—	—
K Sharp	(1) 1445 in 1984	—	—
P J Sharpe	(10) 1039 in 1960	1240 in 1961	2201 in 1962
	1273 in 1964	1091 in 1965	1352 in 1967
	1256 in 1968	1012 in 1969	1149 in 1970
	1320 in 1973		
W B Stott	(5) 1362 in 1957	1036 in 1958	2034 in 1959
	1790 in 1960	1409 in 1961	—
H Sutcliffe	(21) †1839 in 1919	1393 in 1920	1235 in 1921
	1909 in 1922	1773 in 1923	1720 in 1924
	2236 in 1925	1672 in 1926	1814 in 1927
	2418 in 1928	1485 in 1929	1636 in 1930
	2351 in 1931	2883 in 1932	1986 in 1933
	1511 in 1934	2183 in 1935	1295 in 1936
	2054 in 1937	1660 in 1938	1416 in 1939

† First season in First-Class cricket – The record for a debut season.

W H H Sutcliffe	(1) 1193 in 1955	—	—
K Taylor	(6) 1306 in 1959	1107 in 1960	1494 in 1961
	1372 in 1962	1149 in 1964	1044 in 1966
T L Taylor	(2) 1236 in 1901	1373 in 1902	—
S R Tendulkar	(1) 1070 in 1992	—	—
J Tunnicliffe	(12) 1333 in 1895	1368 in 1896	1208 in 1897
	1713 in 1898	1434 in 1899	1496 in 1900
	1295 in 1901	1274 in 1902	1650 in 1904
	1096 in 1905	1232 in 1906	1195 in 1907
C Turner	(1) 1153 in 1934	—	—
G Ulyett	(4) 1083 in 1878	1158 in 1882	1024 in 1885
	1285 in 1887	—	—
M P Vaughan	(4) 1066 in 1994	1235 in 1995	1161 in 1996
	1161 in 1998	—	—
E Wainwright	(3) 1492 in 1897	1479 in 1899	1044 in 1901
W A I Washington	(1) 1022 in 1902	—	—
W Watson	(8) 1331 in 1947	1352 in 1948	1586 in 1952
	1350 in 1953	1347 in 1954	1564 in 1955
	1378 in 1956	1455 in 1957	—
W H Wilkinson	(1) 1282 in 1908	—	—
B B Wilson	(5) 1054 in 1909	1455 in 1911	1453 in 1912
	1533 in 1913	1632 in 1914	—
J V Wilson	(12) 1460 in 1949	1548 in 1950	1985 in 1951
	1349 in 1952	1531 in 1953	1713 in 1954
	1799 in 1955	1602 in 1956	1287 in 1957
	1064 in 1960	1018 in 1961	1226 in 1962
A Wood	(1) 1237 in 1935	—	—
M J Wood	(4) 1080 in 1998	1060 in 2001	1432 in 2003
	1005 in 2005		
N W D Yardley	(4) 1028 in 1939	1299 in 1947	1413 in 1949
	1031 in 1950	—	—

BATSMEN WHO HAVE SCORED OVER 10,000 RUNS

Player	M	I	NO	Runs	HS	Av'ge	100s
H Sutcliffe	602	864	96	38558	313	50.20	112
D Denton	676	1058	61	33282	221	33.38	61
G Boycott	414	674	111	32570	260*	57.85	103
G H Hirst	717	1050	128	32024	341	34.73	56
W Rhodes	883	1195	162	31075	267*	30.08	46
P Holmes	485	699	74	26220	315*	41.95	60
M Leyland	548	720	82	26180	263	41.03	62
L Hutton	341	527	62	24807	280*	53.34	85
D B Close	536	811	102	22650	198	31.94	33
J H Hampshire	456	724	89	21979	183*	34.61	34
J V Wilson	477	724	75	20548	230	31.66	29
D E V Padgett	487	774	63	20306	161*	28.55	29
J Tunnicliffe	472	768	57	19435	243	27.33	22
M D Moxon	277	476	42	18973	274*	43.71	41
A Mitchell	401	550	69	18189	189	37.81	39
P J Sharpe	411	666	71	17685	203*	29.72	23
E Oldroyd	383	509	58	15891	194	35.23	37
J T Brown	345	567	41	15694	311	29.83	23
W Barber	354	495	48	15315	255	34.26	27
R Illingworth	496	668	131	14986	162	27.90	14
D Byas	268	449	42	14398	213	35.37	28
G Ulyett	355	618	31	14157	199*	24.11	15
R J Blakey	339	541	84	14150	223*	30.96	12
A McGrath	242	405	29	14091	211	37.47	34
W Watson	283	430	65	13953	214*	38.22	26
F A Lowson	252	404	31	13897	259*	37.25	30
Lord Hawke	510	739	91	13133	166	20.26	10
R Kilner	365	478	46	13018	206*	30.13	15
D L Bairstow	429	601	113	12985	145	26.60	9
K Taylor	303	505	35	12864	203*	27.37	16
N W D Yardley	302	420	56	11632	183*	31.95	17
R G Lumb	239	395	30	11525	165*	31.57	22
E Wainwright	352	545	30	11092	228	21.53	18
S Haigh	513	687	110	10993	159	19.05	4
E I Lester	228	339	27	10616	186	34.02	24
A A Metcalfe	184	317	19	10465	216*	35.11	25
C White	221	350	45	10376	186	34.01	19
Hon F S Jackson	207	328	22	10371	160	33.89	21
J D Love	247	388	58	10263	170*	31.10	13
A Lyth	161	271	14	10046	251	39.08	22

PLAYERS WHO HAVE SCORED CENTURIES
FOR AND AGAINST YORKSHIRE

Player		For	Venue	Season
C W J Athey (5)	114*	Gloucestershire	Bradford	1984
(10 for Yorkshire)	101	Gloucestershire	Gloucester	1985
	101*	Gloucestershire	Leeds	1987
	112	Sussex	Scarborough	1993
	100	Sussex	Eastbourne	1996
M G Bevan (1)	142	Leicestershire	Leicester	2002
(9 for Yorkshire)				
J B Bolus (2)	114	Nottinghamshire	Bradford	1963
(7 for Yorkshire)	138	Derbyshire	Sheffield	1973
D B Close (1)	102	Somerset	Taunton	1971
(33 for Yorkshire)				
M T G Elliott (1)	125	Glamorgan	Leeds	2004
(1 for Yorkshire)				
P A Gibb (1)	107	Essex	Brentwood	1951
(2 for Yorkshire)				
P A Jaques (1)	222	Northamptonshire	Northampton	2003
(7 for Yorkshire)				
N Kilner (2)	119	Warwickshire	Hull	1932
(2 for Yorkshire)	197	Warwickshire	Birmingham	1933
M J Lumb (1)	135	Nottinghamshire	Scarborough	2013
(8 for Yorkshire)				
P J Sharpe (1)	126	Derbyshire	Chesterfield	1976
(23 for Yorkshire)				

RECORD PARTNERSHIPS FOR YORKSHIRE

1st wkt	555	P Holmes (224*)	and H Sutcliffe (313)	v. Essex at Leyton	1932
2nd wkt	346	W Barber (162)	and M Leyland (189)	v. Middlesex at Sheffield	1932
3rd wkt	346	J J Sayers (173)	and A McGrath (211)	v. Warwickshire at Birmingham	2009
4th wkt	372	J E Root (213)	and J M Bairstow (198)	v. Surrey at Leeds	2016
5th wkt	340	E Wainwright (228)	and G H Hirst (186)	v. Surrey at The Oval	1899
6th wkt	296	A Lyth (251)	and A U Rashid (159*)	v. Lancashire at Manchester,	2014
7th wkt	366*	J M Bairstow (219*)	and T T Bresnan (169*)	v. Durham at Chester-le-Street	2015
8th wkt	292	R Peel (210*)	and Lord Hawke (166)	v. Warwickshire at Birmingham	1896
9th wkt	246	T T Bresnan (116)	and J N Gillespie (123*)	v. Surrey at The Oval	2007
10th wkt	149	G Boycott (79)	and G B Stevenson (115*)	v. Warwickshire at Birmingham	1982

RECORD PARTNERSHIPS AGAINST YORKSHIRE

1st wkt	372	R R Montgomerie (127)	and M B Loye (205)	for Northamptonshire at Northampton	1996
2nd wkt	417	K J Barnett (210*)	and TA Tweats (189)	for Derbyshire at Derby	1997
3rd wkt	523	M A Carberry (300*)	and N D McKenzie (237)	for Hampshire at Southampton	2011
4th wkt	447	R Abel (193)	and T Hayward (273)	for Surrey at The Oval	1899
5th wkt	261	W G Grace (318*)	and W O Moberley (103)	for Gloucestershire at Cheltenham	1876
6th wkt	346	S W Billings (138)	and D I Stevens (237)	for Kent at Leeds	2019
7th wkt	315	D M Benkenstein (151)	and O D Gibson (155)	for Durham at Leeds	2006
8th wkt	178	A P Wells (253*)	and B T P Donelan (59)	for Sussex at Middlesbrough	1991
9th wkt	233	I J L Trott (161*)	and J S Patel (120)	for Warwickshire at Birmingham	2009
10th wkt	132	A Hill (172*)	and M Jean-Jacques (73)	for Derbyshire at Sheffield	1986

CENTURY PARTNERSHIPS FOR THE FIRST WICKET IN BOTH INNINGS

128	108	G Ulyett (82 and 91)	and L Hall (87 and 37)	v. Sussex at Hove	1885
		(First instance in First-Class cricket)			
138	147*	J T Brown (203 and 81*)	and J Tunnicliffe (62 and 63*)	v. Middlesex at Lord's	1896
		(Second instance in First-Class cricket)			
105	265*	P Holmes (51 and 127*)	and H Sutcliffe (71 and 131*)	v. Surrey at The Oval	1926
184	210*	P Holmes (83 and 101*)	and H Sutcliffe (111 and 100*)	v. Nottinghamshire at Nottingham	1928
110	117	L Hutton (95 and 86)	and W Watson (34 and 57)	v. Lancashire at Manchester	1947
122	230	W B Stott (50 and 114)	and K Taylor (79 and 140)	v. Nottinghamshire at Nottingham	1957
136	138	J B Bolus (108 and 71)	and K Taylor (89 and 75)	v. Cambridge University at Cambridge	1962
105	105	G Boycott (38 and 64)	and K Taylor (85 and 49)	v. Leicestershire at Leicester	1963
116	112*	K Taylor (45 and 68)	and J H Hampshire (68 and 67*)	v. Oxford University at Oxford	1964
104	104	G Boycott (117 and 49*)	and R G Lumb (47 and 57)	v. Sussex at Leeds	1974
134	185*	M D Moxon (57 and 89*)	and A A Metcalfe (216* and 78*)	v. Middlesex at Leeds	1988
118	129*	G S Ballance (72 and 73*)	and J J Sayers (139 and 53*)	v. Durham MCCU at Durham	2011

CENTURY PARTNERSHIPS FOR THE FIRST WICKET IN BOTH INNINGS BUT WITH CHANGE OF PARTNER

109		W H H Sutcliffe (82) and F A Lowson (46)	
	143	W H H Sutcliffe (88) and W Watson (52)	v. Canadians at Scarborough, 1954
109		G Boycott (70) and R G Lumb (44)	
	135	G Boycott (74) and J H Hampshire (58)	v. Northamptonshire at Bradford, 1977

CENTURY PARTNERSHIPS

FIRST WICKET (Qualification 200 runs)

555	P Holmes (224*) and H Sutcliffe (313) v. Essex at Leyton, 1932
554	J T Brown (300) and J Tunnicliffe (243) v. Derbyshire at Chesterfield, 1898
378	J T Brown (311) and J Tunnicliffe (147) v. Sussex at Sheffield, 1897
375	A Lyth (230) and A Z Lees (138) v. Northamptonshire at Northampton, 2014
362	M D Moxon (213) and M P Vaughan (183) v. Glamorgan at Cardiff, 1996
351	G Boycott (184) and M D Moxon (168) v. Worcestershire at Worcester, 1985
347	P Holmes (302*) and H Sutcliffe (131) v. Hampshire at Portsmouth, 1920
323	P Holmes (125) and H Sutcliffe (195) v. Lancashire at Sheffield, 1931
315	H Sutcliffe (189) and L Hutton (153) v. Leicestershire at Hull, 1937
315	H Sutcliffe (116) and L Hutton (280*) v. Hampshire at Sheffield, 1939
309	P Holmes (250) and H Sutcliffe (129) v. Warwickshire at Birmingham, 1931
309	C White (186) and M J Wood (115) v. Lancashire at Manchester, 2001
290	P Holmes (179*) and H Sutcliffe (104) v. Middlesex at Leeds, 1925
288	G Boycott (130*) and R G Lumb (159) v. Somerset at Harrogate, 1979
286	L Hutton (156) and F A Lowson (115) v. South Africans at Sheffield, 1951
282	M D Moxon (147) and A A Metcalfe (151) v. Lancashire at Manchester, 1986
281*	W B Stott (138*) and K Taylor (130*) v. Sussex at Hove, 1960
279	P Holmes (133) and H Sutcliffe (145) v. Northamptonshire at Northampton, 1919
274	P.Holmes (199) and H Sutcliffe (139) v. Somerset at Hull, 1923
274	P Holmes (180) and H Sutcliffe (134) v. Gloucestershire at Gloucester, 1927
272	P Holmes (194) and H Sutcliffe (129) v. Leicestershire at Hull, 1925
272	M J Wood (202*) and J J Sayers (115) v. Bangladesh 'A' at Leeds, 2005
270	A Lyth (143) and A Z Lees (108) v. Durham at Leeds, 2014
268	P Holmes (136) and H Sutcliffe (129) v. Essex at Leyton, 1928
267	W Barber (248) and L Hutton (70) v. Kent at Leeds, 1934
265*	P Holmes (127*) and H Sutcliffe (131*) v. Surrey at The Oval, 1926
264	G Boycott (161*) and R G Lumb (132) v. Gloucestershire at Leeds, 1976
253	P Holmes (123) and H Sutcliffe (132) v. Lancashire at Sheffield, 1919
248	G Boycott (163) and A A Metcalfe (122) v. Nottinghamshire at Bradford, 1983
245	L Hutton (152) and F A Lowson (120) v. Lancashire at Leeds, 1952
244	J A Rudolph (149) and J J Sayers (86) v Nottinghamshire at Nottingham, 2009
241	P Holmes (142) and H Sutcliffe (123*) v. Surrey at The Oval, 1929
240	G Boycott (233) and P J Sharpe (92) v. Essex at Colchester, 1971
238*	P Holmes (126*) and H Sutcliffe (105*) v. Cambridge University at Cambridge, 1923
236	G Boycott (131) and K Taylor (153) v. Lancashire at Manchester, 1964
235	P Holmes (130) and H Sutcliffe (132*) v. Glamorgan at Sheffield, 1930
233	G Boycott (141*) and R G Lumb (90) v. Cambridge University at Cambridge, 1973
233	H Halliday (116) and W Watson (108) v. Northamptonshire at Northampton, 1948
231	M P Vaughan (151) and D Byas (90) v. Essex at Chelmsford, 1999
230	H Sutcliffe (129) and L Hutton (163) v. Surrey at Leeds, 1936
230	W B Stott (114) and K Taylor (140*) v. Nottinghamshire at Nottingham, 1957
228	H Halliday (90) and J V Wilson (223*) v. Scotland at Scarborough, 1951
228	G Boycott (141) and R G Lumb (101) v. Gloucestershire at Bristol, 1975
227	P Holmes (110) and H Sutcliffe (119) v. Leicestershire at Leicester, 1928
225	R G Lumb (101) and C W J Athey (125*) v. Gloucestershire at Sheffield, 1980
224	C W J Athey (114) and J D Love (104) v. Warwickshire at Birmingham, 1980
222	W B Stott (141) and K Taylor (90) v. Sussex at Bradford, 1958
221	P Holmes (130) and H Sutcliffe (121) v. Glamorgan at Huddersfield, 1925
221	M D Moxon (141) and A A Metcalfe (73) v. Surrey at The Oval, 1992
221	A Lyth (111) and A Z Lees (121) v. Leeds/Bradford MCCU at Leeds, 2013
219	P Holmes (102) and A Mitchell (130*) v. Somerset at Bradford, 1930
218	M Leyland (110) and H Sutcliffe (235) v. Middlesex at Leeds, 1925
218	R G Lumb (145) and M D Moxon (111) v. Derbyshire at Sheffield, 1981
210*	P Holmes (101*) and H Sutcliffe (100*) v. Nottinghamshire at Nottingham, 1928
210	G Boycott (128) and P J Sharpe (197) v. Pakistanis at Leeds, 1967
209	F A Lowson (115) and D E V Padgett (107) v. Scotland at Hull, 1956

208	A Mitchell (85) and E Oldroyd (111) v. Cambridge University at Cambridge, 1929
207	A Mitchell (90) and W Barber (107) v. Middlesex at Lord's, 1935
206	G Boycott (118) and R G Lumb (87) v. Glamorgan at Sheffield, 1978
204	M D Moxon (66) and A A Metcalfe (162) v. Gloucestershire at Cheltenham, 1990
203	L Hutton (119) and F A Lowson (83) v. Somerset at Huddersfield, 1952
203	M D Moxon (117) and S A Kellett (87) v. Somerset at Middlesbrough, 1992
203	M D Moxon (134) and M P Vaughan (106) v. Matebeleland at Bulawayo, 1996
200*	P Holmes (107*) and H Sutcliffe (80*) v. Oxford University at Oxford, 1930

Note: P Holmes and H Sutcliffe shared 69 century opening partnerships for Yorkshire; G Boycott and R G Lumb 29; L Hutton and F A Lowson 22; M D Moxon and A A Metcalfe 21; J T Brown and J Tunnicliffe 19; H Sutcliffe and L Hutton 15; G Boycott and P J Sharpe 13, and L Hall and G Ulyett 12.

SECOND WICKET (Qualification 200 runs)

346	W Barber (162) and M Leyland (189) v. Middlesex at Sheffield, 1932
343	F A Lowson (183*) and J V Wilson (165) v. Oxford University at Oxford, 1956
333	P Holmes (209) and E Oldroyd (138*) v. Warwickshire at Birmingham, 1922
314	H Sutcliffe (255*) and E Oldroyd (138) v. Essex at Southend-on-Sea, 1924
311	A Z Lees (275*) and P A Jaques (139) v. Derbyshire at Chesterfield, 2013
305	J W.Rothery (134) and D Denton (182) v. Derbyshire at Chesterfield, 1910
302	W Watson (172) and J V Wilson (140) v. Derbyshire at Scarborough, 1948
301	P J Sharpe (172*) and D E V Padgett (133) v. Glamorgan at Swansea, 1971
288	H Sutcliffe (165) and A Mitchell (136) v. Lancashire at Manchester, 1939
280	L Hall (160) and F Lee (165) v. Lancashire at Bradford, 1887
266*	K Taylor (178*) and D E V Padgett (107*) v. Oxford University at Oxford, 1962
264	P A Jaques (152) and K S Williamson (97) v. Durham at Scarborough, 2013
261*	L Hutton (146*) and J V Wilson (110*) v. Scotland at Hull, 1949
260	R G Lumb (144) and K Sharp (132) v. Glamorgan at Cardiff, 1978
258	H Sutcliffe (230) and E Oldroyd (93) v. Kent at Folkestone, 1931
253	B B Wilson (150) and D Denton (200*) v. Warwickshire at Birmingham, 1912
248	H Sutcliffe (200) and M. Leyland (116) v. Leicestershire at Leicester, 1926
244	P. Holmes (138) and E Oldroyd (151*) v. Glamorgan at Cardiff, 1922
243	G Boycott (141) and J D Love (163) v. Nottinghamshire at Bradford, 1976
243	C White (183) and M J Wood (124) v. Glamorgan at Scarborough, 2001
237	H Sutcliffe (118) and D Denton (122) v. Gloucestershire at Leeds, 1919
237	M D Moxon (132) and K Sharp (128) v. Sri Lankans at Leeds, 1988
236	F A Lowson (112) and J V Wilson (157) v. Essex at Leeds, 1950
235	M D Moxon (130) and D Byas (181) v. Cambridge University at Cambridge, 1995
230	L Hutton (180) and A Mitchell (100) v. Cambridge University at Cambridge, 1938
230	M P Vaughan (109) and B Parker (138*) v. Oxford University at Oxford, 1997.
227	M J Wood (102) and M J Lumb (122) v. Leicestershire at Leeds, 2001
225	H Sutcliffe (138) and E Oldroyd (97) v. Derbyshire at Dewsbury, 1928
223	M D Moxon (153) and R J Blakey (90) v. Somerset at Leeds, 1985
222	H Sutcliffe (174) and D Denton (114) v. Kent at Dover, 1919
219	F S Jackson (155) and D Denton (113) v. Middlesex at Bradford, 1899
217	R G Lumb (107) and J D Love (107) v. Oxford University at Oxford, 1978
216	M P Vaughan (105) and D Byas (102) v. Somerset at Bradford, 1994
215	A W Gale (136) and A McGrath (99) v. Lancashire at Manchester, 2008
215	S E Marsh (125*) and A Z Lees (102) v. Surrey at The Oval, 2017
211	J A Rudolph (141) and A McGrath (80) v Nottinghamshire at Leeds, 2010
207	P A Jaques (115) and A McGrath (93) v. Essex at Chelmsford, 2004
206	J Tunnicliffe (102) and F S Jackson (134*) v. Lancashire at Sheffield, 1898
206	H Sutcliffe (187) and M Leyland (90) v. Leicestershire at Leicester, 1931
205	H Sutcliffe (174) and A Mitchell (95) v. Leicestershire at Leicester, 1933
205	G Boycott (148) and P J Sharpe (108) v. Kent at Sheffield, 1970
203	A T Barber (100) and A Oldroyd (143) v. An England XI at Sheffield, 1929
203	J J Sayers (187) and A McGrath (100) v. Kent at Tunbridge Wells, 2007
202*	W Rhodes (115*) and G H Hirst (117*) v. Somerset at Bath, 1906
202	G Boycott (113) and C W J Athey (114) v. Northamptonshire at Northampton, 1978

CENTURY PARTNERSHIPS *(Continued)*

THIRD WICKET (Qualification 200 runs)

346	J J Sayers (173) and A McGrath (211) v. Warwickshire at Birmingham, 2009
323*	H Sutcliffe (147*) and M Leyland (189*) v. Glamorgan at Huddersfield, 1928
317	A McGrath (165) and D S Lehmann (187) v. Lancashire at Leeds, 2002
310	A McGrath (134) and P A Jaques (219) v. Derbyshire at Leeds, 2005
301	H Sutcliffe (175) and M Leyland (180*) v. Middlesex at Lord's, 1939
293*	A A Metcalfe (150*) and P E Robinson (150*) v. Derbyshire at Scarborough, 1990
269	D Byas (101) and R J Blakey (196) v. Oxford University at Oxford, 1991
258*	J T Brown (134*) and F Mitchell (116*) v. Warwickshire at Bradford, 1901
253*	G S Ballance (101*) and J E Root (130*) v. Nottinghamshire at Nottingham, 2019
252	D E V Padgett (139*) and D B Close (154) v. Nottinghamshire at Nottingham, 1959
249	D E V Padgett (95) and D B Close (184) v. Nottinghamshire at Scarborough, 1960
248	C Johnson (102) and J H Hampshire (155*) v. Gloucestershire at Leeds, 1976
247	P Holmes (175*) and M Leyland (118) v. New Zealanders at Bradford, 1927
244	D E V Padgett (161*) and D B Close (144) v. Oxford University at Oxford, 1959
240	L Hutton (151) and M Leyland (95) v. Surrey at Leeds, 1939
237	J A Rudolph (198) and A McGrath (120) v. Worcestershire at Leeds, 2009
236	H Sutcliffe (107) and R Kilner (137) v. Nottinghamshire at Nottingham, 1920
236	M J Wood (94) and D S Lehmann (200) v. Worcestershire at Worcester, 1998
234*	D Byas (126*) and A McGrath (105*) v. Oxford University at Oxford, 1997.
233	L Hutton (101) and M Leyland (167) v. Worcestershire at Stourbridge, 1937
230	D Byas (103) and M J Wood (103) v. Derbyshire at Leeds, 1998
229	L Hall (86) and R Peel (158) v. Middlesex at Lord's, 1889
228	A Mitchell (142) and M Leyland (133) v. Worcestershire at Sheffield, 1933
228	W Barber (141) and M Leyland (114) v. Surrey at The Oval, 1939
228	J V Wilson (132*) and D E V Padgett (115) v. Warwickshire at Birmingham, 1955
226	D E V Padgett (117) and D B Close (198) v. Surrey at The Oval, 1960
224	J V Wilson (110) and D B Close (114) v. Cambridge University at Cambridge, 1955
224	G Boycott (140*) and K Sharp (121) v. Gloucestershire at Cheltenham, 1983
221	A Mitchell (138) and M Leyland (134) v. Nottinghamshire at Bradford, 1933
219	L Hall (116) and W Bates (133) v. Cambridge University at Cambridge, 1884
218	J A Rudolph (127) and A W Gale (121) v. Lancashire at Manchester, 2009
217	A McGrath (144) and J A Rudolph (129) v. Kent at Canterbury, 2008
216	R G Lumb (118) and J H Hampshire (127) v. Surrey at The Oval, 1975
215	A Mitchell (73) and M Leyland (139) v. Surrey at Bradford, 1928
213	E Oldroyd (168) and W Barber (114) v. Glamorgan at Hull, 1929
208	J V Wilson (157*) and E I Lester (112) v. Sussex at Leeds, 1949
206	A McGrath (105) and J A Rudolph (228*) v Durham at Leeds, 2010
205*	E Oldroyd (122*) and M Leyland (100*) v. Hampshire at Harrogate, 1924
205	F S Jackson (124) and D Denton (112) v. Somerset at Taunton, 1897
205	D E V Padgett (83) and D B Close (128) v. Somerset at Bath, 1959
204	M P Vaughan (113) and A McGrath (70) v. Essex at Scarborough, 2001
203	D Denton (132) and J Tunnicliffe (102) v. Warwickshire at Birmingham, 1905
203	A A Metcalfe (216*) and P E Robinson (88) v. Middlesex at Leeds, 1988
201	J Tunnicliffe (101) and T L Taylor (147) v. Surrey at The Oval, 1900
201	H Sutcliffe (87) and W Barber (130) v. Leicestershire at Leicester, 1938
200	M D Moxon (274*) and A P Grayson (100) v. Worcestershire at Worcester, 1994

FOURTH WICKET (Qualification 175 runs)

372	J E Root (213) and J M Bairstow (198) v. Surrey at Leeds, 2016
358	D S Lehmann (339) and M J Lumb (98) v. Durham at Leeds, 2006
330	M J Wood (116) and D R Martyn (238) v. Gloucestershire at Leeds, 2003
312	D Denton (168*) and G H Hirst (146) v. Hampshire at Southampton, 1914
299	P Holmes (277*) and R Kilner (150) v. Northamptonshire at Harrogate, 1921
272	D Byas (138) and A McGrath (137) v. Hampshire at Harrogate, 1996
271	B B Wilson (208) and W Rhodes (113) v. Sussex at Bradford, 1914
259	A Drake (115) and G H Hirst (218) v. Sussex at Hastings, 1911
258	J Tunnicliffe (128) and G H Hirst (152) v. Hampshire at Portsmouth, 1904

258	P E Robinson (147) and D Byas (117) v. Kent at Scarborough, 1989
255	A W Gale (148) and J A Leaning (110) v. Nottinghamshire at Leeds, 2015
254	A W Gale (164) and J M Bairstow (139) v. Worcestershire at Scarborough, 2015
249	W B Stott (143) and G Boycott (145) v. Lancashire at Sheffield, 1963
247*	R G Lumb (165*) and S N Hartley (104*) v. Gloucestershire at Bradford, 1984
247	M Leyland (263) and L Hutton (83) v. Essex at Hull, 1936
238	D S Lehmann (216) and M J Lumb (92) v. Sussex at Arundel, 2002
233	D Byas (120) and P E Robinson (189) v. Lancashire at Scarborough, 1991
231	J E Root (236) and J M Bairstow (186) v. Derbyshire at Leeds, 2013
226	W H Wilkinson (89) and G H Hirst (140) v. Northamptonshire at Hull, 1909
225	C H Grimshaw (85) and G H Hirst (166*) v. Oxford University at Oxford, 1906
212	B B Wilson (108) and G H Hirst (166*) v. Sussex at Hastings, 1913
212	G Boycott (260*) and J H Hampshire (80) v. Essex at Colchester, 1970
211	J V Wilson (120) and W Watson (108) v. Derbyshire at Harrogate, 1951
210*	A Mitchell (150*) and M Leyland (117*) v. Worcestershire at Worcester, 1933
210	E I. Lester (178) and W Watson (97) v. Nottinghamshire at Nottingham, 1952
207	D Byas (213) and C White (107*) v. Worcestershire at Scarborough, 1995
206	J A Rudolph (121) and A W Gale (150) v. Surrey at The Oval, 2008
205*	G Boycott (151*) and P J Sharpe (79*) v. Leicestershire at Leicester, 1964
205	E Oldroyd (121) and R Kilner (117) v. Worcestershire at Dudley, 1922
205	W Watson (162*) and E I Lester (98) v. Somerset at Leeds, 1953
205	A Lyth (111) and J M Bairstow (246) v. Hampshire at Leeds, 2016
204	A W Gale (148) and G S Ballance (90) v. Surrey at Leeds, 2013
201*	J H Hampshire (105*) and D B Close (101*) v. Surrey at Bradford, 1965
203	P A Jaques (160) and G S Ballance (121*) v. Gloucestershire at Bristol, 2012
201	W H H Sutcliffe (181) and L Hutton (120) v. Kent at Canterbury, 1952
200	J V Wilson (92) and W Watson (122) v. Somerset at Taunton, 1950
198	A A Metcalfe (138) and D Byas (95) v. Warwickshire at Leeds, 1989
198	A W Gale (124) and J M Bairstow (95) v. Durham at Chester-le-Street, 2014
197	N W D Yardley (177) and A Coxon (58) v. Derbyshire at Scarborough, 1947
197	A Lyth (248*) and J M Bairstow (118) v. Leicestershire at Leicester, 2012
196	M D Moxon (130) and D L Bairstow (104) v. Derbyshire at Harrogate, 1987
193	A Drake (85) and G H Hirst (156) v. Lancashire at Manchester, 1911
192	J V Wilson (132) and W Watson (105) v. Essex at Bradford, 1955
191	M Leyland (114) and C Turner (63) v. Essex at Ilford, 1938
190	A W Gale (125) and J A Leaning (76) v. Hampshire at West End, Southampton, 2015
188	H Myers (60) and G H Hirst (158) v. Cambridge University at Cambridge, 1910
188	G S Ballance (159) and J A Leaning (69) v. Kent at Canterbury, 2019
187	E Oldroyd (168) and F E Greenwood (104*) v. Glamorgan at Hull, 1929
187	K Taylor (203*) and W B Stott (57) v. Warwickshire at Birmingham, 1961
186	D S Lehmann (193) and D Byas (100) v. Leicestershire at Leicester, 2001
184	J H Hampshire (96) and R Illingworth (100*) v. Leicestershire at Sheffield, 1968
182*	E I Lester (101*) and W Watson (103*) v. Nottinghamshire at Bradford, 1952
180*	G Boycott (207*) and B Leadbeater (50*) v. Cambridge University at Cambridge, 1976
180	J Tunnicliffe (139*) and G H Hirst (108) v. Surrey at The Oval, 1904
179	J H Hampshire (179) and S N Hartley (63) v. Surrey at Harrogate, 1981
179	M D Moxon (171*) and R J Blakey (71) v. Kent at Leeds, 1993
178	E I Lester (186) and J V Wilson (71) v. Warwickshire at Scarborough, 1949
177	J D Love (105*) and J H Hampshire (89) v. Lancashire at Manchester, 1980
175	L Hutton (177) and W Barber (84) v. Sussex at Scarborough, 1939
175	A McGrath (188*) and J A Rudolph (82) v. Warwickshire at Birmingham, 2007

FIFTH WICKET (Qualification 150 runs)

340	E Wainwright (228) and G H Hirst (186) v. Surrey at The Oval, 1899
329	F Mitchell (194) and E Wainwright (153) v. Leicestershire at Leicester, 1899
297	A W Gale (272) and G S Ballance (141) v. Nottinghamshire at Scarborough, 2013
276	W Rhodes (104*) and R Kilner (166) v. Northamptonshire at Northampton, 1921
273	L Hutton (270*) and N W D Yardley (136) v. Hampshire at Bournemouth, 1947

245*	H Sutcliffe (107*) and W Barber (128*) v. Northamptonshire at Northampton, 1939
229	D S Lehmann (193) and C White (79) v. Kent at Canterbury, 2006
217	D B Close (140*) and R Illingworth (107) v. Warwickshire at Sheffield, 1962
213	T Kohler-Cadmore (176) and J A Tattersall (135*) v. Leeds/Bradford MCCU at Weetwood, Leeds, 2019
207	G S Ballance (107) and A U Rashid (180) v. Somerset at Leeds, 2013
198	E Wainwright (145) and R Peel (111) v. Sussex at Bradford, 1896
198	W Barber (168) and K R Davidson (101*) v. MCC at Lord's, 1934
196*	R Kilner (115*) and G H Hirst (82*) v. Gloucestershire at Leeds, 1919
195	M J Lumb (93) and C White (173*) v. Derbyshire at Derby, 2003
194*	Younus Khan (202*) and G L Brophy (100*) v. Hampshire at Southampton, 2007
193	A Mitchell (189) and W Rhodes (88) v. Northamptonshire at Northampton, 1926
193	J D Love (106) and S N Hartley (108) v. Oxford University at Oxford, 1985
192	C W J Athey (114*) and J D Love (123) v. Surrey at The Oval, 1982
191*	L Hutton (271*) and C Turner (81*) v. Derbyshire at Sheffield, 1937
191	M G Bevan (105) and A A Metcalfe (100) v. West Indians at Scarborough, 1995
190*	R J Blakey (204*) and J D Love (79*) v. Gloucestershire at Leeds, 1987
189	J E Root (160) and G S Ballance (87) v. Sussex at Scarborough 2011
188	D E V Padgett (146) and J V Wilson (72) v. Sussex at Middlesbrough, 1960
187	J V Wilson (230) and H Halliday (74) v. Derbyshire at Sheffield, 1952
185	G Boycott (104*) and K Sharp (99) v. Kent at Tunbridge Wells, 1984
182	E Lockwood (208) and E Lumb (40) v. Kent at Gravesend, 1882
182	B B Wilson (109) and W Rhodes (111) v. Sussex at Hove, 1910
182	D B Close (164) and J V Wilson (55) v. Combined Services at Harrogate, 1954
182	A W Gale (126*) and J A Leaning (76) v. Middlesex at Scarborough, 2014
181	A A Metcalfe (149) and J D Love (88) v. Glamorgan at Leeds, 1986
177	Hon F S Jackson (87) and G H Hirst (232*) v. Surrey at The Oval, 1905
176	L Hutton (176*) and A Coxon (72) v. Sussex at Sheffield, 1948
175	A Drake (108) and R Kilner (77) v. Cambridge University at Cambridge, 1913
173	H Sutcliffe (206) and R Kilner (124) v. Warwickshire at Dewsbury, 1925
170	W Rhodes (157) and R Kilner (87) v. Derbyshire at Leeds, 1925
170	J V Wilson (130*) and N W D Yardley (67) v. Lancashire at Manchester, 1954
169	W Watson (147) and A B Sellers (92) v. Worcestershire at Worcester, 1947
169	A T Barber (63) and A Mitchell (122*) v. Worcestershire at Worcester, 1929
167	J M Bairstow (136) and G S Ballance (61) v. Somerset at Taunton 2011
165	E Oldroyd (143) and W Rhodes (110) v. Glamorgan at Leeds, 1922
165	K Sharp (100*) and P Carrick (73) v. Middlesex at Lord's, 1980
159	A A Metcalfe (151) and D L Bairstow (88) v. Northamptonshire at Luton, 1986
159*	J D Love (170*) and D L Bairstow (52*) v. Worcestershire at Worcester, 1979
159	D B Close (128) and R Illingworth (74) v. Lancashire at Sheffield, 1959
159	J H Hampshire (183*) and C Johnson (53) v. Sussex at Hove, 1971
158*	G Boycott (153*) and P E Robinson (74*) v. Derbyshire at Harrogate, 1984
157	T L Taylor (135*) and G H Hirst (72) v. An England XI at Hastings, 1901
157	G H Hirst (142) and F Smith (51) v. Somerset at Bradford, 1903
157	W Barber (87) and N W D Yardley (101) v. Surrey at The Oval, 1937
156	A McGrath (158) and I J Harvey (103) v. Derbyshire at Derby, 2005
155	J M Bairstow (102) and J A Leaning (82) v. Hampshire at Leeds, 2015
153	S N Hartley (87) and M D Moxon (112*) v. Indians at Scarborough, 1986
152	J H Hampshire (83) and S N Hartley (106) v. Nottinghamshire at Nottingham, 1981
151*	G H Hirst (102*) and R Kilner (50*) v. Kent at Bradford, 1913
151	G H Hirst (120) and F Smith (55) v. Kent at Leeds, 1903
151	W Rhodes (57) and R Kilner (90) v. Nottinghamshire at Nottingham, 1925

SIXTH WICKET (Qualification 150 runs)

296	A Lyth (251) and A U Rashid (159*) v. Lancashire at Manchester, 2014
276	M Leyland (191) and E Robinson (124*) v. Glamorgan at Swansea, 1926
252	C White (181) and R J Blakey (109*) v. Lancashire at Leeds, 1996
248	G J Maxwell (140) and A U Rashid (127) v. Durham at Scarborough, 2015
233	M W Booth (210) and G H Hirst (100) v. Worcestershire at Worcester, 1911

229	W Rhodes (267*) and N Kilner (112) v. Leicestershire at Leeds, 1921	
225	E Wainwright (91) and Lord Hawke (127) v. Hampshire at Southampton, 1899	
217*	H Sutcliffe (200*) and A Wood (123*) v. Worcestershire at Sheffield, 1935	
214	W Watson (214*) and N W D Yardley (76) v. Worcestershire at Worcester, 1955	
205	G H Hirst (125) and S Haigh (159) v. Nottinghamshire at Sheffield, 1901	
200	D Denton (127) and G H Hirst (134) v. Essex at Bradford, 1902	
198	M Leyland (247) and W Rhodes (100*) v. Worcestershire at Worcester, 1928	
190	W Rhodes (126) and M Leyland (79) v. Middlesex at Bradford, 1923	
190	J A Rudolph (122) and A U Rashid (86) v. Surrey at The Oval, 2007	
188	W Watson (174) and R Illingworth (53) v. Lancashire at Sheffield, 1955	
188	M P Vaughan (161) and R J Blakey (92) v. Essex at Ilford, 1997.	
188	G S Ballance (111) and A U Rashid (82) v. Warwickshire at Birmingham 2011	
184	R Kilner (104) and M W Booth (79) v. Leicestershire at Leeds, 1913	
183	G H Hirst (131) and E Smith (129) v. Hampshire at Bradford, 1899	
183	W Watson (139*) and R Illingworth (78) v. Somerset at Harrogate, 1956	
178*	D Denton (108*) and G H Hirst (112*) v. Lancashire at Manchester, 1902	
178*	N W D Yardley (100*) and R Illingworth (71*) v. Gloucestershire at Bristol, 1955	
178	E Robinson (100) and D C F Burton (83) v. Derbyshire at Hull, 1921	
178	H Sutcliffe (135) and P A Gibb (157*) v. Nottinghamshire at Sheffield, 1935	
175	G M Fellows (88) and R J Blakey (103) v. Warwickshire at Birmingham, 2002	
174	D S Lehmann (136) and G M Hamilton (73) v. Kent at Maidstone, 1998	
173	T Kohler-Cadmore (81) and A J Hodd (85) v. Somerset at Leeds, 2018	
172	A J Dalton (119*) and D L Bairstow (62) v. Worcestershire at Dudley, 1971	
170*	A U Rashid 103*) and A J Hodd (68*) v. Somerset at Taunton, 2013	
170	A W Gale (101) and T T Bresnan (97) v. Worcestershire at Worcester, 2009	
169	W Barber (124) and H Verity (78*) v. Warwickshire at Birmingham, 1933	
169	R Illingworth (162) and J Birkenshaw (37) v. Indians at Sheffield, 1959	
166	E Wainwright (116) and E Smith (61) v. Kent at Catford, 1900	
166	D B Close (161) and F S Trueman (104) v. Northamptonshire at Northampton, 1963	
162*	G Boycott (220*) and J G Binks (70*) v. Northamptonshire at Sheffield, 1967	
161*	D L Bairstow (100*) and P Carrick (59*) v. Middlesex at Leeds, 1983	
159*	D S Lehmann (187*) and R J Blakey (78*) v. Somerset at Bath, 2001	
159	J M Bairstow (182) and A McGrath (90) v. Leicestershire at Scarborough, 2012	
156	W Rhodes (82*) and E Robinson (94) v. Derbyshire at Chesterfield, 1919	
154	C Turner (84) and A Wood (79) v. Glamorgan at Swansea, 1936	
153*	J A Rudolph (92*) and A U Rashid (73*) v. Worcestershire at Kidderminster, 2007	
153	J A Rudolph (69*) and J M Bairstow (81) v. Warwickshire at Birmingham, 2010	
151	D Denton (91) and W Rhodes (76) v. Middlesex at Sheffield, 1904	
151	G Boycott (152*) and P Carrick (75) v. Warwickshire at Leeds, 1982	
150	G Ulyett (199*) and J M Preston (93) v. Derbyshire at Sheffield, 1887	

SEVENTH WICKET (Qualification 125 runs)

366*	J M Bairstow (219*) and T T Bresnan (169*) v. Durham at Chester-le-Street, 2015	
254	W Rhodes (135) and D C F Burton (142*) v. Hampshire at Dewsbury, 1919	
247	P Holmes (285) and W Rhodes (79) v. Nottinghamshire at Nottingham, 1929	
227	J M Bairstow (246) and L E Plunkett (126) v. Hampshire at Leeds, 2016	
215	E Robinson (135*) and D C F Burton (110) v. Leicestershire at Leicester, 1921	
197	G S Ballance (165*) and T T Bresnan (78) v. Sussex at Hove, 2015	
185	E Wainwright (100) and G H Hirst (134) v. Gloucestershire at Bristol, 1897	
183	G H Hirst (341) and H Myers (57) v. Leicestershire at Leicester, 1905	
183	J A Rudolph (220) and T T Bresnan (101*) v. Warwickshire at Scarborough, 2007	
180	C Turner (130) and A Wood (97) v. Somerset at Sheffield, 1936	
170	G S Blewett (190) and G M Hamilton (84*) v. Northamptonshire at Scarborough, 1999	
168	G L Brophy (99) and A U Rashid (157*) v. Lancashire at Leeds, 2009	
166	R Peel (55) and I Grimshaw (122*) v. Derbyshire at Holbeck, 1886	
162	E Wainwright (109) and S Haigh (73) v. Somerset at Taunton, 1900	
162	R J Blakey (90) and R K J Dawson (87) v. Kent at Canterbury, 2002	
162	A W Gale (149) and G L Brophy (97) v. Warwickshire at Scarborough, 2006	

161	R G Lumb (118) and C M Old (89) v. Worcestershire at Bradford, 1980
160	J Tunnicliffe (158) and D Hunter (58*) v. Worcestershire at Worcester, 1900
157*	F A Lowson (259*) and R Booth (53*) v. Worcestershire at Worcester, 1953
157	K S Williamson (189) and T T Bresnan (61) v. Sussex at Scarborough, 2014
155	D Byas (122*) and P Carrick (61) v. Leicestershire at Leicester.1991.
154*	G H Hirst (76*) and J T Newstead (100*) v. Nottinghamshire at Nottingham, 1908
148	J Rowbotham (113) and J Thewlis (50) v. Surrey at The Oval, 1873
147	E Wainwright (78) and G Ulyett (73) v. Somerset at Taunton, 1893
147	M P Vaughan (153) and R J Harden (64) v. Kent at Scarborough, 1999
143	C White (135*) and A K D Gray (60) v. Durham at Chester-le-Street, 2003
141	G H Hirst (108*) and S Haigh (48) v. Worcestershire at Worcester, 1905
141	J H Hampshire (149*) and J G Binks (72) v. MCC at Scarborough, 1965
140	E Wainwright (117) and S Haigh (54) v. CI Thornton's XI at Scarborough, 1900
140	D Byas (67) and P J Hartley (75) v. Derbyshire at Chesterfield, 1990
138	D Denton (78) and G H Hirst (103*) v. Sussex at Leeds, 1905
136	GH Hirst (93) and S Haigh (138) v. Warwickshire at Birmingham, 1904
136	E Robinson (77*) and A Wood (65) v. Glamorgan at Scarborough, 1931
133*	W Rhodes (267*) and M Leyland (52*) v. Leicestershire at Leeds, 1921
133*	E I Lester (86*) and A B Sellers (73*) v. Northamptonshire at Northampton, 1948
133	D Byas (100) and P W Jarvis (80) v. Northamptonshire at Scarborough, 1992
132	W Rhodes (196) and S Haigh (59*) v. Worcestershire at Worcester, 1904
132	A J Hodd (96*) and Azeem Rafiq (71) v. Nottinghamshire at Scarborough, 2016
131*	D L Bairstow (79*) and A Sidebottom (52*) v. Oxford University at Oxford, 1981
130	P J Sharpe (64) and J V Wilson (134) v. Warwickshire at Birmingham, 1962
128	W Barber (66) and T F Smailes (86) v. Cambridge University at Cambridge, 1938
128	D B Close (88*) and A Coxon (59) v. Essex at Leeds, 1949
126	E Wainwright (171) and R Peel (46) v. Middlesex at Lord's, 1897
126	W Rhodes (91) and G G Macaulay (63) v. Hampshire at Hull, 1925
126	J C Balderstone (58) and J G Binks (95) v. Middlesex at Lord's, 1964
126	J M Bairstow (70) and A U Rashid (59) v. Kent at Canterbury, 2010
125	A B Sellers (109) and T F Smailes (65) v. Kent at Bradford, 1937

EIGHTH WICKET (Qualification 125 runs)

292	R Peel (210*) and Lord Hawke (166) v. Warwickshire at Birmingham, 1896
238	I J Harvey (209*) and T T Bresnan (74) v. Somerset at Leeds, 2005
192*	W Rhodes (108*) and G G Macaulay (101*) v. Essex at Harrogate, 1922
192	A U Rashid (117*) and A Shahzad (78) v. Hampshire at Basingstoke, 2009
180	W Barber (191) and T F Smailes (89) v. Sussex at Leeds, 1935
167	J A Leaning (118) and J A Brooks (109*) v. Lancashire at Manchester, 2017
165	S Haigh (62) and Lord Hawke (126) v. Surrey at The Oval, 1902
163	G G Macaulay (67) and A Waddington (114) v. Worcestershire at Leeds, 1927
159	E Smith (95) and W Rhodes (105) v. MCC at Scarborough, 1901
157	A Shahzad (88) and D J Wainwright (85*) v. Sussex at Hove, 2009
156	G S Ballance (112) and R J Sidebottom (40) v. Leeds/Bradford MCCU at Leeds, 2013
152	W Rhodes (98) and J W Rothery (70) v. Hampshire at Portsmouth, 1904
151	W Rhodes (201) and Lord Hawke (51) v. Somerset at Taunton, 1905
151	R J Blakey (80*) and P J Hartley (89) v. Sussex at Eastbourne, 1996
149	G L Brophy (177*) and R J Sidebottom (61) v. Worcestershire at Worcester 2011
147	J P G Chadwick (59) and F S Trueman (101) v. Middlesex at Scarborough, 1965
146	S Haigh (159) and Lord Hawke (89) v. Nottinghamshire at Sheffield, 1901
144	G L Brophy (85) and D J Wainwright (102*) v. Warwickshire at Scarborough, 2009
138	E Wainwright (100) and Lord Hawke (81) v. Kent at Tonbridge, 1899
137	E Wainwright (171) and Lord Hawke (75) v. Middlesex at Lord's, 1897
135	P W Jarvis (55) and P J Hartley (69) v. Nottinghamshire at Scarborough, 1992
133	R Illingworth (61) and F S Trueman (74) v. Leicestershire at Leicester, 1955
132	G H Hirst (103) and E Smith (59) v. Middlesex at Sheffield, 1904
132	W Watson (119) and J H Wardle (65) v. Leicestershire at Leicester, 1949
131	P E Robinson (85) and P Carrick (64) v. Surrey at Harrogate, 1990
130	E Smith (98) and Lord Hawke (54) v. Lancashire at Leeds, 1904

CENTURY PARTNERSHIPS *(Continued)*

128	H Verity (96*) and T F Smailes (77) v. Indians at Bradford, 1936
128	D L Bairstow (145) and G B Stevenson (11) v. Middlesex at Scarborough, 1980
127	E Robinson (70*) and A Wood (62) v. Middlesex at Leeds, 1928
126	R Peel (74) and E Peate (61) v. Gloucestershire at Bradford, 1883
126	M W Booth (56) and E R Wilson (104*) v. Essex at Bradford, 1913
126	J D Middlebrook (84) and C E W Silverwood (70) v. Essex at Chelmsford, 2001
126	M J Lumb (115*) and D Gough (72) v. Hampshire at Southampton, 2003

NINTH WICKET (Qualification 100 runs)

246	T T Bresnan (116) and J N Gillespie (123*) v. Surrey at The Oval, 2007
192	G H Hirst (130*) and S Haigh (85) v. Surrey at Bradford, 1898
179	R A Hutton (189) and G A Cope (30*) v. Pakistanis at Bradford, 1971
176*	R Moorhouse (59*) and G H Hirst (115*) v. Gloucestershire at Bristol, 1894
173	S Haigh (85) and W Rhodes (92*) v. Sussex at Hove, 1902
171	G S Ballance (194) and J A Brooks (82) v. Worcestershire at Worcester, 2018
167	H Verity (89) and T F Smailes (80) v. Somerset at Bath, 1936
162	W Rhodes (94*) and S Haigh (84) v. Lancashire at Manchester, 1904
161	E Smith (116*) and W Rhodes (79) v. Sussex at Sheffield, 1900
154	R M Pyrah (117) and R J Sidebottom (52) v.Lancashire at Leeds 2011
151	J M Bairstow (205) and R J Sidebottom (45*) v. Nottinghamshire at Nottingham 2011
150	Azeem Rafiq (100) and M J Hoggard (56*) v. Worcestershire at Worcester, 2009
149*	R J Blakey (63*) and A K D Gray (74*) v. Leicestershire at Scarborough, 2002
149	G H Hirst (232*) and D Hunter (40) v. Surrey at The Oval, 1905
146	G H Hirst (214) and W Rhodes (53) v. Worcestershire at Worcester, 1901
144	T T Bresnan (91) and J N Gillespie (44) v. Hampshire at Leeds, 2006
140	A U Rashid (111) and D J Wainwright (104) v. Sussex at Hove, 2008
136	R Peel (210*) and G H Hirst (85) v. Warwickshire at Birmingham, 1896
125*	L Hutton (269*) and A Coxon (65*) v. Northamptonshire at Wellingborough, 1949
124	P J Hartley (87*) and P W Jarvis (47) v. Essex at Chelmsford, 1986
120	G H Hirst (138) and W Rhodes (38) v. Nottinghamshire at Nottingham, 1899
119	A B Sellers (80*) and E P Robinson (66) v. Warwickshire at Birmingham, 1938
118	S Haigh (96) and W Rhodes (44) v. Somerset at Leeds, 1901
114	E Oldroyd (194) and A Dolphin (47) v. Worcestershire at Worcester, 1923
114	N Kilner (102*) and G G Macaulay (60) v. Gloucestershire at Bristol, 1923
113	G G Macaulay (125*) and A Waddington (44) v. Nottinghamshire at Nottingham, 1921
113	A Wood (69) and H.Verity (45*) v. MCC at Lord's, 1938
112	G H Hirst (78) and Lord Hawke (44*) v. Essex at Leyton, 1907
109	Lees Whitehead (60) and W Rhodes (81*) v. Sussex at Harrogate, 1899
108	A McGrath (133*) and C E W Silverwood (80) v. Durham at Chester-le-Street, 2005
106	L E Plunkett (86) and S A Patterson (43) v. Warwickshire at Leeds, 2014
105	J V Wilson (134) and A G Nicholson (20*) v. Nottinghamshire at Leeds, 1962
105	C M Old (100*) and H P Cooper (30) v. Lancashire at Manchester, 1978
105	C White (74*) and J D Batty (50) v. Gloucestershire at Sheffield, 1993
104	L Hall (129*) and R Moorhouse (86) v. Gloucestershire at Clifton, 1888
100	G Pollitt (51) and Lees Whitehead (54) v. Hampshire at Bradford, 1899

TENTH WICKET (Qualification 100 runs)

149	G Boycott (79) and G B Stevenson (115*) v. Warwickshire at Birmingham, 1982
148	Lord Hawke (107*) and D Hunter (47) v. Kent at Sheffield, 1898
144	A Sidebottom (124) and A L Robinson (30*) v. Glamorgan at Cardiff, 1977
121	J T Brown (141) and D Hunter (25*) v. Liverpool & District at Liverpool, 1894
118	Lord Hawke (110*) and D Hunter (41) v. Kent at Leeds, 1896
113	P J Hartley (88*) and R D Stemp (22) v. Middlesex at Lord's, 1996
110	C E W Silverwood (45*) and R D Stemp (65) v. Durham at Chester-le-Street, 1996
109	A Shahzad (70) and R J Sidebottom (45*) v. Worcestershire at Scarborough, 2011
108	Lord Hawke (79) and Lees Whitehead (45*) v. Lancashire at Manchester, 1903
108	G Boycott (129) and M K Bore (37*) v. Nottinghamshire at Bradford, 1973
106	A B Sellers (79) and D V Brennan (30) v. Worcestershire at Worcester, 1948
103	A Dolphin (62*) and E Smith (49) v. Essex at Leyton, 1919
102	D Denton (77*) and D Hunter (45) v. Cambridge University at Cambridge, 1895

FIFTEEN WICKETS OR MORE IN A MATCH

**A complete list of 12, 13 and 14 wickets in a match up to and including 2007
is to be found in the 2008 edition**

W E BOWES (1)

16 for 35 (8 for 18 and 8 for 17) v. Northamptonshire at Kettering, 1935

A DRAKE (1)

15 for 51 (5 for 16 and 10 for 35) v. Somerset at Weston-super-Mare, 1914

T EMMETT (1)

16 for 38 (7 for 15 and 9 for 23) v. Cambridgeshire at Hunslet, 1869

G H HIRST (1)

15 for 63 (8 for 25 and 7 for 38) v. Leicestershire at Hull, 1907

R ILLINGWORTH (1)

15 for 123 (8 for 70 and 7 for 53) v. Glamorgan at Swansea, 1960

R PEEL (1)

15 for 50 (9 for 22 and 6 for 28) v. Somerset at Leeds, 1895

W RHODES (1)

15 for 56 (9 for 28 and 6 for 28) v. Essex at Leyton, 1899

H VERITY (4)

17 for 91 (8 for 47 and 9 for 44) v. Essex at Leyton, 1933
15 for 129 (8 for 56 and 7 for 73) v. Oxford University at Oxford, 1936
15 for 38 (6 for 26 and 9 for 12) v. Kent at Sheffield, 1936
15 for 100 (6 for 52 and 9 for 48) v. Essex at Westcliffe-on-Sea, 1936

J H WARDLE (1)

16 for 112 (9 for 48 and 7 for 64) v. Sussex at Hull, 1954

TEN WICKETS IN A MATCH
(including best analysis)

61	W Rhodes	15 for	56	v Essex	at Leyton	1899
48	H Verity	17 for	91	v Essex	at Leyton	1933
40	G H Hirst	15 for	63	v Leicestershire	at Hull	1907
31	G G Macaulay	14 for	92	v Gloucestershire	at Bristol	1926
28	S Haigh	14 for	43	v Hampshire	at Southampton	1898
27	R Peel	14 for	33	v Nottinghamshire	at Sheffield	1888
25	W E Bowes	16 for	35	v Northamptonshire	at Kettering	1935
25	J H Wardle	16 for	112	v Sussex	at Hull	1954
22	E Peate	14 for	77	v Surrey	at Huddersfield	1881
20	F S Trueman	14 for	123	v Surrey	at The Oval	1960
19	T Emmett	16 for	38	v Cambridgeshire	at Hunslet	1869
17	R Appleyard	12 for	43	v Essex	at Bradford	1951
15	E Wainwright	14 for	77	v Essex	at Bradford	1896
11	R Illingworth	15 for	123	v Glamorgan	at Swansea	1960
10	A Waddington	13 for	48	v Northamptonshire	at Northampton	1920
9	M W Booth	14 for	160	v Essex	at Leyton	1914
9	R Kilner	12 for	55	v Sussex	at Hove	1924
8	W Bates	11 for	47	v Nottinghamshire	at Nottingham	1881
8	G Freeman	13 for	60	v Surrey	at Sheffield	1869
7	E P Robinson	13 for	115	v Lancashire	at Leeds	1939
7	D Wilson	13 for	52	v Warwickshire	at Middlesbrough	1967
6	G A Cope	12 for	116	v Glamorgan	at Cardiff (Sophia Gardens)	1968
6	A Hill	12 for	59	v Surrey	at The Oval	1871

6 T F Smailes	14 for 58	v Derbyshire	at Sheffield	1939
5 P Carrick	12 for 89	v Derbyshire	at Sheffield (Abbeydale Pk)	1983
5 J M Preston	13 for 63	v MCC	at Scarborough	1888
5 E Robinson	12 for 95	v Northamptonshire	at Huddersfield	1927
4 J T Newstead	11 for 72	v Worcestershire	at Bradford	1907
3 T W Foster	11 for 93	v Liverpool & District	at Liverpool	1894
3 G P Harrison	11 for 76	v Kent	at Dewsbury	1883
3 F S Jackson	12 for 80	v Hampshire	at Southampton	1897
3 P W Jarvis	11 for 92	v Middlesex	at Lord's	1986
3 S P Kirby	13 for 154	v Somerset	at Taunton	2003
3 A G Nicholson	12 for 73	v Glamorgan	at Leeds	1964
3 R K Platt	10 for 87	v Surrey	at The Oval	1959
3 A Sidebottom	11 for 64	v Kent	at Sheffield (Abbeydale Pk)	1980
3 R J Sidebottom	11 for 43	v Kent	at Leeds	2000
3 G Ulyett	12 for 102	v Lancashire	at Huddersfield	1889
2 T Armitage	13 for 46	v Surrey	at Sheffield	1876
2 R Aspinall	14 for 65	v Northamptonshire	at Northampton	1947
2 J T Brown (Darfield)	12 for 109	v Gloucestershire	at Huddersfield	1899
2 R O Clayton	12 for 104	v Lancashire	at Manchester	1877
2 D B Close	11 for 116	v Kent	at Gillingham	1965
2 B O Coad	10 for 102	v. Warwickshire	at Birmingham	2017
2 M J Cowan	12 for 87	v Warwickshire	at Birmingham	1960
2 A Coxon	10 for 57	v Derbyshire	at Chesterfield	1949
2 D Gough	10 for 80	v Lancashire	at Leeds	1995
2 G M Hamilton	11 for 72	v Surrey	at Leeds	1998
2 P J Hartley	11 for 68	v Derbyshire	at Chesterfield	1995
2 R A Hutton	11 for 62	v Lancashire	at Manchester	1971
2 E Leadbeater	11 for 162	v Nottinghamshire	at Nottingham	1950
2 K A Maharaj	10 for 127	v. Somerset	at Leeds	2019
2 M A Robinson	12 for 124	v Northamptonshire	at Harrogate	1993
2 M Ryan	10 for 77	v Leicestershire	at Bradford	1962
2 E Smith (Morley)	10 for 97	v MCC	at Scarborough	1893
2 G B Stevenson	11 for 74	v Nottinghamshire	at Nottingham	1980
2 S Wade	11 for 56	v Gloucestershire	at Cheltenham	1886
2 E R Wilson	11 for 109	v Sussex	at Hove	1921
1 A B Bainbridge	12 for 111	v Essex	at Harrogate	1961
1 J Birkenshaw	11 for 134	v Middlesex	at Leeds	1960
1 A Booth	10 for 91	v Indians	at Bradford	1946
1 H P Cooper	11 for 96	v Northamptonshire	at Northampton	1976
1 A Drake	15 for 51	v Somerset	at Weston-Super-Mare	1914
1 L Greenwood	11 for 71	v Surrey	at The Oval	1867
1 P M Hutchison	11 for 102	v Pakistan 'A'	at Leeds	1997
1 L Hutton	10 for 101	v Leicestershire	at Leicester (Aylestone Rd)	1937
1 R Iddison	10 for 68	v Surrey	at Sheffield	1864
1 M Leyland	10 for 94	v Leicestershire	at Leicester (Aylestone Rd)	1933
1 J D Middlebrook	10 for 170	v Hampshire	at Southampton	2000
1 F W Milligan	12 for 110	v Sussex	at Sheffield	1897
1 H Myers	12 for 192	v Gloucestershire	at Dewsbury	1904
1 C M Old	11 for 46	v Gloucestershire	at Middlesbrough	1969
1 D Pickles	12 for 133	v Somerset	at Taunton	1957
1 A U Rashid	11 for 114	v Worcestershire	at Worcester	2011
1 W Ringrose	11 for 135	v Australians	at Bradford	1905
1 C E W Silverwood	12 for 148	v Kent	at Leeds	1997
1 W Slinn	12 for 53	v Nottinghamshire	at Nottingham	1864
1 J Waring	10 for 63	v Lancashire	at Leeds	1966
1 F Wilkinson	10 for 129	v Hampshire	at Bournemouth	1938
1 A C Williams	10 for 66	v Hampshire	at Dewsbury	1919

TEN WICKETS IN AN INNINGS

Bowler				Year
A Drake	10 for 35	v.	Somerset at Weston-super-Mare	1914
H Verity	10 for 36	v.	Warwickshire at Leeds	1931
*H Verity	10 for 10	v.	Nottinghamshire at Leeds	1932
T F Smailes	10 for 47	v.	Derbyshire at Sheffield	1939

*Includes the hat trick.

EIGHT WICKETS OR MORE IN AN INNINGS

(Ten wickets in an innings also listed above)

A complete list of seven wickets in an innings up to and including 2007 is to be found in the 2008 edition

R APPLEYARD (1)

8 for 76 v. MCC at Scarborough, 1951

R ASPINALL (1)

8 for 42 v. Northamptonshire at Northampton, 1947

W BATES (2)

8 for 45 v. Lancashire at Huddersfield, 1878
8 for 21 v. Surrey at The Oval, 1879

M W BOOTH (4)

8 for 52 v. Leicestershire at Sheffield, 1912
8 for 47 v. Middlesex at Leeds, 1912
8 for 86 v. Middlesex at Sheffield, 1913
8 for 64 v. Essex at Leyton, 1914

W E BOWES (9)

8 for 77 v. Leicestershire at Dewsbury, 1929
8 for 69 v. Middlesex at Bradford, 1930
9 for 121 v. Essex at Scarborough, 1932
8 for 62 v. Sussex at Hove, 1932
8 for 69 v. Gloucestershire at Gloucester, 1933
8 for 40 v.Worcestershire at Sheffield, 1935
8 for 18 v. Northamptonshire at Kettering, 1935
8 for 17 v. Northamptonshire at Kettering, 1935
8 for 56 v. Leicestershire at Scarborough, 1936

J T BROWN (Darfield) (1)

8 for 40 v. Gloucestershire at Huddersfield, 1899

P CARRICK (2)

8 for 33 v. Cambridge University at Cambridge, 1973
8 for 72 v. Derbyshire at Scarborough, 1975

R O CLAYTON (1)

8 for 66 v. Lancashire at Manchester, 1877

D B CLOSE (2)

8 for 41 v. Kent at Leeds, 1959
8 for 43 v. Essex at Leeds, 1960

H P COOPER (1)

8 for 62 v. Glamorgan at Cardiff, 1975

EIGHT WICKETS OR MORE IN AN INNINGS *(Continued)*

G A COPE (1)

8 for 73 v. Gloucestershire at Bristol, 1975

M J COWAN (1)

9 for 43 v. Warwickshire at Birmingham, 1960

A COXON (1)

8 for 31 v. Worcestershire at Leeds, 1946

A DRAKE (2)

8 for 59 v. Gloucestershire at Sheffield, 1913
10 for 35 v. Somerset at Weston-super-Mare, 1914

T EMMETT (8)

9 for 34 v. Nottinghamshire at Dewsbury, 1868
9 for 23 v. Cambridgeshire at Hunslet, 1869
8 for 31 v. Nottinghamshire at Sheffield, 1871
8 for 46 v. Gloucestershire at Clifton, 1877
8 for 16 v. MCC at Scarborough, 1877
8 for 22 v. Surrey at The Oval, 1881
8 for 52 v. MCC at Scarborough, 1882
8 for 32 v. Sussex at Huddersfield, 1884

S D FLETCHER (1)

8 for 58 v. Essex at Sheffield, 1988

T W FOSTER (1)

9 for 59 v. MCC at Lord's, 1894

G FREEMAN (2)

8 for 11 v. Lancashire at Holbeck, 1868
8 for 29 v. Surrey at Sheffield, 1869

L GREENWOOD (1)

8 for 35 v. Cambridgeshire at Dewsbury, 1867

S HAIGH (5)

8 for 78 v. Australians at Bradford, 1896
8 for 35 v. Hampshire at Harrogate, 1896
8 for 21 v. Hampshire at Southampton, 1898
8 for 33 v. Warwickshire at Scarborough, 1899
9 for 25 v. Gloucestershire at Leeds, 1912

P J HARTLEY (2)

8 for 111 v. Sussex at Hove, 1992
9 for 41 v. Derbyshire at Chesterfield, 1995

G H HIRST (8)

8 for 59 v. Warwickshire at Birmingham, 1896
8 for 48 v. Australians at Bradford, 1899
8 for 25 v. Leicestershire at Hull, 1907
9 for 45 v. Middlesex at Sheffield, 1907
9 for 23 v. Lancashire at Leeds, 1910
8 for 80 v. Somerset at Sheffield, 1910
9 for 41 v. Worcestershire at Worcester, 1911
9 for 69 v. MCC at Lord's, 1912

EIGHT WICKETS OR MORE IN AN INNINGS *(Continued)*

R ILLINGWORTH (5)

8 for 69 v. Surrey at The Oval, 1954
9 for 42 v. Worcestershire at Worcester, 1957
8 for 70 v. Glamorgan at Swansea, 1960
8 for 50 v. Lancashire at Manchester, 1961
8 for 20 v. Worcestershire at Leeds, 1965

R KILNER (2)

8 for 26 v. Glamorgan at Cardiff, 1923
8 for 40 v. Middlesex at Bradford, 1926

S P KIRBY (1)

8 for 80 v. Somerset at Taunton, 2003

E LEADBEATER (1)

8 for 83 v. Worcestershire at Worcester, 1950

M LEYLAND (1)

8 for 63 v. Hampshire at Huddersfield, 1938

G G MACAULAY (3)

8 for 43 v. Gloucestershire at Bristol, 1926
8 for 37 v. Derbyshire at Hull, 1927
8 for 21 v. Indians at Harrogate, 1932

H MYERS (1)

8 for 81 v. Gloucestershire at Dewsbury, 1904

A G NICHOLSON (2)

9 for 62 v. Sussex at Eastbourne, 1967
8 for 22 v. Kent at Canterbury, 1968

E PEATE (6)

8 for 24 v. Lancashire at Manchester, 1880
8 for 30 v. Surrey at Huddersfield, 1881
8 for 69 v. Sussex at Hove, 1881
8 for 32 v. Middlesex at Sheffield, 1882
8 for 5 v. Surrey at Holbeck, 1883
8 for 63 v. Kent at Gravesend, 1884

R PEEL (6)

8 for 12 v. Nottinghamshire at Sheffield, 1888
8 for 60 v. Surrey at Sheffield, 1890
8 for 54 v. Cambridge University at Cambridge, 1893
9 for 22 v. Somerset at Leeds, 1895
8 for 27 v. South of England XI at Scarborough, 1896
8 for 53 v. Kent at Halifax, 1897

J M PRESTON (2)

8 for 27 v. Sussex at Hove, 1888
9 for 28 v. MCC at Scarborough, 1888

EIGHT WICKETS OR MORE IN AN INNINGS *(Continued)*

W RHODES (18)

9 for 28 v. Essex at Leyton, 1899
8 for 38 v. Nottinghamshire at Nottingham, 1899
8 for 68 v. Cambridge University at Cambridge, 1900
8 for 43 v. Lancashire at Bradford, 1900
8 for 23 v. Hampshire at Hull, 1900
8 for 72 v. Gloucestershire at Bradford, 1900
8 for 28 v. Essex at Harrogate, 1900
8 for 53 v. Middlesex at Lord's, 1901
8 for 55 v. Kent at Canterbury, 1901
8 for 26 v. Kent at Catford, 1902
8 for 87 v. Worcestershire at Worcester, 1903
8 for 61 v. Lancashire at Bradford, 1903
8 for 90 v. Warwickshire at Birmingham, 1905
8 for 92 v. Northamptonshire at Northampton, 1911
8 for 44 v. Warwickshire at Bradford, 1919
8 for 39 v. Sussex at Leeds, 1920
8 for 48 v. Somerset at Huddersfield, 1926
9 for 39 v. Essex at Leyton, 1929

W RINGROSE (1)

9 for 76 v. Australians at Bradford, 1905

E ROBINSON (3)

9 for 36 v. Lancashire at Bradford, 1920
8 for 32 v. Northamptonshire at Huddersfield, 1927
8 for 13 v. Cambridge University at Cambridge, 1928

E P ROBINSON (2)

8 for 35 v. Lancashire at Leeds, 1939
8 for 76 v. Surrey at The Oval, 1946

M A ROBINSON (1)

9 for 37 v. Northamptonshire at Harrogate, 1993

A SIDEBOTTOM (1)

8 for 72 v. Leicestershire at Middlesbrough, 1986

T F SMAILES (2)

8 for 68 v. Glamorgan at Hull, 1938
10 for 47 v. Derbyshire at Sheffield, 1939

G B STEVENSON (2)

8 for 65 v. Lancashire at Leeds, 1978
8 for 57 v. Northamptonshire at Leeds, 1980

F S TRUEMAN (8)

8 for 70 v. Minor Counties at Lord's, 1949
8 for 68 v. Nottinghamshire at Sheffield, 1951
8 for 53 v. Nottinghamshire at Nottingham, 1951
8 for 28 v. Kent at Dover, 1954
8 for 84 v. Nottinghamshire at Worksop, 1962
8 for 45 v. Gloucestershire at Bradford, 1963
8 for 36 v. Sussex at Hove, 1965
8 for 37 v. Essex at Bradford, 1966

EIGHT WICKETS OR MORE IN AN INNINGS *(Continued)*

H VERITY (20)

9 for 60 v. Glamorgan at Swansea, 1930
10 for 36 v. Warwickshire at Leeds, 1931
8 for 33 v. Glamorgan at Swansea, 1931
8 for 107 v. Lancashire at Bradford, 1932
8 for 39 v. Northamptonshire at Northampton, 1932
10 for 10 v. Nottinghamshire at Leeds, 1932
8 for 47 v. Essex at Leyton, 1933
9 for 44 v. Essex at Leyton, 1933
9 for 59 v. Kent at Dover, 1933
8 for 28 v. Leicestershire at Leeds, 1935
8 for 56 v. Oxford University at Oxford, 1936
8 for 40 v. Worcestershire at Stourbridge, 1936
9 for 12 v. Kent at Sheffield, 1936
9 for 48 v. Essex at Westcliff-on-Sea, 1936
8 for 42 v. Nottinghamshire at Bradford, 1936
9 for 43 v. Warwickshire at Leeds, 1937
8 for 80 v. Sussex at Eastbourne, 1937
8 for 43 v. Middlesex at The Oval, 1937
9 for 62 v. MCC at Lord's, 1939
8 for 38 v. Leicestershire at Hull, 1939

A WADDINGTON (3)

8 for 34 v. Northamptonshire at Leeds, 1922
8 for 39 v. Kent at Leeds, 1922
8 for 35 v. Hampshire at Bradford, 1922

E WAINWRIGHT (3)

8 for 49 v. Middlesex at Sheffield, 1891
9 for 66 v. Middlesex at Sheffield, 1894
8 for 34 v. Essex at Bradford, 1896

J H WARDLE (4)

8 for 87 v. Derbyshire at Chesterfield, 1948
8 for 26 v. Middlesex at Lord's, 1950
9 for 48 v. Sussex at Hull, 1954
9 for 25 v. Lancashire at Manchester, 1954

C WHITE (1)

8 for 55 v. Gloucestershire at Gloucester, 1998

A C WILLIAMS (1)

9 for 29 v. Hampshire at Dewsbury, 1919

R WOOD (1)

8 for 45 v. Scotland at Glasgow, 1952

SIX WICKETS IN AN INNINGS AT LESS THAN FOUR RUNS EACH

A complete list of 5 wickets at less than 4 runs each up to and including 2007 is to be found in the 2008 edition

R APPLEYARD (2)

6 for 17 v. Essex at Bradford, 1951
6 for 12 v. Hampshire at Bournemouth, 1954

T ARMITAGE (1)

6 for 20 v. Surrey at Sheffield, 1876

R ASPINALL (1)

6 for 23 v. Northamptonshire at Northampton, 1947

W BATES (5)

6 for 11 v. Middlesex at Huddersfield, 1879
6 for 22 v. Kent at Bradford, 1881
6 for 17 v. Nottinghamshire at Nottingham, 1881
6 for 12 v. Kent at Sheffield, 1882
6 for 19 v. Lancashire at Dewsbury, 1886

A BOOTH (1)

6 for 21 v. Warwickshire at Birmingham, 1946

W E BOWES (4)

6 for 17 v. Middlesex at Lord's, 1934
6 for 16 v. Lancashire at Bradford, 1935
6 for 20 v. Gloucestershire at Sheffield, 1936
6 for 23 v. Warwickshire at Birmingham, 1947

J T BROWN (Darfield) (1)

6 for 19 v. Worcestershire at Worcester, 1899

R.O CLAYTON (1)

6 for 20 v. Nottinghamshire at Sheffield, 1876

A COXON (1)

6 for 17 v. Surrey at Sheffield, 1948

T EMMETT (6)

6 for 7 v. Surrey at Sheffield, 1867
6 for 13 v. Lancashire at Holbeck, 1868
6 for 21 v. Middlesex at Scarborough, 1874
6 for 12 v. Derbyshire at Sheffield, 1878
6 for 19 v. Derbyshire at Bradford, 1881
6 for 22 v. Australians at Bradford, 1882

H FISHER (1)

6 for 11 v. Leicestershire at Bradford, 1932

SIX WICKETS IN AN INNINGS AT LESS THAN FOUR
RUNS EACH *(Continued)*

S HAIGH (10)

6 for 18 v. Derbyshire at Bradford, 1897
6 for 22 v. Hampshire at Southampton, 1898
6 for 21 v. Surrey at The Oval, 1900
6 for 23 v. Cambridge University at Cambridge, 1902
6 for 19 v. Somerset at Sheffield, 1902
6 for 22 v. Cambridge University at Sheffield, 1903
6 for 21 v. Hampshire at Leeds, 1904
6 for 21 v. Nottinghamshire at Sheffield, 1905
6 for 13 v. Surrey at Leeds, 1908
6 for 14 v. Australians at Bradford, 1912

A HILL (2)

6 for 9 v. United South of England XI at Bradford, 1874
6 for 18 v. MCC at Lord's, 1881

G H HIRST (7)

6 for 23 v. MCC at Lord's, 1893
6 for 20 v. Lancashire at Bradford, 1906
6 for 12 v. Northamptonshire at Northampton, 1908
6 for 7 v. Northamptonshire at Northampton, 1908
6 for 23 v. Surrey at Leeds, 1908
6 for 23 v. Lancashire at Manchester, 1909
6 for 20 v. Surrey at Sheffield, 1909

R ILLINGWORTH (2)

6 for 15 v. Scotland at Hull, 1956
6 for 13 v. Leicestershire at Leicester, 1963

F S JACKSON (1)

6 for 19 v. Hampshire at Southampton, 1897

R KILNER (5)

6 for 22 v. Essex at Harrogate, 1922
6 for 13 v. Hampshire at Bournemouth, 1922
6 for 14 v. Middlesex at Bradford, 1923
6 for 22 v. Surrey at Sheffield, 1923
6 for 15 v. Hampshire at Portsmouth, 1924

G G MACAULAY (10)

6 for 10 v. Warwickshire at Birmingham, 1921
6 for 3 v. Derbyshire at Hull, 1921
6 for 8 v. Northamptonshire at Northampton, 1922
6 for 12 v. Glamorgan at Cardiff, 1922
6 for 18 v. Northamptonshire at Bradford, 1923
6 for 19 v. Northamptonshire at Northampton, 1925
6 for 22 v. Leicestershire at Leeds, 1926
6 for 11 v. Leicestershire at Hull, 1930
6 for 22 v. Leicestershire at Bradford, 1933
6 for 22 v. Middlesex at Leeds, 1934

SIX WICKETS IN AN INNINGS AT LESS THAN FOUR RUNS EACH *(Continued)*

E PEATE (5)

6 for 14 v. Middlesex at Huddersfield, 1879
6 for 12 v. Derbyshire at Derby, 1882
6 for 13 v. Gloucestershire at Moreton-in-Marsh, 1884
6 for 16 v. Sussex at Huddersfield, 1886
6 for 16 v. Cambridge University at Sheffield, 1886

R PEEL (4)

6 for 21 v. Nottinghamshire at Sheffield, 1888
6 for 19 v. Australians at Huddersfield, 1888
6 for 22 v. Gloucestershire at Bristol, 1891
6 for 19 v. Leicestershire at Scarborough, 1896

A C RHODES (1)

6 for 19 v. Cambridge University at Cambridge, 1932

W RHODES (12)

6 for 21 v. Somerset at Bath, 1898
6 for 16 v. Gloucestershire at Bristol, 1899
6 for 4 v. Nottinghamshire at Nottingham, 1901
6 for 15 v. MCC at Lord's, 1902
6 for 16 v. Cambridge University at Cambridge, 1905
6 for 9 v. Essex at Huddersfield, 1905
6 for 22 v. Derbyshire at Glossop, 1907
6 for 17 v. Leicestershire at Leicester, 1908
6 for 13 v. Sussex at Hove, 1922
6 for 23 v. Nottinghamshire at Leeds, 1923
6 for 22 v. Cambridge University at Cambridge, 1924
6 for 20 v. Gloucestershire at Dewsbury, 1927

W RINGROSE (1)

6 for 20 v. Leicestershire at Dewsbury, 1903

R J SIDEBOTTOM (1)

6 for 16 v. Kent at Leeds, 2000

W SLINN (1)

6 for 19 v. Nottinghamshire at Nottingham, 1864

G B STEVENSON(1)

6 for 14 v. Warwickshire at Sheffield, 1979

F S TRUEMAN (4)

6 for 23 v. Oxford University at Oxford, 1955
6 for 23 v. Oxford University at Oxford, 1958
6 for 18 v. Warwickshire at Birmingham, 1963
6 for 20 v. Leicestershire at Sheffield, 1968

H VERITY (5)

6 for 11 v. Surrey at Bradford, 1931
6 for 21 v. Glamorgan at Swansea, 1931
6 for 12 v. Derbyshire at Hull, 1933
6 for 10 v. Essex at Ilford, 1937
6 for 22 v. Hampshire at Bournemouth, 1939

SIX WICKETS IN AN INNINGS AT LESS THAN FOUR
RUNS EACH *(Continued)*

A WADDINGTON (2)

6 for 21 v. Northamptonshire at Harrogate, 1921
6 for 21 v. Northamptonshire at Northampton, 1923

S WADE (1)

6 for 18 v. Gloucestershire at Dewsbury, 1887

E WAINWRIGHT (4)

6 for 16 v. Sussex at Leeds, 1893
6 for 23 v. Sussex at Hove, 1893
6 for 18 v. Sussex at Dewsbury, 1894
6 for 22 v. MCC at Scarborough, 1894

J H WARDLE (8)

6 for 17 v. Sussex at Sheffield, 1948
6 for 10 v. Scotland at Edinburgh, 1950
6 for 12 v. Gloucestershire at Hull, 1950
6 for 20 v. Kent at Scarborough, 1950
6 for 23 v. Somerset at Sheffield, 1951
6 for 21 v. Glamorgan at Leeds, 1951
6 for 18 v. Gloucestershire at Bristol, 1951
6 for 6 v. Gloucestershire at Bristol, 1955

D WILSON (3)

6 for 22 v. Sussex at Bradford, 1963
6 for 15 v. Gloucestershire at Middlesbrough, 1966
6 for 22 v. Middlesex at Sheffield, 1966

FOUR WICKETS IN FOUR BALLS

A Drake v. Derbyshire at Chesterfield, 1914

FOUR WICKETS IN FIVE BALLS

F S Jackson v. Australians at Leeds, 1902
A Waddington v. Northamptonshire at Northampton, 1920
G G Macaulay v. Lancashire at Manchester, 1933
P J Hartley v. Derbyshire at Chesterfield, 1995
D Gough v. Kent at Leeds, 1995
J D Middlebrook v. Hampshire at Southampton, 2000

BEST BOWLING ANALYSES IN A MATCH
FOR AND AGAINST YORKSHIRE

Best For Yorkshire:
17 for 91 (8 for 47 and 9 for 44) H Verity v Essex at Leyton, 1933

Against Yorkshire:
17 for 91 (9 for 62 and 8 for 29) H Dean for Lancashire at Liverpool, 1913
(non-championship)

County Championship
16 for 114 (8 for 48 and 8 for 66) G Burton for Middlesex at Sheffield, 1888

Yorkshire versus:

Derbyshire	*For Yorkshire:*	14 for 58 (4 for 11 and 10 for 47)
		T F Smailes at Sheffield, 1939
	Against:	13 for 65 (7 for 33 and 6 for 32)
		W Mycroft at Sheffield, 1879
Most 10 wickets	*For Yorkshire:*	P Carrick and E Peate 4 each
in a match	*Against:*	W Mycroft 3
Durham	*For Yorkshire:*	10 for 101 (6 for 57 and 4 for 44)
		M A Robinson at Durham, 1992
	Against:	10 for 144 (7 for 81 and 3 for 63)
		O D Gibson at Chester-le-Street, 2007
Most 10 wickets	*For Yorkshire:*	M A Robinson 1
in a match	*Against:*	G R Breese and O D Gibson 1 each
Essex	*For Yorkshire:*	17 for 91 (8 for 47 and 9 for 44)
		H Verity at Leyton, 1933
	Against:	14 for 127 (7 for 37 and 7 for 90)
		W Mead at Leyton, 1899
Most 10 wickets	*For Yorkshire:*	W Rhodes 7
in a match	*Against:*	J K Lever, W Mead 2 each
Glamorgan	*For Yorkshire:*	15 for 123 (8 for 70 and 7 for 53)
		R Illingworth at Swansea. 1960
	Against:	12 for 76 (7 for 30 and 5 for 46)
		D J Shepherd at Cardiff, 1957
Most 10 wickets	*For Yorkshire:*	H Verity 5
in a match	*Against:*	D J Shepherd, J S Pressdee 1 each
Gloucestershire	*For Yorkshire:*	14 for 64 (7 for 58 and 7 for 6)
		R Illingworth at Harrogate, 1967
	Against:	15 for 79 (8 for 33 and 7 for 46)
		W G Grace at Sheffield, 1872
Most 10 wickets	*For Yorkshire:*	W Rhodes 8
in a match	*Against:*	E G Dennett 5
Hampshire	*For Yorkshire:*	14 for 43 (8 for 21 and 6 for 22)
		S Haigh at Southampton, 1898
	Against:	12 for 145 (7 for 78 and 5 for 67)
		D Shackleton at Bradford, 1962
Most 10 wickets	*For Yorkshire:*	W Rhodes, E Robinson, H Verity 3 each
in a match	*Against:*	A S Kennedy 3

Yorkshire versus

Kent	*For Yorkshire:*	15 for 38 (6 for 26 and 9 for 12)
		H Verity at Sheffield, 1936
	Against:	13 for 48 (5 for 13 and 8 for 35)
		A Hearne at Sheffield, 1885
Most 10 wickets	*For Yorkshire:*	E Peate and J H Wardle 4 each
in a match	*Against:*	C Blythe 6
Lancashire	*For Yorkshire:*	14 for 80 (6 for 56 and 8 for 24)
		E Peate at Manchester, 1880
	Against:	17 for 91 (9 for 62 and 8 for 29)
		H Dean at Liverpool, 1913 (non-championship)
		14 for 90 (6 for 47 and 8 for 43)
		R Tattersall at Leeds, 1956 (championship)
Most 10 wickets	*For Yorkshire:*	T Emmett 5
in a match	*Against:*	J Briggs 8
Leicestershire	*For Yorkshire:*	15 for 63 (8 for 25 and 7 for 38)
		G H Hirst at Hull, 1907
	Against:	12 for 139 (8 for 85 and 4 for 54)
		A D Pougher at Leicester, 1895
Most 10 wickets	*For Yorkshire:*	G H Hirst 5
in a match	*Against:*	A D Pougher 2
Middlesex	*For Yorkshire:*	13 for 94 (6 for 61 and 7 for 33)
		S Haigh at Leeds, 1900
	Against:	16 for 114 (8 for 48 and 8 for 66)
		G Burton at Sheffield, 1888
Most 10 wickets	*For Yorkshire:*	W Rhodes 5
in a match	*Against:*	J T Hearne 7
Northamptonshire	*For Yorkshire:*	16 for 35 (8 for 18 and 8 for 17)
		W E Bowes at Kettering, 1935
	Against:	15 for 31 (7 for 22 and 8 for 9)
		G E Tribe at Northampton, 1958
Most 10 wickets	*For Yorkshire:*	W E Bowes, G G Macaulay, H Verity,
in a match		A Waddington 3 each
	Against:	G E Tribe 3
Nottinghamshire	*For Yorkshire:*	14 for 33 (8 for 12 and 6 for 21)
		R Peel at Sheffield, 1888
	Against:	14 for 94 (8 for 38 and 6 for 56)
		F Morley at Nottingham, 1878
Most 10 wickets	*For Yorkshire:*	G H Hirst 5
in a match	*Against:*	F Morley, J C Shaw 4 each
Somerset	*For Yorkshire:*	15 for 50 (9 for 22 and 6 for 28)
		R Peel at Leeds, 1895
	Against:	15 for 71 (6 for 30 and 9 for 41)
		L C Braund at Sheffield, 1902
Most 10 wickets	*For Yorkshire:*	G H Hirst 7
in a match	*Against:*	L C Braund 3

BEST BOWLING ANALYSES IN A MATCH
FOR AND AGAINST YORKSHIRE *(continued)*

Yorkshire versus

Surrey | *For Yorkshire:* | 14 for 77 (6 for 47 and 8 for 30)
| | E Peate at Huddersfield, 1881
| *Against:* | 15 for 154 (7 for 55 and 8 for 99)
| | T Richardson at Leeds, 1897

Most 10 wickets | *For Yorkshire:* | W Rhodes 7
in a match | *Against:* | G A Lohmann, T Richardson 6 each

Sussex | *For Yorkshire:* | 16 for 112 (9 for 48 and 7 for 64)
| | J H Wardle at Hull, 1954
| *Against:* | 12 for 110 (6 for 71 and 6 for 39)
| | G R Cox at Sheffield, 1907

Most 10 wickets | *For Yorkshire:* | R Peel, E Wainwright 3 each
in a match | *Against:* | Twelve players 1 each

Warwickshire | *For Yorkshire:* | 14 for 92 (9 for 43 and 5 for 49)
| | H Verity at Leeds, 1937
| *Against:* | 12 for 55 (5 for 21 and 7 for 34)
| | T W Cartwright at Bradford, 1969

Most 10 wickets | *For Yorkshire:* | S Haigh 4
in a match | *Against:* | E F Field 4

Worcestershire | *For Yorkshire:* | 14 for 211 (8 for 87 and 6 for 124)
| | W Rhodes at Worcester, 1903
| *Against:* | 13 for 76 (4 for 38 and 9 for 38)
| | J A Cuffe at Bradford, 1907

Most 10 wickets | *For Yorkshire:* | S Haigh, G G Macaulay 4 each
in a match | *Against:* | N Gifford 2

Australians | *For Yorkshire:* | 13 for 149 (8 for 48 and 5 for 101)
| | G H Hirst at Bradford, 1899
| *Against:* | 13 for 170 (6 for 91 and 7 for 79)
| | J M Gregory at Sheffield, 1919

Most 10 wickets | *For Yorkshire:* | S Haigh 2
in a match | *Against:* | C V Grimmett, F R Spofforth, C T B Turner, H Trumble 2 each

BEST BOWLING ANALYSES IN AN INNINGS
FOR AND AGAINST YORKSHIRE

Best For Yorkshire:
10 for 10 H Verity v Nottinghamshire at Leeds, 1932

Against Yorkshire:
10 for 37 C V Grimmett for Australians at Sheffield, 1930
(non-championship)

County Championship
10 for 51 H Howell for Warwickshire at Birmingham, 1923

Yorkshire versus:

Derbyshire | *For Yorkshire:* | 10 for 47 | T F Smailes at Sheffield, 1939
| *Against:* | 9 for 27 | J J Hulme at Sheffield, 1894
Most 5 wickets | *For Yorkshire:* | S Haigh, E Peat, W Rhodes 11 each
in an innings | *Against:* | W Mycroft 10

Yorkshire versus

Durham

	For Yorkshire:	6 for 37 R D Stemp at Durham, 1994
		6 for 37 J N Gillespie at Chester-le-Street, 2006
	Against:	7 for 58 J Wood at Leeds, 1999
Most 5 wickets	*For Yorkshire:*	D Gough and M J Hoggard 2 each
in an innings	*Against:*	G R Breese, S J E Brown, S J Harmison
		and G Onions 2 each

Essex

	For Yorkshire:	9 for 28 W Rhodes at Leyton, 1899
	Against:	8 for 44 F G Bull at Bradford, 1896
Most 5 wickets	*For Yorkshire:*	W Rhodes 18
in an innings	*Against:*	W Mead 14

Glamorgan

	For Yorkshire:	9 for 60 H Verity at Swansea, 1930
	Against:	9 for 43 J S Pressdee at Swansea, 1965
Most 5 wickets	*For Yorkshire:*	H Verity 12
in an innings	*Against:*	D J Shepherd 6

Gloucestershire

	For Yorkshire:	9 for 25 S Haigh at Leeds, 1912
	Against:	9 for 36 C W L Parker at Bristol, 1922
Most 5 wickets	*For Yorkshire:*	W Rhodes 22
in an innings	*Against:*	T W J Goddard 17

Hampshire

	For Yorkshire:	9 for 29 A C Williams at Dewsbury, 1919
	Against:	8 for 49 O W Herman at Bournemouth, 1930
Most 5 wickets	*For Yorkshire:*	G H Hirst 10
in an innings	*Against:*	A S Kennedy 10

Kent

	For Yorkshire:	9 for 12 H Verity at Sheffield, 1936
	Against:	8 for 35 A Hearne at Sheffield, 1885
Most 5 wickets	*For Yorkshire:*	W Rhodes 12
in an innings	*Against:*	A P Freeman 14

Lancashire

	For Yorkshire:	9 for 23 G H Hirst at Leeds, 1910
	Against:	9 for 41 A Mold at Huddersfield, 1890
Most 5 wickets	*For Yorkshire:*	T Emmett 16
in an innings	*Against:*	J Briggs 19

Leicestershire

	For Yorkshire:	8 for 25 G H Hirst at Hull, 1907
	Against:	9 for 63 C T Spencer at Huddersfield, 1954
Most 5 wickets	*For Yorkshire:*	G H Hirst 15
in an innings	*Against:*	H A Smith 7

Middlesex

	For Yorkshire:	9 for 45 G H Hirst at Sheffield 1907
	Against:	9 for 57 F A Tarrant at Leeds, 1906
Most 5 wickets	*For Yorkshire:*	W Rhodes 18
in an innings	*Against:*	J T Hearne 21

Northamptonshire

	For Yorkshire:	9 for 37 M A Robinson at Harrogate, 1993
	Against:	9 for 30 A E Thomas at Bradford, 1920
Most 5 wickets	*For Yorkshire:*	G G Macaulay 14
in an innings	*Against:*	G E Tribe, W Wells 7 each

Nottinghamshire

	For Yorkshire:	10 for 10 H Verity at Leeds, 1932
	Against:	8 for 32 J C Shaw at Nottingham, 1865
Most 5 wickets	*For Yorkshire:*	W Rhodes 17
in an innings	*Against:*	F Morley 17

Yorkshire versus

Somerset	*For Yorkshire:*	10 for 35	A Drake at Weston-super-Mare, 1914
	Against:	9 for 41	L C Braund at Sheffield, 1902
Most 5 wickets	*For Yorkshire:*	G H Hirst 16	
in an innings	*Against:*	E J Tyler 8	
Surrey	*For Yorkshire:*	8 for 5	E Peate at Holbeck, 1883
	Against:	9 for 47	T Richardson at Sheffield, 1893
Most 5 wickets	*For Yorkshire:*	W Rhodes 17	
in an innings	*Against:*	W Southerton 19	
Sussex	*For Yorkshire:*	9 for 48	J H Wardle at Hull, 1954
	Against:	9 for 34	James Langridge at Sheffield, 1934
Most 5 wickets	*For Yorkshire:*	W Rhodes 14	
in an innings	*Against:*	G R Cox, J A Snow 6 each	
Warwickshire	*For Yorkshire:*	10 for 36	H Verity at Leeds, 1930
	Against:	10 for 51	H Howell at Birmingham, 1923
Most 5 wickets	*For Yorkshire:*	W Rhodes 18	
in an innings	*Against:*	E F Field, W E Hollies 7 each	
Worcestershire	*For Yorkshire:*	9 for 41	G H Hirst at Worcester, 1911
	Against:	9 for 38	J A Cuffe at Bradford, 1907
Most 5 wickets	*For Yorkshire:*	S Haigh, W Rhodes 11 each	
in an innings	*Against:*	R T D Perks 7	
Australians	*For Yorkshire:*	9 for 76	W Ringrose at Bradford, 1905
	Against:	10 for 37	C V Grimmett at Sheffield, 1930
Most 5 wickets	*For Yorkshire:*	R Peel 7	
in an innings	*Against:*	F R Spofforth 7	

HAT-TRICKS

G Freeman v. Lancashire at Holbeck, 1868
G Freeman v. Middlesex at Sheffield, 1868
A Hill v. United South of England XI at Bradford, 1874
A Hill v. Surrey at The Oval, 1880
E Peate v. Kent at Sheffield, 1882
G Ulyett v. Lancashire at Sheffield, 1883
E Peate v. Gloucestershire at Moreton-in-Marsh, 1884
W Fletcher v. MCC at Lord's, 1892
E Wainwright v. Sussex at Dewsbury, 1894
G H Hirst v. Leicestershire at Leicester, 1895
J T Brown v. Derbyshire at Derby, 1896
R Peel v. Kent at Halifax, 1897
S Haigh v. Derbyshire at Bradford, 1897
W Rhodes v. Kent at Canterbury, 1901
S Haigh v. Somerset at Sheffield, 1902
H A Sedgwick v. Worcestershire at Hull, 1906
G Deyes v. Gentlemen of Ireland at Bray, 1907
G H Hirst v. Leicestershire at Hull, 1907
J T Newstead v. Worcestershire at Bradford, 1907
S Haigh v. Lancashire at Manchester, 1909
M W Booth v. Worcestershire at Bradford, 1911
A Drake v. Essex at Huddersfield, 1912

HAT-TRICKS *(Continued)*

M W Booth v. Essex at Leyton, 1912
A Drake v. Derbyshire at Chesterfield, 1914 (4 in 4)
W Rhodes v. Derbyshire at Derby, 1920
A Waddington v. Northamptonshire at Northampton, 1920 (4 in 5)
G G Macaulay v. Warwickshire at Birmingham, 1923
E Robinson v. Sussex at Hull, 1928
G G Macaulay v. Leicestershire at Hull, 1930
E Robinson v. Kent at Gravesend, 1930
H Verity v. Nottinghamshire at Leeds, 1932
H Fisher v. Somerset at Sheffield, 1932 (all lbw)
G G Macaulay v. Glamorgan at Cardiff, 1933
G G Macaulay v. Lancashire at Manchester, 1933 (4 in 5)
M.Leyland v. Surrey at Sheffield, 1935
E Robinson v. Kent at Leeds, 1939
A Coxon v. Worcestershire at Leeds, 1946
F S Trueman v. Nottinghamshire at Nottingham, 1951
F S Trueman v. Nottinghamshire at Scarborough, 1955
R Appleyard v. Gloucestershire at Sheffield, 1956
F S.Trueman v. MCC at Lord's, 1958
D Wilson v. Nottinghamshire at Middlesbrough, 1959
F S Trueman v. Nottinghamshire at Bradford, 1963
D Wilson v. Nottinghamshire at Worksop, 1966
D Wilson v. Kent at Harrogate, 1966
G A Cope v. Essex at Colchester, 1970
A L Robinson v. Nottinghamshire at Worksop, 1974
P W Jarvis v. Derbyshire at Chesterfield, 1985
P J Hartley v. Derbyshire at Chesterfield, 1995 (4 in 5)
D Gough v. Kent at Leeds, 1995 (4 in 5)
C White v. Gloucestershire at Gloucester, 1998
M J Hoggard v. Sussex at Hove, 2009

52 Hat-Tricks: G G Macaulay and F S Trueman took four each, S Haigh and D Wilson three each. There have been seven hat-tricks versus Kent and Nottinghamshire, and six versus Derbyshire.

200 WICKETS IN A SEASON

Bowler	Season	Overs	Maidens	Runs	Wickets	Average
W Rhodes	1900	1366.4	411	3054	240	12.72
W Rhodes	1901	1455.3	474	3497	233	15.00
G H Hirst	1906	1111.1	262	3089	201	15.36
G G Macaulay	1925	1241.2	291	2986	200	14.93
R Appleyard†	1951	1323.2	394	2829	200	14.14

† First full season in First-Class cricket.

100 WICKETS IN A SEASON

Bowler		Wickets taken	Wickets taken	Wickets taken
R Appleyard	(3)	200 in 1951	141 in 1954	110 in 1956
A Booth	(1)	111 in 1946	—	—
M W Booth	(3)	104 in 1912	167 in 1913	155 in 1914
W E Bowes	(8)	117 in 1931	168 in 1932	130 in 1933
		109 in 1934	154 in 1935	113 in 1936
		106 in 1938	107 in 1939	—

293

Bowler		*Wickets taken*	*Wickets taken*	*Wickets taken*
D B Close	(2)	105 in 1949	114 in 1952	—
A Coxon	(2)	101 in 1949	129 in 1950	—
A Drake	(2)	115 in 1913	158 in 1914	—
T Emmett	(1)	112 in 1886	—	—
S Haigh	(10)	100 in 1898	160 in 1900	154 in 1902
		102 in 1903	118 in 1904	118 in 1905
		161 in 1906	120 in 1909	100 in 1911
		125 in 1912	—	—
G H Hirst	(12)	150 in 1895	171 in 1901	121 in 1903
		114 in 1904	100 in 1905	201 in 1906
		169 in 1907	164 in 1908	138 in 1910
		130 in 1911	113 in 1912	100 in 1913
R Illingworth	(5)	103 in 1956	120 in 1961	116 in 1962
		122 in 1964	105 in 1968	—
R Kilner	(4)	107 in 1922	143 in 1923	134 in 1924
		123 in 1925	—	—
G G Macaulay	(10)	101 in 1921	130 in 1922	163 in 1923
		184 in 1924	200 in 1925	133 in 1926
		130 in 1927	117 in 1928	102 in 1929
		141 in 1933	—	—
J T Newstead	(1)	131 in 1908	—	—
A G Nicholson	(2)	113 in 1966	101 in 1967	—
E Peate	(3)	131 in 1880	133 in 1881	165 in 1882
R Peel	(6)	118 in 1888	132 in 1890	106 in 1892
		134 in 1894	155 in 1895	108 in 1896
W Rhodes	(22)	141 in 1898	153 in 1899	240 in 1900
		233 in 1901	174 in 1902	169 in 1903
		118 in 1904	158 in 1905	113 in 1906
		164 in 1907	100 in 1908	115 in 1909
		105 in 1911	117 in 1914	155 in 1919
		156 in 1920	128 in 1921	100 in 1922
		127 in 1923	102 in 1926	111 in 1928
		100 in 1929	—	—
E Robinson	(1)	111 in 1928	—	—
E P Robinson	(4)	104 in 1938	120 in 1939	149 in 1946
		108 in 1947	—	—
T F Smailes	(4)	105 in 1934	125 in 1936	120 in 1937
		104 in 1938	—	—
F S Trueman	(8)	129 in 1954	140 in 1955	104 in 1959
		150 in 1960	124 in 1961	122 in 1962
		121 in 1965	107 in 1966	—
H Verity	(9)	169 in 1931	146 in 1932	168 in 1933
		100 in 1934	199 in 1935	185 in 1936
		185 in 1937	137 in 1938	189 in 1939
A Waddington	(5)	100 in 1919	140 in 1920	105 in 1921
		132 in 1922	105 in 1925	—
E Wainwright	(3)	114 in 1893	157 in 1894	102 in 1896
J H Wardle	(10)	148 in 1948	100 in 1949	172 in 1950
		122 in 1951	169 in 1952	126 in 1953
		122 in 1954	159 in 1955	146 in 1956
		106 in 1957	—	—
D Wilson	(3)	100 in 1966	107 in 1968	101 in 1969

BOWLERS WHO HAVE TAKEN OVER 500 WICKETS

Player	M	Runs	Wkts	Av'ge	Best
W Rhodes	883	57634	3598	16.01	9 for 28
G H Hirst	717	44716	2481	18.02	9 for 23
S Haigh	513	29289	1876	15.61	9 for 25
G G Macaulay	445	30554	1774	17.22	8 for 21
F S Trueman	459	29990	1745	17.12	8 for 28
H Verity	278	21353	1558	13.70	10 for 10
J H Wardle	330	27917	1539	18.13	9 for 25
R Illingworth	496	26806	1431	18.73	9 for 42
W E Bowes	301	21227	1351	15.71	9 for 121
R Peel	318	20638	1311	15.74	9 for 22
T Emmett	299	15465	1216	12.71	9 for 23
D Wilson	392	22626	1104	20.49	7 for 19
P Carrick	425	30530	1018	29.99	8 for 33
E Wainwright	352	17744	998	17.77	9 for 66
D B Close	536	23489	967	24.29	8 for 41
Emmott Robinson	413	19645	893	21.99	9 for 36
A G Nicholson	.282	17296	876	19.74	9 for 62
R Kilner	365	14855	857	17.33	8 for 26
A Waddington	255	16203	835	19.40	8 for 34
T F Smailes	262	16593	802	20.68	10 for 47
E Peate	154	9986	794	12.57	8 for 5
Ellis P Robinson	208	15141	735	20.60	8 for 35
C M Old	222	13409	647	20.72	7 for 20
R Appleyard	133	9903	642	15.42	8 for 76
W Bates	202	10692	637	16.78	8 for 21
G A Cope	230	15627	630	24.80	8 for 73
P J Hartley	195	17438	579	30.11	9 for 41
A Sidebottom	216	13852	558	24.82	8 for 72
M W Booth	144	11017	557	19.17	8 for 47
A Hill	140	7002	542	12.91	7 for 14
Hon F S Jackson	207	9690	506	19.15	7 for 42

BOWLERS UNCHANGED IN A MATCH

(IN WHICH THE OPPONENTS WERE DISMISSED TWICE)

**There have been 31 instances. The first and most recent are listed below.
A complete list is to be found in the 2008 edition.**

First: L Greenwood (11 for 71) and G Freeman (8 for 73) v. Surrey
at The Oval, 1867
Yorkshire won by an innings and 111 runs

Most Recent: E Robinson (8 for 65) and G G Macaulay (12 for 50) v. Worcestershire
at Leeds, 1927
Yorkshire won by an innings and 106 runs

FIELDERS (IN MATCHES FOR YORKSHIRE)

MOST CATCHES IN AN INNINGS

6	E P Robinson	v. Leicestershire	at Bradford, 1938
6	T Kohler- Cadmore		
		v. Kent	at Canterbury, 2019
5	J Tunnicliffe	v. Leicestershire	at Leeds, 1897
5	J Tunnicliffe	v. Leicestershire	at Leicester, 1900
5	J Tunnicliffe	v. Leicestershire	at Scarborough, 1901
5	A B Sellers	v. Essex	at Leyton, 1933
5	D Wilson	v. Surrey	at The Oval, 1969
5	R G Lumb	v. Gloucestershire	at Middlesbrough, 1972

MOST CATCHES IN A MATCH

7	J Tunnicliffe	v. Leicestershire	at Leeds, 1897
7	J Tunnicliffe	v. Leicestershire	at Leicester, 1900
7	A B Sellers	v Essex	at Leyton, 1933
7	E P Robinson	v. Leicestershire	at Bradford, 1938
7	A Lyth	v. Middlesex	at Scarborough, 2014
7	T Kohler-Cadmore		
		v. Hampshire	at West End, Southampton, 2019

MOST CATCHES IN A SEASON

70	J Tunnicliffe	in 1901
70	P J Sharpe	in 1962
61	J Tunnicliffe	in 1895
60	J Tunnicliffe	in 1904
59	J Tunnicliffe	in 1896
57	J V Wilson	in 1955
54	J V Wilson	in 1961
53	J V Wilson	in 1957
51	J V Wilson	in 1951

MOST CATCHES IN A CAREER

665	J Tunnicliffe	(1.40 per match)
586	W Rhodes	(0.66 per match)
564	D B Close	(1.05 per match)
525	P J Sharpe	(1.27 per match)
520	J V Wilson	(1.09 per match)
518	G H Hirst	(0.72 per match)

WICKET-KEEPERS IN MATCHES FOR YORKSHIRE

MOST DISMISSALS IN AN INNINGS

7	(7ct)	D L Bairstow	v. Derbyshire	at Scarborough	1982
6	(6ct)	J Hunter	v. Gloucestershire	at Gloucester	1887
6	(5ct,1st)	D Hunter	v. Surrey	at Sheffield	1891
6	(6ct)	D Hunter	v. Middlesex	at Leeds	1909
6	(2ct,4st)	W R Allen	v. Sussex	at Hove	1921
6	(5ct,1st)	J G Binks	v. Lancashire	at Leeds	1962
6	(6ct)	D L Bairstow	v. Lancashire	at Manchester	1971
6	(6ct)	D L Bairstow	v. Warwickshire	at Bradford	1978
6	(5ct,1st)	D L Bairstow	v. Lancashire	at Leeds	1980
6	(6ct)	D L Bairstow	v. Derbyshire	at Chesterfield	1984
6	(6ct)	R J Blakey	v. Sussex	at Eastbourne	1990
6	(5ct,1st)	R J Blakey	v. Gloucestershire	at Cheltenham	1992
6	(5ct,1st)	R J Blakey	v. Glamorgan	at Cardiff	1994
6	(6ct)	R J Blakey	v. Glamorgan	at Leeds	2003
6	(6ct)	G L Brophy	v. Durham	at Chester-le-Street	2009
6	(6ct)	J M Bairstow	v. Middlesex	at Leeds	2013
6	(6ct)	J M Bairstow	v. Sussex	at Arundel	2014

MOST DISMISSALS IN A MATCH

11	(11ct)	D L Bairstow	v. Derbyshire	at Scarborough	1982
		(Equalled World Record)			
9	(9ct)	J.Hunter	v. Gloucestershire	at Gloucester	1887
9	(8ct,1st)	A Dolphin	v. Derbyshire	at Bradford	1919
9	(9ct)	D L Bairstow	v. Lancashire	at Manchester	1971
9	(9ct)	R J Blakey	v. Sussex	at Eastbourne	1990
8	(2ct,6st)	G Pinder	v. Lancashire	at Sheffield	1872
8	(2ct,6st)	D Hunter	v. Surrey	at Bradford	1898
8	(7ct,1st)	A Bairstow	v. Cambridge University	at Cambridge	1899
8	(8ct)	A Wood	v. Northamptonshire	at Huddersfield	1932
8	(8ct)	D L Bairstow	v. Lancashire	at Leeds	1978
8	(7ct,1st)	D L Bairstow	v. Derbyshire	at Chesterfield	1984
8	(6ct,2st)	D L Bairstow	v. Derbyshire	at Chesterfield	1985
8	(8ct)	R J Blakey	v. Hampshire	at Southampton	1989
8	(8ct)	R J Blakey	v. Northamptonshire	at Harrogate	1993
8	(8ct)	A J Hodd	v. Glamorgan	at Leeds	2012
8	(8ct)	J M Bairstow	v. Middlesex	at Leeds	2013

MOST DISMISSALS IN A SEASON

107	(96ct,11st)	J G Binks, 1960
94	(81ct,13st)	JG Binks, 1961
89	(75ct,14st)	A Wood, 1934
88	(80ct,8st)	J G Binks, 1963
86	(70ct,16st)	J G Binks, 1962
82	(52ct,30st)	A Dolphin, 1919
80	(57ct,23st)	A. Wood, 1935

MOST DISMISSALS IN A CAREER

1186	(863ct,323st)	D Hunter (2.29 per match)
1044	(872ct,172st)	J G Binks (2.12 per match)
1038	(907ct,131st)	D L Bairstow (2.41 per match)
855	(612ct,243st)	A Wood (2.09 per match)
829	(569ct,260st)	A Dolphin (1.94 per match)
824	(768ct, 56st)	R J Blakey (2.43 per match)

YORKSHIRE PLAYERS WHO HAVE COMPLETED THE "DOUBLE"

(all First-Class matches)

Player	Year	Runs	Average	Wickets	Average
M W Booth (1)	1913	1,228	27.28	181	18.46
D B Close (2)	†1949	1,098	27.45	113	27.87
	1952	1,192	33.11	114	24.08
A Drake (1)	1913	1,056	23.46	116	16.93
S Haigh (1)	1904	1,055	26.37	121	19.85
G H Hirst (14)	1896	1,122	28.20	104	21.64
	1897	1,535	35.69	101	23.22
	1901	1,950	42.39	183	16.38
	1903	1,844	47.28	128	14.94
	1904	2,501	54.36	132	21.09
	1905	2,266	53.95	110	19.94
	††1906	2,385	45.86	208	16.50
	1907	1,344	28.38	188	15.20
	1908	1,598	38.97	114	14.05
	1909	1,256	27.30	115	20.05
	1910	1,840	32.85	164	14.79
	1911	1,789	33.12	137	20.40
	1912	1,133	25.75	118	17.37
	1913	1,540	35.81	101	20.13
R Illingworth (6)	1957	1,213	28.20	106	18.40
	1959	1,726	46.64	110	21.46
	1960	1,006	25.79	109	17.55
	1961	1,153	24.53	128	17.90
	1962	1,612	34.29	117	19.45
	1964	1,301	37.17	122	17.45
F S Jackson (1)	1898	1,566	41.21	104	15.67
R Kilner (4)	1922	1,198	27.22	122	14.73
	1923	1,404	32.24	158	12.91
	1925	1,068	30.51	131	17.92
	1926	1,187	37.09	107	22.52
R Peel (1)	1896	1,206	30.15	128	17.50
W Rhodes (16)	1903	1,137	27.07	193	14.57
	1904	1,537	35.74	131	21.59
	1905	1,581	35.93	182	16.95
	1906	1,721	29.16	128	23.57
	1907	1,055	22.93	177	15.57
	1908	1,673	31.56	115	16.13
	1909	2,094	40.26	141	15.89
	1911	2,261	38.32	117	24.07
	1914	1,377	29.29	118	18.27
	1919	1,237	34.36	164	14.42
	1920	1,123	28.07	161	13.18
	1921	1,474	39.83	141	13.27
	1922	1,511	39.76	119	12.19
	1923	1,321	33.02	134	11.54
	1924	1,126	26.18	109	14.46
	1926	1,132	34.30	115	14.86
T F Smailes (1)	1938	1,002	25.05	113	20.84
E Wainwright (1)	1897	1,612	35.82	101	23.06

† First season in First-Class cricket.

†† The only instance in First-Class cricket of 2,000 runs and 200 wickets in a season.

H Sutcliffe (194) and M Leyland (45) hit 102 off six consecutive overs for Yorkshire v. Essex at Scarborough in 1932.

From 1898 to 1930 inclusive, Wilfred Rhodes took no less than 4,187 wickets, and scored 39,969 runs in First-Class cricket at home and abroad, a remarkable record. He also took 100 wickets and scored 1,000 in a season 16 times, and G H Hirst 14 times.

Of players with a qualification of not less than 50 wickets, Wilfred Rhodes was first in bowling in First-Class cricket in 1900, 1901, 1919, 1920, 1922, 1923 and 1926; Schofield Haigh in 1902, 1905, 1908 and 1909; Mr E R Wilson in 1921; G G Macaulay in 1924; H Verity in 1930, 1933, 1935, 1937 and 1939; W E Bowes in 1938; A Booth in 1946; R Appleyard in 1951 and 1955, and F S Trueman in 1952 and 1963.

The highest aggregate of runs made in one season in First-Class cricket by a Yorkshire player is 3,429 by L Hutton in 1949. This total has been exceeded three times, viz: D C S Compton 3,816 and W J Edrich 3,539 in 1947, and 3,518 by T Hayward in 1906. H Sutcliffe scored 3,336 in 1932.

Three players have taken all 10 Yorkshire wickets in an innings. G Wootton, playing for All England XI at Sheffield in 1865, took all 10 wickets for 54 runs. H Howell performed the feat for Warwickshire at Edgbaston in 1923 at a cost of 51 runs; and C V Grimmett, Australia, took all 10 wickets for 37 runs at Sheffield in 1930.

The match against Sussex at Dewsbury on June 7th and 8th, 1894, was brought to a summary conclusion by a remarkable bowling performance on the part of Edward Wainwright. In the second innings of Sussex, he took the last five wickets in seven balls, including the "hat trick". In the whole match he obtained 13 wickets for only 38 runs.

M D Moxon has the unique distinction of scoring a century in each of his first two First-Class matches in Yorkshire — 116 (2nd inns.) v. Essex at Leeds and 111 (1st inns.) v. Derbyshire at Sheffield, June 1981).

In the Yorkshire v. Norfolk match — played on the Hyde Park Ground, Sheffield, on July 14th to 18th, 1834 — 851 runs were scored in the four innings, of which no fewer than 128 were extras: 75 byes and 53 wides. At that time wides were not run out, so that every wide included in the above total represents a wide actually bowled. This particular achievement has never been surpassed in the annals of county cricket.

L Hutton reached his 1,000 runs in First-Class cricket in 1949 as early as June 9th.

W Barber reached his 1,000 runs in 1934 on June 13th. P Holmes reached his 1,000 in 1925 on June 16th, as also did H Sutcliffe in 1932. J T Brown reached his 1,000 in 1899 on June 22nd. In 1905, D Denton reached his 1,000 runs on June 26th; and in 1906 G H Hirst gained the same total on June 27th.

In 1912, D Denton scored over 1,000 runs during July, while M Leyland and H Sutcliffe both scored over 1,000 runs in August 1932.

L Hutton scored over 1,000 in June and over 1,000 runs in August in 1949.

H Verity took his 100th wicket in First-Class cricket as early as June 19th in 1936 and on June 27th in 1935. In 1900, W Rhodes obtained his 100th wicket on June 21st, and again on the same date in 1901, while G H Hirst obtained his 100th wicket on June 28th, 1906.

In 1930, Yorkshiremen (H Sutcliffe and H Verity) occupied the first places by English players in the batting and the bowling averages of First-Class cricket, which is a record without precedent. H Sutcliffe was also first in the batting averages in 1931 and 1932.

G Boycott was the first player to have achieved an average of over 100 in each of two English seasons. In 1971, he scored 2,503 runs for an average of 100.12, and in 1979 he scored 1,538 runs for an average of 102.53.

FIRST-CLASS MATCHES BEGUN AND FINISHED IN ONE DAY

Yorkshire v. Somerset, at Huddersfield, July 9th, 1894.

Yorkshire v. Hampshire, at Southampton, May 27th, 1898.

Yorkshire v. Worcestershire, at Bradford, May 7th, 1900

YORKSHIRE TEST CRICKETERS 1877-2019 (Correct to January 28, 2020)

Player	M.	I	NO	Runs	HS.	Av'ge.	100s	50s	Balls	R	W	Av'ge	Best	5wI	10wM	c/st
APPLEYARD, R ...1954-56	9	9	6	51	19*	17.00	—	—	1,596	554	31	17.87	5-51	1	—	4
ARMITAGE, T 1877	2	3	0	33	21	11.00	—	—	12	15	0	—	—	—	—	0
ATHEY, C W J ...1980-88	23	41	1	919	123	22.97	—	4	—	—	—	—	—	—	—	13
BAIRSTOW, D L ..1979-81	4	7	1	125	59	20.83	—	1	—	—	—	—	—	—	—	12/1
BAIRSTOW, J M ..2012-19	69	121	7	4,020	167*	35.26	6	21	—	—	—	—	—	—	—	181/13
BALLANCE, G S 2013/14-17	23	42	2	1,498	156	37.45	4	7	—	—	—	—	—	—	—	22
BARBER, W 1935	2	4	0	83	44	20.75	—	—	12	5	0	—	—	—	—	1
BATES, W 1881-87	15	26	2	656	64	27.33	—	5	2,364	821	50	16.42	7-28	4	1	9
BINKS, J G 1964	2	4	0	91	55	22.75	—	1	—	—	—	—	—	—	—	8/0
BLAKEY, R J 1993	2	4	0	7	6	1.75	—	—	—	—	—	—	—	—	—	2/0
BOOTH, M W ...1913-14	2	2	0	46	32	23.00	—	—	312	130	7	18.57	4-49	—	—	0
BOWES, W E ...1932-46	15	11	5	28	10*	4.66	—	—	3,655	1,519	68	22.33	6-33	6	—	2
†BOYCOTT, G ...1964-82	108	193	23	8,114	246*	47.72	22	42	944	382	7	54.57	3-47	—	—	33
BRENNAN, D V 1951	2	2	0	16	16	8.00	—	—	—	—	—	—	—	—	—	0/1
BRESNAN, T T .2009-13/14	23	26	4	575	91	26.13	—	3	4,674	2,357	72	32.73	5-48	1	—	8
BROWN, J T ...1894-99	8	16	3	470	140	36.15	1	1	35	22	0	—	—	—	—	7
†CLOSE, D B ...1949-76	22	37	2	887	70	25.34	—	4	1,212	532	18	29.55	4-35	—	—	24
COPE, G A 1977-78	3	3	0	40	22	13.33	—	—	864	277	8	34.62	3-102	—	—	1
COXON, A 1948	1	2	0	19	19	9.50	—	—	378	172	3	57.33	2-90	—	—	0
DAWSON, R K J ..2002-03	7	13	3	114	19*	11.40	—	—	1,116	677	11	61.54	4-134	—	—	3
DENTON, D 1905-10	11	22	1	424	104	20.19	—	1	—	—	—	—	—	—	—	8
DOLPHIN, A. 1921	1	2	0	1	1	0.50	—	—	—	—	—	—	—	—	—	1/0
EMMETT, T 1877-82	7	13	1	160	48	13.33	—	—	728	284	9	31.55	7-68	1	—	9
GIBB, P A 1938-46	8	13	0	581	120	44.69	2	3	—	—	—	—	—	—	—	3/1
GOUGH, D 1994-2003	58	86	18	855	65	12.57	—	2	11,821	6,503	229	28.39	6-42	9	—	13

YORKSHIRE TEST CRICKETERS 1877-2019 (Continued)

Player	M.	I	NO	Runs	HS.	Av'ge.	100s	50s	Balls	R	W	Av'ge	Best	5wI	10wM	c/st
GREENWOOD, A 1877	2	4	0	77	49	19.25	—	—	—	—	—	—	—	—	—	2
HAIGH, S 1899-1912	11	18	3	113	25	7.53	—	—	1,294	622	24	25.91	6-11	1	—	8
HAMILTON, G.M. 1999	1	2	0	0	0	0.00	—	—	90	63	0	—	—	—	—	0
HAMPSHIRE, J H ...1969-75	8	16	1	403	107	26.86	1	2	—	—	—	—	—	—	—	9
†HAWKE, LORD ...1896-99	5	8	1	55	30	7.85	—	—	—	—	—	—	—	—	—	3
HILL, A 1877	2	4	2	101	49	50.50	—	—	340	130	7	18.57	4-27	—	—	1
HIRST, G H ...1897-1909	24	38	3	790	85	22.57	—	5	3,967	1,770	59	30.00	5-48	3	—	18
HOGGARD, M J ..2000-2008	67	92	27	473	38	7.27	—	—	13,909	7,564	248	30.50	7-61	7	1	24
HOLMES, P 1921-32	7	14	1	357	88	27.46	—	4	—	—	—	—	—	—	—	3
HUNTER, J 1884-85	5	7	2	93	39*	18.60	—	—	—	—	—	—	—	—	—	8/3
†HUTTON, L 1937-55	79	138	15	6,971	364	56.67	19	33	260	232	3	77.33	1-2	—	—	57
HUTTON, R.A 1971	5	8	2	219	81	36.50	—	2	738	257	9	28.55	3-72	—	—	9
†ILLINGWORTH, R .1958-73	61	90	11	1,836	113	23.24	2	5	11,934	3,807	122	31.20	6-29	3	—	45
†JACKSON, Hon F S1893-1905	20	33	4	1,415	144*	48.79	5	6	1,587	799	24	33.29	5-52	1	—	10
JARVIS, P W 1988-93	9	15	2	132	29*	10.15	—	—	1,912	965	21	45.95	4-107	—	—	2
KILNER, R 1924-26	9	8	1	233	74	33.28	—	2	2,368	734	24	30.58	4-51	—	—	6
LEADBEATER, E ...1951-52	2	2	0	40	38	20.00	—	—	289	218	2	109.00	1-38	—	—	3
LEYLAND, M 1928-38	41	65	5	2,764	187	46.06	9	10	1,103	585	6	97.50	3-91	—	—	13
LOWSON, F A 1951-55	7	13	0	245	68	18.84	—	2	—	—	—	—	—	—	—	5
LYTH A 2015	7	13	0	265	107	20.38	1	—	6	0	0	—	—	—	—	8
McGRATH, A 2003	4	5	0	201	81	40.20	—	2	102	56	4	14.00	3-16	—	—	3
MACAULAY, G G ..1923-33	8	10	4	112	76	18.66	—	1	1,701	662	24	27.58	5-64	1	—	5
MILLIGAN, F W 1899	2	4	0	58	38	14.50	—	—	45	29	0	—	—	—	—	1
MITCHELL, A 1933-36	6	10	0	298	72	29.80	—	2	6	4	0	—	—	—	—	9
*MITCHELL, F 1899	2	4	0	88	41	22.00	—	—	—	—	—	—	—	—	—	2

For England YORKSHIRE TEST CRICKETERS 1877-2019 (Continued)

Player	M.	I	NO	Runs	HS.	Av'ge.	100s	50s	Balls	R	W	Av'ge	Best	5wI	10wM	c/st
MOXON, M D 1986-89	10	17	1	455	99	28.43	—	3	48	30	0	—	—	—	—	10
OLD, C M 1972-81	46	66	9	845	65	14.82	—	2	8,858	4,020	143	28.11	7-50	4	—	22
PADGETT, D E V 1960	2	4	0	51	31	12.75	—	—	12	8	0	—	—	—	—	0
PEATE, E 1881-86	9	14	8	70	13	11.66	—	—	2,096	682	31	22.00	6-85	2	—	2
PEEL, R 1884-96	20	33	4	427	83	14.72	—	3	5,216	1,715	101	16.98	7-31	5	1	17
PLUNKETT, L E .2005/6-2014	13	20	5	238	55*	15.86	—	—	2,659	1,536	41	37.46	5-64	1	—	3
RASHID, A U ...2015/16-19	19	33	5	540	61	19.28	—	2	3,816	2,390	60	39.83	5-49	2	—	4
RHODES, W 1899-1930	58	98	21	2,325	179	30.19	2	11	8,231	3,425	127	26.96	8-68	6	1	60
ROOT, J E 2012-19/20	92	169	12	7,599	254	48.40	17	48	2,646	1,402	28	50.07	4-87	—	—	114
SHARPE, P J 1963-69	12	21	4	786	111	46.23	1	4	—	—	—	—	—	—	—	17
SHAHZAD, A 2010	1	1	1	5	5	5.00	—	—	102	63	4	15.75	3-45	—	—	2
SIDEBOTTOM, A 1985	1	1	0	2	2	2.00	—	—	112	65	1	65.00	1-65	—	—	1
SIDEBOTTOM, R J .2001-10	22	31	11	313	31	15.65	—	—	4,812	2,231	79	28.24	7-47	5	—	5
SILVERWOOD, CEW 1997-2003	6	7	3	29	10	7.25	—	—	828	444	11	40.36	5-91	1	—	2
SMAILES, T F 1946	1	1	0	25	25	25.00	—	—	120	62	3	20.66	3-44	—	—	0
SMITHSON, G A 1948	2	3	0	70	35	23.33	—	—	—	—	—	—	—	—	—	0
†STANYFORTH, R T 1927-28	4	6	1	13	6*	2.60	—	—	—	—	—	—	—	—	—	7/2
STEVENSON, G B .1980-81	2	2	1	28	27*	28.00	—	—	312	183	5	36.60	3-111	—	—	0
SUTCLIFFE, H 1924-35	54	84	9	4,555	194	60.73	16	23	—	—	—	—	—	—	—	23
TAYLOR, K 1959-64	3	5	0	57	24	11.40	—	—	12	6	0	—	—	—	—	1
TRUEMAN, F S ...1952-65	67	85	14	981	39*	13.81	—	—	15,178	6,625	307	21.57	8-31	17	3	64
ULYETT, G 1877-90	25	39	0	949	149	24.33	1	7	2,627	1,020	50	20.40	7-36	1	—	19
†VAUGHAN M P .1999-2008	82	147	9	5,719	197	41.44	18	18	978	561	6	93.50	2-71	—	—	44
VERITY, H 1931-39	40	44	12	669	66*	20.90	—	3	11,173	3,510	144	24.37	8-43	5	2	30
WADDINGTON, A ...1920-21	2	4	0	16	7	4.00	—	—	276	119	1	119.00	1-35	—	—	1
WAINWRIGHT, E ..1893-98	5	9	0	132	49	14.66	—	—	127	73	0	—	—	—	—	2

YORKSHIRE TEST CRICKETERS 1877-2019 (Continued)

Player	M.	I	NO	Runs	HS.	Av'ge.	100s	50s	Balls	R	W	Av'ge	Best	5wI	10wM	c/st
WARDLE, J H 1948-57	28	41	8	653	66	19.78	2	—	6,597	2,080	102	20.39	7-36	5	1	12
WATSON, W 1951-59	23	37	3	879	116	25.85	2	3	—	—	—	—	—	—	—	8
WHITE, C 1994-2002	30	50	7	1,052	121	24.46	1	5	3,959	2,220	59	37.62	5-32	3	—	14
WILSON, C E M 1899	2	4	1	42	18	14.00	—	—	—	—	—	—	—	—	—	0
WILSON, D 1964-71	6	7	1	75	42	12.50	—	—	1,472	466	11	42.36	2-17	—	—	1
WILSON, E R 1921	1	2	0	10	5	5.00	—	—	123	36	3	12.00	2-28	—	—	0
WOOD, A 1938-39	4	5	1	80	53	20.00	—	1	—	—	—	—	—	—	—	10/1
†YARDLEY, N W D 1938-50	20	34	2	812	99	25.37	—	4	1,662	707	21	33.66	3-67	—	—	14

†Captained England
*Also represented and captained South Africa

For South Africa

Player	M.	I	NO	Runs	HS.	Av'ge.	100s	50s	Balls	R	W	Av'ge	Best	5wI	10wM	c/st
†MITCHELL, F 1912	3	6	0	28	12	4.66	—	—								0

†Captained South Africa

Overseas Players

(Qualification: 20 first-class matches for Yorkshire)

For Australia

Player	M.	I	NO	Runs	HS.	Av'ge.	100s	50s	Balls	R	W	Av'ge	Best	5wI	10wM	c/st
BEVAN, M G 1994-98	18	30	3	785	91	29.07	—	6	1,285	703	29	24.24	6-82	1	1	8
GILLESPIE, J N 1996-2006	71	93	28	1,218	201*	18.73	1	2	14,234	6,770	259	26.13	7-37	8	—	27
JAQUES, P A 2005-2008	11	19	0	902	150	47.47	3	6	—	—	—	—	—	—	—	7
LEHMANN, D S 1999-2004	27	42	2	1,798	177	44.95	5	10	974	412	15	27.46	3-42	—	—	11

For South Africa

Player	M.	I	NO	Runs	HS.	Av'ge.	100s	50s	Balls	R	W	Av'ge	Best	5wI	10wM	c/st
RUDOLPH, J A 2003-12/13	48	83	9	2,622	222*	35.43	6	11	664	432	4	108.00	1-1	—	—	29

For West Indies

Player	M.	I	NO	Runs	HS.	Av'ge.	100s	50s	Balls	R	W	Av'ge	Best	5wI	10wM	c/st
RICHARDSON, R B 1983-84/95	86	146	12	5,949	194	44.39	16	27	66	18	0	—	—	—	—	90

CENTURIES FOR ENGLAND

C W J ATHEY (1)

123 v Pakistan at Lord's, 1987

J M BAIRSTOW (6)

150* v. South Africa at Cape Town, 2016
167* v. Sri Lanka at Lord's, 2016
101 v. New Zealand at Christchurch, 2018

140 v. Sri Lanka at Leeds, 2016
119 v. Australia at Perth, 2017
110 v. Sri Lanka at Colombo (SSC), 2018

G S BALLANCE (4)

104* v. Sri Lanka at Lord's, 2014
256 v. India at Southampton, 2014

110 v. India at Lord's, 2014
122 v. West Indies at North Sound, 2015

G BOYCOTT (22)

113 v. Australia at The Oval, 1964
117 v. South Africa at Port Elizabeth, 1965
246* v. India at Leeds, 1967
116 v. West Indies at Georgetown, 1968
128 v. West Indies at Manchester, 1969
106 v. West Indies at Lord's, 1969
142* v. Australia at Sydney, 1971
119* v. Australia at Adelaide, 1971
121* v. Pakistan at Lord's, 1971
112 v. Pakistan at Leeds, 1971
115 v. New Zealand at Leeds, 1973

112 v West Indies at Port-of-Spain, 1974
107 v. Australia at Nottingham, 1977
191 v. Australia at Leeds, 1977
100* v. Pakistan at Hyderabad, 1978
131 v. New Zealand at Nottingham, 1978
155 v. India at Birmingham, 1979
125 v. India at The Oval, 1979
128* v. Australia at Lord's, 1980
104* v. West Indies at St John's, 1981
137 v. Australia at The Oval, 1981
105 v. India at Delhi, 1981

J T BROWN (1)

140 v. Australia at Melbourne, 1895

D DENTON (1)

104 v. South Africa at Old Wanderers, Johannesburg, 1910

P A GIBB (2)

106 v. South Africa at Old Wanderers, Johannesburg, 1938
120 v. South Africa at Kingsmead, Durban, 1939

J H HAMPSHIRE (1)

107 v. West Indies at Lord's, 1969

L HUTTON (19)

100 v. New Zealand at Manchester, 1937
100 v. Australia at Nottingham, 1938
364 v. Australia at The Oval, 1938
196 v. West Indies at Lord's, 1939
165* v. West Indies at The Oval, 1939
122* v. Australia at Sydney, 1947
100 v. South Africa at Leeds, 1947
158 v. South Africa at Ellis Park, J'b'rg, 1948
123 v. South Africa at Ellis Park, J'b'rg, 1949
101 v. New Zealand at Leeds, 1949

206 v. New Zealand at The Oval, 1949
202* v. West Indies at The Oval, 1950
156* v. Australia at Adelaide, 1951
100 v. South Africa at Leeds, 1951
150 v. India at Lord's, 1952
104 v. India at Manchester, 1952
145 v. Australia at Lord's, 1953
169 v. West Indies at Georgetown, 1954
205 v. West Indies at Kingston, 1954

R ILLINGWORTH (2)

113 v. West Indies at Lord's, 1969

107 v. India at Manchester, 1971

Hon. F S JACKSON (5)

103 v. Australia at The Oval, 1893
118 v. Australia at The Oval, 1899
128 v. Australia at Manchester, 1902

144* v. Australia at Leeds, 1905
113 v. Australia at Manchester, 1905

CENTURIES FOR ENGLAND

M LEYLAND (9)

137 v. Australia at Melbourne, 1929
102 v. South Africa at Lord's, 1929
109 v. Australia at Lord's, 1934
153 v. Australia at Manchester, 1934
110 v. Australia at The Oval, 1934
161 v. South Africa at The Oval, 1935
126 v. Australia at Woolloongabba, Brisbane, 1936
111* v. Australia at Melbourne, 1937
187 v. Australia at The Oval, 1938

A LYTH (1)

107 v. New Zealand at Leeds 2015

W RHODES (2)

179 v. Australia at Melbourne, 1912
152 v. South Africa at Old Wanderers, Johannesburg, 1913

J E ROOT (17)

104 v. New Zealand at Leeds, 2013
200* v. Sri Lanka at Lord's, 2014
149* v. India at The Oval, 2014
134 v. Australia at Cardiff 2015
110 v. South Africa at Johannesburg, 2016
124 v. India at Rajkot, 2016
136 v. West Indies at Birmingham, 2017
124 v. Sri Lanka at Pallekele, 2018
226 v, New Zealand at Hamiton, 2019
180 v. Australia at Lord's, 2013
154* v. India at Nottingham, 2014
182* v. West Indies at St George's, 2015
130 v. Australia at Nottingham, 2015
254 v. Pakistan at Manchester, 2016
190 v. South Africa at Lord's, 2017
125 v. India at The Oval, 2018
122 v. West Indies at Gros Islet, 2019

P J SHARPE (1)

111 v. New Zealand at Nottingham, 1969

H SUTCLIFFE (16)

122 v. South Africa at Lord's, 1924
115 v. Australia at Sydney, 1924
176 v. Australia at Melbourne, 1925 (1st Inns)
127 v. Australia at Melbourne, 1925 (2nd Inns)
143 v. Australia at Melbourne, 1925
161 v. Australia at The Oval, 1926
102 v. South Africa at Old Wanderers, Jbg.1927
135 v. Australia at Melbourne, 1929
114 v. South Africa at Birmingham, 1929
100 v. South Africa at Lord's, 1929
104 v. South Africa at The Oval, 1929 (1st inns)
109* v. South Africa at The Oval, 1929 (2nd inns)
161 v. Australia at The Oval, 1930
117 v. New Zealand at The Oval, 1931
109* v. New Zealand at Manchester, 1931
194 v. Australia at Sydney, 1932

G ULYETT (1)

149 v. Australia at Melbourne, 1882

M P VAUGHAN (18)

120 v. Pakistan at Manchester, 2001
115 v. Sri Lanka at Lord's, 2002
100 v. India at Lord's, 2002
197 v. India at Nottingham, 2002
195 v. India at The Oval, 2002
177 v. Australia at Adelaide, 2002
145 v. Australia at Melbourne, 2002
183 v. Australia at Sydney, 2003
156 v. South Africa at Birmingham, 2003
105 v. Sri Lanka at Kandy, 2003
140 v. West Indies at Antigua, 2004
103 v. West Indies at Lord's (1st inns) 2004
101* v. West Indies at Lord's (2nd inns) 2004
120 v. Bangladesh at Lord's, 2005
166 v. Australia at Manchester,2005
103 v. West Indies at Leeds, 2007
124 v. India at Nottingham, 2007
106 v. New Zealand at Lord's, 2008

CENTURIES FOR ENGLAND *(Continued)*

W WATSON (2)

109 v. Australia at Lord's, 1953	116 v. West Indies at Kingston, 1954

C WHITE (1)

121 v. India at Ahmedabad, 2001

Summary of the Centuries

versus	Total	In England	Away
Australia	43	23	20
Bangladesh	1	1	0
India	18	15	3
New Zealand	13	11	2
Pakistan	6	5	1
South Africa	21	11	10
Sri Lanka	8	5	3
West Indies	21	11	10
Totals	131	82	49

For Australia

J N GILLESPIE (1)

201* v. Bangladesh at Chittagong, 2006

P A JAQUES (3)

100 v. Sri Lanka at Brisbane, 2007	108 v. West Indies at Bridgetown, 2008
150 v. Sri Lanka at Hobart, 2007	

D S LEHMANN (5)

160 v. West Indies at Port of Spain, 2003	129 v. Sri Lanka at Galle, 2004
110 v. Bangladesh at Darwin, 2003	153 v. Sri Lanka at Columbo, 2004
177 v. Bangladesh at Cairns, 2003	

For South Africa

J A RUDOLPH (6)

222* v. Bangladesh at Chittagong, 2003	102 v. Sri Lanka at Galle, 2004
101 v West Indies at Cape Town, 2004	102* v Australia at Perth, 2005
154* v. New Zealand at Auckland, 2004	105* v. New Zealand at Dunedin, 2012

10 WICKETS IN A MATCH FOR ENGLAND

W BATES (1)
14 for 102 (7 for 28 and 7 for 74) v. Australia at Melbourne, 1882

M J HOGGARD (1)
12 for 205 (5 for 144 and 7 for 61) v. South Africa at Johannesburg, 2005

R PEEL (1)
11 for 68 (7 for 31 and 4 for 37) v. Australia at Mancester, 1888

Note: The scorebook for the Australia v. England Test match at Sydney in February 1888
shows that the final wicket to fall was taken by W Attewell, and not by Peel
Peel therefore took 9, and not 10 wickets, in the match
His career totals have been amended to take account of this alteration

W RHODES (1)
15 for 124 (7 for 56 and 8 for 68) v. Australia at Melbourne, 1904

R J SIDEBOTTOM (1)
10 for 139 (4 for 90 and 6 for 49) v. New Zealand at Hamilton, 2008

F S TRUEMAN (3)
11 for 88 (5 for 58 and 6 for 30) v. Australia at Leeds, 1961
11 for 152 (6 for 100 and 5 for 52) v. West Indies at Lord's, 1963*
12 for 119 (5 for 75 and 7 for 44) v. West Indies at Birmingham, 1963*
consecutive Tests

H VERITY (2)
11 for 153 (7 for 49 and 4 for 104) v. India at Chepauk, Madras, 1934
15 for 104 (7 for 61 and 8 for 43) v. Australia at Lord's, 1934

J H WARDLE (1)
12 for 89 (5 for 53 and 7 for 36) v. South Africa at Cape Town, 1957

Summary of Ten Wickets in a Match

versus	Total	In England	Away
Australia	5	3	2
India	1	—	1
New Zealand	1	—	1
Pakistan	—	—	—
South Africa	2	—	2
Sri Lanka	—	—	—
West Indies	2	2	—
Totals	11	5	6

For Australia

M G BEVAN (1)
10 for 113 (4 for 31and 6 for 82) v. West Indies at Adelaide, 1997

5 WICKETS IN AN INNINGS FOR ENGLAND

R APPLEYARD (1)
5 for 51 v. Pakistan at Nottingham, 1954

W BATES (4)
7 for 28 v. Australia at Melbourne, 1882   5 for 31 v. Australia at Adelaide, 1884
7 for 74 v. Australia at Melbourne, 1882   5 for 24 v. Australia at Sydney, 1885

5 WICKETS IN AN INNINGS FOR ENGLAND (Continued)

W E BOWES (6)

6-34	v. New Zealand	at Auckland	1933	5-100	v. South Africa	at Manchester	1935
6-142	v. Australia	at Leeds	1934*	5-49	v. Australia	at The Oval	1938
5-55	v. Australia	at The Oval	1934*	6-33	v. West Indies	at Manchester	1939

consecutive Test matches

T T BRESNAN (1)

5-48   v. India   at Nottingham   2011

T EMMETT (1)

7-68   v. Australia   at Melbourne   1879

D GOUGH (9)

6-49	v. Australia	at Sydney	1995	5-70	v. South Africa	at Johannesburg	1999
5-40	v.New Zealand	at Wellington	1997	5-109	v. West Indies	at Birmingham	2000
5-149	v. Australia	at Leeds	1997	5-61	v. Pakistan	at Lord's	2001
6-42	v.South Africa	at Leeds	1998	5-103	v. Australia	at Leeds	2001
5-96	v. Australia	at Melbourne	1998				

S HAIGH (1)

6-11   v. South Africa   at Cape Town   1909

G H HIRST (3)

5-77	v. Australia	at The Oval	1902	5-58	v. Australia	at Birmingham 1909
5-48	v. Australia	at Melbourne	1904			

M J HOGGARD (7)

7-63	v. New Zealand	at Christchurch	2002	5-73	v. Bangladesh	at Chester-le-Street
5-92	v. Sri Lanka	at Birmingham	2002			2005
5-144	v. South Africa	at Johannesburg	2005*	6-57	v. India	at Nagpur 2006
7-61	v. South Africa	at Johannesburg	2005*	7-109	v. Australia	at Adelaide 2006

Consecutive Test innings

R ILLINGWORTH (3)

6-29	v. India	at Lord's	1967	5-70	v. India	at The Oval 1971
6-87	v. Australia	at Leeds	1968			

Hon F S JACKSON (1)

5-52   v. Australia   at Nottingham   1905

G G MACAULAY (1)

5-64   v. South Africa   at Cape Town   1923

C M OLD (4)

5-113	v. New Zealand	at Lord's	1973	6-54	v. New Zealand	at Wellington 1978
5-21	v. India	at Lord's	1974	7-50	v. Pakistan	at Birmingham 1978

E PEATE (2)

5-43   v. Australia   at Sydney 1882   6-85   v. Australia   at Lord's   1884

R PEEL (5)

5-51	v. Australia	at Adelaide	1884	6-67	v. Australia	at Sydney 1894
5-18	v. Australia	at Sydney	1888	6-23	v. Australia	at The Oval 1896
7-31	v. Australia	at Manchester	1888			

L E PLUNKETT (1)

5-64   v. Sri Lanka   at Leeds   2014

A U RASHID (2)

5-64   v. Pakistan   at Abu Dhabi   2015   5-49   v. Sri Lanka   at Colombo (SSC)   2018

5 WICKETS IN AN INNINGS FOR ENGLAND *(Continued)*

W RHODES (6)

7-17	v. Australia	at Birmingham	1902	7-56	v. Australia	at Melbourne	1904*
5-63	v. Australia	at Sheffield	1902	8-68	v. Australia	at Melbourne	1904*
5-94	v. Australia	at Sydney	1903*	5-83	v. Australia	at Manchester	1909

consecutive Test innings

C E W SILVERWOOD (1)

5-91   v. South Africa   at Cape Town   2000

R J SIDEBOTTOM (5)

5-88	v. West Indies	at Chester-le-Street	2007	5-105	v. New Zealand	at Wellington	2008
				7-47	v. New Zealand	at Napier	2008
6-49	v. New Zealand	at Hamilton	2008	6-47	v. New Zealand	at Nottingham	2008

F S TRUEMAN (17)

8-31	v. India	at Manchester	1952	6-31	v. Pakistan	at Lord's	1962
5-48	v. India	at The Oval	1952	5-62	v. Australia	at Melbourne	1963
5-90	v. Australia	at Lord's	1956	7-75	v. New Zealand	at Christchurch	1963
5-63	v. West Indies	at Nottingham	1957	6-100	v. West Indies	at Lord's	1963*
5-31	v. New Zealand	at Birmingham	1958	5-52	v. West Indies	at Lord's	1963*
5-35	v. West Indies	at Port-of-Spain	1960	5-75	v. West Indies	at Birmingham	1963*
5-27	v. South Africa	at Nottingham	1960	7-44	v. West Indies	at Birmingham	1963*
5-58	v. Australia	at Leeds	1961*	5-48	v. Australia	at Lord's	1964
6-30	v. Australia	at Leeds	1961*				

G ULYETT (1)

7-36   v. Australia   at Lord's   1884

H VERITY (5)

5-33	v. Australia	at Sydney	1933	8-43	v. Australia	at Lord's	1934*
7-49	v. India	at Chepauk, Madras	1934	5-70	v. South Africa	at Cape Town	1939
7-61	v. Australia	at Lord's	1934*				

J H WARDLE (5)

7-56	v. Pakistan	at The Oval	1954	7-36	v. South Africa	at Cape Town	1957*
5-79	v. Australia	at Sydney	1955	5-61	v. South Africa	at Kingsmead Durban	1957*
5-53	v. South Africa	at Cape Town	1957*				

C WHITE (3)

5-57	v. West Indies	at Leeds	2000	5-32	v. West Indies	at The Oval	2000
	5-127	v. Australia	at Perth	2002			

consecutive Test innings

Summary of Five Wickets in an Innings

versus	Total	In England	Away
Australia	42	22	20
Bangladesh	1	1	0
India	8	6	2
New Zealand	11	3	8
Pakistan	6	5	1
South Africa	13	3	10
Sri Lanka	3	2	1
West Indies	11	10	1
Totals	95	52	43

5 WICKETS IN AN INNINGS

M G BEVAN (1)

6-82	v. West Indies	at Adelaide	1997

J N GILLESPIE (8)

5-54	v. South Africa	at Port Elizabeth	1997
7-37	v. England	at Leeds	1997
5-88	v. England	at Perth	1998
5-89	v. West Indies	at Adelaide	2000
6-40	v. West Indies	at Melbourne	2000
5-53	v. England	at Lord's	2001
5-39	v. West Indies	at Georgetown	2003
5-56	v. India	at Nagpur	2004

HAT-TRICKS

W Bates	v. Australia	at Melbourne	1882
D Gough	v. Australia	at Sydney	1998
M J Hoggard	v. West Indies	at Bridgetown	2004
R J Sidebottom	v. New Zealand	at Hamilton	2008

FOUR WICKETS IN FIVE BALLS

C M Old	v. Pakistan	at Birmingham	1978

THREE WICKETS IN FOUR BALLS

R Appleyard	v. New Zealand	at Auckland	1955
D Gough	v. Pakistan	at Lord's	2001

YORKSHIRE PLAYERS WHO PLAYED ALL THEIR TEST CRICKET AFTER LEAVING YORKSHIRE

For England

Player	M.	I	NO	Runs	HS.	Av'ge.	100s	50s	Balls	R	W	Av'ge	Best	5wI	10wM	c/st
BALDERSTONE, J C ..1976	2	4	0	39	35	9.75	—	—	96	80	1	80.00	1:80	—	—	1
BATTY G J 2003/4-16/17	9	12	2	149	38	14.90	—	1	1,714	914	15	60.93	3-55	—	—	3
BIRKENSHAW, J ...1973-74	5	7	0	148	64	21.14	—	1	1,017	469	13	36.07	5:57	1	—	3
BOLUS, J B 1963-64	7	12	0	496	88	41.33	—	4	18	16	0	—	—	—	—	2
†PARKIN, C H 1920-24	10	16	3	160	36	12.30	—	—	2,095	1,128	32	35.25	5:38	2	—	3
RHODES, S J 1994-95	11	17	5	294	65*	24.50	—	1	—	—	—	—	—	—	—	46/3
†SUGG, F H 1888	2	2	0	55	31	27.50	—	—	—	—	—	—	—	—	—	0
WARD, A 1893-95	7	13	0	487	117	37.46	1	3	98	50	0	—	—	—	—	1
WOOD, B 1972-78	12	21	0	454	90	21.61	—	2	—	—	—	—	—	—	—	6

For South Africa

Player	M.	I	NO	Runs	HS.	Av'ge.	100s	50s	Balls	R	W	Av'ge	Best	5wI	10wM	c/st
THORNTON, P G 1902	1	1	1	1	1*	—	—	—	24	20	1	20.00	1:20	—	—	1

†Born outside Yorkshire

CENTURIES
FOR ENGLAND

A WARD (1)
117 v. Australia at Sydney, 1894

5 WICKETS IN AN INNINGS
FOR ENGLAND

J BIRKENSHAW (1)
5 : 57 v. Pakistan at Karachi, 1973

C H PARKIN (2)
5 : 60 v. Australia at Adelaide, 1921
5 : 38 v. Australia at Manchester, 1921

311

YORKSHIRE'S TEST CRICKET RECORDS

R APPLEYARD

Auckland 1954-55: took 3 wickets in 4 balls as New Zealand were dismissed for the lowest total in Test history (26).

C W J ATHEY

Perth 1986-87: shared an opening stand of 223 with B C Broad – England's highest for any wicket at the WACA Ground.

J M BAIRSTOW

Cape Town, January 2016: scored his maiden Test Century (150*). His sixth- wicket partnership of 399 with B A Stokes (258) was the highest in Test cricket and the highest First Class partnership for any wicket at Newlands. There was only one higher partnership for England. This was 411 by P B H May and M C Cowdrey for the fourth wicket against the West Indies at Birmingham in 1957.

Chittagong, October 2016: scored 52 in the first innings, which passed his 1,000 Test runs in a calendar year. He became only the third Yorkshire player to do this after M P Vaughan with 1,481 in 2002 and J E Root 1,385 in 2015. He was only the second Test wicket-keeper to pass this mark. His first scoring shot in the second inning broke a 16-year record set by Zimbabwe's A Flower (1,045 in 2000) to give him the highest total of runs scored in a calendar year by a Test wicket-keeper. His final tally for 2016 was 1,470.

Mohali, November 2016: his third catch of India's first innings (U T Yadav) was his 68th dismissal of the year to pass the previous best in a calendar year (67) by I A Healy (Australia) in 1991 and M V Boucher (South Africa) in 1998. Bairstow's final tally for the calendar year was 70 (66 caught and 4 stumped).

W BATES

Melbourne 1882-83 (Second Test): achieved the first hat-trick for England when he dismissed P S McDonnell, G Giffen and G J Bonnor in Australia's first innings. Later in the match, he became the first player to score a fifty (55) and take 10 or more wickets (14 for 102) in the same Test.

W E BOWES

Melbourne 1932-33: enjoyed the unique satisfaction of bowling D G Bradman first ball in a Test match (his first ball to him in Test cricket).

G BOYCOTT

Leeds 1967: scored 246 not out off 555 balls in 573 minutes to establish the record England score against India. His first 100 took 341 minutes (316 balls) and he was excluded from the next Test as a disciplinary measure; shared in hundred partnerships for three successive wickets.

Adelaide 1970-71: with J H Edrich, became the third opening pair to share hundred partnerships in both innings of a Test against Australia.

Port-of-Spain 1973-74: first to score 99 and a hundred in the same Test.

Nottingham 1977: with A P E Knott, equalled England v. Australia sixth-wicket partnership record of 215 – the only England v. Australia stand to be equalled or broken since 1938. Batted on each day of the five-day Test (second after M L Jaisimha to achieve this feat).

Leeds 1977: first to score his 100th First Class hundred in a Test; became the fourth England player to be on the field for an entire Test.

YORKSHIRE'S TEST CRICKET RECORDS *(Continued)*

G BOYCOTT *(Continued)*

Perth: 1978-79: eighth to score 2,000 runs for England against Australia.

Birmingham 1979: emulated K F Barrington by scoring hundreds on each of England's six current home grounds.

Perth: 1979-80: fourth to carry his bat through a completed England innings (third v. Australia) and the first to do so without scoring 100; first to score 99 not out in a Test.

Lord's 1981: 100th Test for England – second after M C Cowdrey (1968).

The Oval, 1981: second after Hon F S Jackson to score five hundreds v. Australia in England.

Gained three Test records from M C Cowdrey: exceeded England aggregate of 7,624 runs in 11 fewer Tests (Manchester 1981); 61st fifty – world record (The Oval 1981); 189th innings – world record (Bangalore 1981-82).

Delhi, 4.23p.m. on 23 December 1981: passed G St.A Sobers's world Test record of 8,032 runs, having played 30 more innings and batted over 451 hours (cf. 15 complete five-day Tests); his 22nd hundred equalled England record.

J T BROWN

Melbourne 1894-95: his 28-minute fifty remains the fastest in Test cricket, and his 95-minute hundred was a record until 1897-98; his third-wicket stand of 210 with A Ward set a Test record for any wicket.

D B CLOSE

Manchester 1949: at 18 years 149 days he became – and remains – the youngest to represent England.

Melbourne 1950-51: became the youngest (19 years 301 days) to represent England against Australia.

T EMMETT

Melbourne 1878-79: first England bowler to take seven wickets in a Test innings.

P A GIBB

Johannesburg 1938-39: enjoyed a record England debut, scoring 93 and 106 as well as sharing second-wicket stands of 184 and 168 with E Paynter.

Durban 1938-39: shared record England v. South Africa second-wicket stand of 280 with W J Edrich, his 120 in 451 minutes including only two boundaries.

D GOUGH

Sydney 1998-99: achieved the 23rd hat-trick in Test cricket (ninth for England and first for England v. Australia since 1899).

Lord's 2001: took 3 wickets in 4 balls v. Pakistan.

S HAIGH

Cape Town 1898-99: bowled unchanged through the second innings with A E Trott, taking 6 for 11 as South Africa were dismissed for 35 in the space of 114 balls.

J H HAMPSHIRE

Lord's 1969: became the first England player to score 100 at Lord's on his debut in Tests.

A HILL

Melbourne 1876-77: took the first wicket to fall in Test cricket when he bowled N Thompson, and held the first catch when he dismissed T P Horan.

YORKSHIRE'S TEST CRICKET RECORDS *(Continued)*

G H HIRST

The Oval: 1902: helped to score the last 15 runs in a match-winning tenth-wicket partnership with W Rhodes.

Birmingham 1909: shared all 20 Australian wickets with fellow left-arm spinner C Blythe (11 for 102).

M J HOGGARD

Bridgetown 2004: became the third Yorkshire player to take a hat-trick in Test cricket (see W Bates and D Gough). It was the 10th hat-trick for England and the third for England versus West Indies.

L HUTTON

Nottingham 1938: scored 100 in his first Test against Australia.

The Oval 1938: his score (364) and batting time (13 hours 17 minutes – the longest innings in English First-Class cricket) remain England records, and were world Test records until 1958. It remains the highest Test score at The Oval. His stand of 382 with M Leyland is the England second-wicket record in all Tests and the highest for any wicket against Australia. He also shared a record England v. Australia sixth-wicket stand of 216 with J Hardstaff Jr. – the first instance of a batsman sharing in two stands of 200 in the same Test innings. 770 runs were scored during his innings (Test record) which was England's 100th century against Australia, and contained 35 fours. England's total of 903 for 7 declared remains the Ashes Test record.

Lord's 1939: added 248 for the fourth wicket with D C S Compton in 140 minutes.

The Oval 1939: shared (then) world-record third-wicket stand of 264 with W R Hammond, which remains the record for England v. West Indies. Hutton's last eight Tests had brought him 1,109 runs.

The Oval 1948: last out in the first innings, he was on the field for all but the final 57 minutes of the match.

Johannesburg 1948-49: shared (then) world-record first-wicket stand of 359 in 310 minutes with C Washbrook on the opening day of Test cricket at Ellis Park; it remains England's highest opening stand in all Tests.

The Oval 1950: scored England's first 200 in a home Test v. West Indies, and remains alone in carrying his bat for England against them; his 202 not out (in 470 minutes) is the highest score by an England batsman achieving this feat.

Adelaide 1950-51: only England batsman to carry his bat throughout a complete Test innings twice, and second after R Abel (1891-92) to do so for any country against Australia.

Manchester 1951: scored 98 not out, just failing to become the first to score his 100th First Class hundred in a Test match.

The Oval 1951: became the only batsman to be out 'obstructing the field' in Test cricket.

1952: first professional to be appointed captain of England in the 20th Century.

The Oval 1953: first captain to win a rubber after losing the toss in all five Tests.

Kingston 1953-54: scored the first 200 by an England captain in a Test overseas.

R ILLINGWORTH

Manchester 1971: shared record England v. India eighth-wicket stand of 168 with P Lever.

YORKSHIRE'S TEST CRICKET RECORDS *(Continued)*

Hon. F S JACKSON

The Oval 1893: his 100 took 135 minutes, and was the first in a Test in England to be completed with a hit over the boundary (then worth only four runs).

The Oval 1899: his stand of 185 with T W Hayward was then England's highest for any wicket in England, and the record opening partnership by either side in England v. Australia Tests.

Nottingham 1905: dismissed M A Noble, C Hill and J Darling in one over (W01W0W).

Leeds 1905: batted 268 minutes for 144 not out – the first hundred in a Headingley Test.

Manchester 1905: first to score five Test hundreds in England.

The Oval 1905: first captain to win every toss in a five-match rubber.

M LEYLAND

Melbourne 1928-29: scored 137 in his first innings against Australia.

1934: first to score three hundreds in a rubber against Australia in England.

Brisbane 1936-37: scored England's only 100 at 'The Gabba' before 1974-75.

The Oval 1938: contributed 187 in 381 minutes to the record Test total of 903 for 7 declared, sharing in England's highest stand against Australia (all wickets) and record second-wicket stand in all Tests: 382 with L Hutton. First to score hundreds in his first and last innings against Australia.

G G MACAULAY

Cape Town 1922-23: fourth bowler (third for England) to take a wicket (G A L Hearne) with his first ball in Test cricket. Made the winning hit in the fourth of only six Tests to be decided by a one-wicket margin.

Leeds 1926: shared a match-saving ninth-wicket stand of 108 with G Geary.

C M OLD

Birmingham 1978: took 4 wickets in 5 balls in his 19th over (0WW no-ball WW1) to emulate the feat of M J C Allom.

R PEEL

Took his 50th wicket in his ninth Test and his 100th in his 20th Test – all against Australia.

Kingston 1929-30: ended the world's longest Test career (30 years 315 days) as the oldest Test cricketer (52 years 165 days).

W RHODES

Birmingham 1902: his first-innings analysis of 7 for 17 remains the record for all Tests at Edgbaston.

The Oval 1902: helped to score the last 15 runs in a match-winning tenth-wicket partnership with G H Hirst.

Sydney 1903-04: shared record England v. Australia tenth-wicket stand of 130 in 66 minutes with R E Foster.

Melbourne 1903-04: first to take 15 wickets in England v. Australia Tests; his match analysis of 15 for 124 remains the record for all Tests at Melbourne.

Melbourne 1911-12: shared record England v. Australia first-wicket stand of 323 in 268 minutes with J B Hobbs.

YORKSHIRE'S TEST CRICKET RECORDS *(Continued)*

W RHODES *(Continued)*

Johannesburg 1913-14: took his 100th wicket and completed the first 'double' for England (in 44 matches).

Sydney 1920-21: first to score 2,000 runs and take 100 wickets in Test cricket.

Adelaide 1920-21: third bowler to take 100 wickets against Australia.

The Oval 1926: set (then) record of 109 wickets against Australia.

J E ROOT

Chittagong, October 2016: with his score (40) in England's first innings he passed 1,000 runs in a calendar year. He also did this in 2015 (1,385) and became the first Yorkshire player to do this twice. His final tally (1,477) in 2016 left him four short of M P Vaughan's total in 2002

Visakhapatnam, November 2016: Played his 50th Test match, which was also his 100th first-class match

Lord's, July 2017 v. West Indies: His first innings (190) was the highest by an England captain in his first innings in this role.

H SUTCLIFFE

Birmingham 1924: shared the first of 15 three-figure partnerships with J B Hobbs at the first attempt.

Lord's 1924: shared stand of 268 with J B Hobbs, which remains the first-wicket record for all Lord's Tests, and was then the England v. South Africa record.

Sydney 1924-25: his first opening stands against Australia with J B Hobbs realised 157 and 110.

Melbourne 1924-25 (Second Test): with J B Hobbs achieved the first instance of a batting partnership enduring throughout a full day's Test match play; they remain the only England pair to achieve this feat, and their stand of 283 in 289 minutes remains the longest for the first wicket in this series. Became the first to score 100 in each innings of a Test against Australia, and the first Englishman to score three successive hundreds in Test cricket.

Melbourne 1924-25 (Fourth Test): first to score four hundreds in one rubber of Test matches; it was his third 100 in successive Test innings at Melbourne. Completed 1,000 runs in fewest Test innings (12) – since equalled.

Sydney 1924-25: his aggregate of 734 runs was the record for any rubber until 1928-29.

The Oval 1926: shared first-wicket stand of 172 with J B Hobbs on a rain-affected pitch.

The Oval 1929: first to score hundreds in each innings of a Test twice; only England batsman to score four hundreds in a rubber twice.

Sydney 1932-33: his highest England innings of 194 overtook J B Hobbs's world record of 15 Test hundreds.

F S TRUEMAN

Leeds 1952: reduced India to 0 for 4 in their second innings by taking 3 wickets in 8 balls on his debut.

Manchester 1952: achieved record England v. India innings analysis of 8 for 31.

The Oval 1952: set England v. India series record with 29 wickets.

Leeds 1961: took 5 for 0 with 24 off-cutters at a reduced pace v. Australia.

Lord's 1962: shared record England v. Pakistan ninth-wicket stand of 76 with T W Graveney.

YORKSHIRE'S TEST CRICKET RECORDS *(Continued)*

F S TRUEMAN *(Continued)*

Christchurch 1962-63: passed J B Statham's world Test record of 242 wickets; his analysis of 7-75 remains the record for Lancaster Park Tests and for England in New Zealand.

Birmingham 1963: returned record match analysis (12-119) against West Indies in England and for any Birmingham Test, ending with a 6-4 spell from 24 balls.

The Oval 1963: set England v. West Indies series record with 34 wickets.

The Oval 1964: first to take 300 wickets in Tests.

G ULYETT

Sydney 1881-82: with R G Barlow shared the first century opening partnership in Test cricket (122).

Melbourne 1881-82: his 149 was the first Test hundred for England in Australia, and the highest score for England on the first day of a Test in Australia until 1965-66.

M P VAUGHAN

Scored 1481 runs in 2002 – more than any other England player in a calendar year, surpassing the 1379 scored by D L Amiss in 1979. It was the fourth highest in a calendar year.

Scored 633 runs in the 2002-3 series versus Australia – surpassed for England in a five Test series versus Australia only by W R Hammond, who scored 905 runs in 1928-29, H Sutcliffe (734 in 1924-25), J B Hobbs (662 in 1911-12) and G Boycott (657 in 1970-71), when he played in five of the six Tests.

Scored six Test Match centuries in 2002 to equal the record set for England by D C S Compton in 1947.

Lord's 2004: scored a century in each innings (103 and 101*) versus West Indies and so became the third player (after G A Headley and G A Gooch) to score a century in each innings of a Test match at Lord's.

Lord's 2005: only the second player (J B Hobbs is the other) to have scored centuries in three consecutive Test match innings at Lord's. Scored the 100th century for England by a Yorkshire player.

H VERITY

Lord's 1934: took 14 for 80 on the third day (six of them in the final hour) to secure England's first win against Australia at Lord's since 1896. It remains the most wickets to fall to one bowler in a day of Test cricket in England. His match analysis of 15 for 104 was then the England v. Australia record, and has been surpassed only by J C Laker.

W WATSON

Lord's 1953: scored 109 in 346 minutes in his first Test against Australia.

N W D YARDLEY

Melbourne 1946-47: dismissed D G Bradman for the third consecutive innings without assistance from the field. Became the first to score a fifty in each innings for England and take five wickets in the same match.

Nottingham 1947: shared record England v. South Africa fifth-wicket stand of 237 with D C S Compton.

* * *

Facts adapted by Bill Frindall from his *England Test Cricketers – The Complete Record from 1877* (Collins Willow, 1989). With later additions.

TEST MATCHES AT HEADINGLEY, LEEDS 1899-2019

1899 **Australia 172** (J Worrall 76) and **224** (H Trumble 56, J T Hearne hat-trick). **England 220** (A F A Lilley 55, H Trumble 5 for 60) and **19 for 0 wkt.**
Match drawn Toss: Australia

1905 **England 301** (Hon F S Jackson 144*) and **295 for 5 wkts dec** (J T Tyldesley 100, T W Hayward 60, W W. Armstrong 5 for 122). **Australia 195** (W W Armstrong 66, A R Warren 5 for 57) and **224 for 7 wkts** (M A Noble 62).
Match drawn Toss: England

1907 **England 76** (G A Faulkner 6 for 17) and **162** (C B Fry 54). **South Africa 110** (C Blythe 8 for 59) and **75** (C Blythe 7 for 40).
England won by 53 runs Toss: England

1909 **Australia 188** and **207** (S F Barnes 6 for 63). **England 182** (J Sharp 61, J T Tyldesley 55, C G Macartney 7 for 58) and **87** (A Cotter 5 for 38).
Australia won by 126 runs Toss: Australia

1912 **England 242** (F E Woolley 57) and **238** (R H Spooner 82, J B Hobbs 55). **South Africa 147** (S F Barnes 6 for 52) and **159**.
England won by 174 runs Toss: England

1921 **Australia 407** (C G Macartney 115, W W Armstrong 77, C E Pellew 52, J M Taylor 50) and **273 for 7 wkts dec** (T J E Andrew 92). **England 259** (J W H T Douglas 75, Hon L H Tennyson 63, G Brown 57) and **202.**
Australia won by 219 runs Toss: Australia

1924 **England 396** (E H Hendren 132, H Sutcliffe 83) and **60 for 1 wkt.** **South Africa 132** (H W Taylor 59*, M W Tate 6 for 42) and **323** (H W Taylor 56, R H Catterall 56).
England won by 9 wickets Toss: England

1926 **Australia 494** (C G Macartney 151, W M Woodfull 141, A J Richardson 100). **England 294** (G G Macaulay 76, C V Grimmett 5 for 88) and **254 for 3 wkts** (H Sutcliffe 94, J B Hobbs 88).
Match drawn Toss: England

1929 **South Africa 236** (R H Catterall 74, C L Vincent 60, A P Freeman 7 for 115) and **275** (H G Owen-Smith 129). **England 328** (F E Woolley 83, W R Hammond 65, N A Quinn 6 for 92) and **186 for 5 wkts** (F E Woolley 95*).
England won by 5 wickets Toss: South Africa

1930 **Australia 566** (D G Bradman 334, A F Kippax 77, W M Woodfull 50, M W Tate 5 for 124). **England 391** (W R Hammond 113, C V Grimmett 5 for 135) and **95 for 3 wkts.**
Match drawn Toss: Australia

1934 **England 200** and **229 for 6 wkts.** **Australia 584** (D G Bradman 304, W H Ponsford 181, W E Bowes 6 for 142).
Match drawn Toss: England

1935 **England 216** (W R Hammond 63, A Mitchell 58) and **294 for 7 wkts dec** (W R Hammond 87*, A Mitchell 72, D Smith 57). **South Africa 171** (E A B Rowan 62) and **194 for 5 wkts** (B Mitchell 58).
Match drawn Toss: England

1938 **England 223** (W R Hammond 76, W J O'Reilly 5 for 66) and **123** (W J O'Reilly 5 for 56). **Australia 242** (D G Bradman 103, B A Barnett 57) and **107 for 5 wkts.**
Australia won by 5 wickets Toss: England

1947 **South Africa 175** (B Mitchell 53, A Nourse 51) and **184** (A D Nourse 57). **England 317 for 7 wkts dec** (L Hutton 100, C Washbrook 75) and **47 for 0 wkt.**
England won by 10 wickets Toss: South Africa

1948 **England 496** (C Washbrook 143, W .J Edrich 111, L Hutton 81, A V Bedser 79) and **365 for 8 wkts dec** (D C S. Compton 66, C Washbrook 65, L Hutton 57, W J Edrich 54). **Australia 458** (R N Harvey 112, S J E Loxton 93, R R Lindwall 77, K R Miller 58) and **404 for 3 wkts** (A R Morris 182, D G Bradman 173*).
Australia won by 7 wickets Toss: England

1949 **England 372** (D C S Compton 114, L Hutton 101, T B Burtt 5 for 97, J Cowie 5 for 127) and **267 for 4 wkts dec** (C Washbrook 103*, W J Edrich 70). **New Zealand 341** (F B Smith 96, M P Donnelly 64, T E Bailey 6 for 118) and **195 for 2 wkts** (B Sutcliffe 82, F Smith 54*).
Match drawn   Toss: England

1951 **South Africa 538** (E A B Rowan 236, P N F Mansell 90, C B. van Ryneveld 83, R A McLean 67) and **87 for 0 wkt** (E A B Rowan 60*). **England 505** (P B H May 138, L Hutton 100, T E Bailey 95, F A Lowson 58, A M B Rowan 5 for 174).
Match drawn   Toss: South Africa

1952 **India 293** (V L Manjrekar 133, V S Hazare 89) and 165 (D G Phadkar 64, V S Hazare 56). **England 334** (T W Graveney 71, T G Evans 66, Ghulam Ahmed 5 for 100) and **128 for 3 wkts** (R T Simpson 51).
England won by 7 wickets   Toss: India

1953 **England 167** (T W Graveney 55, R R Lindwall 5 for 54) and **275** (W J Edrich 64, D C S Compton 61). **Australia 266** (R N Harvey 71, G B Hole 53, A V Bedser 6 for 95) and **147 for 4 wkts.**
Match drawn   Toss: Australia

1955 **South Africa 171** and **500** (D J McGlew 133, W R Endean 116*, T L Goddard 74, H J Keith 73). **England 191** (D C S Compton 61) and **256** (P B H May 97, T L Goddard 5 for 69, H J Tayfield 5 for 94).
South Africa won by 224 runs   Toss: South Africa

1956 **England 325** (P B H May 101, C Washbrook 98). **Australia 143** (J C Laker 5 for 58) and **140** (R N Harvey 69, J C Laker 6 for 55).
England won by an innings and 42 runs   Toss: England

1957 **West Indies 142** (P J Loader 6 for 36, including hat-trick) and **132.** **England 279** (P B H May 69, M C Cowdrey 68, Rev D S Sheppard 68, F M M Worrell 7 for 70).
England won by an innings and 5 runs   Toss: West Indies

1958 **New Zealand 67** (J C Laker 5 for 17) and **129** (G A R Lock 7 for 51). **England 267 for 2 wkts dec** (P B H May 113*, C A Milton 104*).
England won by an innings and 71 runs   Toss: New Zealand

1959 **India 161** and 149. **England 483 for 8 wkts dec** (M C Cowdrey 160, K F Barrington 80, W G A Parkhouse 78, G Pullar 75).
England won by an innings and 173 runs   Toss: India

1961 **Australia 237** (R N Harvey 73, C C McDonald 54, F S Trueman 5 for 58) and **120** (R N Harvey 53, F S Trueman 6 for 30); **England 299** (M C Cowdrey 93, G Pullar 53, A K Davidson 5 for 63) and **62 for 2 wkts.**
England won by 8 wickets   Toss: Australia

1962 **England 428** (P H Parfitt 119, M J Stewart 86, D A Allen 62, Munir Malik 5 for 128). **Pakistan 131** (Alimuddin 50) and **180** (Alimuddin 60, Saeed Ahmed 54).
England won by an innings and 117 runs   Toss: Pakistan

1963 **West Indies 397** (G St A Sobers 102, R B Kanhai 92, J S Solomon 62) and **229** (B F Butcher 78, G St.A Sobers 52). **England 174** (G A R Lock 53, C C Griffith 6 for 36) and **231** (J M Parks 57, D B Close 56).
West Indies won by 221 runs   Toss: West Indies

1964 **England 268** (J M Parks 68, E R Dexter 66, N J N Hawke 5 for 75) and 229 (K F Barrington 85). **Australia 389** (P J P Burge 160, W M Lawry 78) and **111 for 3 wkts** (I R Redpath 58*).
Australia won by 7 wickets   Toss: England

1965 **England 546 for 4 wkts dec** (J H Edrich 310*, K F Barrington 163). **New Zealand 193** (J R Reid 54) and **166** (V Pollard 53, F J Titmus 5 for 19).
England won by an innings and 187 runs   Toss: England

1966 **West Indies 500 for 9 wkts dec** (G St A Sobers 174, S M Nurse 137). **England 240** (B L D'Oliveira 88, G St A Sobers 5 for 41) and **205** (R W Barber 55, L R Gibbs 6 for 39).
West Indies won by an innings and 55 runs   Toss: West Indies

1967 **England 550 for 4 wkts dec** (G Boycott 246*, B L D'Oliveira 109, K F Barrington 93, T W Graveney 59) and **126 for 4 wkts. India 164** (Nawab of Pataudi jnr 64) and **510** (Nawab of Pataudi jnr 148, A L Wadekar 91, F M Engineer 87, Hanumant Singh 73). **England won by 6 wickets**   Toss: India

1968 **Australia 315** (I R Redpath 92, I M Chappell 65) and **312** (I M Chappell 81, K D Walters 56, R Illingworth 6 for 87). **England 302** (R M Prideaux 64, J H Edrich 62, A N Connolly 5 for 72) and **230 for 4 wkts** (J H Edrich 65). **Match drawn**   Toss: Australia

1969 **England 223** (J H Edrich 79) and **240** (G.St A Sobers 5 for 42). **West Indies 161** and **272** (B F Butcher 91, G S Camacho 71). **England won by 30 runs**   Toss: England

1971 **England 316** (G Boycott 112, B L D'Oliveira 74) and **264** (B L D'Oliveira 72, D L Amiss 56) **Pakistan 350** (Zaheer Abbas 72, Wasim Bari 63, Mushtaq Mohammad 57) and **205** (Sadiq Mohammad 91). **England won by 25 runs**   Toss: England

1972 **Australia 146** (K R Stackpole 52) and **136** (D L Underwood 6 for 45). **England 263** (R Illingworth 57, A A Mallett 5 for 114) and **21 for 1 wkt. England won by 9 wickets**   Toss: Australia

1973 **New Zealand 276** (M G Burgess 87, V Pollard 62) and **142** (G M Turner 81, G G Arnold 5 for 27). **England 419** (G Boycott 115, K W R Fletcher 81, R Illingworth 65, RO Collinge 5 for 74). **England won by an innings and 1 run**   Toss: New Zealand

1974 **Pakistan 285** (Majid Khan 75, Safraz Nawaz 53) and **179. England 183** and **238 for 6 wkts** (J H Edrich 70, K W R Fletcher 67*). **Match drawn**   Toss: Pakistan

1975 **England 288** (D S Steele 73, J H Edrich 62, A W Greig 51, G J Gilmour 6 for 85) and **291** (D S Steele 92). **Australia 135** (P H Edmonds 5 for 28) and **220 for 3 wkts** (R B McCosker 95*, I M Chappell 62). **Match drawn**   Toss: Australia

1976 **West Indies 450** (C G Greenidge 115, R C Fredericks 109, I V A Richards 66, L G Rowe 50) and **196** (C L King 58, R G D Willis 5 for 42). **England 387** (A W Greig 116, A P E Knott 116) and **204** (A W Greig 76*). **West Indies won by 55 runs**   Toss: West Indies

1977 **England 436** (G Boycott 191, A P E Knott 57). **Australia 103** (I T Botham 5 for 21) and **248** (R W Marsh 63). **England won by an innings and 85 runs**   Toss: England

1978 **Pakistan 201** (Sadiq Mohammad 97). **England 119 for 7 wkts** (Safraz Nawaz 5 for 39). **Match drawn**   Toss: Pakistan

1979 **England 270** (I T Botham 137). **India 223 for 6 wkts** (S M Gavaskar 78, D B Vengsarkar 65*). **Match drawn**   Toss: England

1980 **England 143 and 227 for 6 wkts dec** (G A Gooch 55). **West Indies 245. Match drawn**   Toss: West Indies

1981 **Australia 401 for 9 wkts dec** (J Dyson 102, K J Hughes 89, G N Yallop 58, I T Botham 6 for 95) and **111** (R G D Willis 8 for 43). **England 174** (I T Botham 50) and **356** (I T Botham 149*, G R Dilley 56, T M Alderman 6 for 135). **England won by 18 runs**   Toss: Australia

1982 **Pakistan 275** (Imran Khan 67*, Mudassar Nazar 65, Javed Miandad 54) and **199** (Javed Miandad 52, I T Botham 5 for 74). **England 256** (D I Gower 74, I T Botham 57, Imran Khan 5 for 49) and **219 for 7 wkts** (G Fowler 86). **England won by 3 wickets**   Toss: Pakistan

1983 **England 225** (C J Tavaré 69, A J Lamb 58, B L Cairns 7 for 74) and **252** (D I Gower 112*, E J Chatfield 5 for 95). **New Zealand 377** (J G Wright 93, B A Edgar 84, R J Hadlee 75) and **103 for 5 wkts** (R G D Willis 5 for 35). **New Zealand won by 5 wickets**   Toss: New Zealand

320

1984 **England 270** (A J Lamb 100) and **159** (G Fowler 50, M D Marshall 7 for 53). **West Indies 302** (H A Gomes 104*, M A Holding 59, P J W Allott 6 for 61) and **131 for 2 wkts.**
West Indies won by 8 wickets Toss: England

1985 **Australia 331** (A M J Hilditch 119) and **324** (W B Phillips 91, A M J Hilditch 80, K C Wessels 64, J E Emburey 5 for 82). **England 533** (R T Robinson 175, I T Botham 60, P R Downton 54, M W Gatting 53) and **123 for 5 wkts.**
England won by 5 wickets Toss: Australia

1986 **India 272** (D B Vengsarkar 61) and **237** (D B Vengsarkar 102*). **England 102** (R M H Binny 5 for 40) and **128.**
India won by 279 runs Toss: India

1987 **England 136** (D J Capel 53) and **199** (D I Gower 55, Imran Khan 7 for 40). **Pakistan 353** (Salim Malik 99, Ijaz Ahmed 50, N A Foster 8 for 107).
Pakistan won by an innings and 18 runs Toss: England

1988 **England 201** (A J Lamb 64*) and **138** (G A Gooch 50). **West Indies 275** (R A Harper 56, D L Haynes 54, D R Pringle 5 for 95) and **67 for 0 wkt.**
West Indies won by 10 wickets Toss: West Indies

1989 **Australia 601 for 7 wkts dec** (S R Waugh 177*, M A Taylor 136, D M Jones 79, M G Hughes 71, A R Border 66) and **230 for 3 wkts dec** (M A Taylor 60, A R Border 60*). **England 430** (A J Lamb 125, K J Barnett 80, R A Smith 66, T M Alderman 5 for 107) and **191.** (G A Gooch 68, T M Alderman 5 for 44).
Australia won by 210 runs Toss: England

1991 **England 198** (R A Smith 54) and **252** (G A Gooch 154*, C E L Ambrose 6 for 52). **West Indies 173** (I V A Richards 73) and **162** (R B Richardson 68).
England won by 115 runs Toss: West Indies

1992 **Pakistan 197** (Salim Malik 82*) and **221** (Salim Malik 84*, Ramiz Raja 63, N A Mallinder 5 for 50). **England 320** (G A Gooch 135, M A Atherton 76, Waqar Younis 5 for 117) and **99 for 4 wkts.**
England won by 6 wickets Toss: Pakistan

1993 **Australia 653 for 4 wkts dec** (A R Border 200*, S R Waugh 157*, D C Boon 107, M J Slater 67, M E Waugh 52). **England 200** (G A Gooch 59, M A Atherton 55, P R Reiffel 5 for 65) and **305** (A J Stewart 78, M A Atherton 63).
Australia won by an innings and 148 runs Toss: Australia

1994 **England 477 for 9 wkts dec** (M A Atherton 99, A J Stewart 89, G P Thorpe 72, S J Rhodes 65*) and **267 for 5 wkts dec** (G A Hick 110, G P Thorpe 73). **South Africa 447** (P N Kirsten 104, B M McMillan 78, C R Matthews 62*) and **116 for 3 wkts** (G Kirsten 65).
Match drawn Toss: England

1995 **England 199** (M A Atherton 81, I R Bishop 5 for 32) and **208** (G P Thorpe 61). **West Indies 282** (S L Campbell 69, J C Adams 58, B C Lara 53) and **129 for 1 wkt** (C L Hooper 73*).
West Indies won by 9 wickets Toss: West Indies

1996 **Pakistan 448** (Ijaz Ahmed 141, Mohin Khan 105, Salim Malik 55, Asif Mujtaba 51, D G Cork 5 for 113) and **242 for 7 wkts dec** (Inzamam-ul-Haq 65, Ijaz Ahmed sen 52) **England 501** (A J Stewart 170, N V Knight 113, J P Crawley 53).
Match drawn Toss: England

1997 **England 172** (J N. Gillespie 7 for 37) and **268** (N Hussain 105, J P Crawley 72, P R Reiffel 5 for 49). **Australia 501 for 9 wkts dec** (M T G Elliott 199, R T Ponting 127, P R Reiffel 54*, D Gough 5 for 149).
Australia won by an innings and 61 runs Toss: Australia

1998 **England 230** (M A Butcher 116) and **240** (N Hussain 94, S M Pollock 5 for 53, A A Donald 5 for 71). **South Africa 252** (W J Cronje 57, A R C Fraser 5 for 42) and **195** (J N Rhodes 85, B M McMillan 54, D Gough 6 for 42).
England won by 23 runs Toss: England

2000 **West Indies 172** (R R Sarwan 59*, C White 5 for 57) and **61** (A R Caddick 5 for 14). **England 272** (M P Vaughan 76, G A Hick 59).
England won by an innings and 39 runs Toss: West Indies

321

2001 **Australia** 447 (R T Ponting 144, D R Martyn 118, M E Waugh 72, D Gough 5 for 103) and **176 for 4 wkts dec** (R T Ponting 72). **England** 309 (A J Stewart 76*, G D McGrath 7 for 76) and **315 for 4 wkts** (M A Butcher 173*, N Hussain 55).
England won by 6 wickets   Toss: Australia

2002 **India** 628 for 8 wkts dec (S R Tendulkar 193, R S Dravid 148, S C Ganguly 128, S B Bangar 68). **England** 273 (A J Stewart 78*, M P Vaughan 61) and **309** (N Hussain 110.)
India won by an innings and 46 runs   Toss: India

2003 **South Africa** 342 (G Kirsten 130, M Zondeki 59, J A Rudolph 55) and **365** (A J Hall 99*, G Kirsten 60). **England** 307 (M A Butcher 77, M E Trescothick 59, A Flintoff 55) and **209** (M A Butcher 61, A Flintoff 50, J H Kallis 6 for 54.)
South Africa won by 191 runs   Toss: South Africa

2004 **New Zealand** 409 (S P Fleming 97, M H W Papps 86, B B McCullum 54) and **161.** **England** 526 (M E Trescothick 132, G O Jones 100, A Flintoff 94, A J Strauss 62) and **45 for 1 wkt**
England won by 9 wickets   Toss: England

2006 **England** 515 (K P Pietersen 135, I R Bell 119, Umar Gul 5 for 123) and **345** (A J Strauss 116, M E Trescothick 58, C M W Reid 55). **Pakistan** 538 (Mohammad Yousuf 192, Younis Khan 173) and **155**.
England won by 167 runs   Toss: England

2007 **England** 570 for 7 wkts dec (K P Pietersen 226, M P Vaughan 103, M J Prior 75). **West Indies** 146 and 141 (D J Bravo 52).
England won by an innings and 283 runs   Toss: England

2008 **England** 203 and 327 (S C J Broad 67*, A N Cook 60). **South Africa** 522 (A B de Villiers 174, A G Prince 149) and **9 for 0 wkt**.
South Africa won by 10 wickets   Toss: South Africa

2009 **England** 102 (P M Siddle 5 for 21) and 263 (G P Swann 62, S C J Broad 61, M G Johnson 5 for 69). **Australia** 445 (M J North 110, M J Clarke 93, R T Ponting 78, S R Watson 51, S C J Broad 6 for 91).
Australia won by an innings and 80 runs   Toss: England

2010 **Australia** 88 and 349 (R T Ponting 66, M J Clarke 77, S P D Smith 77). **Pakistan** 258 (S R Watson 6-33) and **180-7** (Imran Farhat 67, Azhar Ali 51).
Pakistan won by 3 wickets   Toss: Australia
(This was a Home Test Match for Pakistan)

2012 **South Africa** 419 (A N Petersen 182, G C Smith 52) and **258-9 dec** (J A Rudolph 69, GC Smith 52, S C J Broad 5-69). **England** 425 (K P Pietersen 149, M J Prior 68) and **130-4.**
Match drawn   Toss: England

2013 **England** 354 (J E Root 104, J M Bairstow 64, T A Boult 5-57) and **287-5 dec** (A N Cook 130, I J L Trott 76). **New Zealand** 174 and 220 (L R P L Taylor 70, G P Swann 6-90)
England won by 247 runs   Toss: England

2014 **Sri Lanka** 257 (K C Sangakkara 79, L E Plunkett 5-64) and **457** (K C Sangakkara 55, DPMD Jayawardene 79, A D Mathews 160). **England** 365 (S D Robson 127, G S Ballance 74, I R Bell 64) and **249** (M M Ali 108*, K T G D Prasad 5-50)
Sri Lanka won by 100 runs   Toss: England

2015 **New Zealand** 350 (T W M Latham 84, L Ronchi 88, S C J Broad 5-109) and **454-8 dec** (M J Guptill 70, B B McCullum 55, B J Watling 120, M D Craig 58*). **England** 350 (A Lyth 107, A N Cook 75) and **255** (A N Cook 56, J C Buttler 73)
New Zealand won by 199 runs   Toss: England

2016 **England** 298 (A D Hales 86, J M Bairstow 140). **Sri Lanka** 91 (J M Anderson 5-16) and **119** (B K G Mendis 53, J N Anderson 5-29)
England won by an innings and 88 runs   Toss: Sri Lanka

2017 **England** 258 (J E Root 58, B A Stokes100) and **490-8 dec** (M D Stoneman 52, J E Root 72, D J Malan 61, B A Stokes 58, M M Ali 84, C R Woakes 61*). **West Indies** 427 (K C Brathwaite 134, S D Hope 147, J M Anderson 5-76) and 322-5 (K C Brathwaite 95, S D Hope 118*).
West Indies won by 5 wickets   Toss: England

2018 **Pakistan 174** (Shadab Khan 56) and **134. England 363** (J C Buttler 80*)
England won by an innings and 55 runs Toss: Pakistan

2019 **Australia 179** (M Labuschagne 74, J C Archer 6-45) and **246** (M Labuschagne 80).
England 67 (J R Hazlewood 5-65) and **362-9** (J E Root 77, J L Denly 50,
B A Stokes 135*)
England won by 1 wicket Toss: England

SUMMARY OF RESULTS

ENGLAND	First played	Last played	Played	Won	Lost	Drawn
v. Australia	1899	2019	25	8	9	8
v. India	1952	2002	6	3	2	1
v. New Zealand	1949	2015	8	5	2	1
v. Pakistan	1962	2018	10	6	1	3
v. South Africa	1907	2012	13	6	3	4
v. Sri Lanka	2014	2016	2	1	1	0
v. West Indies	1957	2017	13	5	7	1
Totals	1899	2019	77	34	25	18

SIX HIGHEST AGGREGATES

Runs	Wkts	
1723	31	in 1948 (England 496 and 365 for 8 wkts dec; Australia 458 and 404 for 3 wkts)
1553	40	in 2006 (England 515 and 345; Pakistan 538 and 155)
1497	33	in 2017 (England 258 and 490-8 dec; West Indies 427 and 322-5)
1452	30	in 1989 (Australia 601 for 7 wkts dec and 230 for 3 wkts dec; England 430 and 191)
1409	40	in 2015 (New Zealand 350 and 454 for 8 wkts dec; England 350 and 255)
1350	28	in 1967 (England 550 for 4 wkts dec and 126 for 4 wkts; India 164 and 510)

Note: The highest aggregate prior to the Second World War
| 1141 | 37 | in 1921 (Australia 407 and 272 for 7 wkts dec; England 259 and 202) |

SIX LOWEST AGGREGATES

Runs	Wkts	
423	40	in 1907 (England 76 and 162; South Africa 110 and 75)
463	22	in 1958 (New Zealand 67 and 129; England 267 for 2 wkts)
505	30	in 2000 (West Indies 172 and 61; England 272)
508	30	in 2016 (England 298; Sri Lanka 91 and 119)
553	30	in 1957 (West Indies 142 and 132; England 279)
566	31	in 1972 (Australia 146 and 136; England 263 and 21 for 1 wkt)

SIX HIGHEST TOTALS

653 for 4 wkts dec	Australia v. England, 1993
608 for 8 wkts dec	India v. England, 2002
601 for 7 wkts dec	Australia v. England, 1989
584	Australia v. England, 1934
570 for 7 wkts dec	England v. West Indies, 2007
566	Australia v. England, 1930

SIX LOWEST TOTALS

61	West Indies v. England, 2000
67	New Zealand v. England, 1958
67	England v. Australia, 2019
75	South Africa v. England, 1907
76	England v. South Africa, 1907
87	England v Australia, 1909

SIX HIGHEST INDIVIDUAL SCORES

For England

310*	J H Edrich versus New Zealand, 1965
246*	G Boycott versus India, 1967
226	K P Pietersen versusWest Indies, 2007
191	G Boycott versus Australia, 1977
175	R T Robinson versus Australia, 1985
173*	M A Butcher versus Australia, 2001

For Australia

334	D G Bradman, 1930
304	D G Bradman, 1934
200*	A R Border, 1993
199	M T G Elliott, 1997
182	A R Morris, 1948
181	W H Ponsford, 1934

For Pakistan

192	Mohammad Yousuf, 2006
173	Younis Khan, 2006
141	Ijaz Ahmed, 1996
105	Moin Khan, 1996
99	Salim Malik, 1987
97	Sadiq Mohammad, 1978

For India

193	S R Tendulkar, 2002
148	Nawab of Pataudi jnr, 1967
148	R S Dravid, 2002
133	V L Manjrekar, 1952
128	S C Gangulay, 2002
102*	D B Vengsarkar, 1986

For South Africa

236	E A B Rowan, 1951
182	A N Petersen, 2012
174	A B de Villiers, 2008
149	A G Prince, 2008
133	D J McGlew, 1955
130	G Kirsten, 2003

For New Zealand

120	B J Watling , 2015
97	S P Fleming, 2004
96	F B Smith, 1949
93	J G Wright, 1983
88	L Ronchi, 2015
87	M G Burgess, 1973

For Sri Lanka

160*	A D Mathews, 2014
79	K C Sangakkara, 2014
55	K C Sangakkara, 2014
53*	B K G Mendis, 2016
48	H M R K B Herath, 2014
45	L D Chandimal, 2014
45	F D M Karunaratne, 2014

For West Indies

174	G St.A Sobers, 1966
147	S D Hope, 2017 (1st innings)
137	S M Nurse, 1966
134	K C Brathwaite, 2017
118*	S D Hope, 2017 (2nd innings)
115	C G Greenidge, 1976

S D Hope was the first player to score centuries in both innings of a First Class match at Headingley

HUNDRED BEFORE LUNCH

First day

112*	C G Macartney for Australia, 1926
105*	D G Bradman for Australia, 1930

Third day

102	(from 27* to 129) H G Owen-Smith for South Africa, 1929

CARRYING BAT THROUGH A COMPLETED INNINGS

154* out of 252 G A Gooch, England v. West Indies, 1991

MOST CENTURIES IN AN INNINGS

3	1926	C G Macartney (151), W M Woodfull (141) and A J Richardson for Australia
3	1993	A R Border (200*), S R Waugh (157*) and D C Boon (107) for Australia
3	2002	S R Tendulkar (193), R S Dravid (148) and S C Gangulay (128) for India

MOST CENTURIES IN A MATCH

5	1948	C Washbrook (143) and W J Edrich (111) for England; R N Harvey (112), A R Morris (182) and D G Bradman (173*) for Australia
5	2006	K P Pietersen (135), I R Bell (119) and A J Strauss (116) for England: Younis Khan (173) and Mohammad Yousuf (192) for Pakistan
4	1976	C G Greenidge (115) and R C Fredericks (109) for West Indies; A W Greig (116) and A P E Knott (116) for England
4	1996	Ijaz Ahmed (141) and Moin Khan (105) for Pakistan; A J Stewart (170) and N V Knight (113) for England
4	2002	S R Tendulkar (193), R S Dravid (148) and S C Ganguly (128) for India; N Hussain (110) for England
4	2017	B A Stokes (100) for England; K C Brathwaite (134), S D Hope (147 and 118*) for West Indies

CENTURY PARTNERSHIPS

For England
(six highest)
For the 1st wicket

177	A Lyth (107) and A N Cook (75) v. New Zealand, 2015
168	L Hutton (81) and C Washbrook (143) v. Australia, 1948 (1st inns)
168	G A Gooch (135) and M A Atherton (76) v. Pakistan, 1992
158	M E Trescothick (58) and A J Strauss (116) v. Pakistan, 2006
156	J B Hobbs (88) and H Sutcliffe (94) v. Australia, 1926
153	M E Trescothick (132) and A J Strauss (62) v. New Zealand, 2004

For all other wickets

369	(2nd wkt) J H Edrich (310*) and K F Barrington (163) v. New Zealand, 1965
252	(4th wkt) G Boycott (246*) and B L D'Oliveira (109) v. India, 1967
194*	(3rd wkt) C A Milton (104*) and P B H May (113*) v. New Zealand, 1958
193	(4th wkt) M C Cowdrey (160) and K F Barrington (80) v. India, 1959
187	(4th wkt) P B H May (101) and C Washbrook (98) v. Australia, 1956
181	(3rd wkt) M A Butcher (173*) and N Hussain (55) v. Australia, 2001

For Australia
(six highest)
For the 1st wkt – none

For all other wickets

388	(4th wkt) W H Ponsford (181) and D G Bradman (304), 1934
332*	(5th wkt) A R Border (200*) and S R Waugh (157*), 1993
301	(2nd wkt) A R Morris (182) and D G Bradman (173*), 1948
268	(5th wkt) M T G Elliott (199) and R T Ponting (127), 1997
235	(2nd wkt) W M Woodfull (141) and C G Macartney (151), 1926
229	(3rd wkt) D G Bradman (334) and A F Kippax (77), 1930

For other countries in total
India

249	(4th wkt) S R Tendulkar (193) and S C Ganguly (128), 2002
222	(4th wkt) V S Hazare (89) and V L Manjrekar (133), 1952
170	(2nd wkt) S B Bangar (68) and R S Dravid (148), 2002
168	(2nd wkt) F M Engineer (87) and A L Wadekar (91), 1967
150	(3rd wkt) R S Dravid (148) and S R Tendulkar (193), 2002
134	(5th wkt) Hanumant Singh (73) and Nawab of Pataudi jnr (148), 1967
105	(6th wkt) V S Hazare (56) and D G Phadkar (64), 1952

New Zealand

169	(2nd wkt) M H W Papps (86) and S P Fleming (97), 2004	
121	(5th wkt) B B McCullum (55) and B J Watling (120), 2015	
120	(5th wkt) M P Donnelly (64) and F B Smith (96), 1949	
120	(6th wkt) T W M Latham (84) and L Ronchi (88), 2015	
116	(2nd wkt) J G Wright (93) and M D Crowe (37), 1983	
112	(1st wkt) B Sutcliffe (82) and V J Scott (43), 1949	
106	(5th wkt) M G Burgess (87) and V Pollard (62), 1973	

Pakistan

363	(3rd wkt) Younis Khan (173) and Mohammad Yousuf (192), 2006
130	(4th wkt) Ijaz Ahmed (141) and Salim Malik (55), 1996
129	(3rd wkt) Zaheer Abbas (72) and Mushtaq Mohammed (57), 1971
112	(7th wkt) Asif Mujtaba (51) and Moin Khan (105), 1996
110	(2nd wkt) Imran Farhat (67) and Azhar Ali (51), 2010 v. Australia
100	(3rd wkt) Mudassar Nazar (65) and Javed Miandad (54), 1982
100	(4th wkt) Majid Khan (75) and Zaheer Abbas (48), 1974

South Africa

212	(5th wkt)	A G Prince (149)	and A B de Villiers (174)	2008
198	(2nd wkt)	E A B Rowan (236)	and C B van Ryneveld (83)	1951
176	(1st wkt)	D J McGlew (133)	and T L Goddard (74)	1955
150	(8th wkt)	G Kirsten (130)	and M Zondeki (59)	2003
120	(1st wkt)	A N Petersen (182)	and G C Smith (52)	2012
120	(1st wkt)	J A Rudolph (69)	and G C Smith (52)	2012
117	(6th wkt)	J N Rhodes (85)	and B M McMillan (54)	1998
115	(7th wkt)	P N Kirsten (104)	and B M McMillan (78)	1994
108	(5th wkt)	E A B Rowan (236)	and R A McLean (67)	1951
103	(10th wkt)	H G Owen-Smith (129)	and A J Bell (26*)	1929

Sri Lanka

149	(8th wkt)	A D Mathews (160)	and H M R K B Herath (48)	2014

West Indies

265	(5th wkt)	S M Nurse (137)	and G St A Sobers (174)	1966
246	(4th wkt)	K C Brathwaite (134)	and S D Hope (147)	2017
192	(1st wkt)	R C Fredericks (109)	and C G Greenidge (115)	1976
144	(3rd wkt)	K C Brathwaite (95)	and S D Hope (118*)	2017
143	(4th wkt)	R B Kanhai (92)	and G St A Sobers (102)	1963
118*	(2nd wkt)	C L Hooper (73*)	and B C Lara (48*)	1995
108	(3rd wkt)	G S Camacho (71)	and B F Butcher (91)	1969
106	(1st wkt)	C G Greenidge (49)	and C L Haynes (43)	1984

6 BEST INNINGS ANALYSES

For England

8-43	R G D Willis	v. Australia	1981
8-59	C Blythe	v. South Africa	1907 (1st inns)
8-107	N A Foster	v. Pakistan	1987
7-40	C Blythe	v. South Africa,	1907 (2nd inns)
7-51	G A R Lock	v. New Zealand	1958
7-115	A P Freeman	v. South Africa	1929

For Australia

7-37	J N Gilliespie	1997	
7-58	C G Macartney	1909	
7-76	G D McGrath	2001	
6-33	S R Watson	2010	v. Pakistan
6-85	G J Gilmour	1975	
6-135	T M Alderman	1981	

5 WICKETS IN AN INNINGS

For India (2)

5-40	R M H Binny	1986
5-100	Ghulam Ahmed	1952

For New Zealand (6)

7-74	B L Cairns	1983
5-57	T A Boult	2013
5-74	R O Collinge	1973
5-95	E J Chatfield	1983
5-97	T B Burtt	1949
5-127	J Cowie	1949

For Pakistan (6)

7-40	Imran Khan	1987
5-39	Sarfraz Nawaz	1978
5-49	Imran Khan	1982
5-117	Waqar Younis	1992
5-123	Umar Gul	2006
5-128	Munir Malik	1962

For South Africa

6-17	G A Faulkner	1907
6-92	N A Quinn	1929
6-54	J H Kallis	2003
5-53	S M Pollock	1998
5-69	T L Goddard	1955
5-71	A A Donald	1998
5-94	H J Tayfield	1955
5-174	A M B Rowan	1951

For Sri Lanka

5-50	K T G D Prasad	2014

For West Indies (8)

7-53	M D Marshall	1984
7-70	F M Worrell	1957
6-36	C C Griffith	1963
6-39	L R Gibbs	1996
6-52	C E L Ambrose	1991
5-32	I R Bishop	1995
5-41	G.St.A Sobers	1966
5-42	G.St A Sobers	1969

10 WICKETS IN A MATCH

For England (8)

15-99	(8-59 and 7-40)	C Blythe	v. South Africa	1907
11-65	(4-14 and 7-51)	G A R Lock	v. New Zeland	1958
11-88	(5-58 and 6-30)	F S Trueman	v. Australia	1961
11-113	(5-58 and 6-55)	J C Laker	v. Australia	1956
10-45	(5-16 and 5-29)	J M Anderson	v. Sri Lanka	2016
10-82	(4-37 and 6-45)	D L Underwood	v. Australia	1972
10-115	(6-52 and 4-63)	S F Barnes	v. South Africa	1912
10-132	(4-42 and 6-90)	G P Swann	v. New Zealand	2013
10-207	(7-115 and 3-92)	A P Freeman	v. South Africa	1929

For Australia (3)

11-85	(7-58 and 4-27)	C G Macartney	1909
10-122	(5-66 and 5-56)	W J O'Reilly	1938
10-151	(5-107 and 5-44)	T M Alderman	1989

For New Zealand (1)

10-144	(7-74 and 3-70)	B L Cairns	1983

For Pakistan (1)

10-77	(3-37 and 7-40)	Imran Khan	1987

Note: Best bowling in a match for:

India	7-58	(5-40 and 2-18)	R M H Binney	1986
Sri Lanka	6-125	(1-75 and 5-50)	K T G D Prasad	2014
South Africa	9-75	(6-17 and 3-58)	G A Faulkner	1907
West Indies	9-81	(6 -36 and 3-45)	C C Griffith	1963

HAT-TRICKS

J T Hearne	v. Australia	1899
P J Loader	v. West Indies	1957
S C J Broad	v. Sri Lanka	2014

TEST MATCH AT BRAMALL LANE, SHEFFIELD 1902

1902 **Australia 194** (S F Barnes 6 for 49) and **289** (C Hill 119, V T Trumper 62, W Rhodes 5 for 63) **England 145** (J V Saunders 5 for 50, M A Noble 5 for 51) and **195** (A C MacLaren 63, G L Jessop 55, M A Noble 6 for 52).
Australia won by 143 runs   Toss: Australia

LIST OF PLAYERS AND CAREER AVERAGES IN ALL FIRST-CLASS MATCHES FOR YORKSHIRE 1863-2019

Based on research by John T Potter, Paul E Dyson, Mick Pope and the late Roy D Wilkinson and Anthony Woodhouse

Career records date from the foundation of Yorkshire County Cricket Club in 1863. The Club welcome any help in keeping this list up to date. The compilers do not believe that we should alter the status of matches from that determined when they were played. These averages include the match versus Gentlemen of Scotland in 1878, and exclude those versus Liverpool and District in 1889, 1891, 1892 and 1893 in line with what appear to have been the decisions of the Club.

* Played as an amateur   © Awarded County Cap   § Born outside Yorkshire

Player	Date of Birth	Date of Death (if known)	First Played	Last Played	M	Inns	NO	Runs	HS	Av'ge	100s	Runs	Wkts	Av'ge	Ct/St
Ackroyd, A *	Aug. 29, 1858		1879	1879	1	1	1	7	2*	—	0	7	0	—	0
Allen, S *	Dec. 20, 1893	Oct 9, 1978	1924	1924	1	2	0	8	6	4.00	0	116	2	58.00	0
Allen, W R	Apr 14, 1893	Oct 14, 1950	1921	1925	30	32	10	475	95*	21.59	0	—	0	—	45/21
Ambler, J	Feb 12, 1860	Feb 10 1899	1886	1886	4	7	0	68	25	9.71	0	22	0	—	2
Anderson, G	Jan 20, 1826	Nov 27, 1902	1863	1869	19	31	6	520	99*	20.80	0	—	—	—	19
Anderson, P N	Apr. 28, 1966		1988	1988	1	—	—	—	—	—	0	47	1	47.00	1
Anson, C E *	Oct 14, 1889	Mar 26, 1969	1924	1924	1	2	0	27	14	13.50	0	—	—	—	1
Appleton, C *	May 15, 1844	Feb 26, 1925	1865	1865	3	5	0	56	18	11.20	0	—	—	—	1
Appleyard, R ©	June 27, 1924	Mar 17, 2015	1950	1958	133	122	43	679	63	8.59	0	9,903	642	15.42	70
Armitage, C I *	Apr. 28, 1849	Apr 24, 1917	1873	1878	3	5	0	26	12	5.20	0	29	0	—	0
Armitage, T ©	Apr 25, 1848	Sept 21, 1922	1872	1878	52	85	8	1,053	95	13.67	0	1,614	107	15.08	20
Ash, D L	Feb 18, 1944		1965	1965	3	3	0	22	12	7.33	0	—	0	—	0
Ashman, J R	May 20, 1926		1951	1951	1	—	—	—	—	—	0	116	4	29.00	0
Ashraf, Moin A	Jan 5, 1992		2010	2013	21	19	5	56	10	4.00	0	1,268	43	29.48	2
Aspinall, R ©	Oct 26, 1918	Aug 16, 1999	1946	1950	36	48	8	763	75*	19.07	0	2,670	131	20.38	18
Aspinall, W	Mar 24, 1858	Jan 27, 1910	1880	1880	2	3	0	16	14	5.33	0	—	0	—	2
Asquith, F T	Feb 5, 1870	Jan 11, 1916	1903	1903	1	1	0	0	0	0.00	0	—	0	—	0
Athey, C W J ©	Sept 27, 1957		1976	1983	151	246	21	6,320	134	28.08	10	1,003	21	47.76	144/2
Atkinson, G R	Sept 21, 1830	May 3, 1906	1863	1870	27	38	8	399	44	13.30	0	1,146	54	21.22	14
Atkinson, H T	Feb 1, 1881	Dec 23, 1959	1907	1907	1	2	0	0	0	0.00	0	17	0	—	0
§ Azeem Rafiq	Feb 27, 1991		2009	2017	35	41	4	814	100	22.00	1	2,511	63	39.85	14
Backhouse, E N	May 13, 1901	Nov 1, 1936	1931	1931	1	1	0	2	2	2.00	0	4	0	—	0
Badger, H D *	Mar 7, 1900	Aug 10, 1975	1921	1922	2	4	2	6	6*	3.00	0	145	6	24.16	1
Bainbridge, A B §	Oct 15, 1932		1961	1963	5	10	0	93	24	9.30	0	358	20	17.90	3

LIST OF PLAYERS AND CAREER AVERAGES IN ALL FIRST-CLASS MATCHES FOR YORKSHIRE (Continued)

Player	Date of Birth	Date of Death (if known)	First Played	Last Played	M	Inns	NO	Runs	HS	Av'ge	100s	Runs	Wkts	Av'ge	Ct/St
Baines, F E *	June 18, 1864	Nov 17, 1948	1888	1888	1	1	0	—	0	0.00	0	—	—	—	—
Bairstow, A	© Aug 14, 1868	Dec 7, 1945	1896	1900	24	24	10	69	12	4.92	0	—	—	—	41/18
Bairstow, D L	© Sept 1, 1951	Jan 5, 1998	1970	1990	429	601	113	12,985	145	26.60	9	192	6	32.00	907/131
Bairstow, J M	**© Sept 26, 1989**		**2009**	**2018**	**92**	**146**	**22**	**6,343**	**246**	**51.15**	**15**	**1**	**0**	**—**	**246/10**
Baker, G R	Apr 18, 1862	Feb 6, 1938	1884	1884	7	11	1	42	13	4.20	0	43	0	—	5
Baker, R *	July 3, 1849	June 21, 1896	1874	1875	3	5	1	45	22	11.25	0	790	37	21.35	3
Balderstone, J C	Nov 16, 1940	Mar 6, 2000	1961	1969	68	81	6	1,332	82	17.76	0				24
§ Ballance, G S	**© Nov 22, 1989**		**2008**	**2019**	**117**	**188**	**20**	**7,913**	**203***	**47.10**	**26**	**143**	**0**	**—**	**67**
Barber, A T *	© June 17, 1905	Mar 10, 1985	1929	1930	42	54	3	1,050	100	20.58	1				40
Barber, W	Apr 18, 1901	Sept 10, 1968	1926	1947	354	495	48	15,315	255	34.26	27	404	14	28.85	169
Barraclough, E S	Mar 30, 1923	May 21, 1999	1949	1950	2	4	2	43	24*	21.50	0				0
Bates, W	Nov 19, 1855	Jan 8, 1900	1877	1887	202	331	12	6,499	136	20.37	8	10,692	637	16.78	163
Bates, W E	© Mar 5, 1884	Jan 17, 1957	1907	1913	113	167	15	2,634	81	17.32	0	136	4	34.00	64
Batty, G J	Oct 13, 1977		1997	1997	1	2	0	18	18	9.00	0	57	2	28.50	0
Batty, J D	May 15, 1971		1989	1994	64	67	20	703	51	14.95	0	5,286	140	37.75	25
Bayes, G W	Feb 27, 1884	Dec 6, 1960	1910	1921	18	24	11	165	36	12.69	0	1,534	48	31.95	7
Beaumont, J	Oct 14, 1916	Nov 15, 2003	1946	1947	28	46	6	716	60	17.90	0	236	9	26.22	11
Beaumont, J	Sept 16, 1854	May 1, 1920	1877	1878	5	9	3	60	24	10.00	0	50	2	25.00	1
Bedford, H	July 17, 1907	July 5, 1968	1928	1928	5	5	1	57	30*	14.25	0	179	8	22.37	1
Bedford, R	Feb 24, 1879	July, 1939	1903	1903	2	2	1	38	38	38.00	0	117	2	58.50	—
Bell, J T	June 16, 1895	Aug 8, 1974	1921	1923	7	8	1	125	54	17.85	0				6
Berry, John	Jan 10, 1823	Feb 26, 1895	1864	1867	18	32	2	492	78	16.40	0	149	8	18.62	12
Berry, Joseph	Nov 29, 1829	Apr 20, 1894	1863	1874	3	4	0	68	31	17.00	0				1
Berry, P J	Dec 28, 1966		1986	1990	7	5	1	76	31*	19.00	0	401	7	57.28	6
§ Bess, D M	**© July 22, 1997**		**2019**	**2019**	**4**	**5**	**1**	**156**	**91***	**39.00**	**0**	**234**	**7**	**33.42**	**4**
Best, T L	Aug 26, 1981		2010	2010	9	9	0	86	44	9.55	0	793	18	44.05	4
Betts, G	Sept 19, 1841	Sept 26, 1902	1873	1874	2	4	1	56	44*	18.66	0				—
§ Bevan, M G	© May 8, 1970		1995	1996	32	56	8	2,823	160*	58.81	9	720	10	72.00	24
§ Binks, J G	© Oct 5, 1935		1955	1969	491	587	128	6,745	95	14.69	0				872/172
Binns, J	Mar 31, 1870	Dec 8, 1934	1898	1898	1	1	0	4	4	4.00	0	66	0	—	0/3

LIST OF PLAYERS AND CAREER AVERAGES IN ALL FIRST-CLASS MATCHES FOR YORKSHIRE (Continued)

Player	Date of Birth	Date of Death (if known)	First Played	Last Played	M	Inns	NO	Runs	HS	Av'ge	100s	Runs	Wkts	Av'ge	Ct/St
Bird, H D	Apr 19, 1933		1956	1959	14	25	2	613	181*	26.65	1	—	—	—	3
Birkenshaw, J	Nov 13, 1940		1958	1960	30	42	7	588	42	16.80	0	1,819	69	26.36	21
Birtles, T J D	Oct 26, 1886	Jan 13, 1971	1913	1924	37	57	11	876	104	19.04	1	20	0	—	19
Blackburn, J D H *	Oct 27, 1924	Feb 19, 1987	1956	1956	1	2	0	18	15	9.00	0	—	—	—	0
Blackburn, J S	Sept 24, 1852	July 8, 1922	1876	1877	6	11	1	102	28	10.20	0	173	7	24.71	4
§ Blackburn, W E *	Nov 24, 1888	June 3, 1941	1919	1920	10	13	6	26	6*	3.71	0	1,113	45	24.73	9
§ Blain J A R	Jan 4, 1979		2004	2010	15	17	0	137	28*	13.70	0	1,312	38	34.52	4
Blake, W	Nov 29, 1854	Nov 28, 1931	1880	1880	2	3	0	44	21	14.66	0	17	1	17.00	0
Blakey, R J ©	Jan 15, 1967		1985	2003	339	541	84	14,150	223*	30.96	12	68	1	68.00	768/56
Blamires, E		Mar 22, 1886	1877	1877	1	2	0	23	17	11.50	0	82	5	16.40	0
§ Blewett, G S ©	Oct 28, 1971		1999	1999	12	23	1	655	190	31.19	1	212	5	42.40	5
Bloom, G R	Sept 13, 1941		1964	1964	1	2	1	2	2	2.00	0	—	—	—	2
Bocking, H	Dec 10, 1835	Feb 22, 1907	1865	1865	1	1	0	14	11	7.00	0	—	—	—	0
Boden, J G *	Dec 27, 1848	Jan 3, 1918	1878	1878	1	1	0	6	6	6.00	0	—	—	—	0
Bolton, B C *	Sept 23, 1861	Nov 18, 1910	1890	1891	4	6	0	25	11	4.16	0	252	13	19.38	2
Bolus, J B ©	Jan 31, 1934		1956	1962	107	179	18	4,712	146*	29.26	7	407	13	31.30	45
Booth, A	Nov 3, 1902	Aug 17, 1974	1931	1947	36	36	16	114	29	5.70	0	1,684	122	13.80	10
Booth, M W ©	Dec 10, 1886	July 1, 1916	1908	1914	144	218	31	4,244	210	22.69	4	11,017	557	19.77	114
Booth, P A	Sept 5, 1965		1982	1989	23	29	9	193	33*	9.65	0	1,517	35	43.34	7
Booth, R	Oct 1, 1926		1951	1955	65	76	28	730	53*	15.20	0	—	—	—	79/29
Bore, M K	June 2, 1947		1969	1977	74	78	21	481	37*	8.43	0	4,866	162	30.03	27
Borrill, P D	July 4, 1951		1971	1971	2	2	1	—	7	—	0	61	1	—	0
Bosomworth W E	Mar 8, 1847	June 7, 1891	1872	1880	4	7	1	20	7	3.33	0	140	9	15.55	2
Bottomley, I H *	Apr 9, 1855	Apr 23, 1922	1878	1880	9	12	0	166	32	13.83	0	75	1	75.00	0
Bottomley, T	Dec 26, 1910	Feb 19, 1977	1934	1935	6	7	0	142	51	20.28	0	188	1	188.00	5
Bower, W H	Oct 17, 1857	Jan 31, 1943	1883	1883	1	2	0	10	5	5.00	0	—	—	—	0
Bowes, W E ©	July 25, 1908	Sept 4, 1987	1929	1947	301	257	117	1,251	43*	8.93	0	21,227	1,351	15.71	118
Boycott, G ©	Oct 21, 1940		1962	1986	414	674	111	32,570	260*	57.85	103	665	28	23.75	200
Brackin, T	Jan 5, 1859	Oct 7, 1924	1882	1882	3	6	0	12	9	2.00	0	—	—	—	0
§ Brathwaite, K C	Dec 1, 1992		2017	2017	2	4	0	40	18	10.00	0	—	—	—	1

LIST OF PLAYERS AND CAREER AVERAGES IN ALL FIRST-CLASS MATCHES FOR YORKSHIRE (Continued)

Player	Date of Birth	Date of Death (if known)	First Played	Last Played	M	Inns	NO	Runs	HS	Av'ge	100s	Runs	Wkts	Av'ge	Ct/St
Brayshay, P B *	Oct 14, 1916	July 6, 2004	1952	1952	2	3	0	20	13	6.66	0	104	3	34.66	0
Brearley, H *	June 26, 1913	Aug 14, 2007	1937	1937	1	2	0	17	9	8.50	0	—	—	—	0
Brennan, D V *	Feb 10, 1920	Jan 9, 1985	1947	1953	204	221	66	1,653	47	10.66	0	—	—	—	280/100
Bresnan, T T *	**Feb 28, 1985**		**2003**	**2019**	**163**	**232**	**35**	**5,594**	**169***	**28.39**	**5**	**13,663**	**445**	**30.70**	**89**
Britton, G	Feb 7, 1843	Jan 3, 1910	1867	1867	1	3	0	3	3	1.50	0	—	—	—	0
Broadbent, A	June 7, 1879	July 19, 1958	1909	1910	3	5	0	66	29	13.20	0	252	5	50.40	1
Broadhead, W B	May 31, 1903	Apr 2, 1986	1929	1929	1	2	0	5	5	2.50	0	—	—	—	0
Broadhurst, M	June 20, 1974		1991	1994	5	3	0	7	6	2.33	0	231	7	33.00	0
Brook, H C	**Feb 22, 1999**		**2016**	**2019**	**28**	**47**	**0**	**1,027**	**124**	**21.85**	**2**	**132**	**1**	**132.00**	**15**
Brook, J W	Feb 1, 1897		1923	1923	1	1	0	0	0*	0.00	0	—	—	—	0
Brooke, B	Mar 3, 1930		1950	1950	2	4	0	16	14	4.00	0	191	2	95.50	0
§ Brooks, J A	June 4, 1984		2013	2018	81	102	34	1,229	31*	18.07	0	8,341	316	26.39	21
§ Brophy, G L	Nov 26, 1975		2006	2012	73	112	12	3,012	177*	30.12	3	6	0	—	176/15
Broughton, P N	Oct 22, 1935		1956	1956	6	5	2	19	12	6.33	0	365	16	22.81	4
Brown, A	June 10, 1854		1872	1872	2	3	0	9	3	3.00	0	47	3	15.66	4
Brown, J T (Driffield) ©	Aug 20, 1869	Nov 2, 1900	1889	1904	345	567	41	15,694	311	29.83	23	5,183	177	29.28	188
Brown, J T (Darfield) ©	Nov 24, 1874	Nov 4, 1904	1897	1903	30	32	3	333	37*	11.48	0	2,071	97	21.35	18
Brown, W	Nov 19, 1876	July 27, 1945	1902	1908	2	2	1	2	2	2.00	0	84	4	21.00	0
Brownhill, T	Oct 10, 1838	Jan 6, 1915	1863	1871	14	20	3	185	25	10.88	0	—	—	—	7
Brumfitt, J *	Feb 18, 1847	Mar 16, 1907	1871	1871	1	1	0	9	9	9.00	0	—	—	—	0
Buller, J S	Aug 23, 1909	Apr 7, 1970	1930	1930	1	2	0	5	5	2.50	0	—	—	—	2
Bulmer, J R L	Dec 28, 1867	Jan 20, 1917	1891	1891	1	2	0	0	0	0.00	0	79	1	79.00	0
Burgess, T	Oct 1, 1859	Feb 15, 1922	1895	1895	1	2	1	0	0*	0.00	0	—	—	—	2
Burgin, E	Jan 4, 1924	Nov 16, 2012	1952	1953	12	10	3	92	32	13.14	0	795	31	25.64	2
Burman, J	Oct 5, 1838	May 14, 1900	1867	1867	1	2	1	1	1*	1.00	0	—	—	—	0
Burnet, J R * ©	Oct 11, 1918	Mar 9, 1999	1958	1959	54	75	6	889	54	12.88	0	26	1	26.00	7
§ Burrows, W	Aug 18, 1855	May 29, 1893	1880	1880	6	10	0	82	23	8.20	0	—	—	—	2
Burton, D C F *	Sept 13, 1887	Sept 24, 1971	1907	1921	104	130	15	2,273	142*	19.76	0	—	—	—	44
Burton, R C *	Apr 11, 1891	Apr 30, 1971	1914	1914	2	2	0	47	47	23.50	0	73	6	12.16	2
Butterfield, E B *	Oct 22, 1848	May 6, 1899	1870	1870	1	2	0	18	10	9.00	0	—	—	—	0

LIST OF PLAYERS AND CAREER AVERAGES IN ALL FIRST-CLASS MATCHES FOR YORKSHIRE (Continued)

Player	Date of Birth	Date of Death (if known)	First Played	Last Played	M	Inns	NO	Runs	HS	Av'ge	100s	Runs	Wkts	Av'ge	Ct/St
© Byas, D	Aug 26, 1963		1986	2001	268	449	42	14,398	213	35.37	28	727	12	60.58	351
Byrom, J L *	July 20, 1851	Aug 24, 1931	1874	1874	2	4	0	19	11	4.75	0	—	—	—	1
Callis, E	Nov 8, 1994		2016	2017	2	3	1	131	84	65.50	0	—	—	—	1
Cammish, J W	May 21, 1921		1954	1954	2	1	0	0	0	0.00	0	155	3	51.66	0
© Carrick, P	July, 16 1952		1970	1993	425	543	102	9,994	131*	22.66	3	30,530	1,018	29.99	183
Carter, Rev E S *	Feb 3, 1845	May 23, 1923	1876	1881	14	21	2	210	39*	11.05	0	104	8	13.00	4
Cartman, W H	June 20, 1861	Jan 16, 1935	1891	1891	3	6	0	57	49	9.50	0	—	—	—	0
Carver, K	Mar 26, 1996		2014	2018	8	13	6	108	20	15.42	0	543	18	30.16	4
Cawthray, G	Sept 28, 1913	Jan 5, 2001	1939	1952	4	6	0	114	30	19.00	0	304	4	76.00	2
Chadwick, J P G	Nov 8, 1934		1960	1965	6	9	3	106	59	17.66	0	67	2	33.50	7
Chapman, A	Dec 27, 1851	June 26, 1909	1876	1879	14	23	4	148	29	7.78	0	17	1	17.00	7
Chapman, C A	June 8, 1971		1990	1998	8	13	2	238	80	21.63	0	—	—	—	13/3
Charlesworth, A P	Feb 19, 1865	May 11, 1926	1894	1895	7	12	1	241	63	21.90	0	—	—	—	2
§ Chichester-Constable, R C J *	Dec 21, 1890	May 26, 1963	1919	1919	1	1	0	0	0	0.00	0	6	0	—	0
Clarkson, A	Sept 5, 1939		1963	1963	6	8	1	80	30	11.42	0	92	5	18.40	5
Claydon, H M	Dec 24, 1891	Oct 17, 1980	1914	1919	4	6	0	39	15	6.50	0	176	3	58.66	1
§ Claydon, M E	May 21, 1982		2005	2006	3	2	0	38	19	19.00	0	263	3	87.66	0
§ Clayton, R O	Jan 1, 1844	Nov 26, 1901	1870	1879	70	115	23	992	62	10.78	0	2,478	153	16.19	26
§ Cleary, M F	July 19, 1980		2005	2005	2	2	0	23	12	11.50	0	250	8	31.25	0
Clegg, H	Dec 8, 1850	Dec 30, 1920	1881	1881	6	8	1	63	25*	9.00	0	—	—	—	2
Clifford, C C	July, 5, 1942		1972	1972	11	12	4	39	12*	4.87	0	666	26	25.61	5
Close, D B	Feb 24, 1931	Sept 14, 2015	1949	1970	536	811	102	22,650	198	31.94	33	23,489	967	24.29	564
Clough, G D	May 23, 1978		1998	1998	1	2	0	34	33	17.00	0	11	0	—	0
© **Coad, B O**	**Jan 10, 1994**		**2016**	**2019**	**36**	**48**	**16**	**487**	**35**	**15.21**	**0**	**3043**	**145**	**20.98**	**1**
Collinson, R W *	Nov 6, 1875	Dec 26, 1963	1897	1897	2	3	0	58	34	19.33	0	—	—	—	0
Cooper, H P	Apr 17, 1949		1971	1980	98	107	29	1,159	56	14.85	0	6,327	227	27.87	60
Cooper, P E *	Feb 19, 1885	May 21, 1950	1910	1910	1	2	0	0	0	0.00	0	—	—	—	0
© Cope, G A	July 23, 1947		1966	1980	230	249	89	2,241	78	14.00	0	15,627	630	24.80	64
Corbett, A M	Nov 25, 1855	Oct 7, 1934	1881	1881	1	2	0	0	0	0.00	0	—	—	—	1

LIST OF PLAYERS AND CAREER AVERAGES IN ALL FIRST-CLASS MATCHES FOR YORKSHIRE (Continued)

Player	Date of Birth	Date of Death (if known)	First Played	Last Played	M	Inns	NO	Runs	HS	Av'ge	100s	Runs	Wkts	Av'ge	Ct/St
Coverdale, S P	Nov 20, 1954	—	1973	1980	6	4	0	31	18	7.75	0	—	—	—	11/4
Coverdale, W *	July 8, 1862	Sept 23, 1934	1888	1888	2	2	0	2	1	1.00	0	—	—	—	2
Cowan, M J	© June 10, 1933	Nov 7, 1998	1953	1962	91	84	48	170	19*	4.72	0	6,389	266	24.01	37
Cownley, J M	Feb 24, 1929	—	1952	1952	2	2	1	19	19	19.00	0	119	1	119.00	0
Coxon, A	© Jan 18, 1916	Jan 22, 2006	1945	1950	142	182	33	2,747	83	18.43	0	9,528	464	20.53	124
Craven, V J	July 31, 1980	—	2000	2004	33	55	6	1,206	81*	24.61	0	584	15	38.93	18
Crawford, G H	Dec 15, 1890	June 28, 1975	1914	1926	9	8	0	46	21	5.75	0	541	21	25.76	3
Crawford, M G *	July 30, 1920	Dec 2, 2012	1951	1951	1	2	0	22	13	11.00	0	—	—	—	1
Creighton, E	July 9, 1859	Feb 17, 1931	1888	1888	4	8	2	33	10	5.50	0	181	10	18.10	0
Crick, H	Jan 29, 1910	Feb 10, 1960	1937	1947	8	10	0	88	20	8.80	0	—	—	—	18/4
Crookes, R	Oct 9, 1846	Nov 15, 1897	1879	1879	4	6	2	32	20	8.00	0	14	0	—	0
Crossland, S M	Aug 16, 1851	April 11, 1906	1883	1886	1	2	1	2	2*	2.00	0	—	—	—	3/5
Crowther, A	Aug 1, 1878	June 4, 1946	1905	1905	4	6	2	0	0	0.00	0	—	—	—	1
Cuttell, W	Jan 28, 1835	June 10, 1896	1863	1871	15	27	6	271	56	12.90	0	596	36	16.55	4
Dalton, A J	Mar 14, 1947	—	1969	1972	21	31	2	710	128	24.48	3	—	—	—	6
§ Darnton, T	Feb 12, 1836	Oct 18, 1874	1864	1868	13	22	1	314	81*	14.95	0	349	12	29.08	18
Davidson, K R	Dec 24, 1905	Dec 25, 1954	1933	1935	30	46	5	1,331	128	32.46	2	—	—	—	3
Dawes, J	Feb 14, 1836	Not known	1865	1865	5	9	2	93	28*	13.28	0	196	5	39.20	3
Dawood, I	July 23, 1976	—	2004	2005	20	31	7	636	75	26.50	0	—	—	—	46/3
Dawson, E	May 1, 1835	Dec 1, 1888	1863	1874	16	25	1	224	87	9.33	0	—	—	—	5
Dawson, R K J	© Aug 4, 1980	—	2001	2006	72	106	9	2,179	87	22.46	0	6,444	157	41.04	39
Dawson, W A *	Dec 3, 1850	Mar 6, 1916	1870	1870	1	2	0	25	25	12.50	0	—	—	—	1
Day, A G *	Sept 20, 1865	Oct 16, 1908	1885	1888	6	10	0	78	67	7.80	0	—	—	—	3
Dennis, F	© June 11, 1907	Nov 21, 2000	1928	1933	89	100	28	1,332	67	18.50	0	4,517	156	28.95	58
Dennis, S J	© Oct 18, 1960	—	1980	1988	67	62	24	338	53*	8.89	0	5,548	173	32.06	19
Denton, D	© July 4, 1874	Feb 16, 1950	1894	1920	676	1,058	61	33,282	221	33.38	61	957	34	28.14	360/1
Denton, J	Feb 3, 1865	July 19, 1946	1887	1888	15	24	0	222	24	9.25	0	—	—	—	6
Dewse, H	Feb 23, 1836	July 8, 1910	1873	1873	1	2	0	14	12	7.00	0	15	0	—	1
Deyes, G	Feb 11, 1878	Jan 11, 1963	1905	1907	17	24	4	44	12	2.20	0	944	41	23.02	6
Dick, R D *	Apr 16, 1889	Dec 14, 1983	1911	1911	1	1	0	2	2	2.00	0	37	2	18.50	1

Player	Date of Birth	Date of Death (if known)	First Played	Last Played	M	Inns	NO	Runs	HS	Av'ge	100s	Runs	Wkts	Av'ge	Ct/St
Dobson, A	Feb 22, 1854	Sept 17, 1932	1879	1879	2	3	0	1	1	0.33	0	106	0	—	1
Doidge, M J	July 2, 1970	—	1990	1990	2	—	—	—	—	—	—	—	0	—	—
Dolphin, A	© Dec 24, 1885	Oct 23, 1942	1905	1927	427	446	157	3,325	66	11.50	0	28	1	28.00	569/260
Douglas, J S	Apr 4, 1903	Dec 27, 1971	1925	1934	23	26	8	125	19	6.94	0	1,310	49	26.73	14
Drake, A *	© Apr 16, 1884	Feb 14, 1919	1909	1914	156	244	24	4,789	147*	21.76	3	8,623	479	18.00	93
Drake, J	Sept 1, 1893	May 22, 1967	1923	1924	3	4	1	21	10	7.00	0	117	1	117.00	1
Driver, J	May 16, 1861	Dec 10, 1946	1889	1889	2	4	1	24	8	8.00	0				2
Dury, T S *	June 12, 1854	Mar 20, 1932	1878	1881	13	24	1	329	46	14.30	0	21	0	—	2
Dyson, W L	Dec 11, 1857	May 1, 1936	1887	1887	2	4	0	8	6	2.00	0				3
Earnshaw, W	Sept 20, 1867	Nov 24, 1941	1893	1896	6	7	3	44	23	11.00	0				6/2
Eastwood, D	Mar 30, 1848	May 11, 1903	1870	1877	29	51	2	591	68	12.06	0	349	11	31.72	16
Eckersley, R	Sept 4, 1925	May 30, 2009	1945	1945	1	1	0	9	9*	—	0	62	0	—	0
Elam, F W *	Sept 13, 1871	Mar 19, 1943	1900	1902	2	3	1	48	28	24.00	0				0
§ Elliott, M T G	Sept 28, 1971		2002	2002	5	10	4	487	127	54.11	1	77	1	77.00	7
Ellis, J E	Nov 10, 1864	Dec 1, 1927	1888	1892	11	15	6	14	4*	1.55	0				11/10
Ellis, S *	Nov 23, 1851	Oct 28, 1930	1880	1880	2	3	0	12	9	4.00	0				2
Elms, J E	Dec 24, 1874	Nov 1, 1951	1905	1905	1	2	0	20	20	10.00	0	28	1	28.00	1
Elstub, C J	Feb 3, 1981		2000	2002	6	7	6	28	18*	28.00	0	356	9	39.55	2
Emmett, T	© Sept 3, 1841	June 29, 1904	1866	1888	299	484	65	6,315	104	15.07	1	15,465	1,216	12.71	179
Farrar, A	Apr 29, 1883	Dec 25, 1954	1906	1906	1	1	0	2	2	2.00	0				1
Fearnley, M C	Aug 21, 1936	July 7, 1979	1962	1964	3	4	2	19	11*	9.50	0	133	6	22.16	0
Featherby, W D	Aug 18, 1888	Nov 20, 1958	1920	1920	2	—	—	—	—	—	—	12	0	—	0
Fellows, G M	July 30, 1978		1998	2003	46	71	6	1,526	109	23.47	1	1,202	32	37.56	23
Fiddling, K	Oct 13, 1917	June 19, 1992	1938	1946	18	24	6	182	25	10.11	0				24/13
§ Finch, A J	© Nov 17, 1986		2014	2015	8	10	1	415	110	46.11	1	40	1	40.00	11
Firth, A *	Sept 3, 1847	Jan 16, 1927	1869	1869	1	1	0	4	4	4.00	0				0
Firth, Rev E B *	Apr 11, 1863	July 25, 1905	1894	1894	1	1	0	1	1	1.00	0				0
§ Firth, E L *	Mar 7, 1886	Jan 8, 1949	1912	1912	2	4	0	43	37	13.75	0				1
Firth, J	June 26, 1917	Sept 6, 1981	1949	1950	8	8	5	134	67*	44.66	0				14/2

LIST OF PLAYERS AND CAREER AVERAGES IN ALL FIRST-CLASS MATCHES FOR YORKSHIRE (Continued)

Player	Date of Birth	Date of Death (if known)	First Played	Last Played	M	Inns	NO	Runs	HS	Av'ge	100s	Runs	Wkts	Av'ge	Ct/St
Fisher, H ...... ©	Aug 3, 1903	Apr 16, 1974	1928	1936	52	58	14	681	76*	15.47	0	2,621	93	28.18	22
Fisher, I D	Mar 31, 1976		1996	2001	24	32	9	545	68	23.69	0	1,382	43	32.13	1
Fisher, M D	**Nov 9, 1997**		**2015**	**2019**	**11**	**15**	**3**	**240**	**47***	**20.00**	**0**	**945**	**26**	**36.34**	**8**
Flaxington, S	Oct 14, 1860	Mar 10, 1895	1882	1882	4	8	0	121	57	15.12	0	—	—	—	1
§ Fleming, S P	Apr 1, 1973		2003	2003	7	14	2	469	98	39.08	0	—	—	—	13
Fletcher, S D ...... ©	June 8, 1964		1983	1991	107	91	31	414	28*	6.90	0	7,966	234	34.04	25
Fletcher, W	Feb 16, 1866	June 1, 1935	1892	1892	5	8	1	80	31*	11.42	0	157	7	22.42	4
Foord, C W	June 11, 1924	July 8, 2015	1947	1953	51	34	16	114	35	6.33	0	3,412	126	27.07	19
Foster, E	Nov 23, 1873	April 16, 1956	1901	1901	1	1	0	2	2	2.00	0	27	0	—	0
Foster, M J	Sept 17, 1972		1993	1994	5	7	1	165	63*	27.50	0	150	6	25.00	6
§ Foster, T W *	Nov 12, 1871	Jan 31, 1947	1894	1895	14	20	5	138	25	9.20	0	952	58	16.41	6
Fraine, W A R	**June 13, 1996**		**2019**	**2019**	**8**	**15**	**1**	**393**	**106**	**28.07**	**1**	—	—	—	**8**
Frank, J *	Dec 27, 1857	Oct 22, 1940	1881	1881	1	2	0	10	7	5.00	0	17	1	17.00	3
Frank, R W * ...... ©	May 29, 1864	Sept 9, 1950	1889	1903	18	28	4	298	58	12.41	0	9	0	—	8
Freeman, G	July 27, 1843	Nov 18, 1895	1865	1880	32	54	2	752	53	14.46	0	2,079	209	9.94	16
Gale, A W ...... ©	Nov 28, 1983		2004	2016	149	235	17	7,726	272	35.44	19	238	1	238.00	46
Geldart, C J	Dec 17, 1991		2010	2011	2	2	0	51	34	25.50	0	—	—	—	1
Gibb, P A * ...... ©	July 11, 1913	Dec 7, 1977	1935	1946	36	54	7	1,545	157*	32.87	2	82	3	27.33	25/8
Gibson, B P **	Mar 31, 1996		2011	2011	1	1	0	—	1*	—	0	—	—	—	6/0
Gibson, R	Jan 22, 1996		2016	2016	1	1	0	0	0	0.00	0	42	1	42.00	0
§ Gifkins, C J *	Feb 19, 1856	Jan 31, 1897	1880	1880	2	3	0	30	23	10.00	0	—	—	—	0
Gilbert, C R	Apr 16, 1984		2007	2007	1	1	0	64	64	64.00	0	11	0	—	0
Gill, F	Sept 3, 1883	Nov 1, 1917	1906	1906	2	4	0	18	11	4.50	0	—	—	—	0
§ Gillespie, J N ...... ©	April 19, 1975		2006	2007	26	34	11	640	123*	27.82	1	2,013	59	34.11	4
Gillhouley, K	Aug 8, 1934		1961	1961	24	31	7	323	56*	13.45	0	1,702	77	22.10	16
Gough, D	Sept 18, 1970		1989	2008	146	188	29	2,922	121	18.37	1	12,487	453	27.56	30
Goulder, A	Aug 16, 1907	June 11, 1986	1929	1929	2	1	0	3	3	3.00	0	90	3	30.00	0
§ Gray, A K D	May 19, 1974		2001	2004	18	26	3	649	104	28.21	1	1,357	30	45.23	16

** At 15 years and 27 days on April 27, 2011, First Day of Yorkshire's match v. Durham MCCU, he became the youngest ever English First Class cricketer.

Player	Date of Birth	Date of Death (if known)	First Played	Last Played	M	Inns	NO	Runs	HS	Av'ge	100s	Runs	Wkts	Av'ge	Ct/St
Grayson, A P	Mar 31, 1971		1990	1995	52	80	10	1,958	100	27.97	1	846	13	65.07	36
Greenwood, A *	Aug 20, 1847	Feb 12, 1889	1869	1880	95	166	12	2,762	91	17.93	0	9	0	—	33
Greenwood, F E *	© Sept 28, 1905	July 30, 1963	1929	1932	57	66	8	1,558	104*	26.86	1	36	2	18.00	37
Greenwood, L	July 13, 1834	Nov 1, 1909	1864	1874	50	84	12	885	83	12.29	0	1,615	85	19.00	24
Grimshaw, C H	May 12, 1880	Sept 25, 1947	1904	1908	54	75	7	1,219	85	17.92	0	221	7	31.57	42
Grimshaw, I	May 4, 1857	Jan 18, 1911	1880	1887	125	194	14	3,354	129*	18.63	4	—	—	—	76/3
Guy S M	Nov 17, 1978		2000	2011	37	52	6	742	52*	16.13	0	8	0	—	98/12
Haggas, S	Apr 18, 1856	Mar 14, 1926	1878	1882	31	47	3	478	43	10.86	0	—	—	—	10
Haigh S	© Mar 19, 1871	Feb 27, 1921	1895	1913	513	687	110	10,993	159	19.05	4	29,289	1,876	15.61	276
Hall, B	Sept 16, 1929	Feb 27, 1989	1952	1952	1	2	0	14	10	7.00	0	55	1	55.00	1
Hall, C H	Apr 5, 1906	Dec 11, 1976	1928	1934	23	22	9	67	15*	5.15	0	1,226	45	27.24	11
§ Hall, J	Nov 11, 1815	Apr 17, 1888	1863	1863	1	2	0	4	2	2.00	0	—	—	—	2
Hall, L	© Nov 1, 1852	Nov 19, 1915	1873	1894	275	477	58	9,757	160	23.28	9	781	15	52.06	173
Halliday, H	Feb 9, 1920	Aug 27, 1967	1938	1953	182	279	18	8,361	144	32.03	12	3,119	101	30.88	140
Halliley, C	Dec 5, 1852	Mar 23, 1929	1872	1872	3	5	0	23	5	4.60	0	—	—	—	2
Hamer, A	Dec 8, 1916	Nov 3, 1993	1938	1938	2	3	1	3	1	1.50	0	64	1	64.00	2
§ Hamilton, G M	© Sept 16, 1974		1994	2003	73	108	18	2,228	125	24.75	1	5,479	222	24.68	25
Hampshire, A W	Oct 4, 1950		1975	1975	1	2	0	18	17	9.00	0	—	—	—	1
Hampshire, J	Oct 5, 1913	May 23, 1997	1937	1937	3	2	0	5	3	2.50	0	109	5	21.80	1
Hampshire, J H	© Feb 10, 1941	March 11, 2017	1961	1981	456	724	89	21,979	183*	34.61	34	1,108	24	46.16	367
§ Handscomb, P S P	Apr 26, 1991		2017	2017	9	14	1	441	101*	33.92	1	—	—	—	7
Hannon-Dalby, O J	June 20, 1989		2008	2012	24	25	10	45	11*	3.00	0	1,938	43	45.06	2
§ Harbord, W E *	Dec 15, 1908	July 28, 1992	1929	1935	16	22	2	470	58	23.50	0	—	—	—	7
§ Harden, R J	Aug 16, 1965		1999	2000	12	22	2	411	109	20.55	1	—	—	—	2
Hardisty, C H	© Dec 15, 1885	Sept 29, 1990	1906	1909	12	21	2	439	69	23.10	0	—	—	—	18
§ Hargreaves, H S	Mar 22, 1912	Mar 2, 1968	1934	1938	38	55	5	991	84	19.82	0	—	—	—	18
§ Harrison, S J	Oct 23, 1978		2012	2012	18	20	6	51	23	3.64	0	1,145	55	20.81	3
Harris, W	Nov 21, 1861	May 23, 1923	1884	1887	4	8	2	45	25	7.50	0	195	8	24.37	1
Harrison, G P	© Feb 11, 1862	Sept 14, 1940	1883	1892	59	87	26	407	25	6.67	0	3,276	226	14.49	36
Harrison, H	Jan 26, 1885	Feb 11, 1962	1907	1907	2	1	1	4	4*	—	0	39	2	19.50	1

LIST OF PLAYERS AND CAREER AVERAGES IN ALL FIRST-CLASS MATCHES FOR YORKSHIRE (Continued)

Player	Date of Birth	Date of Death (if known)	First Played	Last Played	M	Inns	NO	Runs	HS	Av'ge	100s	Runs	Wkts	Av'ge	Ct/St
Harrison, W H	May 27, 1863	July 15, 1939	1888	1888	3	6	1	12	6	2.40	0	—	—	—	0
Hart, H W *	Sept 21, 1859	Nov 2, 1895	1888	1888	1	2	0	6	6	3.00	0	32	2	16.00	0
Hart, P R	Jan 12, 1947		1981	1981	3	2	0	23	11	4.60	0	140	2	70.00	1
Hartington, H E	Sept 18, 1881	Feb 16, 1950	1910	1911	10	10	4	51	16	8.50	0	764	23	33.21	2
Hartley, P J	© Apr 18, 1960		1985	1997	195	237	51	3,844	127*	20.66	0	17,438	579	30.11	60
Hartley, S N	Mar 18, 1956		1978	1988	133	199	27	4,193	114	24.37	4	2,052	42	48.85	47
§ Harvey, I J	Apr 10, 1972		2005	2005	20	31	2	1,045	209*	36.03	2	1,218	37	32.91	12
Hatton, A G	Mar 25, 1937		1960	1961	3	5	1	4	4*	—	0	202	6	33.66	0
§ Hawke, Lord *	Aug 16, 1860	Oct 10, 1938	1881	1911	510	739	91	13,133	166	20.26	10	16	0	—	159
Hayley, H	Feb 22, 1860	June 3, 1922	1884	1898	7	12	1	122	24	11.09	0	48	3	—	3
Haywood, W J	Feb 25, 1841	Jan 7, 1912	1878	1878	1	2	0	7	7	3.50	0	14	1	14.00	0
§ Head, T M	Dec 29, 1993		2016	2016	1	2	0	56	54	28.00	0	14	0	—	0
Hicks, J	Dec 10, 1850	June 10, 1912	1872	1876	15	25	3	313	66	14.22	0	17	0	—	12
Higgins, J	Mar 13, 1877	Nov 9, 1954	1901	1905	9	14	5	93	28*	10.33	0	—	—	—	10/3
Hill, A	Nov 15, 1843	Aug 28, 1910	1871	1882	140	223	25	1,705	49	8.61	0	7,002	542	12.91	91
Hill, H *	Nov 29, 1858	Aug 14, 1935	1888	1891	14	27	2	337	34	13.48	0	—	—	—	10
Hill, L G *	Nov 2, 1860	Aug 27, 1940	1882	1882	1	2	0	13	8	6.50	0	—	—	—	1
Hirst, E T *	May 6, 1857	Oct 26, 1914	1877	1888	21	33	2	328	87*	10.58	0	—	—	—	7
Hirst, E W *	Feb 27, 1855	Oct 24, 1933	1881	1881	2	3	0	33	28	11.00	0	3	0	—	1
Hirst, G H	© Sept 7, 1871	May 10, 1954	1891	1921*	717	1,050	128	32,024	341	34.73	56	44,716	2,481	18.02	518
Hirst, T H	May 21, 1865	Apr 3, 1927	1899	1899	1	1	1	5	5*	—	0	27	0	—	0
§ Hodd, A J	© Jan 12, 1984		2012	2018	57	79	10	1,803	96*	26.13	0	14	0	—	165/11
Hodgson, D M	Feb 26, 1990		2014	2015	2	3	0	72	35	24.00	0	—	—	—	2
Hodgson, G	July 24, 1938		1964	1964	1	1	0	4	4	4.00	0	—	—	—	0/2
Hodgson, I	Nov 15, 1828	Nov 24, 1867	1863	1866	21	35	14	164	21*	7.80	0	1,537	88	17.46	11
Hodgson, L J	Jun 29, 1986		2009	2010	3	3	0	99	34	33.00	0	158	2	79.00	1
Hodgson, P	Sept 21, 1935	Mar 30, 2015	1954	1956	13	6	2	33	8*	8.25	0	648	22	29.45	6
Hoggard, M J	© Dec 31, 1976		1996	2009	102	120	34	956	89*	11.11	0	8,956	331	27.05	23
Holdsworth, W E N	Sept 17, 1928	July 31, 2016	1952	1953	27	26	12	111	22	7.92	0	1,598	53	30.15	7
Holgate, G	June 23, 1839	July 11, 1895	1865	1867	12	19	0	174	38	9.15	0	—	—	—	17/1

LIST OF PLAYERS AND CAREER AVERAGES IN ALL FIRST-CLASS MATCHES FOR YORKSHIRE (Continued)

Player	Date of Birth	Date of Death (if known)	First Played	Last Played	M	Inns	NO	Runs	HS	Av'ge	100s	Runs	Wkts	Av'ge	Ct/St
Holmes, P ©............	Nov 25, 1886	Sept 3, 1971	1913	1933	485	699	74	26,220	315*	41.95	60	124	1	124.00	319
Horner, N F	May 10, 1926	Dec 24, 2003	1950	1950	2	4	0	114	43	28.50	0	—	—	—	2
Houseman I J	Oct 12, 1969		1989	1991	5	2	1	18	18	18.00	0	311	3	103.66	0
Hoyle, T H	Mar 19, 1884		1919	1919	1	3	0	7	7	3.50	0	—	—	—	0/1
Hudson, B	June 29, 1851		1880	1880	3	4	0	13	5	3.25	0	—	—	—	2
Hunter, D ©............	Feb 23, 1860	Nov 11, 1901	1888	1909	517	681	323	4,177	58*	11.66	0	43	0	—	863/323
Hunter, J	Aug 3, 1855	Jan 4, 1891	1878	1888	143	213	61	1,183	60*	7.78	0	—	—	—	207/102
Hutchison, P M ©......	June 9, 1977		1996	2001	39	39	23	187	30	11.68	0	3,244	143	22.68	8
Hutton, L ©............	June 23, 1916	Sept, 6, 1990	1934	1955	341	527	62	24,807	280*	53.34	85	4,221	154	27.40	278
Hutton, R A ©........	Sept 6, 1942		1962	1974	208	287	45	4,986	189	20.18	4	10,254	468	21.91	160
Iddison, R	Sept 15, 1834	Mar 19, 1890	1863	1876	72	108	15	1,916	112	20.60	0	1,540	102	15.09	70
Illingworth, R ©......	June 8, 1932		1951	1983	496	668	131	14,986	162	27.90	14	26,806	1,431	18.73	286
§ Imran Tahir	Mar 27, 1979		2007	2007	1	2	0	5	5	2.50	0	141	0	—	0
Ingham, P G	Sept 28, 1956		1979	1981	8	14	0	290	64	20.71	0	—	—	—	0
Inglis, J W	Oct 19, 1979		2000	2000	1	2	0	4	2	2.00	0	—	—	—	0
§ Inzamam-ul-Haq	Mar 3, 1970		2007	2007	3	4	0	89	51	22.25	0	—	—	—	5
Jackson, Hon F S * ©..	Nov 21, 1870	Mar 9, 1947	1890	1907	207	328	22	10,371	160	33.89	21	9,690	506	19.15	129
Jackson, S R *	July 15, 1859	July 19, 1941	1891	1891	1	2	0	9	9	4.50	0	—	—	—	0
Jacques, T A *	Feb 19, 1905	Feb 23, 1995	1927	1936	28	20	7	162	35*	12.46	0	1,786	57	31.33	12
Jakeman, F	Jan 10, 1921	May 17, 1986	1946	1947	10	16	2	262	51	13.71	0	—	—	—	3
James, B	Apr 23, 1934	May 26, 1999	1954	1954	4	5	3	22	11*	11.00	0	—	—	—	3
§ Jaques, P A ©........	May 3, 1979		2004	2013	53	82	3	4,039	243	51.12	11	228	8	28.50	46
Jarvis, P W ©........	June 29, 1965		1981	1993	138	160	46	1,898	80	16.64	0	11,990	449	26.70	36
Johnson, C	Sept 5, 1947		1969	1979	100	152	14	2,960	107	21.44	2	265	4	66.25	50
Johnson, J	May 16, 1916	Jan 16, 2011	1936	1939	3	3	2	5	4*	5.00	0	27	5	5.40	1
Johnson, M	Apr 23, 1958		1981	1981	4	4	2	2	2	1.00	0	301	7	43.00	1
Joy, J	Dec 29, 1825	Sept 27, 1889	1863	1867	3	5	0	107	74	21.40	—	5	0	—	3
Judson, A	July 10, 1885	Apr 8, 1975	1920	1920	1							5	0	—	
§ Katich, S M	Aug 21, 1975		2002	2002	1	2	0	37	21	18.50	0	25	0	—	1

LIST OF PLAYERS AND CAREER AVERAGES IN ALL FIRST-CLASS MATCHES FOR YORKSHIRE (Continued)

Player	Date of Birth	Date of Death (if known)	First Played	Last Played	M	Inns	NO	Runs	HS	Av'ge	100s	Runs	Wkts	Av'ge	Ct/St
Kaye, Harold S *	May 9, 1882	Nov 6, 1953	1907	1908	18	25	1	243	37	10.12	0	—	—	—	9
Kaye, Haven	June 11, 1846	Jan 24, 1892	1872	1873	8	14	0	117	33	8.35	0	—	—	—	3
Keedy, G	Nov 27, 1974		1994	1994	1	1	0	1	1	1.00	0	—	—	—	0
§ Keighley, W G * ©	Jan 10, 1925	June 14, 2005	1947	1951	35	51	5	1,227	110	26.67	1	18	0	—	12
Kellett, S A	Oct 16, 1967		1989	1995	86	147	10	4,204	125*	30.68	2	7	0	—	74
Kennie, G	May 17, 1904	Apr 11, 1994	1927	1927	1	1	0	6	3	3.00	0	7	—	—	1
Kettleborough, R A	Mar 15, 1973		1994	1997	13	19	2	446	108	26.23	1	153	3	51.00	9
Kilburn, S	Oct 16, 1868	Sept 25, 1940	1896	1896	1	1	0	8	8	8.00	0	—	—	—	0
Kilner, N	July 21, 1895	Apr 28, 1979	1919	1923	73	73	7	1,253	112	18.98	2	—	—	—	34
Kilner, R ©	Oct 17, 1890	Apr 5, 1928	1911	1927	365	478	46	13,018	206*	30.13	15	14,855	857	17.33	231
King, A M	Oct 8, 1932		1955	1955	1	2	0	12	12	12.00	0	12	0	—	0
Kippax, P J	Oct 15, 1940		1961	1962	4	5	0	37	17	7.40	0	279	8	34.87	0
§ Kirby, S P ©	Oct 4, 1977		2001	2004	47	61	14	342	57	7.27	0	5,143	182	28.25	11
8 Kohler-Cadmore, T ©	Apr 19, 1994		2017	2019	24	40	3	1,569	176	42.40	5	—	—	—	38
§ Kruis, G J ©	May 9, 1974		2005	2009	54	64	31	617	50*	18.69	0	5,431	154	35.26	11
§ Lambert, G A	Jan 4, 1980		2000	2000	2	3	2	6	3*	6.00	0	133	4	33.25	1
Lancaster, W W	Feb 4, 1873	Dec 30, 1938	1895	1895	7	10	0	163	51	16.30	0	29	0	—	7
§ Landon, C W *	May 30, 1850	Mar 5, 1903	1878	1882	9	13	0	51	18	3.92	0	74	0	—	1
§ Law, W *	Apr 9, 1851	Dec 20, 1892	1871	1873	4	7	0	51	22	7.28	0	—	—	—	3
Lawson, M A K	Oct 24, 1985		2004	2007	15	21	5	197	44	12.31	0	1,699	42	40.45	7
Leadbeater, M A K ©	Aug 14, 1943		1966	1979	144	236	27	5,247	140*	25.10	1	5	1	5.00	80
Leadbeater, E	Aug 15, 1927	Apr 17, 2011	1949	1956	81	94	29	898	91	13.81	0	5,657	201	28.14	49
Leadbeater, H *	Dec 31, 1863	Oct 9, 1928	1884	1890	6	10	2	141	65	17.62	0	11	0	—	4
§ Leaning, J A ©	Oct 18, 1993		2013	2019	68	108	11	2,955	123	30.46	4	455	8	56.87	52
Leatham, G A B *	Apr 30, 1851	June 19, 1932	1874	1886	12	18	5	61	14	4.69	0	—	—	—	21/7
Leather, R S *	Aug 17, 1880	Jan 3, 1913	1906	1906	1	2	0	19	14	9.50	0	—	—	—	0
Lee, C	Mar 17, 1924	Sept 4, 1999	1952	1952	2	4	0	98	74	24.50	0	—	—	—	1
Lee, F ©	Nov 18, 1856	Sept 13, 1896	1882	1890	105	182	10	3,622	165	21.05	3	—	—	—	53/1
Lee, G H	Aug 24, 1854	Oct 4, 1919	1879	1879	1	2	0	13	9	6.50	0	—	—	—	0

339

Player	Date of Birth	Date of Death (if known)	First Played	Last Played	M	Inns	NO	Runs	HS	Av'ge	100s	Runs	Wkts	Av'ge	Ct/St
Lee, Herbert	July 2, 1856	Feb 4, 1908	1885	1885	5	6	0	20	12	3.33	0	—	—	—	2
Lee, J E *	Mar 23, 1838	Apr 2, 1880	1867	1867	2	3	0	9	6	3.00	0	—	—	—	1
Lee, J E	Dec 23, 1988		2006	2009	2	3	1	24	21*	12.00	0	149	2	74.50	1
Lees, A Z	Apr 14, 1993		2010	2018	82	140	11	4,528	275*	35.10	11	77	2	38.50	56
Legard, A D *	June 19, 1878	Aug 15, 1939	1910	1910	4	5	0	50	15	10.00	0	26	0	—	1
§ Lehmann, D S	Feb 5, 1970		1997	2006	88	137	8	8,871	339	68.76	26	1,952	61	32.00	35
§ Lehmann, J S	Jul 8, 1992		2016	2016	2	8	0	384	116	54.85	1	—	—	—	
Lester, E I	Feb 18, 1923	Mar 23, 2015	1945	1956	228	339	27	10,616	186	34.02	24	160	3	53.33	106
Leyland, M	July 20, 1900	Jan 1, 1967	1920	1946	548	720	82	26,180	263	41.03	62	11,079	409	27.08	204
Lilley, A E	Apr 17, 1992		2011	2011	1	2	1	0	0	0.00	0	34	1	28.00	0
Linaker, L	Apr 8, 1885	Nov 17, 1961	1909	1909	1	2	0	0	0	0.00	0	28	1	28.00	2
Lister, B	Dec 9, 1850	Dec 3, 1919	1874	1878	7	11	1	36	10	3.60	0	—	—	—	2
Lister, J *	May 14, 1930	Jan 28, 1991	1954	1954	2	4	0	35	16	8.75	0	—	—	—	2
§ Lister-Kaye, K A *	Mar 27, 1892	Feb 28, 1955	1928	1928	2	2	1	13	7*	13.00	0	64	1	64.00	2
Lockwood, E	Apr 4, 1845	Dec 19, 1921	1868	1884	214	364	29	7,789	208	23.25	6	2,265	141	16.06	164/2
Lockwood, H	Oct 20, 1855	Feb 18, 1930	1877	1882	16	27	4	408	90	16.32	0	37	0	—	8
Lodge, J T	Apr 16, 1921	July 9, 2002	1948	1948	2	3	0	48	30	16.00	0	17	0	—	1
Loten, T W	Oct 12, 1997		2018	2019	2	3	1	33	20*	16.50	0	85	4	21.25	1
Logan, J E G	Jan 8, 1999		2019	2019	1	1	0	58	58	58.00	0	—	—	—	
Love, J D	Apr 22, 1955		1975	1989	247	388	58	10,263	170*	31.10	13	835	12	69.58	123
Lowe, G E	Jan 12, 1877	Aug 15, 1932	1902	1902	1	1	0	5	5*	5.00	0	—	—	—	1
Lowe J R	Oct 19, 1991		2010	2010	1	2	1	5	5*	5.00	0	15	0	—	
Lowson, F A	July 1, 1925	Sept 8, 1984	1949	1958	252	404	31	13,897	259*	37.25	30	84	8	10.50	180
§ Lucas, D S	Aug 19, 1978		2005	2005	1	1	1	—	—	—	—	—	—	—	5
Lumb, E *	Sept 12, 1852	Apr 5, 1891	1872	1886	14	23	4	311	70*	16.36	0	—	—	—	5
§ Lumb, M J	Feb 12, 1980		2000	2006	78	135	12	4,194	144	34.09	8	199	5	39.80	43
Lumb, R G	Feb 27, 1950		1970	1984	239	395	30	11,525	165*	31.57	22	5	0	—	129
Lupton, A W *	Feb 23, 1879	Apr 14, 1944	1908	1927	104	79	15	668	43	10.43	0	88	0	—	25
Lynas, G G	Sept 7, 1832	Dec 8, 1896	1867	1867	2	3	1	4	4*	2.00	0	—	—	—	2
Lyth, A	Sept 25, 1987		2007	2019	161	271	14	10,046	251	39.08	22	1,552	33	47.03	219

LIST OF PLAYERS AND CAREER AVERAGES IN ALL FIRST-CLASS MATCHES FOR YORKSHIRE (Continued)

Player	Date of Birth	Date of Death (if known)	First Played	Last Played	M	Inns	NO	Runs	HS	Av'ge	100s	Runs	Wkts	Av'ge	Ct/St
Macaulay, G G ◎	Dec 7, 1897	Dec 13, 1940	1920	1935	445	430	112	5,717	125*	17.97	3	30,554	1,774	17.22	361
McGrath, A	Oct 6, 1975		1995	2012	242	405	29	14,091	211	37.47	34	4,652	128	36.34	168
McHugh, F P	Nov 15, 1925		1949	1949	3	1	0	0	0	0.00	0	147	4	36.75	1
§ Maharaj, K A	Feb 7, 1990		2017	2019	5	9	0	239	85	26.55	0	719	38	18.92	1
§ Marsh, S E	Jul 9, 1983		2017	2017	2	3	1	225	125*	112.50	1	—	—		—
Marshall, S E	July 10, 1849		1874	1874	1	2	0	2	1	1.00	0	11	0	—	1
§ Martyn, D R	Oct 21, 1971		2003	2003	2	3	1	342	238	171.00	1	—	—		2
Mason, A	May 2, 1921	Mar 22, 2006	1947	1950	18	19	3	105	22	6.56	0	1,473	51	28.88	6
Maude, E *	Dec 31, 1839	July 2, 1876	1866	1866	2	2	0	17	16	8.50	0	—	—		2
§ Maxwell, G J	Oct 14, 1988		2015	2015	4	7	1	244	140	40.66	1	144	4	36.00	3
Metcalfe, A A ◎	Dec 25, 1963		1983	1995	184	317	19	10,465	216*	35.11	25	344	3	114.66	72
Micklethwait, W H *	Dec 13, 1885	Oct 7, 1947	1911	1911	1	1	0	44	44	44.00	0	—	—		—
Middlebrook, J D	May 13, 1977		1998	2015	29	38	3	534	84	15.25	0	1,899	66	28.77	1
Middlebrook, W	May 23, 1858	Apr 26, 1919	1888	1889	17	27	7	88	19*	4.40	0	895	50	17.90	17
Midgley, C A *	Nov 13, 1877	June 24, 1942	1906	1906	4	6	2	115	59*	28.75	0	149	8	18.62	3
Milburn, S M	Sept 29, 1972		1992	1995	6	8	2	22	7	3.66	0	431	14	30.78	0
§ Milligan, F W * ◎	Mar 19, 1870	Mar 31, 1900	1894	1898	81	113	10	1,879	74	18.24	0	2,736	112	24.42	40
Mitchell, A ◎	Sept 13, 1902	Dec 25, 1976	1922	1945	401	550	69	18,189	189	37.81	39	291	5	58.20	406
Mitchell, F *	Aug 13, 1872	Oct 11, 1935	1894	1904	83	125	5	4,104	194	34.20	10	16	1	16.00	52
Monks, G D	Sept 3, 1929		1952	1952	1	1	0	3	3	3.00	0	—	—		1
Moorhouse, R ◎	Sept 7, 1866	Jan 7, 1921	1888	1899	206	315	45	5,217	113	19.32	3	1,232	43	28.65	92
§ Morkel, M	Oct 6, 1984		2008	2008	1	2	0	8	8	4.00	0	33	1	33.00	0
Morris, A C	Oct 4, 1976		1995	1997	16	23	4	362	60	17.23	0	508	9	56.44	12
Mosley, H	Mar 8, 1850	Nov 29, 1933	1881	1881	2	2	0	1	1	0.25	0	34	3	11.33	1
Motley, A *	Feb 5, 1858	Sept 28, 1897	1879	1879	2	2	1	10	8*	10.00	0	135	7	19.28	1
Mounsey, J T ◎	Aug 30, 1871	Apr 6, 1949	1891	1897	92	145	21	1,939	64	15.63	0	444	10	44.40	45
Moxon, M D ◎	May 4, 1960		1981	1997	277	476	42	18,973	274*	43.71	41	1,213	22	55.13	190
Myers, H	Jan 2, 1875	June 12, 1944	1901	1910	201	289	46	4,450	91	18.31	0	7,095	282	25.15	106
Myers, M	Apr 12, 1847	Dec 8, 1919	1876	1878	22	40	4	537	49	14.91	0	20			11

LIST OF PLAYERS AND CAREER AVERAGES IN ALL FIRST-CLASS MATCHES FOR YORKSHIRE (Continued)

Player	Date of Birth	Date of Death (if known)	First Played	Last Played	M	Inns	NO	Runs	HS	Av'ge	100s	Runs	Wkts	Av'ge	Ct/St
§ Naved-ul-Hasan, Rana	Feb 28, 1978		2008	2009	11	16	3	207	32	15.92	0	1,018	26	39.15	3
Naylor, J E	Dec 11, 1930	June 27, 1996	1953	1953	1	1	0					88	0		1
Newstead, J T ©	Sept 8, 1877	Mar 25, 1952	1903	1913	96	128	17	1,791	100*	16.13	1	5,555	297	18.70	75
Nicholson, A G ©	June 25, 1938	Nov 3, 1985	1962	1975	282	267	125	1,667	50	11.73	0	17,296	876	19.74	85
Nicholson, N G	Oct 17, 1963		1988	1989	5	8	3	134	56*	26.80	0	25	0		5
Oates, William	Jan 1, 1852	Dec 9, 1940	1874	1875	7	13	7	34	14*	5.66	0				5/1
Oates, W F	June 11, 1929	May 15, 2001	1956	1956	3	3	0	20	9	6.66	0				
Old, C M ©	Dec 22, 1948		1966	1982	222	262	56	4,785	116	23.22	5	13,409	647	20.72	131
Oldham, S	July 26, 1948		1974	1985	59	39	18	212	50	10.09	0	3,849	130	29.60	18
Oldroyd, E ©	Oct 1, 1888	Dec 27, 1964	1910	1931	383	509	58	15,891	194	35.23	37	1,658	42	39.47	203
§ Olivier, D ©	May 9, 1992		2019	2019	14	17	11	130	24	21.66	0	1458	47	31.02	3
Oyston, C	May 12, 1869	July 15, 1942	1900	1909	15	21	8	96	22	7.38	0	872	31	28.12	3
Padgett, D E V ©	July 20, 1934		1951	1971	487	774	63	20,306	161*	28.55	29	208	6	34.66	250
Padgett, G H	Oct 9, 1931		1952	1952	6	7	4	56	32*	18.66	0	336	4	84.00	5
Padgett, J	Nov 21, 1860	Aug 2, 1943	1882	1889	6	9	0	92	22	10.22	0				2
Parker, B	June 23, 1970		1992	1998	44	71	10	1,839	138*	30.14	2	3	0		19
Parkin, C H	Feb 18, 1886	June 15, 1943	1906	1906	1	1	0	0	0	0.00	0	25	2	12.50	0
Parratt, J	Mar 24, 1859	May 6, 1905	1888	1890	2	2	0	11	11	5.50	0	75	1	75.00	4
§ Parton, J W	Jan 31, 1863	Jan. 30, 1906	1889	1889	1	2	0	16	14	8.00	0	4	1	4.00	0
§ Patel, A Y ©	Oct 21, 1988		2019	2019	2	2	1	20	20	20.00	0	231	2	115.50	0
Patterson, S A ©	Oct 3, 1983		2005	2019	155	186	43	2,354	63*	16.46	0	11,454	409	28.00	31
Pearson, H E	Aug 7, 1851	July 8, 1903	1878	1880	4	7	5	31	10*	15.50	0	90	5	18.00	1
Pearson, J H	May 14, 1915	May 13, 2007	1934	1936	3	3	0	54	44	18.00	0				
Peate, E ©	Mar 2, 1855	Mar 11, 1900	1879	1887	154	226	61	1,793	95	10.86	0	9,986	794	12.57	97
Peel, R ©	Feb 12, 1857	Aug 12, 1941	1882	1897	318	510	42	9,322	210*	19.91	6	20,638	1,311	15.74	141
Penny, J H	Sept 29, 1856	July 29, 1902	1891	1891	1	1	0	8	8*		0	31	2	15.50	1
Pickles, J H	Jan 30, 1966		1985	1992	58	76	21	1,336	66	24.29	0	3,638	83	43.83	24
Pickles, C S	Nov 16, 1935		1957	1960	41	40	20	74	12	3.70	0	2,062	96	21.47	10
§ Pillans, M W	Jul 4, 1991		2018	2019	2	2	0	11	8	5.50	0	189	2	94.50	2

LIST OF PLAYERS AND CAREER AVERAGES IN ALL FIRST-CLASS MATCHES FOR YORKSHIRE (Continued)

Player	Date of Birth	Date of Death (if known)	First Played	Last Played	M	Inns	NO	Runs	HS	Av'ge	100s	Runs	Wkts	Av'ge	Ct/St
Pinder, G	July 15, 1841	Jan 15, 1903	1867	1880	125	199	44	1,639	57	10.57	0	325	19	17.10	145/102
Platt, R K	© Dec 26, 1932		1955	1963	96	103	47	405	57*	7.23	0	6,389	282	22.65	35
Plunkett, L E	Apr 6, 1985		2013	2017	36	51	7	1,241	126	28.20	1	2,925	98	29.84	20
Pollard, D	Aug 7, 1835	Mar 26, 1909	1865	1865	1	2	0	3	3	1.50	0	19	0	—	0
Pollitt, G	June 3, 1874	May 19, 1942	1899	1899	1	1	0	51	51	51.00	0	—	—	—	1
§ Poysden, J E	**Aug 8, 1991**		**2018**	2018	**3**	**5**	**2**	**25**	**20***	**8.33**	**0**	**259**	**7**	**37.00**	**0**
Prest, C H *	Dec 9, 1841	Mar 4, 1875	1864	1864	2	4	0	57	31	14.25	0	—	—	—	3
Preston, J M	© Aug 23, 1864	Nov 26, 1890	1885	1889	79	134	11	1,935	93	15.73	0	3,232	178	18.15	36
Pride, T	July 23, 1864	Feb 16, 1919	1887	1887	1	1	0	1	1	1.00	0	—	—	—	4/3
Priestley, I M	Sept 25, 1967		1989	1989	2	4	2	25	23	12.50	0	119	4	29.75	1
Pullan, P	Mar 29, 1857	Mar 3, 1901	1884	1884	1	1	0	14	14	14.00	0	5	0	—	1
§ Pujara, C A	Jan 25, 1988		2015	2015	4	6	1	264	133*	52.80	1	5	0	—	2
Pyrah, R M	© Nov 1, 1982		2004	2015	51	61	8	1,621	134*	30.58	3	2527	55	45.94	22
§ Radcliffe, E J R H * ©	Jan 27, 1884	Nov 23, 1969	1909	1911	64	89	13	826	54	10.86	0	134	2	67.00	21
Ramage, A	Nov 29, 1957		1979	1983	23	22	9	219	22	16.84	0	1,649	44	37.47	1
Ramsden, G	Mar 2, 1983		2000	2000	1	—	—	0	0*	—	0	—	—	—	0
Randhawa, G S	Jan 25, 1992		2011	2011	1	1	0	5	5	5.00	0	68	1	68.00	0
Raper, J R S *	Aug 9, 1909	Mar 9, 1997	1936	1947	3	4	0	24	15	6.00	0	62	2	31.00	0
Rashid, A U	**Feb 17, 1988**		**2006**	**2017**	**140**	**196**	**33**	**5,620**	**180**	**34.47**	**10**	**14,136**	**420**	**33.65**	**70**
§ Raval, J A	© May 22, 1988		2018	2018	4	7	0	84	21	12.00	0	—	—	—	3
Rawlin, J A	Oct 4, 1897	Jan 11, 1943	1927	1936	8	10	1	72	35	8.00	0	498	21	23.71	3
Rawlin, J T	Nov 10, 1856	Jan 19, 1924	1880	1885	27	36	2	274	31	8.05	0	258	11	23.45	13
Rawlinson, E B	Apr 10, 1837	Feb 17, 1892	1867	1875	37	68	5	991	55	15.73	0	62	5	12.40	16
Read, J	Feb 2, 1998		2016	2016	1	1	0	14	14	14.00	0	—	—	—	4
Redfearn, J	May 13, 1862	Jan 14, 1931	1890	1890	1	1	0	5	5	5.00	0	—	—	—	0
Render, G W A	Jan 5, 1887	Sept 17, 1922	1919	1919	1	1	0	5	5	5.00	0	—	—	—	0
Revis, M L	**Nov 15, 2001**		**2019**	**2019**	**1**	**2**	**0**	**9**	**8**	**4.50**	**0**	—	—	—	**1**
Rhodes, A C	© Oct 14, 1906	May 21, 1957	1932	1934	61	70	19	917	64*	17.98	0	3,026	107	28.28	45
§ Rhodes, H E *	Jan 11, 1852	Sept 10, 1889	1878	1883	10	16	1	269	64	17.93	0	—	—	—	1
Rhodes, S J	June 17, 1964		1981	1984	3	2	1	41	35	41.00	0	—	—	—	3

LIST OF PLAYERS AND CAREER AVERAGES IN ALL FIRST-CLASS MATCHES FOR YORKSHIRE (Continued)

Player	Date of Birth	Date of Death (if known)	First Played	Last Played	M	Inns	NO	Runs	HS	Av'ge	100s	Runs	Wkts	Av'ge	Ct/St
Rhodes, Wilfred .....©	Oct 29, 1877	July 8, 1973	1898	1930	883	1,195	162	31,075	267*	30.08	46	57,634	3,598	16.01	586
Rhodes, William	Mar 4, 1883	Aug 5, 1941	1911	1911					1*		0	40			0
§ Rhodes, W M H	Mar 2, 1995		2015	2016	15	25	2	689	95	29.95	0	551	16	34.43	8
Richardson, J A *	Aug 4, 1908	Apr 2, 1985	1936	1947	7	12	2	308	61	30.80	0	90	2	45.00	3
§ Richardson, R B .....©	Jan 12, 1962		1993	1994	23	39	1	1,310	112	34.47	1	23	1	23.00	18
§ Richardson, S A	Sept 5, 1977		2000	2003	13	23	2	377	52	17.95	0				11
Riley, H	Aug 17, 1875	Nov 6, 1922	1895	1900	4	5	1	36	25*	9.00	0	54	1	54.00	1
Riley, M *	Apr 5, 1851	June 1, 1899	1878	1882	17	28	1	361	92	13.37	0	10			3
Ringrose, W	Sept 2, 1871	Sept 14, 1943	1901	1906	57	66	9	353	23	6.19	0	3,224	155	20.80	25
Robinson, A L .....©	Aug 17, 1946		1971	1977	84	69	31	365	30*	9.60	0	4,927	196	25.13	48
Robinson, B L H	May 12, 1858	Dec 14, 1909	1879	1879	1	2		5	4	2.50	0	20	1	20.00	0
Robinson, Edward *	Dec 27, 1862	Sept 3, 1942	1887	1887	1	2		23	23*	23.00	0				0
Robinson, Emmott .....©	Nov 16, 1883	Nov 17, 1969	1919	1931	413	455	77	9,651	135*	25.53	7	19,645	893	21.99	318
Robinson, E P	Aug 10, 1911	Nov 10, 1998	1934	1949	208	253	46	2,596	75*	12.54	0	15,141	735	20.60	189
Robinson, M A .....©	Nov 23, 1966		1991	1995	90	93	36	240	23	4.21	0	6,866	218	31.49	17
Robinson, P E	Aug 3, 1963		1984	1991	132	217	31	6,668	189	25.84	7	238	1	238.00	96
Robinson, W	Nov 29, 1851	Aug 14, 1919	1876	1877	1	1		151	68	11.61	0				3
Roebuck C G	Aug 14, 1991		2010	2010	1	1	0	23	23	23.00	0				0
Root, J E .....©	Dec 30, 1990		2010	2019	47	78	9	3,119	236	45.20	7	827	17	48.64	28
Roper, E *	Apr 8, 1851	Apr 27, 1921	1878	1880	5	7	1	85	68	14.16	0				2
Rothery, J W	Sept 5, 1876	June 2, 1919	1903	1910	150	236	18	4,614	161	21.16	3	44	2	22.00	45
Rowbotham, J	July 8, 1831	Dec 22, 1899	1863	1876	94	162	9	2,624	113	17.15	3	37	3	12.33	52
§ Rudolph J A	May 4, 1981		2007	2011	68	112	8	5,429	228*	52.20	18	311	1	311.00	79
Rudston, H	Nov 22, 1878	Apr 14, 1962	1902	1907	21	30	0	609	164	20.30	0				3
Ryan, M .....©	June 23, 1933	Nov 16, 2015	1954	1965	150	149	58	682	26*	7.49	0	9,466	413	22.92	59
Ryder, L	Aug 28, 1900	Jan 24, 1955	1924	1924	2	2	1	1	1	1.00	0	151	4	37.75	2
Sanderson B W	Jan 3, 1989		2008	2010	3	2	1	6	6	6.00	0	190	6	31.66	0
Savile, G *	Apr 26, 1847	Sept 4, 1904	1867	1874	5	7	2	140	65	20.00	0				2
Sayers, J J .....©	Nov 5, 1983		2004	2013	97	161	13	4,855	187	32.80	9	166	6	27.66	60

LIST OF PLAYERS AND CAREER AVERAGES IN ALL FIRST-CLASS MATCHES FOR YORKSHIRE (Continued)

Player	Date of Birth	Date of Death (if known)	First Played	Last Played	M	Inns	NO	Runs	HS	Av'ge	100s	Runs	Wkts	Av'ge	Ct/St
Schofield, C J	Mar 21, 1976		1996	1996	1	1	0	25	25	25.00	0	112	5	22.40	0
Schofield, D	Oct 9, 1947		1970	1974	3	4	4	13	6*	—	0	27	2	13.50	1
Scott, E	July 6, 1834	Dec 3, 1898	1864	1864	1	1	0	8	8	8.00	0	—	—	—	0
Sedgwick, H A	Apr 8, 1883	Dec 28, 1957	1906	1906	3	5	2	53	34	17.66	0	327	16	20.43	1
Sellers, Arthur * ©	May 31, 1870	Sept 25, 1941	1890	1899	49	88	5	1,643	105	18.88	2	84	2	42.00	40
Sellers, A B * ©	Mar 5, 1907	Feb 20, 1981	1932	1948	334	437	51	8,949	204	23.18	4	653	8	81.62	264
Shackleton, W A	Mar 9, 1908	Nov 16, 1971	1928	1934	5	6	0	49	25	8.16	0	130	6	21.66	3
Shahzad, Ajmal ©	July 27, 1985		2006	2012	45	58	14	1,145	88	26.02	0	4,196	125	33.56	5
Sharp, K ©	Apr. 6, 1959		1976	1990	195	320	35	8,426	181	29.56	11	836	12	69.66	95
§ Sharpe, C M *	Sept 6, 1851	June 25, 1935	1875	1875	1	1	0	15	15	15.00	0	17	0	—	0
Sharpe, P J ©	Dec 27, 1936	May 19, 2014	1958	1974	411	666	71	17,685	203*	29.72	23	140	2	70.00	526
Shaw C	Feb 17, 1964		1984	1988	61	58	27	340	31	10.96	0	4,101	123	33.34	9
Shaw, James	Mar 12, 1865	Jan 22, 1921	1896	1897	3	3	0	8	7	2.66	0	181	7	25.85	2
Shaw, Joshua ©	Jan 3, 1996		2016	2019	8	11	2	144	42	16.00	0	617	12	51.41	1
Sheepshanks, E R *	Mar 22, 1910	Dec 31, 1937	1929	1929	1	1	0	26	26	26.00	0	—	—	—	0
Shepherd, D A *	Mar 10, 1916	May 29, 1998	1938	1938	1	1	0	0	0	0.00	0	—	—	—	0
Shotton, W	Dec 1, 1840	May 26, 1909	1865	1874	2	4	0	13	7	3.25	0	—	—	—	0
Sidebottom, A ©	Apr 1, 1954		1973	1991	216	249	50	4,243	124	22.33	1	13,852	558	24.82	60
Sidebottom, R J ©	Jan 15, 1978		1997	2017	137	172	55	1,674	61	14.30	0	10,128	450	22.50	37
Sidgwick, R *	Aug 7, 1851	Oct 23, 1933	1882	1882	9	13	0	64	17	4.92	0	—	—	—	7
Silverwood, C E W * ©	Mar 5, 1975		1993	2005	131	179	33	2,369	80	16.22	0	11,413	427	27.62	30
Silvester, S	Mar 12, 1951		1976	1977	6	7	4	30	14	10.00	0	313	12	26.08	2
Simpson, E T B *	Mar 5, 1867	Mar 20, 1944	1889	1889	1	2	0	1	1	0.50	0	—	—	—	0
§ Sims, Rev H M *	Mar 15, 1853	Oct 5, 1885	1875	1877	5	10	1	109	35*	12.11	0	—	—	—	2
Slinn, W	Dec 13, 1826	June 17, 1888	1863	1864	9	14	3	22	11	2.00	0	742	48	15.45	5
Smailes, T F ©	Mar 27, 1910	Dec 1, 1970	1932	1948	262	339	42	5,686	117	19.14	3	16,593	802	20.68	153
Smales, K	Sept 15, 1927	Mar 10, 2015	1948	1950	13	19	3	165	45	10.31	0	766	22	34.81	4
Smith, A F	Mar 7, 1847	Jan 6, 1915	1868	1874	28	49	4	692	89	15.37	0	—	—	—	11
Smith, E (Morley) * ©	Oct 19, 1869	April 9, 1945	1888	1907	154	234	18	4,453	129	20.61	2	6,278	248	25.31	112

LIST OF PLAYERS AND CAREER AVERAGES IN ALL FIRST-CLASS MATCHES FOR YORKSHIRE (Continued)

Player	Date of Birth	Date of Death (if known)	First Played	Last Played	M	Inns	NO	Runs	HS	Av'ge	100s	Runs	Wkts	Av'ge	Ct/St
Smith, E (Barnsley)	July 11, 1888	Jan 2, 1972	1914	1926	16	21	5	169	49	10.56	0	1,090	46	23.69	5
Smith, Fred (Yeadon)	Dec 18, 1879	Oct 20, 1905	1903	1903	13	19	1	292	55	16.22	0	292	2	22.50	3
Smith, Fred (Idle)	Dec 26, 1885	Not known	1911	1911	1	1	0	11	11	11.00	0	45	2	22.50	0
Smith, G	Jan 19, 1875	Jan 16, 1929	1901	1906	2	1	0	7	7	7.00	0	62	0	—	3
Smith, J	Mar 23, 1833	Feb 12, 1909	1865	1865	2	3	0	28	16	9.33	0	72	6	12.00	3
Smith, N	Apr 1, 1949	Mar 4, 2003	1970	1971	8	11	5	82	20	13.66	0	—	—	—	14/3
Smith, R	Apr 6, 1944		1969	1970	5	8	3	99	37*	19.80	0	—	—	—	0
Smith, Walter	Aug 19, 1845	June 2, 1926	1874	1874	5	9	0	152	59	16.88	0	—	—	—	3
§ Smith, William	Nov 1, 1839	Apr 19, 1897	1865	1874	11	19	3	260	90	16.25	0	—	—	—	8
Smithson, G A	© Nov 1, 1926	Sept 6, 1970	1946	1950	39	60	5	1,449	169	26.34	2	84	1	84.00	21
Smurthwaite, J	Oct 17, 1916	Oct 20, 1989	1938	1939	7	9	5	29	20*	7.25	0	237	12	19.75	4
Sowden, A	Dec 1, 1853	July 5, 1921	1878	1887	8	11	0	137	37	12.45	0	22	0	—	1
Squire, D	Dec 31, 1864	Apr 28, 1922	1893	1893	1	2	0	0	0	0.00	0	25	0	—	0
Squires, P J	Aug 4, 1951		1972	1976	49	84	8	1,271	70	15.72	0	32	0	—	14
Stanley, H C *	Feb 16, 1888	May 18, 1934	1911	1913	8	13	0	155	42	11.92	0	—	—	—	6
§ Stanyforth, R T *	May 30, 1892	Feb 20, 1964	1928	1928	3	3	0	26	10	8.66	0	—	—	—	2
§ Starc, M A	Jan 30, 1990		2012	2012	2	2	1	28	28*	—	0	153	7	21.85	0
Stead, B	June 21, 1939	Apr 15, 1980	1959	1959	2	3	0	8	8	2.66	0	115	7	16.42	0
§ Stemp, R D	© Dec 11, 1967		1993	1998	104	135	36	1,267	65	12.79	0	8,557	241	35.50	49
Stephenson, J	June 5, 1832	July 5, 1898	1863	1873	36	61	5	803	67	14.33	0	—	—	—	30/27
Stephenson, J S *	© Nov 10, 1903	Oct 7, 1975	1923	1926	16	19	2	182	60	10.70	0	65	0	—	6
Stevenson, G B *	© Dec 16, 1955		1973	1986	177	217	32	3,856	115*	20.84	2	13,254	464	28.56	73
Stott, W B	Feb 18, 1934		1952	1963	187	309	19	9,168	186	31.61	17	112	7	16.00	91
Stringer, P M	Feb 23, 1943		1967	1969	19	17	8	101	15*	11.22	0	696	32	21.75	7
Stuchbury, S	June 22, 1954		1978	1981	3	3	2	7	7	7.00	0	236	8	29.50	0
§ Sugg, F H	Jan 11, 1862	May 29, 1933	1883	1883	8	12	4	80	13*	10.00	0	—	—	—	4/1
§ Sugg, W	May 21, 1860	May 21, 1933	1881	1881	1	1	0	9	9	9.00	0	—	—	—	0
Sullivan, J H B *	Sept 21, 1890	Feb 8, 1932	1912	1912	1	2	0	41	26	20.50	0	43	0	—	0
Sutcliffe, H	© Nov 24, 1894	Jan 22, 1978	1919	1945	602	864	96	38,558	313	50.20	112	381	8	47.62	402

LIST OF PLAYERS AND CAREER AVERAGES IN ALL FIRST-CLASS MATCHES FOR YORKSHIRE (Continued)

Player	Date of Birth	Date of Death (if known)	First Played	Last Played	M	Inns	NO	Runs	HS	Av'ge	100s	Runs	Wkts	Av'ge	Ct/St
Sutcliffe, W H H * ©	Oct 10, 1926	Sept 16, 1998	1948	1957	177	273	34	6,247	181	26.13	6	152	6	25.33	80
Swallow, I G	Dec 18, 1962		1983	1989	61	82	18	1,296	114	20.25	1	3,270	64	51.09	28
§ Swanepoel, P J	Mar 30, 1977		2003	2003	2	3	0	20	17	6.66	0	129	3	43.00	1
§ Tait, T	Oct 7, 1872		1898	1899	2	3	1	7	3	3.50	0	—	—	—	
Tasker, J * ©	Feb 4, 1887	Sept 6, 1954	1912	1913	31	43	4	586	67	15.02	0	—	—	—	14
Tattersall, G *	Apr 21, 1882	Aug 24, 1975	1905	1905	1	2	0	26	26	13.00	0	—	—	—	0
Tattersall, J A *	**Dec 15, 1994**		**2018**	**2019**	**22**	**34**	**3**	**1,008**	**135**	**32.51**	**1**	**—**	**—**	**—**	**55/4**
Taylor, C R	Feb 21, 1981		2001	2008	16	27	3	416	52*	17.33	0	—	—	—	8
Taylor, H	Dec 18, 1900	Oct 28, 1988	1924	1925	9	13	0	153	36	11.76	0	—	—	—	1
Taylor, H S	Dec 11, 1856	Nov 16, 1896	1879	1879	3	5	0	36	22	7.20	0	—	—	—	1
Taylor, J	Apr 2, 1850	May 27, 1924	1880	1881	9	13	1	107	44	8.91	0	—	—	—	4
Taylor, K ©	Aug 21, 1935		1953	1968	303	505	35	12,864	203*	27.37	16	3,680	129	28.52	146
Taylor, N S	June 2, 1963		1982	1983	8	6	2	10	10	2.50	0	720	22	32.72	10
Taylor, T L * ©	May 25, 1878	Mar. 16, 1960	1899	1906	82	122	10	3,933	156	35.11	8	195	4	48.75	47/2
§ Tendulkar, S R ©	Apr 24, 1973		1992	1992	16	25	2	1,070	100*	46.52	1	—	—	—	10
Thewlis, H	Aug 31, 1865	Nov 30, 1920	1888	1888	2	4	0	21	10	5.25	0	—	—	—	
Thewlis, John Sen.	Mar 11, 1828	Dec 29, 1899	1863	1875	44	80	3	1,280	108	16.62	1	—	—	—	21/1
Thewlis, John Jun.	Sept 21, 1850	Aug 9, 1901	1879	1879	3	4	0	21	12	5.25	0	—	—	—	0
Thompson, J A	**Oct 9, 1996**		**2019**	**2019**	**2**	**3**	**0**	**36**	**34**	**12.00**	**0**	**105**	**5**	**21.00**	**0**
Thornicroft, N D	Jan 23, 1985		2002	2007	7	10	4	50	30	8.33	0	545	16	34.06	2
Thornton, G	July 20, 1854	Apr 18, 1915	1877	1881	3	4	0	21	16	5.25	0	—	—	—	2
Thornton, G *	Dec 24, 1867	Jan 31, 1939	1891	1891	3	4	0	21	9*	5.25	0	74	2	37.00	2
Thorpe, G	Feb 20, 1834	Mar 2, 1899	1864	1864	1	2	1	14	14	14.00	0	—	—	—	0
Threapleton, J W	July 20, 1857	July 30, 1918	1881	1881	1	1	1	8	8*	—	0	—	—	—	2/1
Tinsley, H J	Feb 20, 1865	Dec 10, 1938	1890	1891	9	13	0	56	15	4.30	0	57	4	14.25	1
Tinsley, R A J	June 24, 1952		1974	1975	2	4	0	22	12	5.50	0	—	—	—	
Towse, A D	Apr 22, 1968		1988	1988	1	1	0	1	1	1.00	0	50	3	16.66	2
Trueman, F S ©	Feb 6, 1931	July 1, 2006	1949	1968	459	533	81	6,852	104	15.15	3	29,890	1,745	17.12	325
Tunnicliffe, J ©	Aug 26, 1866	July 11, 1948	1891	1907	472	768	57	19,435	243	27.33	22	388	7	55.42	665

LIST OF PLAYERS AND CAREER AVERAGES IN ALL FIRST-CLASS MATCHES FOR YORKSHIRE (Continued)

Player	Date of Birth	Date of Death (if known)	First Played	Last Played	M	Inns	NO	Runs	HS	Av'ge	100s	Runs	Wkts	Av'ge	Ct/St
Turner, A	Sept 2, 1885	Aug 29, 1951	1910	1911	9	16	1	163	37	10.86	0	—	—	—	7
Turner, B	July 25, 1938	Dec 27, 2015	1960	1961	2	4	2	7	3*	3.50	0	47	4	11.75	7
Turner, C ©	Jan 11, 1902	Nov 19, 1968	1925	1946	200	266	32	6,132	130	26.20	2	5,320	173	30.75	181
Turner, F I	Sept 3, 1894	Oct 18, 1954	1924	1924	5	7	0	33	12	4.71	0	—	—	—	2
Tyson, C T	Jan 24, 1889	Apr 3, 1940	1921	1921	3	5	2	232	100*	77.33	1	—	—	—	1
Ullathorne, C E	Apr 11, 1845	May 2, 1904	1868	1875	27	46	8	283	28	7.44	0	—	—	—	19
Ulyett, G ©	Oct 21, 1851	June 18, 1898	1873	1893	355	618	31	14,157	199*	24.11	15	8,181	457	17.90	235
§ Usher, J	Feb 26, 1859	Aug 9, 1905	1888	1888	1	2	0	7	5	3.50	0	31	2	15.50	1
van Geloven, J	Jan 4, 1934	Aug 21, 2003	1955	1955	3	2	1	17	16	17.00	0	224	6	37.33	2
§ Vaughan, M P ©	Oct 29, 1974		1993	2009	151	267	14	9,160	183	36.20	20	4,268	92	46.39	55
§ Verelst, H W * ©	July 2, 1846	Apr 5, 1918	1868	1869	3	4	1	66	33*	22.00	0	—	—	—	1
Verity, H ©	May 18, 1905	July 31, 1943	1930	1939	278	294	77	3,898	101	17.96	1	21,353	1,558	13.70	191
Waddington, A ©	Feb 4, 1893	Oct 28, 1959	1919	1927	255	250	65	2,396	114	12.95	0	16,203	835	19.40	222
Wade, S ©	Feb 8, 1858	Nov 5, 1931	1886	1890	65	11	20	1,438	74*	15.80	0	2,498	133	18.78	31
Wainwright D J	Mar 21, 1985		2004	2011	29	36	11	914	104*	35.56	0	2,480	69	35.94	6
Wainwright, E ©	Apr 8, 1865	Oct 28, 1919	1888	1902	352	545	30	11,092	228	21.53	18	17,744	998	17.77	327
Waite, M J ♦	**Dec 24, 1995**		**2017**	**2019**	**8**	**11**	**1**	**160**	**42**	**16.00**	**0**	**582**	**19**	**30.63**	**21**
Wake, W R *	May 21, 1852	Mar 14, 1896	1881	1881	3	3	0	13	11	4.33	0	583	23	25.34	2
Walker, A *	June 22, 1844	May 26, 1927	1863	1870	9	16	1	138	26	9.20	0	74	1	74.00	3
Walker, C	June 27, 1919	Dec 3, 1992	1947	1948	5	9	2	268	91	38.28	0	71	2	35.50	3
Walker, T	Apr 3, 1854	Aug 28, 1925	1879	1880	14	22	2	179	30	8.95	0	7	0	—	1
Waller, C	Dec 3, 1864	Dec 11, 1937	1893	1894	3	4	0	17	13	4.25	0	70	4	17.50	3
Wallgate, L *	Nov 12, 1849	May 9, 1887	1875	1878	3	3	0	9	6	3.00	0	17	1	17.00	3
Ward, A	Nov 21, 1865	Jan 6, 1939	1886	1886	4	7	1	41	22	6.83	0	1	0	—	0
Ward, J	Aug 31, 1881	Feb 28, 1948	1903	1903	1	1	0	0	0	0.00	0	16	0	—	0
Ward, H P *	Jan 20, 1899	Dec 16, 1946	1920	1920	1	1	1	10	10*	—	0	—	—	—	1

LIST OF PLAYERS AND CAREER AVERAGES IN ALL FIRST-CLASS MATCHES FOR YORKSHIRE (Continued)

Player	Date of Birth	Date of Death (if known)	First Played	Last Played	M	Inns	NO	Runs	HS	Av'ge	100s	Runs	Wkts	Av'ge	Ct/St
Wardall, T A ©	Apr 19, 1862	Dec 20, 1932	1884	1894	43	73	2	1,003	106	14.12	2	489	23	21.26	25
Wardlaw, I	Jun 29, 1985		2011	2012	4	3	2	31	17*	31.00	0	368	4	92.00	2
Wardle, J H ©	Jan 8, 1923	July 23, 1985	1946	1958	330	418	57	5,765	79	15.96	0	27,917	1,539	18.13	210
Waring, J S	Oct 1, 1942		1963	1966	28	27	15	137	26	11.41	0	1,122	53	21.16	17
Waring, S *	Nov 4, 1838		1870	1870	1	1	0	9	9	9.00	0	—	—	—	0
Washington, W A I	Dec 11, 1879	Oct 20, 1927	1900	1902	44	62	6	1,290	100*	23.03	1	—	—	—	18
Watson, H	Sept 26, 1880	Nov 24, 1951	1908	1914	29	35	11	141	41	5.87	0	—	—	—	46/10
Watson, W ©	Mar 7, 1920	Apr 24, 2004	1939	1957	283	430	65	13,953	214*	38.22	26	75	0	—	170
Waud, B W *	June 4, 1837	May 31, 1889	1863	1864	6	10	1	165	42	18.33	0	—	—	—	2
Webster, C	June 9, 1838	Jan 6, 1881	1868	1868	3	5	1	30	10	7.50	0	—	—	—	1
Webster, H H	May 8, 1844	Mar 5, 1915	1868	1868	2	3	0	10	10	3.33	0	—	—	—	0
§ Weekes, L C	July 19, 1971		1994	2000	2	2	0	20	10	10.00	0	191	10	19.10	1
West, J	Oct 16, 1844	Jan 27, 1890	1868	1876	38	64	13	461	41	9.03	0	853	53	16.09	14
Wharf, A G	June 4, 1975		1994	1997	7	9	1	186	62	23.25	0	454	11	41.27	2
Whatmough, F J	Dec 4, 1856	June 3, 1904	1878	1882	7	11	1	51	20	5.10	0	111	5	22.20	4
Wheater, C H *	Mar 4, 1860	May 11, 1885	1880	1880	2	4	1	45	27	15.00	0	—	—	—	3
White, Sir A W * ©	Oct 14, 1877	Dec 16, 1945	1908	1920	55	128	28	1,457	55	14.57	0	7	0	—	50
White, C ©	Dec 16, 1969		1990	2007	221	350	45	10,376	186	34.01	19	7,649	276	27.71	140
Whitehead, J P	Sept 3, 1925	Aug 15, 2000	1946	1951	37	38	17	387	58*	18.42	0	2,610	96	27.47	11
Whitehead, Lees ©	Mar 14, 1864	Nov 22, 1913	1889	1904	119	172	38	2,073	67*	15.47	0	2,408	99	24.32	68
Whitehead, Luther	June 25, 1869	Jan 17, 1931	1893	1893	2	4	0	21	13	5.25	0	—	—	—	0
Whiteley, J P	Feb 28, 1955		1978	1982	45	38	17	231	20	11.00	0	2,410	70	34.42	21
Whiting, C P	Apr 18, 1888	Jan 14, 1959	1914	1920	6	10	2	92	26	11.50	0	416	15	27.73	2
Whitwell, J F *	Feb 22, 1869	Nov 6, 1932	1890	1890	1	2	0	8	4	4.00	0	11	1	11.00	0
§ Whitwell, W F *	Dec 12, 1867	Apr 12, 1942	1890	1890	10	14	2	67	26	5.58	0	518	25	20.72	2
Widdup, S	Nov 10, 1977		2000	2001	11	18	1	245	44	14.41	0	22	1	22.00	5
Wigley, D H	Oct 26, 1981		2002	2002	5	6	2	19	15	19.00	0	116	1	116.00	0
§ Wilkinson, A J A *	May 28, 1835	Dec 11, 1905	1865	1868	5	6	0	129	53	21.50	0	57	0	—	1

Player	Date of Birth	Date of Death (if known)	First Played	Last Played	M	Inns	NO	Runs	HS	Av'ge	100s	Runs	Wkts	Av'ge	Ct/St
Wilkinson, F	May 23, 1914	Mar 26, 1984	1937	1939	14	14	1	73	18*	5.61	0	590	26	22.69	12
Wilkinson, H * ©	Dec 11, 1877	Apr 15, 1967	1903	1905	48	75	3	1,382	113	19.19	1	121	3	40.33	19
Wilkinson, R	Nov 11, 1977		1998	1998	1	1	0	9	9	9.00	0	35	1	35.00	0
Wilkinson, W H ©	Mar 12, 1881	June 4, 1961	1903	1910	126	192	14	3,812	103	21.41	1	971	31	31.32	93
§ Willey, D J ©	Feb 28, 1990		2016	2019	13	18	2	298	46	18.62	0	1015	30	33.83	3
Williams, A C	Mar 1, 1887	June 1, 1966	1911	1919	12	14	10	95	48*	23.75	0	678	30	22.60	6
§ Williamson. K S ©	Aug 8, 1990		2013	2018	19	32	3	1,292	189	44.55	1	475	11	43.18	20
Wilson, B B ©	Dec 11, 1879	Sept 14, 1957	1906	1914	185	308	12	8,053	208	27.50	15	278	2	139.00	53
Wilson, C E M * ©	May 15, 1875	Feb 8, 1944	1896	1899	9	13	3	256	91*	25.60	0	257	12	21.41	3
Wilson, D ©	Aug 7, 1937	July 21, 2012	1957	1974	392	502	85	5,788	83	13.88	0	22,626	1,104	20.49	235
Wilson, E R *	Mar 25, 1879	July 21, 1957	1899	1923	66	72	18	902	104*	15.70	0	3,106	197	15.76	30
Wilson, Geoffrey * ©	Aug 21, 1895	Nov 29, 1960	1919	1924	92	94	14	983	70	12.28	0	11	0	—	33
Wilson, G A *	Feb 2, 1916	Sept 24, 2002	1936	1939	15	25	5	352	55*	17.60	0	138	1	138.00	7
Wilson, John *	June 30, 1857	Nov 11, 1931	1887	1888	4	5	1	17	13*	4.25	0	165	12	13.75	3
Wilson, J P *	Apr 3, 1889	Oct 3, 1959	1911	1912	9	14	1	81	36	6.23	0	24	1	24.00	2
Wilson, J V	Jan 17, 1921	June 5, 2008	1946	1962	477	724	75	20,548	230	31.66	29	313	3	104.33	520
Wood, A ©	Aug 25, 1898	Apr 1, 1973	1927	1946	408	481	80	8,579	123*	21.39	1	33	1	33.00	612/243
Wood, B	Dec 26, 1942		1964	1964	5	7	1	63	35	12.60	0			—	4
Wood, C H	July 23, 1934	June 28, 2006	1959	1959	4	4	1	22	10	7.33	0	319	11	29.00	4
Wood, G W	Nov 18, 1862	Dec 4, 1948	1895	1895	2	2	0	2	2	1.00	0			—	0/1
Wood, H *	Mar 22, 1855	July 31, 1941	1879	1880	10	16	1	156	36	10.40	0	212	10	21.20	8
Wood, J H *			1881	1881	2	1	0	14	14	14.00	0			—	0
Wood, M J ©	Apr 6, 1977		1997	2007	128	222	20	6,742	207	33.37	16	27	2	13.50	113
Wood, R	June 3, 1929	May 22, 1990	1952	1956	22	18	4	60	17	4.28	0	1,346	51	26.39	5
Woodford, J D	Sept 9, 1943		1968	1972	38	61	2	1,204	101	20.40	1	185	4	46.25	12
Woodhead, F E *	May 29, 1868	Aug 25, 1943	1893	1894	4	8	0	57	18	7.12	0			—	3
Woodhouse, W H *	Apr 16, 1856	Mar 4, 1938	1884	1885	9	13	0	218	63	16.76	0			—	6
Wormald, A	May 10, 1855	Feb 6, 1940	1885	1891	7	11	3	161	80	20.12	0			—	10/2

LIST OF PLAYERS AND CAREER AVERAGES IN ALL FIRST-CLASS MATCHES FOR YORKSHIRE (Continued)

Player	Date of Birth	Date of Death (if known)	First Played	Last Played	M	Inns	NO	Runs	HS	Av'ge	100s	Runs	Wkts	Av'ge	Ct/St
Worsley, W A * ....©	Apr 5, 1890	Dec 4, 1973	1928	1929	60	50	4	722	60	15.69	0	—	—	—	32
Wrathmell, L F	Jan 22, 1855	Sept 16, 1928	1886	1886	1	2	0	18	17	9.00	0	—	—	—	0
Wright, R	July 19, 1852	Jan 2, 1891	1877	1877	2	4	1	28	22	9.33	0	—	—	—	0
Wright, T J *	Mar 5, 1900	Nov 7, 1962	1919	1919	1	1	0	12	12	12.00	0	—	—	—	0
Yardley, N W D * ...©	Mar 19, 1915	Oct 3, 1989	1936	1955	302	420	56	11,632	183*	31.95	17	5,818	195	29.83	220
Yeadon, J	Dec 10, 1861	May 30, 1914	1888	1888	3	6	2	41	22	10.25	0	—	—	—	5/3
§ Younus Khan ....©	Nov 29, 1977		2007	2007	13	19	2	824	217*	48.47	3	342	8	42.75	11
§ Yuvraj Singh	Dec 12, 1981		2003	2003	7	12	2	145	56	14.50	0	130	3	43.33	12

In the career averages it should be noted that the bowling analysis for the second Cambridgeshire innings at Ashton-under-Lyne in 1865 has not been found. G R Atkinson took 3 wickets, W Cuttell 2, G Freeman 4 and R Iddison 1. The respective bowling averages have been calculated excluding these wickets.

351

MOST FIRST-CLASS APPEARANCES FOR YORKSHIRE

Matches	Player	Matches	Player
883	W Rhodes (1898-1930)	477	J V Wilson (1946-1962)
717	G H Hirst (1891-1929)	472	J Tunnicliffe (1891-1907)
676	D Denton (1894-1920)	459	F S Trueman (1949-1968)
602	H Sutcliffe (1919-1945)	456	J H Hampshire (1961-1981)
548	M Leyland (1920-1947)	445	G G Macaulay (1920-1935)
536	D B Close (1949-1970)	429	D L Bairstow (1970-1990)
517	D Hunter (1888-1909)	427	A Dolphin (1905-1927)
513	S Haigh (1895-1913)	425	P Carrick (1970-1993)
510	Lord Hawke (1881-1911)	414	G Boycott (1962-1986)
496	R Illingworth (1951-1983)	413	E. Robinson (1919-1931)
491	† J G Binks (1955-1969)	411	P J Sharpe (1958-1974)
487	D E V Padgett (1951-1971)	408	A Wood (1927-1946)
485	P Holmes (1913-1933)	401	A Mitchell (1922-1945)

† Kept wicket in 412 consecutive Championship matches 1955-1969

MOST TOTAL APPEARANCES FOR YORKSHIRE
(First-Class, Domestic List A and t20)

Matches	Player	Matches	Player
883	W Rhodes (1898-1930)	513	S Haigh (1895-1913)
832	D L Bairstow (1970-1990)	510	Lord Hawke (1881-1911)
729	P Carrick (1970-1993)	502	P J Sharpe (1958-1974)
719	R J Blakey (1985-2004)	485	P Holmes (1913-1933)
717	G H Hirst (1891-1929)	477	J V Wilson (1946-1962)
690	J H Hampshire (1961-1981)	472	J Tunnicliffe (1891-1907)
678	G Boycott (1962-1986)	470	F S Trueman (1949-1968)
676	D Denton (1894-1920)	467	J D Love (1975-1989)
602	H Sutcliffe (1919-1945)	453	D Wilson (1957-1974)
583	A McGrath (1995-2012)	452	A Sidebottom (1973-1991)
581	D Byas (1986-2001)	445	G G Macaulay(1920-1935)
568	D B Close (1949-1970)	443	C M Old (1966-1982)
548	M Leyland (1920-1947)	427	A Dolphin (1905-1927)
546	C White (1990-2007)	414	P J Hartley (1985-1997)
544	D E V Padgett (1951-1971)	413	E Robinson (1919-1931)
537	R Illingworth (1951-1983)	408	A Wood (1927-1946)
521	J G Binks (1955-1969)	402	A G Nicholson (1962-1975)
517	D Hunter (1888-1909)	401	A Mitchell (1922-1945)
514	M D Moxon (1980-1997)		

ONE DAY RECORDS SECTION

Yorkshire County Cricket Club thanks Statistician JOHN T. POTTER, who in 2014 revamped and streamlined Yorkshire's One-Day Records Section. John's symbols in the pages that follow are:

$ = Sunday and National Leagues, Pro 40, Clydesdale Bank 40 and Yorkshire Bank 40

\# = Benson & Hedges Cup

+ = Gillette Cup, NatWest Trophy, Cheltenham & Gloucester Trophy, Friends Provident Trophy and Royal London Cup

LIST A
WINNERS OF THE GILLETTE CUP, NATWEST TROPHY, CHELTENHAM & GLOUCESTER TROPHY FRIENDS PROVIDENT TROPHY AND ROYAL LONDON ONE-DAY CUP

Yorkshire's Position

GILLETTE CUP

1963	Sussex	Quarter-Final
1964	Sussex	Round 2
1965	**Yorkshire**	**Winner**
1966	Warwickshire	Round 2
1967	Kent	Quarter-Final
1968	Warwickshire	Round 2
1969	**Yorkshire**	**Winner**
1970	Lancashire	Round 1
1971	Lancashire	Round 2
1972	Lancashire	Round 1
1973	Gloucestershire	Round 1
1974	Kent	Quarter-Final
1975	Lancashire	Round 2
1976	Northamptonshire	Round 1
1977	Middlesex	Round 2
1978	Sussex	Quarter-Final
1979	Somerset	Quarter-Final
1980	Middlesex	Semi-Final

NATWEST TROPHY

1981	Derbyshire	Round 1
1982	Surrey	Semi-Final
1983	Somerset	Round 2
1984	Middlesex	Round 1
1985	Essex	Round 2
1986	Sussex	Quarter-Final
1987	Nottinghamshire	Quarter-Final
1988	Middlesex	Round 2
1989	Warwickshire	Round 2
1990	Lancashire	Quarter-Final

Yorkshire's Position

1991	Hampshire	Round 1
1992	Northamptonshire	Round 2
1993	Warwickshire	Quarter-Final
1994	Worcestershire	Round 2
1995	Warwickshire	Semi-Final
1996	Lancashire	Semi-Final
1997	Essex	Quarter-Final
1998	Lancashire	Round 2
1999	Gloucestershire	Semi-Final
2000	Gloucestershire	Round 4

CHELTENHAM & GLOUCESTER TROPHY

2001	Somerset	Quarter-Final
2002	**Yorkshire**	**Winner**
2003	Gloucestershire	Round 4
2004	Gloucestershire	Semi-Final
2005	Hampshire	Semi-Final
2006	Sussex	North 7 (10)

FRIENDS PROVIDENT TROPHY

2007	Durham	North 5 (10)
2008	Essex	Semi-Final
2009	Hampshire	Group C 3 (5)

ROYAL LONDON ONE-DAY CUP

2014	Durham	Quarter-Final
2015	Gloucestershire	Semi-Final
2016	Warwickshire	Semi-Final
2017	Nottinghamshire	Quarter-Final
2018	Hampshire	Semi-Final

WINNERS OF THE NATIONAL AND SUNDAY LEAGUES, PRO 40, CLYDESDALE BANK 40 AND YORKSHIRE BANK 40 1969-2014

	SUNDAY LEAGUE	*Yorkshire's Position*
1969	Lancashire	8th
1970	Lancashire	14th
1971	Worcestershire	15th
1972	Kent	4th
1973	Kent	2nd
1974	Leicestershire	=6th
1975	Hampshire	=5th
1976	Kent	15th
1977	Leicestershire	=13th
1978	Hampshire	7th
1979	Somerset	=4th
1980	Warwickshire	=14th
1981	Essex	=7th
1982	Sussex	16th
1983	**Yorkshire**	**1st**
1984	Essex	=14th
1985	Essex	6th
1986	Hampshire	8th
1987	Worcestershire	=13th
1988	Worcestershire	8th
1989	Lancashire	11th
1990	Derbyshire	6th
1991	Nottinghamshire	7th
1992	Middlesex	15th

		Yorkshire's Position
1993	Glamorgan	9th
1994	Warwickshire	5th
1995	Kent	12th
1996	Surrey	3rd
1997	Warwickshire	10th
1998	Lancashire	9th

NATIONAL LEAGUE

1999	Lancashire	5th Div 1
2000	Gloucestershire	2nd Div 1
2001	Kent	6th Div 1
2002	Glamorgan	4th Div 1
2003	Surrey	8th Div 1
2004	Glamorgan	4th Div 2
2005	Essex	8th Div 2
2006	Essex	9th Div 2
2007	Worcestershire	6th Div 2
2008	Sussex	2nd Div 2
2009	Sussex	7th Div 1

CLYDESDALE BANK 40

2010	Warwickshire	Group B 1 (7) (Semi-Final)
2011	Surrey	Group A 6 (7)
2012	Hampshire	Group C 5 (7)
2013	Nottinghamshire	Group C 6 (7)

BENSON & HEDGES WINNERS 1972-2002

		Yorkshire's Position
1972	Leicestershire	Final
1973	Kent	Group N 3 (5)
1974	Surrey	Quarter-Final
1975	Leicestershire	Quarter-Final
1976	Kent	Group D 3 (5)
1977	Gloucestershire	Group D 3 (5)
1978	Kent	Group D 4 (5)
1979	Essex	Semi-Final
1980	Northamptonshire	Group B 4 (5)
1981	Somerset	Quarter-Final
1982	Somerset	Group A 5 (5)
1983	Middlesex	Group B 5 (5)
1984	Lancashire	Semi-Final
1985	Leicestershire	Group B 3 (5)
1986	Middlesex	Group B 3 (5)
1987	**Yorkshire**	**Winner**

		Yorkshire's Position
1988	Hampshire	Group B 4 (5)
1989	Nottinghamshire	Group C 3 (5)
1990	Lancashire	Group C 3 (5)
1991	Worcestershire	Semi-Final
1992	Hampshire	Group C 5 (5)
1993	Derbyshire	Round One
1994	Warwickshire	Round One
1995	Lancashire	Quarter-Final
1996	Lancashire	Semi-Final
1997	Surrey	Quarter-Final
1998	Essex	Semi-Final
1999	Gloucestershire	Final
2000	Gloucestershire	Quarter-Final
2001	Surrey	Semi-Final
2002	Warwickshire	Quarter-Final

Season	Played	Won	Lost	Tie	N R	Abd	Season	Played	Won	Lost	Tie	N R	Abd
1963	2	1	1	0	0	0	1993	21	10	10	0	1	0
1964	1	0	1	0	0	0	1994	19	11	8	0	0	1
1965	4	4	0	0	0	1	1995	27	15	11	0	1	1
1966	1	0	1	0	0	0	1996	27	18	9	0	0	0
1967	2	1	1	0	0	0	1997	25	14	10	1	0	1
1968	1	0	1	0	0	0	1998	25	14	10	0	1	0
1969	19	12	7	0	0	2	1999	23	13	10	0	0	0
1970	17	5	10	0	2	0	2000	24	13	10	0	1	0
1971	15	5	10	0	0	2	2001	26	13	13	0	0	0
1972	25	15	8	0	2	1	2002	27	16	11	0	0	1
1973	21	14	7	0	0	0	2003	18	6	12	0	0	0
1974	22	12	9	0	1	1	2004	23	13	8	0	2	0
1975	22	12	10	0	0	0	2005	22	8	14	0	0	0
1976	22	9	13	0	0	0	2006	15	4	10	0	1	2
1977	19	5	10	0	4	2	2007	17	8	7	0	2	1
1978	22	10	11	0	1	2	2008	18	10	4	1	3	0
1979	21	12	6	0	3	3	2009	16	6	9	0	1	0
1980	23	9	14	0	0	0	2010	13	10	3	0	0	0
1981	19	9	8	0	2	3	2011	12	5	7	0	0	0
1982	23	7	14	1	1	1	2012	11	4	7	0	0	1
1983	19	11	7	0	1	3	2013	13	4	9	0	0	0
1984	23	10	13	0	0	0	2014	10	6	4	0	0	0
1985	19	9	9	0	1	3	2015	10	5	3	0	2	0
1986	22	11	9	1	1	1	2016	10	5	4	0	1	0
1987	24	14	9	0	1	2	2017	10	6	3	0	1	0
1988	21	9	9	0	3	1	2018	9	6	3	0	0	1
1989	23	10	13	0	0	0	2019	8	2	3	2	0	0
1990	22	13	9	0	0	1							
1991	24	13	10	0	1	0		998	495	455	6	41	40
1992	21	8	13	0	0	2							

Abandoned matches are not included in the list of matches played.

ABANDONED LIST A MATCHES (40)

1965	v. South Africa at Bradford
1969 (2)	v. Warwickshire at Harrogate $
	v. Lancashire at Manchester $
1971 (2)	v. Gloucestershire at Sheffield $
	v. Somerset at Weston-Super-Mare $
1972	v. Sussex at Leeds $
1974	v. Warwickshire at Leeds $
1977 (2)	v. Warwickshire at Birmingham $
	v. Surrey at Leeds $
1978 (2)	v. Essex at Bradford $
	v. Gloucestershire at Hull $
1979 (3)	v. Leicestershire at Middlesbrough $
	v. Kent at Huddersfield $
	v. Worcestershire at Worcester $
1981 (3)	v. Warwickshire at Birmingham $
	v. Lancashire at Leeds #
	v. Sussex at Hove $
1982	v. Glamorgan at Bradford $
1983 (3)	v. Derbyshire at Chesterfield #
	v. Surrey at Leeds $
	v. Essex at Chelmsford $

1985 (3)	v. Derbyshire at Scarborough $
	v. Warwickshire at Birmingham $
	v. Lancashire at Leeds $
1986	v. Kent at Canterbury $
1987 (2)	v. Sussex at Hull $
	v. Hampshire at Leeds $
1988	v. Northamptonshire at Northampton $
1990	v. Glamorgan at Newport $
1992 (2)	v. Sussex at Hove $
	v. Durham at Darlington $
1994	v. Essex at Leeds $
1995	v. Derbyshire at Chesterfield #
1997	v. Sussex at Scarborough $
2002	v. Nottinghamshire at Nottingham $
2006 (2)	v. Nottinghamshire at Leeds +
	v. Derbyshire at Derby $
2007	v. Warwickshire at Birmingham +
2012	v. Northamptonshire at Leeds $
2018	v. Nottinghamshire at Leeds +

ANALYSIS OF LIST A RESULTS V. ALL TEAMS 1963-2019
DOMESTIC MATCHES

Opponents	Played	HOME				AWAY				Abd
		Won	Lost	Tied	N. R	Won	Lost	Tied	N. R	
Derbyshire	65	20	9	1	1	20	9	1	4	4
Durham	31	10	5	0	1	7	7	0	1	1
Essex	47	12	12	0	0	11	12	0	0	3
Glamorgan	39	9	8	0	0	9	13	0	0	2
Gloucestershire	55	12	12	0	2	8	19	0	2	2
Hampshire	45	11	9	0	1	9	15	0	0	1
Kent	55	13	11	0	1	10	20	0	0	2
Lancashire	64	10	17	0	2	15	18	0	2	3
Leicestershire	68	20	16	0	0	13	16	1	2	1
Middlesex	48	14	4	0	3	9	16	0	2	0
Northamptonshire	60	18	11	0	3	20	7	0	1	2
Nottinghamshire	60	19	8	1	2	10	17	0	3	3
Somerset	54	13	14	0	1	11	15	0	0	1
Surrey	56	12	15	0	0	11	18	0	0	2
Sussex	46	11	11	0	1	11	12	0	0	5
Warwickshire	63	11	18	1	2	13	17	1	0	6
Worcestershire	65	13	20	0	2	17	13	0	0	1
Bedfordshire	1	0	0	0	0	1	0	0	0	0
Berkshire	2	0	0	0	0	2	0	0	0	0
Cambridgeshire	3	2	0	0	0	1	0	0	0	0
Cheshire	1	0	0	0	0	1	0	0	0	0
Combined Universities	3	0	2	0	0	1	0	0	0	0
Devon	4	0	0	0	0	4	0	0	0	0
Dorset	1	0	0	0	0	1	0	0	0	0
Durham (M C)	3	1	1	0	0	1	0	0	0	0
Herefordshire	1	0	0	0	0	1	0	0	0	0
Ireland	4	3	0	0	0	1	0	0	0	0
Minor Counties	11	6	0	0	0	5	0	0	0	0
Netherlands	4	1	1	0	0	1	1	0	0	0
Norfolk	2	1	0	0	0	1	0	0	0	0
Northumberland	1	1	0	0	0	0	0	0	0	0
Scotland	16	8	0	0	0	8	0	0	0	0
Shropshire	2	0	0	0	0	1	1	0	0	0
Unicorns	4	2	0	0	0	2	0	0	0	0
Wiltshire	1	0	0	0	0	1	0	0	0	0
Yorkshire Cricket Board	1	0	0	0	0	1	0	0	0	0
Total	**986**	**253**	**204**	**3**	**22**	**238**	**246**	**3**	**17**	**39**
			OTHER MATCHES							
Australia	3	0	1	0	2	0	0	0	0	0
Bangladesh A	1	1	0	0	0	0	0	0	0	0
South Africa	0	0	0	0	0	0	0	0	0	1
South Africa A	1	0	0	0	1	0	0	0	0	0
Sri Lanka A	3	0	3	0	0	0	0	0	0	0
West Indies	1	1	0	0	0	0	0	0	0	0
West Indies A	1	0	1	0	0	0	0	0	0	0
Young Australia	1	1	0	0	0	0	0	0	9	0
Zimbabwe	1	1	0	0	0	0	0	0	0	0
Total	**12**	**4**	**5**	**0**	**3**	**0**	**0**	**0**	**0**	**1**
Grand Total	**998**	**257**	**209**	**3**	**25**	**238**	**246**	**3**	**17**	**40**

Abandoned matches are not included in the list of matches played.

LIST A HIGHEST AND LOWEST SCORES BY AND AGAINST YORKSHIRE
PLUS INDIVIDUAL BEST BATTING AND BOWLING

The lowest score is the lowest all-out total or the lowest score at completion of the allotted overs, 10-over matches not included

Yorkshire versus:

Derbyshire

		By Yorkshire		Against Yorkshire	
Highest Score:	In Yorkshire	349:7	at Leeds 2017 +	334:8	at Leeds 2017 +
	Away	288:6	at Derby 2002 #	268:8	at Chesterfield 2010 $
Lowest Score:	In Yorkshire	117	at Huddersfield 1978 $	87	at Scarborough 1973 $
	In Yorkshire	132	at Chesterfield 1986 $	127	at Chesterfield 1972 #
Best Batting:	In Yorkshire	P S P Handscomb 140	at Leeds 2017 +	W L Madsen 112	at Leeds 2017 +
	Away	M J Wood 115*	at Derby 2002 #	C J Adams 109*	at Derby 1997 $
Best Bowling:	In Yorkshire	S A Patterson 6-32	at Leeds 2010 $	F E Rumsey 4-20	at Bradford 1973 #
	Away	C W J Athey 5-35	at Chesterfield 1981 $	C J Tunnicliffe 5-24	at Derby 1981 #

Durham

		By Yorkshire		Against Yorkshire	
Highest Score:	In Yorkshire	339:4	at Leeds 2017 +	335:5	at Leeds 2017 +
	Away	328:4	at Chester-le-Street 2018 +	281:7	at Chester-le-Street 2016 +
Lowest Score:	In Yorkshire	133	at Leeds 1995 $	121	at Scarborough 1997 $
	Away	122	at Chester-le-Street 2007 $	136	at Chester-le-Street 1996 $
Best Batting:	In Yorkshire	J M Bairstow 174	at Leeds 2017 +	W Larkins 114	at Leeds 1993 $
	Away	T Kohler-Cadmore 164	at Chester-le-Street 2018 +	J P Maher 124*	at Chester-le-Street 2006 +
Best Bowling:	In Yorkshire	C White 4-18	at Scarborough 1997 $	S J E Brown 4-20	at Leeds 1995 $
	Away	C E W Silverwood 4-26	at Chester-le-Street 1996 $	P D Collingwood 4-31	at Chester-le-Street 2000 #

Essex

		By Yorkshire		Against Yorkshire	
Highest Score:	In Yorkshire	290:6	at Scarborough 2014 +	291:5	at Scarborough 2014 +
	Away	307:3	at Chelmsford 1995 +	285:8	at Chelmsford 2008 +
Lowest Score:	In Yorkshire	54	at Leeds 2003 $	108	at Leeds 1996 $
	Away	119:8	at Colchester 1987 $	123	at Colchester 1974 $
Best Batting:	In Yorkshire	J A Leaning 111*	at Scarborough 2014 +	R N ten Doeschate 119*	at Scarborough 2014 +
	Away	A W Gale 125*	at Chelmsford 2010 $	N Hussain 136*	at Chelmsford 2002 #
Best Bowling:	In Yorkshire	G B Stevenson 4-20	at Barnsley 1977 #	R E East 6-18	at Hull 1969 $
	Away	A L Robinson 4-31	at Leyton 1976 $	R E East 5-20	at Colchester 1979 $

Yorkshire versus:

Glamorgan

		By Yorkshire			Against Yorkshire	
Highest Score:	In Yorkshire	253:4	at Leeds 1991 $		216:6	at Leeds 2013 $
	Away	257	at Colwyn Bay 2013 $		285:7	at Colwyn Bay 2013 $
Lowest Score:	In Yorkshire	139	at Hull 1981 $		83	at Leeds 1987 +
	Away	93-8	at Swansea 1985 $		90	at Neath 1969 $
Best Batting:	In Yorkshire	96	A A Metcalfe	at Leeds 1991 $	97*	G P Ellis at Leeds 1976 $
	Away	141*	M D Moxon	at Cardiff 1991 #	127	A R Butcher at Cardiff 1991 #
Best Bowling:	In Yorkshire	5-22	P Carrick	at Leeds 1991 $	5-26	D S Harrison at Leeds 2002 $
	Away	6-40	R J Sidebottom	at Cardiff 1998 $	5-16	G C Holmes at Swansea 1985 $

Gloucestershire

		By Yorkshire			Against Yorkshire	
Highest Score:	In Yorkshire	263:9	at Leeds 2015 +		269	at Leeds 2009 +
	Away	262:7	at Bristol 1996 $		294:6	at Cheltenham 2010 $
Lowest Score:	In Yorkshire	115	at Leeds 1973 $		91	at Scarborough 2001 $
	Away	133	at Cheltenham 1999 $		90	at Tewkesbury 1972 $
Best Batting:	In Yorkshire	118	J A Rudolph	at Leeds 2009 +	146*	S Young at Leeds 1997 $
	Away	100*	J D Love	at Gloucester in 1985 $	143*	C M Spearman at Bristol 2004 $
	In Yorkshire	100*	R J Blakey	at Cheltenham 1990 $		
Best Bowling:	In Yorkshire	5-42	N D Thornicroft	at Leeds 2003 $	5-33	M C J Ball at Leeds 2003 $
	Away	4-25	R D Stemp	at Bristol 1996 $	5-42	M C J Ball at Cheltenham 1999 $

Hampshire

		By Yorkshire			Against Yorkshire	
Highest Score:	In Yorkshire	259:4	at Middlesbrough 1985 $		257:6	at Middlesbrough 1985 $
	Away	264:2	at Southampton 1995 $		348:9	at West End, Southampton, 2018 +
Lowest Score:	In Yorkshire	74:9	at Hull 1970 $		50	at Leeds 1991 #
	Away	118	at Southampton 1990 +		133	at Bournemouth 1976 $
Best Batting:	In Yorkshire	104*	D Byas	at Leeds 1999 #	155*	B A Richards at Hull 1970 $
	Away	97*	M G Bevan	at Southampton 1995 $	171	J M Vince at West End, Southampton, 2018 +
Best Bowling:	In Yorkshire	5-16	G M Hamilton	at Leeds 1998 $	5-33	A J Murtagh at Huddersfield 1977 $
	Away	5-33	A U Rashid	at Southampton 2014 +	5-31	D W White at Southampton 1969 $

358

LIST A HIGHEST AND LOWEST SCORES BY AND AGAINST YORKSHIRE PLUS INDIVIDUAL BEST BATTING AND BOWLING (Continued)

Yorkshire versus:

Kent

		By Yorkshire			Against Yorkshire		
Highest Score:	In Yorkshire	299:3		at Leeds 2002 $	232:8		at Leeds 2011 $
	Away	263:3		at Maidstone 1998 $	266:5		at Maidstone 1998 $
Lowest Score:	In Yorkshire	75		at Leeds 1995 $	133		at Leeds 1974 $
					133		at Leeds 1979 #
Best Batting:	Away	114		at Canterbury 1978 #	105	M H Denness	at Canterbury 1969 $
	In Yorkshire	130*	R J Blakey	at Scarborough 1991 $	118*	M H Denness	at Scarborough 1976 $
	Away	102	A McGrath	at Canterbury 2001 $	118*	C J Tavare	at Canterbury 1981 +
Best Bowling:	In Yorkshire	4-15	A G Nicholson	at Leeds 1974 $	6-32	M T Coles	at Leeds 2012 $
	Away	6-18	D Wilson	at Canterbury 1969 $	5-25	B D Julien	at Canterbury 1971 +

Lancashire

		By Yorkshire			Against Yorkshire		
Highest Score:	In Yorkshire	310		at Leeds 2019 +	311:6		at Leeds 2019 +
	Away	379:7		at Manchester 2018 +	363		at Manchester 2018 +
Lowest Score:	In Yorkshire	81		at Leeds 1998 $	68		at Leeds 2000 $
	In Yorkshire	81		at Leeds 2002 #			
Best Batting:	Away	125		at Manchester 1973 #	84		at Manchester 2016 +
	In Yorkshire	111*	D Byas	at Leeds 1996 $	102*	N J Speak	at Leeds 1992 $
	Away	144	A Lyth	at Manchester 2018 +	141*	B J Hodge	at Manchester 2007 +
Best Bowling:	In Yorkshire	5-25	C White	at Leeds 2000 #	6-25	G Chapple	at Leeds 1998 $
	Away	4-18	G S Blewett	at Manchester 1999 +	5-49	M Watkinson	at Manchester 1991 #

Leicestershire

		By Yorkshire			Against Yorkshire		
Highest Score:	In Yorkshire	379:7		at Leeds 2019 +	302:7		at Leeds 2008 $
	Away	376:3		at Leicester 2016 +	298:9		at Leicester 1997 $
Lowest Score:	In Yorkshire	93		at Leeds 1998 $	141		at Hull 1975 $
	Away	89:9		at Leicester 1989 $	53		at Leicester 2000 $
Best Batting:	In Yorkshire	156	G S Ballance	at Leeds 2019 +	108	N E Briers	at Bradford 1984 $
	Away	176	T M Head	at Leicester 2016 +	108	E J H Eckersley	at Leicester 2013 $
Best Bowling:	In Yorkshire	5-29	M W Pillans	at Leeds 2019 +	5-24	C W Henderson	at Leeds 2004 $
	Away	5-16	S Stuchbury	at Leicester 1982 $	4-25	J Ormond	at Leicester 2001 #

LIST A HIGHEST AND LOWEST SCORES BY AND AGAINST YORKSHIRE
PLUS INDIVIDUAL BEST BATTING AND BOWLING (Continued)

Yorkshire versus:

Middlesex

		By Yorkshire		Against Yorkshire	
Highest Score:	In Yorkshire	271:7	at Scarborough 1990 $	245:8	at Scarborough 2010 $
	Away	275:4	at Lord's 2011 $	273:6	at Southgate 2004 $
Lowest Score:	In Yorkshire	148	at Leeds 1974 $	23	at Leeds 1974 $
	Away	90	at Lord's 1964 +	107	at Lord's 1979 #
Best Batting:	In Yorkshire	124* J A Rudolph	at Scarborough 2010 $	104 P N Weekes	at Leeds 1996 +
	Away	116 A A Metcalfe	at Lord's 1991	125* O A Shah	at Southgate 2004 $
Best Bowling:	In Yorkshire	4-6 R Illingworth	at Hull 1983 $	4-24 N G Cowans	at Leeds 1986 +
	Away	4-28 H P Cooper	at Lord's 1979 #	5-44 T M Lamb	at Lord's 1975 #

Northamptonshire

		By Yorkshire		Against Yorkshire	
Highest Score:	In Yorkshire	314:8	at Scarborough 2016 +	314:4	at Leeds 2007 +
	Away	341:3	at Northampton 2006 +	351	at Northampton 2019 +
Lowest Score:	In Yorkshire	129	at Leeds 2000 $	127	at Huddersfield 1974 $
	Away	112	at Northampton 1975 $	109	at Northampton 2000 $
Best Batting:	In Yorkshire	125 A Lyth	at Scarborough 2016 +	132 U Afzaal	at Leeds 2007 +
	Away	152* G S Ballance	at Northampton in 2017 +	161 D J G Sales	at Northampton 2006 +
Best Bowling:	In Yorkshire	5-38 C M Old	at Sheffield 1972 $	5-16 B S Crump	at Bradford 1969 $
	Away	5-29 P W Jarvis	at Northampton 1992 $	5-15 Sarfraz Nawaz	at Northampton 1975 $

Nottinghamshire

		By Yorkshire		Against Yorkshire	
Highest Score:	In Yorkshire	352:6	at Scarborough 2001 $	251:5	at Scarborough 1996 $
				251:9	at Scarborough 2016 +
	Away	280:4	at Nottingham 2007 +	291:6	at Nottingham 2004 +
Lowest Score:	In Yorkshire	147	at Scarborough 1998 +	66	at Bradford 1969 $
	Away	140	at Nottingham 1975 $	134:8	at Nottingham 1973 $
Best Batting:	In Yorkshire	191 D S Lehmann	at Scarborough 2001 $	101 M J Harris	at Hull 1973 #
	Away	103 R B Richardson	at Nottingham 1993 $	123 D W Randall	at Nottingham 1987 $
Best Bowling:	In Yorkshire	5-17 A G Nicholson	at Hull 1972 $	5-41 C L Cairns	at Scarborough 1996 $
	Away	4-12 C M Old	at Nottingham 1977 $	5-30 F D Stephenson	at Nottingham 1991 #

LIST A HIGHEST AND LOWEST SCORES BY AND AGAINST YORKSHIRE
PLUS INDIVIDUAL BEST BATTING AND BOWLING (Continued)

Yorkshire versus:

		Somerset	By Yorkshire		Against Yorkshire		
Highest Score:	In Yorkshire	283:9		at Scarborough 2002 $	338:5		at Leeds 2013 $
	Away	343:9		at Taunton 2005 $	345:4		at Taunton 2005 $
Lowest Score:	In Yorkshire	110		at Scarborough 1977 $	103		at Sheffield 1972 $
	Away	120		at Taunton 1992 #	63		at Taunton 1965 +
Best Batting:	In Yorkshire	127	J A Rudolph	at Scarborough 2007 $	113	R T Ponting	at Scarborough 2004 $
	Away	148	A McGrath	at Taunton 2006 $	140*	P D Trego	at Taunton 2013 $
Best Bowling:	In Yorkshire	6-36	A G Nicholson	at Sheffield 1972 $	4-10	I T Botham	at Scarborough 1979 $
	Away	6-15	F S Trueman	at Taunton 1965 +	5-27	J Garner	at Bath 1985 $

		Surrey					
Highest Score:	In Yorkshire	289:9		at Leeds 2017 +	375:4		at Scarborough 1994 $
	Away	334:5		at The Oval 2005 $	329:8		at The Oval 2009 +
Lowest Score:	In Yorkshire	76		at Harrogate 1970 +	90		at Leeds 1996 $
	Away	128:8		at The Oval 1971 $	134		at The Oval 1969 +
Best Batting:	In Yorkshire	118*	J D Love	at Leeds 1987 $	136	M A Lynch	at Bradford 1985 $
	Away	146	G Boycott	at Lord's 1965 +	177	S A Newman	at The Oval 2009 +
Best Bowling:	In Yorkshire	5-25	D Gough	at Leeds 1998 $	7-33	R D Jackman	at Harrogate 1970 +
	Away	5-29	R Illingworth	at Lord's 1965 +	5-22	R D Jackman	at The Oval 1978 $

		Sussex					
Highest Score:	In Yorkshire	302:4		at Scarborough 2011 $	267		at Scarborough 2011 $
	Away	270		at Hove 1963 +	292		at Hove 1963 +
Lowest Score:	In Yorkshire	89:7		at Huddersfield 1969 $	85		at Bradford 1972 #
	Away	89		at Hove 1998 $	108		at Hove 1971 $
Best Batting:	In Yorkshire	132*	J A Rudolph	at Scarborough 2011 $	129	A W Greig	at Scarborough 1976 $
	Away	111*	J H Hampshire	at Hastings 1973 $	103	L J Wright	at Hove 2012 $
Best Bowling:	In Yorkshire	5-34	G M Hamilton	at Scarborough 2000 $	4-15	Imran Khan	at Sheffield 1985 $
	Away	5-13	D Gough	at Hove 1994 $	4-10	M H Yardy	at Hove 2011 $

361

LIST A HIGHEST AND LOWEST SCORES BY AND AGAINST YORKSHIRE PLUS INDIVIDUAL BEST BATTING AND BOWLING *(Continued)*

Yorkshire versus:

Warwickshire

		By Yorkshire		Against Yorkshire	
Highest Score:	In Yorkshire	274:3	at Leeds 2003 $	283:6	at Leeds 2016 +
	Away	281:8	at Birmingham 2017 +	309-3	at Birmingham 2005 $
Lowest Score:	In Yorkshire	158	at Scarborough 2012 $	59	at Leeds 2001 $
	Away	56	at Birmingham 1995 $	158:9	at Birmingham 2003 $
Best Batting:	In Yorkshire	139* S P Fleming	at Leeds 2003 $	118 I J L Trott	at Leeds 2016 +
	Away	100* J H Hampshire	at Birmingham 1975 $	137 I R Bell	at Birmingham 2005 $
Best Bowling:	In Yorkshire	5-31 M D Moxon	at Leeds 1991 #	4-16 N M Carter	at Scarborough 2012 $
	Away	4-27 H P Cooper	at Birmingham 1973 $	7-32 R G D Willis	at Birmingham 1981 #

Worcestershire

		By Yorkshire		Against Yorkshire	
Highest Score:	In Yorkshire	346:9	at Leeds 2018 +	350:6	at Leeds 2018 +
	Away	346:6	at Worcester 2015 +	342	at Worcester 2017 +
Lowest Score:	In Yorkshire	88	at Leeds 1995 #	86	at Leeds 1969 $
	Away	90	at Worcester 1987 $	122	at Worcester 1975 $
Best Batting:	In Yorkshire	101 M G Bevan	at Scarborough 1995 $	113* G A Hick	at Scarborough 1995 $
		101 C A Pujara	at Leeds 2018 $	115 Younis Ahmed	at Worcester 1980 #
	Away	142 G Boycott	at Worcester 1980 #		
Best Bowling:	In Yorkshire	7-15 R A Hutton	at Leeds 1969 $	5-36 Kabir Ali	at Leeds 2002 $
	Away	6-14 H P Cooper	at Worcester 1976 $	5-25 W D Parnell	at Worcester 2019 +

Bedfordshire +

		By Yorkshire		Against Yorkshire	
Highest Score:	Away	212:6	at Luton 2001	211:9	at Luton 2001
Best Batting:	Away	88 D S Lehmann	at Luton 2001	34 O J Clayton	at Luton 2001
Best Bowling:	Away	4-39 R J Sidebottom	at Luton 2001	4-54 S R Rashid	at Luton 2001

Berkshire +

		By Yorkshire		Against Yorkshire	
Highest Score:	Away	131:3	at Reading 1983	128:9	at Reading 1983
Lowest Score:	Away			105	at Finchampstead 1988
Best Batting:	Away	74* A A Metcalfe	at Finchampstead 1988	29 G R J Roope	at Reading 1983
Best Bowling:	Away	5-27 G B Stevenson	at Reading 1983	1-15 M Lickley	at Reading 1983

LIST A HIGHEST AND LOWEST SCORES BY AND AGAINST YORKSHIRE PLUS INDIVIDUAL BEST BATTING AND BOWLING (*Continued*)

Yorkshire versus:

Cambridgeshire +

	By Yorkshire		Against Yorkshire	
Highest Score: In Yorkshire	177:1	at Leeds 1986	176:8	at Leeds 1986
Away	299:5	at March 2003	214:8	at March 2003
Lowest Score: In Yorkshire			176:8	at Leeds 1986
Away	299:5	at March 2003	214:8	at March 2003
Best Batting: In Yorkshire	75 M D Moxon	at Leeds 1986	85 J D R Benson	at Leeds 1986
Away	118* M J Wood	at March 2003	53 N T Gadsby	at March 2003
Best Bowling: In Yorkshire	3-11 A G Nicholson	at Castleford 1967	2-8 D H Fairey	at Castleford 1967
Away	3-37 A K D Gray	at March 2003	3-53 Ajaz Akhtar	at March 2003

Cheshire +

	By Yorkshire		Against Yorkshire	
Highest Score: Away	160:0	at Oxton 1985	159:7	at Oxton 1985
Best Batting: Away	82* M D Moxon	at Oxton 1985	46 K Teasdale	at Oxton 1985
Best Bowling: Away	2-17 G B Stevenson	at Oxton 1985		

Combined Universities

	By Yorkshire		Against Yorkshire	
Highest Score: In Yorkshire	197:8	at Leeds 1990	200:8	at Leeds 1990
Away	151:1	at Oxford 1980	150:7	at Oxford 1980
Lowest Score: In Yorkshire	197:8	at Leeds 1990	200:8	at Leeds 1990
Away	151:1	at Oxford 1980	150:7	at Oxford 1980
Best Batting: In Yorkshire			63 S P James	at Leeds 1990
Away	74* C W J Athey	at Oxford 1980	63 J O D Orders	at Oxford 1980
Best Bowling: In Yorkshire	3-34 P J Hartley	at Leeds 1990	3-44 M E W Brooker	at Barnsley 1976
Away	2-43 H P Cooper	at Oxford 1980	1-16 C J Ross	at Oxford 1980

Devon +

	By Yorkshire		Against Yorkshire	
Highest Score: Away	411:6	at Exmouth 2004	279:8	at Exmouth 2004
Lowest Score: Away	259:5	at Exmouth 2002	80	at Exmouth 1998
Best Batting: Away	160 M J Wood	at Exmouth 2004	83 P M Roebuck	at Exmouth 1994
Best Bowling: Away	4-26 D S Lehmann	at Exmouth 2002	2-42 A O F Le Fleming	at Exmouth 1994

LIST A HIGHEST AND LOWEST SCORES BY AND AGAINST YORKSHIRE
PLUS INDIVIDUAL BEST BATTING AND BOWLING (*Continued*)

Yorkshire versus:

		By Yorkshire			Against Yorkshire		
Dorset +							
Highest Score:	Away	101:2		at Bournemouth 2004	97		at Bournemouth 2004
Best Batting:	Away	71*	M J Wood	at Bournemouth 2004	23	C L Park	at Bournemouth 2004
Best Bowling:	Away	4-18	C E W Silverwood	at Bournemouth 2004	2-31	D J Worrad	at Bournemouth 2004
Durham M C C +							
Highest Score:	In Yorkshire	249:6		at Middlesbrough 1978	138:5		at Middlesbrough 1978
	Away	214:6		at Chester-le-Street 1979	213:9		at Chester-le-Street 1979
Lowest Score:	In Yorkshire	135		at Harrogate 1973	136:7		at Harrogate 1973
	Away				213:9		at Chester-le-Street 1979
Best Batting:	In Yorkshire	110	J H Hampshire	at Middlesbrough 1978	52	N A Riddell	at Middlesbrough 1978
	Away	92	G Boycott	at Chester-le-Street 1979	52	Wasim Raja	at Chester-le-Street 1979
Best Bowling:	In Yorkshire	4-9	C M Old	at Middlesbrough 1978	5-15	B R Lander	at Harrogate 1973
	Away	3-39	H P Cooper	at Chester-le-Street 1979	2-35	B L Cairns	at Chester-le-Street 1979
Herefordshire +							
Highest Score:	Away	275:8		at Kington 1999	124:5		at Kington 1999
Best Batting:	Away	77	G S Blewett	at Kington 1999	39	R D Hughes	at Kington 1999
Best Bowling:	Away	2-22	G M Hamilton	at Kington 1999	2-41	C W Boroughs	at Kington 1999
Ireland +							
Highest Score:	In Yorkshire	299:6		at Leeds 1995	228:7		at Leeds 1995
	Away	202:4		at Belfast 2005	201:7		at Belfast 2005
Lowest Score:	In Yorkshire	249		at Leeds 1997	53		at Leeds 1997
	Away				201:7		at Belfast 2005
Best Batting:	In Yorkshire	113	C White	at Leeds 1995	82	S J S Warke	at Leeds 1995
	Away	58	M P Vaughan	at Belfast 2005	59	E J G Morgan	at Belfast 2005
Best Bowling:	In Yorkshire	7-27	D Gough	at Leeds 1997	3-26	P McCrum	at Leeds 1997
	Away	4-43	C White	at Belfast 2005	1-29	W K McCallan	at Belfast 2005

LIST A HIGHEST AND LOWEST SCORES BY AND AGAINST YORKSHIRE
PLUS INDIVIDUAL BEST BATTING AND BOWLING (Continued)

Yorkshire versus:

Minor Counties

		By Yorkshire		Against Yorkshire	
Highest Score:	In Yorkshire	309:5	at Leeds 1997	206:6	at Leeds 1988
	Away	218:3	at Scunthorpe 1975	182	at Scunthorpe 1975
		218:9	at Jesmond 1979		
Lowest Score:	In Yorkshire	309:5	at Leeds 1997	109	at Leeds 1974
	Away	218:3	at Scunthorpe 1975	85	at Jesmond 1979
		218:9	at Jesmond 1979		
Best Batting:	In Yorkshire	109* A McGrath	at Leeds 1997	80* J D Love	at Leeds 1991
	Away	83* G Boycott	at Chester-le-Street 1973	61 N A Folland	at Jesmond 1989
Best Bowling:	In Yorkshire	6-27 A G Nicholson	at Middlesbrough 1972	3-37 S Oakes	at Leeds 1997
	Away	5-32 S Oldham	at Scunthorpe 1975	3-27 I E Conn	at Jesmond 1989

Netherlands $

		By Yorkshire		Against Yorkshire	
Highest Score:	In Yorkshire	204:6	at Leeds 2010	200:8	at Leeds 2010
	Away	158:5	at Rotterdam 2010	154:9	at Rotterdam 2010
Lowest Score:	In Yorkshire	188:9	at Leeds 2011	190:8	at Leeds 2011
	Away	123	at Amsterdam 2011	154:9	at Amsterdam 2011
Best Batting:	In Yorkshire	83* J A Rudolph	at Leeds 2010	62 M G Dighton	at Leeds 2010
	Away	46* J M Bairstow	at Rotterdam 2010	34 P W Borren	at Rotterdam 2010
Best Bowling:	In Yorkshire	3-34 S A Patterson	at Leeds 2010	3-26 Mudassar Bukhari	at Leeds 2011
	Away	4-24 R M Pyrah	at Rotterdam 2010	3-28 Mudassar Bukhari	at Amsterdam 2011

Norfolk +

		By Yorkshire		Against Yorkshire	
Highest Score:	In Yorkshire	106:0	at Leeds 1990	104	at Leeds 1990
	Away	167	at Lakenham 1969	78	at Lakenham 1969
Lowest Score:	In Yorkshire			104	at Leeds 1990
	Away	167	at Lakenham 1969	78	at Lakenham 1969
Best Batting:	In Yorkshire	56* M D Moxon	at Leeds 1990	25 R Finney	at Leeds 1990
	Away	55 J H Hampshire	at Lakenham 1969	21 G J Donaldson	at Lakenham 1969
Best Bowling:	In Yorkshire	3-8 P Carrick	at Leeds 1990		
	Away	3-14 C M Old	at Lakenham 1969	6-48 T I Moore	at Lakenham 1969

LIST A HIGHEST AND LOWEST SCORES BY AND AGAINST YORKSHIRE
PLUS INDIVIDUAL BEST BATTING AND BOWLING (Continued)

Yorkshire versus:

Northumberland +

		By Yorkshire		Against Yorkshire	
Highest Score:	In Yorkshire	138: 2	at Leeds 1992	137	at Leeds 1992
Best Batting:	In Yorkshire	38	S A Kellett	at Leeds 1992	47 G R Morris	at Leeds 1992
Best Bowling:	In Yorkshire	3-18	M A Robinson	at Leeds 1992	2-22 S Greensword	at Leeds 1992

Scotland

		By Yorkshire		Against Yorkshire	
Highest Score:	In Yorkshire	317:5	at Leeds 1986 #	244	at Leeds 2008 +
	Away	259:8	at Edinburgh 2007 +	217	at Edinburgh 2007 +
Lowest Score:	In Yorkshire	228:6	at Bradford 1981 #	142	at Leeds 1996 #
	Away	199:8	at Edinburgh 2004 $	129	at Glasgow 1995 #
Best Batting:	In Yorkshire	118* J D Love	at Bradford 1981 #	73 I L Philip	at Leeds 1989 +
	Away	91 A A Metcalfe	at Glasgow 1987 #	78 J A Beukes	at Edinburgh 2005 $
Best Bowling:	In Yorkshire	5-28 C E W Silverwood	at Leeds 1996 #	2-22 P J C Hoffman	at Leeds 2006 +
	Away	4-20 R K J Dawson	at Edinburgh 2004 $	3-42 Asim Butt	at Linlithgow 1998 #

Shropshire +

		By Yorkshire		Against Yorkshire	
Highest Score:	Away	192	at Telford 1984	229:5	at Telford 1984
Lowest Score:	Away	192	at Telford 1984	185	at Wellington 1976
Best Batting:	Away	59 J H Hampshire	at Wellington 1976	80 Mushtaq Mohammad	at Telford 1984
Best Bowling:	Away	3-17 A L Robinson	at Wellington 1976	3-26 Mushtaq Mohammad	at Telford 1984

Unicorns $

		By Yorkshire		Against Yorkshire	
Highest Score:	In Yorkshire	266:6	at Leeds 2013	234	at Leeds 2013
	Away	191:5	at Chesterfield 2013	189-9	at Chesterfield 2013
Lowest Score:	In Yorkshire			150:6	at Leeds 2012
	Away			184	at Scarborough 2012
Best Batting:	In Yorkshire	139 G S Ballance	at Leeds 2013	107 M S Lineker	at Leeds 2013
	Away	103* G S Ballance	at Scarborough 2012	83* T J New	at Scarborough 2012
Best Bowling:	In Yorkshire	5-22 J A Leaning	at Leeds 2013	2-25 R J Woolley	at Leeds 2012
	Away	3-34 R M Pyrah	at Chesterfield 2013	2-31 W W Lee	at Chesterfield 2013

LIST A HIGHEST AND LOWEST SCORES BY AND AGAINST YORKSHIRE PLUS INDIVIDUAL BEST BATTING AND BOWLING (*Continued*)

Yorkshire versus:

		By Yorkshire		Against Yorkshire	
Wiltshire +					
Highest Score:	Away	304:7	at Trowbridge 1987	175	at Trowbridge 1987
Best Batting:	Away	85 A A Metcalfe	at Trowbridge 1987	62 J J Newman	at Trowbridge 1987
Best Bowling:	Away	4-40 K Sharp	at Trowbridge 1987	2-38 R C Cooper	at Trowbridge 1987
Yorkshire Cricket Board +					
Highest Score:	Away	240:5	at Harrogate 2000	110	at Harrogate 2000
Best Batting:	Away	70 M P Vaughan	at Harrogate 2000	31 R A Kettleborough	at Harrogate 2000
Best Bowling:	Away	5-30 D Gough	at Harrogate 2000	1-25 A E McKenna	at Harrogate 2000
Australians					
Highest Score:	In Yorkshire	188	at Leeds 1989	297:3	at Leeds 1989
Lowest Score:	In Yorkshire	140	at Bradford 1972	297:3	at Leeds 1989
Best Batting:	In Yorkshire	105 G Boycott	at Bradford 1972	172 D C Boon	at Leeds 1989
Best Bowling:	In Yorkshire	2-23 D Wilson	at Bradford 1972	3-30 D J Colley	at Bradford 1972
Bangladesh A					
Highest Score:	In Yorkshire	198	at Leeds 2013	191	at Leeds 2013
Best Batting:	In Yorkshire	47* L E Plunkett	at Leeds 2013	69 Anamul Haque	at Leeds 2013
Best Bowling:	In Yorkshire	5-30 Azeem Rafiq	at Leeds 2013	3-25 Elias Sunny	at Leeds 2013
South Africa A					
Highest Score:				129:4	at Leeds 2017
Best Batting:				56* K Zonda	at Leeds 2017
Best Bowling:	In Yorkshire	2-16 S A Patterson	at Leeds 2017		
Sri Lanka A					
Highest Score:	In Yorkshire	249	at Leeds 2014	275:9	at Leeds 2014
Lowest Score:	In Yorkshire	179:7	at Leeds 2004		
Best Batting:	In Yorkshire	81 A W Gale	at Leeds 2007	100 L D Chandimal	at Leeds 2014
Best Bowling:	In Yorkshire	5-51 A Shahzad	at Leeds 2007	4-42 S Prasanna	at Leeds 2014

367

LIST A HIGHEST AND LOWEST SCORES BY AND AGAINST YORKSHIRE PLUS INDIVIDUAL BEST BATTING AND BOWLING (Continued)

Yorkshire versus:

		By Yorkshire		Against Yorkshire		
West Indians						
Highest Score:	In Yorkshire	253-4	A McGrath	242		at Scarborough 1995
Best Batting:	In Yorkshire	106	A McGrath	54	R B Richardson	at Scarborough 1995
Best Bowling:	In Yorkshire	3-42	G M Hamilton	3-48	R Dhanraj	at Scarborough 1995
West Indians A						
Highest Score:	In Yorkshire	139	M J Wood	140-2		at Leeds 2002
Best Batting:	In Yorkshire	48	M J Wood	57	D Ganga	at Leeds 2002
Best Bowling:	In Yorkshire	1-31	C J Elstub	4-24	J J C Lawson	at Leeds 2002
Young Australians						
Highest Score:	In Yorkshire	224-6	M P Vaughan	156		at Leeds 1995
Best Batting:	In Yorkshire	76	M P Vaughan	51	A C Gilchrist	at Leeds 1995
Best Bowling:	In Yorkshire	5-32	A C Morris	2-21	S Young	at Leeds 1995
Zimbabwe						
Highest Score:	In Yorkshire	203-7		202		at Sheffield 1982
Best Batting:	In Yorkshire	98*	G Boycott	53	D A G Fletcher	at Sheffield 1982
Best Bowling:	In Yorkshire	3-47	P W Jarvis	3-30	D A G Fletcher	at Sheffield 1982

LIST A HIGHEST TEAM TOTALS

BY YORKSHIRE

411:6	v.	Devon at Exmouth	2004 +
379:7	v.	Lancashire at Manchester	2018 +
379:7	v.	Leicestershire at Leeds	2019 +
376:3	v.	Leicestershire at Leicester	2016 +
352:6	v.	Nottinghamshire at Scarboough	2001 $
349:7	v.	Derbyshire at Leeds	2017 +
346:9	v.	Worcestershire at Leeds	2018 +
345:5	v.	Nottinghamshire at Leeds	1996 +
345:6	v.	Worcestershire at Worcester	2015 +
343:9	v.	Somerset at Taunton	2005 $
341:3	v.	Northamptonshire at Northampton	2006 +
339:4	v.	Durham at Leeds	2017 +
334:5	v.	Surrey at The Oval	2005 $
330:6	v.	Surrey at The Oval	2009 +
328:4	v.	Durham at Chester-le-Street	2018 +
325:7	v.	Lancashire at Manchester	2016 +
324:7	v.	Lancashire at Manchester	2014 +
318:7	v.	Leicestershire at Leicester	1993 $
317:4	v.	Surrey at Lord's	1965 +
317:5	v.	Scotland at Leeds	1986 #
314:8	v.	Northamptonshire at Scarboough	2016 +
310:5	v.	Leicestershire at Leicester	1997 +
310	v.	Lancashire at Leeds	2019 +
309:5	v.	Minor Counties at Leeds	1997 #
307:3	v.	Essex at Chelmsford	1995 +
307:4	v.	Somerset at Taunton	2002 $
304:7	v.	Wiltshire at Trowbridge	1986 +

AGAINST YORKSHIRE

375:4	for Surrey at Scarborough	1994 $
363	for Lancashire at Manchester	2018 +
351	for Northamptonshire at Northampton	2019 +
350:6	for Worcestershire at Leeds	2018 +
348:9	for Hampshire at West End	2018 +
345:4	for Somerset at Taunton	2005 $
342	for Worcestershire at Worcester	2017 +
339:7	for Northamptonshire at Northampton	2006 +
338:5	for Somerset at Leeds	2013 $
335:5	for Durham at Leeds	2017 +
334:8	for Derbyshire at Leeds	2017 +
329:8	for Surrey at The Oval	2009 +
325:7	for Northamptonshire at Northampton	1992 $
314:4	for Northamptonshire at Leeds	2007 +
313:7	for Surrey at Leeds	2017 +
311:6	for Lancashire at Leeds	2019 +
310:7	for Northamptonshire at Scarboough	2016 +
309:3	for Warwickshire at Birmingham	2005 $
308:6	for Surrey at The Oval	1995 $
306:8	for Somerset at Taunton	2002 $
302:7	for Leicestershire at Leeds	2008 $
298:9	for Leicestershire at Leicester	1997 $
297:3	for Australians at Leeds	1989
294:6	for Gloucestershire at Cheltenham	2010 $
293:7	for Worcestershire at Worcester	2019 +
293:9	for Lancashire at Manchester	1996 +
293:9	for Leicestershire at Leicester	2018 +
292	for Sussex at Hove	1963 +

LIST A HIGHEST INDIVIDUAL SCORES

BY YORKSHIRE

191	D S Lehmann	v.	Nottinghamshire at Scarborough	2001 $
175	T M Head	v.	Leicestershire at Leicester	2016 +
174	J M Bairstow	v.	Durham at Leeds	2017 +
164	T Kohler-Cadmore	v.	Durham at Chester-le-Street	2018 +
160	M J Wood	v.	Devon at Exmouth	2004 +
156	G S Ballance	v.	Leicestershire at Leeds	2019 +
152 *	G S Ballance	v.	Northamptonshire at Northampton	2017 +
148	C White	v.	Leicestershire at Leicester	1997 $
148	A McGrath	v.	Somerset at Taunton	2006 +
146	G Boycott	v.	Surrey at Lord's	1965 +
144	A Lyth	v.	Lancashire at Manchester	2018 +
142	G Boycott	v.	Worcestershire at Worcester	1980 #
141*	M D Moxon	v	Glamorgan at Cardiff	1991 #
140	P S P Handscomb	v.	Derbyshire at Leeds	2017 +
139*	S P Fleming	v.	Warwickshire at Leeds	2003 $
139	G S Ballance	v.	Unicorns at Leeds	2013 $

AGAINST YORKSHIRE

177	S A Newman	for	Surrey at The Oval	2009 +
172	D C Boon	for	Australia at Leeds	1989
171	J M Vince	for	Hampshire at West End	2018 +
161	D J G Sales	for	Northamptonshire at Northampton	2006 +
155*	B A Richards	for	Hampshire at Hull	1970 $
146*	S Young	for	Gloucestershire at Leeds	1997 $
143*	C M Spearman	for	Gloucestershire at Bristol	2004 $
141*	B J Hodge	for	Lancashire at Manchester	2007 +
140*	P D Trego	for	Somerset at Taunton	2013 $
137*	M Klinger	for	Gloucestershire at Leeds	2015 +
137	I R Bell	for	Warwickshire at Birmingham	2005 $
136*	N Hussain	for	Essex at Chelmsford	2002 #
136	M A Lynch	for	Surrey at Bradford	1985 $
135*	D J Bicknell	for	Surrey at The Oval	1989 +
133	A D Brown	for	Surrey at Scarborough	1994 $

MOST RUNS IN LIST A MATCHES

742	v.	Lancashire at Manchester	2018 +	Y 379:7	L 363
696	v.	Worcestershire at Leeds	2018 +	W 350:6	Y 346:9
690	v.	Devon at Exmouth	2004 +	Y 411:6	D 279:8
688	v.	Somerset at Taunton	2005 $	S 345:4	Y 343:9
683	v.	Derbyshire at Leeds	2017 +	Y 349:7	D 334:8
680	v.	Northamptonshire at Northampton	2006 +	Y 342:3	N 339:7
674	v.	Durham at Leeds	2017 +	D 335:5	Y: 339-4
659	v.	Surrey at The Oval	2009 +	S 329:8	Y 330:6
633	v.	Worcestershire at Worcester	2017 +	W 342	Y 291
625	v.	Surrey at The Oval	2005 $	Y 334:5	S 291
624	v.	Northamptonshire at Scarborough	2016 +	N 310:7	Y 314:8
621	v.	Lancashire at Leeds	2019 +	L 311:6	Y 310
613	v.	Somerset at Taunton	2002 $	Y 307:4	S 306:8
605	v.	Leicestershire at Leeds	2008 $	Y 303:4	L 302:7
604	v.	Surrey at The Oval	1995 $	S 308:6	Y 296:6
602	v.	Surrey at Leeds	2017 +	S 313:7	Y 289:9
601	v.	Lancashire at Manchester	2014 +	Y 324:7	L 277

LIST A BEST BOWLING

BY YORKSHIRE

7-15	R A Hutton	v.	Worcestershire at Leeds	1969	$
7-27	D Gough	v.	Ireland at Leeds	1997	+
6-14	H P Cooper	v.	Worcestershire at Worcester	1975	$
6-15	F S Trueman	v.	Somerset at Taunton	1965	+
6-18	D Wilson	v.	Kent at Canterbury	1969	$
6-27	A G Nicholson	v.	Minor Counties at Middlesbrough	1972	#
6-27	P W Jarvis	v.	Somerset at Taunton	1989	$
6-32	S A Patterson	v.	Derbyshire at Leeds	2010	$
6-36	A G Nicholson	v.	Somerset At Sheffield	1972	$
6-40	R J Sidebottom	v.	Glamorgan at Cardiff	1998	$
5-13	D Gough	v.	Sussex at Hove	1994	$
5-16	S Stuchbury	v.	Leicestershire at Leicester	1982	$
5-16	G M Hamilton	v.	Hampshire at Leeds	1998	$
5-17	A G Nicholson	v.	Nottinghamshire at Hull	1972	$
5-18	P W Jarvis	v.	Derbyshire at Leeds	1990	$

AGAINST YORKSHIRE

7-32	R G D Willis	for	Warwickshire at Birmingham	1981	#
7-33	R D Jackman	for	Surrey at Harrogate	1970	+
6-15	A A Donald	for	Warwickshire at Birmingham	1995	$
6-18	R E East	for	Essex at Hull	1969	$
6-25	G Chapple	for	Lancashire at Leeds	1998	$
6-32	M T Coles	for	Kent at Leeds	2012	$
6-48	T I Moore	for	Norfolk at Lakenham	1969	+
5-15	B R Lander	for	Durham M C at Harrogate	1973	+
5-15	Sarfraz Nawaz	for	Northamptonshire at Northampton	1975	$
5-16	B S Crump	for	Northamptonshire at Bradford	1969	$
5-16	G C Holmes	for	Glamorgan at Swansea	1985	$
5-20	R E East	for	Essex at Colchester	1979	$
5-22	R D Jackman	for	Surrey at The Oval	1978	$
5-24	C J Tunnicliffe	for	Derbyshire at Derby	1981	#
5-24	C W Henderson	for	Leicestershire at Leeds	2004	$

LIST A ECONOMICAL BOWLING

BY YORKSHIRE

11-9-3-1	C M Old	v.	Middlesex at Lord's	1979	#
8-5-3-3	A L Robinson	v.	Derbyshire at Scarborough	1973	$

AGAINST YORKSHIRE

8-4-6-2	P J Sainsbury	for	Hampshire at Hull	1970	$
8-5-6-3	M J Procter	for	Gloucestershire at Cheltenham	1979	$

LIST A MOST EXPENSIVE BOWLING

BY YORKSHIRE

9-0-87-1	T T Bresnan	v.	Somerset at Taunton	2005	$

AGAINST YORKSHIRE

12-1-96-0	M E Waugh	for	Essex at Chelmsford	1995	+

LIST A HAT-TRICKS FOR YORKSHIRE (4)

P W Jarvis v. Derbyshire at Derby 1982 $ D Gough v. Ireland at Leeds 1997 +
D Gough v. Lancashire at Leeds 1998 $ C White v. Kent at Leeds 2000 $

LIST A MAN-OF-THE-MATCH AWARDS (137)

M D Moxon	12	M P Vaughan	5	M J Wood	3
G Boycott	11	A Sidebottom	4	R J Blakey	2
D L Bairstow	8	C E W Silverwood	4	G L Brophy	2
C White	8	D Byas	3	P Carrick	2
A A Metcalfe	7	D Gough	3	R A Hutton	2
J H Hampshire	6	P J Hartley	3	L E Plunkett	2
D S Lehmann	6	J D Love	3	P J Sharpe	2
C W J Athey	5	A McGrath	3	G B Stevenson	2
M G Bevan	5	C M Old	3		

One each: T T Bresnan, D B Close, M T G Elliott, G M Fellows, S D Fletcher,
G M Hamilton, S N Hartley, P M Hutchinson, R Illingworth, C Johnson, S A Kellett,
B Leadbeater, M J Lumb, A G Nicholson, S Oldham, S A Patterson, R M Pyrah,
P E Robinson, R D Stemp, F S Trueman and D Wilson.

ALL LIST A CENTURIES 1963-2019 (117)

C W J ATHEY (2)

118	v.	Leicestershire	at Leicester	1978 $
115	v.	Kent	at Leeds	1980 +

D L BAIRSTOW (1)

103 *	v.	Derbyshire	at Derby	1981 #

J M BAIRSTOW (2)

114	v.	Middlesex	at Lord's	2011 $
174	v.	Durham	at Leeds	2017 +

G S BALLANCE (4)

139	v.	Unicorns	at Leeds	2013 $
103 *	v.	Unicorns	at Scarborough	2012 $
152 *	v.	Northamptonshire	at Northampton	2017 +
156	v.	Leicestershire	at Leeds	2019 $

M G BEVAN (2)

103 *	v	Gloucestershire	at Middlesbrough	1995 $
101	v	Worcestershire	at Scarborough	1995 $

G BOYCOTT (7)

146	v	Surrey	at Lord's	1965 +
142	v	Worcestershire	at Worcester	1980 #
108 *	v	Northamptonshire	at Huddersfield	1974 $
106	v	Northamptonshire	at Bradford	1984 #
105	v	Australians	at Bradford	1972
104 *	v	Glamorgan	at Colwyn Bay	1973 $
102	v	Northamptonshire	at Middlesbrough	1977 #

R J BLAKEY (3)

130	v	Kent	at Scarborough	1991 $
105 *	v	Warwickshire	at Scarborough	1992 $
100 *	v	Gloucestershire	at Cheltenham	1990 $

H C BROOK (1)

103	v. Leicestershire	at Leeds	2019 +

D BYAS (5)

116 *	v. Surrey	at The Oval	1996 #
111 *	v. Lancashire	at Leeds	1996 $
106 *	v. Derbyshire	at Chesterfield	1993 $
104 *	v. Hampshire	at Leeds	1999 #
101 *	v. Nottinghamshire	at Leeds	1994 $

M T G ELLIOTT (3)

128 *	v. Somerset	at Lord's	2002 +
115 *	v. Kent	at Leeds	2002 $
109	v. Leicestershire	at Leicester	2002 $

S P FLEMING (1)

139 *	v. Warwickshire	at Leeds	2003 $

M J FOSTER (1)

118	v. Leicestershire	at Leicester	1993 $

A W GALE (2)

125 *	v. Essex	at Chelmsford	2010 $
112	v. Kent	at Canterbury	2011 $

J H HAMPSHIRE (7)

119	v. Leicestershire	at Hull	1971 $
114 *	v. Northamptonshire	at Scarborough	1978 $
111 *	v. Sussex	at Hastings	1973 $
110	v. Durham M C	at Middlesbrough	1978 +
108	v. Nottinghamshire	at Sheffield	1970 $
106 *	v. Lancashire	at Manchester	1972 $
100 *	v. Warwickshire	at Birmingham	1975 $

P S P HANDSCOMB (1)

140	v. Derbyshire	at Leeds	2017 +

T M HEAD (1))

175	v. Leicestershire	at Leicester	2016 +

P A JAQUES (1)

105	v. Sussex	at Leeds	2004 $

S A KELLETT (2)

118 *	v. Derbyshire	at Leeds	1992 $
107	v. Ireland	at Leeds	1995 +

T KOHLER-CADMORE (1)

164	v. Durham	at Chester-le-Street	2018 +

J A LEANING (2)

131 *	v. Leicestershire	at Leicester	2016 +
111 *	v. Essex	at Scarborough	2014 +

A Z LEES (1)

102	v. Northamptonshire	at Northampton	2014 +

D S LEHMANN (8)

191	v. Nottinghamshire	at Scarborough	2001	$
119	v. Durham	at Leeds	1998	#
118 *	v. Northamptonshire	at Northampton	2006	+
105	v. Glamorgan	at Cardiff	1995	+
104	v. Somerset	at Taunton	2002	$
103	v. Derbyshire	at Leeds	2001	#
103	v. Leicestershire	at Scarborough	2001	$
102 *	v. Derbyshire	ar Derby	1998	#

J D LOVE (4)

118 *	v. Scotland	at Bradford	1981	#
118 *	v. Surrey	at Leeds	1987	$
104 *	v. Nottinghamshire	at Hull	1986	$
100 *	v. Gloucestershire	at Gloucester	1985	$

R G LUMB (1)

101	v. Nottinghamshire	at Scarborough	1976	$

A LYTH (5)

144	v. Lancashire	at Manchester	2018	+
136 §	v. Lancashire	at Manchester	2016	+
132*	v. Leicestershire	at Leicester	2018	+
125 §	v. Northamptonshire	at Scarborough	2016	+
109 *	v. Sussex	at Scarborough	2009	$

(§ consecutive days)

A McGRATH (7)

148	v. Somerset	at Taunton	2006	$
135 *	v. Lancashire	at Manchester	2007	+
109 *	v. Minor Counties	at Leeds	1997	#
106	v. West Indies	at Scarborough	1995	
105 *	v. Scotland	at Leeds	2008	+
102	v. Kent	at Canterbury	2001	$
100	v. Durham	at Leeds	2007	+

G J MAXWELL (1)

111	v. Worcestershire	at Worcester	2015	+

A A METCALFE (4)

127 *	v. Warwickshire	at Leeds	1990	+
116	v. Middlesex	at Lord's	1991	$
115 *	v. Gloucestershire	at Scarborough	1984	$
114	v. Lancashire	at Manchester	1991	#

M D MOXON (7)

141 *	v. Glamorgan	at Cardiff	1991	#
137	v. Nottinghamshire	at Leeds	1996	+
129 *	v. Surrey	at The Oval	1991	$
112	v. Sussex	at Middlesbrough	1991	$
107 *	v. Warwickshire	at Leeds	1990	+
106 *	v. Lancashire	at Manchester	1986	#
105	v. Somerset	at Scarborough	1990	$

C A PUJARA (1)

101	v.	Worcestershire	at Leeds	2018 +

R B RICHARDSON (1)

103	v.	Nottinghamshire	at Nottingham	1993 $

J A RUDOLPH (9)

132 *	v.	Sussex	at Scarborough	2011 $
127	v.	Somerset	at Scarborough	2007 $
124 *	v.	Middlesex	at Scarborough	2010 $
120	v.	Leicestershire	at Leeds	2008 $
118	v.	Gloucestershire	at Leeds	2009 +
106	v.	Warwickshire	at Scarborough	2010 $
105	v.	Derbyshire	at Chesterfield	2010 $
101 *	v.	Essex	at Chelmsford	2010 $
100	v.	Leicestershire	at Leeds	2007 +

K SHARP (3)

114	v.	Essex	at Chelmsford	1985 $
112 *	v.	Worcestershire	at Worcester	1985 $
105 *	v.	Scotland	at Leeds	1984 #

S R TENDULKAR (1)

107	v.	Lancashire	at Leeds	1992 $

M P VAUGHAN (3)

125 *	v.	Somerset	at Taunton	2001 #
116 *	v.	Lancashire	at Manchester	2004 +
116 *	v.	Kent	at Leeds	2005 $

C WHITE (5)

148	v.	Leicestershire	at Leicester	1997 $
113	v.	Ireland	at Leeds	1995 +
112	v.	Northamptonshire	at Northampton	2006 +
101 *	v.	Durham	at Chester-le-Street	2006 +
100 *	v.	Surrey	at Leeds	2002 +

D J WILLEY (1)

131	v.	Lancashire	at Manchester	2018 +

M J WOOD (5)

160	v.	Devon	at Exmouth	2004 +
118 *	v.	Cambridgeshire	at March	2003 +
115 *	v.	Derbyshire	at Derby	2002 #
111	v.	Surrey	at The Oval	2005 $
105 *	v.	Somerset	at Taunton	2002$

YOUNUS KHAN (1)

100	v.	Nottinghamshire	at Nottingham	2007 +

LIST A PARTNERSHIPS OF 150 AND OVER 1963-2019 (51)

274	3rd wkt	T M Head (175)	and J A Leaning (131*)	v. Leicestershire at Leicester 2016+
242*	1st wkt	M D Moxon (107*)	and A A Metcalfe (127*)	v. Warwickshire at Leeds 1990 +
235	2nd wkt	A Lyth (144)	and D J Willey (131)	v. Lancashire at Manchester 2018 +
233*	1st wkt	A W Gale (125*)	and J A Rudolph (101*)	v. Essex at Chelmsford 2010 $
213	1st wkt	M D Moxon (141*)	and A A Metcalfe (84)	v. Glamorgan at Cardiff 1991 #
211*	1st wkt	M D Moxon (93*)	and A A Metcalfe (94*)	v. Warwickshire at Birmingham 1987 #
211	4th wkt	H C Brook (103)	and G S Ballance (156)	v. Leicestershire at Leeds 2019 +
207	4th wkt	S A Kellett (107)	and C White (113)	v. Ireland at Leeds 1995 +
202	2nd wkt	G Boycott (87)	and C W J Athey (115)	v. Kent at Leeds 1980 +
201	1st wkt	J H Hampshire (86)	and C W J Athey (118)	v. Leicestershire at Leicester 1978 $
198*	4th wkt	M T G Elliott (115*)	and A McGrath (85*)	v. Kent at Leeds 2002 $
195	1st wkt	A Lyth (84)	and A Z Lees (102)	v. Northamptonshire at Northampton 2014 $
192	2nd wkt	G Boycott (146)	and D B Close (79)	v. Surrey at Lord's 1965 +
190	1st wkt	G Boycott (89*)	and R G Lumb (101)	v. Nottinghamshire at Scarborough 1976 $
190	5th wkt	R J Blakey (96)	and M J Foster (118)	v. Leicestershire at Leicester 1993 $
189	2nd wkt	J M Bairstow (174)	and J E Root (55)	v. Durham at Leeds 2017 +
186	1st wkt	G Boycott (99)	and J H Hampshire (92*)	v. Gloucestershire at Scarborough 1975 $
186	1st wkt	G S Blewett (71)	and D Byas (104*)	v. Hampshire at Leeds 1999 #
184	3rd wkt	M P Vaughan (70)	and D S Lehmann (119)	v. Durham at Leeds 1998 #
181	5th wkt	M T G Elliott (109)	and A McGrath (78)	v. Leicestershire at Leicester 2002 $
176	3rd wkt	R J Blakey (86)	and S R Tendulkar (107)	v. Lancashire at Leeds 1992 $
176	2nd wkt	T Kohler-Cadmore (164)	and C A Pujara (82)	v. Durham at Chester-le-Street 2018 +
172	2nd wkt	D Byas (86)	and D S Lehmann (99)	v. Kent at Maidstone 1998 $
172	3rd wkt	A McGrath (38)	and D S Lehmann (191)	v. Nottinghamshire at Scarborough 2001 $
171	1st wkt	M D Moxon (112)	and A A Metcalfe (68)	v. Sussex at Middlesbrough 1991 $
170	4th wkt	M J Wood (105*)	and D S Lehmann (104)	v. Somerset at Taunton 2002 $
170	1st wkt	A W Gale (89)	and J A Rudolph (120)	v. Leicestershire at Leeds 2008 $
167*	6th wkt	M G Bevan (95*)	and R J Blakey ((80*)	v. Lancashire at Manchester 1996 #
167*	1st wkt	C White (100*)	and M J Wood (57*)	v. Surrey at Leeds 2002 +
167	1st wkt	M D Moxon(64)	and A A Metcalfe (116)	v. Middlesex at Lord's 1991 $
167	1st wkt	M J Wood (65)	and S P Fleming (139*)	v. Warwickshire at Leeds 2003 $
166	1st wkt	M D Moxon (82*)	and A A Metcalfe (70)	v. Northamptonshire at Leeds 1988 #
165	1st wkt	M D Moxon (80)	and D Byas (106*)	v. Derbyshire at Chesterfield 1993 $
165	1st wkt	M D Moxon (70)	and D Byas (88*)	v. Northamptonshire at Leeds 1993 $
164*	2nd wkt	G Boycott (91*)	and C W J Athey (79*)	v. Worcestershire at Worcester 1981 $

164	3rd wkt	A McGrath (105*)	and J A Rudolph (82)	v. Scotland at Leeds	2008 +
164	3rd wkt	J A Rudolph (84)	and A McGrath (73)	v. Glamorgan at Scarborough	2008 $
161	1st wkt	M D Moxon (74)	and A A Metcalfe (85)	v. Wiltshire at Trowbridge	1987 +
160*	1st wkt	G Boycott (70*)	and M D Moxon (82*)	v. Cheshire at Oxton	1985 +
160*	5th wkt	G M Fellows (80*)	and C White (73*)	v. Surrey at Leeds	2001 +
160*	3rd wkt	A Lyth (60*)	and G S Ballance (103*)	v. Unicorns at Scarborough	2012 $
160	1st wkt	G Boycott (67)	and J H Hampshire (84)	v. Warwickshire at Birmingham	1973 $
159	2nd wkt	G Boycott (92)	and D B Close (96)	v. Surrey at The Oval	1969 +
157	2nd wkt	K Sharp (71)	and R J Blakey (79)	v. Worcestershire at Worcester	1990 $
157	1st wkt	T Kohler-Cadmore (79)	and A Lyth (78)	v. Derbyshire at Leeds	2019 +
156	4th wkt	P S P Handscomb (140)	and G S Ballance (63)	v. Derbyshire at Leeds	2017 +
155*	1st wkt	A Lyth (67*)	and A Z Lees (69*)	v. Derbyshire at Scarborough	2014 +
154*	2nd wkt	J H Hampshire (111*)	and B Leadbeater (57*)	v. Sussex at Hove	1973 $
153	4th wkt	Younus Khan (100)	and A W Gale ((69*)	v. Nottinghamshire at Nottingham	2007 +
153	1st wkt	A Lyth (132*)	and T Kohler-Cadmore (74)	v. Leicestershire at Leicester	2018 +
150*	5th wkt	S N Hartley (67*)	and J D Love (82*)	v. Hampshire at Middlesbrough	1983 $

LIST A HIGHEST PARTNERSHIPS FOR EACH WICKET

1st wkt	242*	M D Moxon (107*)	and A A Metcalfe (127*)	v Warwickshire at Leeds	1990 +
2nd wkt	235	A Lyth (144)	and D J Willey (131)	v. Lancashire at Manchester	2018 +
3rd wkt	274	T M Head (175)	and J A Leaning (131*)	v.Leicestershire at Leicester	2016+
4th wkt	211	H C Brook (103)	and G S Ballance (156)	v.Leicestershire at Leeds	2019 +
5th wkt	190	R J Blakey (96)	and M J Foster (118)	v. Leicestershire at Leicester	1993 $
6th wkt	167*	M G Bevan (95*)	and R J Blakey ((80*)	v. Lancashire at Manchester	1996 #
7th wkt	149*	J D Love (118*)	and C M Old (78*)	v. Scotland at Bradford	1981 +
8th wkt	89	R J Blakey (60)	and R K J Dawson (41)	v. Leicestershire at Scarborough	2002 $
9th wkt	88	S N Hartley (67)	and A Ramage (32*)	v. Middlesex at Lord's	1982 $
10th wkt	80*	D L Bairstow (103*)	and M Johnson (4*)	v. Derbyshire at Derby	1981 #

C W J ATHEY (1)

5-35	v	Derbyshire	at Chesterfield	1981 $

AZEEM RAFIQ (1)

5-30	v	Bangladesh A	at Leeds	2013

M G BEVAN (1)

5-29	v	Sussex	at Eastbourne	1996 $

P CARRICK (2)

5-22	v	Glamorgan	at Leeds	1991 $
5-40	v	Sussex	at Middlesbrough	1991 $

H P COOPER (2)

6-14	v	Worcestershire	at Worcester	1975 $
5-30	v	Worcestershire	at Middlesbrough	1978 $

D GOUGH (4)

5-13	v	Sussex	at Hove	1994 $
7-27	v	Ireland	at Leeds	1997 +
5-25	v	Surrey	at Leeds	1998 $
5-30	v	Yorkshire C B	at Harrogate	2000 +

G M HAMILTON (2)

5-16	v	Hampshire	at Leeds	1998 $
5-34	v	Sussex	at Scarborough	2000 $

P J HARTLEY (4)

5-36	v	Sussex	at Scarborough	1993 $
5-38	v	Worcestershire	at Worcester	1990 $
5-43	v	Scotland	at Leeds	1986 #
5-46	v	Hampshire	at Southampton	1990 +

M J HOGGARD (3)

5-28	v	Leicestershire	at Leicester	2000 $
5-30	v	Northamptonshire	at Northampton	2000 $
5-65	v	Somerset	at Lord's	2002 +

R A HUTTON (1)

7-15	v	Worcestershire	at Leeds	1969 $

R ILLINGWORTH (1)

5-29	v	Surrey	at Lord's	1965 +

P W JARVIS (3)

6-27	v	Somerset	at Taunton	1989 $
5-18	v	Derbyshire	at Leeds	1990 $
5-29	v	Northamptonshire	at Northampton	1992 $

J A LEANING (1)

5-22	v	Unicorns	at Leeds	2013 $

A C MORRIS (1)

5-32	v	Young Australia	at Leeds	1995

M D MOXON (1)

5-31	v	Warwickshire	at Leeds	1991 #

A G NICHOLSON (4)

6-27	v	Minor Counties	at Middlesbrough	1972 #
6-36	v	Somerset	at Sheffield	1972 $
5-17	v	Nottinghamshire	at Hull	1972 $
5-24	v	Derbyshire	at Bradford	1975 #

C M OLD (2)

5-33	v	Sussex	at Hove	1971 $
5-38	v	Northamptonshire	at Sheffield	1972 $

S OLDHAM (1)

5-32	v	Minor Counties	at Scunthorpe	1975 #

S A PATTERSON (2)

6-32	v	Derbyshire	at Leeds	2010 $
5-24	v	Worcestershire	at Worcester	2015 +

M W PILLANS (1)

5-29	v	Leicestershire	Leeds	2019 +

A U RASHID (1)

5-33	v	Hampshire	at Southampton	2014 +

A SHAHZAD (1)

5-51	v	Sri Lanka A	at Leeds	2007

C SHAW (1)

5-41	v	Hampshire	at Bournemouth	1984 $

A SIDEBOTTOM (2)

5-27	v	Worcestershire	at Bradford	1985 #
5-27	v	Glamorgan	at Leeds	1987 +

R J SIDEBOTTOM (2)

6-40	v	Glamorgan	at Cardiff	2003 $
5-42	v	Leicestershire	at Leicester	2003 $

C E W SILVERWOOD (1)

5-28	v	Scotland	at Leeds	1996 #

G B STEVENSON (4)

5-27	v	Berkshire	at Reading	1983 +
5-28	v	Kent	at Canterbury	1978 #
5-41	v	Leicestershire	at Leicester	1976 $
5-50	v	Worcestershire	at Leeds	1982 #

S STUCHBURY (1)

5-16	v	Leicestershire	at Leicester	1982 $

N D THORNICROFT (1)

5-42	v	Gloucestershire	at Leeds	2003 $

F S TRUEMAN (1)

6-15	v	Somerset	at Taunton	1965 +

C WHITE (2)

5-19	v	Somerset	at Scarborough	2002 $
5-25	v	Lancashire	at Leeds	2000 #

D WILSON (2)

6-18	v	Kent	at Canterbury	1969 $
5-25	v	Lancashire	at Bradford	1972 #

ALL LIST A PLAYERS WHO HAVE TAKEN 4 WICKETS
IN AN INNINGS 1963-2019 (167) AND BEST FIGURES

11	C M Old	4-9	v	Durham M C	at Middlesbrough	1978 +
10	C White	4-14	v	Lancashire	at Leeds	2000 $
		4-14	v	Surrey	at The Oval	2005 $
9	A Sidebottom	4-15	v	Worcestershire	at Leeds	1987 #
8	P W Jarvis	4-13	v	Worcestershire	at Leeds	1986 $
8	D Gough	4-17	v	Nottinghamshire	at Nottingham	2000 #
8	G B Stevenson	4-20	v	Essex	at Barnsley	1977 #
7	S D Fletcher	4-11	v	Kent	at Canterbury	1988 $
6	C E W Silverwood	4-11	v	Leicestershire	at Leicester	2000 $
6	H P Cooper	4-18	v	Leicestershire	at Leeds	1975 +
5	S Oldham	4-13	v	Nottinghamshire	at Nottingham	1989 #
5	R M Pyrah	4-24	v	Netherlands	at Rotterdam	2010 $
4	P Carrick	4-13	v	Derbyshire	at Bradford	1983 $
4	R K J Dawson	4-13	v	Derbyshire	at Derby	2002 #
4	T T Bresnan	4-25	v	Somerset	at Leeds	2005 $
4	G M Hamilton	4-27	v	Warwickshire	at Birmingham	1995 $
3	R A Hutton	4-18	v	Surrey	at The Oval	1972 $
3	A G Nicholson	4-15	v	Kent	at Leeds	1974 $
3	P J Hartley	4-21	v	Scotland	at Glasgow	1995 #
3	A L Robinson	4-25	v	Surrey	at The Oval	1974 $
3	R D Stemp	4-25	v	Gloucestershire	at Bristol	1996 $
3	M P Vaughan	4-27	v	Gloucestershire	at Bristol	2000 $
3	S A Patterson	4-28	v	Worcestershire	at Worcester	2011 $
3	A U Rashid	4-38	v	Northamptonshire	at Northampton	2012 $
2	M K Bore	4-21	v	Sussex	at Middlesbrough	1970 $
		4-21	v	Worcestershire	at Worcester	1970 $
2	J D Woodford	4-23	v	Northamptonshire	at Northampton	1970 $
		4-23	v	Warwickshire	at Middlesbrough	1971 $
2	G J Kruis	4-17	v	Derbyshire	at Leeds	2007 $
2	D Wilson	4-22	v	Nottinghamshire	at Bradford	1969 $
2	V J Craven	4-22	v	Kent	at Scarborough	2003 $
2	M A Robinson	4-23	v	Northamptonshire	at Leeds	1993 $
2	S N Hartley	4-32	v	Derbyshire	at Leeds	1989 #
2	A U Rashid	4-38	v	Northamptonshire	at Northampton	2012 $
2	A McGrath	4-41	v	Surrey	at Leeds	2003 $
2	D J Willey	4-47	v	Derbyshire	at Derby	2018 +
1	R Illingworth	4-6	v	Middlesex	at Hull	1983 $
1	M Johnson	4-18	v	Scotland	at Bradford	1981 #
1	G S Blewett	4-18	v	Lancashire	at Manchester	1999 +
1	G M Fellows	4-19	v	Durham	at Leeds	2002 $
1	A P Grayson	4-25	v	Glamorgan	at Cardiff	1994 $
1	C J Elstub	4-25	v	Surrey	at Leeds	2001 $
1	D S Lehmann	4-26	v	Devon	at Exmouth	2002 +
1	C Shaw	4-29	v	Middlesex	at Leeds	1988 +
1	A G Wharf	4-29	v	Nottinghamshire	at Leeds	1996 #
1	F S Trueman	4-30	v	Nottinghamshire	at Middlesbrough	1963 —
1	J D Batty	4-33	v	Kent	at Scarborough	1991 $
1	P M Hutchinson	4-34	v	Gloucestershire	at Gloucester	1998 $
1	A K D Gray	4-34	v	Kent	at Leeds	2002 $

1	A Shahzad	4-34	v	Middlesex	at Lord's	2010 $
1	P M Stringer	4-35	v	Derbyshire	at Sheffield	1969 $
1	C S Pickles	4-36	v	Somerset	at Scarborough	1990 $
1	M J Hoggard	4-39	v	Surrey	at Leeds	2000 #
1	R J Sidebottom	4-39	v	Bedfordshire	at Luton	2001 +
1	K Sharp	4-40	v	Wiltshire	at Trowbridge	1987 +
1	T L Best	4-46	v	Essex	at Chelmsford	2010 $
1	Azeem Rafiq	4-47	v.	Lancashire	at Leeds	2017 $
1	A C Morris	4-49	v	Leicestershire	at Leicester	1997 $
1	L E Plunkett	4-52	v	Kent	Canterbury	2016 +
1	D B Close	4-60	v	Sussex	at Hove	1963 +
1	B O Coad	4-63	v.	Derbyshire	at Leeds	2017 +
1	M J Waite	4-65	v.	Worcestershire	at Worcester	2017 +

Roses centuries by the sea

Yorkshire's Director of Cricket, Martyn Moxon, was one of three centuries the last time Yorkshire hosted Lancashire in a County Championship match at Scarborough.

The *Roses* rivals will, this June, face each other at North Marine Road for the first time since September 1991, when opener Moxon posted a second-innings 115 in a 48-run victory.

David Byas, with 120, and Phil Robinson, 189, underpinned a first-innings 501-6 declared before Peter Hartley took five wickets in a reply of 403-7 declared. Moxon's 115 then led to a third declaration on 244-6, setting the *Red Rose* 343 on the final day.

Lancashire were bowled out for 294, Darren Gough matching Hartley's earlier five-for, but they were 129-8 before Ian Austin hit a blistering 101 to add 165 for the last two wickets.

Player	M	Inns	NO	Runs	HS	Av'ge	100s	50s	Runs	Wkts	Av'ge	Ct/St
Ashraf, M A ...	22	6	4	3	3*	1.50	0	0	895	23	38.91	4
Athey, C W J ...	140	129	14	3,662	118	31.84	2	25	431	19	22.68	46
Azeem Rafiq ...	30	21	8	222	52*	17.07	0	1	1,160	41	28.29	12
Bairstow, D L ..	403	317	71	5,180	103*	21.05	1	19	17	0	—	390/31
Bairstow, J M ..	43	39	4	1,051	174	30.02	2	3	0	0	—	33/3
Baker, T M	4	1	0	3	3	3.00	0	0	89	4	22.25	3
Balderstone, J C	13	11	2	173	46	19.22	0	0	38	2	19.00	3
Ballance, G S ..	67	62	9	2,853	156	53.83	4	18	0	0	—	23
Batty, J D	38	16	7	50	13*	5.55	0	0	1,297	42	30.88	18
Berry, P J	1	0	0	0	0	—	0	0	28	0	—	0
Best, T L	5	1	1	8	8*	—	0	0	166	10	16.60	1
Bevan, M G	48	45	12	2,110	103*	63.93	2	19	540	28	19.28	11
Binks, J G	30	21	2	247	34	13.72	0	0	0	0	—	26/8
Birkhead, B D ..	1	0	0	0		—	0	0	0	0	—	1
Blain, J A R	15	8	3	34	11*	6.80	0	0	462	14	33.00	3
Blakey, R J	373	319	84	7,361	130*	31.32	3	35	0	0	—	369/59
Blewett, G S ...	17	17	0	345	77	20.29	0	2	196	11	17.81	7
Booth, P A	5	2	1	7	6*	7.00	0	0	147	3	49.00	1
Bore, M K	55	24	10	90	15	6.42	0	0	1,600	50	32.00	15
Boycott, G	264	255	38	8,699	146	40.08	7	63	1,095	25	43.80	92
Bresnan, T T ..	181	130	31	2,124	95*	21.45	0	8	6,536	196	33.34	52
Broadhurst, M ..	1	0	0	0		—	0	0	27	0	—	0
Brook, H C	15	12	1	343	103	31.18	1	1	19	0	—	4
Brooks, J A	12	4	1	7	6	2.33	0	0	461	15	30.73	3
Brophy, G L ...	68	57	12	1,240	93*	27.55	0	9	0	0	—	67/14
Byas, D	313	301	35	7,782	116*	29.25	5	44	659	25	26.36	128
Callis, E	1	1	0	0	0	0.00	0	0	0	0	—	0
Carrick, P	304	206	53	2,159	54	14.11	0	2	7,408	236	31.38	70
Carver, K	15	4	4	52	35*	—	0	0	440	14	31.42	2
Chapman, C A ..	10	7	4	94	36*	31.33	0	0	0	0	—	7
Claydon, M E ..	7	2	0	15	9	7.50	0	0	293	8	36.62	0
Cleary, M F	4	3	1	50	23*	25.00	0	0	159	2	79.50	0
Close, D B	32	31	2	631	96	21.75	0	3	475	23	20.65	14
Coad, B O	17	6	5	15	9	15.00	0	0	748	20	37.40	5
Cooper, H P ...	142	74	34	483	29*	12.07	0	0	4,184	177	23.63	26
Cope, G A	37	20	13	96	18*	13.71	0	0	1,020	24	42.50	9
Coverdale, S P .	3	3	2	18	17*	18.00	0	0	0	0	—	3
Craven, V J	42	39	5	580	59	17.05	0	2	353	21	16.80	14
Dalton, A J	17	16	1	280	55	18.66	0	1	0	0	—	7
Dawood, I	25	20	4	260	57	16.25	0	1	0	0	—	18/8
Dawson, R K J ..	92	58	12	431	41	9.36	0	0	2,784	91	30.59	31
Dennis, S J	56	24	11	114	20	8.76	0	0	1,736	42	41.33	7
Elliott, M T G ..	6	6	3	394	128*	131.33	3	0	0	0	—	0
Elstub, C J	10	4	4	6	4*	—	0	0	290	12	24.16	0
Fellows, G	95	79	15	1,342	80*	20.96	0	6	836	22	38.00	27
Fisher, I D	28	12	3	68	20	7.55	0	0	708	29	24.41	6
Fisher, M D ...	27	14	9	201	36*	40.20	0	0	1,039	27	38.48	7
Fleming, S P ...	7	7	1	285	139*	47.50	1	1	0	0	—	3
Fletcher, S D ..	129	32	18	109	16*	7.78	0	0	4,686	164	28.57	34
Foster, M J	20	14	1	199	118	15.30	1	0	370	6	61.66	6
Fraine, W A R ..	8	8	0	0		—	0	0	0	0	—	6
Gale, A W	125	116	11	3,256	125*	31.00	2	17	0	0	—	24

Player	M	Inns	NO	Runs	HS	Av'ge	100s	50s	Runs	Wkts	Av'ge	Ct/St
Gibson, R	6	4	1	19	9	6.33	0	0	158	5	31.60	1
Gilbert, C R ...	5	4	0	55	37	13.75	0	0	199	8	24.87	2
Gillespie, J N ..	18	4	1	29	15*	9.66	0	0	601	18	33.38	6
Gough, D	214	120	33	1,280	72*	14.71	0	1	6,798	291	23.36	43
Gray, A K D ...	31	19	7	130	30*	10.83	0	0	843	25	33.72	8
Grayson, A P ..	66	49	8	587	55	14.31	0	1	1,441	39	36.94	19
Guy, S M	32	23	4	282	40	14.84	0	0	0	0	—	35/11
Hamilton, G M .	101	70	18	1,059	57*	20.36	0	2	2,803	121	23.16	15
Hampshire, A W	4	3	0	3	3	1.00	0	0	0	0	—	1
Hampshire, J H .	234	223	24	6,296	119	31.63	7	36	26	1	26.00	69
Hannon-Dalby, O J	5	1	1	21	21*	—	0	0	202	5	40.40	3
Handscomb, P S P	9	9	1	504	140	63.00	1	3	0	0	—	5
Harden, R J	19	16	2	230	42	16.42	0	0	0	0	—	1
Hartley, P J	219	145	49	1,609	83	16.76	0	4	7,476	283	26.41	40
Hartley, S N ...	171	154	31	2,815	83*	22.88	0	13	2,153	67	32.13	52
Harvey, I J	28	27	2	637	74	25.48	0	3	950	30	31.66	8
Head, T M	4	4	0	277	175	69.25	1	1	0	0	—	1
Hodd, A J	32	23	5	368	69*	20.44	0	1	0	0	—	39/8
Hodgson, D M .	12	10	1	272	90	30.22	0	3	0	0	—	10/2
Hodgson, L J ..	6	2	0	9	9	4.50	0	0	161	4	40.25	1
Hoggard, M J ..	83	28	19	41	7*	4.55	0	0	2,682	118	22.72	7
Hutchison, P M .	32	11	8	18	4*	6.00	0	0	844	43	19.62	3
Hutton, R A	107	80	25	1,075	65	19.54	0	4	3,000	128	23.43	27
Illingworth, R ..	41	15	11	171	45	42.75	0	0	793	40	19.82	14
Ingham, P G	12	10	4	312	87*	52.00	0	2	0	0	—	4
Inzamam ul Haq	3	3	0	69	53	23.00	0	1	0	0	—	0
Jaques, A	43	42	2	1,588	105	39.70	1	13	0	0	—	16
Jarvis, P W	144	74	28	529	42	11.50	0	0	4,684	213	21.99	33
Johnson, C	129	102	22	1,615	73*	20.18	0	4	28	2	14.00	33
Johnson, M	14	6	3	34	15*	11.33	0	0	455	12	37.91	2
Katich, S M ...	3	3	2	79	40*	79.00	0	0	0	0	—	2
Kellett, S A	56	51	3	1,207	118*	25.14	2	4	16	0	—	13
Kettleborough, R A	10	6	3	71	28	23.66	0	0	72	3	24.00	4
Kirby, S P	29	12	3	38	15	4.22	0	0	1,061	24	44.20	6
Kohler -Cadmore, T ..	17	16	0	762	164	47.62	1	6	0	0	—	16
Kruis, G J	55	22	11	138	31*	12.54	0	0	1,793	62	28.91	9
Lawson, M A K .	4	4	0	30	20	7.50	0	0	141	3	47.00	1
Leadbeater, B ..	105	100	19	2,245	90	27.71	0	11	95	5	19.00	26
Leaning, J A ...	47	40	7	1,024	131*	31.03	2	5	204	7	29.14	24
Lee, J E	4	0	0	0	0	—	0	0	116	7	16.57	0
Lees, A Z	42	39	2	1,109	102	29.97	1	8	0	0	—	15
Lehmann, D S .	130	126	20	5,229	191	49.33	8	38	1,990	79	25.18	41
Lester, E I	1	1	0	0	0	0.00	0	0	0	0	—	0
Loten, T W ..	1	0	0	0	—	—	0	0	0	0	—	0
Love , J D	220	203	33	4,298	118*	25.28	4	18	129	5	25.80	44
Lucas, D S	5	2	0	40	32	20.00	0	0	187	3	62.33	1
Lumb, M J	104	98	8	2,606	92	28.95	0	18	28	0	—	31
Lumb, R G	137	123	13	2,784	101	25.30	1	16	0	0	—	21
Lyth, A	121	114	8	3,574	144	35.41	5	18	373	6	62.16	53
McGrath, A	275	253	39	7,220	148	33.73	7	44	2,514	79	31.82	91
Maxwell, G J ...	8	7	1	312	111	52.00	1	2	144	3	48.00	4
Metcalfe, A A ..	194	189	15	5,584	127*	32.09	4	36	44	2	22.00	44
Middlebrook, J D	18	11	3	61	15*	7.62	0	0	530	13	40.76	5

Player	M	Inns	NO	Runs	HS	Av'ge	100s	50s	Runs	Wkts	Av'ge	Ct/St
Milburn, S M ..	4	2	1	14	13*	14.00	0	0	118	2	59.00	1
Miller, D A	3	3	0	45	44	15.00	0	0	0	0	—	3
Morris, A C	27	17	5	212	48*	17.66	0	0	464	21	22.09	5
Moxon, M D ...	237	229	21	7,380	141*	35.48	7	49	1,202	34	35.35	77
Nicholson, A G .	120	46	22	155	15*	6.45	0	0	2,951	173	17.05	16
Nicholson, N G .	2	2	1	1	1*	1.00	0	0	0	0	—	2
Old, C M	221	169	38	2,572	82*	19.63	0	10	5,841	308	18.96	56
Oldham, S	106	40	21	192	38*	10.10	0	0	3,136	142	22.08	17
Olivier, D	**5**	**3**	**3**	**17**	**8***	**—**	**0**	**0**	**262**	**2**	**131.00**	**1**
Padgett, D E V .	57	54	3	1,069	68	20.96	0	2	25	1	25.00	13
Parker, B	73	61	8	965	69	18.20	0	1	18	0	—	12
Patterson, S A .	**94**	**39**	**20**	**248**	**25***	**13.05**	**0**	**0**	**3,436**	**118**	**29.11**	**17**
Pickles, C S	71	48	20	375	37*	13.39	0	0	2,403	63	38.14	23
Pillans, M W ..	**7**	**5**	**1**	**54**	**31**	**13.50**	**0**	**0**	**344**	**16**	**21.50**	**2**
Plunkett, L E ...	28	21	10	327	53	29.72	0	1	1,060	33	32.12	17
Poysden, J E ..	**8**	**4**	**1**	**2**	**1**	**0.66**	**0**	**0**	**303**	**6**	**50.50**	**0**
Pyrah, R M	114	75	20	978	69	17.78	0	2	3,572	133	26.85	35
Pujara, C A	8	8	1	370	101	52.85	1	3	0	0	—	4
Ramage, A	34	17	8	134	32*	14.88	0	0	1,178	30	39.26	3
Ramsden, G	1	0	0	—	—	—	0	0	26	2	13.00	0
Rana Naved -ul-Hasan	17	16	1	375	74	25.00	0	3	681	26	26.19	5
Rashid, A U ...	**107**	**75**	**22**	**1,063**	**71**	**20.05**	**0**	**1**	**3,986**	**137**	**29.09**	**34**
Read, J	1	0	0	—	—	—	0	0	0	0	—	1
Rhodes, S J	2	1	0	6	6	6.00	0	0	0	0	—	3
Rhodes, W M H	21	17	2	252	46	16.80	0	0	364	11	33.09	8
Richardson. R B	28	28	6	993	103	45.13	1	8	0	0	—	5
Richardson, S A	1	1	0	7	7	7.00	0	0	0	0	—	0
Robinson, A L ..	92	36	19	127	18*	7.47	0	0	2,588	105	24.64	14
Robinson, M A .	89	30	16	41	7	2.92	0	0	2,795	91	30.71	7
Robinson, O E ..	3	2	2	16	12*	—	0	0	66	0	—	4
Robinson, P E ..	135	123	15	2,738	78*	25.35	0	14	0	0	—	47
Root, J E	**23**	**22**	**3**	**747**	**83**	**39.31**	**0**	**5**	**280**	**7**	**40.00**	**10**
Rudolph, J A ...	65	62	10	3,090	132*	59.42	9	19	37	0	—	32
Ryan, M	3	2	1	7	6*	7.00	0	0	149	5	29.80	3
Sadler, J L	1	1	0	19	19	19.00	0	0	0	0	—	0
Sanderson, B W	10	2	1	14	12*	14.00	0	0	247	8	30.87	5
Sayers, J	31	30	2	594	62	21.21	0	5	79	1	79.00	2
Scofield, D	3	1	0	0	0	0.00	0	0	111	2	55.50	1
Shahzad. A	30	22	7	243	59*	16.20	0	1	1,182	34	34.76	7
Sharp, K	206	191	18	4,776	114	27.60	3	28	48	4	12.00	68
Sharpe, P J	91	86	4	1,515	89*	18.47	0	8	11	0	—	53
Shaw, C	48	20	10	127	26	12.70	0	0	1,396	58	24.06	8
Sidebottom, A .	236	131	47	1,279	52*	15.22	0	1	6,918	260	26.60	51
Sidebottom, R J .	113	51	22	303	30*	10.44	0	0	3,631	124	29.28	24
Silverwood, C E W	166	94	33	892	61	14.62	0	4	5,212	224	23.26	25
Smith, N	7	2	1	5	5	5.00	0	0	0	0	—	2
Smith, R	3	2	0	17	17	8.50	0	0	0	0	—	1
Squires, P J	56	48	5	708	79*	16.46	0	3	4	0	—	10
Starc, M A	4	2	2	5	4*	—	0	0	181	8	22.62	1
Stemp, R D	88	28	10	118	23*	6.55	0	0	2,996	100	29.96	14
Stevenson, G B .	217	158	23	1,710	81*	12.66	0	2	6,820	290	23.51	38
Stott, W B	2	2	0	30	30	15.00	0	0	0	0	—	0

Player	M	Inns	NO	Runs	HS	Av'ge	100s	50s	Runs	Wkts	Av'ge	Ct/St
Stringer, P M ...	11	8	6	29	13*	14.50	0	0	256	15	17.06	0
Stuchbury, S ...	22	8	4	21	9*	5.25	0	0	677	29	23.34	2
Swallow, I G ...	8	5	3	37	17*	18.50	0	0	198	2	99.00	5
Swanepoel, P J .	3	2	2	9	8*	—	0	0	100	3	33.33	0
Tattersall, J A .	**15**	**11**	**2**	**375**	**89**	**41.66**	**0**	**4**	**0**	**0**	**—**	**16/3**
Taylor, C R	6	5	0	102	28	20.40	0	0	0	0	—	0
Taylor, K	10	10	0	135	30	13.50	0	0	168	11	15.27	3
Taylor, N S	1	0	0	0	0	—	0	0	45	1	45.00	1
Tendulkar, S R .	17	17	2	540	107	36.00	1	1	167	6	27.83	3
Thompson, J A	**1**	**0**	**0**	**0**	—	—	**0**	**0**	**43**	**0**	**—**	**0**
Thornicroft, N D	14	7	4	52	20	17.33	0	0	591	17	34.76	3
Townsley, R A J	5	4	1	81	34	27.00	0	0	62	0	—	1
Trueman, F S ...	11	9	1	127	28	15.87	0	0	348	21	16.57	5
Vaughan, M P ..	183	178	13	4,966	125*	30.09	3	29	1,860	60	31.00	56
Wainman, J C ..	4	3	1	51	33	25.50	0	0	201	5	40.20	1
Wainwright, D ...	48	21	13	150	26	18.75	0	0	1,427	38	37.55	16
Waite, M E	**13**	**11**	**3**	**278**	**71**	**34.75**	**0**	**1**	**522**	**16**	**32.62**	**0**
Wardlaw, I	17	10	4	56	18	9.33	0	0	686	24	28.58	3
Waring, J	1	1	1	1	1*	—	0	0	11	0	—	0
Warner, J D ...	**1**	**0**	**0**	**0**	—	—	**0**	**0**	**32**	**0**	**—**	**0**
Warren, A C ...	1	1	0	3	3	3.00	0	0	35	1	35.00	0
Wharf, A G	6	1	1	2	2*	—	0	0	176	8	22.00	1
White, C	292	266	39	6,384	148	28.12	5	28	6,120	248	24.67	84
Whiteley, J P ...	6	4	0	19	14	4.75	0	0	195	2	97.50	1
Widdup, S	4	4	0	49	38	12.25	0	0	0	0	—	2
Wigley, D H ...	1	1	0	0	0	0.00	0	0	38	0	—	0
Willey, D J	**20**	**16**	**2**	**448**	**131**	**32.00**	**1**	**2**	**808**	**33**	**24.48**	**5**
Williamson, K A	13	11	0	279	70	25.36	0	1	42	1	42.00	6
Wilson, D	61	47	8	430	46	11.02	0	0	1,527	76	20.09	22
Wood, G L	1	1	0	26	26	26.00	0	0	0	0	—	0
Wood, M J	145	134	14	3,270	160	27.25	5	14	76	3	25.33	57
Woodford, J D ..	72	57	14	890	69*	20.69	0	2	1,627	77	21.12	25
Younus Khan ...	11	8	0	248	100	31.00	1	0	144	2	72.00	5
Yuvraj Singh ...	9	9	0	196	50	21.77	0	1	197	3	65.66	1

LIMITED-OVERS INTERNATIONAL MATCHES
AT NORTH MARINE ROAD, SCARBOROUGH 1976-1978

1976 **England 202 for 8 wkts** (55 overs) (G D Barlow 80*, A M E Roberts 4 for 32).
West Indies 207 for 4 wkts (41 overs) (I V A Richards 119*).
West Indies won by 6 wickets **Award: I V A Richards**

1978 **England 206 for 8 wkts** (55 overs) (G A Gooch 94, B L Cairns 5 for 28).
New Zealand 187 for 8 wkts (55 overs) (B E Congdon 52*).
England won by 19 runs **Award: G A Gooch**

For England

YORKSHIRE ONE-DAY INTERNATIONAL CRICKETERS 1971-2019 (Correct to October 18, 2019)

Player	M	I	NO	Runs	HS	Av'ge	100s	50s	Balls	Runs	W	Av'ge	Best	4wI	Ct/St
ATHEY, C W J ..1980-88	31	30	3	848	142*	31.40	2	4	—	—	—	—	—	0	16
BAIRSTOW, D L ..1979-84	21	6	3	206	23*	14.71	0	0	—	—	—	—	—	0	17/4
BAIRSTOW, J M ..2011-19	74	68	8	2,861	141*	47.68	9	11	—	—	—	—	—	0	33/3
BALLANCE, G S ..2013-14/15	16	15	1	297	79	21.21	0	2	—	—	—	—	—	0	8
BLAKEY, R J ..1992-93	3	2	0	25	25	12.50	0	0	—	—	—	—	—	0	2/1
BOYCOTT, G ..1971-81	36	34	4	1,082	105	36.06	1	9	168	105	5	21.00	2-14	0	5
BRESNAN, T T ..2006-15	85	64	20	871	80	19.79	0	0	4,221	3,813	109	34.98	5-48	4	20
COPE, G A ..1977-78	2	1	1	1	1*	—	0	0	112	35	2	17.50	1-16	0	0
GOUGH, D ..1994-2006	158	87	38	609	46*	12.42	0	0	8,422	6,154	234	26.29	5-44	10	24
HAMPSHIRE, J H ..1971-72	3	3	1	48	25*	24.00	0	0	—	—	—	—	—	0	5
HOGGARD, M J ..2001-06	26	6	2	17	7	4.25	0	0	1,306	1,152	32	36.00	5-49	1	5
JARVIS, P W ..1988-93	16	8	2	31	16*	5.16	0	0	879	672	24	28.00	5-35	2	1
LOVE, J D ..1981	3	3	0	61	43	20.33	0	0	—	—	—	—	—	0	1
McGRATH, A ..2003-04	14	12	2	166	52	16.60	0	1	228	175	4	43.75	1-13	0	4
MOXON, M D ..1985-88	8	8	0	174	70	21.75	0	1	—	—	—	—	—	0	5
OLD, C M ..1973-81	32	25	7	338	51*	18.77	0	1	1,755	999	45	22.20	4-8	2	8
PLUNKETT, L E 2005/6-2019	89	50	19	646	56	20.83	0	1	4,137	4,010	135	29.70	5-52	7	24
RASHID, A U ..2009-19	99	43	12	588	69	18.96	0	0	4,851	4,547	143	31.79	5-27	9	30
ROOT, J E ..2012/13-19	143	135	21	5,856	133*	51.36	16	33	1,410	1,364	22	62.00	3-52	0	74
SHAHZAD, A ..2010-11	11	8	2	39	9	6.50	0	0	588	490	17	28.82	3-41	0	4
SIDEBOTTOM, R J ..2001-10	25	18	8	133	24	13.30	0	0	1,277	1,039	29	35.82	3-19	0	6
SILVERWOOD, C E W 1996-2001	7	4	3	17	12	4.25	0	0	306	244	6	40.66	3-43	0	0
STEVENSON, G B ..1980-81	4	4	0	28	28*	43.00	0	0	192	125	7	17.85	4-33	1	2
VAUGHAN, M P ..2001-07	86	83	19	1,982	90*	27.15	0	16	796	649	16	40.56	4-22	0	25
WHITE, C ..1994-2003	51	41	10	568	57*	15.77	0	1	2,364	1,726	65	26.55	5-21	1	12
WILLEY, D J ..2015-2019	46	27	5	279	50	18.60	0	1	1,971	1,889	52	36.32	4-34	2	21
For Scotland															
BLAIN, J A R ..1999-2009	33	25	6	284	41	14.94	0	0	1,329	1,173	41	28.60	5-22	4	8
HAMILTON, G M ..1999-2010	38	38	3	1,231	119	35.17	2	7	220	160	3	53.33	2-36	0	6/1
WARDLAW, I ..2012/14/15	22	14	8	21	7*	3.50	0	0	1,108	1,036	36	28.77	4-22	2	1

YORKSHIRE PLAYERS WHO PLAYED ALL THEIR ONE-DAY INTERNATIONAL CRICKET AFTER LEAVING YORKSHIRE

For England

Player	M	I	NO	Runs	HS	Av'ge	100s	50s	Balls	Runs	W	Av'ge	Best	4wI	Ct/St
BATTY, G J 2002-09	10	8	2	30	17	5.00	0	0	440	366	5	73.20	2-40	—	4
CLOSE, D B 1972	3	3	0	49	43	16.33	0	0	18	21	0	—	—	—	1
GRAYSON, A P ...2000-01	2	2	0	6	6	3.00	0	0	90	60	3	20.00	3-40	—	1
ILLINGWORTH, R .1971-72	3	2	0	5	4	2.50	0	0	130	84	4	21.00	3-50	—	1
LUMB, M J 2013/14	3	3	0	165	106	55.00	1	0	—	—	—	—	—	—	1
RHODES, S J 1989-95	9	8	2	107	56	17.83	0	1	—	—	—	—	—	—	9/2
WHARF, A G 2004-05	13	5	3	19	9	9.50	0	0	584	428	18	23.77	4-24	1	1
WOOD, B 1972-82	13	12	2	314	78*	31.40	0	2	420	224	9	24.88	2-14	—	6

Overseas Players
(Qualification: 24 List A matches for Yorkshire)

For Australia

Player	M	I	NO	Runs	HS	Av'ge	100s	50s	Balls	Runs	W	Av'ge	Best	4wI	Ct/St
BEVAN, M G ...1994-2004	232	196	67	6,912	108*	53.58	6	46	1,966	1,655	36	45.97	3-36	—	128
HARVEY, I J .1997/98-2004	73	51	11	715	48*	17.87	0	0	3,279	2,577	85	30.31	4-16	4	17
JAQUES, P A ...2006-2007	6	6	0	125	94	20.83	0	1	—	—	—	—	—	—	3
LEHMANN, D S .1996-2005	117	101	22	3,078	119	38.96	4	17	1,793	1,445	52	27.78	4-7	1	26

For South Africa

Player	M	I	NO	Runs	HS	Av'ge	100s	50s	Balls	Runs	W	Av'ge	Best	4wI	Ct/St
RUDOLPH, J A 2003-06	43	37	6	1,157	81	37.32	0	7	24	26	0	—	—	—	11

For West Indies

Player	M	I	NO	Runs	HS	Av'ge	100s	50s	Balls	Runs	W	Av'ge	Best	4wI	Ct/St
RICHARDSON, R B 1983-96	224	217	30	6,248	122	33.41	5	44	58	46	1	46.00	1-4	—	75

YORKSHIRE PLAYERS IN WORLD CUPS FOR ENGLAND

BATTING AND FIELDING

Player	Seasons	M	I	NO	Runs	HS	100s	50s	Avge	SR	ct/st
J M Bairstow	2019	11	11	0	532	111	2	2	48.36	92.84	9
G S Ballance	2015	4	4	0	36	10	0	0	9.00	50.70	1
G Boycott	1979	5	5	1	92	57	0	1	23.00	42.90	0
T T Bresnan	2011	7	5	1	41	20*	0	0	10.25	82.00	0
D Gough	1996										
	&1999	11	6	2	95	26*	0	0	23.75	73.07	2
C M Old	1975										
	&1979	9	7	2	91	51*	0	1	18.20	122.97	2
A U Rashid	2019	11	5	1	45	25	0	0	11.25	118.42	3
J E Root *	2015										
	&2019	17	16	2	758	121	3	3	54.14	88.03	20
A Shahzad	2011	2	2	1	7	6*	0	0	7.00	140.00	0
M P Vaughan	2003										
	&2007	14	14	0	348	79	0	3	24.85	71.02	3
C White	1996										
	&2003	7	5	1	92	35	0	0	23.00	98.92	1

* Joe Root's catching tally is an England record. Collingwood has 13, so he is way out in front. Only Ricky Ponting, of Australia, on 28, is ahead.

BOWLING

Player	Overs	Mdns	Runs	Wkts	Avge	BpW	Best	4wi	RPO
G Boycott	27	1	94	5	18.80	32.40	2-14	0	3.48
T T Bresnan	63	5	309	9	34.33	42.00	5-48	1	4.90
D Gough	99.4	8	430	15	28.66	39.86	4-34	1	4.31
C M Old	90.3	18	243	16	15.18	33.93	4- 8	1	2.68
A U Rashid	92	0	526	11	47.81	50.18	3-54	0	5.71
J E Root	19	0	111	3	37.00	38.00	2-27	0	5.84
A Shahzad	18	0	96	3	32.00	36.00	3-43	0	5.33
M P Vaughan	30	0	128	4	32.00	45.00	3-39	0	4.26
C White	51.3	6	202	9	22.44	34.33	3-33	0	3.91

Paul E Dyson

LIMITED-OVERS INTERNATIONAL MATCHES
AT HEADINGLEY, LEEDS 1973-2019

1973 **West Indies 181** (54 overs) (R B Kanhai 55). **England 182 for 9 wkts** (54.3 overs) (M H Denness 66).
England won by 1 wicket   **Award: M H Denness**

1974 **India 265** (53.5 overs) (B P Patel 82, A L Wadekar 67). **England 266 for 6 wkts** (51.1 overs) (J H Edrich 90).
England won by 4 wickets   **Award: J H Edrich**

1975 **Australia 278 for 7 wkts** (60 overs) (R Edwards 80*). **Pakistan 205** (53 overs) (Majid Khan 65, Asif Iqbal 53, D K Lillee 5 for 34).
Australia won by 73 runs   **Award: D K Lillee**

1975 **East Africa 120** (55.3 overs). **India 123 for 0 wkt** (29.5 overs) (S M Gavaskar 65* F M Engineer 54*).
India won by 10 wickets   **Award: F M Engineer**

1975 **England 93** (36.2 overs) (G J Gilmour 6 for 14). **Australia 94 for 6 wkts** (28.4 overs).
Australia won by 4 wickets   **Award: G J Gilmour**

1979 **Canada 139 for 9 wkts** (60 overs). **Pakistan 140 for 2 wkts** (40.1 overs) (Sadiq Mohammed 57*).
Pakistan won by 8 wickets   **Award: Sadiq Mohammed**

1979 **India 182 (55.5 overs)** (S M Gavaskar 55). **New Zealand 183 for 2 wkts** (57 overs) (B A Edgar 84*).
New Zealand won by 8 wickets   **Award: B A Edgar**

1979 **England 165 for 9 wkts** (60 overs). **Pakistan 151** (56 overs) (Asif Iqbal 51, M Hendrick 4 for 15)
England won by 14 runs   **Award: M Hendrick**

1980 **West Indies 198** (55 overs) (C G Greenidge 78). **England 174** (51.2 overs) (C J Tavaré 82*).
West Indies won by 24 runs   **Award: C J Tavaré**

1981 **Australia 236 for 8 wkts** (55 overs) (G M Wood 108). **England 165** (46.5 overs) (R M Hogg 4 for 29).
Australia won by 71 runs   **Award: G M Wood**

1982 **India 193** (55 overs) (Kapil Dev 60, I T Botham 4 for 56). **England 194 for 1 wkt** (50.1 overs) (B Wood 78*, C J Tavaré 66).
England won by 9 wickets   **Award: B Wood**

1983 **West Indies 252 for 9 wkts** (60 overs) (H A Gomes 78). **Australia 151** (30.3 overs) (W W Davis 7 for 51).
West Indies won by 101 runs   **Award: W W Davis**

1983 **Pakistan 235 for 7 wkts** (60 overs) (Imran Khan 102*, Shahid Mahboob 77, A L F de Mel 5 for 39). **Sri Lanka 224** (58.3 overs) (S Wettimuny 50, Abdul Qadir 5 for 44).
Pakistan won by 11 runs   **Award: Abdul Qadir**

1983 **Sri Lanka 136** (50.4 overs). **England 137 for 1 wkt** (24.1 overs) (G Fowler 81*).
England won by 9 wickets   **Award: R G D Willis**

1986 **New Zealand 217 for 8 wkts** (55 overs) (J J Crowe 66). **England 170** (48.2 overs).
New Zealand won by 47 runs   **Award: J J Crowe**

1988 **England 186 for 8 wkts** (55 overs). **West Indies 139** (46.3 overs).
England won by 47 runs   **Award: D R Pringle**

1990 **England 295 for 6 wkts** (55 overs) (R A Smith 128, G A Gooch 55). **New Zealand 298 for 6 wkts** (54.5 overs) (M J Greatbatch 102*, J G Wright 52, A H Jones 51).
New Zealand won by 4 wickets   **Award: M J Greatbatch**

1990 **England 229** (54.3 overs) (A J Lamb 56, D I Gower 50). **India 233 for 4 wkts** (53 overs) (S V Manjrekar 82, M Azharuddin 55*)
India won by 6 wickets   **Award: A Kumble**

1996 **India 158** (40.2 overs). **England 162 for 4 wkts** (39.3 overs) (G P Thorpe 79*).
England won by 6 wickets   **Award: G P Thorpe**

1997 **Australia 170 for 8 wkts** (50 overs).**England 175 for 4 wkts** (40.1 overs) (G P Thorpe 75*, A J Hollioake 66*).
England won by 6 wickets   **Award: G P Thorpe**

1998 **South Africa 205 for 8 wkts** (50 overs) (S M Pollock 56). **England 206 for 3 wkts** (35 overs) (A D Brown 59, N V Knight 51).
England won by 7 wickets   **Award: A D Brown**

1999 **Pakistan 275 for 8 wkts** (50 overs) (Inzamam-ul-Haq 81, Abdur Razzaq 60). **Australia 265** (49.5 overs) (M G Bevan 61, Wasim Akram 4-40).
Pakistan won by 10 runs   **Award: Inazmam-ul-Haq**

1999 **Zimbabwe 175** (49.3 overs) (M A Goodwin 57). **New Zealand 70 for 3 wkts** (15 overs).
No result   **No Award**

1999 **South Africa 271 for 7 wkts** (50 overs) (H H Gibbs 101, D J Cullinan 50). **Australia 275 for 5 wkts** (49.4 overs) (S R. Waugh 120*, R T Ponting 69).
Australia won by 5 wickets   **Award: S R Waugh**

2001 **England 156 (45.2 overs)** (B C Hollioake 53, Waqar Younis 7 for 36). **Pakistan 153 for 4 wkts** (39.5 overs) (Abdur Razzaq 75).
Pakistan won — England conceding the match following a pitch invasion.
                                                            Award: Waqar Younis

2002 **Sri Lanka 240 for 7 wkts** (32 overs) (S T Jayasuriya 112). **England 241 for 7 wkts** (31.2 overs) (M E Trescothick 82).
England won by 3 wkts   **Award: S T Jayasuriya**

2003 **England 81 for 4 wkts. Zimbabwe** did not bat.
No result   **No Award**

2004 **West Indies 159** (40.1 overs). **England 160 for 3 wkts** (22 overs) (M E Trescothick 55).
England won by 7 wickets   **Award: S J Harmison**

2005 **Bangladesh 208 for 7 wkts** (50 overs) (Belim 81, A Flintoff 4-29). **England 209 for 5 wkts** (38.5 overs) (A J Strauss 98)
England won by 5 wickets   **Award: A J Strauss**

Australia 219 for 7 wkts (50 overs) (P D Collingwood 4-34). **England 221 for 1 wkt** (46 overs) (M E Trescothick 104*, M P Vaughan 59*).
England won by 9 wickets   **Award: M E Trescothick**

2006 **England 321 for 7 wkts** (50 overs) (M E Trescothick 121, S L Malinga 4-44). **Sri Lanka 324 for 2 wkts** (37.3 overs) (S T Jayasuriya 152, W U Tharanga 109).
Sri Lanka won by 8 wickets   **Award: S T Jayasuriya**

2007 **India 324 for 6 wkts** (50 overs) (Yuvraj Singh 72, S R Tendulkar 71, S C Ganguly 59, G Gambhir 51). **England 242 for 8 wkts** (39 overs) (P D Collingwood 91*)
India won by 38 runs *(D/L Method)*   **Award: S C Ganguly**

2008 **England 275 for 4 wkts** (50 overs) (K P Pietersen 90*, A Flintoff 78). **South Africa 255** (J H Kallis 52).
England won by 20 runs   **Award: K P Pietersen**

2009 **England v. West Indies**   **Match abandoned without a ball bowled**

2010 **Pakistan 294 for 8 wkts** (50 overs) (Kamran Akmal 74, Asad Shafiq 50, S C J Broad 4-81). **England 295 for 6 wkts** (A J Strauss 126, I J L Trott 53)
England won by 4 wickets   **Award: A J Strauss**

2011 **Sri Lanka 309 for 5 wkts** (50 overs) (D P M D Jayawardene 144, K C Sangakkara 69) **England** 240 all out (E J G Morgan 52)
Sri Lanka won by 69 runs   **Award: D P M D Jayawardene**

2012 **England v. West Indies**   **Match abandoned without a ball bowled**

2013 **England v. Australia**   **Match abandoned without a ball bowled**

2014 **England 294 for 7 wkts** (50 overs) (J E Root 113). **India** 253 all out (48.4 overs) (R A Jadeja 87)
England won by 41 runs
Award: J E Root

2015 **Australia 299 for 7 wkts** (50 overs) (G J Bailey 75, G J Maxwell 85, M S Wade 50*). **England 304 for 7 wkts** (48.2 overs) (E J G Morgan 92, P J Cummins 4-49)
England won by 3 wickets
Award: E J G Morgan

2016 **Pakistan 247 for 8 wkts** (50 overs) (Azhar Ali 80, Imad Wasim 57*); **England 252 for 6 wkts** (48 overs) (B A Stokes 69, J M Bairstow 61)
England won by 6 wickets
Award: J M Bairstow

2017 **England 339 for 6 wkts** (50 overs) (A D Hales 61, E J G Morgan 107, M M Ali 77*). **South Africa** 267 (45 overs) (H M Amla 72, F du Plessis 67, C R Woakes 4-38)
England won by 72 runs
Award M M Ali

2018 **India 256 for 8 wkts** (50 overs) (V Kohli 71). **England 260 for 2 wkts** (44.3 overs) (J E Root 100*, E J G Morgan 88*)
England won by 8 wickets
Award: A U Rashid

2019 **England 351 for 9 wkts** (50 overs) (J E Root 84, E J G Morgan 76, Shaheen Afridi 4-82). **Pakistan** 297 (46.5 overs) (Babar Azam 80, Sarfaraz Ahmed 97, C R Woakes 5-54)
England won by 54 runs
Award: C R Woakes

2019 **Sri Lanka 232 for 9 wkts** (50 overs) (A D Mathews 85*). **England** 212 (47 overs) (B A Stokes 82*, S L Malinga 4-43)
Sri Lanka won by 20 runs
Award: S L Malinga

2019 **Afghanistan 227 for 9 wkts** (50 overs) (Shaheen Afridi 4-47). **Pakistan 230 for 7 wkts** (49.4 overs)
Pakistan won by 3 wickets
Award: Imad Wasim

2019 **West Indies 311 for 6 wkts** (50 overs) (E Lewis 58, S D Hope 77). **Afghanistan** 288 (50 overs) (Rahmat Shah 62, Ikram Ali Khil 86, C R Brathwaite 4-63)
West Indies won by 23 runs
Award: S D Hope

2019 **Sri Lanka 264 for 7 wkts** (50 overs) (A D Mathews 113). **India 265 for 3 wkts** (43.3 overs) (K L Rahul 111, R G Sharma 103)
India won by 7 wickets
Award: R G Sharma

SUMMARY OF RESULTS

ENGLAND	Played	Won	Lost
v. Australia	5	3	2
v. Bangladesh	1	1	0
v. India	7	5	2
v. New Zealand	2	0	2
v. Pakistan	5	4	1
v. South Africa	3	3	0
v. Sri Lanka	5	2	3
v. West Indies	4	3	1
v. Zimbabwe	1*	0	0
Totals	33	21	11

*No result. In addition to two matches v. West Indies abandoned and one match v. Australia abandoned

AFGHANISTAN	Played	Won	Lost
v. Pakistan	1	0	1
v. West Indies	1	0	1
Totals	2	0	2

AUSTRALIA	Played	Won	Lost
v. England	5	2	3
v. Pakistan	2	1	1
v. South Africa	1	1	0
v. West Indies	1	0	1
Totals	9	4	5

In addition to one match abandoned

BANGLADESH	Played	Won	Lost
v. England	1	0	1

INDIA	Played	Won	Lost
v. England	7	2	5
v. East Africa	1	1	0
v. New Zealand	1	0	1
v. Sri Lanka	1	1	0
Totals	10	4	6

NEW ZEALAND	Played	Won	Lost
v. England	2	2	0
v. India	1	1	0
v. Zimbabwe	1*	0	0
Totals	4	3	0

*No result

PAKISTAN	Played	Won	Lost
v. Afghanistan	1	1	0
v. Australia	2	1	1
v. Canada	1	1	0
v. England	5	1	4
v. Sri Lanka	1	1	0
Totals	10	5	5

SOUTH AFRICA	Played	Won	Lost
v. Australia	1	0	1
v. England	2	0	2
Totals	3	0	3

SRI LANKA	Played	Won	Lost
v. England	5	3	2
v. India	1	0	1
v. Pakistan	1	0	1
Totals	7	3	4

WEST INDIES	Played	Won	Lost
v. Afghanistan	1	1	0
v. Australia	1	1	0
v. England	4	1	3
Totals	6	3	3

In addition to two matches abandoned

SUMMARY OF RESULTS *(Continued)*

ZIMBABWE	Played	Won	Lost
v. England	1*	0	0
v. New Zealand	1*	0	0
Totals	2*	0	0

*No result

CANADA	Played	Won	Lost
v. Pakistan	1	0	1

EAST AFRICA	Played	Won	Lost
v. India	1	0	1

CENTURIES

152	S J Jayasuriya	for Sri Lanka	v. England	2006
144	D P M D Jayawardene	for Sri Lanka	v. England	2011
128	R A Smith	for England	v. New Zealand	1990
126	A J Strauss	for England	v. Pakistan	2010
121	M E Trescothick	for England	v. Sri Lanka	2006
120*	S R Waugh	for Australia	v. South Africa	1999
113	J E Root	for England	v. India	2014
113	A M Mathews	for Sri Lanka	v. India	2019
112	S J Jayasuriya	for Sri Lanka	v. England	2002
111	K L Rahul	for India	v. Sri Lanka	2019
109	W U Tharanga	for Sri Lanka	v. England	2006
108	G M Wood	for Australia	v. England	1981
104*	M E Trescothick	for England	v. Australia	2005
103	R G Sharma	for India	v. Sri Lanka	2019
102*	Imran Khan	for Pakistan	v. Sri Lanka	1983
102*	M J Greatbatch	for New Zealand	v. England	1990
101	H H Gibbs	for South Africa	v. Australia	1999
100*	J E Root	for England	v. India	2018

4 WICKETS IN AN INNINGS

7-36	Waqar Younis	for Pakistan	v. England	2001
7-51	W W Davis	for West Indies	v. Australia	1983
6-14	G J Gilmour	for Australia	v. England	1975
5-34	D K Lillee	for Australia	v. Pakistan	1975
5-39	A L F de Mel	for Sri Lanka	v. Pakistan	1983
5-44	Abdul Qadir	for Pakistan	v. Sri Lanka	1983
5-54	C R Woakes	for England	v. Pakistan	2019
4-15	M Hendrick	for England	v. Pakistan	1979
4-29	R M Hogg	for Australia	v England	1981
4-29	A Flintoff	for England	v. Bangladesh	2005
4-34	P D Collingwood	for England	v. Australia	2005
4-38	C R Woakes	for England	v. South Africa	2017
4-40	Wasim Akram	for Pakistan	v. Australia	1999
4-43	S L Malinga	for Sri Lanka	v. England	2019
4-44	S L Malinga	for Sri Lanka	v. England	2006
4-47	Shaheen Afridi	for Pakistan	v. Afghanistan	2019
4-49	P J Cummins	Australia	v. England	2015
4-56	I T Botham	for England	v. India	1982
4-81	S J C Broad	for England	v. Pakistan	2010

YORKSHIRE T20i CRICKETERS 2003-2019 (Correct to November 12, 2019)

For England

Player	M	I	NO	Runs	HS	Av'ge	100s	50s	Balls	Runs	W	Av'ge	Best	4wI	Ct/St
BAIRSTOW, J M ...2011-19	34	29	6	603	68	26.21	0	3	—	—	—	—	—	0	30
BRESNAN, T T ..2006-13/14	34	22	9	216	47*	16.61	0	0	663	837	24	36.95	3-10	0	10
PLUNKETT, L E ...2006-19	22	11	4	42	18	6.00	0	0	476	627	25	25.08	3-21	0	7
RASHID, A U ...2009-19	40	15	8	51	9*	7.28	0	0	798	1000	39	25.64	3-11	0	10
ROOT, J E ...2012-19	32	30	5	893	90*	35.72	0	5	84	139	6	23.16	2- 9	0	18
SHAHZAD, A ...2010-11	3	1	1	0	0*	—	0	0	66	97	3	32.33	2-38	0	1
VAUGHAN, M P" ...2005-7	2	2	0	27	27	13.50	0	0	—	—	—	—	—	0	0
WILLEY, D J ...2015-19	28	19	7	166	29*	13.83	0	0	557	761	34	22.38	4- 7	1	12

For Scotland

Player	M	I	NO	Runs	HS	Av'ge	100s	50s	Balls	Runs	W	Av'ge	Best	4wI	Ct/St
BLAIN, J A R ...2007-8	6	3	1	4	3*	2.00	0	0	120	108	6	18.00	2-23	0	1
HAMILTON, G M ...2007-10	12	8	0	90	32	11.25	0	0	—	—	—	—	—	0	3
WARDLAW, I 2012/13-13/14	4	1	0	1	1	1.00	0	0	96	145	9	16.11	4-40	0	0

YORKSHIRE PLAYERS WHO PLAYED ALL THEIR T20i CRICKET AFTER LEAVING YORKSHIRE

For England

Player	M	I	NO	Runs	HS	Av'ge	100s	50s	Balls	Runs	W	Av'ge	Best	4wI	Ct/St
BATTY, G J ...2009	1	1	0	4	4	4.00	0	0	18	17	0	—	—	0	0
GOUGH, D ...2005-06	2	0	0	0	—	—	0	0	41	49	3	16.33	3-16	0	0
LUMB, M J ...2010-13/14	27	27	1	552	63	21.23	0	3	—	—	—	—	—	0	8
SIDEBOTTOM, R J ...2007-10	18	1	1	5	5*	—	0	0	367	437	23	19.00	3-16	0	5

Overseas Players
(Qualification: 20 t20 matches for Yorkshire)

For South Africa

Player	M	I	NO	Runs	HS	Av'ge	100s	50s	Balls	Runs	W	Av'ge	Best	4wI	Ct/St
RUDOLPH, J A ...2006	1	1	1	6	6*	—	0	0	—	—	—	—	—	0	0

		Yorkshire's Position			*Yorkshire's Position*
2003	Surrey	Group N 2 (6)	2012	Hampshire	Final
2004	Leicestershire	Group N 5 (6)	2013	Northamptonshire	Group N 6 (6)
2005	Somerset	Group N 4 (6)	2014	Warwickshire	Group N 5 (9)
2006	Leicestershire	Quarter-Final	2015	Lancashire	Group N 8 (9)
2007	Kent	Quarter-Final	2016	Northamptonshire	Semi-Final
2008	Middlesex	Group N 3 (6)	2017	Nottinghamshire	Group N 5 (9)
2009	Sussex	Group N 5 (6)	2018	Worcestershire	Group N 5 (9)
2010	Hampshire	Group N 6 (9)	2019	Essex	Group N 5 (9)
2011	Leicestershire	Group N 6 (9)			

SEASON-BY-SEASON RECORD OF ALL T20 MATCHES
PLAYED BY YORKSHIRE 2003-2019

Season	Played	Won	Lost	Tie	N R	Abd	Season	Played	Won	Lost	Tie	N R	Abd
2003	5	3	2	0	0	0	2012/13	6	2	3	0	1	0
2004	5	2	3	0	0	0	2013	10	2	7	1	0	0
2005	8	3	5	0	0	0	2014	11	6	5	0	0	3
2006	9	4	4	0	1	0	2015	14	5	8	1	0	0
2007	8	4	4	0	0	1	2016	15	8	6	0	1	1
2008	9	5	3	1	0	1	2017	12	6	5	1	0	2
2009	10	4	6	0	0	0	2018	16	8	8	0	0	0
2010	16	6	9	1	0	0	2019	10	4	5	1	0	4
2011	15	6	7	0	2	1							
2012	12	9	2	0	1	1		191	87	92	6	6	14

ANALYSIS OF T20 RESULTS V. ALL TEAMS 2003-2019
DOMESTIC MATCHES

Opponents	Played	HOME Won	Lost	Tied	N. R	AWAY Won	Lost	Tied	N. R	Abd
Derbyshire	29	8	8	0	0	8	4	0	1	0
Durham	32	10	4	1	0	7	9	0	1	1
Essex	1	0	0	0	0	0	1	0	0	0
Glamorgan	1	0	0	0	0	1	0	0	0	0
Hampshire	1	0	0	0	0	0	1	0	0	0
Lancashire	28	8	5	1	0	4	9	1	0	4
Leicestershire	22	5	5	0	0	4	7	1	0	1
Northamptonshire	13	4	3	0	0	4	1	1	0	3
Nottinghamshire	30	6	7	0	1	4	12	0	0	2
Sussex	2	0	0	0	0	1	1	0	0	0
Warwickshire	14	4	3	1	0	1	3	0	2	2
Worcestershire	10	4	2	0	0	1	3	0	0	1
Total	**183**	**49**	**37**	**3**	**1**	**35**	**51**	**3**	**4**	**14**

Abandoned matches are not included in the list of matches played.

ANALYSIS OF T20 RESULTS V. ALL TEAMS 2003-2019 *(Cont)*
OTHER MATCHES

Opponents	Played	HOME				AWAY				
		Won	Lost	Tied	N. R	Won	Lost	Tied	N. R	Abd
Uva	1	0	0	0	0	1	0	0	0	0
Trinidad and Tobago	1	0	0	0	0	1	0	0	0	0
Sydney Sixers	1	0	0	0	0	0	1	0	0	0
Mumbai	1	0	0	0	0	0	0	0	1	0
Highveld	1	0	0	0	0	0	1	0	0	0
Chennai	1	0	0	0	0	0	1	0	0	0
Lahore Qalandars	1	0	0	0	0	0	1	0	0	0
Hobart Hurricanes	1	0	0	0	1	0	0	0	0	0
Total	**8**	**0**	**0**	**0**	**0**	**3**	**4**	**0**	**1**	**0**
Grand Total	**191**	**49**	**37**	**3**	**1**	**38**	**55**	**3**	**5**	**14**

ABANDONED T20 MATCHES (14)

2007	v. Lancashire at Leeds	2017	v. Northamptonshire at Northampton
2008	v. Leicestershire at Leeds		v. Warwickshire at Birmingham
2011	v. Northamptonshire at Leeds	2019	v. Nottinghamshire at Leeds
2012	v. Lancashire at Manchester		v. Northamptonshire at Northampton
2014	v. Warwickshire at Birmingham		v. Lancashire at Manchester
	v. Lancashire at Leeds		v. Durham at Leeds
	v. Worcestershire at Worcester		
2016	v. Nottinghamshire at Leeds		

T20 HIGHEST TEAM TOTALS

BY YORKSHIRE

260-4	v.	Northamptonshire at Leeds	2017
255:2	v.	Leicestershire at Leicester	2019
233-6	v.	Worcestershire at Leeds	2017
227-5	v.	Nottinghamshire at Leeds	2017
223-5	v.	Nottinghamshire at Nottingham	2017
226:8	v.	Birmingham Bears at Leeds	2018
223:6	v.	Durham at Leeds	2016
215:6	v.	Northamptonshire at Leeds	2016
213:7	v.	Worcestershire at Leeds	2010
212:5	v.	Worcestershire at Leeds	2012
211:6	v.	Leicestershire at Leeds	2004
210:3	v.	Derbyshire at Derby	2006
209:4	v.	Nottinghamshire at Leeds	2015
207:7	v.	Nottinghamshire at Nottingham	2004
202:8	v.	Lancashire at Manchester	2015
200:3	v.	Durham at Leeds	2018
200:3	v.	Birmingham Bears at Birmingham	2019
200:5	v.	Nottinghamshire at Leeds	2014

T20 HIGHEST TEAM TOTALS

AGAINST YORKSHIRE

231:6	for Lancashire at Manchester	2015
225:5	for Nottinghamshire at Nottingham	2017
222:6	for Derbyshire at Leeds	2010
221:3	for Leicestershire at Leeds	2004
215:6	for Nottinghamshire at Nottingham	2011
215:6	for Durham at Chester-le-Street	2013
212:5	for Nottinghamshire at Nottingham	2018
210:7	for Nottinghamshire at Nottingham	2004
208:7	for Worcestershire at Worcester	2010
207:5	for Derbyshire at Leeds	2019
207:6	for Lancashire at Manchester	2005
201:4	for Leicestershire at Leicester	2019
201:5	for Nottinghamshire at Leeds	2014
204:7	for Lancashire at Manchester	2016
196:7	for Worcestershire at Leeds	2017
195:8	for Derbyshire at Leeds	2005
195:4	for Nottinghamshire at Nottingham	2006
193:5	for Sussex at Hove	2007

T20 HIGHEST INDIVIDUAL SCORES

BY YORKSHIRE

161	A Lyth	v.	Northamptonshire at Leeds	2017
118	D J Willey	v.	Worcestershire at Leeds	2017
109	I J Harvey	v.	Derbyshire at Leeds	2005
108*	I J Harvey	v.	Lancashire at Leeds	2004
102*	J M Bairstow	v	Durham at Chester-le-Street	2014
101*	H H Gibbs	v.	Northamptonshire at Northampton	2010
96*	M J Wood	v.	Nottinghamshire at Nottingham	2004
96*	T Kohler-Cadmore	v.	Leicestershire at Leicester	2019
94*	T Kohler-Cadmore	v.	Birmingham Bears at Birmingham	2019
92*	G J Maxwell	v.	Nottinghamshire at Leeds	2015
92*	J E Root	v.	Lancashire at Manchester	2016
92*	A Lyth	v.	Durham at Leeds	2018
92	P A Jaques	v.	Leicestershire at Leeds	2004
92	J M Bairstow	v.	Durham at Leeds	2015
91	A W Gale	v.	Nottinghamshire at Leeds	2009
89	A J Finch	v.	Nottinghamshire at Leeds	2014
88	A J Finch	v.	Lancashire at Manchester	2014
87	A Lyth	v.	Durham at Leeds	2017

T20 HIGHEST INDIVIDUAL SCORES

AGAINST YORKSHIRE

111	D L Maddy	for	Leicestershire at Leeds	2004
101	S G Law	for	Lancashire at Manchester	2005
101	A D Hales	for	Nottinghamshire at Nottingham	2017
100*	G M Smith	for	Derbyshire at Leeds	2008
100	Sohail Akhtar	for	Lahore Qalandars at Abu Dhabi	2018
97	B J Hodge	for	Leicestershire at Leicester	2003
96*	A B McDonald	for	Leicestershire at Leeds	2011
94	L E Bosman	for	Derbyshire at Leeds	2010
91*	G Clark	for	Durham at Leeds	2015
91*	R A Whiteley	for	Worcestershire at Leeds	2015
91	M A Ealham	for	Nottinghamshire at Nottingham	2004
91	P Mustard	for	Durham at Chester-le-Street	2013
91	M H Wessels	for	Worcestershire at Leeds	2019
90*	S R Patel	for	Nottinghamshire at Leeds	2015
90*	B A Stokes	for	Durham at Leeds	2018
88*	P D Collingwood	for	Durham at Chester-le-Street	2017
85	A Flintoff	for	Lancashire at Leeds	2004
83	J Moss	for	Derbyshire at Leeds	2005

T20 BEST BOWLING

BY YORKSHIRE

6-19	T T Bresnan	v.	Lancashire at Leeds	2017
5-11	J W Shutt	v.	Durham at Chester-le-Street	2019
5-16	R M Pyrah	v.	Durham at Scarborough	2011
5-19	Azeem Rafiq	v.	Northamptonshire at Leeds	2017
5-22	M D Fisher	v.	Derbyshire at Leeds	2015
5-21	J A Brooks	v.	Leicestershire at Leeds	2013
5-31	A Lyth	v.	Nottinghamshire at Nottingham	2019
4-18	M A Ashraf	v.	Derbyshire at Derby	2012
4-18	D J Willey	v.	Northamptonshire at Leeds	2019
4-19	A U Rashid	v.	Durham at Leeds	2017
4-20	R M Pyrah	v.	Durham at Leeds	2008
4-20	A U Rashid	v.	Leicestershire at Leeds	2010
4-21	R M Pyrah	v.	Worcestershire at Leeds	2011
4-21	B W Sanderson	v.	Derbyshire at Derby	2011
4-21	J A Brooks	v.	Derbyshire at Leeds	2013
4-23	Rana Naved	v.	Nottinghamshire at Leeds	2009
4-24	A U Rashid	v.	Nottinghamshire at Nottingham	2008
4-25	R J Sidebottom	v.	Durham at Chester-le-Street	2012

T20 BEST BOWLING

AGAINST YORKSHIRE

4- 9	C K Langeveldt	for	Derbyshire at Leeds	2008
4-17	L V van Beek	for	Derbyshire at Leeds	2019
4-19	K H D Barker	for	Warwickshire at Birmingham	2010
4-19	J S Patel	for	Warwickshire at Leeds	2014
4-19	R Rampaul	for	Derbyshire at Chesterfield	2018
4-19	M R J Watt	for	Derbyshire at Chesterfield	2019
4-21	J Needham	for	Derbyshire at Leeds	2009
4-23	A J Hall	for	Northamptonshire at Northampton	2011
4-23	M W Parkinson	for	Lancashire at Leeds	2017
4-25	J A Morkel	for	Derbyshire at Chesterfield	2013
4-25	I G Butler	for	Northamptonshire at Leeds	2014
4-25	M A Wood	for	Durham at Birmingham	2016
4-31	Shakib al Hasan	for	Worcestershire at Worcester	2011
4-32	C A Ingram	for	Glamorgan at Cardiff	2016
4-37	K K Jennings	for	Durham at Chester-le-Street	2015
4-38	S J Harmison	for	Durham at Leeds	2008
3- 3	J K H Naik	for	Leicestershire at Leeds	2011
3- 6	B J Hodge	for	Leicestershire at Leicester	2003

T20 ECONOMICAL BOWLING

BY YORKSHIRE

4-0-11-5	J W Shutt	v. Durham at Chester-le-Street	2019

AGAINST YORKSHIRE

4-0-9-4	C K Langeveldt	for Derbyshire at Leeds	2008

T20 MOST EXPENSIVE BOWLING

BY YORKSHIRE

4-0-65-2	M J Hoggard	v. Lancashire at Leeds	2005

AGAINST YORKSHIRE

4-0-77-0	B W Sanderson	for Northamptonshire at Leeds	2017

T20 MAN OF THE MATCH AWARDS (89)

A W Gale	8	Azeem Rafiq	4	A J Finch	2
A Lyth	7	J M Bairstow	3	H H Gibbs	2
A McGrath	6	I J Harvey	3	P A Jaques	2
D J Willey	6	J A Leaning	3	A Z Lees	2
T T Bresnan	5	D A Miller	3	M J Lumb	2
T Kohler-Cadmore	5	A U Rashid	3		
R M Pyrah	5	K S Williamson	3		

One each: G S Ballance, J A Brooks, M E Claydon, M D Fisher, S P Fleming, D S Lehmann, G J Maxwell, J E Root, J A Rudolph, B W Sanderson, J J Sayers, A Shahzad, J W Shutt, D J Wainwright and C White

T20 HIGHEST AND LOWEST SCORES BY AND AGAINST YORKSHIRE PLUS INDIVIDUAL BEST BATTING AND BOWLING

The lowest score is the lowest all-out score or the lowest score at completion of the allotted overs, five-over matches not included.

Yorkshire versus:

Derbyshire

		By Yorkshire	Against Yorkshire
Highest Score:	In Yorkshire	198:4 at Leeds 2005	222:5 at Leeds 2010
	Away	210:3 at Derby 2006	170:5 at Chesterfield 2018
Lowest Score:	In Yorkshire	102 at Leeds 2018	124 at Chesterfield 2014
	Away	109 at Derby 2012	119:7 at Leeds 2007
Best Batting:	In Yorkshire	109 I J Harvey at Leeds 2005	100* G M Smith at Leeds 2008
	Away	79* A W Gale at Chesterfield 2009	71* B A Godleman at Chesterfield 2018
Best Bowling:	In Yorkshire	5-22 M D Fisher at Leeds 2015	4-9 C K Langeveldt at Leeds 2008
	Away	4-18 M A Ashraf at Derby 2012	4-19 R Rampaul at Chesterfield 2018
			4-19 M R J Watt at Chesterfield 2019

Durham

		By Yorkshire	Against Yorkshire
Highest Score:	In Yorkshire	223:6 at Leeds 2016	191:6 at Leeds 2015
	Away	186:8 at Chester-le-Street 2014	215:6 at Chester-le-Street 2013
Lowest Score:	In Yorkshire	95 at Leeds 2014	116:8 at Leeds 2009
	Away	90:9 at Chester-le-Street 2009	98 at Chester-le-Street 2006
Best Batting:	In Yorkshire	92 J M Bairstow at Leeds 2015	91* G Clark at Leeds 2015
	Away	102* J M Bairstow at Chester-le-Street 2014	91 P Mustard at Chester-le-Street 2013
Best Bowling:	In Yorkshire	5-16 R M Pyrah at Scarborough 2011	4-38 S J Harmison at Leeds 2008
	Away	5-11 J W Shutt at Chester-le-Street 2019	4-25 M A Wood at Birmingham 2016

Essex

		By Yorkshire	Against Yorkshire
Highest Score:	Away	143:7 at Chelmsford 2006	149:5 at Chelmsford 2006
Best Batting:	Away	43 G L Brophy at Chelmsford 2006	48* J S Foster at Chelmsford 2006
Best Bowling:	Away	2-22 A Shahzad at Chelmsford 2006	2-11 T J Phillips at Chelmsford 2006

Glamorgan

		By Yorkshire	Against Yorkshire
Highest Score:	Away	180:8 at Cardiff 2016	90 at Cardiff 2016
Best Batting:	Away	79 D J Willey at Cardiff 2016	26 J A Rudolph at Cardiff 2016
Best Bowling:	Away	4-26 A U Rashid at Cardiff 2016	4-32 C A Ingram at Cardiff 2016

T20 HIGHEST AND LOWEST SCORES BY AND AGAINST YORKSHIRE PLUS INDIVIDUAL BEST BATTING AND BOWLING *(Continued)*

The lowest score is the lowest all-out score or the lowest score at completion of the allotted overs, five-over matches not included.

Yorkshire versus:

Hampshire

		By Yorkshire		Against Yorkshire	
Highest Score:	Away	140:6	at Cardiff 2012	150:6	at Cardiff 2012
Best Batting:	Away	72*	D A Miller at Cardiff 2012	43	J H K Adams	at Cardiff 2012
Best Bowling:	Away	2-20	R J Sidebottom at Cardiff 2012	3-26	C P Wood	at Cardiff 2012

Lancashire

		By Yorkshire		Against Yorkshire	
		Against Yorkshire			
Highest Score:	In Yorkshire	185:8	at Leeds 2015	186:6	at Leeds 2015
	Away	202:8	at Manchester 2015	231:4	at Manchester 2015
Lowest Score:	In Yorkshire	111:8	at Leeds 2009	131:9	at Leeds 2004
	Away	97	at Manchester 2005	104:3	at Manchester 2003
Best Batting:	In Yorkshire	108*	I J Harvey at Leeds 2004	85	A Flintoff	at Leeds 2004
	Away	92*	J E Root at Manchester 2016	101	S G Law	at Manchester 2005
Best Bowling:	In Yorkshire	6-19	T T Bresnan at Leeds 2017	4-23	M W Parkinson	at Leeds 2017
	Away	3-15	Azeem Rafiq at Manchester 2011	3-10	D G Cork	at Manchester 2005

Leicestershire

		By Yorkshire		Against Yorkshire	
Highest Score:	In Yorkshire	211:6	at Leeds 2004	221:3	at Leeds 2004
	Away	255:2	at Leicester 2019	201:4	at Leicester 2019
Lowest Score:	In Yorkshire	134	at Leeds 2006	113:9	at Leeds 2013
	Away	105	at Leicester 2013	147:9	at Leicester 2012
Best Batting:	In Yorkshire	92	P A Jaques at Leeds 2004	111	D L Maddy	at Leeds 2004
	Away	96 *	T Kohler-Cadmore at Leicester 2019	97	B J Hodge	at Leicester 2003
Best Bowling:	In Yorkshire	5-21	J A Brooks at Leeds 2013	3-3	J K H Naik	at Leeds 2011
	Away	3-42	L E Plunkett at Leicester 2017	3-6	B J Hodge	at Leicester 2003

T20 HIGHEST AND LOWEST SCORES BY AND AGAINST YORKSHIRE PLUS INDIVIDUAL BEST BATTING AND BOWLING (Continued)

The lowest score is the lowest all-out score or the lowest score at completion of the allotted overs, five-over matches not included.

Yorkshire versus:

		By Yorkshire		Against Yorkshire	
	Northamptonshire				
Highest Score:	In Yorkshire	260:4	at Leeds 2017	165:7	at Leeds 2014
	Away	181:3	at Northampton 2014	180:5	at Northampton 2010
Lowest Score:	In Yorkshire	162:7	at Leeds 2014	107	at Leeds 2019
	Away	144	at Northampton 2011	132:7	at Northampton 2011
Best Batting:	In Yorkshire	161	A Lyth at Leeds 2017	65	R E Levi at Leeds 2017
	Away	101*	H H Gibbs at Northampton 2010	76	R E Levi at Northampton 2014
Best Bowling:	In Yorkshire	5-19	Azeem Rafiq at Leeds 2017	4-25	I G Butler at Leeds
	Away	3-15	T T Bresnan at Northampton 2016	4-23	A J Hall at Northampton 2011
	Nottinghamshire				
Highest Score:	In Yorkshire	227:5	at Leeds 2017	201:4	at Leeds 2014
	Away	223:5	at Nottingham 2017	225:5	at Nottingham 2017
Lowest Score:	In Yorkshire	141:8	at Leeds 2008	155:6	at Leeds 2009
	Away	112:7	at Nottingham 2010	136:6	at Nottingham 2008
Best Batting:	In Yorkshire	92*	G J Maxwell at Leeds 2015	90*	S R Patel at Leeds 2015
	Away	96*	M J Wood at Nottingham 2004	101	A D Hales at Nottingham 2017
Best Bowling:	In Yorkshire	4-23	Rana Naved-ul-Hasan at Leeds 2009	3-38	J T Ball at Leeds 2014
	Away	5-31	A Lyth at Nottingham 2019	3-16	H F Gurney at Nottingham 2016
	Sussex				
Highest Score:	Away	172:6	at Cardiff 2012	193:5	at Hove 2007
Lowest Score:	Away	155	at Hove 2007	136:8	at Cardiff 2012
Best Batting:	Away	68*	J M Bairstow at Cardiff 2012	80*	C D Nash at Cardiff 2012
Best Bowling:	Away	2-22	T T Bresnan at Cardiff 2012	3-22	S B Styris at Cardiff 2012

T20 HIGHEST AND LOWEST SCORES BY AND AGAINST YORKSHIRE PLUS INDIVIDUAL BEST BATTING AND BOWLING (Continued)

The lowest score is the lowest all-out score or the lowest score at completion of the allotted overs, five-over matches not included.

Yorkshire versus:

		By Yorkshire	Against Yorkshire
Warwickshire			
Highest Score:	In Yorkshire	226:8 at Leeds 2018	177:4 at Leeds 2019
	Away	200:3 at Birmingham 2019	158:2 at Birmingham 2018
Lowest Score:	In Yorkshire	121:9 at Leeds 2010	145 at Leeds 2015
	Away	131 at Birmingham 2010	181:5 at Birmingham 2019
Best Batting:	In Yorkshire	76* T Kohler-Cadmore at Leeds 2014	69* L J Evans at Leeds 2014
	Away	94* T Kohler-Cadmore at Birmingham 2019	64* S R Hain at Birmingham 2019
Best Bowling:	In Yorkshire	3-21 T T Bresnan at Leeds 2017	4-19 J S Patel at Leeds 2014
	Away	3-25 S A Patterson at Birmingham 2010	4-19 K H D Barker at Birmingham 2010
Worcestershire			
Highest Score:	In Yorkshire	233:6 at Leeds 2017	196:7 at Leeds 2017
	Away	187:7 at Worcester 2010	208:7 at Worcester 2010
Lowest Score:	In Yorkshire	117 at Leeds 2015	109 at Leeds 2010
	Away	142 at Worcester 2011	183:7 at Worcester 2011
Best Batting:	In Yorkshire	118 D J Willey at Leeds 2017	91* R A Whiteley at Worcester 2011
	Away	40 G S Ballance at Worcester 2018	91 M H Wessels at Worcester 2011
			56 A N Kervezee at Worcester 2011
Best Bowling:	In Yorkshire	4-21 R M Pyrah at Leeds 2011	3-29 B L d'Oliveira at Leeds 2015
	Away	3-30 A Shahzad at Worcester 2011	4-31 Shakib al Hasan at Worcester 2011
Chennai			
Highest Score:	Away	140:6 at Durban 2012	141:6 at Durban 2012
Best Batting:	Away	58 G S Ballance at Durban 2012	47 S Badrinath at Durban 2012
Best Bowling:	Away	3-23 I Wardlaw at Durban 2012	2-12 J A Morkel at Durban 2012
Highveld			
Highest Score:	Away	131:7 at Johannesburg 2012	134:5 at Johannesburg 2012
Best Batting:	Away	31 P A Jaques at Johannesburg 2012	32 Q de Kock at Johannesburg 2012
Best Bowling:	Away	2-21 S A Patterson at Johannesburg 2012	2-23 A M Phangiso at Johannesburg 2012

T20 HIGHEST AND LOWEST SCORES BY AND AGAINST YORKSHIRE
PLUS INDIVIDUAL BEST BATTING AND BOWLING (Continued)

The lowest score is the lowest all-out score or the lowest score at completion of the allotted overs, five-over matches not included.

Yorkshire versus:

Hobart Hurricanes

	By Yorkshire		Against Yorkshire	
Highest Score:	Away	144:1	at Abu Dhabi 2018	140:7	at Abu Dhabi 2018
Best Batting:	Away	72* T Kohler-Cadmore	at Abu Dhabi 2018	38 C P Jewell	at Abu Dhabi 2018
Best Bowling:	Away	2-29 K Carver	at Abu Dhabi 2018	1-24 J Clark	at Abu Dhabi 2018

Lahore Qalandars

	By Yorkshire		Against Yorkshire	
Highest Score:	Away	184:5	at Abu Dhabi 2018	189:4	at Abu Dhabi 2018
Best Batting:	Away	37 H C Brook	at Abu Dhabi 2018	100 Sohail Akhtar	at Abu Dhabi 2018
Best Bowling:	Away	2-26 J E Poysden	at Abu Dhabi 2018	2-36 Shaheen Shah Afridi	at Abu Dhabi 2018

Mumbai

	By Yorkshire		Against Yorkshire	
Highest Score:	Away			156: 6	at Cape Town 2012
Best Batting:	Away			37 D R Smith	at Cape Town
Best Bowling:	Away	2-36 Azeem Rafiq	at Cape Town 2012		

Sydney Sixers

	By Yorkshire		Against Yorkshire	
Highest Score:	Away	96:9	at Cape Town 2012	98:2	at Cape Town 2012
Best Batting:	Away	25 J E Root	at Cape Town 2012	43* M J Lumb	at Cape Town 2012
Best Bowling:	Away	1-21 Azeem Rafiq	at Cape Town 2012	3-22 M A Starc	at Cape Town 2012

Trinidad and Tobago

	By Yorkshire		Against Yorkshire	
Highest Score:	Away	154:4	at Centurion 2012	148:9	at Centurion 2012
Best Batting:	Away	64* G S Ballance	at Centurion 2012	59 D Ramdin	at Centurion 2012
Best Bowling:	Away	3-13 R J Sidebottom	at Centurion 2012	1-16 K Y G Ortley	at Centurion 2012

Uva

	By Yorkshire		Against Yorkshire	
Highest Score:	Away	151:5	at Johannesburg 2012	150:7	at Johannesburg 2012
Best Batting:	Away	39* D A Miller	at Johannesburg 2012	29 S H T Kandamby	at Johannesburg 2012
Best Bowling:	Away	2-29 M A Ashraf	at Johannesburg 2012	3-32 E M D Y Munaweera	at Johannesburg 2012

T20 PARTNERSHIPS OF 100 AND OVER 2003-2019 (25)

150	2nd wkt	A Lyth	(66)	and D J Willey	(79)	v. Northamptonshire at Northampton 2018
137*	2nd wkt	A W Gale	(60*)	and H H Gibbs	(76*)	v. Durham at Leeds 2010
131	1st wkt	A Lyth	(78)	and P A Jaques	(64)	v. Derbyshire at Leeds 2012
129	2nd wkt	A W Gale	(91)	and M P Vaughan	(41*)	v. Nottinghamshire at Leeds 2009
129	2nd wkt	T Kohler-Cadmore	(46)	and D J Willey	(80)	v. Lancashire at Leeds 2018
127	1st wkt	A Lyth	(161)	and T Kohler-Cadmore	(41)	v. Northamptonshire at Leeds 2017
124	2nd wkt	I J Harvey	(109)	and P A Jaques	(37)	v. Derbyshire at Leeds 2005
124	2nd wkt	A Lyth	(161)	and D J Willey	(40)	v. Northamptonshire at Leeds 2017
121	3rd wkt	J A Rudolph	(56)	and A McGrath	(59)	v. Leicestershire at Leicester 2008
121	2nd wkt	T Kohler-Cadmore	(96*)	and N Pooran	(67)	v. Leicestershire at Leicester 2019
116	1st wkt	A W Gale	(70)	and P A Jaques	(48)	v. Leicestershire at Leeds 2012
116	1st wkt	A Lyth	(69)	and T Kohler-Cadmore	(96*)	v. Leicestershire at Leicester 2019
110*	4th wkt	A Lyth	(92*)	and J A Tattersall	(53*)	v. Durham at Leeds 2018
108	2nd wkt	I J Harvey	(108*)	and P A Jaques	(39)	v. Lancashire at Leeds 2004
108	2nd wkt	A Lyth	(59)	and H H Gibbs	(39)	v. Worcestershire at Leeds 2010
106	2nd wkt	D J Willey	(74)	and A Z Lees	(35)	v. Northamptonshire at Leeds 2016
104	1st wkt	A W Gale	(43)	and J A Rudolph	(61)	v. Leicestershire at Leicester 2009
104	2nd wkt	A Z Lees	(63)	and J A Leaning	(60*)	v. Warwickshire at Leeds 2015
104	1st wkt	A Lyth	(68)	and T Kohler-Cadmore	(40)	v. Worcestershire at Leeds 2019
103*	5th wkt	G S Ballance	(64*)	and A U Rashid	(33*)	v. Trinidad & Tobago at Centurion 2012/13
103	1st wkt	A W Gale	(65*)	and J A Rudolp	(53)	v. Leicestershire at Leicester 2010
102	1st wkt	T Kohler-Cadmore	(94*)	and A Lyth	(42)	v. Birmingham Bears at Birmingham 2019
101	2nd wkt	M J Wood	(57)	and M J Lumb	(55)	v. Nottinghamshire at Leeds 2003
101	3rd wkt	A J Hodd	(70)	and G J Maxwell	(92*)	v. Nottinghamshire at Leeds 2015
100	4th wkt	A Z Lees	(59)	and J A Leaning	(64)	v. Northamptonshire at Northampton 2016

T20 HIGHEST PARTNERSHIPS FOR EACH WICKET

1st wkt	131	A Lyth	(78)	and P A Jaques	(64)	v. Derbyshire at Leeds 2012
2nd wkt	150	A Lyth	(66)	and D J Willey	(79)	v. Northamptonshire at Northampton 2018
3rd wkt	121	J A Rudolph	(56)	and A McGrath	(59)	v. Leicestershire at Leicester 2008
4th wkt	100	A Z Lees	(59)	and J A Leaning	(64)	v. Northamptonshire at Northampton 2016
5th wkt	103*	G S Ballance	(64*)	and A U Rashid	(33*)	v. Trinidad & Tobago at Centurion 2012/13
6th wkt	76	J E Root	(92*)	and L E Plunkett	(22)	v. Lancashire at Manchester 2016
7th wkt	68*	T T Bresnan	(45*)	and A U Rashid	(29*)	v. Warwickshire at Leeds 2014
8th wkt	54	T T Bresnan	(51)	and J D Middlebrook	(29*)	v. Lancashire at Manchester 2015
9th wkt	33*	A U Rashid	(5*)	and D Gough	(20*)	v. Lancashire at Leeds 2008
10th wkt	28*	A U Rashid	(28*)	and G J Kruis	(12*)	v. Durham at Chester-le-Street 2009

ALL WHO HAVE TAKEN 4 WICKETS IN AN INNINGS (22)

M A ASHRAF (1)

4-18	v. Derbyshire	at Derby	2012

AZEEM RAFIQ (1)

5-19	v. Northamptonshire	at Leeds	2017

T T BRESNAN (1)

6-19	v. Lancashire	at Leeds	2017

J A BROOKS (2)

5-21	v. Leicestershire	at Leeds	2013
4-21	v. Derbyshire	at Leeds	2013

M D FISHER (1)

5 22	v. Derbyshire	at Leeds	2015

A LYTH (1)

5-31	v. Nottinghamshire	at Nottingham	2019

C J MCKAY (1)

4-33	v. Derbyshire	at Leeds	2010

RANA NAVED-UL-HASAN (1)

4-23	v. Nottinghamshire	at Leeds	2009

S A PATTERSON (1)

4-30	v. Lancashire	at Leeds	2010

R M PYRAH (3)

5-16	v. Durham	at Scarborough	2011
4-20	v. Durham	at Leeds	2006
4-21	v. Worcestershire	at Leeds	2011

A U RASHID (5)

4-19	v. Durham	at Leeds	2017
4-20	v. Leicestershire	at Leeds	2011
4-24	v. Nottingham	at Nottingham	2008
4-26	v. Lancashire	at Leeds	2011
4-26	v. Glamorgan	at Cardiff	2016

B W SANDERSON (1)

4-21	v. Derbyshire	at Derby	2011

J W SHUTT (1)

5-11	v. Durham	at Chester-le-Street	2019

R J SIDEBOTTOM (1)

4-25	v. Durham	at Chester-le-Street	2012

D J WILLEY

4-18	v. Northamptonshire	at Leeds	2019

CAREER AVERAGES FOR YORKSHIRE

ALL t20 MATCHES 2003-2019

Player	M	Inns	NO	Runs	HS	Av'ge	100s	50s	Runs	Wkts	Av'ge	Ct/St
Ashraf, M A ...	17	1	0	4	4	4.00	0	0	462	17	27.17	1
Azeem Rafiq ...	95	37	24	153	21*	11.76	0	0	2,489	102	24.40	36
Bairstow, J M .	**63**	**58**	**11**	**1,231**	**102***	**26.19**	**1**	**4**	**0**	**0**	**—**	**27/8**
Ballance, G S ..	**79**	**68**	**8**	**1,390**	**79**	**23.16**	**0**	**4**	**0**	**0**	**—**	**43**
Bess, D M	6	3	1	8	5*	4.00	0	0	174	4	43.50	0
Best, T L	8	3	2	10	10*	10.00	0	0	243	7	34.71	4
Blakey, R J	7	5	1	119	32	29.75	0	0	0	0	—	5/1
Bresnan, T T ..	**118**	**91**	**35**	**1,208**	**51**	**21.57**	**0**	**1**	**2,918**	**118**	**24.72**	**41**
Brook, H C ...	**17**	**17**	**4**	**367**	**44**	**28.23**	**0**	**0**	**13**	**0**	**—**	**7**
Brooks, J A	23	0	0	0	—	—	0	0	582	22	26.45	11
Brophy, G L ...	54	46	9	717	57*	19.37	0	2	0	0	—	25/7
Carver, K	10	2	1	2	2	2.00	0	0	208	8	26.00	5
Claydon, M E ..	7	2	2	14	12*	—	0	0	188	5	37.60	2
Coad, B O	**8**	**2**	**1**	**3**	**2***	**—**	**0**	**0**	**194**	**7**	**27.71**	**5**
Craven, V J ...	6	6	4	76	44*	38.00	0	0	67	0	—	3
Dawood, I	11	8	3	44	15	8.80	0	0	0	0	—	5/2
Dawson, R K J .	22	8	3	71	22	14.20	0	0	558	24	23.25	7
Finch, A J	16	16	0	332	89	20.75	0	2	24	1	24.00	16
Fisher, M D ...	**23**	**6**	**4**	**33**	**17***	**16.50**	**0**	**0**	**659**	**23**	**28.65**	**7**
Fleming, S P ...	4	4	0	62	58	15.50	0	1	0	0	—	1
Fraine, W A R .	**4**	**3**	**1**	**30**	**16**	**15.00**	**0**	**0**	**0**	**0**	**—**	**6**
Gale, A W	104	97	8	2,260	91	25.39	0	16	0	0	—	30
Gibbs, H H	15	15	3	443	101*	36.91	1	2	0	0	—	8
Gibson, R	3	2	0	32	18	16.00	0	0	30	0	—	1
Gilbert, C R ...	13	9	2	107	38*	15.28	0	0	0	0	—	7
Gillespie, J N ..	17	4	2	14	8*	7.00	0	0	422	17	24.82	5
Gough, D	17	7	3	42	20*	10.50	0	0	416	16	26.00	2
Gray, A K D ...	8	3	0	17	13	5.66	0	0	211	9	23.44	4
Guy, S M	10	6	1	44	13	8.80	0	0	0	0	—	4
Hamilton, G M .	3	3	1	41	41*	20.50	0	0	0	0	—	1
Handscomb, P S P	7	6	0	97	31	16.16	0	0	0	0	—	3/3
Hannon-Dalby, O J	2	0	0	0	—	—	0	0	58	3	19.33	0
Harvey, I J	10	10	1	438	109	48.66	2	2	258	10	25.80	4
Head, T M	4	4	0	113	40	28.25	0	0	4	0	—	0
Hodd, A J	26	17	4	147	70	11.30	0	1	0	0	—	9/6
Hodgson, D M .	16	14	2	213	52*	17.75	0	1	0	0	—	9/1
Hodgson, L J ...	2	1	1	39	39*	—	0	0	59	2	29.50	1
Hoggard, M J ...	15	2	1	19	18	19.00	0	0	472	13	36.30	4
Jaques, P A	34	32	3	907	92	31.27	0	6	15	0	—	5
Kirby, S P	3	0	0	0	—	—	0	0	119	4	29.75	1
Kohler-Cadmore, T												
	36	36	4	1,116	96*	34.87	**0**	**10**	**0**	**0**	**—**	**18**
Kruis, G J	20	5	3	41	22	20.50	0	0	486	19	25.57	6
Lawson, M A K .	2	1	1	4	4*	—	0	0	87	3	29.00	1
Leaning, J A ...	52	45	11	952	64	28.00	0	2	45	1	45.00	25
Lees, A Z	37	36	2	857	67*	25.20	0	4	0	0	—	12
Lehmann, D S ..	9	9	3	252	48	42.00	0	0	180	8	22.50	4
Lumb, M J	26	26	3	442	84*	19.21	0	4	65	3	21.66	8
Lyth, A	**111**	**102**	**3**	**2,619**	**161**	**26.45**	**1**	**14**	**342**	**18**	**19.00**	**53**
McGrath, A	66	61	12	1,403	73*	28.63	0	8	698	23	30.34	26

Player	M	Inns	NO	Runs	HS	Av'ge	100s	50s	Runs	Wkts	Av'ge	Ct/St
McKay, C J	8	6	3	54	21*	18.00	0	0	258	10	25.80	1
Maharaj, K A ...	5	2	2	10	10*	—	0	0	126	2	63.00	2
Marsh, S E	11	11	4	289	60*	41.28	0	2	0	0	—	1
Maxwell, G J ...	12	12	1	229	92*	20.81	0	1	264	12	22.00	6
Middlebrook, J D	4	2	2	33	29*	—	0	0	101	4	25.25	1
Miller, D A	14	13	4	457	74*	50.77	0	4	0	0	—	7
Olivier, D	**5**	**2**	**0**	**2**	**1**	**1.00**	**0**	**0**	**191**	**6**	**31.83**	**0**
Patterson, S A .	**63**	**9**	**4**	**9**	**3***	**1.80**	**0**	**0**	**1,811**	**61**	**29.68**	**10**
Pillans, M W ..	**5**	**1**	**0**	**8**	**8**	**8.00**	**0**	**0**	**118**	**3**	**39.33**	**1**
Plunkett, L E ..	42	31	10	353	36	16.80	0	0	1,146	44	26.04	13
Pooran, N	**3**	**3**	**0**	**122**	**67**	**40.66**	**0**	**1**	**0**	**0**	**—**	**2**
Poysden, J E ..	**3**	**0**	**0**	**0**	**—**	**—**	**0**	**0**	**73**	**3**	**24.33**	**1**
Pyrah, R M	105	71	21	593	42	11.86	0	0	2,315	108	21.43	40
Rana												
Naved-ul-Hasan	8	8	2	63	20*	10.50	0	0	159	11	14.45	2
Rashid, A U ...	**103**	**63**	**20**	**577**	**36***	**13.41**	**0**	**0**	**2,668**	**110**	**24.25**	**34**
Rhodes, W M H	18	16	3	128	45	9.84	0	0	283	13	21.76	2
Robinson, O E ..	7	3	0	5	3	1.66	0	0	162	6	27.00	3
Root, J E	**33**	**29**	**7**	**633**	**92***	**28.77**	**0**	**4**	**269**	**4**	**67.25**	**11**
Rudolph, J A ..	39	35	5	710	61	23.66	0	3	145	6	24.16	7
Sanderson, B W	4	0	0	0	0	—	0	0	74	6	12.33	0
Sarfraz Ahmed .	5	4	0	53	42	13.25	0	0	0	0	—	3/1
Sayers, J J	17	14	0	253	44	18.07	0	0	0	0	—	5
Shahzad, A	22	16	4	129	20	10.75	0	0	576	17	33.88	5
Shaw, J	5	2	1	1	1	1.00	0	0	138	2	69.00	1
Shutt, J W	**7**	**2**	**1**	**0**	**0***	**0.00**	**0**	**0**	**164**	**10**	**16.40**	**2**
Sidebottom, R J .	40	16	10	87	16*	14.50	0	0	1,069	42	25.45	9
Silverwood, C E W	9	5	2	32	13*	10.66	0	0	264	7	37.71	4
Starc, M A	10	2	1	0	0*	0.00	0	0	218	21	10.38	1
Swanepoel, P J .	2	1	1	2	2*	—	0	0	60	3	20.00	1
Tattersall, J A .	**24**	**17**	**5**	**301**	**53***	**25.08**	**0**	**1**	**0**	**0**	**—**	**16/4**
Taylor, C R	2	2	1	10	10*	10.00	0	0	0	0	—	0
Thompson, J A	**18**	**13**	**7**	**113**	**50**	**18.83**	**0**	**1**	**436**	**12**	**36.33**	**4**
Vaughan, M P ..	16	16	1	292	41*	19.46	0	0	81	1	81.00	2
Wainman, J C ..	2	1	1	12	12*	—	0	0	49	1	49.00	0
Wainwright, D J	26	9	6	23	6*	7.66	0	0	551	21	26.23	9
Waite, M J	**6**	**3**	**3**	**34**	**19***	**—**	**0**	**0**	**81**	**2**	**40.50**	**3**
Wardlaw, I	10	1	1	1	1	—	0	0	179	5	35.80	0
Warren, A C ...	2	0	0	0	—	—	0	0	70	4	17.50	0
White, C	33	31	0	570	55	18.38	0	2	132	2	66.00	8
Willey, D J	**43**	**41**	**1**	**1,240**	**118**	**31.00**	**1**	**7**	**1,132**	**38**	**29.78**	**17**
Williamson, K S	12	11	0	302	65	27.45	0	1	37	3	12.33	3
Wood, M J	15	15	3	328	96*	27.33	0	2	32	2	16.00	11
Younus Khan ...	2	2	0	55	40	27.50	0	0	32	2	16.00	0
Yuvraj Singh ...	5	5	0	154	71	30.80	0	1	51	5	10.20	0

SECOND ELEVEN CHAMPIONSHIP 1959-1961 AND 1975-2019

SUMMARY OF RESULTS BY SEASON

Season	Played	Won	Lost	Drawn	Tied	Abandoned	Position in Championship
1959	10	4	1	5	0	0	7
1960	10	1	3	6	0	0	14
1961	9	2	2	5	0	1	11
1975	14	4	0	10	0	0	4
1976	14	5	5	4	0	0	5
1977	**16**	**9**	**0**	**7**	**0**	**1**	**1**
1978	15	5	2	8	0	1	4
1979	16	5	0	11	0	0	3
1980	14	5	2	7	0	1	5
1981	16	2	3	11	0	0	11
1982	16	2	3	11	0	0	14 =
1983	11	5	1	5	0	3	2
1984	**15**	**9**	**3**	**3**	**0**	**0**	**1**
1985	14	3	3	8	0	1	12
1986	16	5	1	10	0	0	5
1987	**15**	**5**	**2**	**8**	**0**	**1**	**1 =**
1988	16	4	1	11	0	0	9
1989	17	2	3	12	0	0	9 =
1990	16	1	6	9	0	0	17
1991	**16**	**8**	**1**	**7**	**0**	**0**	**1**
1992	17	5	2	10	0	0	5
1993	17	6	1	10	0	0	3
1994	17	6	2	9	0	0	2
1995	17	7	1	9	0	0	5
1996	17	6	3	8	0	0	4
1997	16	8	5	3	0	1	2
1998	15	4	2	9	0	1	9
1999	16	3	5	8	0	1	14
2000	14	5	2	7	0	1	5
2001	12	8	2	2	0	1	2
2002	12	5	1	6	0	0	3
2003	**10**	**7**	**1**	**2**	**0**	**0**	**1**
2004	7	2	0	5	0	1	8
2005	12	2	4	6	0	0	10
2006	14	6	4	4	0	0	3
2007	12	4	5	3	0	0	10
2008	12	4	4	4	0	2	5
2009	9	5	0	4	0	0	(Group A) 2
2010	9	2	4	3	0	0	(Group A) 8
2011	9	0	4	4	1	0	(Group A) 10
2012	7	1	2	4	0	2	(North) 9
2013	9	3	4	2	0	0	(North) 4
2014	9	2	1	6	0	0	(North) 4
2015	9	2	4	3	0	0	(North) 7
2016	9	2	3	4	0	0	(North) 5
2017....	8	2	0	6	0	1	(North) 4
2018....	9	3	1	5	0	0	(North) 5
2019............ ..	8	3	1	4	0	0	(North) 2
Totals	618	199	112	305	1	19	

Matches abandoned without a ball bowled are not counted as matches played. The 1976 match between Yorkshire and Northamptonshire at Bradford was cancelled after the fixtures had been published. The Championship was divided into two groups from 2009, each team playng each other once. The two group winners play for the Championship.

ANALYSIS OF RESULTS AGAINST EACH OPPONENT

County	Played	Won	Lost	Drawn	Tied	Abandoned	First Played
Derbyshire	60	14	8	38	0	3	1959
Durham	35	11	6	18	0	2	1992
Essex	13	9	2	2	0	0	1990
Glamorgan	40	11	3	26	0	2	1975
Gloucestershire	10	3	3	4	0	0	1990
Hampshire	12	4	1	7	0	0	1990
Kent	26	5	4	17	0	1	1981
Lancashire	72	14	19	39	0	3	1959
Leicestershire	34	15	8	10	1	1	1975
MCC Young Cricketers	8	4	1	3	0	0	2005
MCC Universities	4	1	1	2	0	0	2011
Middlesex	18	7	2	9	0	0	1977
Northamptonshire	52	16	6	30	0	2	1959
Nottinghamshire	61	17	13	31	0	4	1959
Scotland	2	1	0	1	0	0	2007
Somerset	18	9	3	6	0	0	1988
Surrey	36	9	9	18	0	2	1976
Sussex	16	6	5	5	0	0	1990
Warwickshire	65	24	13	28	0	0	1959
Worcestershire	44	21	6	17	0	0	1961
Totals	626	201	113	311	1	20	

Note: Matches abandoned are not included in the total played.

Largest Victory An innings and 230 runs v. Glamorgan at Headingley, 1986
Largest Defeat An innings and 124 runs v. Gloucestershire at Bradford, 1994
Narrowest Victory By 1 run v. Lancashire at Old Trafford, 2003
Narrowest Defeat By 8 runs v. Derbyshire at Harrogate, 1982

Highest Total
By Yorkshire: 585 for 8 wkts dec v. Lancashire at Scarborough, 2017
Against Yorkshire: 567 for 7 wkts dec by Middlesex at RAF Vine Lane, Uxbridge, 2000

Lowest Total
By Yorkshire 66 v Nottinghamshire at Trent College, 2016
Against Yorkshire: 36 by Lancashire at Elland, 1979

Highest Match Aggregate
1,470 for 39 wkts v. Gloucestershire at Cheltenham, 2001

Highest Individual Score
For Yorkshire: 273* by R J Blakey v. Northamptonshire at Northampton, 1986
Against Yorkshire: 235 by O A Shah for Middlesex at Leeds, 1999

Century in Each Innings
For Yorkshire: C White 209* and 115* v. Worcestershire at Worcester, 1990
(The only instance of two unbeaten centuries in the same match)
K Sharp 150* and 127 v. Essex at Elland, 1991
A A Metcalfe 109 and 136* v. Somerset at North Perrott, 1994
R A Kettleborough 123 and 192* v. Nottinghamshire at Todmorden, 1996
C R Taylor 201* and 129 v. Sussex at Hove, 2005
A W Gale 131 and 123 v. Somerset at Taunton, 2006
J J Sayers 157 and 105 v. Lancashire at Leeds, 2007

410

Century in Each Innings *(Continued)*

Against Yorkshire: N Nannan 100 and 102* for Nottinghamshire at Harrogate, 1979
G D Lloyd 134 and 103 for Lancashire at Scarborough, 1989
A J Swann 131 and 100 for Northamptonshire at York, 1998
G J Kennis 114 and 114 for Somerset at Taunton, 1999

Most Career Runs

B Parker 7,450 in 122 matches (average 40.48)

Best Bowling in an Innings

For Yorkshire: 9 for 27 by G A Cope v. Northamptonshire at Northampton, 1979
Against Yorkshire: 8 for 15 by I Folley for Lancashire at Heywood, 1983

Best Bowling in a Match

For Yorkshire: 13 for 92 (6 for 48 and 7 for 44) by M K Bore v. Lancashire
at Harrogate, 1976
Against Yorkshire: 13 for 100 (7 for 45 and 6 for 55) by N J Perry for Glamorgan
at Cardiff, 1978

Most Career Wickets

Paul A Booth 248 in 85 matches, average 29.33

Totals of 450 and over

By Yorkshire (30)

Score	Versus	Ground	Season
585 for 8 wkts dec	Lancashire	Scarborough	2017
538 for 9 wkts dec	Worcestershire	Stamford Bridge	2007
534 for 5 wkts dec	Lancashire	Stamford Bridge	2003
530 for 8 wkts dec	Nottinghamshire	Middlesbrough	2000
526 for 8 wkts dec	MCC Young Cricketers	High Wycombe	2017
514 for 3 wkts dec	Somerset	Taunton	1988
509 for 4 wkts dec	Northamptonshire	Northampton	1986
508	Durham	Riverside	2017
502	Derbyshire	Chesterfield	2003
501 for 5 wkts dec	MCC Young Cricketers	Stamford Bridge	2009
497	Derbyshire	Chesterfield	2005
495 for 5 wkts dec	Somerset	Taunton	2006
488 for 8 wkts dec	Warwickshire	Harrogate	1984
486 for 6 wkts dec	Glamorgan	Leeds	1986
480	Leicestershire	Market Harborough	2013
476 for 3 wkts dec	Glamorgan	Gorseinon	1984
475 for 9 wkts dec	Nottinghamshire	Nottingham	1995
474 for 3 wkts dec	Glamorgan	Todmorden	2003
474	Durham	Stamford Bridge	2003
470	Lancashire	Leeds	2006
469	Warwickshire	Castleford	1999
462	Scotland	Stamford Bridge	2007
461 for 8 wkts dec	Essex	Stamford Bridge	2006
459 for 3 wkts dec	Leicestershire	Oakham	1997
459 for 6 wkts dec	Glamorgan	Bradford	1992
457 for 9 wkts dec	Kent	Canterbury	1983
456 for 5 wkts dec	Gloucestershire	Todmorden	1990
456 for 6 wkts dec	Nottinghamshire	York	1986
454 for 9 wkts dec	Derbyshire	Chesterfield	1959
452 for 9 wkts dec	Glamorgan	Cardiff	2005

Totals of 450 and over

Against Yorkshire (14)

Score	For	Ground	Season
567 for 7 wkts dec	Middlesex	RAF Vine Lane, Uxbridge	2000
555 for 7 wkts dec	Derbyshire	Stamford Bridge	2002
530 for 9 wkts dec	Leicestershire	Hinckley	2015
525 for 7 wkts dec	Sussex	Hove	2005
502 for 4 wkts dec	Warwickshire	Edgbaston Community Foundation Sports Ground	2016
493 for 8 wkts dec	Nottinghamshire	Lady Bay, Nottingham	2002
488 for 8 wkts dec	Warwickshire	Castleford	1999
486	Essex	Chelmsford	2000
485	Gloucestershire	North Park, Cheltenham	2001
477	Lancashire	Headingley	2006
471	Warwickshire	Clifton Park, York	2010
458	Lancashire	Bradford	1997
454 for 7 wkts dec	Lancashire	Todmorden	1993
450 for 7 wkts (inns closed)	Derbyshire	Bradford	1980

Completed Innings under 75

By Yorkshire (6)

Score	Versus	Ground	Season
66	Nottinghamshire	Trent College	2016
67	Worcestershire	Barnt Green (1st inns)	2013
68	Worcestershire	Barnt Green (2nd inns)	2013
69	Lancashire	Heywood	1983
72	Leicestershire	Kibworth	2019
74	Derbyshire	Chesterfield	1960
74	Nottinghamshire	Bradford	1998

Against Yorkshire (10)

Score	By	Ground	Season
36	Lancashire	Elland	1979
49	Leicestershire	Leicester	2008
50	Lancashire	Liverpool	1984
60	Derbyshire	Bradford	1977
60	Surrey	Sunbury-on-Thames	1977
62	MCC YC	High Wycombe	2005
64	Nottinghamshire	Brodsworth	1959
66	Leicestershire	Lutterworth	1977
72	Sussex	Horsham	2003
74	Worcestershire	Barnsley	1978

Individual Scores of 150 and over (68)

Score	Player	Versus	Ground	Season
273*	R J Blakey	Northamptonshire	Northampton	1986
238*	K Sharp	Somerset	Taunton	1988
233	P E Robinson	Kent	Canterbury	1983
230	T Kohler-Cadmore	Derbyshire	York	2017
221*	K Sharp	Gloucestershire	Todmorden	1990
219	G M Hamilton	Derbyshire	Chesterfield	2003
218*	A McGrath	Surrey	Elland	1994
212	G S Ballance	MCC Young Cricketers	Stamford Bridge	2009
209*	C White	Worcestershire	Worcester	1990
205	C R Taylor	Glamorgan	Todmorden	2003
204	B Parker	Gloucestershire	Bristol	1993
203	A McGrath	Durham	Headingley	2005
202*	J M Bairstow	Leicestershire	Oakham	2009
202	A Z Lees	Durham	Riverside	2017
202	M J Wood	Essex	Stamford Bridge	2006
201*	C R Taylor	Sussex	Hove	2005
200*	D Byas	Worcestershire	Worcester	1992
200*	A McGrath	Northamptonshire	Northampton	2012
192*	R A Kettleborough	Nottinghamshire	Todmorden	1996
191	P E Robinson	Warwickshire	Harrogate	1984
191	M J Wood	Derbyshire	Rotherham	2000
191	M J Lumb	Nottinghamshire	Middlesbrough	2000
189*	C S Pickles	Gloucestershire	Bristol	1991
186	A McGrath	MCC Universities	York	2011
184	J D Love	Worcestershire	Headingley	1976
183	A W Gale	Durham	Stamford Bridge	2006
174	G L Brophy	Worcestershire	Stamford Bridge	2007
173	S N Hartley	Warwickshire	Edgbaston	1980
173	A A Metcalfe	Glamorgan	Gorseinon	1984
173	B Parker	Sussex	Hove	1996
173	R A Kettleborough	Leicestershire	Oakham School	1997
173	T Kohler-Cadmore	Northamptonshire	Desborough	2018
172	A C Morris	Lancashire	York	1995
170*	R A J Townsley	Glamorgan	Harrogate	1975
169	J E Root	Warwickshire	York	2010
168	M J Wood	Leicestershire	Oakham School	1997
166	A A Metcalfe	Lancashire	York	1984
166	C A Chapman	Northamptonshire	York	1998
165*	A Lyth	Durham	Stamford Bridge	2006
165	J J Sayers	Sussex	Hove	2006
164*	A W Gale	Leicestershire	Harrogate	2002
164	J C Balderstone	Nottinghamshire	Harrogate	1960
163*	J E Root	Leicestershire	Oakham	2009
163	A A Metcalfe	Derbyshire	Chesterfield	1992
162*	D Byas	Surrey	Scarborough	1987
162*	R Gibson	Leicestershire	York	2016
161	H C Brook	Lancashire	Scarborough	2017
160	A A Metcalfe	Somerset	Bradford	1993
157*	W A R Fraine	Worcestershire	Kidderminster	2019
157	J J Sayers	Lancashire	Headingley	2007
155	S M Guy	Derbyshire	Chesterfield	2005
154*	C R Taylor	Surrey	Whitgift School	2005
153*	A A Metcalfe	Warwickshire	Bingley	1995

413

Individual Scores of 150 and over *(Continued)*

Score	Player	Versus	Ground	Season
153	C White	Worcestershire	Marske-by-the-Sea	1991
153	R A Stead	Surrey	Todmorden	2002
152	A A Metcalfe	Gloucestershire	Bristol	1993
151*	P E Robinson	Nottinghamshire	York	1986
151*	S J Foster	Kent	Elland	1992
151*	J J Sayers	Durham	Stamford Bridge	2004
151	P J Hartley	Somerset	Clevedon	1989
151	A McGrath	Somerset	Elland	1995
151	V J Craven	Glamorgan	Todmorden	2003
150*	K Sharp	Essex	Elland	1991
150*	G M Fellows	Hampshire	Todmorden	1998
150*	S M Guy	Nottinghamshire	Headingley	2005
150*	J A Leaning	Worcestershire	Worcester	2011
150	K Sharp	Glamorgan	Ebbw Vale	1983
150	S N Hartley	Nottinghamshire	Worksop	1988
150	C R Taylor	Derbyshire	Chesterfield	2003

7 Wickets in an Innings (31)

Analysis	Player	Versus	Ground	Season
9 for 27	G A Cope	Northamptonshire	Northampton	1977
9 for 62	M K Bore	Warwicshire	Scarborough	1976
8 for 33	B O Coad	MCC Young Cricketers	York	2018
8 for 53	S J Dennis	Nottinghamshire	Nottingham	1983
8 for 57	M K Bore	Lancashire	Manchester	1977
8 for 79	P J Berry	Derbyshire	Harrogate	1991
7 for 13	P Carrick	Northamptonshire	Marske-by-the-Sea	1977
7 for 21	S Silvester	Surrey	Sunbury-on-Thames	1977
7 for 22	J A R Blain	Surrey	Purley	2004
7 for 32	P W Jarvis	Surrey	The Oval	1984
7 for 34	P Carrick	Glamorgan	Leeds	1986
7 for 37	P M Hutchison	Warwickshire	Coventry	2001
7 for 39	G M Hamilton	Sussex	Leeds	1995
7 for 40	M K Bore	Worcestershire	Old Hill	1976
7 for 44	M K Bore	Lancashire	Harrogate	1976
7 for 44	J P Whiteley	Worcestershire	Leeds	1979
7 for 51	J D Middlebrook	Derbyshire	Rotherham	2000
7 for 53	J P Whiteley	Warwickshire	Birmingham	1980
7 for 55	C White	Leicestershire	Bradford	1990
7 for 58	K Gillhouley	Derbyshire	Chesterfield	1960
7 for 58	P J Hartley	Lancashire	Leeds	1985
7 for 63	M J Hoggard	Worcestershire	Harrogate	1998
7 for 65	M K Bore	Nottinghamshire	Steetley	1976
7 for 70	J D Batty	Leicestershire	Bradford	1992
7 for 71	J D Batty	Hampshire	Harrogate	1994
7 for 81	K Gillhouley	Lancashire	Scarborough	1960
7 for 84	I J Houseman	Kent	Canterbury	1989
7 for 88	I G Swallow	Nottinghamshire	Nottingham	1983
7 for 90	A P Grayson	Kent	Folkestone	1991
7 for 93	D Pickles	Nottinghamshire	Nottingham	1960
7 for 94	K Gillhouley	Northamptonshire	Redcar	1960

12 Wickets in a Match (6)

Analysis		Player	Versus	Ground	Season
13 for 92	(6-48 and 7-44)	M K Bore	Lancashire	Harrogate	1976
13 for 110	(7-70 and 6-40)	J D Batty	Leicestershire	Bradford	1992
13 for 111	(4-49 and 9-62)	M K Bore	Warwickshire	Scarborough	1976
12 for 69	(5-32 and 7-37)	P M Hutchison	Warwickshire	Coventry	2001
12 for 120	(5-39 and 7-81)	K Gillhouley	Lancashire	Scarborough	1960
12 for 162	(5-78 and 7-84)	I J Houseman	Kent	Canterbury	1989

Hat-tricks (4)

Player	Versus	Ground	Season
I G Swallow	Warwickshire	Harrogate	1984
S D Fletcher	Nottinghamshire	Marske-by-the-Sea	1987
I G Swallow	Derbyshire	Chesterfield	1988
M Broadhurst	Essex	Southend-on-Sea	1992

Second Eleven Performance Of The Year Award

The Trophy was instituted in 2013 to reward a Second Eleven performance with either bat or ball that stood out from the ordinary and turned the course of the game.

2013	M D Fisher	6-25	v. Leicestershire (One-Day Trophy)	
				Grace Road, Leicester
2014	J A Leaning	102	v. Nottinghamshire (T20)	Trent College, Nottingham
2015	M J Waite	143	v. Lancashire (Friendly)	Scarborough
2016	W M H Rhodes	137		
		and 114*	v Lancashire (Friendly)	Liverpool
2017	J W Jack Shutt	4-19	v. Middlesex in the Trophy Final	Headingley
		and 4-12	v. Derbyshire in the T20	Alvaston and Boulton
		to secure two victories.		
2018	J H Wharton	162	v. Leicestershire (Friendly)	Kibworth CC
		in only his second Second Eleven match.		
2019	M L Revis	177	v Sussex (Friendly)	Hove

ANNUAL REPORT
and
Statement of Account
for the year ended
December 31, 2019

CHAIRMAN'S STATEMENT

ROBIN SMITH

This is my last report to members, and it has two contrasting headlines. On the field Yorkshirehad a somewhat unsatisfactory year, but on the financial front an outstandingly successful one as a consequence of the staging of four World Cup matches and an Ashes Test.

Our cricket performance in the 2019 season was disappointing. We failed to advance beyond the group stages in both white-ball competitions, and finished fifth in the Championship.

The Championship season had started with high hopes, and progressed satisfactorily until the September resumption at Taunton, at which point we stood fourth and still had an arithmetical chance of topping the table. Defeat at Taunton, followed by an even worse defeat by Kent at Emerald Headingley, put an end to our hopes and resulted in us finishing fifth in the Championship. Sadly, the Kent defeat remained uppermost in our minds as the season drew to its close, despite splendid innings by Tom KohlerCadmore and newcomer Tom Loten at Edgbaston in the rain-affected drawn final game of the season.

The closed season has seen a thorough review of all aspects of our cricket resources and performance, of which fuller details can be found in the Director of Cricket's report. I am confident that Martyn Moxon's and Andrew Gale's plans are sound, and I believe that members can expect some competitive performances in the coming season. The additions of Keshav Maharaj and Ravichandran Ashwin will strengthen the bowling, and Dawid Malan's arrival will make a difference to the top order. Nicholas Pooran will also return. Add in the established players and the developing youngsters, and there is every prospect of the coming season delivering a broad panoply of cricket entertainment and success.

Notwithstanding a somewhat qualified season for Yorkshire on the field, the year will be long remembered by all cricket followers as an exceptional one, rather as 1981 — the year of the Botham/Willis *Ashes* victory — is to this day. The final day of the Australia Test saw Ben Stokes's magnificent innings (not to mention Jack Leach's single run!) procuring the most improbable and tense of England wins to the delight of a full ground. I sat next to the Australian Chairman of Selectors throughout, and our respective reactions to the Stokes winning boundary were in sharp contrast!

I hope I was as magnanimous in victory as he was gracious in defeat! Four successful World Cup matches, with the ground full to capacity, were also efficiently delivered, and thereby Emerald Headingley's reputation as a world-class international venue was enhanced. The completion of the new Emerald Stand on time and within budget, itself an outstanding achievement for our Operations team led by Sam Hinchliffe, made a huge contribution to this outcome, and I pay tribute to all involved, including the main contractor, Caddick Construction and, not least, Leeds City Council, whose leader, Judith Blake, supplied support and encouragement throughout as well as the breakthrough which secured the funding.

The Emerald Stand has become the home of a new joint venture hospitality-and-events business with Leeds Rugby. Since the stand's completion it has hosted a large and varied number of events, many unconnected with cricket and rugby. For instance, more Christmas parties of outside commercial institutions were held at the ground than ever before by a considerable margin. Emerald Headingley's reputation as the entertainment venue of choice in the region has grown significantly during the year, and we are confident that the newly established joint venture will make material contributions to the Club in the years ahead. I might add that Emerald Headingley constitutes an asset of abiding value to Leeds and to Yorkshire, and members should be proud of its major contribution to our region.

Off the field there were three notable developments. First, the opening of the new Emerald Stand to which I have already referred. Second, the delivery of a £5m-plus profit before tax, the largest by far in the Club's history. Third, the repayment of £3.8m of debt, the result of which is apparent on the balance sheet. Full details of the Club's financial performance during the year are set out in the Finance Director's report. I should add that at the end of the year agreement was reached with the trustees of the Graves Trusts for the refinancing of the Club's debt for a further period of five years, and I extend to the trustees the Club's profound appreciation of the support they have given to us over the past five years and for their willingness to continue that support. Without it we would not have been able to develop the ground as we have, nor to deliver an unsurpassed cricket experience to so many. Our thanks are due to our Director of Finance, Paul Hudson, for leading the refinancing negotiations on the Club's behalf and to his team for their consistent and timely delivery of accurate figures and reports throughout the year.

Despite this positive financial picture there are some negatives ahead. In 2020 and 2024 Emerald Headingley will not stage a Test match, which means broadly that income in those years may be insufficient to sustain debt repayments. Prudent management of all aspects of the Club will therefore continue to be an imperative for the foreseeable future, with the eyes of all involved being focused on debt reduction.

Members will be aware of the progress made in Yorkshire by Women's and Girls' cricket under the direction of Jane Hildreth, and I do ask all to peruse her report with great care. This is the first year in which the Club's Annual Report has included a report on the women's game, which reflects the fact that women's cricket is an integral part of the Club's affairs and one which is growing in importance. I encourage members to take every opportunity to watch a game in the coming season. They will not be disappointed.

The coming year will see the introduction of the new *The Hundred* competition, with men's and women's games being played over the same period. The Northern Superchargers men will play at Emerald Headingley and the women at York and South Northumberland. With the controversy behind us I trust that all Yorkshire members will give this competition their support, and thereby help it to be the success which the whole English game needs, notably red-ball cricket.

This report would be incomplete without a reference to the two other institutions, namely the Yorkshire Cricket Board (YCB) and the Yorkshire Cricket Foundation (YCF). Together with the Club they constitute Yorkshire Cricket, a brand and an endeavour which crosses the county, both geographically and in terms of the breadth of its offering. The YCB governs all recreational cricket, and its responsibilities include that most crucial of activities, the development of talented young cricketers. YCF, now 10 years old, is the Club's charity. It is active in the fields of heritage, including the Club's museum, education, participation and health and well-being.

The ECB has introduced new governance guidelines following an exercise in which board member Katherine Mathew played an influential part, for which our thanks are due. The result is some recommended changes to our Rules, with an explanatory memorandum, which I ask you to support. In passing, I mention that your Club introduced new corporatestyle governance with new Rules in 2003, which created a balanced board containing executives and non-executives, novel in the cricket world at the time. This has worked well, and it is gratifying to note that the game is now catching up!

In September it was announced to the great pleasure of Yorkshire cricket followers that a knighthood was to be conferred by Her Majesty the Queen on our former captain and opening batsman, Sir Geoffrey Boycott. At the end of the year the awards in the New Year's Honours List of an MBE to England Captain Joe Root and a CBE to former Chairman Colin Graves were announced. I extend our warmest congratulations to them all for these well-deserved honours.

This is my last report to you as your Chairman as I plan to retire from the board on the conclusion of the AGM. I shall do so with mixed feelings. On the one hand, after 20 years on the board and two stints as Chairman I am quite looking forward to a stress-free summer of cricket-watching! On the other hand, I have hugely enjoyed my involvement over the years with so many excellent people, all committed to the endeavour of keeping Yorkshire in the forefront of English cricket, and I shall miss them all. I have derived great satisfaction from seeing the Club's progress over those years.

Twenty years ago, the Club did not own Emerald Headingley and was in a financially precarious position. Today, the Club owns the ground and has redeveloped it to worldclass standards. Emerald Headingley is now widely regarded as in the front rank of Test grounds. In addition, it has evolved a business model which will enable its outstanding debt to be repaid over the coming years. Most important of all, it has a team of employees, ably led by our Chief Executive, Mark Arthur, who are characterised by greater enthusiasm, energy and purpose than I have seen in any organisation with which I have been connected throughout my career. It has been a privilege and a pleasure to have played my small part alongside them, and I extend my heartfelt thanks to them all.

Finally, my warmest appreciation and thanks are due to all our members. Notwithstanding some pretty strong headwinds at times and many disappointments, you have stood firm in your support, and I am truly grateful. I hope that you will be richly rewarded by success on the field in the coming years, coupled with a steadily improving financial position.

ROBIN SMITH TD DL
Chairman
The Yorkshire
County Cricket Club

CHIEF EXECUTIVE'S REPORT

We have just completed an amazing year in the history of Yorkshire Cricket. We have been journeying towards the potential of 2019 for quite some time, but it was absolutely essential that we delivered a positive financial outcome, and we did.

It is special when a ground hosts an *Ashes* series for the first time in 10 years, as well as an ODI, and four ICC World Cup matches. On top of that, halfway through the season, we opened the 4,400-seater Emerald Stand which houses the Emerald Suite, a unique facility in World Sport.

MARK ARTHUR

I would like to commend the executive team, which is the best group of people that I have ever worked with, for delivering on the promise that 2019 would be an incredible year at Emerald Headingley.

I have stated, since I became your Chief Executive, that we would always put cricket first as a Club. We are all aware that we have been a transitioning Club on the field for a few years now. Despite that, our season started off reasonably well, only to trail off at the end of the year. With three County Championship matches to play we still had an outside chance of winning the title. If rain had not intervened with the Hampshire match at Emerald Headingley and the Warwickshire match at Edgbaston the final Championship table might have looked different. The One Day Cup and the Vitality T20 Blast campaigns never really got going, so on the domestic front it was not one of our better seasons.

During the winter months Martyn Moxon and Andrew Gale have put together a squad that should be competitive in all three competitions. We welcome Dawid Malan on a four-year contract, who will bring experience and international ability to our top order, and Ravi Ashwin, who will join us for Championship cricket once his IPL commitments have concluded. It is a larger squad than normal as we want to have plenty of cover for international call-ups, the Hundred and, of course, the inevitable crop of injuries sustained during a busy season. There will certainly be healthy competition for places in the first team, and match-winning performances will be required in the second eleven in order to stake a claim. I wish Steve Patterson in the Championship and One Day Cup, and David Willey, our captain for the T20 Vitality Blast, every success for the upcoming campaigns.

The Emerald Headingley Test of 2019 has to go down as one of the best Test matches ever staged, with Ben Stokes delivering mission impossible. For me, this was a perfect finale to a remarkable year for the Club, witnessed by millions of people around the world. In years to come more people than our capacity will state that they were there! It can only have enhanced our reputation.

However, we do need to continually improve the facilities at Emerald Headingly in order to compete for hosting the best international matches beyond 2024. The ECB have set up a new facilities fund for counties to apply for in order to make improvements to their grounds. Your Board will be looking to prioritise funding applications that both fit the criteria for the ECB funding policy and the needs of Yorkshire CCC. I hope to be able to update members at the AGM.

Our outgrounds, Scarborough CC and York CC, both earned enormous praise for their staging of matches in 2019 and are the envy of other counties. Every county wants to play at Scarborough, and Scarborough has been rewarded with their first *Roses* match for nearly 30 years. Given a decent forecast, we are expecting bumper crowds. York CC, having hosted theor first-ever County Championship match in 2019, are hosting a "Festival of Cricket" this season with two 50-over matches and two women's Hundred matches in an 11-day period.

2020 sees the dawn of a new era for cricket with the introduction of The Hundred. We will be hosting the Northern Superchargers, both men and women, at Emerald Headingley and York. There will be some great cricketers participating which should provide wonderful entertainment for everyone.

We have a strong sense of community at Yorkshire and our charitable arm, the Yorkshire Cricket Foundation, has been recognised by winning two national awards: Best Volunteer Programme of the Year and Best Community Programme for the Inspirational Women's project at Bradford Park Avenue. The YCF now has 22 full time members of staff and hundreds of volunteers.

The success of the Club off the field in 2019 was truly a team effort. There are too many individuals to thank in this report, but I would like to highlight the contributions of YCCC Board, Leeds City Council, Caddick Construction HSBC, the Graves Family Trust, Leeds Rugby, Sodexo, the YCB, The Emerald Group, The Emerald Foundation and Mazars. Mazars has been our Principal Partner for six years. They originally sponsored the Club in 2014 for a three-year term, but extended for a further three years and have been part of our recent success on and off the field. We remain the best of friends.

I hope you are looking forward to the season as much as I am.ason.

MARK ARTHUR
Chief Executive
Yorkshire County Cricket Club

DIRECTOR OF PROFESSIONAL CRICKET'S REPORT

County Championship

Although we finished one place lower in 2019 than the previous two years, we played a lot better cricket, winning five games and drawing a further five. There were some disappointing results along the way, none more so than the game against Kent at Emerald Headingley. There were also some outstanding results, both individually and as a team.

MARTYN MOXON

We went into the final three games with an outside chance of winning the Championship, and a great chance of securing a top three spot. Defeats at Taunton and at home to Kent, along with bad weather at Edgbaston, left us with a feeling of disappointment. Finishing poorly left a negative feeling, going into the winter, as opposed to the previous two years, where we had finished strongly, and I think that hid the fact that we actually played better cricket over the season.

Gary Ballance was once again the stand-out player in the Championship, scoring 975 runs. Will Fraine, in his first season for the Club, came into the team and started to make the opening spot his own before his season-ending injury. The hundred he scored against Surrey at Scarborough really highlighted his potential. There were also a number of other young players who gained more experience and, although there was still some inconsistency they have shown what they are capable of at first-team level.

Keshav Maharaj proved to be a hugely successful signing, and he contributed to several victories. Not only did he take 38 wickets in five games, he also scored valuable runs batting at number eight, which helped the balance of the side. Aside from the on-field performances, he was a great help off the pitch with the advice he gave to our own young spinners. He was the ideal overseas professional, and consequently we are delighted to be able to bring him back for the opening two County Championship games of 2020. Although his availability is limited, hopefully he can help us get off to a good start to the season.

As you will know, we have secured the services of Ravi Ashwin for at least eight Championship games following the IPL. Ravi is a top international performer, and is very willing to pass on his own knowledge and experience to our players, which will be great for their development.

There will be up to four games without an overseas player, which will give our own players the opportunity to stake their claim. The signings of Keshav and Ravi are obviously short-term measures, but we need to look at who is going to bowl spin for us in the longer term. This period will help us to assess that conundrum.

We have talked over the last three years about a transitional period, where we wanted to give our younger players opportunities and to learn more about their capabilities. I think we are now in a position to push on and really challenge for trophies again.

I believe we have shown our intent with the signings of Keshav and Ravi, but even more so in the acquisition of Dawid Malan. We are absolutely delighted to welcome Dawid. He is a player of high quality, who can perform in all formats and will give us the experience we require going forward.

These acquisitions, along with the development of our own players over the last couple of years, give us a strong squad on paper. As we all know you don't win on paper, and we still have to perform. Nevertheless, I think we can look forward to the season with excitement.

Limited-Overs Cricket

Our one-day results were largely disappointing last season, more so because we got ourselves into winning positions on a number of occasions but made mistakes at crucial times. The fact that we tied three games and lost a game by one run shows how different it could have been, but if we're being brutally honest we generally played below our capabilities. The disruption of losing Matthew Fisher, Adil Rashid and Josh Poysden impacted upon our plans, and the weather certainly didn't help with four no-results.

We have spent a lot of time this winter continuing to work on individual skills, but also on decision-making under pressure.

Again, I think we have shown our intent in the T20 by signing Nicholas Pooran for at least the first 11 games. He made a favourable impression in his short stay last season, and we look forward to having him here for an extended period this season.

With the start of The Hundred the 50-over competition will give opportunities to players who may not normally get a chance to play first-eleven cricket. We will not be signing an overseas player for this competition, and look forward to seeing how our players perform in what will be a highly competitive competition.

2nd XI, Academy and Under-17s

Generally, our younger players gained valuable experience in 2019 and showed a growing maturity in their performances.

The 2nd XI came third in the Championship, but were only two points off the leaders. In white-ball cricket winning the group in the 50-over competition along with a fifth-place finish in the T20 resembles a reasonable season.

The Academy side came seventh in the Yorkshire League North, which was a good result for a young side, and there were plenty of great individual performances. The Under-17s also performed well, and we were delighted to have a number of players pushing on for higher honours. Three of our Academy players (Finlay, Bean, Harry Duke and George Hill) have represented England at Under-19s level over the last year. Opening batsman Matthew Revis, at the age of just 17, made his first-class debut against Kent, and a host of Academy players earned a place in the second team. As ever, consistency is key for them.

Contract Changes

The ECB and PCA have brought in a change to the types of contracts Counties are able to offer their players. In the past, once a player has come off the Academy we have used a Senior Academy and Junior Pro contract as stepping stones to achieving full professional status. Our only options now are to offer either a rookie contract or a triallist before we have to offer a player full professional terms. There have been some concerns raised by the counties on the effect of these changes and, at the time of writing, discussions are still taking place with a view to tweaking the system to ensure that we give players the best chance of progressing within the game.

Thank you

First of all, I'd like to thank the groundstaff at Emerald Headingley and around the county who have done a fantastic job in a year of increasing demands on pitches. Congratulations to the team at Emerald Headingley who earned an award and national recognition for their County Championship pitches.

As ever, I'd like to thank the Board, my support team and all of the staff at the Club for their support, but most of all to you, our supporters for whom we will hopefully give some great entertainment this season.

MARTYN MOXON
Director of Professional Cricket
Yorkshire County Cricket Club

FINANCE DIRECTOR'S REPORT

This has been an exceptional year financially, which has delivered a significant impact on our funding. Overall, we have generated earnings before interest, tax, depreciation and amortisation of £6,451,000 (2018:£515,000) in the financial year. These results are due in large part to two specific events that occurred during the year.

Firstly, the staging of four World Cup matches generated a one-off receipt of £1m that was distributed to all first-class counties, together with payments to stage the four matches of an additional £600,000. In addition, we received a small bonus on successful delivery. We were also able

PAUL HUDSON

to sell a large volume of corporate hospitality for the matches and generated strong pouring rights income.

Secondly, the *Ashes* was undoubtedly the standout financial highlight of the year, generating £4.7m in ticket sales, bolstered by another £1.9m of corporate hospitality revenue and pouring rights income.

As I reported last year the catering and pouring rights have now reverted to the Club. This has clearly been a key new income stream, which produced a revenue of £611,000 in this first complete year.

Operating costs have increased over the prior year, due to the new stand and cost of operating the catering operation.

The new Emerald stand was brought into operation during the year, and we have started to make operating-lease payments over the 40-year term. Following the 40-year term the ownership of part of the stand will revert to the Club. The first year's payment is £607,000, of which this year's results include the period from August 31, 2019, when the charging arrangement started.

The balance sheet has continued to strengthen as a result of the *Ashes* and the World Cup. You will recall that during 2018 we repaid £1.8m of debt, which has been followed up this year by a further £3.8m repayment. The ability to repay debt over the last two financial years has marked a long-awaited return to reducing the debt and hence interest burden that the Club has built up with the purchasing of the ground and development of facilities. Our loans, borrowings and overdrafts net of cash have now been reduced to £18,340,000 from a year-end peak at December 31, 2016, of £24,636,000.

We have also seen a reduction in deferred income during the year, and this is predominantly as a result of a change in makeup of international cricket at Emerald Headingley Stadium in 2020 compared to 2019.

We are now aware of the new funding structure of the game, from the ECB. We have incorporated this into our financial plans, and have agreed a new term on our loans from the Colin Graves family trusts. This was planned, as discussed at last year's AGM, and the term takes us through to 2024. During this period, the Club remains able to continue to operate in a normal year at a broadly break-even level. This is after the funding of a significant interest cost. The ability to make further significant debt repayments remains dependant on major matches or other one-off events.

The 2020 year sees us without a Test match, and as such will be a very difficult year. We plan to make no major loan repayments during the year as we deliver two international T20s. Whilet these make a modest return they are not of such a significant scale that debt repayments are envisaged.

In summary, from a financial perspective, this has been a significant year for the Club. We have made inroads into debt repayment, and now have a platform from which we can move forward in a managed way.

PAUL HUDSON
Director of Finance
Yorkshire County Cricket Club

White Rose for Ravi Ashwin

Indian spinner Ravi Ashwin has arrived in Yorkshire with quite a reputation behind him.

Ashwin, who will play a minimum of eight County Championship matches from mid-summer onwards, has taken just over 1,000 wickets across all three formats in his professional career, while his 564 wickets with red ball and white made him the leading international wicket-taker through the most recent decade.

"I'm thrilled to be joining Yorkshire, a club with a wonderful history and a fantastic fan base," he said. "I think our team looks extremely talented with some superb pace bowlers and exciting batsmen. Hopefully, my role as the spinner will be a key feature in helping the team to achieve success."

RECENT FINANCIAL TRENDS

	2019	2018	2017	2016	2015
	£000	£000	£000	£000	£000
Income:					
International ticket and hospitality revenue	10,484	2,498	2,686	2,399	2,441
Domestic ticket and hospitality revenue	1,095	999	932	1,005	836
Subscriptions	812	828	742	740	652
England and Wales Cricket Board	2,536	2,119	3,152	2,638	2,481
Commercial income	3,001	2,353	1,998	1,881	1,905
Other	118	118	150	131	50
Total Income	**17,996**	**8,915**	**9,660**	**8,794**	**8,365**
Cost of sales	(4,229)	(2,095)	(2,208)	(2,109)	(1,993)
Cricket expenses	(3,500)	(3,386)	(3,326)	(3,055)	(3,168)
Overheads	(3,817)	(2,920)	(2,982)	(2,554)	(2,610)
EBITDA	**6,451**	**515**	**1,144**	**1,076**	**594**
Interest	(680)	(797)	(805)	(794)	(639)
Depreciation	(590)	(556)	(513)	(465)	(435)
Capital grants release	253	190	188	186	177
Surplus/(deficit) before exceptional items	**5,434**	**(648)**	**14**	**3**	**(302)**
Exceptional items	—	—	(68)	—	781
Surplus/(deficit) before taxation	**5,434**	**(648)**	**(54)**	**3**	**479**
Loans, borrowing and overdrafts net of cash	**18,340**	**20,636**	**22,942**	**24,636**	**24,055**

CORPORATE GOVERNANCE

The Board is accountable to the Club's members for good corporate governance, and this statement describes how the principles of governance are applied.

THE BOARD

The Board is responsible for approving Club policy and strategy. It meets bi-monthly, or more frequently if business needs require, and has a schedule of matters specifically reserved to it for decision, including all significant commercial issues and all capital expenditure.

The Executive Management Team supply the Board with appropriate and timely information, and Board Members are free to seek any further information they consider necessary. The Board has formed various committees to assist in the governance of the Club's affairs.

NOMINATIONS COMMITTEE

The Nominations and Governance Committee is formally constituted with written terms of reference, which are defined in the Club Rules and reviewed regularly. It is chaired by the Chairman, and the other members of the committee are the President, Secretary and one Non-Executive board member, currently Katherine Mathew.

AUDIT, GOVERNANCE AND RISK COMMITTEE

The Audit, Governance and Risk Committee meets to provide oversight of the financial reporting process, the audit process, systems of internal controls and compliance with laws and regulations. It is chaired by Stephen Willis, and meets with the external auditors as part of this process. The other members of the committee are Katherine Mathew and Neil Hartley.

REMUNERATION COMMITTEE

The Remuneration Committee assists the Board in developing and administering a fair remuneration policy for the Club and determining remuneration of senior employees. It is chaired by Stephen Willis, and the other members of the committee are Robin Smith and Hanif Malik.

MEMBERS' COMMITTEE

The Club encourages effective communication with its members, and the Members' Committee, as defined in the Club Rules, is appointed for that purpose.

INTERNAL CONTROL

The Board acknowledges its responsibility to maintain a sound system of internal control relating to operational, financial and compliance controls and risk management to safeguard the members' interests and the Club's assets, and will regularly review its effectiveness. Such a system, however, is designed to manage and meet the Club's particular needs and mitigate the risks to which it is exposed, rather than eliminate the risk of failure to achieve business objectives, and can provide only reasonable and not absolute assurance against material mis-statement or loss. The Club considers the key components to provide effective internal control and improve business efficiency are:

- Regular meetings with senior management to review and assess progress made against objectives and deal with any problems which arise from such reviews.

- A financial reporting system of annual budgets, periodic forecasts and detailed monthly reporting which includes cash-flow forecasts. Budgets and forecasts are reviewed and approved by the Board.

- A management and organisation structure exists with defined responsibilities and appropriate authorisation limits and short lines of communication to the Non-Executive Chairman.

- A Senior Independent Director is appointed by the Board, whose role is to serve as a sounding board for the Chairman and act as an intermediary for other directors. The position is currently held by Stephen Willis.

BOARD MEMBERS' RESPONSIBILITIES

The Board Members are responsible for preparing the annual report and the financial statements in accordance with applicable law and regulations. Co-operative and Community Benefit Society law requires the Board Members to prepare financial statements for each financial year. Under that law the Board Members have elected to prepare the financial statements in accordance with United Kingdom Generally Accepted Accounting Practice (United Kingdom Accounting Standards and applicable law). Under Co-operative and Community Benefit Society law the Board Members must not approve the financial statements unless they are satisfied that they give a true and fair view of the state of affairs of the Club and of the income and expenditure of the Club for that period.

In preparing these financial statements the Board Members are required to:

- select suitable accounting policies and then apply them consistently;
- make judgements and accounting estimates that are reasonable and prudent;
- prepare the financial statements on the going-concern basis unless it is inappropriate to presume that the Club will continue in business.

The Board Members are responsible for keeping adequate accounting records that are sufficient to show and explain the Club's transactions and disclose with reasonable accuracy at any time the financial position of the Club and enable them to ensure that the financial statements comply with the Co-operative and Community Benefit Societies Act 2014.

They are also responsible for safeguarding the assets of the Club and hence for taking reasonable steps for the prevention and detection of fraud and other irregularities.

DISCLOSURE OF INFORMATION TO AUDITOR

The members of the Board who held office at the date of approval of the Annual Report and Accounts confirm that, so far as they are aware, there is no relevant information of which the Club's auditor is unaware; or each member has taken all the steps that he ought to have taken as a member to make himself aware of any relevant audit information or to establish that the Club's auditor is aware of that information.

INDEPENDENT AUDITORS' REPORT

TO THE MEMBERS OF THE YORKSHIRE COUNTY CRICKET CLUB

Opinion

We have audited the financial statements of Yorkshire County Cricket Limited (the 'Club') for the year ended December 31, 2019, which comprise the Income And Expenditure Account, the Balance Sheet, Cash Flow Statement, Statement of Changes in Equity and notes to the financial statements, including a summary of significant accounting policies. The financial reporting framework that has been applied in their preparation is applicable law and United Kingdom Accounting Standards, including FRS 102 The Financial Reporting Standard applicable in the UK and Republic of Ireland (United Kingdom Generally Accepted Accounting Practice).

In our opinion the financial statements:

- give a true and fair view of the state of the Club's affairs as at December 31, 2019, and of its income and expenditure for the year then ended;
- have been properly prepared in accordance with United Kingdom Generally Accepted Accounting Practice; and
- have been prepared in accordance with the requirements of the Cooperative and Community Benefit Societies Act 2014.

Basis for opinion

We conducted our audit in accordance with International Standards on Auditing (UK) (ISAs (UK)) and applicable law. Our responsibilities under those standards are further described in the Auditor's Responsibilities for the Audit of the Financial Statements section of our report. We are independent of the Club in accordance with the ethical requirements that are relevant to our audit of the financial statements in the UK, including the FRC's Ethical Standard, and we have fulfilled our other ethical responsibilities in accordance with these requirements. We believe that the audit evidence we have obtained is sufficient and appropriate to provide a basis for our opinion.

Conclusions relating to going concern

We have nothing to report in respect of the following matters in relation to which the ISAs (UK) require us to report to you where:

- the board members' use of the going-concern basis of accounting in the preparation of the financial statements is not appropriate; or
- the board members have not disclosed in the financial statements

any identified material uncertainties that may cast significant doubt about the Club's ability to continue to adopt the going-concern basis of accounting for a period of at least twelve months from the date when the financial statements are authorised for issue.

Other information

The other information which comprises the Chairman's Report, Chief Executive Report, Director of Cricket's Report, President, Board Members, Staff and Players, Director of Finance's Report, Corporate Governance Statement, AGM Minutes, Members' Committee Report, Board Attendance and Players' Appearances for 2019, Yorkshire Cricket Foundation Manager's Report, Archives Committee Report and Notice of AGM and Agenda. Our opinion on the financial statements does not cover the other information and, except to the extent otherwise explicitly stated in our report, we do not express any form of assurance conclusion thereon.

In connection with our audit of the financial statements our responsibility is to read the other information and, in doing so, consider whether the other information is materially inconsistent with the financial statements or our knowledge obtained in the audit or otherwise appears to be materially mis-stated. If we identify such material inconsistencies or apparent material mis-statements we are required to determine whether there is a material mis-statement in the financial statements or a material mis-statement of the other information. If, based on the work we have performed, we conclude that there is a material mis-statement of this other information we are required to report that fact.

Matters on which we are required to report by exception

In the light of the knowledge and understanding of the Club and its environment obtained in the course of the audit we have not identified material mis-statements in the directors' report.

We have nothing to report in respect of the following matters where the Cooperative and Community Benefit Societies Act 2014 requires us to report to you if, in our opinion:

- adequate accounting records have not been kept, or returns adequate for our audit have not been received from branches not visited by us; or
- the financial statements are not in agreement with the accounting records and returns; or
- we have not received all the information and explanations we require for our audit.

Responsibilities of the board

As explained more fully in the board members' responsibilities statement, the directors are responsible for the preparation of the financial statements and for being satisfied that they give a true and fair view, and for such internal control as the board members determine is necessary to enable the preparation of financial statements that are free from material mis-statement, whether due to fraud or error.

In preparing the financial statements the board members are responsible for assessing the Club's ability to continue as a going concern, disclosing, as applicable, matters related to going concern and using the going-concern basis of accounting unless the directors either intend to liquidate the Club or to cease operations, or have no realistic alternative but to do so.

Auditors responsibilities for the audit of the financial statements

Our objectives are to obtain reasonable assurance about whether the financial statements as a whole are free from material mis-statement, whether due to fraud or error, and to issue an auditor's report that includes our opinion. Reasonable assurance is a high level of assurance, but is not a guarantee that an audit conducted in accordance with ISAs (UK) will always detect a material mis-statement when it exists. Mis-statements can arise from fraud or error and are considered material if, individually or in the aggregate, they could reasonably be expected to influence the economic decisions of users taken on the basis of these financial statements.

A further description of our responsibilities for the audit of the financial statements is located on the Financial Reporting Council's website at: *http://www.frc.org.uk/auditorsresponsibilities*. This description forms part of our auditor's report.

Use of our report

This report is made solely to the Club's members, as a body, in accordance with Section 87 of the Co-operative and Community Benefit Societies Act 2014. Our audit work has been undertaken so that we might state to the company's members those matters we are required to state to them in an auditor's report and for no other purpose. To the fullest extent permitted by law we do not accept or assume responsibility to anyone other than the company and the company's members, as a body, for our audit work, for this report, or for the opinions we have formed.

CHRIS BUTT (Senior Statutory Auditor) for and on behalf of Garbutt & Elliott Audit Limited

Statutory Auditor
Chartered Accountants
33 Park Place, Leeds LS1 2RY

February 7, 2020

433

INCOME AND EXPENDITURE ACCOUNT
for the year ended December 31, 2019

	Note	2019 £	2018 £
Income			
International ticket and hospitality revenue		10,483,782	2,498,366
Domestic ticket and hospitality revenue		1,095,209	999,030
Subscriptions		811,815	828,003
England and Wales Cricket Board		2,536,345	2,119,265
Commercial income		3,001,265	2,352,790
Other income		67,900	117,781
		17,996,316	8,915,235
Cost of sales			
International match and hospitality expenditure		3,362,414	1,264,173
Domestic match and hospitality costs (home fixtures)		561,569	586,517
Commercial costs		304,533	244,150
		(4,228,516)	(2,094,840)
Cricket expenses			
Staff remuneration and employment expenses		2,714,761	2,585,810
Match expenses (away fixtures)		227,138	225,638
Development expenses		415,522	443,700
Other cricket expenses		142,574	130,433
		(3,499,995)	(3,385,581)
Overheads			
Infrastructure and ground operations		1,514,962	1,191,570
Commercial		1,100,589	799,445
Administration		962,387	729,940
Ticket and membership office		238,949	198,701
		(3,816,887)	(2,919,656)
Earnings before interest, tax, depreciation and amortisation		6,450,918	515,158
Interest		(680,183)	(797,485)
Depreciation	5	(590,049)	(555,648)
Release of capital grants	10	252,971	190,315
		(1,017,261)	(1,162,818)
(Deficit)/Surplus before exceptional item and taxation		(647,660)	13,727
Exceptional item		—	(67,699)
Surplus/(Deficit) Before Taxation		5,433,657	(647,660)
Taxation	4,11	(1,031,832)	286,804
Surplus/(Deficit) after taxation		4,401,825	(360,856)

BALANCE SHEET

as at December 31, 2019

	Note	2019 £	2019 £	2018 £	2018 £
Assets employed:					
Investments	14		**50**		50
Fixed assets	5		**29,687,706**		28,852,481
Current assets:					
Stocks		**132,212**		104,211	
Debtors	6	**1,357,568**		2,826,391	
Cash at bank and in hand		**319,778**		1,817,901	
		1,809,558		4,748,503	
Creditors: amounts falling due within one year	7	**(5,707,027)**		(12,997,845)	
Net current liabilities			**(3,897,469)**		(8,249,342)
Total assets less current liabilities			**25,790,287**		20,603,189
Funded by:					
Creditors: amounts falling due after more than one year	8		**19,411,006**		18,766,152
Provision for liabilities			**15 450,000**		316,546
Deferred Income — capital grants	10		**4,894,634**		4,887,669
			24,755,640		23,970,367
Capital and Reserves					
Called up share capital	12		**214**		228
Capital redemption reserve			**676**		662
Income and expenditure account			**1,033,757**		(3,368,068)
			1,034,647		(3,367,178)
			25,790,287		20,603,189

These accounts were approved by the Board on February 7, 2020.

ROBIN SMITH, Chairman

PAUL HUDSON, Club Secretary

CASH FLOW STATEMENT
for the year ended December 31, 2019

	Note	2019 £	2018 £
Cash flows from Operating Activities			
Surplus/(Deficit) for the year		4,401,825	(360,856)
Adjustments for:			
Deprecation of tangible assets		586,510	555,648
Loss on disposal of tangible fixed asset		3,539	—
Loan interest payable		680,183	797,485
Capital grants released		(252,971)	(190,315)
Taxation		1,031,832	(286,804)
Decrease (Increase) in trade and other debtors		570,445	(992,192)
(Increase)/Decrease in stocks		(28,001)	12,947
(Decrease)/Increase in creditors		(2,851,025)	4,180,098
Interest paid		(680,183)	(797,485)
Net cash inflow from operating activities		3,462,154	2,918,526
Cash flows from investing activities			
Purchase of tangible fixed assets	5	(1,430,774)	(713,387)
Sale of tangible fixed assets	5	5,500	—
Capital grants received	10	259,936	100,000
Net cash outflow from investing activities		(1,165,338)	(613,387)
Cash flows from financing activities			
Repayment of borrowings		(3,725,565)	(1,128,085)
Repayment of finance lease liabilities		(69,374)	(704,430)
Net cash outflow from financing activites		(3,794,939)	(1,832,515)
(Decrease)/Increase in cash in the period		(1,498,125)	472,624
Cash and cash equivalents at January 1		1,817,901	1,345,277
Cash and cash equivalents at December 31		319,778	1,817,901

STATEMENT OF CHANGES IN EQUITY
for the year ended December 31, 2019

	Called Up Share Capital £	Capital Redemption Reserve £	Income and Expenditure Account £	Total £
Balance at January 1, 2018	210	680	(3,007,212)	(3,006,322)
Additional share capital for new members	18	(18)	—	—
Defi cit for the year after taxation	—	—	(360,856)	(360,856)
Balance at December 31, 2018	228	662	(3,368,068)	(3,367,178)
Balance at January 1, 2019	228	662	(3,368,068)	(3,367,178)
Reduction in share capital for new members	(14)	14	—	—
Surplus for the year after taxation	—	—	4,401,825	4,401,825
Balance at December 31, 2019	214	676	1,033,757	1,034,647

NOTES TO THE ACCOUNTS

for the year ended December 31, 2019

1. Accounting policies

These financial statements were prepared in accordance with Financial Reporting Standard 102. The Financial Reporting Standard applicable in the UK and Republic of Ireland ("FRS 102") as issued in August 2014 and the Co-Operative and Community Benefit Societies Act 2014. The amendments to FRS 102 issued in July 2015 have been applied. The presentation currency of these financial statements is sterling.

Under section 100 of the Co-operative and Community Benefit Societies Act 2014 neither The Yorkshire Cricket Foundation nor Headingley North-South Stand Limited meet the definition of a subsidiary. The Co-operative and Community Benefit Societies Act 2014 only requires a consolidation to be prepared where investments meet the definition of a subsidiary. In addition, under section 9.3(g) of FRS 102 an entity is exempt from preparing consolidated financial statements if not required by the applicable statutory framework (in this case, Co-operative and Community Benefit Societies Act 2014). As such, no consolidated accounts have been prepared.

(a) Income

All income is accounted for on an accruals basis except for donations which are accounted for in the year of receipt.

Income represents amounts receivable from the Club's principal activities. Income is analysed between international ticket and hospitality revenue, domestic ticket and hospitality revenue, subscriptions, England and Wales Cricket Board, commercial and other income:

International ticket and hospitality revenue

Relate to amounts received from ticket sales and hospitality directly attributable to staging international cricket matches in Yorkshire.

Domestic ticket and hospitality revenue

Relate to amounts received from ticket sales and hospitality directly attributable to staging domestic cricket matches in Yorkshire.

Subscriptions

Subscription income comprises amounts receivable from members in respect of the current season. Subscriptions received in respect of future seasons is treated as deferred income.

England and Wales Cricket Board (ECB)

ECB income relates to fees receivable, including performance-related elements, in the current season distributed from central funds in accordance with the First Class Memorandum of Understanding. ECB fees received in respect of future seasons are treated as deferred income. ECB distributions receivable to fund capital projects are treated as deferred income, and are released to the Income and Expenditure Account by equal installments over the expected useful lives of the relevant assets in accordance with accounting policy (c) Fixed assets and depreciation.

Commercial Income

Commercial income relates to amounts received from stadium naming rights, ground advertising, retail operations, catering guarantees, indoor cricket-centre facility hire, dinners and other events. Advertising income received in respect of future seasons is treated as deferred income.

Other Income

Other income relates to amounts received from sundry items which mainly consists of donations, car parking and any other income not falling into the above categories.

(b) Investments in jointly controlled entity

Investments in jointly controlled entities are carried at cost less impairment.

(c) Fixed assets and depreciation

All expenditure in connection with the development of Emerald Headingley Cricket Ground and the related facilities has been capitalised. Finance costs relating to and incurred during the period of construction were also capitalised. Depreciation is only charged once a discrete phase of the development is completed.

Depreciation is calculated to write down the cost of fixed assets by equal annual installments over their expected useful lives.

The periods generally applicable are:

Emerald Headingley Cricket Ground and Cricket Centre

Buildings	Carnegie Pavilion	125 years
	Other buildings	10-50 years
Fixtures		4 years
Plant & Equipment		4-10 years
Office equipment		2-4 years

Freehold land is not depreciated.

All other expenditure on repairs to Emerald Headingley Cricket Ground and other grounds is written off as and when incurred.

(d) Carnegie Pavilion

The Club's contribution towards the design and build cost of the Carnegie Pavilion is £3m, of which £1.5m is payable over 20 years under a 125-year lease agreement. The £3m, together with the associated legal, professional and capital fit-out costs of the areas within the Pavilion that the Club occupies, have been capitalised and are being depreciated over the 125-year lease term. The £1.5m, payable under the lease agreement has been treated as a finance lease within the financial statements with the capital element reported within Creditors (Finance leases), and the interest element charged to the Income and Expenditure Account on a straightline basis over the 20-year term.

(e) Stocks

Stocks represent goods for resale and are stated at the lower of cost and net realisable value.

(f) Grants

Capital grants relating to the development of Emerald Headingley Cricket Ground (including the Yorkshire Cricket Museum) and Cricket Centre are included within the Balance Sheet as deferred income, and are released to the Income and Expenditure Account by equal installments over the expected useful lives of the relevant assets in accordance with accounting policy (c) Fixed asets and depreciation.

Grants of a revenue nature are credited to the Income and Expenditure Account in the same period as their related expenditure.

(g) Trade and other debtors/creditors

Trade and other debtors are recognised initially at transaction price less attributable transaction costs. Trade and other creditors are recognised initially at transaction price plus attributable transaction costs. Subsequent to initial recognition they are measured at amortised cost using the effective interest method, less any impairment losses in the case of trade debtors. Short-term instruments have an amortised cost materially equal to transaction price unless otherwise stated.

(h) Interest-bearing borrowings classified as basic financial instruments

Interest-bearing borrowings are recognised initially at the present value of future payments discounted at a market rate of interest. Subsequent to initial recognition, interest-bearing borrowings are stated at amortised cost using the effective interest method, less any impairment losses.

(i) Cash and cash equivalents

For the purpose of presentation in the cash-flow statement cash and cash equivalents include cash in hand, deposits with financial institutions which are subject to an insignificant risk of change in value, and bank overdrafts. Bank overdrafts are presented as current borrowings in the balance sheet.

(j) Taxation

Tax on the surplus or deficit for the year comprises current and deferred tax. Tax is recognised in the income-and-expenditure account except to the extent that it relates to items recognised directly in equity or other income, in which case it is recognised directly in equity or other income.

Current tax is the expected tax payable or receivable on the taxable income or deficit for the year, using tax rates enacted or substantively enacted at the balance-sheet date, and any adjustment to tax payable in respect of previous years.

Deferred tax is provided in full using the balance-sheet liability method. A deferred tax asset is recognised where it is probable that future taxable income will be sufficient to utilise the available relief. Tax is charged or credited to the income statement except when it relates to items charged or credited directly to equity, in which case the tax is also dealt with in equity. Deferred tax liabilities and assets are not discounted.

2. Financial Position

Going concern

The financial statements are prepared on a going-concern basis which the board members believe to be appropriate for the following reasons. The Club meets its day-to -day working capital requirements through an overdraft facility, which is repayable on demand in addition to loans from the Graves Family Trusts and HSBC. Details of the loans and the overdraft aturity analysis which impact on the financial position can be found in Note 8.

The Club is in a a net current-liability position of £3.9m (2018:£8.2m) and net assets of £1.0m (2018 — net liabilities of £3.4m) at December 31, 2019. These positions include deferred income of £3.2m, of which £0.9m is long term (2018:£7.6m of which none was long term) which relates primarily to the advance ticket sales of the two IT20 games England will play against Australia and Pakistan in 2020 along with membership subscriptions for 2020. The Board have prepared cash-flow forecasts which show the Club will continue to operate within its current facilities and pay creditors as they fall due for at least the next 12 months from the date of approval of the accounts. The next financial year remains a difficult one for the Club with the lack of a Test Match, but with the introduction of The Hundred and the new County Partnership Agreement (CPA) with the ECB bringing an increased cash inflow from central ECB funding the Club still expect to be profitable during the year.

The new CPA, along with the allocation of international cricket matches to be played at Emerald Headingley Stadium, have helped to provide a degree of certainty over funding through to 2024, and this has been used as the basis for refinancing the debt with the Graves Family Trusts during 2019. This includes deferring capital repayments until the latter half of 2022, when the Club is expecting to go on sale with tickets for the next Ashes Test to be played at Emerald Headingley in 2023. This should help to ensure that the Club remains broadly cash neutral during 2020.

This cash-flow forecast also assumes the renewal of the Club's current overdraft facility of £0.35m (2018: £0.5m) upon its annual expiry in May 2020 under the normal course of business, which has been the case since the facilities were last restructured in 2015. In the unlikely event that the facility is not renewed mitigating actions would be taken to remain within the new facility.

Based on the indications above the Board Members are confident that the Club will have sufficient funds to continue to meet its liabilities as they fall due for at least 12 months from the date of approval of the accounts, and therefore have prepared the accounts on a going-concern basis.

3. Staff Numbers and Costs

The average number of persons employed by the Club (including directors) during the year, analysed by category, was as follows:

	2019	2018
Players (including Academy and Yorkshire Diamonds)	45	43
Non-playing full-time staff	50	51
Seasonal and casual staff	18	15
	113	109

The aggregate payroll costs of these persons were as follows:

	£	£
Wages and salaries	3,819,423	3,549,883
Social security costs	402,502	375,773
Contribution to pension plans	260,535	263,951
	4,482,460	4,189,607

The total compensation of key management personnel (including Board members) as defined on the staff list in the year amounted to £856,983 (2018: £654,025). Non-Executive Board members receive no remuneration.

	2019 £	2018 £
4. Taxation		
Surplus/(deficit) for the year after taxation	**4,401,825**	(360,856)
Total tax (expense)/credit	**(1,031,832)**	286,804
Surplus/(deficit) for the year before taxation	**5,433,658**	(647,660)
Tax at 19.00% (2018: 19.00%)	**(1,032,395)**	123,056
Expenses not deductible for taxation purposes	**(6,983)**	(950)
Reduction in tax rate on deferred tax balances	**14,234**	113,243
Fixed asset permanent differences	**(8,936)**	(73,069)
Non taxable income	**61,287**	98,536
Adjustments in respect of prior periods	**(59,039)**	25,988
Total tax credit/(expense)	**(1,031,832)**	286,804

The Club has utilised corporation-tax losses brought forward in the year, and therefore the tax charge represents movements in deferred tax only.

A reduction in the UK corporation tax rate from 19% to 17% (effective April 1, 2020) was substantively enacted on September 6, 2016. This will reduce the Club's future current tax charge accordingly. The deferred tax asset and liability as at December 31, 2019, has been calculated based on these rates.

5. Fixed assets (See next page)

6. Debtors

	2019 £	2018 £
Trade debtors	**731,662**	1,284,504
Deferred tax asset (see Note 11)	**325,000**	1,223,378
Other debtors	**300,906**	318,509
	1,357,568	2,526,391

7. Creditors: amounts falling due within one year

	2019 £	2018 £
ECB fl oodlight loan (see Note 8)	**—**	100,000
ECB Scarborough loan (see Note 8)	**40,000**	—
C J Graves Accumulation and Maintenance Trust Loan (see Note 8)	**—**	1,750,000
J Graves Accumulation and Maintenance Trust Loan (see Note 8)	**—**	1,750,000
Trade creditors	**1,341,578**	1,053,258
Finance leases (see Note 13)	**75,000**	88,124
Social security and other taxes	**293,216**	350,293
Other creditors	**134,633**	65,761
Accruals	**1,495,407**	236,020
Deferred income	**2,327,193**	7,604,389
	5,707,027	12,997,845

	Cricket Centre		Emerald Headingley Cricket Ground					
	Freehold Land and Buildings £	Plant & Equipment £	Freehold Land and Buildings £	Plant and Equipment £	Improvements to Leasehold Property £	Office Equipment £	Assets in the course of construction £	Total £
Cost								
At January 1, 2019	608,624	798,891	27,121,542	5,281,372	4,453,421	492,354	573,789	39,329,993
Additions			500,000	908,259		22,515		1,430,774
Disposals	(34,877)		(34,877)	(18,876)		(149,493)		(203,246)
Transfers				573,789			(573,789)	—
At December 31, 2019	608,624	798,891	27,586,665	6,744,544	4,453,421	365,376		40,557,521
Depreciation								
At January 1, 2019	209,516	773,527	3,695,229	4,977,674	367,219	454,347		10,477,512
Charged in the year	17,914	4,774	316,401	177,517	42,523	27,382		586,510
Written off on disposal			(34,877)	(9,837)		(149,493)		(194,207)
At December 31, 2019	227,430	778,301	3,976,753	5,145,354	409,742	332,236		10,869,815
Net book value								
At December 31, 2019	381,194	20,590	23,609,912	1,599,190	4,043,679	33,140		29,687,706
At December 31, 2018	399,108	25,364	23,426,313	303,698	4,086,202	38,007	573,789	28,852,481

During 2017 the construction of the new shared stand with Leeds Rugby commenced, together with the constructions of the new Leeds Rugby South Stand. Work was completed in 2019 for the two projects, financed by Legal and General Pension Limited. The two Clubs are funding certain fit-out costs themselves. Upon completion of the fit-out amounts capitalised have been transferred from Assets in the Course of Construction to Plant and Equipment and depreciated over a 10-year term. The costs are being directly incurred and capitalised by Legal and General Pensions Limited. The assets are then leased to Leeds City Council over a 42-year term. The cricket interest is then leased by Leeds City Council to Headingley North-South Stand (Cricket) Limited, company number 10750426, being a wholly owed subsidiary of Headingley North-South Limited, company number 10747361. The Club's interest in Headingley North-South Stand Limited is disclosed in Note 14. In August 2019 the Club commenced to pay a license fee for the use of the stand, as set out in Note 13. The Club's total incurred cost on the fit-out of the stand was £1.32m, and is included within Plant and Equipment.

441

	2019 **£**	2018 £
8. Creditors: amounts falling due after more than one year		
HSBC Bank Loan (see below)	**2,569,014**	2,569,014
ECB Floodlight Loan (see below)	**—**	100,000
ECB Scarborough Cricket Club Loan (see below)	**—**	40,000
CJ Graves Accumulation and Maintenance Trust Loan (see below)	**4,703,500**	4,703,500
J Graves Accumulation and Maintenance Trust Loan (see below)	**4,703,500**	4,703,500
CJ Graves 1999 Settlement Trust Loan (see below)	**5,500,000**	5,500,000
Debentures	**319,750**	345,315
Deferred income	**866,669**	—
Finance leases (see Note 13)	**748,573**	804,823
	19,411,006	18,766,152

Loan, borrowing and overdraft maturity analysis:		
In one year or less or on demand	**115,000**	3,688,124
In more than one year but not more than two years	**2,644,014**	15,122,000
In more than two years but not more than five years	**15,451,750**	2,794,014
In more than five years	**448,573**	850,138
	18,659,337	22,454,276

Loan descriptions

During 2017 the loan from HSBC Bank plc was renegotiated to extend the period over which capital repayments are made. A £500k repayment was made in October 2018 with the balance to be repaid in instalments during 2021. The loan still carries an interest rate charge of 2% above the Bank of England base rate. The Club has also given a First Legal Charge to HSBC Bank plc over the Cricket Centre known as 41/43 St Michael's Lane, Headingley, Leeds and a Third Legal Charge over the property known as Emerald Headingley Cricket Ground, St Michael's Lane, Leeds, in respect of the bank loan and overdrafts. HSBC Bank plc also has a fixed and floating charge over all of the assets of the Club, subject to the Legal Charges referred to above.

C J Graves Accumulation & Maintenance and J Graves Accumulation & Maintenance Trusts loans were renegotiated during the year to extend the period over which capital repayments are made. The loans currently stand at £4.7m, each bearing an interest rate of 4.875% plus any rise in Bank of England base rate above 0.75%. Capital repayments of £1.75m per Trust were made in 2019, and further repayments are due to be paid in 2022 and 2023 with the outstanding balance repaid by October 31, 2024. The two Trusts have been granted by the Club joint First Legal Charge over the property known as Emerald Headingley Cricket Ground, St Michael's Lane, Leeds, and joint Second Legal Charge over the Cricket Centre known as 41/43 St Michael's Lane, Headingley, Leeds.

A further £5.5m of debt has also been incurred from the C J Graves 1999 Settlement Trust, and this was also renegotiated in 2019. This loan bears an interest rate of 0% while Mr C J Graves is the Chair of the ECB before reverting to an interest rate of 4.875% plus any rise in Bank of England base rate above 0.75%. Capital repayment of this loan is due to begin in 2022 with further payments in 2023 before the outstanding balance is repaid on October 31, 2024. The Club has granted Second Legal Charge over the property known as Emerald Headingley Cricket Ground, St Michael's Lane, Leeds, nd Third Legal Charge over the property known as the Cricket Centre, St Michael's Lane, Leeds.

An additional loan was made available by the ECB towards the cost of installing the floodlights at Headingley Cricket Ground. The total available loan is £700k, of which all was drawn down in 2015. A balance of £200k was owing at the end of 2018, and this has been repaid during the year. The current policy of the ECB is to award a capital grant of the same value as the repayment resulting in no cash outflow for the club.

The ECB has also made available a £40k loan for capital improvements at Scarborough

Cricket Club and this will be repaid in 2020 by way of a capital funding payment from the ECB. YCCC has lent this money to Scarborough Cricket Club to enable them to carry out the work on the same basis that the money has been borrowed. This debtor forms part of the Other Debtors line in Note 6, and the transactions have created no cash inflow or outflow and no impact on the Income and Expenditure Account.

9. Financial instruments

	2019 £	2018 £
Assets measured at cost less impairment		
Trade debtors	731,662	1,284,504
Other debtors	300,906	318,509
Cash at bank and in hand	319,778	1,817,901
Liabilities measured at amortised cost		
Term loans	17,476,014	21,216,014
Debentures	319,750	345,315
Finance leases	823,573	892,947
Loan commitments measured at cost less impairment		
Trade creditors	1,341,578	1,053,258
Social security and other taxes	293,216	350,293
Other creditors	134,633	65,761
Accruals	1,495,407	236,020

10. Deferred income - capital grants

At 1 January 1, 2019	4,887,669	4,977,984
Received in year	259,936	100,000
Released to Income and Expenditure Account	(252,971)	(190,315)
At December 31,2019	4,894,634	4,887,669

11. Deferred tax asset

At January 1, 2019	906,832	620,028
Charge/(Credit) to Income and Expenditure Account for the year (see Note 4)	(1,031,832)	286,804
At December 31, 2019 (see Note 6)	(125,000)	906,832
Included within debtors (see Note 6)	325,000	1,223,378
Included within provisions for liabilities	(450,000)	(316,546)
	(125,000)	906,832

The elements of recognised deferred tax are as follows:

Difference between accumulated depreciation and capital allowances	(450,000)	(317,211)
Tax losses	325,000	1,223,377
Short term timing differences	—	666
	(125,000)	906,832

12. Share capital

Allotted, called up and fully paid Ordinary shares of 5p each	214	228

During the year there was a reduction in qualifying members of 271. The total number of qualifying members at December 31, 2019, was 4,286 (2018:4,557). Each member of the Club owns one Ordinary share, and the rights attached thereto are contained within the Club's rules which can be found on the Club's website, or from the Secretary on request.

13. Leasing commitments

Finance lease liabilities are payable as follows:

Minimum Lease Payment	**2019**	2018
	£	£
In one year or less	**75,000**	88,124
Between two and five years	**300,000**	300,000
More than five years	**448,573**	504,823
	823,573	892,947

The Club currently has one finance lease which is with Leeds Beckett University relating to the Carnegie Pavilion. This lease is for 125 years, with lease payments being made for 20 years until 2030, after which a peppercorn rate is due. Non-cancellable operating lease rentals are payable as follows:

Non-cancellable operating-lease rentals are payable as follows:

Minimum Lease Payment	**2019**	2018
	£	£
In one year or less	**456,240**	230,192
Between two and five years	**1,298**	397,708
	457,538	627,900

Operating lease payments amounting to £232,303 (2018:£37,199) were recognised as an expense in the Income and Expenditure. In August 2019 the Club began to pay a license fee for use of the redeveloped North-South Stand and incurred a cost of £195,329 to December 2019. The license is to be renewed annually at the discretion of the Club.

14. Investments

	50	50
Cost: at January 1	**50**	50
Addition	**—**	—
Cost: at December 31	**50**	50

The Club holds 50% of the ordinary share capital of Headingley North-South Stand Limited (HNSS), company number 10747361 of Emerald Headingley Stadium St. Michael's Lane, Headingley, Leeds LS6 3BR. This company has been incorporated to facilitate the redevelopment of the North South Stand.

15. Provision for liabilities

Deferred tax (see Note 11)	**450,000**	316,546

16. Related Party Transactions

By way of the Articles of Association of The Yorkshire Cricket Foundation (YCF), the Club has the power to appoint two trustees to the board of the YCF. During the year Mark Arthur and Robin Smith were Board Members and Trustees of the YCF. During 2019 the YCF awarded non-capital grants of £15,962 (2018: £29,533) to the Club. The balance owed to the Club at December 31, 2019, was £59 (2018:£9,914) and this forms part of the trade debtors balance at the year end.

Mark Arthur was also Board Member and Director of the Yorkshire Cricket Board (YCB). During 2019 the Club invoiced sales to the YCB of £92,056 (2018:£99,526) in return for goods or services. All invoices have been either settled in cash or form part of the trade debtors balance at the year end. The balance owed at December 31, 2019, was £2,720 (2018: £8,805). The Club has also received invoices from the YCB of £32,745 (2018: £nil). All invoices have been either settled in cash or form part of the trade creditors balance at the year end. The amount owed at December 31, 2019, was £9,476 (2018:£nil).

The Club is a founding member of Park Avenue Bradford Limited (PABL) along with the

YCF and YCB, a private company limited by guarantee, with an investment of £nil. Mark Arthur acted as a Board Member and director of both the Club and PABL while Paul Hudson and Andrew Dawson acted as Board Members of PABL and employees of the Club. During 2019 the Club invoiced sales to PABL of £1,016 (2018:£nil) in return for goods or services. These invoices are included in the trade debtors balance at December 31, 2019.

The Club invested £50 by way of paid-up share capital in Headingley North-South Limited (HNSS) (see Note 14). Mark Arthur, Paul Hudson and Andrew Dawson all acted as directors of this company alongside their roles with the Club. Costs of £1,461,039 (2018: £688,547) were received by the Club from HNSS in 2019, and were all settled in cash during the year, leaving no balance owing at December 31, 2019 (2018: £338,416).

Headingley North-South Stand (Cricket) Limited (HNSS Cricket) is a wholly owned subsidiary of HNSS. During the year the Club incurred costs of £259,395 (2018:£nil) from HNSS Cricket and all were settled in cash during the year.

Robin Smith was a Non-Executive Director of the Bartlett Group (Holdings) Limited. Costs of £3,006 (2018: £3,006) were incurred by the Club from one of its subsidiaries and were settled in cash during the year.

17. Pensions

The Club operates defined contribution pension schemes for the benefit of certain employees. The employee and employer contributions during the year were £347,292 (2018: £356,810). The assets of these schemes are administered in funds independent from those of the Club and of this £57,256 was unpaid at the end of the year (2018: £3,915).

18. Audit Fee

The Club paid its auditor £17,500 (2018:£20,000) in respect of the audit of these Financial Statements.

MEMBERS' COMMITTEE
CHAIRMAN'S REPORT

The following served on the Members' Committee during the year.

Chairman:	**Graeme Greenfield**
Elected Members:	**Charlotte Evers**
	Pauline Beesley
	John Morris
	Howard Ray
Appointed Members:	**Graeme Greenfield**
	Richard Levin
	Chris Woodthorpe
	Andrew Kilburn
In Attendance:	**Robin Smith,** Board Chairman
	Mark Arthur, Chief Executive
	Andy Dawson, Commercial Director

The year started on a sad note. John Morris, who had been elected to the committee at the 2019 AGM, sadly passed away before taking up his position.

There were seven full committee meetings during the year. Each meeting is appropriately recorded with the detailed minutes subsequently being submitted to the main Board. The openness and accessibility of the Board continues and, as Chair of the Members' Committee I continue to attend the full board meetings to ensure that our members' views are represented.

GRAEME GREENFIELD

There has been an excellent relationship between the members of the committee and the Board members who attend the meetings. Many of the suggestions made at meetings have been actioned during recent years. During the season there have also been a number of events directed at greater member involvement, in addition to the three full Forum meetings at Headingley.

The opening event was Meet the Players after the close of play. Unfortunately, the weather disrupted the event, but the hardy members who stayed enjoyed spending time with the players.

It was great to see the Emerald Stand completed and open for business during the season. A large number of members took up the opportunity to tour the facilities, and the stand has proved a popular viewing spot for many — including me!

A further innovation was the presentation of the members' Player of the Season Award taking place in the Long Room. The presentation was open to all members and I hope continues for many years.

The committee have continued to challenge the Club on the team performance in both red and white ball cricket, we and are united in our strength of feeling about some of the facilities at Scarborough. The County Championship game at York was eagerly anticipated, and those attending were not disappointed. We look forward to returning to York in August, and who can fail to be excited by the prospects of a *Roses* match at Scarborough?

I would encourage all members to attend the Forum meetings in 2020. It is your opportunity to ask questions of the Board members and YCCC staff who attend. Items discussed at the forums and subsequent feedback have resulted in positive action taken for the benefit of the members.

The Club has committed to the refurbishment of the Long Room and a review of the catering options. We hope this will result in an improved experience next season.

There is no need to wait until a Forum to share your comments and views as committee members are happy to speak to you throughout the season. Alternatively, please send us an email at:

ycccmemberscommitee@gmail.com

In conclusion, I would like to express my sincere appreciation to all my committee colleagues this year for their love of the game and particularly Yorkshire County Cricket Club. They continue to give up their free time for the benefit of all members, and all have made a great contribution to Membership Committee meetings this year.

I would like to offer special thanks to Andrew Kilburn who is stepping down as an appointed member. Andrew has made a valuable contribution to the committee over a number of years, and will be missed.

Once again it has been a privilege to be Chairman of the Members' Committee, and I look forward to hearing your views in the coming season, either at Forums or during the tea interval in the Long Room at most county games at Emerald Headingley.

GRAEME GREENFIELD
Chairman,
Members' Committee
Yorkshire County Cricket Club